PENGUIN BOOKS

THE PENGUIN GUIDE TO THE MONUMENTS OF INDIA

VOLUME ONE: BUDDHIST, JAIN, HINDU

Dr George Michell has a Bachelor of Architecture degree from Melbourne University and a PhD in Indian Archaeology from the London School of Oriental and African Studies. His lecturing and research have taken him all over South Asia, and he has most recently headed a field-work team at the medieval Hindu imperial capital of Vijayanagara. He has also organized several exhibitions and edited their catalogues, including *In the Image of Man: 2000 years of Indian Sculpture and Painting*, held at the Hayward Gallery in 1982. He has written several books, including *The Hindu Temple* and *Brick Temples of Bengal*.

Also published:

THE PENGUIN GUIDE TO THE MONUMENTS OF INDIA

VOLUME TWO: ISLAMIC, RAJPUT, EUROPEAN

by Philip Davies

D0543476

THE PENGUIN GUIDE TO THE

MONUMENTS OF INDIA

VOLUME ONE

BUDDHIST, JAIN, HINDU

GEORGE MICHELL

PENGUIN BOOKS

PENGUIN BOOKS

Published by the Penguin Group
27 Wrights Lane, London W8 5TZ, England
Viking Penguin Inc., 40 West 23rd Street, New York, New York 10010, USA
Penguin Books Australia Ltd, Ringwood, Victoria, Australia
Penguin Books Canada Ltd, 2801 John Street, Markham, Ontario, Canada L3R 1B4
Penguin Books (NZ) Ltd, 182–190 Wairau Road, Auckland 10, New Zealand

Penguin Books Ltd, Registered Offices: Harmondsworth, Middlesex, England

First published by Viking 1989
Published in Penguin Books 1990

1 3 5 7 9 10 8 6 4 2

Copyright © George Michell, 1989
All rights reserved

Filmset in Linotron 202 Bembo
by Wyvern Typesetting Ltd, Bristol

Made and printed in Great Britain by Butler & Tanner Ltd.
Frome and London

Frontispiece Sanchi, Stupa 1, detail of gateway post with lotuses and ducks, 1st century]

CONTENTS

PREFACE

India preserves one of the world's great artistic traditions, a heritage of art, architecture and sculpture that goes back more than two thousand years. Unlike ancient civilizations such as those of China, Egypt, Greece or even Mexico, that of India is still very much alive. Buddhist, Jain and Hindu temples are not merely archaeological monuments; they are active places of worship where carvings and mural paintings are objects of devotion as well as objects of art. The continuity of religious traditions in India means that ancient shrines are still animated by their ritual and mythical context.

To write a guidebook to India's sacred monuments is to cover an area and a time-span almost equivalent to the whole of Western European architecture from the period of ancient Rome to the present day. While few authors would venture to cover the buildings of Europe over some two and a half thousand years in a single volume, guidebooks on India do not hesitate to attempt an equally impossible task. A comparison of Karnataka, India, with West Germany gives an idea of the scale of the task. Not only are they equivalent in size but they also probably have the same large number of ancient buildings and sites. Because of the sheer scale and volume of work involved, most existing guidebooks on India have given even the major monuments inadequate coverage; other less familiar but not necessarily less interesting sites are omitted altogether. It is this situation that has prompted the authors to conceive the idea of two completely new and comprehensive guides.

Overall Aims

The two volumes of *The Penguin Guide to the Monuments of India* are intended as handbooks to all the major monuments of India. Volume II describes the Islamic, Rajput and European buildings, while this volume deals with the Buddhist, Jain and Hindu temples and their art. In both volumes all of the country is covered, from Ladakh in the Himalayas to Kanyakumari at the southernmost tip of the peninsula, and from Assam in the east to Dwarka on the westernmost promontory of Gujarat. The time-span is equally encompassing, beginning with the earliest monuments in the 3rd century BC and ending with those which have been erected in the present century. (Two prehistoric sites in western India dating from the 2nd millennium BC have also been included.) Since Volume II deals with the architecture of the Muslim and European periods there is a chronological overlap between the two guides; in fact, some sites appear in both guides. Volume I, however, is confined to shrines and temples, including those which were built or renovated during later times. As such, it reflects the persistence of religious and artistic traditions in India down to the present day.

The Penguin Guides to the Monuments of India have been designed to complement more conventional travel books, the best of which are *India: A Travel Survival Kit* (Melbourne: Lonely Planet Publications, 1987) and *India in Luxury* by Louise Nicholson (London: Century, 1985). Here the visitor will find essential data on hotels, restaurants and shopping as well as on the logistics of travel. *The Penguin Guides* present information about sites and buildings which are only sketchily covered in other such publications. Much of the information is presented for the first time in a format intended for the traveller. The regional maps are the most detailed yet to appear in a work of this kind; many of the site maps have been specially commissioned.

The first part of this volume is a general introduction to the religious, social and artistic background of India's sacred monuments. The aim is to provide sufficient data to permit the traveller to appreciate the buildings and their sculptures or paintings with some comprehension of their ritual and mythical context. Obviously, these chapters are condensations of a vast and complex subject that encompasses a considerable diversity of practices and beliefs. However, there has been an attempt to cover all relevant aspects, without engulfing the reader in too many Indian names and technical terms. A list of recent publications is included for those who wish to pursue their interests in more detail.

The bulk of the volume is contained in the second part, which is a gazetteer of the monuments. This is divided into six regions, each with a historical summary in which the sites are chronologically arranged. The site descriptions which follow are arranged alphabetically and a map for each region locates these sites. The maps have been fully annotated to indicate access roads as well as the nearest town from which a bus may be taken, or the appropriate railway station or airport. So that the traveller can plan his itinerary in conjunction with the sites described in Volume II, these too have been indicated.

This volume includes an explanation of all Indian words, whether architectural terms or names of deities or dynasties. An index to all of the sites is also provided, cross-referenced with volume II.

Visiting the Monuments

Many ancient sites come under the protection of the archaeological authorities, either of the Government of India or of the State, whose custodians are usually in attendance. Some sites are fenced in and a small fee is charged for entering. Visiting hours are normally from 8.00 a.m. to 5.00 p.m., if not longer, and there is no day of the week when any site closes. Photography with a hand-held camera is usually permitted, unless some archaeological or restoration work is in progress. However, the use of tripod and/or flash requires permission from the archaeological authorities in New Delhi or the State capital; this demands time and patience. Unless a shrine or temple is currently in use for worship, visitors will not be required to remove their shoes. Local guides are available at many sites.

Other monuments which are 'living' shrines come under the management of temple committees, whose regulations are to be respected. Like other worshippers, visitors are required to dress appropriately. Shoes, hats and leather articles may have to be deposited at the gateway to a temple, where a custodian will charge a small fee. Access into the sacred precinct may be restricted in two ways. The times of visiting may be governed by the hours of worship, visitors being discouraged from entering during the main ceremonies; the temple may also close for some hours at the hottest time of the day. It may not be possible to penetrate all the way into the sanctuary, though this procedure differs considerably from one temple to another. In Kerala, on the western coast of southern India, for example, almost no temple will admit non-Hindus. In contrast, some religious institutions encourage visitors to directly approach the deity and make offerings. Local priests acting as guides may assist the visitor.

Museums are included in this volume since they are the repositories of sculptures and architectural fragments from ancient temple sites. Museums are generally closed on one day of the week and on public holidays. There is a small entrance charge and perhaps also an additional fee for taking photographs. Guidebooks are not always available.

ACKNOWLEDGEMENTS

In writing such an ambitious work as this, the author has had to rely on the good will of many friends and scholars. General editorial direction at Penguin was provided first by Catriona Luckhurst, under whom the project was conceived and initiated, and then by Tessa Strickland, who ably steered the two volumes through the various editorial and production stages. Lesley Levene performed the herculean task of checking all of the text, and of ensuring that the two volumes worked effectively together. Melanie Gibson, Gail Hinich and Eleanor Schwartz patiently read parts of the manuscript and offered helpful criticism. The volume has been designed by Jessica Smith, and Fiona Jackson assisted in the picture research.

Gathering data for the gazetteer sections was an arduous and frustrating task since some regions and many ancient sites lacked adequate publications. Fortunately, the author benefited from the accumulated knowledge of several colleagues, who were extremely generous with their information. They include M. A. Dhaky, Suresh Jadhav, B. L. Nagarch, R. Nagaswamy, S. Nagaraju and Foy Nissen in India; Bruno Dagens, Anna L. Dallapiccola and Philip Denwood in Europe; and, in the US, Frederick Asher, Susan and John Huntington, Michael Meister, Walter Spink and Philip Wagoner. A number of friends undertook to check parts of the gazetteer on their travels in India: in particular, Norman Braden, John Copland, Jo and Peter Meyer and Deanna Petherbridge.

If this guide has any semblance of completeness it is because of the invaluable contributions of these many colleagues and friends. However, the author does not hesitate to take full responsibility for any inaccuracies and confusions which may have occurred. These are almost impossible to avoid in such a comprehensive survey of India's monuments. In the hope that a second edition of this volume might one day appear, the author would appreciate receiving notification of any mistakes. Correspondence may be directed to the publishers in London.

Preparing maps of the various sites was in itself a major task. Jean Deloche, Arthur Duff, Niels Gutschow, Adam Hardy, A. P. Jamkhedkar and Jan Pieper provided some maps. Others were specially commissioned from Shyambhu Mitra and Snehal Shah, who travelled around different parts of India exercising their cartographic skills in the field. Their maps appear here for the first time. In London, Nigel White devoted himself to the labour of interpreting the maps, standardizing their conventions and redrawing them for publication; K. S. Ravindran was responsible for the building plans. While photographs came from diverse sources, the American Institute of Indian Studies in Varanasi was particularly helpful in making its archives available.

Over a period of almost three years it has been a pleasure to work closely together with Philip Davies, author of the second volume of *The Penguin Guide to the Monuments of India*. A more sympathetic and helpful co-author could hardly be imagined. Then there was the companionship of John M. Fritz, visiting various sites and museums in India, and also at the desk in London. Without his constant encouragement and patience the work would only have been completed with a great deal more difficulty.

George Michell

PART ONE

INTRODUCTION

Himalayan landscape, Ladakh

ONE

REGIONS AND CULTURES

Each region of India is in itself a country; the vast extent of the subcontinent and its large population have prevented any overall cultural uniformity. Yet social and religious systems were evolved at an early stage and continue to act as cohesive forces. The interaction between these diversifying and unifying cultural tendencies lies at the core of India's vital civilization.

The Land

Cut off from the rest of Asia by the encircling ranges of the Himalayas and protruding as a peninsula into the ocean which bears its name, India is isolated as a subcontinent. It is also subcontinental in scale, being no less than 3,200 km (2,000 miles) from north to south and almost the same distance from east to west. Although India's extent is characterized by a wide variety of terrain, there is the common climatic experience of a violent monsoon in the summer months (June–September).

The Indian Himalayas contain the highest peaks in the world; these are linked together in a continuous chain of ridges that defines the northern peripheries of the subcontinent. Narrow valleys intrude into these mountains, some of which open up to form isolated regions, such as that of central Kashmir. Other valleys are remotely located beyond the first ridges in arid zones which extend into the Tibetan region further north.

Two great river-systems have their origins in the Himalayas: the Indus flows southwards to the Arabian Sea, while the Ganga and Yamuna rivers flow eastwards, eventually combining with the Brahmaputra to form one great water-way that ends its journey in the Bay of Bengal. These riverine landscapes are generally flat and featureless. The Indus passes through sandy desert, part of which extends into western India, the country's most arid region; the Brahmaputra and lower Ganga flow through the wettest zone, which is in the east.

Central India has large expanses of wooded low ridges, bordered on the north by the Vindhya hills and on the south by the westward-flowing Narmada and Tapti rivers. South of this region is the Deccan, the elevated plateau of the peninsula which is dramatically punctuated by granite and sandstone outcrops. This plateau is cut off from the Arabian Sea to the west by forested ridges known as ghats; on the east, another line of ghats descends to the Bay of Bengal. The Deccan is traversed by the eastward-flowing Godavari and Krishna rivers; their fertile coastal deltas contrast with the dry plateau.

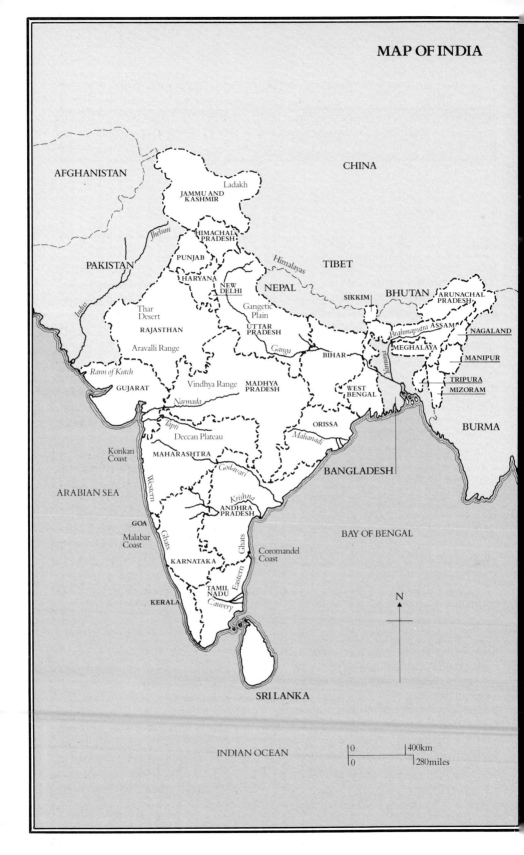

Map of India showing regions and natural features

Southern India is generally wetter and more varied in elevation than the Deccan; rugged granite hills are a constant feature. The Cauvery, which is the principal river of the region, fans out into a fertile delta along the eastern Coromandel coast. The western Malabar coast, the wettest zone in this region, is bounded by wooded mountains; these define the limits of coastal Kerala and Kannara. The two coasts meet at Kanyakumari, the southernmost tip of the peninsula.

Regional Cultures

India's history is one of repeated invasions by peoples from the north-west, their passage across the plains of the north and their eventual absorption into the general population. The first known group of foreigners were the Aryans, who arrived in the middle of the 2nd millennium BC; after them came the Kushanas in the 1st century AD, the Hunas in the 6th century and then waves of Muslims from the end of the 12th century onwards. Striking ethnic and cultural contrasts existed between these peoples and the indigenous populations. Even so, the invaders were eventually integrated, as were their diverse beliefs and practices.

But differences also existed among the indigenous peoples. India's densely populated river valleys and coastal deltas are separated from each other by vast expanses of mountains, forests and dry territories, the less attractive areas for habitation. Much of the population has always been concentrated in these different fertile regions, each with its own distinctive languages, religious practices and even artistic traditions.

Peoples of northern, central, eastern and western India, as well as of the northern Deccan, speak languages which all belong to the Indo-Aryan group, having their common origin in the language originally introduced by the Aryans. These languages have given their names to the modern states of India, such as Bengal, Gujarat and Maharashtra. But there are also Urdu and its derivative Hindi, which reflect the centuries of Persian influence in northern India (see Volume II). In contrast, southern India is dominated by indigenous languages of the Dravidian group; these have given their names to the modern states of Karnataka and Tamil Nadu.

There is a proliferation of religious traditions, some of them tribal in origin, which focus on local deities. Rituals and festivals sometimes pertain only to a particular place of worship which has its own sacred geography. Holy sites may be the summit of a rocky hill, a spreading tree, a river bank or a cave. These are considered the auspicious places where divine forces are likely to manifest themselves. The connection between this mythical landscape and the development of religious cults is obvious everywhere. Temple architecture provides numerous examples of the transformation of a sacred place into a sacred building: the holy mountains of Girnar and Satrunjaya in western India or the tree shrine at Bodhgaya in eastern India are among the best known of countless examples. The changes of cult that may occur over the centuries at a particular site indicate the pervasive influence of the sacred locality. There is also a regional limitation to mainstream religious developments. Buddhism and Jainism, for instance, have never spread to all of the different parts of the country and are today mostly confined to the northern and western zones respectively.

Over more than two millennia, India's artistic traditions have been dominated by regional techniques and styles. Temple forms differ strikingly from eastern to western India, and from the northern plains to the southern zone. Regional styles frequently affect the overall layout of religious buildings, as well as the details of their exteriors and interiors. Sculptors and paintings also display local influences, attesting to the long-established guilds of artists and craftsmen in the different parts of the country. In zones such as the Himalayan valleys of northern India, the riverine delta of eastern India or the coastal tract of southern India, architectural forms reflect the impact of local climate.

Cohesive Forces

There have always been movements of people from one part of the country to another, and this has provided opportunities over the centuries for the intermingling of cultures, beliefs and artistic traditions. In this way, regional cultures have contributed to a national culture which finds its most characteristic expression in social and religious forms. Though political fragmentation is the most common historical tendency, Indian civilization has achieved coherence through a common social and religious experience.

Religious beliefs are based on an ancient social system that was first developed by the Aryans after they had settled in India. Society, according to the Aryans, was to be constructed according to a strict hierarchy, with dominating groups or castes. At the top of this social scheme are the brahmin priests and kshatriya warriors; lower down the social scale are the merchants, free peasants and labourers. There have been repeated reactions to this division of humanity: the Buddhist and Jain religions which grew up in the 5th century BC are sometimes interpreted as expressions of social reform, as are certain later Hindu sects. However, history has demonstrated the ultimate failure of these reactions: to this day the caste system, with its clearly defined strata of different groups, each assigned its own duty or dharma, has prevailed.

A religious system dominated by brahmin priests and teachers still survives in India. While there are innumerable differences in the means and objects of worship, India's unifying religious experience is the living tradition embraced by the term Hinduism. The beliefs and practices that constitute Hinduism have no single doctrinal basis; yet they are bound together by the common acknowledgement of the authority of the ancient Aryan scriptures. Sanskrit, the language in which these scriptures were composed, has been meticulously preserved through the centuries as the sacred and intellectual medium of communication.

Regional Histories

The history of India as recorded in chronicles and inscriptions is an unending list of dynasties, rulers, battles and intrigues; yet there are overriding patterns. The earliest states were geographically determined by fertile zones such as river valleys and coastal deltas which could support large populations. Among the many examples of these regional kingdoms are those of the 4th–3rd-century BC Magadhas in the Ganga and Yamuna river valleys, the 10th–12th century Cholas in the Cauvery river basin and their contemporaries, the Eastern Gangas, in the

Mahanadi river delta of Orissa in eastern India. The histories of the different regions reveal a succession of dynasties, one taking over from the other in order to benefit from local resources and accumulated wealth. In this respect, each region of India has its own separate chronology. (These regional histories are summarized in the introductions to each of the six gazetteer sections.)

From time to time, the resources of other zones proved an irresistible attraction. History recounts the warring campaigns of kings who attempted to extend their territories into neighbouring territories. But despite the claims of these ambitious figures, only occasionally was more than one zone brought under the control of a single ruler; regional states were rarely transformed into pan-regional empires. The Mauryas in the 3rd century BC, the Guptas in the 3rd–5th centuries, the Pratiharas in the 8th–10th centuries and the Vijayanagara kings in the 14th–17th centuries were the more successful of these pan-regional empires. (For Muslim empires, most notably that of the Mughals in the 16th–17th centuries, see Volume II.)

Regional states are better understood in terms of their dynastic centres than the extents of their boundaries. While frontiers were usually ill defined, capitals and their immediate environs tended to remain constant since there was usually a correlation between royal residence and population density. Only a well-watered locality capable of sustaining a large number of people could serve as the capital of a ruling dynasty. The agricultural resources concentrated in such areas were necessary to support the king's army and his courtly and military retinues. Here, religious and artistic traditions could flourish under the sustained sponsorship of the king himself and those in his service.

Where military considerations were paramount, the king's capital had to be strategically located. Rocky outcrops capable of being converted into fortified citadels served as dynastic headquarters, as, for example, at Gwalior and Chitorgarh in central and western India respectively. Elsewhere, it was the remote locations of capitals, as in Kashmir or Ladakh, that shielded kingdoms from the disruptive invasions of the plains below.

The king's influence was extended beyond the capital and its immediate environs by a complex network of power relationships. Lesser centres and outlying regions were mostly governed by local rulers or chieftains who were linked with the capital through effective political alliances. The conflict between the central authority of the capital and these lesser rulers forms a constant topic in Indian history; inevitably, some of these feudatories found opportunities to seize control of the centre, thereby elevating their influence from a local to a regional level. The emergence of the Eastern Gangas in eastern India or the Nayakas in southern India is a successful illustration of this historical process.

Pilgrims bathing in the Ganga at Varanasi

TWO

RELIGIOUS DEVELOPMENTS

India preserves a bewildering range of beliefs and cults in which a vast array of divinities and mythological beings receives worship. To begin with, it is necessary to distinguish between clearly defined doctrines, such as those of Buddhism and Jainism, and the amalgam of cults and devotional movements which makes up the religion known best as Hinduism. Yet Buddhism, Jainism and Hinduism are not entirely separate religions; interaction over more than two thousand years means that there are overlapping beliefs and practices. Sikhism is a comparatively recent religion which to some extent bridges the gap between Hinduism and Islam.

The Indus Civilization

Religious traditions are traceable back to the civilization of the Indus valley region which flourished in the 3rd–2nd millennia BC. The artefacts that were discovered at the urban sites of Mohenjodaro and Harappa, now in Pakistan, provide clues about the possible beliefs of these prehistoric peoples. Cult figurines, especially 'goddesses', inscribed seals and models of animals suggest that there may have been the worship of the female principle, as well as a concern for the preservation of life, including that of certain animals, plants and trees. Objects representing male and female sexual emblems indicate a celebration of human fertility. The exact nature of beliefs, however, remains obscure since the script associated with these artefacts has yet to be deciphered.

Regularly laid-out streets lined with brick structures have been uncovered by archaeologists at Mohenjodaro and Harappa, and to a lesser extent at Kalibangan and Lothal in western India. While no religious monument has been identified with any certainty, it is possible that the Great Bath at Mohenjodaro may have served a ceremonial purpose; the so-called 'granaries', consisting of clusters of square brick platforms, may also have been connected with religious rituals.

The Aryans

The Indus civilization had already collapsed by the middle of the 2nd millennium BC when the Aryan peoples entered India through the mountain passes in the north-west. While the archaeological remains associated with these invaders are restricted to pottery fragments, the Aryans introduced a distinctive religion which they set down in a body of literature known as the Vedas. These were written in an early form of Sanskrit, the language that survives to the present day as the sacred script common to all Indian religions.

The Rig Veda is the oldest Aryan text and it is still regarded as the source for later Hindu literature. The priests of the Vedas are known as brahmins; they offer sacrifices to the gods on behalf of the community. The 1,028 hymns of the Rig Veda are addressed to a pantheon of divinities that is dominated by powerful male figures associated with the heavens. Indra, the greatest Vedic deity, fulfils the dual function of war god and weather god.

The texts composed in the centuries following the Vedas, such as the Brahmanas and the Upanishads, reveal the growing power of the brahmin priests, who imbued the mystery of the sacrifice with cosmic significance. From the pantheon of the Vedas, the creator is transformed into a single divinity or godhead. In the Upanishads, this godhead is further identified with atman, the 'self' or spirit, which is formless but all-powerful and ever-present.

An important belief developed in the later Vedic texts is that of samsara, the soul's transmigration from one generation to the next. Samsara is closely linked with the idea of karma, the result of one lifetime's deeds affecting those of the next. While karma explains the mystery of man's suffering, it offers little hope for ultimate peace and happiness. According to this view, humans are trapped in an unending sequence of lifetimes. The desired state of bliss, which is the ultimate aim of all religious endeavour, is nirvana, which is perceived as the extinction of personal identity, or moksha, the final release.

Buddhism

The history of the Buddhist religion is bound up with the life of Buddha, the teacher who lived from 563 to 483 BC in the plains beneath the Himalayan foothills in eastern India. Buddha was the leading exponent of a reform movement that reacted against the Aryan social system. His teachings, which were more con-cerned with practical instruction than with mystical speculation, grew out of his quest for a rationally enlightened experience. Buddha had practised penance and experienced the futility of mystical speculation before he achieved insight into the causes of human suffering and the way to remove them. He propounded an Eightfold Path of right conduct to eliminate the burden of human suffering.

Later Buddhist scriptures illuminate the life of Gautama, who was born as the son of a Shakya prince. He left his family at the age of twenty-nine and spent many years as a wandering ascetic until he experienced an enlightenment; after this event he was known as Enlightened One or Buddha. He gave his first sermon at Sarnath, outside Varanasi in central India, and over the next fifty years toured many parts of the country preaching and converting. He organized increasing numbers of followers into the ascetic order known as the Sangha, and he met many kings, including the Magadha ruler of Rajgir in eastern India.

After his death, a council of five hundred Buddhists was convened at Rajgir to edit the corpus of his sermons so that his teachings could be authentically preserved. A schism took place at the second council at Vaisali in central India. The Old Ones, or Theravada, insisted on maintaining the ascetic ideal of the Sangha, while reformers wanted to broaden the concept of the Sangha to include lay followers. This new movement was the origin of Mahayana, the Great Vehicle school of Buddhism, which looked down on the old order, which it called Hinayana, the Lesser Vehicle.

In the 3rd century BC, Buddhism became one of the state doctrines of the Maurya emperor Ashoka, who ruled from Pataliputra (modern Patna) in eastern India. Monuments commemorating Buddha and his teachings were erected at holy sites associated with the life of the Master, where they were regularly visited by pilgrims. Stone columns inscribed with royal edicts were set up at these and other locations, such as Dhauli in eastern India and Girnar in western India. Ashoka even sent ambassadors to Nepal and Sri Lanka to propagate the new religion; in this way, Buddhism spread beyond India.

After the decline of the Mauryas, Buddhism continued to flourish under the 1st-century-BC Shunga rulers of central India and the 1st–3rd century Kushana rulers of Gandhara in the north-west (now Pakistan) and Mathura in central India. By this time, commemorative monuments were no longer restricted to the holy sites of the Master and the remote locations of the Sangha; even dynastic centres were adorned with Buddhist structures. Royal patronage continued into the 4th–5th centuries under the Guptas of northern and central India, and the Ikshvakus and Vakatakas of

Ajanta, Cave 26, the Parinirvana of Buddha, 5th century

the Deccan. Nagarjunakonda, capital of the Ikshvakus, was an important religious centre endowed with numerous monastic establishments.

While Buddhism expanded in influence it underwent internal changes. By the first centuries of the Christian era the Great Vehicle had established itself as the dominant force. Mahayana doctrine evolved a series of Buddhas and Buddha-like saviours, known as Bodhisattvas, who were especially popular since they helped the worshipper, whether monk or lay follower, in his quest for enlightenment. Mahayana monasteries functioning as universities, as at Nalanda in eastern India, attracted students from all over the country, and even beyond, who came to study under famous teachers. It was through this movement of students and teachers that Mahayana doctrines spread in the 3rd–4th centuries to western and southern India, and even to South-East Asia and the Himalayan valleys. By the 5th–6th centuries, the traditions of the Great Vehicle reached the Far East, where they profoundly affected Chinese culture.

As the Great Vehicle developed ever more complicated doctrines it began to lose its appeal; simultaneously, Hinduism gained in popularity. Mahayana theology was repeatedly revised to accommodate an increasing number of mythical and semi-divine beings. This elaborated pantheon partly coincided with that of Hinduism, and there was less and less distinction between the two religions; inevitably, Mahayana declined. Chinese pilgrims touring India in the 7th century reported that the Great Vehicle was almost extinct except for a few religious sites in eastern India. By the end of the 12th century, Buddhism had effectively vanished from the land of its origin.

But Mahayana traditions did not entirely die out; they were preserved in remote zones such as the Himalayan valleys. The Great Vehicle flourished in neighbouring Tibet, where sacred texts were brought from India to be translated and studied. Tibetan monasteries benefited from the patronage of local rulers; as these leaders expanded their territories, so too did Mahayana spread. By the 16th century, Tibetan versions of the Great Vehicle were introduced into eastern and northern India through the lower valleys of the Himalayas. Buddhist institutions were founded, often as citadels on the summits of steep ridges. Mahayana traditions flourished in these fortified monasteries, and have continued to do so to the present day.

Since the 19th century there has been a revival of Buddhism in India under the sponsorship of Buddhist countries such as Burma, Sri Lanka and, most recently, Japan. The holy sites have been restored and commemorative monuments and rest-houses for pilgrims constructed. With the recent desecration of monasteries in Tibet, there has been an influx of Buddhist refugees from this mountain kingdom. Among them was the Dalai Lama, the spiritual leader of the Tibetans, who now lives permanently in India. New monasteries have been erected and Tibetan Buddhism is now enjoying a renewal of its ancient Mahayana traditions.

Jainism

Among the religious teachers who were contemporary with Buddha in the 5th century BC in eastern India was Vardhamana. Known to his followers as

Mahavira, the Great Hero, he was born in about 540 BC. For thirty years he taught in the same region as did Buddha; he was even patronized by the same kings. He died of self-starvation near Rajgir in about 468 BC.

Jainism, the religion founded by Mahavira, has a different history to Buddhism even though it began in a similar way, with a doctrine of teachings followed by those who had renounced their worldly ties. While Jainism succeeded in establishing itself firmly and permanently in different parts of the country, it never spread beyond India.

Like early Buddhism, Jain doctrines were designed to be taught and practised by ascetics. Unlike Buddhism, however, Jainism never developed beyond this stage; it scrupulously preserved its original doctrines and practices. Mahavira was considered to be the last of a series of spiritual leaders referred to as Conquerors or Jinas; more generally, they were known as Tirthankaras, or Ford-Makers, a title in which the completion of a spiritual journey is compared to the crossing of a river. In time, like the Great Vehicle of Buddhism, there was an elaboration of Mahavira's doctrine and a variety of semi-divine beings were incorporated from Hindu cults. Even so, Jainism never gave up its ascetic basis. Perhaps for this reason, it remained the religion of only a small proportion of the country's population.

The patronage of Jainism is traceable back to the 3rd century BC during the Maurya period; monuments associated with the reign of Ashoka are still preserved in eastern India. A serious famine at this time led to a migration of Jain monks to the Deccan, where they established important religious centres. Out of this dispersal arose the great schism of Jainism, which, as in Buddhism, was based on conflicting interpretations of the founder's teachings. The sect which flourished in the Deccan insisted on the retention of nudity, which had been established by Mahavira; accordingly they were known as Space-Clad or Digambara. The other sect, which remained in eastern India, allowed followers to wear white garments; they called themselves White-Clad or Shvetambara. This schism did not become final until about the 1st century, and although there were never any fundamental doctrinal differences between these two schools of Jainism, the division has persisted down to the present day.

Jainism soon spread throughout India. Shvetambara monuments are known to have existed alongside Buddhist ones in the Mathura region of central India in the 1st–2nd centuries. This sect found much support among the rulers of western India, and gained a position of great prominence during the reign of the Solankis in the 11th–12th centuries; many fine Jain temples dating from this era are still in use for worship. The support of the Shvetambaras by local chiefs was unaffected by the Muslim occupation of the region in the 15th–16th centuries, and western India continues to be the home of the Shvetambaras. Important pilgrimage sites are located at the summits of holy mountains at Girnar and Satrunjaya. Despite the emphasis on monastic discipline, the Jains of this region developed into a wealthy mercantile community and acted as patrons of temple architecture over many centuries.

The Digambaras of the Deccan and southern India are less numerous. In the 9th–10th centuries they benefited from the patronage of the Rashtrakutas and Western Gangas. From this period dates Shravana Belgola, the principal pilgrimage site of the region.

Beginnings of Hinduism

While the origins of Hinduism may be sought in prehistory, the religion as it is known today is not nearly so ancient. The movements of devotional theism that lie at the core of Hinduism date only from the centuries immediately preceding the Christian era. The outstanding feature of these movements is the worship of a personal deity who takes the form of a particular god or goddess. The adoration of such a deity is known as bhakti; the path of love and self-effacing submission to the godhead is believed to bring about the fulfilment of all desires, even the ultimate emancipation from the cycle of samsara.

The deities upon whom this religion concentrates are essentially syncretistic creations: they have their mixed origins in the earlier pantheon of the Vedas and in the folk cults of which there is little record in early literature. Paramount among these non-Vedic divinities are the nature spirits associated with sacred mountains, caves, trees and flowers, as well as totemic gods with animal-like features and ferocious natures. Other popular cults focus on local figures whose heroic deeds are celebrated in epic poems. Hinduism owed its popularity to the accumulation of an increasing number of these spirits, gods and heroes. In time, even Buddhism and Jainism were infected by this process.

By the 1st–2nd centuries, the major cults of Hinduism had emerged which were to dominate the beliefs and practices of the majority of Indians up to the present day. At the same time, there was a host of minor divinities and spirits who were no less important for human affairs. Elaborate rituals and ceremonies were evolved for worshipping these gods; myths and popular legends flourished.

The Epics and Puranas

An enormous body of Hindu literature has been produced in Sanskrit. Although the Vedas, Brahmanas and Upanishads are regarded as the most sacred of India's religious texts, the scriptures of popular Hinduism are the Epics, the Puranas or 'Ancient Stories' and the books of Sacred Law. As these were not set down in writing until long after their composition, the period to which they belong cannot be accurately determined; many of these texts are tentatively dated to the first centuries of the Christian era.

The Epics express the richness of contrasting cultural traditions. The Mahabharata and Ramayana were originally secular stories, but they also developed a religious character. The most celebrated portion of the Epics is the Bhagavad Gita in the Mahabharata; this poem is universally held to be a definitive statement of devotional Hinduism. The story of Krishna is as well known as the Mahabharata and Ramayana. Told in countless variations, the episodes associated with the childhood and youth of this god are among the best loved in all devotional Hindu literature.

The Puranas represent another popular aspect of Hindu literature. They are compilations of legends and religious instruction which, in their present form, do not precede the 4th–5th centuries even though they incorporate older material. Sthalapuranas written in regional languages set down the local myths of a particular holy site. For those who cannot read, there is a whole class of popular reciters who travel from village to village, commenting in regional languages on the Epics and Puranas.

Cults of Hinduism

A vast pantheon of divinities unfolds in the myths and legends of Hinduism. Even so, the history of this religion at its highest devotional level is bound up with the simultaneous development of two cults which focus on the gods Shiva and Vishnu. Worshippers of Shiva belong to the Shaiva cult; similarly, Vishnu worshippers belong to the Vaishnava cult. The Shakti cult, which concentrates on the worship of various goddesses, is also of importance, though only occasionally did this achieve independence from the cults of the male deities. Shiva, Vishnu and Shakti are compound creations with a wide range of powers and richly paradoxical personalities. Nor are these cults mutually exclusive; worshippers of Shiva consider Vishnu a minor deity, while in the cult of Vishnu, Shiva is a secondary emanation. These male deities are passive and shadowy figures in the Shakti cult.

There is little overall conflict between the different cults of Hinduism; the reason for this peaceful coexistence is the belief that the ultimate godhead lies beyond the divisions of cult and that the worship of Shiva, Vishnu or Shakti leads to the same goal. From the inclusive viewpoint fostered by some schools of Hindu philosophy, these cult deities are all aspects of the divine in different forms. Such an attitude promotes harmony between the cults; as a result, Shiva and Vishnu are sometimes worshipped together, and Shakti is revered in conjunction with Shiva. Occasionally there is also the concept of a triad of divinities in which the god Brahma is introduced as the creator; in this trinity, Vishnu acts as the preserver and Shiva as the destroyer.

The principal Hindu cults developed alongside a wide range of minor mythological figures, sometimes of only local significance and not always of great antiquity. Many of these lesser beings are incorporated into the major cults by being labelled as an aspect or emanation of Shiva, Vishnu or Shakti. In time, some of these minor beings were transformed into important deities, while others disappeared altogether.

Development of Hinduism

Many of the principal Hindu divinities appear for the first time in the art of the Kushana rulers of central India in the 1st–3rd centuries. That these Hindu cults had an earlier history is suggested by isolated sculptures, such as the 1st-century-BC Shiva emblem at Gudimallam in southern India. The earliest shrines dedicated to Shiva and Vishnu are no earlier than the 3rd–5th century Gupta period in central India. The following centuries witness a proliferation of Hindu sacred art in all parts of the country. As Buddhism waned in influence, the cults of Shiva and Vishnu were taken up by kings, lesser rulers and governors, who dedicated temples to both these gods. Only rarely did patrons sponsor the worship of a single deity; the typical religious site of the 8th–9th centuries has a number of shrines or temples dedicated to different aspects of both Shiva and Vishnu. Surya temples were also erected at this time, as at Martand in northern India and Osian in western India.

The climax of this first phase of Hindu sacred architecture is reached in the 10th–11th centuries with a series of royal monuments dedicated to Shiva; among the many examples are the temples of the Chandellas at Khajuraho in central India, of the Somavamshis at Bhubaneshwar in eastern India, of the Solanakis at Prabhas Patan in western India and of the Cholas at Thanjavur in southern India. But Vishnu temples are also known at these and other sites, demonstrating the continued popularity of this other cult deity. The elaborate sculpture programmes of such monuments incorporated a large number of different gods and semi-divine beings. In this way, the worship of the temple deity, whether Shiva or Vishnu, could encompass the entire pantheon of Hinduism. More unusual are the shrines devoted to Shakti; in her various forms, she more often appears as a consort to the male god. Particular royal figures sometimes promoted the worship of a particular divinity: thus, for example, the 13th-century Surya temple at Konarak in eastern India and the contemporary Nataraja complex at Chidambaram in southern India.

The development of Hindu cults during these centuries was stimulated by saintly teachers, or Acharyas, whose doctrines crystallized the popular bhakti movement. Abhinavagupta in Kashmir in northern India and Shankara in the Deccan were of particular importance for the development of Shaiva philosophy; Ramanuja stimulated the Vaishnava movement in southern India. Parallel to the work of these historical teachers was the emergence of quasi-mythical figures such as the sixty-three Shaiva saints, known as the Nayanars, and the twelve Alvars, who were Vaishnava saints. These saintly poets and musicians expressed the religious ardour of the times; their hymns are among the most popular scriptures of Hinduism. There are also instances of particular historical figures being transformed into semi-divine beings who were then worshipped. Kannappar, the devotee of Shiva at Kalahasti in southern India, is a typical example.

While the invasions of the Muslim armies seriously disrupted royal sponsorship of temple art, Hinduism continued to develop, and many new religious centres were established in the 15th–16th centuries. Shiva temples from this period include royal monuments at Eklingji in western India, Vijayanagara in the Deccan and Kanchipuram in southern India. All of these regions were controlled by Hindu kings who maintained their independence in the face of Muslim opposition. Other more peripheral zones continued to preserve Hindu traditions, as demonstrated by royal temples at Mandi in the Kulu valley in northern India and Gauhati in Assam in eastern India. As Muslim influence waned in the 17th–18th centuries some regions were once again dominated by Hindu rulers. The Marathas in the Deccan and the Mallas in eastern India, for instance, erected temples to various Hindu divinities in territories which had previously been under Muslim control.

A particular feature of Hinduism during the Muslim period is the increased popularity of Krishna; this deity was promoted by the teachings of saintly figures such as Vallabha in southern India and Chaitanya in eastern India. The shrine at Nathdwara in western India was developed into an important pilgrimage centre after a sculpture of Krishna was rescued from Muslim desecration. At the temple at Puri in eastern India a tribal deity was transformed into Krishna, an aspect of Vishnu. This process was carried out under the direct orders of the kings of Orissa, who converted the local cult of Jagannatha into a state religion.

In southern India, the temple became a receptacle for a wide range of divinities; the typical sacred complex was a vast enclosure in which a number of shrines were erected, each housing a different deity, both male and female. In this way, both Shiva and Vishnu as well as their attendant goddesses and saintly worshippers could all be accommodated within a single precinct. The royal patrons of these complexes enjoyed the prestige of sponsoring a monument which incorporated almost the entire Hindu pantheon.

Sikhism

In order to counter the Muslim forces of northern India, a group of military leaders known as Sikhs took control of the Punjab in the 16th century; in doing so they converted to a new religion which has come to be known as Sikhism. Like their Muslim adversaries, Sikhs worship a holy book, the Adi Granth, which sets down the teachings of Nanak, their first spiritual leader. The religion propounded by Nanak is essentially monotheistic, since it focuses on a single but invisible godhead. In this respect, Sikhism is influenced by Islam; even so, its social system remains much closer to that of Hinduism.

The spiritual leaders of Sikhism are known as Gurus. Arjan, the fifth Guru, founded the temple at Amritsar, which is the holiest Sikh shrine; the original Adi Granth is kept here. The spread of the faith was much opposed by the Muslims, who persecuted many Sikhs; Arjan himself was martyred in 1606. The Sikhs are organized into a martial community, with rites of initiation and an army to defend their faith; according to his religious obligations, a Sikh must never cut his hair and as a warrior he must always wear a sword. Gurudwaras or Sikh sanctuaries with rest-houses for the faithful have been established in all the towns of the Punjab, and more recently in cities elsewhere in the country.

Ajanta, Cave 1, Padmapani, 5th century

THREE

BUDDHIST AND JAIN SAVIOURS

In Buddhist cosmology each era is distinguished by a number of enlightened beings or Buddhas. In the present cycle there have already been four Buddhas, the last being Shakyamuni; a fifth Buddha has yet to appear. For Jains, each era consists of a period of improvement and one of decline; there are twenty-four saviours or Tirthankaras. At present the world is declining and the last Tirthankara has already passed away; true knowledge is rapidly disappearing.

The Life of Buddha

Over the centuries the story of Buddha's life has been embellished with many non-historical episodes; it is now embedded in myth and legend. Buddha's birth was announced in a dream that came to Maya, the chief queen of the Shakya king Shuddhodhana. A floating white elephant approached Maya and impregnated her with the future saviour. Wise men prophesied that she had conceived a son who would become a Chakravartin or Universal Sovereign. The child was born in the grove called Lumbini, not far from the town of Kapilavastu (Piprahwa) in central India.

Siddhartha was the boy's name, but in later Buddhist literature he was more commonly known by his family name of Gautama. His youthful days were spent in the sheltered comfort of the palace; he learned the arts required of a prince and enjoyed unbounded prosperity and pleasures. Yet Gautama was not inwardly happy, especially after he witnessed the Four Signs planted by the gods. Conducted around the royal park by Channa, his faithful charioteer, Gautama saw an aged man, a sick man, a corpse and finally a wandering holy man. Gautama became obsessed with the riddle of life and death: how could man escape the tragedy of samsara, with its unavoidable consequence of eternal misery? Renunciation was the only answer. That night he roused Channa and rode away from the palace. Far from the city, Gautama stripped off his jewellery and garments and put on a hermit's robe; with a sword he cut off his hair, which rose miraculously to heaven, much to the rejoicing of the gods.

Thus did Gautama become a wandering ascetic. Soon he was a forest hermit entirely dedicated to meditation, penance and the rigours of self-mortification. Still he was not satisfied. One day, when he was about thirty-five years old, Gautama seated himself beneath a tree, at a site later known as Bodhgaya in eastern India, determined not to rise before solving the mystery of suffering. There he sat in meditation, resisting the temptations and violent storms of Mara, the evil spirit.

When Mara called on Gautama to produce evidence of his sincerity, he touched the ground with his hand and the earth itself spoke in witness. Eventually left alone, Gautama sank into the deepest state of meditation. At the dawning of the forty-ninth day he arrived at the truth; he had become Buddha, the Enlightened One. He had discovered the secret of sorrow and understood why the world was full of suffering; he also knew what man must do to attain happiness. He remained another seven weeks beneath the Tree of Wisdom (bodhi), accepting rice cooked in milk offered by the maiden Sujata.

At first Buddha hesitated to proclaim his new wisdom, but at the insistence of the gods he travelled to Varanasi in central India; he preached his first sermon in the deer park known as Sarnath to the north of the city. In this sermon, which is represented by dharmachakra, the Wheel of Law, Buddha outlined his doctrine of the Four Great Truths. Sorrow is inherent in life; it invariably arises from 'thirst' or desire. Only by eliminating desire can man be released from sorrow; this may be achieved by following the Noble Eightfold Path of right conduct in vision, thought, speech, action, giving, striving, vigilance and meditation. If followed diligently, this Middle Path will inevitably lead to nirvana.

Buddha rapidly became the leading spiritual teacher of his day. He journeyed from town to town, preaching the doctrine of the Middle Path and attracting increasing numbers of followers. Many stories are told of Buddha's conversions; he even tamed a wild elephant sent to trample him by Devadatta, his jealous cousin. Among the miracles that he performed was the feat of levitation at Sravasti in central India to meet the challenge from rival teachers. For over forty years, Buddha's reputation grew, and the Sangha increased in size and influence.

Buddha spent his last rainy season near Vaisali in eastern India. He then travelled to Kusinagara in central India, where he lay down on his side. 'All things decay; strive diligently!' he commanded before dying. His death was the Great Nirvana or Parinirvana. Buddha's sorrowing disciples cremated his body and the ashes were dispersed.

Jataka Stories

One of the early beliefs of Buddhism was that the Master was the last in a long series of transmigrations as an Enlightened Being or Bodhisattva. In these previous births as a prince, an animal or even a bird, the Bodhisattva performed many deeds of kindness and rescue before achieving his final birth as Gautama. The stories of these previous births of the Bodhisattva are known as Jatakas; they are among the most popular legends of early Buddhism. The following are some of the best-known Jatakas.

The hero of the Chhaddanta Jataka is a six-tusked elephant. Out of jealous rage, one of the elephant's two wives managed to be born again as a beautiful maiden. She married the king of Varanasi and persuaded him to engage a hunter to bring her Chhaddanta's tusks. Though wounded, Chhaddanta pitied the hunter and even helped him saw off his own tusks. At the sight of these, the queen died of remorse.

In the Mahakapi Jataka, the Bodhisattva as a monkey lived with his animal retinue on the fruits of a mango tree beside the Ganga river. But these fruits were also desired by the king of Varanasi. About to be killed by the king's followers, the Bodhisattva used his body as a bridge across the water so that the other animals could escape. A rival monkey took this opportunity to kill the Bodhisattva. The king, moved at the Bodhisattva's self-sacrifice, gently lifted down his corpse.

In the Ruru Jataka, the Bodhisattva appears as a golden deer who rescues a drowning man. Ungratefully, the man reported to his king the place where this deer could be hunted. However, before the king could shoot the Bodhisattva, the deer informed the king of his retainer's misdeed. The Bodhisattva is also a deer in the Nigrodhamriga Jataka, where he was trapped with other deer in the king's park; he offered himself for slaughter instead of a pregnant doe who had been selected. At this self-sacrifice, the king granted immunity to all the deer.

As a serpent king in the Samkhapala Jataka, the Bodhisattva lay on an ant-hill, where he was maltreated by a party of men. Alara, a householder, took pity on him and delivered him from persecution by offering money to the men. In turn, Samkhapala entertained his rescuer with great pleasures. The Bodhisattva hero of the Champeyya Jataka is also a naga king. He was captured and had to perform for a snake-charmer in the presence of the king of Varanasi. The king's wife took pity on him and had him released.

Another popular Jataka relates the story of the Bodhisattva as Prince Vessantara, who was banished from his kingdom together with his wife and two children. Living in a forest hermitage, the prince gave away all of his possessions, including even his children and his wife, to satisfy the needs of others. In recognition of his unbounded generosity, the family was eventually reunited by the gods.

In the Mahajanaka Jataka, the Bodhisattva as a prince was shipwrecked on an island, where he married Sivali. Eventually, he decided to renounce the world; Sivali attempted unsuccessfully to dissuade him. In the Sama Jataka, the Bodhisattva cared for his blind parents. One day he was accidentally killed with a poisoned arrow shot by the king of Varanasi, who was out hunting. Full of remorse, the king offered his services to the parents. In time, the boy was miraculously restored to life.

The Bodhisattva Ideal

As Buddhism developed into the Great Vehicle or Mahayana, the devotional focus of the religion was broadened to incorporate an increasing number of enlightened saviours. While there were several past appearances of Buddha in Bodhisattva form, a future incarnation was also imagined; this was Maitreya. By extension, Bodhisattvas were believed to exist during the present era, working continuously for the welfare of all living things. Conceived as celestial beings of immeasurable charity and compassion, Bodhisattvas delayed their own extinction into nirvana so as to serve mankind. Bodhisattvas could be adored and prayed to since their mission was to respond to all appeals.

According to the Mahayana doctrine, the heavens were populated with mighty forces of goodness represented by a host of Bodhisattvas. The chief of these from the earthly point of view was Avalokiteshvara, the Lord Who Looks Down; he is also known as Padmapani, the Lotus-Bearer. The special attribute of this Bodhisattva is compassion; his helping hand reaches out to all Buddhist worshippers. Another important Bodhisattva is Manjushri; his particular activity is to stimulate understanding, and he holds a sword to combat error and falsehood. Vajrapani, a sterner Bodhisattva, is the foe of sin and evil, and he holds a thunderbolt. In contrast, Maitreya, the future Buddha, is gentle and serene.

Although the Great Vehicle admits that the universe is full of sorrow, it is fundamentally optimistic. The world contains much good and every living thing is potentially a Bodhisattva, capable of gaining nirvana and achieving a Buddha-like nature. As an extension of the Bodhisattva ideal, there is the notion that Buddha was not a mere man but an earthly expression of a divine being. Buddha as Amitabha, Immeasurable Glory, is the presiding deity of the Mahayana heaven. He also manifests the compassion of the Bodhisattva; at his touch, lotuses open to give birth to countless blessed beings. Amitabha, Gautama and Avalokiteshvara play a dominant role in Mahayana theology because they belong to this region of the universe and to this period of cosmic time.

There is also the concept of five Buddhas who are each identified with a directional paradise: thus Akshobhya (east), Amitabha (west), Amogasiddhi (north), Ratnasambhava (south) and Vairochana, who is a central figure. These celestial beings are accompanied by diverse consorts, attendants and fierce guardians, who are often grouped together into complicated pantheons.

Tirthankara Stories

Parshvanatha and Mahavira, the only Tirthankaras for whom any historicity is claimed, are believed to be the last two of a series of twenty-four Jain saviours. Other Tirthankaras who are particularly popular are the first of the series, known as Adinatha or Rishabhanatha, as well as Neminatha and Parshvanatha, the twenty-second and twenty-third respectively.

The lives of the Tirthankaras are described in considerable detail in Jain sacred literature. The legends of the different saviours follow a standard pattern, which is surprisingly similar to that adopted for Buddha's life. Tirthankara stories invariably begin with the previous births of the saviour as well as his appearance in the dreams of his mother prior to his birth. Then come the episodes connected with the youth of the Tirthankara as a young prince, especially the tales of the young saviour taking different forms to win games against his adversaries or to crush his opponents. The next great event is the renunciation in which the youthful hero gives away his possessions; he leaves the palace and takes up the practice of austerities. The moment of enlightenment is described in some detail since it represents the moment of spiritual transformation. The final episode relates the death or nirvana of the Tirthankara.

The most important Jain myth is the story of Mahavira. This begins with his previous lives before he descended to earth to be born as the son of the mortal woman Trishala. According to tradition, Mahavira had already achieved the status of Tirthankara before being born. His birth was announced by a number of auspicious motifs that appeared to Trishala in her dreams; these included an elephant, a lion, a garland, the moon, the sun, a tree, a lotus lake, a heap of jewels and a smokeless fire.

In his youth Mahavira was bathed by the god Indra. On one occasion, which is frequently depicted, a god decided to shatter Mahavira's courage by taking the form of a serpent, but the young hero merely picked up the snake and threw it to one side. The enraged god then took the form of a playful opponent and the two fought. Eventually the god appeared in his true form and revered Mahavira.

At the age of thirty, after his parents had died, Mahavira took off his princely attire and shaved his head. He left the palace and began his quest for salvation by practising various austerities. At first he wore a single garment which he never changed; later he laid this aside and spent the rest of his life naked. While meditating he was attacked by serpents, bulls and other animals who were created by hostile gods; cowherds beat the ascetic with their whips and even stuck spikes into his ears; a beautiful girl was sent to distract him.

In the thirteenth year of these penances Mahavira successfully achieved enlightenment and became a Jina or Conqueror. He soon gained a great reputation and a large following. For thirty years he travelled around central and eastern India propounding his doctrine of enlightenment before dying of self-starvation and thereby achieving eternal nirvana.

Another popular Jain story relates the life of Bahubali, the son of the first Tirthankara. After his father's renunciation, Bahubali's elder brother, Bharata, began to conquer the universe, though this was resisted by Bahubali. The result was a duel between the two brothers. Just as he was about to defeat his brother, Bahubali became aware of the futility of the struggle and renounced the world. As an ascetic, he practised severe penances, standing naked in the open, lost in meditation. So long did he maintain this position that a thicket of vines climbed up his limbs, enveloping his legs and arms; his hair grew long until it hung down over his shoulders. He is depicted in this stance at Shravana Belgola in southern India in what is the largest free-standing figural sculpture in India.

Khajuraho, Kandariya Mahadeva Temple, wall sculptures, 11th century

FOUR

HINDU GODS AND GODDESSES

A vast panorama of male and female deities, semi-divine beings and quasi-mythical heroes and saints unfolds in the popular epics and legends of Hinduism. This rich diversity of celestial personalities is only occasionally ordered into a systematic pantheon, which varies considerably according to the cult affiliation of the principal divinity. Themes of cosmic creation and destruction underlie all of these myriad appearances and emanations, since gods and goddesses are constantly engaged in an eternal struggle with evil forces.

Creation and Destruction

As in Buddhist and Jain cosmologies, Hindu views of the universe are also cyclical. One era follows another in a repetitive sequence which inevitably spirals downwards, both morally and spiritually. Eventually, a great fire consumes all that exists and the universe is dissolved in the cosmic ocean. This destruction does not signal the end of the cyclic process; it is merely a prelude to the re-creation of the universe and the beginning of a new cosmic era.

A single era of creation–destruction is sometimes described as one day in the life of Brahma, the active creator of the universe; alternatively, the blinking of an eyelid of the god Vishnu may encompass a complete human life-span. In this way, Hindu mythology expresses the relationship between divine and human time-scales.

The cycle of creation–destruction is also related to concepts of light and darkness as personified by the gods and demons. The complex themes of Hindu mythology are dominated by the conflict between good and evil. Since time is cyclical not linear, neither good nor evil can triumph for long. Deities fight ongoing battles against demons and other powerfully opposed forces, but they are also related in some way to their adversaries. The conflict between good and evil is expressed as a continuous tension; there is no final resolution.

This dependent relationship between opposing forces is vividly illustrated in the celebrated creation myth of the churning of the milky ocean. According to this story, the serpent Shesha wrapped himself conveniently around the column-like mountain that stood in the ocean that preceded all creation. The gods grasped the head of the serpent and the demons the tail. By alternately pulling and pushing Shesha, a twisting motion was set up by which the mountain churned the ocean. This produced all that exists in the universe, including amrita, the prized nectar of immortality.

Fertility and Prosperity

'The gods always play where groves are, near rivers, mountains and springs, and in towns with pleasure gardens,' advises the Brihatsamhita, an ancient text on astronomy. The landscape is imbued with a potential sanctity: mountain tops, caves, rivers, springs, lakes and trees are all places where gods, goddesses and semi-divine beings manifest themselves. These deities are identified with their geographical settings as mountain gods, river goddesses or tree spirits. Such divinities embody the beneficial forces of nature as expressed through fertility and good fortune. They appear repeatedly at the gateways and doorways of sacred monuments, their auspicious powers providing an effective barrier against all evil. Nor are these deities worshipped only by Hindus: Buddhists and Jains also pay them respect.

Chief among these nature divinities are the yakshas and their king, Kubera. These creatures are associated with prosperity since they watch over the riches of the earth. They protect the household from negative influences by serving as guardians and door-keepers or dvarapalas; in these roles they are provided with clubs and other weapons. In Jainism, the yakshas and their consorts appear as attendants of the Tirthankaras.

Related to the yakshas are the mischievous and playful imps known as ganas. Their lord, Ganesha or Ganapati, is the son of the Hindu goddess Parvati. Ganesha is of great importance because he is the remover of all obstacles. His invocation is essential at the commencement of any undertaking, such as building a house, writing a book or performing a religious ceremony. The elephant head by which the god is most easily recognized and the tiny rat that accompanies him are symbols of his ability to overcome obstructions, both large and small.

Yakshis and apsarases comprise another important category of folk deities: these auspicious females are identified with animals, trees and sacred waters. As an aspect of fertility, the yakshi often appears as a beautiful female embracing a tree which she gently kicks, a gesture by which she imparts her fruitful energy to the tree. Yakshis are accompanied by a particular animal or even a child, as is Ambika, the mother goddess in Jainism. The yakshis and their male companions, the yakshas, engage in warm embraces; such intimacy becomes sexual in frank depictions of copulation.

Similar to the yakshis are the apsarases, the courtesans of the gods and the heavenly dancers; they are the perfect dispensers of sensual delights and erotic bliss. Ganga and Yamuna embody the purifying powers of the sacred rivers; they are ubiquitous themes at doorways. Ganga is heavenly in origin; she winds around the sacred mountain of Shiva and descends to earth at the insistence of King Bhagiratha.

Another popular deity is Shri or Lakshmi, the goddess of beauty and fortune. Though she is sometimes considered the consort of Vishnu, she is also worshipped for her own powers to confer material abundance. Her identification with the lotus flower indicates her aquatic nature, for she was born from the life-giving forces of the immortal ocean. The goddess of knowledge and art, Sarasvati, is also of aquatic origin; she is the patroness of speech, song and wisdom. On occasions, Sarasvati appears as the consort of the god Brahma.

The serpent deities known as nagas are also of importance among these nature divinities. Dwelling in the underground recesses, nagas are the keepers of the life energy that is stored in springs, wells and pools; they bestow prosperity, heal sickness and grant wishes. As such, they are held in great awe and veneration.

Aspects of Shiva

In his developed form, the popular Hindu god Shiva arose out of the commingling of many separate deities. As the Great Lord (Maheshvara or Mahadeva) and the supreme principle of the universe, Shiva is worshipped for his essential characteristic of energy, which is interpreted as a direct expression of the inner workings of the cosmos. This energy dominates the diverse aspects and mythological appearances of the god; it is manifested in the guise of fertility or as a force of destruction; it is even inwardly directed to achieve the powerful meditation that characterizes the god in his ascetic role. Sexuality and asceticism are both typical of the god's personality.

Shiva is worshipped most directly in the form of an erect phallus, known as the linga. This cult of phallus worship forcefully expresses the creative energy of the god but is also accorded a profound theological significance. Shiva is also worshipped as Pashupati, Lord of Animals, and is generally accompanied by the bull Nandi. In his destructive aspect, the god directs his energy outwards to annihilate demons and the enemies of his worshippers. Shiva is the god of the battlefield, the cremation grounds and the inauspicious crossroads, where he is accompanied by ghosts, evil spirits, dwarf-like imps or ganas, and dogs. It is in this form that Shiva is known as Bhairava, the destroyer of forces that threaten the well-being of the gods.

No less characteristic of Shiva is his role as the originator and exponent of various artistic accomplishments. He is the Lord of the Dance, Nataraja, pacing out the cosmic steps of destruction–creation, the most vivid symbolic expression of his energy. In complete contrast, Shiva is also the ascetic seated among the peaks of his sacred mountain, Kailasa; here, his energy is directed inwards as he meditates upon the nature of the universe. In this aspect, Shiva is usually accompanied by his consort Parvati, the daughter of the Himalayas. In yet another manifestation, the god is the lord of mental and physical Yoga, the repository of all knowledge.

Incarnations of Vishnu

This god is the embodiment of the qualities of mercy and goodness. Vishnu preserves the balance between the ordered and the disruptive forces of the cosmos. He is also responsible for the creation of the universe and its final destruction. According to a celebrated cosmic myth, Vishnu sleeps in the primeval ocean upon the serpent Shesha, dreaming the scheme of the universe. From his navel a lotus stalk emerges, opening into a flower to reveal Brahma, the god actually concerned with the task of creation.

The cult of Vishnu owes its inception to a monotheistic devotional movement that promoted the notion of a composite god who appeared in a number of different incarnations. Vishnu combines the man-god Vasudeva–Krishna with the creator-god Narayana known in the Vedas. Vishnu rides on Garuda, the eagle, and his consort is the goddess Shri or Lakshmi.

The doctrine of incarnations forms an important part of the cult of Vishnu. The term avatara, literally 'descent', is applied to Vishnu's appearance on earth in the form of an animal or man, or a combination of both, to preserve the well-being of mankind. The number of incarnations is usually fixed as ten. The first three avataras of fish, tortoise and boar present Vishnu as the hero of myths concerned with the creation of earth and its rescue from floods in times of crisis. Vishnu as the tortoise supports the column-like mountain in the myth of the churning of the cosmic ocean. As Varaha the boar, Vishnu raises the earth, personified by the goddess Bhu, from the clutches of the serpent demon who had held her captive at the bottom of the ocean.

As the cult of Vishnu developed, other incarnations were added, such as Narasimha, the man-lion, in which Vishnu appears in a revengeful and terrifying form, and the Vamana or dwarf incarnation, in which the god transforms himself into the giant Trivikrama, who paces out the universe in three great strides.

In the following three incarnations of Parashurama, Rama and Krishna, Vishnu comes to live among men as a warrior prince. Rama is the hero of the Ramayana, one of the most popular Hindu epics (see p. 42). Krishna, around whom a vast mass of legends has been gathered, is the charioteer of Arjuna, one of the five heroic Pandava brothers in the other popular Hindu epic, the Mahabharata. In this guise, Krishna delivers the celebrated sermon of the Bhagavad Gita, one of the most beautifully composed religious texts of Hinduism. Krishna is also the child-god, the youthful lover of the gopis, who tend the cows, and also the wise ruler. His story is told in the Krishnalila, where it forms the subject of much romantic poetry and art (see p. 43).

The last two incarnations of Vishnu are Buddha and Kalki. The inclusion of Buddha was originally intended to discredit Buddhists by depicting them as the victims of a false form of Vishnu. As Kalki, Vishnu appears as a man riding a horse, heralding the destruction of the present era.

Forms of Shakti

The worship of the female principle in India can be traced to a remote past and a cult of a goddess may have existed among pre-Aryan peoples. Female emblems dating back to these early phases of Indian civilization represent the yoni, which is the female counterpart of the phallic linga. In later centuries, these female emblems came to be worshipped as manifestations of Shakti or Devi, the Great Mother.

In Hinduism, as in certain schools of Mahayana Buddhism, a goddess is often considered to be the embodiment of male strength; as such, she is described as his Energy or Shakti. This goddess, who is mother of all, embodies the child-bearing, nourishing and maternal principles and is connected with the life-giving waters and lotus flowers. The variety of names and alternative forms that she assumes demonstrates her all-embracing nature.

The idea of Shakti as the creative energy of the god causes her to be associated with Shiva, with whom she develops her most characteristic features. The eternal Hindu couple Shiva–Shakti is represented by the conjunction of the male and female sexual emblems, the linga and the yoni. In Buddhism, the sexual union of the Bodhisattva with his appropriate female saviour or Tara expresses the same idea. Also of importance in this goddess cult is her multiple appearance as a group of mothers, the Matrikas, who are the personified energies of the principal gods.

According to a corpus of particular Hindu myths, Shakti is the combined energies of all the gods, who created her and equipped her with weapons so that she might destroy Mahisha, the buffalo demon whose power threatened the heavens. In her forceful and destructive role she is Durga, who rides the lion or tiger, pursuing evil throughout the universe. She becomes the fearful Chamunda or Kali, the embodiment of the negative principle, the symbol of death. In these terrifying forms she is sometimes considered the presiding deity of famine or diseases such as smallpox. Similarly fierce goddesses inhabit the Mahayana Buddhist pantheon, which incorporates a wide range of demonesses and sorceresses or dakinis.

In her peaceful aspect as Parvati, known also as Gauri or Uma, Shakti is worshipped as the consort of Shiva. Here, she personifies the passive, benevolent and philosophical nature of her lord. This peaceful goddess is also popular in Buddhism, where she expresses the merciful qualities of the Bodhisattva.

Some sects of Hindus and Buddhists worship Shakti as the ultimate principle of the universe. These sects are known as Tantric, after their scriptures, the Tantras. Cosmic energy is personified by the goddess Kundalini, who is likened to the coiled serpent that activates the chakras or nodes of energy located along the spine. The highest chakra in the head or brain is represented as a thousand-petalled lotus in the centre of which occurs the final union of Shiva and Shakti. In another of her Tantric forms, Shakti appears as a group of yoginis who possess magical powers. Shakti is also represented in diagrammatic form as a mystical pattern or yantra. Shri Yantra, which is one of the most common diagrams, consists of nine intersecting triangles within a square frame; the four triangles pointing up symbolize the male principle, while the female principle is indicated by the five triangles pointing down.

Other Deities

As well as Shiva, Vishnu and Shakti, there are other important deities, some of which also appear in Buddhism and Jainism, demonstrating the shared traditions of these different religions.

Perhaps the only god who approaches the popularity of the major Hindu cults is the solar divinity, Surya. The sun is worshipped as the supreme soul, the creator of the universe and the source of all life. Surya rides a chariot which is drawn across the sky by seven horses under the guidance of Aruna, the personification of dawn. There are also the nine 'planets', the Navagrahas, which include both the sun and moon. These planets form the basis upon which horoscopes are cast: as such, they play an important role in everyday life. Chandra, the moon god, is identified with soma, the essence of life, and with amrita, the beverage of immortality.

While the god Brahma is sometimes connected with the act of creating the universe, he is mostly subservient to the other deities, for whom he performs various sacrifices. There is also the eternally youthful and chaste battle god, the head of the celestial armies; he is known as Karttikeya, Kumara, Skanda or Subrahmanya, and rides on a peacock. Legends give different accounts of the birth of this deity, who is believed in some myths to have grown from Shiva's semen that fell into the Ganga, and in others to have been brought up by the six stars of the Pleiades constellation.

The Dikpalas are the regents of the eight directions of space and are also popular in Jainism. Some of the Dikpalas are important Vedic deities: thus Indra, the lord of the heavens, holding a thunderbolt and riding on the elephant; Agni, the fire god; and Varuna, the embodiment of the waters, accompanied by an aquatic monster. Another Dikpala is Yama, the lord of death, who is recognized by the noose with which he drags his victims into the underworld.

The Ramayana

Of the two great Hindu epics, the Ramayana is more important for sacred art. The narrative is a vast poem of more than 24,000 couplets; it exists both in a Sanskrit version by Valmiki and in translations in the different regional languages. Though Rama is believed to be an avatara of Vishnu, this identification with the godhead is a later addition; his portrayal is more human than religious in character.

The main characters of the story are Dasharatha, the king of Ayodhya, and his four sons, who are Rama, the oldest, Bharata, Lakshmana and Shatrughna, by three wives. The four sons attend the court of King Janaka, where Rama wins the hand of Janaka's daughter Sita in an archery contest. Rama and Sita are married and live happily at the court of Dasharatha. When Dasharatha grows old and it is time to choose the heir, he is reminded by his second queen, Kaikeyi, of a promise to grant her a boon. She demands that her own son, Bharata, become the heir. Reluctantly, Dasharatha complies, and Rama and Sita together with Lakshmana are banished to the forest. When Dasharatha dies from grief, Bharata rules the kingdom, but only as regent for the exiled Rama.

In the following scenes, Rama, Lakshmana and Sita dwell as hermits with the forest sages. Bharata visits Rama and begs him to return; Rama refuses. The heroes encounter demons, especially the ogress Shurpanakha, whose nose is cut off by Lakshmana. Shurpanakha's brother is Ravana, the wicked king of Sri Lanka, and he plots his revenge. Ravana assumes the form of a golden deer which diverts Rama and Lakshmana away from the hermitage. Then, posing as an old man, Ravana grabs Sita and abducts her in his aerial chariot. The bird Jatayu tries to intercept Ravana but is struck down; before dying, Jatayu relates the fate of Sita to the hero brothers.

While wandering through the forest in search of Sita, Rama and Lakshmana meet Sugriva, the monkey chief, and his general, Hanuman. They help Sugriva to recover his kingdom. Hanuman, a favourite character in the story, discovers Sita in captivity and brings her Rama's ring as a mark of trust. With the aid of the monkey allies, Rama and Lakshmana cross over to Sri Lanka, where after a long and heated battle they defeat Ravana. Sita is rescued and the couple reunited.

The final chapters describe Rama's rejection of Sita. Since she had dwelt in the palace of Ravana, her purity was in question. She throws herself on a funeral pyre, but the fire god, Agni, refuses to accept her body, thus proving her innocence. After their return to Ayodhya, Rama is crowned, to live long and righteously. But Rama is forced to banish Sita, who takes refuge in a forest hermitage, where she gives birth to twins. As final demonstration of her innocence she calls on her earth mother to swallow her up and she disappears. Soon after this Rama returns to heaven to merge with the god Vishnu.

Krishnalila

Vishnu's incarnation as Krishna forms the subject for another popular narrative, which is among the best-loved stories in Indian literature. It is known in a variety of versions, one of the most widespread being the Gita Govinda, which was composed by the poet Jayadeva at the beginning of the 13th century.

During the rule of the wicked King Kamsa, Krishna is born at Mathura in central India as the son of a humble woman, Devaki. Since it has been prophesied that Kamsa will be killed by one of Devaki's sons, Kamsa sets out to destroy all of her children. But Krishna and his brother Balarama are saved and are brought up away from Mathura by the cowherd Nanda and his wife, Yashoda. As a child, the god is full of mischief. He steals butter, kicks his guardians' cart and drags a stone mortar to which he is chained, thereby uprooting two trees and liberating two brothers who had been imprisoned there by a curse. He kills the ogress Putana by sucking at her breast; he also vanquishes the whirlwind demon, subdues the wicked serpent Kaliya by dancing on his hoods and fights the crane demon.

Then follow numerous episodes describing the romantic adolescent dallying with the gopis, who tend the cows; his favourite is Radha. Krishna conceals the clothes of the bathing gopis and then hides up a tree. He lifts up Govardhana mountain with one finger to shelter the flocks from Indra's storm; he drinks in the flames of a forest fire to save the herds.

When he comes of age, Krishna returns to Mathura, at which the gopis faint in grief. On his way, he fights the bull, horse and elephant demons; he wrestles with bodyguards to gain admittance to the palace of Kamsa. When Krishna arrives at Kamsa's throne he pulls him down and kills him. Krishna then makes Rukmini his chief queen and rules in peace from his new capital at Dwarka in western India.

Krishna's adventures at this stage in his career include the destruction of demons all over the country. Throughout the Mahabharata he appears as the friend and adviser of the Pandava brothers; he preaches the great sermon of the Bhagavad Gita to Arjuna before the battle which is the climax of the epic story.

After seeing the Pandavas safely installed, Krishna returns to Dwarka, but evil besets the city. In time, Krishna is forced to abandon his kingdom; he is eventually shot by a hunter who mistakes him for a deer. The city of Dwarka is then swallowed by the sea.

Shravana Belgola, monolithic Gommateshvara image, 10th century

FIVE

SACRED ART

The sculptures and mural paintings of India's religious monuments give visual form to superhuman powers while constantly expressing the auspicious and protective forces of nature. Long-standing artistic conventions govern the forms and details of figures, animals and plants; the result is a strictly controlled but vivid iconography.

Votive Images

Images of saviours or deities that serve as the principal objects of devotion are invariably located within the sanctuaries of shrines and temples. They may also be placed in wall niches or at gateways and doorways. Votive images are sometimes shown together with other gods, goddesses and semi-divine beings; they are accompanied by their consorts and attendants.

Whether carved or painted, these figures follow well-defined conventions. Such control is considered necessary if a sculpture or a mural is to be satisfactorily identified with the sacred presence. Figural art is dominated by ancient texts which set out rules for image-making; these guide both the artist and the worshipper through the bewildering array of saviours, divinities and other mythological beings.

A well-executed image follows the proportional measurements prescribed in the texts; the face-length, or tala, is usually given as the regulating module. Further classification is based upon facial expression, bodily posture, hand gesture, emblems held in the hands, costume, ornament and even colour. The result of this rigorous codification is an overall standardization of figural forms. Within such constraints, however, Indian sculptors and painters were able to express considerable artistry.

Figural Conventions

Particular physical types have been developed in Indian art. For male figures, the shoulders and chest are broad, the waist slim, but the stomach slightly overflows the belt; the limbs are solid and somewhat cylindrical. For female figures, jewellery, heavy spherical breasts, narrow waist, ample hips and a graceful posture are preferred. Heads are fully modelled, sometimes with triple folds at the neck and elongated earlobes. There is no attempt to portray details of physical anatomy such as musculature; rather, it is the quality of prana, the inwardly held breath, that is conveyed. This breath is identified with the essence of life, the control of which is the object of religious discipline. The celestial beings of Buddhist, Jain and Hindu art have their bodies tautly drawn, as if containing a pressure from within. The protruding stomach of minor divinities conveys prosperity and well-being, as in the pot-bellied figures of Kubera and Ganesha. In contrast, the emaciated and skeletal bodies of Shiva and Kali express terror and horror.

In order to communicate superhuman qualities, figural art frequently multiplies the heads and arms. Mythology provides explanations for these departures from human anatomy. The four heads of Brahma were created so that god could gaze incestuously in all directions upon his daughter. Karttikeya's six heads indicate his celestial origins in the six stars of the Pleiades constellation. Shiva is also sometimes depicted with multiple heads. At Elephanta in the Deccan the god's peaceful and destructive personalities are depicted in the side heads that flank the central impassive face.

Bodhisattva figures of the Mahayana pantheon, as well as most Hindu divinities, generally have four or more arms. Some of the hands carry emblems, while others make meaningful gestures. Whenever a god takes 'human' form, as in Vishnu's incarnations as Parashurama, Rama and Krishna, there are no duplicated heads and arms. 'Human' forms are also preferred for Buddhist and Jain saviours, as well as for images of quasi-mythical saints and teachers.

Of particular interest are the composite images. Harihara, in which Shiva and Vishnu are joined together, is depicted as a male figure with four arms; each half-figure displays the emblems and characteristic headdress of one god. Ardhanarish-vara is a composite image, one side of which represents Shiva, the other Parvati. The resulting figure presents a curious appearance with only one breast and a single female hip and shoulder.

Posture, Gesture and Expression

Though standing figures constitute the largest category of votive images, there are also seated figures. These are usually shown in padmasana, the meditation posture, with the soles of the feet turned up, or with one or both legs hanging down. Deities sit on a double-petalled lotus, which is a symbol of divine perfection, or on a royal throne with lion-like supports.

Standing postures are inflected by tilting the axis of the body; the favourite mode employs three bends (tribhanga) of the head, torso and legs. But the principal cult figures are often static; the Tirthankaras, in particular, are characterized by their rigidly erect or seated postures. Among the reclining images are Buddha's Parinirvana and Vishnu on the serpent Shesha.

Sacred figures become more animated when depicted in attitudes of destruction and hunting. Provocative postures, expressive of an undisguised sexuality, are common, particularly for goddesses and female attendants, dancers and musicians. That there was a close connection between figural art and sacred dance is obvious in images of Shiva pacing out the steps of creation–destruction, or of the same god performing his victory dance upon the prostrate body of his victim.

Mudras, the gestures of the hands, are particularly significant in India's sacred art. Buddhist and Jain figures were the first to express the importance of hand gestures, and this practice was developed in later Hindu art. The positions of the fingers and thumbs express the essential nature of saviours and deities, in both their benign and fearful aspects. The uplifted outward-facing palm bestows grace upon the worshipper; the downward palm signifies submission. The palms laid one upon the other in the lap signify meditation; the fingers held together as if untying an invisible knot indicate the act of teaching.

Facial expressions of divine figures are mostly introspective, detached and other-worldly; meditating faces generally have the eyelids fully lowered. This calm expression is sometimes retained even when deities are engaged in violent pursuits, thus contrasting with energetic bodily postures. Fierce facial expressions portray destructive moods; the eyes protrude in a demonic stare, the opened mouth displays fangs and the tongue drips blood. But for the majority of sacred figures there is a constant facial type. In goddesses, the face is rather full, with fish-shaped eyes above which are the eyebrows in the contour of an arched bow; the nose is sharply defined and the lips are full. The facial type for male deities is often similar, there being little attempt to distinguish male and female.

Costume and Headdress

Early Buddhist figures depict the Master as a monk with coiled hair. Buddha is simply attired in a long robe, sometimes with fluted pleatings, through which the body is clearly visible; there is a small top-knot on the head. The circular halo behind the head signifies Buddha's celestial nature; it is ornamented with lotus designs and even flames. Tirthankaras are similarly depicted with coiled hair and haloes. Digambara saints are shown completely naked; Bahubali is recognized by the creepers that wind round his undressed limbs. Jain figures are sometimes distinguished by the diamond-like tuft of hair known as shrivatsa in the middle of the chest. Other naked figures include Shiva as Bhikshatanamurti, the wandering beggar. As Dakshinamurti, Shiva is dressed in the simple attire of a holy man with the sacred thread of the brahmin passing across one shoulder.

More usually, deities are richly attired in royal costume and headdress. Some Bodhisattvas have pleated costumes bedecked with elaborate jewelled belts, necklaces, arm-bands and flowing tassels. Crowns are also worn; Maitreya, for instance, is identified by the miniature seated Buddha figure set into his headdress. Hindu deities also appear in royal attire, with jewelled belts, bracelets and earrings. Costumes for male figures often flow outwards in pleats and tassels. Although females may be shown mostly unclothed, they are still festooned with jewels and hair ornaments.

Vishnu wears a tall cylindrical crown with a disc-like halo attached to the rear. Shiva's hair is long, matted and mostly piled up; it is sometimes decorated with a small skull, a crescent moon and a miniature female figure that represents the goddess Ganga. The ears are dissimilar, one being long and pendulous with a large earring hanging from it; a third eye is placed vertically in the centre of the forehead. Shiva is sometimes draped with snakes, which serve him as scarves, bracelets and belts. He is decked in the skin of the tiger or the elephant that he has just killed; he even wears garlands of human skulls. Of unusual interest is the costume of Surya, who wears foreign boots and a long cloak.

Emblems

As physical appearance does not distinguish one figure from another, identification usually relies upon the emblems held in the hands or placed beneath the feet. On occasions these emblems are venerated as independent objects: the footprints, or pada, of Buddha represent the Master's presence; those of Vishnu are worshipped as divine.

Compassionate Bodhisattvas hold emblems which indicate their perfected knowledge, such as the lotus flower, rosary of beads, water pot or book. The sword and the thunderbolt symbolize their constant battle against evil and delusion. The thunderbolt is also the emblem of the Vajrayana school of Tantric Buddhism.

In the cult of Shiva, the linga or phallic emblem represents the procreative energy of the god. In his quasi-human form, Shiva is provided with different weapons, in particular the three-pronged trishula. He also carries the rattling drum, half-skull begging-bowl and noose to suggest his connection with death. Two emblems of Vishnu are imbued with a special significance. The shankha, or conch shell, serves as a symbol of eternal space and the heavenly atmosphere; when blown, it produces the sound of the primeval waters. The chakra, or wheel-like discus, represents eternal time and the power to destroy all things. Figures guarding the sanctuaries of Shiva and Vishnu display the same emblems as those held by their respective deities.

Variety and arrangement of emblems are also important. In addition to the ten incarnations of Vishnu, this god also appears in twenty-four forms, which can only be distinguished by the different combination of two emblems and two hand gestures. There are many other emblems: for example, ritual instruments, such as rosaries, ladles, water pots and thunderbolts; musical instruments, both stringed and percussive; flowers and mirrors expressive of female beauty; and a wide range of war and hunting weapons, including bows and arrows, swords, spears, clubs and daggers.

Emblems are sometimes transformed into human form; Vishnu's attendant figures are personifications of the conch and the discus. Lingas are adorned with one or four human faces, indicating the outward radiation of Shiva's energy. Known as mukhalingas, these emblems are striking examples of the intermingling of figural and symbolic forms.

Hybrid Figures

Combinations of human, animal and bird features result in a remarkable series of hybrid figures. The fierce guardians of Mahayana Buddhism and many Hindu deities are depicted with human bodies and animal heads, or with animal bodies and human heads. As the fish and tortoise, Vishnu is a hybrid creature with a human head attached to a fish or tortoise body. In the god's Varaha and Narasimha incarnations, these human and animal components are reversed; the god has the head of a boar or of a lion upon a human body. As Vaikuntha, Vishnu displays boar and lion heads on either side of a central human head. Kalki, the last of Vishnu's incarnations, sometimes appears as a horse-headed human figure.

Semi-divine beings and fantastic creatures also take hybrid forms. Paramount among these are the nagas or serpents, whose divine nature is indicated by multiple cobra heads. Human and reptilian aspects are sometimes combined, with a human figure sheltered by a canopy of hoods. Buddha is protected from Mara's evil temptations by Muchalinda; Vishnu sleeps upon the coils of Shesha.

The mythological bird Garuda is the traditional enemy of the serpents and sometimes holds a pair of these in his eagle-like claws. Garuda mostly appears in hybrid form, with a human torso and bird beak, wings and claws. Among the other hybrid creatures are the kinnaras with wings, bird-like feet and plumed tails; their human hands play stringed instruments. Pot-bellied ganas often have animal heads; they are typically depicted in playful and obscene postures. The lord of the ganas, Ganesha, is distinguished by his elephant head with a broken tusk, all that remained after he had hurled part of it in anger at the moon.

Buddhist and Jain Narratives

Illustrations of the lives of Buddha and Mahavira are generally confined to isolated episodes. In fact, Buddha never appears in early Indian art since Buddhist theology at first prevented the worship of the Master as a celestial figure; instead, pictorial devices were invented to indicate key episodes. The nativity is symbolized by Lakshmi in her lotus pond; more commonly, Maya clutches the branch of an overhanging tree in the act of giving birth. A riderless horse sheltered by a parasol indicates the departure of Buddha from the palace. After he cuts off his hair, this rises to heaven as an object of veneration. An empty seat beneath the bodhi tree, surrounded by the evil host of Mara or by devotees, represents Buddha in meditation at Bodhgaya. A throne associated with a spoked disc, sometimes elevated on a column, refers to the first sermon at Sarnath. A staircase leading to heaven, in the presence of assembled worshippers, and a platform seemingly floating on the waters indicate the miracles that Buddha performed, such as that of levitation. The stupa adored by worshippers, including even elephants, commemorates Buddha's death. Battle scenes suggest the wars over the Master's relics.

In later Buddhist art the Master himself is shown; but these narratives are also restricted in scope. Panels depict Buddha as a young prince in the palace; leaving the palace on horseback; seated beneath the bodhi tree; receiving the first meal after his enlightenment; and subduing the wicked elephant sent by Devadatta. Meditating and teaching images of the Master are the most common. The Parinirvana is occasionally the subject of a separate composition, as in the monumental reclining figure of the Master at Ajanta in the Deccan.

The numerous legends that have gathered around the lives of the Tirthankaras resemble those of Buddha. As in Buddhist art, Jain narrative scenes do not attempt to depict a continuous story; rather, there is the representation of key events, such as the birth of the saviour, his early life, the renunciation of worldly goods, the life of the wandering ascetic and the meditation beneath a tree that leads to enlightenment despite all manner of vividly portrayed temptations. The final scene is always that of the saviour's death in which a prostrate figure is surrounded by mourning disciples.

Ettumanur, Mahadeva Temple, 16th century

Rescue and Destruction

Among the countless images of Hindu deities, certain compositions focus on moments of miraculous appearance or intervention. Vishnu riding on Garuda descends to earth to deliver an elephant devotee who had become trapped by a wicked serpent king in a lotus pond. As Varaha, Vishnu steps out of the cosmic waters with one great stride to rescue the earth, which is personified as the diminutive goddess Bhudevi. In another incarnation, Vishnu transforms himself from a dwarf mendicant into Trivikrama, the cosmic giant who paces out the triple steps of the cosmos; this act is indicated by one leg kicked up high.

Popular representations of Shiva show him in the various myths. He leaps out of a linga to save Markandeya, the youthful devotee who is shown clutching the linga so as not to be dragged off by Yama, the regent of death. Shiva appears from another linga to settle a dispute between Vishnu and Brahma, who are sometimes shown as a boar and a goose respectively, attempting to judge the linga's height. In yet another myth, Shiva assists Ganga to descend to earth by receiving her in the matted tresses of his hair. This act is suggested by a small female figure in a strand of the god's hair.

Angry and terrifying images portray deities destroying their demonic adversaries. As Narasimha, Vishnu breaks out of a column to pounce upon the wicked Hiranyakashipu, whose entrails he then savagely devours. As Tripurantaka, Shiva appears in his chariot, lifting his bow to shoot arrows at the demon of the triple cities. The god slaughters the elephant and tiger demons, and then performs his triumphant dance holding out the animal skins. He raises his trident before energetically thrusting it into the small figure of Andhaka.

Further illustrations of this violent theme are provided by depictions of Shakti. In a popular myth, the goddess Durga rides her lion and wields a long sword as she advances on Mahisha, the buffalo demon. She is also shown slaying Mahisha in different ways: she picks up the animal by its tail before cutting off its head; she thrusts a trident deep into its body, which she fixes with her foot; she stands victorious on the decapitated buffalo head.

Sensuality and Sexuality

Themes of fecundity are considered auspicious in Indian art; maidens affirming life in all of its abundance are among the most popular and animated subjects. Posed in seductive and alluring postures, beautiful young girls are depicted with full breasts, narrow waists and ample hips; they smile pleasurably and gaze invitingly outwards. As the heavenly apsarases, they bridge the gap between gods and men, being the consorts of divinities and the seducers of humans. Turning and twisting, they transfer their generative powers to trees, which they gently kick while clutching on to a branch. As Ganga and Yamuna they embody the life-giving forces of the magical rivers.

Attendants, animals and birds are all incorporated into this theme of female sensuality. Maidens hold parrots or are accompanied by peacocks, emblems of female beauty. They are teased by monkeys, feign terror when they discover a scorpion or pick thorns out of their upturned feet.

Maidens are often depicted in intimate embrace with their male companions. Couples tenderly hold and kiss each other beneath trees; they fly through the air, their clothes billowing outwards. They copulate in an astonishing variety of sexual positions. Such an irrepressible sensuality is imbued with magical purpose; it reinforces the life-giving powers of nature. Some sexual acts, such as those shown on the temples at Khajuraho in central India, involve acrobatic postures achieved only with the aid of assistants. Sexual scenes of maidens coupling with bearded sages, warriors and even animals may refer to the ritual practices of unorthodox Hindu cults.

Music and Dance

Performances of music and dance are an integral part of religious life. In response to such activities, temple art abounds in the representations of these entertainments. Celestial orchestras include male drummers, who beat a variety of instruments, and also singers and players of stringed instruments. The participants are either human or hybrid kinnaras or ganas. Musicians accompany the gods when they dance; Shiva, for instance, is sometimes surrounded by a complete orchestra.

Beautiful maidens dance in a variety of poses that emphasize their seductive nature and their generative energy; they hold small drums, cymbals and snakes. They may appear as large free-standing dancers or as rows of miniature figures, all swaying in coordinated rhythms. Temple art sometimes illustrates dance postures according to the descriptions in dance manuals. Within the gateways at Chidambaram in southern India there are more than one hundred sculpted figures, each shown in a different dance posture.

King and Court

Courtly receptions, hunting and war are common motifs on friezes of basements, walls and beams. Such themes blend with mythical narratives and epic scenes, but they also form independent subjects. Elephants and horses in procession indicate a royal presence. The animals are richly bridled and ornamented; they are attended by riders and footmen. In military campaigns, they become magnificent war animals accompanied by soldiers bearing swords, shields and staffs. Soldiers are sometimes shown in displays of martial arts, but only rarely is there an actual battle scene. Royal figures and courtiers appear in military processions; they ride on horses or are carried in palanquins together with their retinues and armed guards. Hunting expeditions form part of the forest episodes in Jatakas and Ramayana narratives, but they also appear independently as scenes of royal privilege. Hunters armed with arrows and swords pursue deer, boar, tigers and other animals.

Coronations and courtly receptions, though less common, are another important royal motif. The king is surrounded by courtiers and consorts; he receives visiting dignitaries, reviews his troops, practises archery, converses with priests, is entertained by dancers and enjoys the attentions of his women. Such scenes become independent subjects in monuments closely connected with a particular royal sponsor, as at Konarak in eastern India.

Kingly and courtly donors are often shown in the act of paying homage to a temple deity. Dressed in full regalia, complete with elaborate crowns and jewelled costumes, such figures have their hands brought together in attitudes of reverence. They gaze fervently towards the image which is the object of their devotion.

Animals and Birds

Animals and birds play an important role in Indian art, both in their own right and as vahanas or 'vehicles' for saviours, gods and goddesses. As such, these fauna are not only a means of transportation but they also symbolize an essential aspect of the divine personality. Nandi is fully expressive of Shiva's sexuality; the seated bull is depicted naturalistically, often decked with bells and garlands. The lion or tiger mount of Durga embodies her fierce strength and is sometimes shown in an aggressive rearing posture. The river goddesses appear with their aquatic emblems, Ganga with the makara monster and Yamuna with the tortoise. Lakshmi is accompanied by elephants and lotuses; Sarasvati has a graceful swan.

Animals and birds help to identify the gods. Brahma is recognized by the goose, the elephant indicates Indra and the peacock belongs to Karttikeya. Ganesha is accompanied by a miniature rat who cannot possibly support his ample body. Animal mounts are the most convenient means of distinguishing the twenty-four Tirthankaras: for example, Adinatha stands on the bull, Ajitanatha on the elephant, Parshvanatha on the serpent and Mahavira on the lion.

As an extension of natural fauna, there exists a whole range of fantastic beasts in sacred art. Among the most common of these are the kirttimukhas, the lion-like monster masks with protruding eyes and flame-like tufts of hair; from their open mouths issue bands of jewels and garlands. The makara is an aquatic monster with an elephant head, crocodile body, tusks and scroll-like fins; it has a profusely foliated tail that hangs down and sometimes also miniature riders. More ferocious are the vyalas or yalis. These animals have lion bodies; their heads combine protruding eyes, long elephant-like snouts and curved horns. They are often shown as magnificent beasts, prancing out of control.

Plant Life

Motifs derived from vegetation are among the most popular accessory themes of sacred art. Flowers, leaves, stalks and stylized foliage appear in a seemingly limitless variety of designs. Throughout, this vegetal ornamentation evokes the generative processes of nature; the lotus floating on the watery surface serves as a ubiquitous emblem of perfection.

The most common plant is the lotus flower, which usually appears as an undulating stalk with symmetrically disposed leaves and flowers. Sometimes interwoven into lotus designs are miniature animals, birds and human figures, illustrating the teeming world of nature. Lotus petals and fully open lotuses with central buds are also popular. Lotuses are sometimes combined with geometric or multi-lobed motifs to create elaborate ceiling compositions.

This naturalism is transformed by invention into fantasy. Dense sprays of foliation and scrollwork, or even tufts of foliation, are all derived from the watery roots and stalks of the lotus plant. Representations of water pots, either overflowing with foliage or with sprays of foliation issuing from the sides, are symbols of nature's fecundity.

Puri, Jagannatha Temple, chariot festival

SIX

PRIESTS AND PILGRIMS

For the ordinary devotee in India, whether Buddhist, Jain or Hindu, the contemplation of divine forces in visible form is the most popular means of worship. This usually takes place in a temple or shrine, where devotees approach an image of the saviour, god or goddess. Priests are an indispensable part of worship; as ritual specialists their services are required on most occasions. But the worship of divine forces does not always require the setting of a temple or shrine; ascetic devotees are trained to turn their gaze inwards to concentrate on an inner image of the saviour or divinity.

Priestly Duties

As experts in sacred texts and devotional practice, temple priests are responsible for controlling the ritual life of the monument. They determine which social groups might be admitted into the sacred precinct, how they should be attired and what items they might offer to the godhead. Appropriate ceremonies of worship, whether daily, weekly or annual, are defined by priests down to the most minute detail. So too are the prayers to be recited, the music to be sung and even the costumes, jewellery and crowns that are to be worn by votive images. As the timings of all ritual events have to be fixed, priests have to consult with astrologers.

The temple is usually the centre of intellectual life in the community. Priests are required to give instruction in sacred lore, as well as grammar, astrology and mathematics. Colleges are attached to some temples expressly for the purpose of instructing young men. But there is also scope for popular education; spacious halls are settings for recitations of sacred texts, the singing of hymns and devotional chanting.

In the patronage of the arts, temple priests are responsible for directly commissioning architects and craftsmen; they also play a crucial role in the actual construction of the monument since they give advice and guidance to workmen whenever required. They perform ceremonies at crucial stages in the work, or when some accident requires atonement; they supervise consecration ceremonies, such as the purification of the site, the initial tracing of the ground plan, the setting of the crowning finial and the installation of the votive image within the sanctuary.

Temple Puja

Direct contact with the godhead is fundamental to religious life in India. Rituals are intended to promote an identification of the worshipper with the godhead. Those who are able to achieve a unity of self and godhead gain merit and access to the path that leads to liberation.

Religious literature emphasizes the willingness of saviours and deities to manifest themselves to humans; stories relate myths which explain these different appearances of the godhead. Images are only receptacles for divine forces on particular occasions. Saviours, gods and goddesses condescend to manifest themselves to aid the limited imagination of the worshipper, who may otherwise be unable to perform devotional rites. Sculptures and paintings represent the different forms of these celestial figures.

Like the image itself, the temple too is a temporary receptacle for divine forces that appear there in the forms imagined by the worshipper. Temple images or emblems can only be identified with divine presence after they have been prepared for worship by elaborate rites of consecration. Thereafter, appropriate rituals are essential to guarantee the continued manifestation of superhuman forces.

Worship of an image is known as puja. This is conceived as an evocation, reception and entertainment of the saviour, god or goddess as a royal guest. Ritual procedures are strictly codified in religious texts such as Shastras and Agamas, some of which date back to the early centuries of the Christian era. Though rituals and ceremonies in present-day India have not altered essentially from those practised in earlier periods, they have become increasingly elaborate; even so, puja for different saviours and deities follows the same basic patterns.

At the core of all devotional rituals is the opportunity for the worshipper to communicate visually with the image. This auspicious sight of the godhead is known as darshana; it is the moment when the devotee makes direct contact with the godhead. No matter how intricate the procedures of puja, the climax of all the rites is the viewing of the divine presence in a particular manifestation.

Priestly Worship

Before ceremonies in a shrine or temple can begin, the priests who are to perform the rituals must first be prepared. Bathing and other acts of purification are necessary to promote the transformation by which priests identify themselves with the object of worship. At the ceremony there is no need for any onlookers; rituals are performed on behalf of the community whose welfare is represented on these occasions.

Priestly ritual for an ordinary day consists of a number of celebrations, usually at sunrise, noon, sunset and midnight. The ceremonies begin with the reverential opening of the doors of the sanctuary which houses the image or emblem of the deity. The priest salutes the guardian figures presiding over the threshold of the sanctuary and sounds the bells and clasps his hands together in a reverential attitude before entering the chamber to attract the attention of the godhead. The priest then expresses his intention of worship and asks the divinity for consent. Hymns are recited to persuade the godhead to take visible form by inhabiting the image or emblem; once this takes place, the priest is able to converse with the divine presence. This he does by using magical verbal formulas known as mantras, and symbolic hand gestures or mudras. Such means enable the priest to draw himself into direct contact with the object of his devotions.

The saviour, god or goddess, who is otherwise considered asleep, is then awakened. Due attention is paid to the comfort of the divine presence and to the preparation of vessels and ingredients necessary for worship. The image is bathed and dressed, and anointed with oils, camphor and sandalwood. Once suitably attired, the image may be entertained by moving flames and even mirrors. Food is offered, especially cooked rice, and also milk, curd, clarified butter, honey and coconut. The image is adorned with flowers, usually in garlands. The priest may perform the rite of pradakshina, which venerates the image by circumambulating it several times in an auspicious clockwise direction. Finally, the sanctuary door is closed as the deity is once more considered to be asleep. In this manner a typical priestly ceremony is completed, to be regularly repeated during the day according to prescribed practice.

Private Worship

Other than these priestly operations, there are opportunities for private worship. Individuals visit the shrine or temple to make offerings to the saviour or deity, to recite prayers and to perform suitable circumambulations. Such private worship usually takes place in the intervals between the regular ceremonies when the godhead gives audience to the priest. Generally, a priest is employed by private worshippers; larger religious institutions display boards advertising priestly charges and the appropriate offerings for different ceremonies.

Private worship may be undertaken as the result of simple piety, or for some specific purpose, such as the hope of securing divine assistance in times of distress or sickness. Vows and presentation of offerings by the general public are an important part of temple activities. Ceremonies such as marriage, the investiture of the sacred thread for brahmin boys, which is the commencement of their religious life, oaths for law cases and even the signing of business contracts also take place in the presence of the saviour or deity. Devotees who wish to approach the image are first required to purify themselves by bathing. They then present their offerings directly to the image of the godhead, or hand them to the priest, who places them in front of the image while reciting hymns and prayers on their behalf.

Some forms of worship are more congregational in character. Performances of sacred songs and dances take place in front of a seated audience, as do recitals of mythological stories or the exposition of religious texts by learned brahmins.

Festivals

Public ceremonies of a spectacular nature occur regularly throughout the year in every important Buddhist, Jain or Hindu establishment. Some of these festivals are widely observed all over India, such as Durga Puja (September–October) or Shivaratri (February–March), both of which celebrate important cult deities. Other festivals are linked more closely with the local manifestation of a divinity at a particular shrine or temple.

Festivals may commemorate the birthday of the saint or god, the anniversary of the miraculous appearance of the deity or the 'marriage' of the god with the goddess. On such occasions, the image of the deity may be brought out of the sanctuary to be displayed in a more public place, such as an open hall or courtyard.

If the image is of a male deity he may be joined by his female consort. Together they are seated on a throne or a swinging seat, and are offered particular delicacies and entertained with performances of music and dance. There may even be animal sacrifices, such as the slaughter of a buffalo or goat to placate the goddess Durga.

Public processions of the temple deity form an important part of temple festivals. On these occasions the image is brought outside the sacred precinct to become visible to all, especially to those groups who may not usually be permitted darshana within the building. Devotees have the opportunity of directly presenting flowers, fruits and other offerings to the processional deity while it is conveyed through the village or town in a palanquin or a wheeled chariot. The most spectacular of these chariot festivals is that at Puri in eastern India, where three chariots, each carrying a divinity, are pulled up and down the main street by crowds of fervent devotees.

While the processional image is not often the same as that permanently housed within the sanctuary, it is ceremonially identified with it. Great attention is lavished on the chariot, which is often adorned with carvings, garlands and banners; sometimes it has a tower or multi-storey roof which imitates that of the temple itself. Processional images are also placed in boats to float on the ocean, a river or a temple tank before being submerged. Sometimes such images are conveyed from one minor shrine to another in order to 'visit' other deities. Such processional routes ritually define the sacred boundaries of a town and its immediate environs. In some regions, temple deities are carried long distances to shrines at other towns; here the processional routes define much larger territories.

Not all festivals have to have a processional image; sometimes the pretext for the occasion is the invisible manifestation of the godhead. A certain moment that is determined by astrologers may become the focus for all manner of ceremonies. The great Kumbha Mela at Allahabad, for instance, which is held only once every twelve years, draws the largest crowds of any festival in India. The climax of this religious occasion is the bath taken by devotees at the confluence of the sacred Ganga and Yamuna rivers.

Festivals are often linked with the agricultural life of the region, since they may coincide with the planting or harvesting of a crop, or the exchange of commodities at a fair or market. Festivals provide opportunities for the mingling of stories and legends which may be expressed in performances of music, dance and drama. The Dasara festival (September–October) is marked by enactments of episodes from the Ramayana epic; the exuberant Holi festival (February–March) celebrates the end of the cool season by relating the exploits of Krishna.

Pilgrimage

Natural features in the landscape define the holy sites of India, which are referred to as tirthas, or fords, thereby associating these sites with rivers, lakes, springs and tanks. Other typical tirthas are mountain tops, caves and trees. Shrines and temples are located at tirthas so as to benefit from the auspicious presence of sacred forces that are manifested in the landscape.

Pilgrimages to Buddhist, Jain and Hindu holy sites are generally motivated by the reward of purification of the soul, and the attainment of perpetual bliss. Devotees travel extensively, sometimes in large groups, to mountain tops, river banks, hot-water springs and natural caverns. Pilgrims may make a journey at any time, or they may wish their trip to coincide with an important religious festival.

Circuits of auspicious sites are followed by visits to a number of localities in a sequence prescribed by pilgrimage manuals. In the area around Vrindavan in central India, for example, Vaishnava devotees make the round of spots linked with the mythology of Krishna. Buddhist pilgrims make a circuit of holy sites in eastern India connected with the life of the Master; similarly, Jains in western India visit the holy mountains at Abu, Girnar and Satrunjaya, which are associated with the lives of the Tirthankaras or their followers.

Tirthas define the sacred geography of India. The four holy cities of Hinduism demarcating the cardinal directions are Hardwar in northern India, Puri in eastern India, Dwarka in western India and Kanchipuram in southern India. At Varanasi in central India, it is possible to perform a symbolic tour of all India by visiting a succession of shrines, each of which is identified with a sacred site in a different part of the country. Other holy spots are connected with the mythology of a particular divinity. Shiva's luminous energy, for example, is believed to appear miraculously at twelve holy sites known as Jyotirlingas.

Ascetic Practices

Prominent among India's pilgrims are ascetic devotees. The typical ascetic depends upon gifts from the laity for his food, clothing and shelter. He lives exclusively in a religious environment set apart from the ordinary world; he renounces the goal of earning a living. The greatest number of ascetics are affiliated with a particular religious order; others retreat to forest hermitages or wander continuously without any fixed abode.

Spiritual power is recognized as the outcome of self-control and selfless action. In Hinduism, the striving to achieve these ends is often highly individual; each ascetic or sadhu must determine his own salvation, even if he is guided by a spiritual teacher or guru. Vows of celibacy, poverty, vegetarianism and abstinence from intoxicants are common to all ascetics, whether Buddhist, Jain or Hindu. The ascetic may be versed in religious precepts and philosophy, which he expounds to his followers; alternatively, he may have taken a vow of silence.

At the core of all ascetic practice is the training by which all mental and physical states are controlled. Yoga, as these disciplines are generally known, encompasses a wide range of exercises and acts of self-discipline. The courses of training advocated in yoga emphasize the different physical postures and control of breath that are employed as an aid to mental discipline. There is the concentration on a yantra or magical diagram to focus the mind and to promote elevated states of consciousness. There may also be the contemplation of a mantra, or magical syllable, that signifies the cult affiliation of the ascetic sect.

Monastic Orders

The founders of Buddhism and Jainism are the first great ascetic figures in India; their teachings inspired monastic orders which are still active today. But there are also important Hindu ascetics, such as Shankara, the 9th-century teacher who set down the philosophical precepts which provided the basis for the first Hindu monastic sect.

In ancient Buddhism and Jainism, monastic life was strictly codified; in later Mahayana traditions, such as those still practised in the Himalayan valleys, as well as in Hinduism, such procedures have been maintained. In this respect, monastic life in the different religions presents a relatively uniform pattern.

A novice is generally admitted at an early age, but he can only qualify for full membership after a long course of study. Rites of admission are usually simple; they involve putting on the appropriate yellow, orange or white robes of the order, ceremonially shaving the head, wearing beads or carrying a rosary, and sometimes marking the forehead with the distinctive motif of the sect, such as the three horizontal lines for Shaiva ascetics. The pronouncement of fundamental vows is important since these are repeated on numerous occasions; they are commonly directed against violence, falsehood, stealing, copulation and attachment. Such precepts define the pure, chaste and impoverished life which is the ascetic ideal. The intention is to avoid committing any physical or mental sin, which would result in the loss of spiritual power. Such vows are not necessarily taken for a whole lifetime; resolutions may apply for only a limited duration, as in certain Buddhist orders where boys spend some months in a monastery after leaving school.

Though each novice or junior has his teacher, the ascetic monk is essentially a member of a free community. There is no central authority to regulate monasteries or to enforce uniformity; each ascetic order is a law unto itself, guided only by the precepts of the founder. At the head of the order is the chief monk, who is usually appointed in a democratic fashion by members of the institution. As spiritual leader of the monastery he formulates the ritual policy of the institution, fixing the appropriate details of worship. The everyday business of the order is usually the responsibility of a committee of senior ascetics; important decisions, such as the admission or expulsion of members, can sometimes be made only by this body. Other matters are discussed at meetings attended by all of the members. At such assemblies, the long list of monastic regulations may be recited; individuals may have to confess any breaches that they have committed. This ceremony usually concludes with suitable devotions, presided over by the head of the order.

Among the essential duties of the ascetic monk is the offering of prayers to the saviour or divinity to which the order is dedicated. There is also the need to preserve a pure and detached nature at all times, and to contemplate the higher spiritual realm through meditation. All of these activities are regulated by a strict daily routine. Of particular importance is the time allotted for withdrawal to the private cell. At such times, the ascetic has to practise deep concentration; he is trained to observe his own actions so as to progress steadily through ascending spiritual stages. Other more mundane tasks, such as cooking, cleaning and teaching, are also expected of the ascetic monk.

Retreat

Pursuing meditation outside the temple or monastery generally means leaving society and living in a forest hermitage. In India this retreat to the natural habitat is interpreted as a spiritual return. Though there is never more than a small number of ascetics who actually live in forests, the idea of the spiritually powerful forest sage or rishi pervades all religious literature. Some of these ascetics receive pilgrims at their remote hermitages; others shun any contact with the outside world. After their death, the forest retreats where these ascetics meditated may continue to be revered by their followers.

Four stages of life are described in traditional Hindu texts. The ideal man passes from student to householder, the second stage. On realizing that the pleasures of the world are merely transitory, he leaves his occupation and possessions in the hands of his grown sons and embarks with his wife upon the life of a hermit. Liberated from the concerns of the everyday world, he is concerned only with a search for true knowledge. Yet this third stage is but a preparation for the fourth and final stage, that of the wandering beggar or sannyasi.

Ascetics with no fixed abode wander from one village to the next. They display emblems appropriate to the deity which they worship, such as the trident, which signifies devotion to Shiva. They are sometimes scantily clad or even completely naked; their hair is long and matted. They smear their bodies with ash and cow dung; they may even abuse their bodies and fast for long periods. They defy pain and discomfort by standing immobile in the sun, by stretching out on beds of spikes, by walking on fire and by completely burying themselves in the ground. They carry portable altars of their chosen saviour or divinity; they drag themselves along the ground long distances towards their favoured shrines. While such austerities may be undertaken in fulfilment of a private vow, they do not represent the requirements of a monastic order. Here, the progression towards a spiritual goal is transformed into an eternal pilgrimage with no final resting place.

Bhubaneshwar, Lingaraja Temple, detail of tower, 11th century

SEVEN

SACRED ARCHITECTURE

India's religious buildings take a variety of forms, most notably the stupa, the vihara and the temple; but these are not distinguished according to religious cult. Indian sacred architecture is based on symbolic and formal principles that are common to all of the religions. These principles are laid down in architectural manuals known as Shastras that were compiled over the centuries by priests rather than by architects. The Shastras give information on building forms and techniques, as well as essential astronomical and astrological data which permit sacred monuments to be related to the heavens.

Time and Number

In the spatial continuum that links the human world to that of the gods, architectural forms make specific reference to cosmic patterns. The sacred monument in India is symbolically identified with the temporal and formal structure of the universe. The moment for each stage of the building operation, beginning with the laying-out of the building plan on the ground, has to be precisely determined. This introduces the relation between time and building in which the observations of heavenly bodies bear upon sacred architecture. Astronomy and astrology are never truly distinguished in Indian thought; they provide the basis for fixing the appropriate moments when all important activities take place. The Brihatsamhita, for example, which is one of the earliest sources of information about temple building, is actually a treatise on astronomy with a chapter on architecture. Not only is the moment in time determined at which the plan of the sacred monument is laid out but the plan itself is a product of astronomical calculations. From a knowledge of the heavens derives the symbolism of the cardinal points of the compass, which are dictated by the course of the sun. The plan of the sacred monument is strictly coordinated with the cardinal directions; building masses are most frequently dominated by an east–west axis aligned with the rising and setting sun.

Since number is considered an expression of universal order, other sections of the Shastras are devoted to proportional measurement, which links the sacred monument with the mathematical structure of the cosmos. That number has a special significance in Indian architecture is demonstrated by the term vimana, meaning 'well-measured', which is often used to designate a temple. Detailed chapters in the Shastras describe schemes that mathematically coordinate each part of the building. The controlling module is usually derived from the dimensions of the sanctuary, or of the image enshrined there.

While a correctly proportioned building is considered to be in harmony with the principles of universal order, such a building can also bring perfection to the community. One Shastra assures the architect that if he masters the mathematics of his building, then harmony will reign throughout the world. Other Shastras insist that only work completed according to the rules can gain the desired merit for the patron and worshipper.

Regulating Mandalas

Another way in which the sacred monument is connected with schemes of cosmic order is through geometric diagrams known as mandalas; these diagrams reproduce the pattern of the universe.

Indian cosmology imagines an infinite series of universes, each isolated from the other and suspended in empty space, the medium that precedes all creation. According to one view, the universe is ovoid in shape; it is described as the egg of the creator god, Brahma. This cosmic egg is divided into zones or regions, one of which represents the abode of human beings; above are the heavens, while beneath are the nether worlds. At the centre of this scheme is Meru, the pillar-like mountain that separates the earth from the heavens. Around Meru revolve the sun, moon and stars; the continents, rivers and oceans are also disposed in a concentric fashion around this axial mountain. To the south of Meru is the continent upon which human beings dwell; this has a rose-apple tree (jambu) as its distinctive flora and is therefore known as Jambudvipa. Maps of Jambudvipa are geometrically organized, with concentric rings guarded by 'gateways' at the cardinal directions. Such charts are commonly used by architects to regulate the plans of sacred buildings.

Other mandala schemes are based upon a square divided into a number of smaller squares by a grid of intersecting lines. This mandala also serves as a symbolic pantheon of the gods, since each of the smaller squares is the seat of a particular deity. The central square, which is usually enlarged, is occupied by a prominent divinity. Arranged all around are the planetary divinities and the guardians of the eight directions of space. The courses and recurring time-sequences of the heavenly bodies are thus incorporated into the building mandala.

The mandala is sometimes overlaid with the figure of Mahapurusha, the Cosmic Man who displays all of universal creation on his outstretched body. In a further extension of this biological notion of universal order, the Cosmic Man is transformed into the trunk of a gigantic tree, supporting the cosmos in its ample branches.

The Stupa

The earliest architectural form in India to be linked with a religious cult is the stupa, originally a hemispherical funerary mound. The first known stupas were erected to enshrine the cremated remains of Buddha and his disciples; stupas were also associated with Mahavira. In time, stupas came to commemorate the teachings of Buddha or Mahavira even if they housed the relics of other teachers. Memorial

Amaravati, Stupa, relief panel, 2nd–3rd century; Madras, Government Museum

stupas were erected at all of the Buddhist and Jain holy sites; they were also incorporated into religious and monastic complexes as votive objects. In Tibetan Buddhist establishments, memorial stupas or chortens continue to be built.

The earliest surviving stupas date from the period of Ashoka in the 3rd century BC. In the following centuries, these and other stupas were enlarged by adding successive layers of brick and stone. These early stupas, such as that at Sanchi in central India, consist of hemispheres of earth and rubble raised on low cylindrical bases and faced with bricks or brick-like stones. Miniature stone railings at the summit of the mound demarcate a square zone with a stone mast in the middle; this supports a finial with one or more umbrella-like tiers. The mast also marks the position of the relic casket that is set deep into the mass of the hemisphere; this casket generally contains ashes and charred bones, fragments of gold leaf and other precious items.

Since the principal rite of worship is to perform pradakshina by circumambulating the monument, the stupa is generally surrounded by a paved pathway. In more elaborate schemes this pathway is delimited by a fence with posts and railings, interrupted only by gateways. While the hemispherical mass of the stupa is unadorned, a wealth of emblems and narrative scenes is carved on to the posts and railings. The gateways consist of simple arrangements of architraves supported on two posts, in imitation of timber models.

Over the centuries, stupa forms gradually changed. The cylindrical drum supporting the hemispherical mass was heightened to incorporate niches with votive Buddhist figures. Basements were sometimes transformed into multi-storey constructions with flights of access steps. The hemisphere itself became increasingly bulbous in shape, and the finial came to resemble a slender spire with ring-like markings. Smaller stupas were added, clustering around the base of the central stupa; miniature portable stupas were manufactured in terracotta or metal to serve as reminders of the monument.

Stupas are imbued with a specific cosmological symbolism. The hemispherical mass refers to the dome of heaven; the mast at the summit is identified with the cosmic axis, and the finial of umbrella-like tiers with the ascending heavens of the gods. This finial is also interpreted as the trunk of a cosmic tree; representations of stupas sometimes even have spreading branches emerging from their summits.

As he performs pradakshina around the stupa, the worshipper repeats the rotational movement of the celestial bodies. The cardinal directions are indicated by gateways on the east, north, south and west. In a further extension of this cosmic symbolism, there is the notion of the stupa as a wheel or disc. The wheel is the regulator of cosmic time and the measure of the universe; the wheel-like disc indicates the sun. Some stupa plans are even structurally akin to wheels, with radiating 'spokes' of masonry containing earthen infill. The stupa can also be identified with the unfolding lotus, which is the perfect blossom and the seat of the gods; accordingly, stalks and petals of the cosmic flower adorn the drum and hemisphere.

Chaitya Halls

The other important sacred monument in early Indian architecture is the chaitya hall. This follows a standard layout, not unlike that of a Christian church, with a long hall divided into a central nave and side aisles by two rows of columns. The chief object of worship is the votive stupa positioned at the end of the nave and surrounded by a passageway that follows the circular outlines of the stupa. The resulting part-circular plan resembles the apse of a church and is thus termed apsidal-ended. The other outstanding features of these chaitya halls are the horseshoe-shaped openings above the entrances and the ribbed vaults over the central naves.

The earliest chaitya halls were free-standing timber structures, but these are known only through rock-cut copies. The carved details of these artificially excavated sanctuaries imitate timber models; teak ribs and screens were even inserted into the rock to suggest the original wooden construction. While the overall layout of the chaitya hall remained constant throughout its evolution, its façade changed considerably. The earliest examples, dating back to the 2nd century BC, had timber screens with doors and windows; these were later replaced by stone walls into which doorways and horseshoe-shaped windows were cut. While windows gradually decreased in size, they became increasingly ornate. Porches were added and niches housing Buddha images adorned the outer walls.

Buddhist and Hindu temple architecture in later centuries sometimes imitates chaitya halls. Sanctuaries have part-circular ends and are even completely circular or elliptical in plan.

Viharas

A specific building type known as the vihara was developed in early Buddhism to house monks and other ascetic groups. Viharas follow a standard pattern, with small residential cells opening off a square or rectangular court. In the middle of one side is the entrance; the cell opposite usually accommodates a votive stupa or Buddha image.

Like the chaitya halls, the earliest viharas were rock-cut; but brick remains of structural monasteries have survived from later centuries. While the overall vihara plan remained constant, the focal shrine was enlarged and projected forwards; it was even surrounded by a passageway for pradakshina and was approached through an antechamber or porch. In more elaborate schemes, a stupa or image shrine was built in the middle of a court and surrounded by small cells.

Monastic complexes were essentially groups of viharas, as at Ajanta in the Deccan or at Nalanda in eastern India. Residential complexes were grouped together, sometimes in a linear fashion, together with stupas, shrines for worship and meeting halls. Associated features included kitchens and dining-halls, libraries and stores.

Temple Plans

The most characteristic form of India's sacred architecture is the temple; this is conceived as a receptacle for an image of the saviour or deity who is worshipped there. This votive image is housed in the sanctuary, which is known as the garbhagriha or womb-chamber, a term referring to the place that contains the ritual kernel of the temple.

The garbhagriha coincides with the centre of the regulating mandala, its most powerful point; it also dictates the arrangement of the other architectural elements. The most important of these is the regulating axis of the temple, most often laid out on an east–west line. Doorways are often positioned along this axis so that it is possible to see right through the building into the middle of the sanctuary. Only in this way can the worshipper experience darshana as he moves towards the saviour or deity. In his progression inwards, the devotee passes through a succession of spaces. In the simplest schemes, the sanctuary is entered directly from the outside, through only a small porch or verandah. The ritually vulnerable threshold is transformed into an elaborate doorway. In more complex schemes, one or more halls (mandapas) are aligned on the principal axis to provide a transition from the outer doorway to that of the sanctuary. These mandapas vary from confined chambers to vast open spaces with numerous columns divided into aisles. Immediately preceding the garbhagriha is a small antechamber which marks the point beyond which only the priest can pass.

Secondary axes are sometimes also provided. Side porches and doorways permit access from other directions; subsidiary shrines house less important votive images. Occasionally, two or three sanctuaries of the same size open off a common mandapa.

Rituals of worship demand that the devotee perform pradakshina. As a result, a narrow passageway is often provided on three sides of the sanctuary. Niches in the outer walls of the garbhagriha contain votive images; those niches on an axis with the centre of the garbhagriha are generally enlarged and project outwards. This architectural emphasis coincides with powerful lines of influence that are believed to radiate outwards in four directions from the centre of the garbhagriha. In a western Indian variant of this scheme, quadruple images within the garbhagriha are approached through four doorways.

Temple Elevations

In its vertical elevation, the temple is conceived as a mountain. Mythological peaks such as Meru and Kailasa are used as names for temples, as at Ellora in the Deccan and at Kanchipuram in southern India. A temple so designated is a symbolic replica of the sacred place of the gods.

The tower rises directly above the garbhagriha, its summit being positioned over the middle of the sanctuary. In this way, the highest point of the elevation is coordinated with the innermost point in the plan. The vertical axis implied by such an alignment is a powerful projection of the sacredness that radiates upwards from the garbhagriha. That this towered form was conceived as a mountain is indicated by the term shikhara, meaning peak or crest; horizontal tiers or storeys are sometimes labelled bhumi, which indicates earth or soil.

The development of temple towers, whether curved or multi-storeyed, demonstrates a constant desire to create structures of ever increasing height and complexity. Multiple towered elements suggest a range of peaks; multi-storey towers rising in diminishing tiers create an exaggerated soaring perspective. The finials that adorn the summit, especially the amalaka or ribbed fruit motif and the kalasha or water pot, are auspicious emblems of purity and good fortune.

The walls of sanctuaries and halls are enlivened by rhythmic projections which expand outwards in the middle of each side. The elevation is conceived dynamically, the outer surfaces restlessly moving forwards and backwards, as well as upwards into the tower itself. Architectural elements are deeply cut to emphasize these changes of plane. Wall basements or plinths are composed of sets of different mouldings, including those with curved or pot-like profiles. The walls are usually divided by pilasters into regularly spaced bays or niches. Ornate designs serve as pediments above the niches into which carved panels depicting saviours, deities and other divine beings are inserted. But sculptures are not necessarily confined to niches; the entire wall surface is sometimes covered with figures and foliage decoration. At the top of the walls is an eave and sometimes also a parapet with miniature replica roof forms.

Portions of the temple elevation are partly open, either as porches to shelter entrance doorways or as verandahs with colonnades and even balcony seating. The columns here are elaborately treated, especially the brackets, which may be fashioned as maidens or embracing couples. Porches and verandahs are overhung by an angled or curved eave, deeply undercut on the inside.

Identical elements used on different scales and in different applications unify the various parts of the temple elevation, from the basement to the tower. For example, the horseshoe-shaped arch, originally derived from the windows of chaityas, appears on the front of temple towers as a dominant motif; it is repeated in smaller versions and is fragmented into half-arches. Combinations of these motifs produce complicated meshes of arch-like patterns. Even the overall shape of the curvilinear tower is repeated in miniature as a decorative device. Another instance of this process is the barrel-vaulted roof form which is used at the top of the towers of southern Indian temples. Smaller representations of these vaulted forms adorn the ascending storeys of the tower itself or are used in pediments.

Temple Interiors

Compared to their exuberant and elaborately sculpted exteriors, temple interiors are invariably plain and massive. The confined and cave-like garbhagrihas are dark since no natural light is permitted to enter. Progression through the temple interior, from the entrance porch to the sanctuary doorway, is a transition from light to darkness, from visual complexity to simplicity. Doorways flanked by guardian figures protect the devotee as he progresses inwards; since each threshold marks an increased state of sanctity it has to be adorned with semi-divine beings and auspicious emblems.

Additional visual interest is provided by the columns that define the aisles of the mandapas that precede the garbhagriha. Shafts and brackets are fashioned into intricate forms and are embellished with figural and plant motifs. Ceiling panels, especially those above the central bays of the mandapa, are elaborate compositions with flying figures or deities.

Temple Complexes

Temples often stand in the middle of a paved court which is delimited by high walls and entered through one or more gateways. Subsidiary shrines for minor divinities are sometimes located in the four corners of the court; one of these shrines may be dedicated to the female consort of the male deity who is worshipped in the main temple. Other structures include storerooms, kitchens and residential quarters for priests and pilgrims; there are also lamp-columns, flag-posts and small altars. Sometimes the enclosure walls are lined with a colonnade or a row of small shrines.

Of particular importance in the temple complex are the mandapas inside which accessory activities take place. In larger precincts, these mandapas are extended until they occupy a large proportion of the overall temple. In southern India, the need for increased space was solved by adding a second court which completely surrounded the first one; over the centuries this process was repeated several times until the temple complex consisted of a number of enclosures, one within the other, and each defined by its own rectangle of high walls. The vast areas contained within these walls are filled with secondary shrines, mandapas, colonnades and other utilitarian structures.

One or more gateways provide access into the temple court; the most important of these is usually aligned with the main entrance to the temple inside. The most spectacular development of the gateway is in southern India, where towered gopuras rise higher and higher until they completely overshadow the towered shrine.

Another feature of the temple complex is the tank for bathing, which is situated within the compound or just outside the walls. Fed by rain water, channels or even springs, the temple tank has stepped sides, to facilitate access to the water, and occasionally also a pavilion in the middle.

Timber Origins

Though India's early wooden architecture has not survived, techniques derived from this tradition influenced later rock-cut and masonry monuments. Among the timber, bamboo, and thatch elements that were preserved in later architecture are circular or part-circular plans, curved doorways and window openings, and domed and barrel-vaulted roof forms.

The earliest rock-cut Buddhist and Jain sanctuaries had timber-like ceilings with cross-beams and rafters; actual teak ribs were even inserted into the stone vaults. Clearly, these artificial caves were intended as copies of timber structures. Stone posts and rails that surrounded stupas also imitated timber originals, even to the details of jointing; so too did the stone gateways with curved architraves known as toranas. Masonry details of temples were often wooden in origin: projecting blocks on basements and cornices were derived from the ends of timber beams; doorways had jambs and lintels of timber designs. Towers with curved profiles and roofs with barrel-vaulted or dome-like tops were also wooden in origin, as were the curved cornices and hut-like roofs of brick temples in Bengal in eastern India, or the sloping stone roofs of temples in coastal southern India.

Some completely wooden structures have survived the corrosive effects of India's climate. In the Himalayan valleys and in Kerala, temples have carved timber doorways, columns and beams; angled wooden brackets support sloping tiled roofs, which sometimes rise in ascending tiers.

Cutting into Rock

Excavated sanctuaries for Buddhist and Jain sects date back to the 3rd–2nd centuries BC. These artificial grottoes imitated structural architecture, together with monolithic columns, brackets, doorways and windows. Iron chisels and mallets were the main cutting tools. First of all, the outline of the façade was incised on to the rock. The workmen generally began by driving a tunnel into the rock beneath the place where the ceiling would be; this tunnel was then widened and deepened. The masons who did the rough work were followed by artisans who cleaned and polished the surface. Another method of working was to divide the rock face into square blocks. Deep grooves were cut between these blocks, which were then hewn off. When the first layer was removed, the process was repeated until the required depth was achieved.

Some later examples of rock-cut architecture imitated free-standing buildings. At Mamallapuram in southern India, granite boulders were cut into monolithic copies of temples. The most impressive monolithic monument is the Kailasa temple already referred to at Ellora. Here, a great ditch was excavated into a cliff exposing a solid mass of rock; this was then hewn into a free-standing monolithic temple, complete in all of its architectural details, from the mouldings of the basement to the dome-like roof of the tower.

Rock-cut techniques also influenced structural practice. The building was conceived as a solid mass composed of stone blocks laid without mortar. This was chiselled away by masons to reveal the precise outlines of the elevation. Because of this method, stone joints did not always coincide with structural elements; the same was true for images and decorative motifs which were sometimes carved across the joints. In this respect, the structural temple was conceived as a sculpted monolith, the chief endeavour of the craftsman being to carve the building surface.

Stone Construction

The most characteristic feature of temple construction in India is the combination of vertical and horizontal stonework. Stability is achieved by columns, cross-beams and lintels which are held together by their sheer weight; iron clamps are only occasionally used. Openings are generally spanned with a single lintel; interior spaces are roofed by horizontal stone slabs, sometimes the openings are extended by the use of corbelled blocks which project progressively outwards to diminish the space.

Engineering principles are mostly rudimentary: roofs or ceilings of dome-like appearance are built with overlapping horizontal stone courses; soaring towers with complex silhouettes are constructed with hollow corbelled interiors; complicated arch-like shapes are created by carving rather than by constructing.

Stone blocks were often brought large distances from distant quarries to the building site. The most convenient means of transport were wooden rollers drawn by elephants or barges floating along rivers and canals. At the site, roughly shaped blocks were hoisted into position by rope pulleys on scaffolding; earthen or timber ramps facilitated the positioning of particularly heavy blocks.

Tirumala, Venkateshvara Temple, portrait sculptures of Krishnadeva Raya and two queens, 16th century.

EIGHT

PATRONS AND ARTISTS

The direct relationship between religious architecture and political forces is expressed in the royal patronage of sacred monuments. But patronage was not restricted to kings; courtiers, military officials and wealthy individuals also had opportunities to make donations so that they too might benefit from the divine blessings of the saviour or god. The economic life of monasteries and temples was based on income from grants and the investment of this in land; as they developed into wealthy institutions, they acted as employers and patrons.

Kings and Gods

The ideal Indian ruler, whatever his religious affiliation, was the upholder of traditional law and the agent of moral well-being and prosperity. While a king was expected to assert his military power and to display his wealth whenever possible, he was also responsible for the spiritual welfare of the people. Rulers protected gods so that they in turn might benefit from divine protection. The role of the king in this partnership with the divine was that of worshipper. As chief sacrificer, the king erected new temples, generously endowing them with gifts and grants of income to ensure the continuity of worship. He was rewarded in his endeavours by blessings from the saviour or deity which guaranteed victory, welfare and prosperity. These blessings were then passed on by the king to the population.

Inscriptions from all periods record the substantial royal investment in Buddhist, Jain and Hindu monuments. Only after patronizing an indigenous but powerful saintly figure or divinity could kings hope to gain sufficient influence to increase their territorial possessions. Displays of royal patronage in temple construction, donation and ceremonies were an indispensable means of achieving legitimacy in the eyes of the population. Such acts of sponsorship were of importance both for emerging dynasties in their attempts to secure control over newly won territories and for established rulers who continued to be plagued by insecurities and threats.

Each ruling dynasty associated itself with a saviour or deity who was considered the guardian of the royal household. Such protective divinities were used in regal signatures and seals; they were worshipped at shrines at the capital and at other strategic centres; they even appeared on war banners and shields. In this way, gods were visibly incorporated into the king's world. The ruler also made frequent pilgrimages to deities in outlying temples; he even had sacred images moved to temples that were especially built for them at his capital.

Temples to particular deities grew up in the capitals of the different dynasties, or at sacred places within the kingdom. Many of the major Hindu gods were patronized at one time or another by royal figures, but certain deities were adopted as protective divinities. The 4th–5th-century Gupta rulers of central India built shrines for the Varaha and Narasimha incarnations of Vishnu. Later kings adopted Shiva as their tutelary deity; temples enshrining lingas were erected by the 11th-century Paramara ruler at Bhojpur in central India and by the contemporary Chola king at Gangaikondacholapuram in southern India. Narasimha, the Eastern Ganga ruler of Orissa in the 13th century, promoted Surya as his personal divinity.

A further demonstration of the close connection between kings and temple deities is the coincidence of their names. Rulers adopted the titles of gods and, in turn, gods were given regal titles. Royal rites were similar to temple rituals, and sacred imagery was pervaded with a distinctly regal iconography. By such means, the celestial realm of the divinity was incorporated into the terrestrial domain of the king himself.

Temple Patrons

Almost every large-scale sacred building in India is connected with an influential patron. Because of the prestige accorded to temple patronage, men who held high positions of administrative power, whether on a provincial, district or village level, competed with each other in the construction of shrines and temples. But the king always served as a model; others merely emulated his acts of piety and generosity.

The erection of a Buddhist stupa or a Hindu temple was frequently the expression of sincere piety inspired by the assurance of both eternal and temporal rewards. 'Let him who wishes to enter the worlds that are reached by meritorious deeds or piety and charity build a temple to the gods', states one ancient text, while another promises the temple patron 'peace, wealth, grain and sons'.

But sponsorship was also a visible statement of the ambitions and economic resources of the patron. The stupas and stone columns set up by Ashoka in the 3rd century BC, for example, asserted his imperial presence as well as publicizing his conversion to Buddhism. Much later, in the 16th century, the Vijayanagara kings renovated all of the important Hindu temples in those parts of the Deccan and southern India that came under their control. The towering gopuras which rose above the entrances to their temples were obvious emblems of royal power and piety.

Sometimes the royal patron was directly involved with the construction of the sacred monument. Narasimha, the Eastern Ganga ruler already referred to, took a personal interest in the Surya temple at Konarak; he was portrayed in carved panels on the temple itself in the role of worshipper. Sacred monuments also served as memorials of important political events, such as coronations and military victories. Rajendra, the 11th-century Chola ruler, erected an impressive temple at Gangaikondacholapuram to commemorate his successful march northwards to the Ganga river; he even had himself depicted on the temple as a saint kneeling before the deity to receive a victory wreath. That temples could serve as records of royal activities is suggested by the appearance of royal themes in temple sculpture, but only occasionally was sacred art dominated by courtly episodes. Exceptional examples are the panels on the 8th-century Vaikuntha Perumal temple at Kanchipuram in southern India which illustrate the complete genealogy of the Pallava dynasty, and the friezes on the outer walls of the 15th-century Ramachandra complex at Vijayanagara in the Deccan which record the processions of the king's elephants, horses, soldiers and courtly women.

Regal sponsorship of religious monuments is a thing of the past, even though royal figures continue to participate in the ceremonies of temple festivals. Patronage is now mostly in the hands of wealthy families and individuals. The Vaishnava temples in many of India's large cities erected by the Birla family are among the best-known examples. Institutions such as universities also sponsor large-scale temples, such as that which dominates the campus at Varanasi in central India.

Dynasties and Building Styles

Whenever political stability coincided with the accumulation of sufficient resources, patronage of sacred architecture increased. Religious monuments sponsored by the king and those in his service were usually built in related styles, even if they differed in scale. For this reason, a dynastic label is usually adopted for the different architectural and artistic styles. That these styles were actually related to dynasties is proved by inscriptions which testify to the direct sponsorship of the temple by members of the royal household. This is not to suggest that kings were actually involved with the process of architectural design and the execution of carvings, but rather that their constant patronage permitted local art traditions to flourish in the region where they ruled.

But artistic continuity also existed beyond the king's domain. Since patronage operated at different levels, building traditions could be sustained where lesser sponsors continued to commission. In this way, styles continued to evolve. Sometimes artistic traditions outlived the career of one dynasty, to be taken up by successive rulers. The Gupta style, which was first enunciated in the monuments and sculptures of these 4th–5th-century rulers of central India, survived into subsequent centuries, affecting the monuments of later kings. The term post-Gupta is sometimes applied to describe the style of 6th–7th-century monuments of this region. Feudatories adopted the building styles of their overlords and then maintained them when they had the opportunity of seizing power. Monuments of the 16th-century Vijayanagara kings and their successors, the Nayakas in southern India, can hardly be distinguished since dynastic transition is not directly mirrored in architectural or sculptural style. In Gujarat in western India during the period of Muslim rule in the 15th–16th centuries, temple styles evolved continuously under the patronage of Jain merchants; obviously, a dynastic appellation would be inappropriate in this case.

Despite these and other instances of the lack of coincidence of royal histories and artistic traditions, dynastic labels remain the most convenient means of identifying temple styles. (A chart correlating the dynasties with monuments appears on pp. 86–93.)

Temples as Patrons

Sources of wealth for religious institutions consisted mainly of donations from royal patrons and private individuals. These were received by the temple in the form of money, valuable objects, livestock or income from grants of land, including whole villages and their inhabitants. As grants accumulated, temples became wealthy and could afford to become employers and act as patrons themselves. Since this wealth was usually invested in land, temples came to function as landlords. From the produce of the land derived the income upon which the economic life of the institution was based. Projects of cultivation and irrigation were embarked upon, and land was usually leased out to tenants. These leases, and indeed all economic transactions of the temple, were entered upon in the name of the deity.

Usually, strict and efficient control was exercised by religious institutions over the tenants; units of measurement, for example, were fixed to weigh grain that was brought in. Tenants were helped by the temple in times of want and there are records of loans being made and credit extended to needy cultivators. Holders of temple land were permitted to keep only a proportion of the produce, but they benefited from the protection of the temple and sometimes even enjoyed exemption from paying state taxes.

As temples provided work and the means of livelihood for a large number of people they exerted a considerable influence upon the economic life of the region. Religious institutions entered into contracts with individuals who undertook to supply specified goods and services at stated periods: for example, clarified butter for burning lamps, flowers for garlands, rice for offerings and the feeding of brahmins, and sandal-paste and incense for adorning images. An inscription on the 11th-century temple at Thanjavur in southern India lists no fewer than six hundred employees, including dancing girls, musicians, dance teachers, accountants, parasol-bearers, lamp-lighters, sprinklers of water, potters, astrologers, tailors, jewel-stitchers, carpenters, washermen and cleaners.

Religious institutions also acted as patrons of the arts and of knowledge, contributing to the cultural and intellectual life of the region. Performances of music, dance and theatre, which played a vital role in ceremonies and festivals, were directly commissioned. Ancient texts were compiled and copied, and sometimes translated into regional languages; learned teachers were invited to expound the scriptures; schools with resident students were founded and maintained. This process is still very much alive. The Venkateshvara temple at Tirumala in southern India, reputed to be the richest religious institution in the country, has an active cultural programme. Funds provided by the temple help to support a local university, a publishing house and a museum. Less wealthy shrines also act as sponsors, expending considerable sums of money at festival time to accommodate and feed brahmins and other visitors.

Builders and Craftsmen

The architects, artists and craftsmen who worked on sacred monuments were organized into groups which functioned like guilds. Families and individuals were united into cohesive social groups which exercised control over the social life of their members, and even acted on occasions as guardians of widows and orphans. Guilds regulated the transference of knowledge, ensuring that techniques were handed down from one generation to the next. They fixed rules of work and wages and set standard prices for work completed. Guilds became wealthy and powerful, and even made donations to sacred monuments. Members of guilds travelled from one region to another to work on different projects; in this way, artistic traditions spread throughout the country.

The overall directors of the building project were the chief architect, known as the sutradhara, and the superintendent of works; also of significance were the head stonemason and the chief image-maker. There were workmen for every skill: masons to cut the stones to size, artisans to fashion them into architectural forms and sculptors to execute the final chiselling. Specialists carried out particular jobs, such as laying out the building plan, marking out the plumb and square lines which regulated the carving, grinding the polishing materials, carving the bands of friezes and mixing the coloured pigments for paintwork. Leading master-sculptors designed and executed the principal images of the sanctuary and its outer walls; lesser artisans added the carved details. Women were employed for lighter tasks such as cleaning and polishing stones. Work was usually assigned on the basis of contracts for separate operations; each contract had a different leader for each task.

Workmen and their families often settled in camps around the building site; they had their meals in a common mess. Construction generally occupied only part of the year; during the rainy season the work halted and workmen were given leave. Holidays were celebrated when the patron came on a visit or when an important part of the building was completed. Officials maintained law and order, while administrators settled any disputes.

Large-scale temple construction continues into the modern era. The Somanatha temple at Prabhas Patan in western India that was desecrated by the Muslims on several occasions has now been entirely rebuilt. Architects and sculptors have faithfully copied the original 12th-century monument, complete in all of its sculpted details, thus demonstrating that artistic traditions are still very much alive in the region. In southern India at Srirangam, for example, the great Ranganatha temple has been extensively renovated. Work on the largest of its 17th-century towered gopuras was only completed in 1987. Even though modern concrete was used instead of brick, the exuberant plaster sculptures that adorn each of the storeys are in keeping with the original conception.

Anonymity of Artists

Like the artists of medieval Europe, those of India are mostly anonymous. But the overall lack of information about architects, sculptors and painters, especially for the earlier period, does not mean that artists lacked social status. The Shastras, which have already been mentioned in reference to building practice, provide information on the technical and religious training that the artist has to undergo before executing his work. These manuals make it clear that the artist is considered as a ritual practitioner; he has to undergo rites of purification and mental preparation in order to visualize correctly the appropriate forms. The suppression of the artist's personality is considered essential to the success of the creative process.

Chariot wheel carved onto terrace, 13th century

But from time to time artists have asserted their importance. Inscriptions on some monuments record the names of the architects or of the craftsmen who carved the various panels. Sculpted brackets on the 12th-century temple at Belur in southern India, for instance, are each provided with a label which mentions the artist, his family and place of origin. Almost all the 18th–19th-century brick temples of Bengal in eastern India have an inscribed wall plaque giving the names of the patron of the building, the chief architect and the master-craftsmen; even the overall cost of the project may be set down.

As older temples continue to be renovated and new ones erected, there is a continuous demand for master-architects and craftsmen. Temples in traditional southern Indian styles, for example, are commissioned by wealthy Tamil communities in many cities of the country, and even elsewhere in Asia, Africa, Europe and North America. Artists with national and sometimes international reputations are brought from southern India to execute this work.

FURTHER READING

The list of suggested volumes is restricted to general works; only the most recent publication date is given. Detailed bibliographies are included in many of these books.

1. Regions and Cultures

Hermann Kulke and Dietmar Rothermund, *A History of India*, New Delhi: Manohar Publications, 1986.

Richard Lannoy, *The Speaking Tree: A Study of Indian Culture and Society*, Oxford: Oxford University Press, 1971.

R.C. Majumdar, ed., *History and Culture of the Indian People*, Volumes I–VIII, Bombay: Bharatiya Vidya Bhavan, 1951–77.

Clarence Maloney, *Peoples of South Asia*, New York: Holt, Rinehart & Winston, 1974.

2. Religious Developments

A.L. Basham, *The Wonder That Was India*, London: Sidgwick & Jackson, 1985.

Heinz Bechert and Richard Gombrich, eds., *The World of Buddhism*, London: Thames & Hudson, 1984.

Nirad C. Chaudhuri, *Hinduism: A Religion to Live By*, New Delhi: B.I. Publications, 1979.

William de Bary, ed., *Sources of Indian Tradition*, New York: Columbia University Press, 1958. (Original sources in translation.)

Jan Gonda, *Visnuism and Sivaism: A Comparison*, London: Athlone, 1970.

David L. Snellgrove, *Indo-Tibetan Buddhism: Indian Buddhists and Their Tibetan Successors*, London: Serindia, 1987.

3. Buddhist and Jain Saviours

Edward Conze, *Buddhism, Its Essence and Development*, New York: Harper & Row, 1975.

Jyotindra Jain and Eberhard Fischer, *Jain Iconography*, 2 volumes, Leiden: E.J. Brill, 1978.

Edward J. Thomas, *The Life of Buddha as Legend and History*, London: Routledge & Kegan Paul, 1975.

4. Hindu Gods and Goddesses

Alain Danielou, *Hindu Polytheism*, London: Routledge & Kegan Paul, 1964.

John Dowson, *A Classical Dictionary of Hindu Mythology and Religion, Geography, History and Literature*, Calcutta: Rupa & Co., 1982.

Diana L. Eck, *Banaras: City of Light*, New York: Alfred A. Knopf, 1982.

Wendy O'Flaherty, *Hindu Myths: A Sourcebook Translated from the Sanskrit*, Harmondsworth: Penguin Books, 1975.

Margaret and James Stutley, *A Dictionary of Hinduism: Its Mythology, Folklore and Development 1500 BC–AD 1500*, New Delhi: Heritage Publishers, 1986.

5. Sacred Art

J.C. Harle, *The Art and Architecture of the Indian Subcontinent*, Harmondsworth: Penguin Books, 1986.

Susan L. and John C. Huntington, *The Art of Ancient India*, New York and Tokyo: Weatherhill, 1985.

Calambur Sivaramamurti, *The Art of India*, New York: Harry N. Abrams, 1977.

Heinrich Zimmer, *Myths and Symbols in Indian Art and Civilization*, New York: Harper & Brothers, 1962.

—, *Form and Yoga in the Sacred Images of India*, Princeton: Princeton University Press, 1984.

6. Priests and Pilgrims

Surinder Moihan Bhardwaj, *Hindu Places of Pilgrimage in India*, Berkeley and Los Angeles: University of California Press, 1973.

Carl Diehl, *Instrument and Purpose: Studies in Rites and Rituals in South India*, Lund: C. W. K. Gleerup, 1956.

Sukumar Dutt, *Buddhist Monks and Monasteries of India: Their History and Their Contribution to Indian Culture*, London: Allen & Unwin, 1962.

Diana L. Eck, *Darsan: Seeing the Divine Image in India*, Chambersburg: Anima Books, 2nd edition, 1985.

7. Sacred Architecture

Percy Brown, *Indian Architecture (Buddhist and Hindu Periods)*, Bombay: Taraporevala, 1976.

Stella Kramrisch, *The Hindu Temple*, Delhi and Varanasi: Motilal Banarsidass, 1980.

George Michell, *The Hindu Temple: An Introduction to Its Meanings and Forms*, Chicago: The University of Chicago Press, 1988.

Debala Mitra, *Buddhist Monuments*, Calcutta: Sahitya Samsad, 1971.

Adrian Snodgrass, *The Symbolism of the Stupa*, Ithica: Cornell University Southeast Asia Program, 1985.

8. Patrons and Artists

Alice Boner and S. R. Sharma, 'Economic and organizational aspects of the building operations of the Sun Temple at Konarka', *Journal of the Economic and Social History of the Orient*, XIII, 3, Leiden, 1970.

Vidya Dehejia, ed., *Royal Patrons and Great Temple Art*, Bombay: Marg, 1988.

B. Stein, 'The economic functions of a medieval south Indian temple', in *All the King's Mana: Papers on Medieval South Indian History*, Madras: New Era, 1984.

PART TWO

GAZETTEER OF MONUMENTS

HOW TO USE THE GAZETTEER

The sites included in this gazetteer are grouped into six regions, from northern India to southern India. These regions coincide only partly with modern state boundaries since they are based on geographical and historical divisions. Each region is preceded by an illustrated introduction that surveys the development of sacred architecture and art over more than two thousand years. Sites indicated in **bold** are marked on the detailed regional map that follows the introduction. This map shows modern roads, railways and airports, as well as nearby cities and towns where accommodation is available.

The sites indicated in **bold** are also described separately in the regional gazetteers, in which they are organized alphabetically. Almost three hundred sites have been selected, according to the importance of their monuments, beginning with the earliest surviving examples and continuing up to the modern era. The selection of monuments is intended to be representative of all significant regional forms and historical styles. Even within a single site, there has often been a choice of monuments. The relative interest of gazetteer entries is suggested by their comparative lengths.

Throughout, there is an emphasis on basic information. City maps and site plans are provided wherever possible; individual buildings are described in detail, especially their architectural and sculptural forms. Architectural terminology has been simplified; a glossary (see pp. 493–5) explains both English and Indian terms.

Names of deities, saints, heroes, rulers, dynasties, etc., in Sanskrit and other Indian languages, have been spelt without diacritical marks, to facilitate pronunciation; a complete glossary of these names is provided on pp. 496–511. Cities, towns and sites are spelt according to modern convention. For this reason, a discrepancy sometimes occurs between temple deity and place name (as in the Tarakanatha sanctuary at Tarakeswar).

Dates are indicated by century only, unless there is a precise historical record ('4th–5th century' is a broadly estimated date; '4th–5th centuries' suggests a building phase spread over two hundred years); if not otherwise indicated, all dates are AD.

The historical chart on pp. 86–93 records the principal dynasties of Indian rulers from the 6th century BC onwards. The chart is separated into four blocks, each of six hundred years; it is also divided into the six regions of the gazetteer. Sites with principal monuments appear *beneath* the associated dynasties, except where these encompass two adjacent regions. Sites with monuments spanning different periods appear more than once.

Since sculptures and architectural fragments have been removed from many ancient sites, museums are also included in the gazetteer. As in the regional introductions, sites indicated in **bold** are described separately in the gazetteer (but not always in the same region in which the museum itself is located). There has been no attempt to describe the layouts of museum collections; pieces are generally described in chronological sequence, with accession number provided wherever available.

Some cities and towns are treated more fully in Volume II, which deals with the monuments of the Muslim and European periods. Cross-references are indicated in the relevant gazetteer entries. Sites in the index marked with an asterisk (★) also appear in Volume II.

HISTORICAL CHART   600 – 0 BC

		600 BC	500 BC	400 BC
NORTHERN INDIA				
CENTRAL INDIA				
EASTERN INDIA		Kushinagara, Piprahwa, Sravasti **MAGADHA RULERS** Rajgir, Vaisali		
WESTERN INDIA				
THE DECCAN				
SOUTHERN INDIA				
		600 BC	500 BC	400 BC

300 BC	200 BC	100 BC	0	
				NORTHERN INDIA
				CENTRAL INDIA
Ahichhatra, Kausambi, Patna, Sanchi, Sarnath	Bharhut, Kausambi Sanchi, Vidisha			
MAURYAS ——	**SHUNGAS**			EASTERN INDIA
Barabar, Dhauli Lauriya Nandangarh	Bodhgaya, Tamluk			
	CHEDIS Khandagiri and Udayagiri, Sisupalgarh			
MAURYAS Bairat, Junagadh				WESTERN INDIA
	SATAVAHANAS Ajanta, Amaravati, Bhaja, Guntupalle, Pitalkhora			THE DECCAN
				SOUTHERN INDIA
300 BC	200 BC	100 BC	0	

HISTORICAL CHART   0 – 600 AD

		0	100 AD	200 AD
NORTHERN INDIA				
CENTRAL INDIA		**KUSHANAS** Mat, Mathura, Sonkh		
EASTERN INDIA				
WESTERN INDIA				Junagadh
THE DECCAN		**SATAVAHANAS** Bedsa, Junnar, Amaravati, Kanheri, Nasik, Pandu Lena, Ter	**KSHATRAPAS** Karli,	Junnar **IKSHVAKUS** Nagarjunakonda, Sankaram
SOUTHERN INDIA				
		0	100 AD	200 AD

00 AD	400 AD	500 AD	600 AD	
				NORTHERN INDIA
				CENTRAL INDIA
GUPTAS Bhitargaon, Bhumara, Deogarh, Dhamnar, Eran, Mathura Nachna, Pawaya, Sanchi, Sarnath, Tigawa, Udayagiri				
				EASTERN INDIA
		MAITRAKAS Bileshwar, Gop		WESTERN INDIA
VAKATAKAS Ajanta, Aurangabad, Ramtek		**KALACHURIS** Elephanta, Jogeshwari **EARLY CHALUKYAS** Badami		THE DECCAN
				SOUTHERN INDIA
300 AD	400 AD	500 AD	600 AD	

HISTORICAL CHART   600 – 1200 AD

	600 AD	700 AD	800 AD
NORTHERN INDIA			
	KARKOTAS Martand, Mulbekh, Paraspora		**UTPALAS** Avantipur,
	HUNAS Kanauj	**PRATIHARAS** Amrol, Badoh Pathari, Batesara, Gwalior, Gyaraspur, Naresar, Terahi	
CENTRAL INDIA			Bheraghat, Chandrehi **HAIHAYAS** Rajim, Sirpur
EASTERN INDIA	**SHAILODBHAVAS** Bhubaneshwar	**BHAUMA KARA** Bhubaneshwar, Simhanatha	**SOMAVAMSHI** Bhubaneshwar,
	LATE GUPTAS Aphsad, Bodhgaya, Mundesvari, Sultanganj		
	PALAS Antichak, Bangarh, Nalanda	Bodhgaya, Kurkihar, Lalitagiri, Ratnagiri, Udayagiri	
WESTERN INDIA		**PRATIHARAS** Abaneri, Osian	
	MAITRAKAS Samalaji	Roda	
THE DECCAN		**KONDAVIDUS** Bhairavakonda, Undavalli	**EASTERN CHALUK** Biccavolu, Samalkot
	RASHTRAKUTAS Ellora		Kukku
	EARLY CHALUKYAS Aihole, Alampur, Mahakuta, Pattadakal, Satyavolu		
SOUTHERN INDIA	**PALLAVAS** Mandagappatu, Mamallapuram, Kanchipuram, Narttamalai Panamalai, Tiruttani, Uttaramerur		
	PANDYAS Kalugumalai, Namakkal, Sittanavasal, Tiruchirapalli		
	600 AD	700 AD	800 AD

0 AD	1000 AD	1100 AD		
				NORTHERN INDIA
...ayar, Srinagar				
...ajaura, Brahmaur, Chamba, ...gatsukh, Jageshwar, Masrur				
PARAMARAS				**CENTRAL INDIA**
Bhojpur, Nemawar, Udayapur	**KACHHAPAGHATAS**			
	Gwalior, Kadwaha, Suhania			
CHANDELLAS				
...hajuraho				
				EASTERN INDIA
...haurasi, Khiching				
EASTERN GANGAS				
...Mukhalingam		Puri		
	CHAHAMANAS			**WESTERN INDIA**
...adoli, Jagat, Kiradu	Jhalrapatan, Menal			
SOLANKIS				
Abu, Kumbharia, Modhera		Ghumli, Sejakpur, Patan, Prabhas Patan, Siddhpur, Taranga		
		KAKATIYAS		**THE DECCAN**
		Hanamkonda		
	YADAVAS			
	Ambarnath, Anwa, Balsane, Kolhapur, Sinnar			
	LATE CHALUKYAS			
	Dambal, Ittagi, Kuruvatti, Lakkundi			
		KADAMBAS		
		Degamve		
NOLAMBAS				**SOUTHERN INDIA**
...aralaguppe, Hemavati, Nandi				
WESTERN GANGAS	**HOYSALAS**			
...ambadahalli, Shravana Belgola	Belur, Dodda Gaddavahalli, Halebid			
CHOLAS				
...ilaiyur, Kodumbalur, Kumbakonam, Thanjavur, ...angaikondacholapuram, Darasuram		**CHERAS**		
		Trichur		
0 AD	1000 AD	1100 AD		

HISTORICAL CHART   1200–1800 AD

	1200 AD	1300 AD	1400 AD
NORTHERN INDIA			
CENTRAL INDIA			
EASTERN INDIA	**EASTERN GANGAS** Bhubaneshwar, Konarak, Simhachalam (Deccan)		**GAJAPATIS** Bhubaneshwar, Puri
WESTERN INDIA	**CHAHAMANAS** Bijolia **SOLANKIS** Abu, Bhadreshwar, Girnar, Vadnagar		**SISODIYAS, RATHOR** Eklingji, Ranakpur, Chitorg **AHMAD SHAHIS** Abhapur, Abu, Adalaj
THE DECCAN	**KAKATIYAS** Palampet, Ghanpur, Warangal **YADAVAS** Ratanvadi		
SOUTHERN INDIA	**HOYSALAS** Somnathpur, Harnahalli **CHOLAS** Chidambaram, Tribhuvanam, Tiruvarur **CHERAS** Peruvanam	**VIJAYANAGARA** Sringeri, Penukonda, Kanchipuram, Kumbakonam,	

| | 1200 AD | 1300 AD | 1400 AD |

...0 AD	1600 AD	1700 AD	1800 AD	
NAMGYALS Basgo, Hemis, Leh, Shey, Spituk				NORTHERN INDIA
	PAHARIS Manali, Mandi, Pandoh	Sarahan		
	SIKHS Amritsar	Patiala		
	MUGHALS Vrindavan	Varanasi		CENTRAL INDIA
		BURDWAN RAJAS Bansberia, Kalna		EASTERN INDIA
	MALLAS Bishnupur			
OCH ...uhati, Udaipur	**AHOM** Sibsagar			
D OTHER RAJPUTS ...almer, Ahar, Amber, Bikaner, Mandor, Nathdwara				WESTERN INDIA
		GAEKWARS Dwarka		
	MARATHAS Mahuli, Nasik, Pandharpur, Trimbak			THE DECCAN
...ayanagara, Ahobilam, Srisailam, Tadpatri ...ahasti, Lepakshi, Somapalem, Srirangam, Tirumala, Vellore		**WADIYARS** Mysore		SOUTHERN INDIA
	NAYAKAS Madurai, Srirangam, Srimushnam, Kanchipuram, Tiruvannamalai	**SETHUPATHIS** Suchindram, Rameshwaram		
		CHETIARS Bhatkal, Mudabidri		
	TRAVANCORE RAJAS Ettumanur, Vaikom	Chengannur, Trivandrum		
...00 AD	1600 AD	1700 AD	1800 AD	

NORTHERN INDIA

NINE

NORTHERN INDIA

New Delhi, northern Uttar Pradesh, Punjab, Haryana, Himachal Pradesh, Jammu and Kashmir

Introduction

Almost no monuments of any antiquity are preserved in the plains of northern India due to the totally destructive impact of the Muslim invaders. But an idea of the rich artistic heritage that must have existed in this region is given by the wealth of Buddhist and Hindu remains surviving in the foothills and valleys of the western Himalayas (northern Uttar Pradesh, Himachal Pradesh, and Jammu and Kashmir). This heritage is extremely varied, testifying to artistic contacts with central and eastern India, as well as with the Gandhara region in northern Pakistan and Afghanistan in earlier centuries, and with Tibet and China in later times.

Most ancient Buddhist monuments, like the stupa on Shankaracharya Hill overlooking **Srinagar**, have completely vanished; others survive in fragmentary form only. Dismantled portions of earlier structures were incorporated into later Muslim projects, such as the 3rd-century-BC Maurya columns brought to Kotla Firuz Shah (**New Delhi**), or were buried, like the 2nd-century railing pieces imported from **Mathura** in central India (recently discovered at **Sanghol** in the Punjab).

Foundations are preserved of Buddhist structures at **Harwan** and **Ushkur** in the central Kashmir valley; terracotta figurines and tiles from these sites are dated to the 3rd–5th centuries. Other terracotta finds come from the ruins of a large monastery at **Akhnur**. Stone sculptures were discovered among the 8th–9th-century

dilapidated Buddhist structures at **Pandrethan**, south-east of **Srinagar**.

During the Karkota period, especially in the reign of the 8th-century ruler Lalitaditya, the central Kashmir valley became the setting of a brilliant intellectual and artistic culture. **Paraspora**, Lalitaditya's capital, is indicated by the foundations of large Buddhist edifices. A magnificent Surya temple was erected under the patronage of the same ruler at **Martand**. Though now ruined, this monument remains the masterpiece of Kashmir architecture. Earlier classical influences (Corinthian columns, pilasters and cornices) transmitted through Afghanistan and Pakistan were combined with indigenous features (trilobed niches within steeply gabled roofs). The impressive scale of the temple and its colonnaded courtyard was also inspired by classical models.

During the succeeding Utpala period, Hindu temple traditions in the central Kashmir valley continued to evolve. At **Avantipur**, the capital of the 9th-century ruler Avantivarman, two ruined temples displayed the same overall conception as the **Martand** monument. Another similar complex from the same era still stands at **Bunniyar**. Later projects from the 11th–12th centuries were considerably smaller in scale. Temples at **Payar** and **Pandrethan** (**Srinagar**) have single chambers with steeply gabled masonry pediments and roofs.

Overleaf Himalayan panorama, Ladakh

At the same time, Hindu temple architecture flourished elsewhere in the western Himalayas; examples in the Kangra, Kulu and Chamba valleys testify to the influence of central Indian traditions. The earlier temples of this group date from the 9th–10th centuries and are stylistically linked to Pratihara monuments. At **Bajaura**, **Brahmaur**, **Jagatsukh** and **Jageshwar**, small square sanctuaries were contained within soaring curved towers. Niches on three sides once housed sculptures (preserved only at **Bajaura**); above the entrance porches are large projections with carvings. Characteristic of the Pratihara style were the pot and foliage column capitals, the door frames ornamented with miniature figures and foliation, the meshes of arch-like motifs above niches and in bands on the towers, and the amalaka motifs at the summits (concealed by later projecting wooden roofs). The unique rock-cut shrines at **Masrur** are further examples of Pratihara monuments.

The later evolution of these traditions, from the 13th century onwards, is demonstrated by temples at **Baijnath**, **Chamba** and **Mandi**. Sanctuary walls were divided into double tiers of niches surmounted by tower-like pediments; most of the carved detail, unfortunately, has disappeared.

Coexisting with this stone architecture was a timber tradition of which there are only a few early examples still standing. These shrines were mostly modest structures with sloping tiled roofs, sometimes arranged in ascending tiers and supported on angled brackets. At **Brahmaur** and **Chatrarhi**, carved wooden doorways, columns, beams and ceilings survive from the 8th–9th centuries; sculptures resemble contemporary practice in the central Kashmir valley. Later wood carving is preserved at **Manali** and **Udaipur**. There are examples of other smaller temples with multi-tiered towers at **Dhiri** and **Pandoh**.

A variation of this indigenous timber style is seen in temples of the Sutlej valley. At **Behna**, a sloping roof and a multi-tiered tower were combined together; doorways and brackets were carved. Also belonging to this region are shrines raised on towers. Those at **Sarahan** were constructed of masonry bonded with wooden logs; the overhanging sanctuaries have gabled roofs and projecting balconies.

Many of these stone and wooden shrines house important metal images. At **Brahmaur**, **Chamba**, **Chatrarhi**, **Jageshwar** and **Udaipur**, for example, inlaid brass figures dating from the 7th century onwards reveal a tradition closely related to post-Gupta styles in central and eastern India.

As in other parts of India, later temple architecture in the 18th and 19th centuries was strongly influenced by contemporary Islamic traditions; this is particularly true of Sikh gurudwaras. Of all the Sikh shrines, that at **Amritsar** is the most important. This was built in a late-Mughal style that affected both its overall form and its sumptuous ornamentation. Less elaborate but comparable shrines were erected at **Patiala**; a modern example is to be found in **New Delhi**.

A 19th-century revivalist approach is represented by the temple in **Jammu**, where curved towers deriving from central Indian architecture were adopted. A fusion of Mughal and revivalist features is found in the many pilgrimage shrines in the region: for example, on the upper reaches of the Ganga at **Hardwar** and **Rishikesh**; beneath the holy peaks of the Himalayas at **Badrinath** and **Kedarnath**; and at **Kurukshetra**, one of the sites associated with the Mahabharata epic.

Beyond the first high range of the Himalayas are the arid valleys of Ladakh, Zanskar and Lahul, mostly elevated above 3,000 m (9,750 ft). Commercially and culturally, this zone was closely linked with Tibet and China, at least after the 8th–9th centuries, as demonstrated by the rock-cut images at **Mulbekh** on the principal trade route. Mahayana

Buddhism in its Tibetan form still flourishes here, having been introduced into the region in the 11th century by the monk Rinchen Bzangpo and his followers. Subsequent religious leaders (lamas) and local rulers of the Namgyal dynasty continued to promote Tibetan Buddhism under its different Kagyupa (Red Cap) and Gelugpa (Yellow Cap) sects, particularly after the 16th century.

The upper reaches of the Indus, Doda and Spiti rivers are overlooked by numerous monastic establishments (gompas), many of which are still active. These consist of clusters of assembly halls (lhakhangs) and temples (dukhangs) that enshrine Mahayana divinities; other structures include residences, stores and kitchens. Memorial stupas (chortens) and walls of carved stones (manis) are other characteristic features. Buildings are generally of whitewashed mud brick, with elaborately carved wooden columns, beams and balconies; flat roofs are often tiled with stones. Of particular interest are the brightly coloured murals covering the walls and ceilings; large-scale plaster sculptures are also generally painted.

Of the earlier monasteries dating from the 11th century onwards, that at **Alchi** is unsurpassed for the glory of its paintings. These fully illustrate the Mahayana pantheon, with its innumerable divinities, guardians, saints, teachers and attendants. These remarkably well-preserved paintings are related to contemporary traditions in central and eastern India. Other examples of early wall paintings are seen at **Lamayuru** and **Tabo**. At the latter monastery, finely modelled plaster sculptures have also survived.

Slightly later are the 13th–15th-century paintings in the cave temples at **Saspol** and in the halls of the **Karsha** complex. During this period, Tibetan iconographic and stylistic features were increasingly adopted. After the 16th century, when most of the other monasteries in the region were established, Tibetan influences predominated. Paintings and sculptures at **Basgo**, **Hemis**, **Phiyang**, **Shey** and **Spituk** provide abundant evidence of Tibetan Buddhist art in northern India. Today, monasteries continue to be renovated, as at **Leh**, **Phiyang** and other sites in the region (also at **Pemayangtse** and **Rumtek** in Sikkim, and **Tawang** in Arunachal Pradesh in eastern India). Artists working in traditional Tibetan styles continue to adorn the interiors of halls and shrines.

Opposite above Martand, Surya Temple, 8th century

Opposite below Pendrethan (Srinagar), Shiva Temple, 12th century

Opposite above Jagheshwar, Temples, 9th–10th centuries
Opposite below Masrur, Rock-cut Temples, 9th–10th century
Above Chamba, Lakshmi Narayana Temple, 14th century

Left Dhingri (Manali), Hidimba Devi Temple, 16th century

Below Behna, Mahadeva Temple, 16th–17th century

Opposite above Amritsar, Golden Temple, 18th century

Opposite below New Delhi, Lakshmi Narayana Temple, 20th century

Shey, Gompa, 16th–17th century

Opposite Leh, Chorten, 17th–18th century

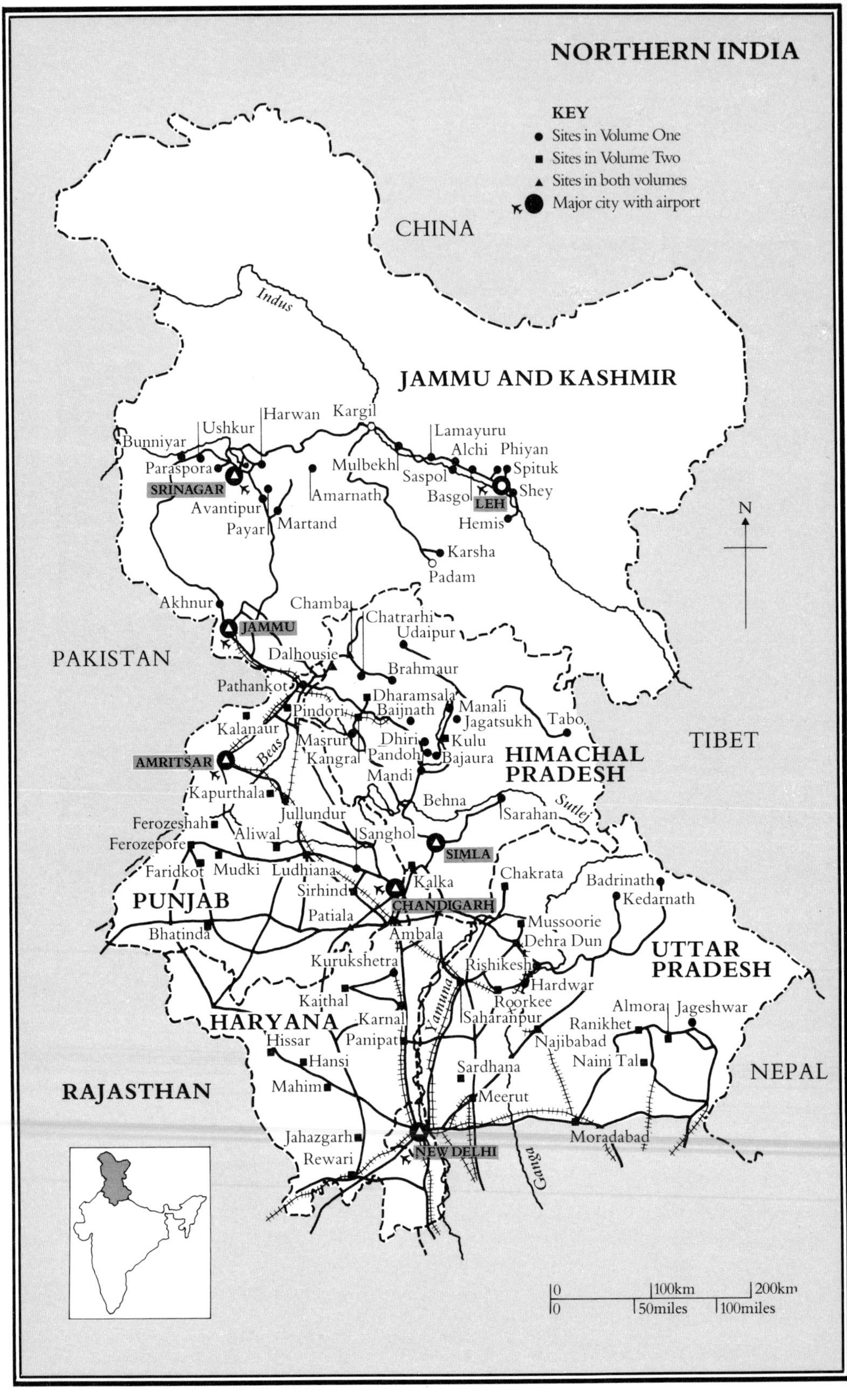

NORTHERN INDIA

KEY
- ● Sites in Volume One
- ■ Sites in Volume Two
- ▲ Sites in both volumes
- ✈● Major city with airport

CHINA

Indus

JAMMU AND KASHMIR

N

Bunniyar · Ushkur · Harwan · Kargil · Lamayuru · Alchi · Phiyan
Paraspora · Spituk
SRINAGAR · Mulbekh · Saspol · Basgo · **LEH** · Shey
Avantipur · Amarnath · Hemis
Payar · Martand
Karsha
Padam

Akhnur · Chamba · Chatrarhi · Udaipur
JAMMU · Dalhousie · Brahmaur
PAKISTAN · Pathankot · Dharamsala · Manali · Tabo
Pindori · Baijnath · Jagatsukh · **TIBET**
Kalanaur · Masrur · Dhiri · Kulu
AMRITSAR · Kangra · Pandoh · Bajaura · **HIMACHAL**
· Mandi · **PRADESH**
Kapurthala · Behna · *Sutlej*
Ferozeshah · Jullundur · Sarahan
Ferozepore · Aliwal · Sanghol
Faridkot · Mudki · Ludhiana · **SIMLA**
PUNJAB · Sirhind · Kalka · Chakrata · Badrinath
Patiala · **CHANDIGARH** · Kedarnath
Bhatinda · Ambala · Mussoorie · **UTTAR**
Kurukshetra · Dehra Dun · **PRADESH**
Kaithal · Rishikesh · Roorkee · Hardwar
Karnal · Saharanpur · Almora · Jageshwar
HARYANA · Panipat · Ranikhet
Hissar · Najibabad · **NEPAL**
Hansi · Sardhana · Naini Tal
Mahim · Meerut
RAJASTHAN · *Yamuna* · *Ganga*
Jahazgarh · Moradabad
Rewari · **NEW DELHI**

| 0 | | 100km | | 200km |
| 0 | 50miles | | 100miles | |

AKHNUR

The ruins of a large Buddhist monastery are found at this site on the bank of the Chenab river. Among the sculptures that were discovered here are numerous fine terracotta heads dating from the 6th century and which are clearly influenced by Gupta traditions of central India. Several of these figurines are exhibited in museums at **Chandigarh** and **Jammu**.

ALCHI

The temples comprising the Choskor complex at Alchi are the most important early Buddhist monuments in Ladakh. Five shrines partly obscured by residences stand in a large courtyard. Three chortens define a path leading to the dukhang, the nucleus of the complex. Throughout, timber balconies, doorways and windows are set in mud-covered rock walls; flat roofs are covered with stone tiles. Much of the woodwork is finely carved and painted. Interior plastered walls and ceilings are covered with paintings of the Mahayana pantheon; stucco figures are larger than life-size. The condition of these murals is remarkable; the original brilliant colours are almost perfectly preserved. While it is likely that these paintings were restored in the 15th–16th century, their iconography and style indicate an earlier date.

Sumtsek, late 11th century

Architecturally and artistically, this is the most interesting monument at Alchi. The triple-storey temple has openings in the middle of each floor that permit light to enter from the topmost chamber. The ground level is laid out on a stepped plan, with a chorten in the middle surrounded by four columns. These columns, as well as those on the exterior, have brackets incised with flowing foliation. Sculpted

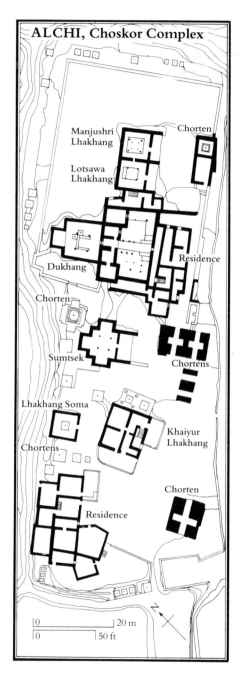

ALCHI, Choskor Complex

Manjushri Lhakhang
Lotsawa Lhakhang
Chorten
Dukhang
Chorten
Residence
Sumtsek
Chortens
Lhakhang Soma
Khaiyur Lhakhang
Chortens
Chorten
Residence

0   20 m
0   50 ft

Buddha images sit in trefoil niches above the elaborately carved beams. The walls are covered with painted figures and mandalas notable for their vibrant reds and blues.

Double-height niches on three sides house large standing figures more than 4 m (13 ft) high: thus, Manjushri (east), Maitreya (north) and Avalokiteshvara (west). These brightly painted Bodhisattvas are remarkable for the rich detail of their headdresses and costumes; miniature medallions on the robes contain scenes from the lives of the Master and his disciples. The walls of the niches in which these Bodhisattvas stand have rows of miniature devotees, sages, Buddhas, consorts and celestials; sculptures of attendant figures are also found here. Seated Bodhisattva images surrounded by hundreds of miniature replicas are seen on the flanking walls. Over the entrance (south) is a large blue Mahakala figure striding vigorously across a corpse.

The walls of the second and third levels of the temple are completely covered with large mandalas. These follow a standard scheme: within a large circle, a square with four 'gateways' contains numerous miniature seated Bodhisattvas, goddesses, attendants, guardians and lotus petals arranged in a strict hierarchical sequence. Between the mandalas are goddesses and guardians. The ceilings too are painted, mostly with lotus medallions, miniature figures (including horsemen) and stylized foliation.

Dukhang, late 11th century

Concealed by a house, this temple is entered through a courtyard partly roofed by a colonnade. A chorten is suspended over the central pathway leading to the door of the shrine; its hollow interior is adorned with murals. The doorway itself is elaborately carved with miniature Bodhisattva figures, attendants and guardians. Angled struts over the porch have lobes containing rampant lions and composite animals.

The interior of the temple has a niche at the rear (north) housing a large Vairochana image together with attendants,

all executed in plaster. The other three walls are each painted with two circular mandalas containing squares with 'gateways'. These depict Vairochana, surrounded by the four Tathagatas, subsidiary female divinities, Bodhisattvas and guardian figures. In the middle of the south wall is a painting of striding Mahakala beneath a smaller mandala. More restrained in its colouristic effects than the Sumtsek, this temple may have been intended for the use of monks only.

Lhakhang Soma, 12th–13th century

This small square chamber contains a chorten in the middle; two columns with lion-faced brackets support the roof. The west wall is dominated by three painted mandalas which progressively increase in size from left to right; the other walls have large images of Vairochana (north) or Buddha (east) surrounded by multiple Bodhisattvas, attendants and guardians. On the lower part of the south wall are scenes from the life of Buddha; over the doorway is the usual Mahakala figure.

Lotsawa Lhakhang and Manjushri Lhakhang, 12th–13th century

These two small, square shrines adjoin each other; both have four centrally placed columns supporting raised roofs over the central bays. Seated in the middle of the Manjushri Lhakhang is a large shrine with four images of the Bodhisattva (recent date); a seated Buddha is located at the rear (north) of the adjacent shrine. The paintings in these two temples resemble those of the Lhakhang Soma but are not as well preserved. The interiors are dominated by miniature Buddhas, Bodhisattvas, goddesses and guardians arranged both in mandalas and horizontal rows. Similar figures are also found in the clerestory of the Lotsawa Lhakhang.

AMARNATH

Magnificently located in a glacial valley at an elevation of 4,175 m (13,700 ft), this holy Hindu site is reached only after several days of climbing. The object of worship here is a cave containing a natural ice formation; this is worshipped by devotees as a Shiva linga known as Amaranatha. At the time of the full moon in July–August, thousands of devotees make a pilgrimage to this cave.

AMRITSAR

The chief focus of Sikh history and culture, Amritsar is celebrated for the Golden Temple, the holiest of Sikh gurudwaras. Here the Adi Granth, the Original Book, is kept and read. The religious importance of Amritsar dates from the early 16th century, when Nanak, the first Sikh Guru, founded the new religion. Under succeeding Gurus, especially Arjan (1581–1606), the Adi Granth was compiled and a large temple founded. The practice of regular readings and recitals of Sikh scriptures was also established at this time.

(For the British monuments of the city see Volume II.)

Hari Mandir (Golden Temple), 18th century and later

The present shrine replaces several earlier structures. It stands in the middle of a large rectangular tank (Amrita Sarovar or Pool of Nectar) reached by a marble causeway on the west. Surrounding the

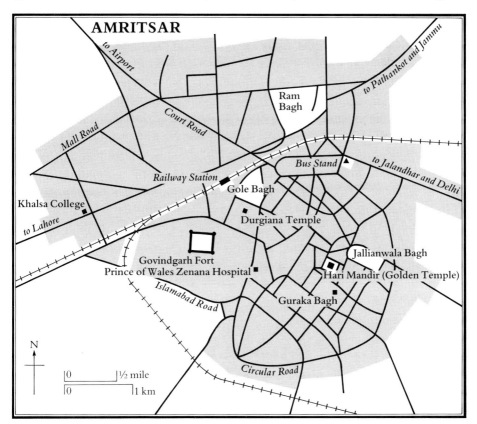

AMRITSAR

to Airport
to Pathankot and Jammu
Ram Bagh
Court Road
Mall Road
to Jalandhar and Delhi
Bus Stand
Railway Station
Gole Bagh
Khalsa College
to Lahore
Durgiana Temple
Jallianwala Bagh
Govindgarh Fort
Prince of Wales Zenana Hospital
Hari Mandir (Golden Temple)
Islamabad Road
Guraka Bagh
N
0 ½ mile
0 1 km
Circular Road

tank are offices, stores, dining-hall, kitchen, guesthouse and watchtowers. The main gateway on the north (Darshani Darwaza) is marked by a clocktower. On the west is the Ahal Takht, a domed building which serves as the seat of the supreme Sikh council. A tree nearby shades the spot where Arjan meditated.

In the middle of the pond stands the triple-storey temple, its doors and balconies open to the four directions. On the ground floor is the shrine containing the Adi Granth; the book rests on a sumptuous throne that is covered by a jewelled canopy. Singers take turns declaiming verses from the book; each evening it is taken in holy procession to the Ahal Takht. On the upper levels are a treasury housing the canopy and other processional items, and a small mirrored hall used for meditation.

The marble building is much influenced by late-Mughal architecture. Colonnades, niches, balconies, parapets, turrets and the central petalled dome are all typical of contemporary mosques and palaces. The exterior is completely gilded with gold leaf; inlaid marble, carved woodwork, ivory mosaic and embossed gold and silverwork adorn the interior. Murals illustrate scenes from the lives of the Sikh Gurus.

Guraka Bagh (Garden of the Guru)

This contains fruit trees, a tank and a number of pavilions, including the Tower of Baba Atal (son of the sixth Guru). The monument is capped by a small petalled dome; within, wall paintings depict episodes from the life of Nanak. The Kaulsar tank commemorates the devotion of a Muslim girl who converted to the Sikh religion.

AVANTIPUR

This site represents the capital of Avanti-varman (c. 855–83), the first ruler of the Utpala dynasty of Kashmir. Two ruined Hindu temples are found here.

Avantisvamin Temple, 9th century

This temple is an important example of the later Kashmir style. As at **Martand**, the principal shrine is set within a large, rectangular court entered through a gateway on the west. Only the lower portions of the colonnade have survived; even so, a richly decorated classical style is evident in the pilasters, the niches with trilobed openings and the gabled pediments. The basements of six minor shrines are preserved at the corners of the courtyard; a raised floor area is positioned in front (west) of the principal sanctuary. The broad staircase leading up to the sanctuary is flanked by a high basement; among the sculptures on its sides are seated Vishnu with two consorts, and some unidentified royal figures. While little of the shrine itself still stands, its overall layout, with a central sanctuary and projecting porches on each side, is clear.

More exists of the gateway, with its two porches raised on a high basement. Exuberant carving (badly worn) includes friezes and medallions of figures, birds and animals, and niches with gable-like pediments containing images of Ganga (north) and Yamuna (south).

Among the large assortment of antiquities discovered in the excavations here are several sculptures now displayed at the Sri Pratap Singh Museum, **Srinagar**.

Avantishvara Temple, 9th century

This temple was conceived on a grand scale but was probably never completed. The damage and spoilage suffered here are greater than those of the Avantisvamin temple, with which it is almost identical in layout. Only the basement of the main shrine now stands; attached to this are the outlines of four minor shrines. The colonnade is more or less reduced to its basement; more is visible of the gateway.

BADRINATH

This celebrated Hindu pilgrimage site is situated in a valley dominated by two lofty peaks, Nar Parbet and Narayana Parbet. The temple of Badrinatha is said to have been founded by Shankara, the 9th-century philosopher; but the present stone building is a recent structure. Above the sanctuary rises an unadorned curved tower with shallow projections; at the summit is an overhanging wooden roof. The mandapa also has a gabled roof, but a recent extension is provided with a dome. The gateway is built in a revivalist Mughal style.

A short distance below the temple are pools supplied by water from thermal springs.

BAIJNATH

Vaidyanatha Temple, 1204 and later

This is one of the best-preserved Hindu stone temples in the Kangra valley. Its sanctuary walls are divided both horizontally and vertically into niches; above rises a soaring tower with an amalaka and a pot finial at the summit. Facing west, a later mandapa (mostly rebuilt) adjoins the sanctuary; miniature shrines, complete with their own towers, are inserted into the corners. Among the sculptures in the mandapa there are a Harihara panel and a dancing Shiva carved on a column. Gracefully posed figures of Ganga and Yamuna flank the sanctuary doorway. Several other large panels date from the 13th–14th century.

BAJAURA

Vishveshvara Mahadeva Temple,
late 9th century

This Hindu stone temple is one of the best preserved in the Kulu valley. Its overall form and decoration illustrate the influence of contemporary Pratihara traditions from central India.

The sanctuary has projecting shrines on three sides and a porch on the front (east), each surmounted by a pyramidal roof. These roofs are adorned with tower-like motifs and large arched niches containing triple heads of Shiva, the god to whom the temple is dedicated. Rising above is the curved shaft of the central tower, which is divided into horizontal sections, with an amalaka at the summit. The doorways are flanked by pilasters with pot and foliage capitals, and figures of river goddesses; miniature shrine-like motifs are carved on the lintels. Of interest are the images housed in the niches, especially Durga (north), Ganesha (south) and Vishnu (west). Among the loose sculptures that were found nearby is an 8th-century image of Vishvarupa; other pieces have been removed to the State Museum, **Simla**.

BASGO

The ruins of this impressive Buddhist citadel crown a dramatic spur of rock overlooking the upper Indus valley. Basgo served as a royal residence on several occasions between the 15th and 17th centuries; it was also besieged by the Tibetan and Mongol armies. Two Buddhist temples and a small shrine surrounded by numerous chortens still stand. Beyond the village are mani walls of heaped stones incised with Buddha figures, lotus flowers, mantras and other auspicious emblems.

Maitreya Temple, 16th century

This temple occupies an isolated rocky point. It was constructed by one of the Namgyal rulers. Here paintings in the Tibetan style are preserved. On the right of the entrance doorway, under the protection of Vajrapani, is a representation of the royal founder and his family; to the left are episodes illustrating the life of Shakyamuni. A large sculpture of Maitreya protrudes above the painted ceiling at the rear of the hall; smaller Bodhisattva figures appear at either side. On each side of the two lateral walls are painted images of Buddha, Vajrapani, Avalokiteshvara and monks of the Kagyupa sect.

Serzang (Gold and Copper) Temple, 17th century

The temple owes its name to the copy of the Buddhist canon partly written in gold, silver and copper letters that is kept here. Murals depict Buddha figures, including Vairochana.

BEHNA

Mahadeva Temple, 16th–17th century

This is one of the largest gable-roofed Hindu temples in the Sutlej valley. The mandapa and corridor around the sanctuary are open on all sides; benches with leaning back-rests are positioned at the peripheries. Angled struts support the overhanging stone-tiled roof, which is steeply gabled in two tiers. Rising over the sanctuary is an open construction of two superimposed balconies; the upper balcony is provided with a timber-tiled conical roof and a metal pot-like finial.

There are elaborate carvings on the cedar balconies and internal columns. Window recesses flanking the sanctuary doorway have friezes of animals and stylized foliation. Leaning against the recess to the right are 8th–9th-century stone sculptures of Vishnu and Lakshmi.

A collection of brass masks of the god Shiva is housed in the sanctuary; these possibly date from the 12th–13th century.

BRAHMAUR

Lakshana Devi Temple, 9th century

This is one of the most important early wooden Hindu temples in the Chamba valley. Though substantially rebuilt in recent times, the temple preserves elaborately carved timber elements of an early date. The outer doorway is surrounded by miniature figures of erotic couples, river goddesses and the Navagrahas. Within the large trefoil niche above is a triple-headed Vishnu figure seated on Garuda. Scrollwork and foliate patterns surround the sanctuary doorway. Within the mandapa, richly carved columns, capitals and brackets support beams and raised ceilings on rotated square designs.

A large metal image of Durga is housed in the shrine; the goddess holds up the buffalo demon by its tail.

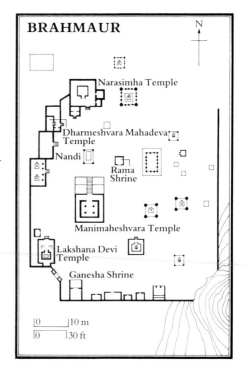

Narasimha and Manimaheshvara Temples, 10th century

These Hindu stone buildings illustrate the later evolution of the Pratihara temple style. The sanctuaries are contained within soaring towers, the uppermost portions of which are concealed beneath overhanging wooden roofs. Small wall niches are mostly empty. Over the entrances, projections with carved decoration have tower-like motifs; the towers are otherwise without ornament.

Among the brass sculptures here are seated images of Narasimha and Ganesha; an almost life-size Nandi is enshrined within an open pavilion opposite the Manimaheshvara temple. Together with the Durga figure in the Lakshana Devi temple, these sculptures are dated to the 8th century.

BUNNIYAR

Vishnu Temple, 9th century

Despite its dilapidation and worn stonework, this is an important Hindu example of the early-Kashmir style. An almost square enclosure is defined by a colonnade with classical pilasters and intermediate trilobed niches; a gateway with two porches is situated on the east. Within the enclosure is a small temple raised high on a double plinth. The projecting porches on each side are flanked by classical pilasters and surmounted by trilobed openings. Nothing is preserved of the roof, presumably once gabled in two tiers. The original Vishnu image within the sanctuary is now replaced by a set of small lingas.

CHAMBA

The towered Hindu stone temples in this town illustrate the influence of central Indian traditions, especially of the 9th–10th-century Pratihara period. Walls of the typical Chamba temple have projections with miniature niches (mostly empty). The curved tower continues these wall projections, but the upper portions are concealed beneath overhanging wooden roofs (later additions). Of particular interest are the metal images enshrined in several of these temples.

(For the other monuments of the town see Volume II.)

Lakshmi Narayana Complex, mostly 14th century

Situated opposite the palace of the Chamba rulers, this is the most important temple of the town. Several shrines, columns and a tank are contained within a long walled compound that is divided into four courts arranged on ascending levels. The principal sanctuary, which gives its name to the complex, faces the entrance on the north; the detached mandapa in front is a later addition.

The Gauri Shankara shrine within the third court dates partly from the 11th century. Large images of Shiva, Parvati

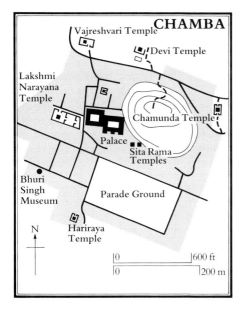

CHAMBA

Vajreshvari Temple

Devi Temple

Lakshmi Narayana Temple

Chamunda Temple

Palace

Sita Rama Temples

Bhuri Singh Museum

Parade Ground

Hariraya Temple

N

| 0 | 600 ft |
| 0 | 200 m |

and Nandi are enshrined within the sanctuary; these brass sculptures are all inlaid with silver and copper.

Hariraya Temple, 14th century

This temple contains a fine 9th–10th-century brass sculpture of Vaikuntha, 1·4 m (4½ ft) high. This aspect of Vishnu is recognizable by the triple heads.

Bhuri Singh Museum

14th–15th-century stone sculptures from nearby sites are exhibited here. These include a Vaikuntha image as well as smaller brass figures and masks.

CHANDIGARH

(For the city and its monuments see Volume II.)

Government Museum and Art Gallery

This collection is notable for the large number of antiquities from the Gandhara region of north-western Pakistan. Most of these schist sculptures and stucco fragments date from the 2nd–3rd centuries. They depict standing and seated Buddhist figures, and scenes from the life of the Master. Among the most impressive figures are three princely Maitreya images with superbly detailed headdresses, costumes and jewellery (2069, 2342, 2353), a seated meditating Buddha with a fully modelled head (41) and narrative panels (432.87, 590). Architectural fragments from Gandhara are carved with devotees, Buddhist episodes, Jataka stories and Hellenistic motifs.

Terracotta heads from the 4th–6th-century sites of **Akhnur** and **Ushkur** are on display. There is also a selection of Hindu and Jain sculptures from local sites.

Of interest is a group of 9th–10th-century images from Agroha, especially standing Shiva and Parvati (47) and two standing Vishnu figures (36.85, 37). Bronzes from nearby sites are also displayed.

CHATRARHI

Shakti Devi Temple, partly 8th–9th century

Though mostly rebuilt, this Hindu temple houses a sanctuary and colonnade that preserve early examples of carved woodwork. As at **Brahmaur**, these sculptures demonstrate the influence of post-Gupta traditions from central India. Cedar columns are fashioned with pot and foliage motifs; flying figures adorn the brackets. The doorway has scrollwork and other decorative motifs, as well as miniature divinities, ganas and animals.

Enshrined within the sanctuary is a large 8th-century brass image of Devi; the goddess is richly adorned with jewels and a crown. There are also attendant figurines and brass masks of Shiva.

DHIRI

Brahma Temple, 16th–17th century

This is a typical example of traditional Hindu temple architecture in the Kulu valley. Though the building was substantially renovated in recent times, it preserves its original form. Over the square sanctuary rises a triple series of sloping roofs. The lower two roofs are pyramidal and covered with blue slate; the upper roof, which is coated with timber tiles, is conical. The walls of timber-bonded masonry contrast with the carved wooden struts and fringes (recently replaced).

HARDWAR

One of the holy cities of Hinduism, Hardwar is built on the west bank of the Ganga at a point where the river flows out of the hills into the plains. Here too the Ganges Canal begins, drawing water away from the main river; the entrance to the canal is guarded by two stone lions. A hydroelectric station is located nearby.

While there are no ancient monuments at Hardwar, the city attracts saints, pilgrims and devotees who come in large numbers to bathe in the Ganga. (The water here is considered so holy that it is transported all over the country to be used in purification ceremonies.) As at **Allahabad** and **Varanasi**, visitors seek salvation, atonement for their sins and merit in their next birth. Every twelve years a great Kumbha Mela attracts thousands of pilgrims, especially sadhus, who leave their mountain retreats to bathe here. The town is provided with numerous institutions and rest-houses. Several spots in the vicinity, including **Rishikesh** 24 km (15 miles) upstream, are renowned for their religious establishments.

Hardwar is connected with the well-known myth of the descent of the Ganga. At the insistence of Bhagiratha, a king who wished to liberate the souls of his ancestors, the celestial river was persuaded to descend to earth to purify the ashes of the dead. To protect the earth from the shattering impact of the waters, Shiva agreed to receive Ganga in his matted hair; thereafter, the river flowed peacefully on earth. This legend is only one of several that link Hardwar with Ganga; numerous episodes from the Mahabharata epic are also set here.

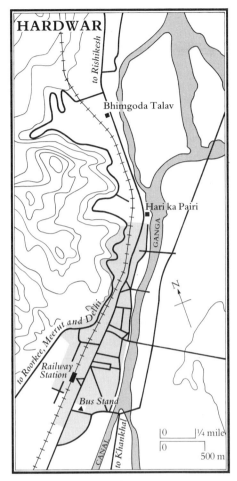

Hari ka Pairi

This ghat is where most pilgrims come to bathe. Regarded as a heavenly staircase, the bank displays the footprints of Vishnu; opposite is a modern clocktower. The temples here are dedicated to various deities and date from no earlier than the 19th century. Curved and clustered towers rise over small sanctuaries; open pavilions, often octagonal in plan, multi-lobed arches and domes with lotus petals indicate the influence of late-Mughal architecture.

Bhimgoda Talav

This holy tank 3 km (2 miles) upstream is associated with Bhima, the Pandava hero of the Mahabharata.

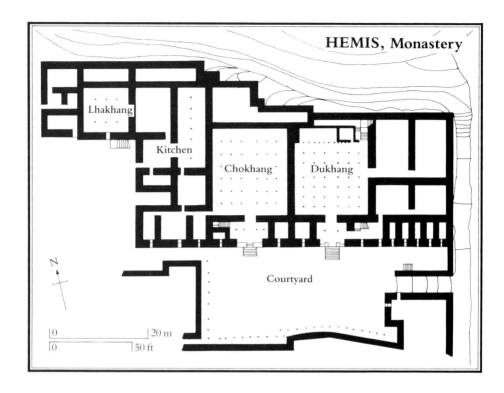

HEMIS, Monastery

Lhakhang

Kitchen

Chokhang

Dukhang

Courtyard

Khankhal

3 km (2 miles) downstream is this sacred point, believed to be the site where Shiva's wife Sati sacrificed herself.

Gurukul

Still further downstream is a cluster of large-scale religious establishments. These include the Ved Mandir, an elaborate revivalist building with curved towers and turrets.

HARWAN

Of this important 4th–5th-century Buddhist site in the central valley of Kashmir, only the foundations of stone terraces and structures are visible. The most interesting feature is an apsidal-ended temple with a circular shrine. This stood in a courtyard paved with terracotta tiles; benches for seating all around were also covered with tiles. These tiles have moulded decoration, with a large variety of motifs including human figures. Several tiles from this site are displayed in the Sri Pratap Singh Museum, **Srinagar**.

HEMIS

This secluded Buddhist monastery in Ladakh was founded by Senge Namgyal, a celebrated 17th-century ruler, for the Tibetan Kagyupa sect. It was added to in subsequent centuries and is now one of the wealthiest monasteries in the western Himalayas. It is especially renowned for its summer festival with mask dances. Every twelve years a gigantic cloth thangka is displayed here.

The complex is entered through a gate on the east which leads into a large courtyard, the setting of the festival activities.

Stones inserted into the walls of the colonnade (south side of court) are painted with saintly figures. On the north side are two assembly halls, which are approached by steep steps which lead to verandahs with brightly coloured columns and carved brackets. Paintings here have recently been restored; these depict ferocious guardians and a Wheel of Life. The left hall (chokhang), used for winter ceremonies, has the central portion of its ceiling raised up. The altar and area behind are adorned with figures and thangkas; there are also brass and silver chortens and an image of Tara. The right hall (dukhang) has murals dating from the 18th century; these portray aggressive deities, including Hevajra and Samvara. Another smaller, older shrine on the western side of the complex preserves murals dating from the 16th–18th centuries.

At the upper level there are a number of shrines, the most important being the lhakhang. Here, a metal statue of the first head monk of the monastery is kept,

together with the silver chorten containing his remains. There are also 9th–11th-century brass images of standing and seated Buddha figures from Kashmir, thangkas, masks and costumes. The southern face of the upper floor has projecting balconies that overlook the court beneath.

JAGATSUKH

Mahesha Temple, 8th century

This small Hindu shrine in the Kulu valley is a typical Pratihara monument. The small square sanctuary has three delicate and ornate niches in its outer walls. On the front, the decorated doorway is sheltered by a porch, the columns of which have fluted shafts with pot and foliage capitals. The curved tower is divided into horizontal mouldings; a large amalaka is positioned at the summit. Over the porch, the projection contains a

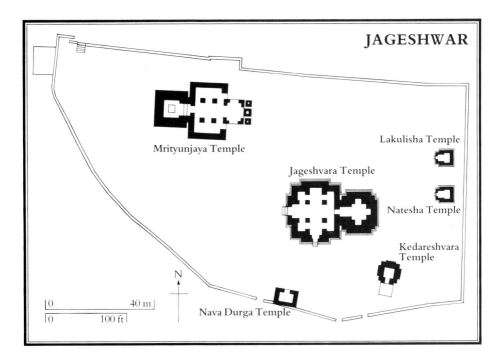

JAGESHWAR

Mrityunjaya Temple

Lakulisha Temple

Jageshvara Temple

Natesha Temple

Kedareshvara Temple

N

0   40 m

0   100 ft

Nava Durga Temple

triple-headed bust of Shiva and a seated image of the god, both set into arch-like frames.

Several loose sculptures indicate the presence of other temples, now dismantled.

JAGESHWAR (map p. 117)

Numerous 9th–8th-century Hindu stone temples typical of the Pratihara period stand at this site. Walls and curved towers are provided with shallow projections; towers are divided into slender horizontal mouldings. The amalakas at the summits are concealed within later overhanging wooden roofs.

Natesha Temple, 9th century

This shrine is typical of the smaller examples. The outer walls are plain except for small niches surmounted by triangular pediments. The doorway has finely carved motifs, including sculptures of the river goddesses. Above is a large projection with a triple-headed bust of Shiva and a dancing image of the god; a lion sits on top.

Mrityunjaya Temple, 10th century

This is the largest and best-preserved temple at the site. It is adorned with Shiva sculptures on its outer walls and tower; the triple heads of the deity are also carved on to the front (east) projection of the tower. The most interesting feature of the interior is the decorated sanctuary doorway.

Nava Durga Temple, 9th–10th century

This rectangular shrine with a vaulted roof now serves as a sculpture store. Among the metal images is a large 9th–10th-century figure, possibly the portrait of a royal patron.

JAMMU

(For the city and its civic monuments see Volume II.)

Raghunatha Mandir, 1857

Inaugurated by the local ruler Ranbir Singh, this sacred Hindu complex is the focus of the religious and cultural life of the town. The temple consists of seventeen shrines, each with a steeply angled tower unadorned except for shallow projections on each side. Over the principal central shrine, the tower has a curved profile. Fluted wall pilasters and shallow niches with lobed arches indicate the influence of late-Mughal architecture.

The principal sanctuary is dedicated to Rama, the patron deity of the Dogra kings; the niches in the outer walls contain the Navagrahas and the Dikpalas. A portrait of the royal patron and an imposing sculpture of Hanuman flank the entrance. Subsidiary mandapas contain innumerable shalagramas brought from the bed of the Narmada river in the northern Deccan. Other shrines house images of the incarnations of Vishnu, as well as of Surya and Shiva.

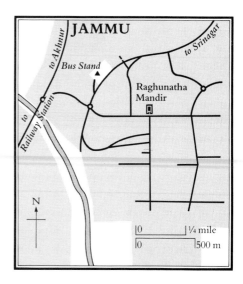

Dogra Art Gallery

Among the sculptures from various local sites are 6th-century terracotta heads from **Akhnur**.

KARSHA

This Buddhist monastery of the Tibetan Gelugpa sect is the largest in the Zanskar valley. Monastic life focuses on the main courtyard near the top of the complex; this is reached by a narrow zigzag path. Here are two assembly halls (lhakhangs) and a number of temples. Another larger temple, the Labrang, is situated half-way down the hill; there is a Maitreya shrine at the lower end of the complex. Other religious buildings and the ruins of a fort are located on the summit of a hill west of the main monastery, from which they are separated by a gorge. Another Maitreya temple beneath the fort is surrounded by a few houses and chortens. Throughout the monastery there are fine examples of mural paintings and sculptures depicting a range of Mahayana deities. Some of these date back to the 13th–14th centuries; others are more recent.

Lower Dukhang, 17th–18th century

Left of the entrance is a sculpture of Maitreya. Almost the whole of the left wall is occupied by racks housing Tibetan manuscripts and a collection of metal images. The mural on the rear wall depicts scenes from the life of Shakyamuni; these are executed in the later Tibetan style permeated with Chinese motifs, such as the details of landscape and of domestic life. These motifs do not appear in the paintings on the right wall, where Avalokiteshvara, Tara and Manjushri are represented.

Labrang, 14th–15th century

The surviving murals in this temple depict five different male divinities as well as Prajnaparamita. Against the right wall is a large sculpture of Maitreya, more than 4 m (13 ft) high, as well as a smaller Avalokiteshvara figure.

Avalokiteshvara Temple, 17th–18th century

This temple is remarkable for its well-preserved murals depicting Mahayana deities and mandalas; low down on the walls are scenes of monks and lay people and illustrations of houses and horses. An eleven-headed Avalokiteshvara image stands in a central niche. The walls at either side are adorned with figures of Manjushri (left) and Vajrapani (right), both with attendant goddesses.

KEDARNATH

Situated at an elevation of 3,580 m (11,750 ft), this celebrated Hindu pilgrimage spot in the high Himalayas is dedicated to Shiva. According to tradition, Shankara, the great philosopher, died here in about 820. Despite the antiquity of the site, the Kedareshvara temple here is of recent date. The sanctuary is contained within an unadorned curved tower with shallow projections and a timber roof at the summit. The projecting mandapa is gabled; its façade displays bands of curved ornamentation and decorated niches.

KURUKSHETRA

This Hindu site is celebrated in literature as the battle-ground of the Kauravas and Pandavas, scene of the climactic episode of the Mahabharata epic. A vast rectangular tank, the Brahmasagar, is a favourite spot for pilgrims, who come here in large numbers to bathe. The tank is surrounded by ghats and shrines.

(For the Islamic monuments nearby see Volume II.)

LAMAYURU

Perched on a rocky crag overlooking the Indus river, this Buddhist monastery belongs to the Tibetan Kagyupa sect. It was founded in the 11th century but was partly destroyed in the 19th century. The monastery preserves paintings in which Indian and Tibetan styles are mixed.

The oldest temple in the complex is dominated by a large Vairochana image seated on a lion-throne. The murals here date from the 11th–12th century but are in poor condition. They include four friezes of Buddha on the rear wall, a mandala of Vairochana and an eleven-headed image of Avalokiteshvara.

The imposing dukhang has been recently decorated with brightly coloured paintings of wrathful deities. A small grotto in the right wall houses stucco images of monks. On the upper storey there are four small rooms, two for the head lama, one containing printing blocks and the last a shrine for protective divinities.

LEH

Capital of Ladakh since the 16th century, Leh is built on an elevated plain only a short distance from the Indus river. The town was once a major stopping-point on the trade route linking Kashmir with Tibet and China. Leh is overlooked by a palace built on a hill north-east of the town; higher up are a fort and Buddhist monastery. Within the town there are several other Buddhist establishments and chortens, mostly neglected. The Sankar Gompa is 2 km (1½ miles) to the north.

Tsemo Gompa, 16th century and later

The Maitreya temple of this monastery is celebrated for its colossal three-storey-high image of Bodhisattva flanked by figures of Avalokiteshvara (right) and Manjushri (left). The walls have been repainted recently. The Gonkhang temple to the guardian divinities was founded by the Namgyal rulers at the beginning of the 16th century. A portrait of Tashi Namgyal, the royal patron, is positioned to the left of the entrance; there are also protective divinities in terrifying aspects. Other dominant figures are Mahakala with six arms and a fierce divinity riding a dog.

Royal Palace, 17th century

This is contemporary with the famed Potala palace at Lhasa in Tibet. The nine-storey building has sloping buttressed walls and projecting wooden balconies at different levels. The palace is now unoccupied.

Mani Walls, 17th–18th centuries

These walls were erected as memorials to deceased royal figures. Almost 500 m (1,650 ft) long, the walls contain many hundreds of Tibetan inscriptions carved

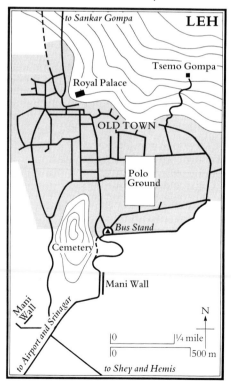

on to boulders. Beyond the walls stand numerous chortens.

Sankar Gompa, 17th–18th centuries

This modest monastic establishment is the residence of the chief lama of **Spituk**. A number of sculptures are housed here, including a bronze image of Tsongkhapa, the 15th-century founder of the Gelugpa sect; other small bronzes are of Tibetan origin. The verandah below the principal hall is decorated with murals of a recent date; these illustrate scenes of monastic life and of Buddhas and guardian figures.

Soma Gompa, 1957

This new monastery within the town was built to commemorate the 2,500th anniversary of the birth of Buddha. The principal hall contains an image of Shakyamuni brought from Tibet.

MANALI

Hidimba Devi Temple, 1553 and later

This Hindu temple stands in a sacred cedar forest near to the village of Dunghri, 2 km (1½ miles) west of Manali. Its sanctuary is built over a rocky crevice covered by a large rock that is worshipped as a manifestation of Durga; an image of this goddess is also enshrined here. The divinity is popularly worshipped throughout the region; on festival occasions the goddess is even transported to Kulu to 'visit' the god Raghunatha.

The temple is characterized by its 24-m-high (79 ft) tower. This consists of three tiers of square roofs covered with timber tiles; the conical roof is clad in metal. The unadorned walls of mud-covered stonework contrast with the carved wooden doorway, probably an original feature. This is elaborately decorated with miniature depictions of the goddess, attendants, animals and

stylized foliation. On the beams above the doorway appear the Navagrahas, female dancers and isolated scenes from the Krishna story.

MANDI

Trilokanatha Temple, 1520

This Hindu sanctuary is the focus of a group of shrines overlooking the Beas river. These illustrate the later evolution of stone temple architecture in the western Himalayas. In this example, the sanctuary is contained within a curved tower; the adjoining square mandapa is roofed with a pyramid of stone tiles. Little original sculptural ornamentation is preserved. A characteristic feature is the use of tower-like elements at the corners of the mandapa walls and above the niches.

Within the compound stand several smaller shrines dating from the 11th century.

Memorials

Outside the old city is a walled enclosure containing more than one hundred memorial stone slabs. These commemorate kings and other members of the royal household, including queens and concubines. The earliest examples date from the 13th–14th century; the latest is of King Bhavani Sen, who died in 1912.

MARTAND

Surya Temple, 8th century

This Hindu temple to the sun deity is situated on a lofty plateau commanding a superb view over the central valley of Kashmir. Despite its general dilapidation, the large scale of the monument and the grandeur of its conception are still impressive. It remains the masterpiece of

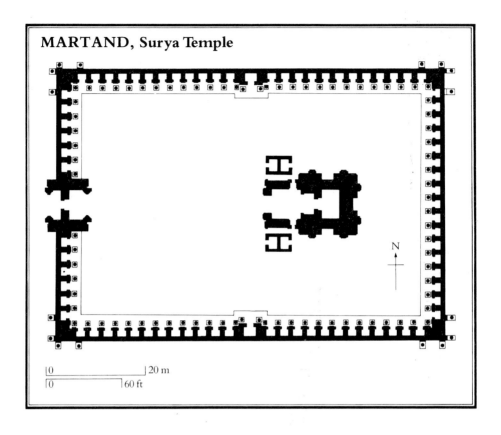

MARTAND, Surya Temple

0 _____ 20 m

0 _____ 60 ft

the early-Kashmir temple style, the work of Lalitaditya (c. 724–60), the most powerful and renowned monarch of the Karkota dynasty.

Throughout, the impact of classical architecture is evident, especially in the basement and cornice mouldings, pilasters and pediments. However, gabled roofs characteristic of the western Himalayas and traditional Hindu themes are also present. This blend of imported and indigenous architectural elements is a feature of the monument.

The temple is located at one end of a large rectangular court, which is entered through a gateway (mostly ruined) in the middle of the western side. The court is defined by a colonnade of fluted classical columns, some more than 4 m (13 ft) high. Between these are deep niches with trilobed openings flanked by pilasters; the central niches on each side are enlarged.

The temple itself consists of a principal sanctuary and two minor shrines raised on a high plinth. A broad flight of steps leads up to the main entrance on the west. Badly eroded panels in niches of various shapes are set into the plinth. The sanctuary is approached through an antechamber, the walls of which preserve damaged images of Ganga (north) and Vishnu (south) set in trilobed niches with gable-like pediments. The porches projecting in the middle of each side are flanked by classical pilasters; doorways are framed by ornamented jambs and lintels, now badly worn. Large trilobed openings within gabled pediments were created from massive corbelled blocks, many of which have now fallen. Nothing remains of the roof, presumably once gabled in two tiers.

MASRUR

Fifteen towered Hindu shrines dating from the 9th–10th century have been excavated out of solid rock. Despite their eroded condition, stylistic links with the Pratihara traditions of central India are evident.

The doorway to the main shrine is surrounded by bands of foliation with miniature figurative panels; the image of Shiva carved on to the lintel is earlier than the panels of Rama, Lakshmana and Sita installed within the sanctuary. Pilasters display the characteristic pot and foliage capitals. Niches are surmounted by elongated pediments with meshes of arch-like motifs; similar motifs adorn the curvilinear tower that rises above.

While almost no original sculptures are preserved at Masrur, several loose panels have been removed to the State Museum, **Simla**.

MULBEKH

Rock-cut Sculpture, 8th–9th century

This ancient stopping-point on the trade route between **Srinagar** and **Leh** is celebrated for the enormous rock-cut relief of the Buddhist saviour Maitreya. Carved on to the face of a solitary pinnacle, this 9-m-high (30 ft) sculpture depicts the standing four-armed Bodhisattva with elaborate headdress and jewels. The stiff posture and rounded modelling suggest contacts with contemporary artistic traditions in the central valley of Kashmir.

NEW DELHI

While not one monument prior to the arrival of the Muslims at the end of the 12th century survives intact within the city and its environs, there is substantial evidence of earlier occupation. This is provided by excavated finds in the Purana Qila, as well as by earlier architectural fragments incorporated into later Muslim projects, as at Mehrauli and Kotla Firuz Shah. (For Islamic and British monuments see Volume II.)

Religious architecture in the modern era is represented by numerous examples in the city. Among the larger shrines are the Birla Mandir and the Sikh gurudwara.

Purana Qila

The earliest artefacts discovered in the excavations within this Muslim fort date back to the 1st millennium BC. The presence of painted grey pottery fragments has encouraged some interpreters to identify the Purana Qila with Indraprastha, the capital of the Pandava heroes of the Mahabharata epic. A settlement contemporary with these finds, however, has yet to be located.

Continuous stratification begins in the 3rd-century-BC Maurya period. Typical finds are earthenware pottery with a glassy surface, punch-marked coins, human and animal terracotta figurines and inscribed terracotta seals. Wells lined with terracotta rings have also been exposed. Evidence of habitation from the 2nd century BC to the 3rd century AD is provided by rubble and burnt brick walls. Characteristic artefacts include red earthenware pottery, copper currency and terracotta plaques with semi-divine figures. Isolated coins and terracotta figurines belong to the Gupta era.

In the 12th century, the site was fortified by the Chahamana rulers, who constructed rubble ramparts with gates and houses of rubble and brick. Pottery and coins are common finds from these later levels.

Lakshmi Narayana Temple, 1938

Financed by the industrialist Raja Baldeo Birla, this temple is one of the most popular Hindu shrines within the city; it is

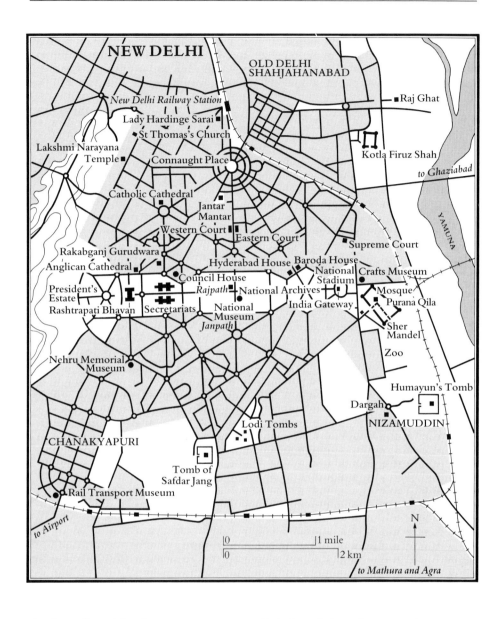

New Delhi map showing: NEW DELHI, OLD DELHI SHAHJAHANABAD, New Delhi Railway Station, Raj Ghat, Lady Hardinge Sarai, St Thomas's Church, Lakshmi Narayana Temple, Connaught Place, Kotla Firuz Shah, to Ghaziabad, Catholic Cathedral, Jantar Mantar, Western Court, Eastern Court, Supreme Court, YAMUNA, Rakabganj Gurudwara, Hyderabad House, Baroda House, Anglican Cathedral, Council House, National Stadium, Crafts Museum, President's Estate, Rajpath, National Archives, Mosque, Purana Qila, Rashtrapati Bhavan, Secretariats, National Museum, India Gateway, Sher Mandel, Janpath, Zoo, Nehru Memorial Museum, Humayun's Tomb, Dargah, NIZAMUDDIN, CHANAKYAPURI, Lodi Tombs, Tomb of Safdar Jang, Rail Transport Museum, to Airport, 0 1 mile, 0 2 km, N, to Mathura and Agra

the focus for celebrations commemorating the birth of Krishna.

The temple is designed in the Orissan style, with tall curved towers capped by large amalakas. The exterior is faced with the white marble and red sandstone typical of Delhi's Mughal architecture. The interior court is overlooked by two-storey verandahs on three sides; there are gardens and fountains at the rear.

Rakabganj Gurudwara, 20th century

This Sikh shrine marks the spot where Tej Bahadur, the ninth Guru, was cremated in 1675. The Guru was executed at the order of the Mughal emperor Aurangzeb when he refused to embrace Islam.

Despite its modern date, the design of this white marble shrine is typical of the late-Mughal period, with multi-lobed arches, projecting balconies, corner octagonal pavilions and a central raised chamber capped with a fluted dome. Smaller domed pavilions are positioned at the four corners of the platform on which the shrine is elevated.

National Museum

Since its foundation in 1949, this museum has grown to house a large collection of sculptures from almost all periods of Indian art.

The prehistoric civilization of the Indus valley, dating from the 3rd–2nd millennium BC, is represented by several important pieces from Harappa and Mohenjodaro. These include miniature stone sculptures of a male head (910) and torso (187.9042), as well as the celebrated statuette of a dancer (69884.987) and a bronze figurine of a dancing girl (5721.195). Among the other artefacts of this civilization are terracotta figurines and toys, decorated storage jars, gold jewellery and stone seals engraved with a variety of motifs.

From the earliest historical era of Indian sculpture, a few 3rd-century-BC Maurya figurines from **Mathura**, including a terracotta goddess (60.291), are on display. Belonging to the later Shunga period are terracotta and stone figures and plaques. These include a miniature scene of a couple seated on a throne from **Kausambi** (067). There is also a stone column carved with nagas and yakshis from Pauni (L77.1), as well as a relief depicting lovers from **Pitalkhora** (64.174). The gateway fragment from **Sanchi** has a seated mythical beast (76.614). A frieze from **Bharhut** shows elephants in undulating lotus stalks (66.168). Buddhist narrative reliefs and other motifs carved on to limestone panels from **Amaravati** are on loan from the British Museum, London.

Kushana sculptures dating from the 1st–2nd centuries, mostly from **Mathura**, are represented by an unusual double-sided panel depicting courtly scenes of drunken revelry and erotic pursuit (2800). Small railing pillars are carved with maidens in different postures. There is also a Jain votive plaque with auspicious emblems (J249). Buddhist art of the period includes a large headless Bodhisattva (A40); this may be compared with a smaller but more complete example from **Ahichhatra** (59.530/1). Among the other Buddhist figures are a seated image (L55.25) and a fine head (49.13/2). An unusual free-standing sculpture of Lakshmi has a pot and lotuses carved on to the back (3/6/87).

2nd–4th-century Ikshvaku limestone panels from **Nagarjunakonda** illustrate the evolution of early Buddhist art in the Deccan. One example depicts a stupa with flying celestials above (50.25); another combines together narrative episodes such as the casting of the horoscope, Buddha's birth, the first steps, the presentation of the child and the visit of Asita (50.17). Seven other episodes from the Master's life form a long frieze (50.18).

Gandharan art from north-western Pakistan belonging to the 2nd–3rd centuries includes numerous schist panels and heads as well as several Buddha and Bodhisattva figures: standing Maitreya (48.3/55), for example. Of note is the scene of Buddha preaching within an arched frame surrounded by miniature figures (48.3/40). Artefacts discovered at Taxila in Gandhara include silver bowls, ivory combs and a fine gold necklace (49.262/6).

The 3rd–5th-century Gupta period is represented by many fine Buddhist figures from **Sarnath**, such as standing Lokanatha (B8/14.53), standing Buddha (B21/59.527), the head of Buddha (47.20) and the torso of a Bodhisattva with a deerskin over the shoulder (59.527/5). One narrative panel combines Maya's dream, the enlightenment of the Master and the first sermon (49.114). Of Hindu epic subjects there are Lakshmana disfiguring Shurpanakha (51.178), Krishna kicking the cart (51.80) and scenes of lovers enjoying music (51.184), all from **Deogarh**. Cult icons include a single-faced linga from Khoh (76.223) and a linga combined with images of Surya and Brahma (71.211). From **Mathura** comes the torso of an imposing crowned Vishnu image (SR242). The seated gana from Nagpur, complete with a headdress and rotund stomach, is in exceptionally fine condition (L77.2). As for other themes, there is a fine panel of flying figures from Sondani (51.94), an armed rider on a vyala from **Sarnath** (49.115) and a double-lion capital from **Gwalior** (51.59).

Also displayed are several exceptional examples of Gupta terracotta art, particularly the large free-standing images of Ganga and Yamuna from **Ahichhatra** (L1–2). Narrative panels also come from the same site, such as Vikrama riding the centaur goddess, Urvashi (62.239).

To the post-Gupta styles of the 7th century belong several female figures from **Udaipur** and **Samalaji**. Two Early Chalukya ceiling panels from **Aihole** depict couples with billowing drapery flying through the clouds (L55.22–23). There is also a standing Harihara image from **Badami** (78.1005). Belonging to the 8th–9th centuries is a Rashtrakuta image of Ganga from **Ellora** (78.1010).

Southern sculptures, the earliest of which are from the 7th–8th-century Pallava era, are represented by an impressive seated Vishnu (59.153/106), seated Jyeshtha (59.153/357) and two large Rama figures shooting arrows (74/218–219), all from **Kanchipuram**. To the succeeding Chola period belong two pairs of guardian figures and also a slender standing Vishnu from Pashupatikovil (55.77/6). Typical of later Vijayanagara sculpture are the 16th-century figures of Parvati (59.153/168).

Returning to central and northern Indian styles, various seated and standing divinities datable to the 10th–12th centuries are on display. Among the finest are a Pratihara Trivikrama image of Vishnu (L143), a standing Parvati with attendant

figures from Baijnath (53.14) and a bust of a four-headed Tara image from **Sarnath** (47.32). The Chahamana basalt panel of Vishnu, in which the god stands in a frame surrounded by incarnations and other figures (L39), was discovered in the vicinity of the Quwwat-ul-Islam mosque. Contemporary western Indian examples include a finely detailed marble image of Sarasvati from **Bikaner** (1.6/278), an elegant polished basalt icon of Neminatha from Narhad (69.132) and a maiden playing with a ball from **Nagda** (71.L/5).

Pala and Sena sculptures from eastern India date from the 9th–12th centuries. These are represented by two fine standing Bodhisattva figures from **Nalanda** (49.148, 59.528) and several small Buddhist plaques. Hindu divinities, such as Surya (63.945), Vishnu (79.474) and Durga slaying Mahisha (63.936), are also exhibited. A female bracket figure carrying a water pot comes from Mahanadi (55.9). There is a fine selection of 12th–13th-century Orissan sculptures. These include an impressive standing Surya figure from **Konarak** (50.178), seated Varunani (50.179) and an unusual series of panels depicting Narasimha, the royal patron of the **Konarak** temple, worshipping (50.182), discoursing (50.180), seated in a swing (50.185) and practising archery (50.186).

Contemporary Deccan styles include a massive Late Chalukya lintel with Shiva dancing in the middle, flanked by deities, makaras and flying celestials, all carved in exuberant relief (50.159); another similar lintel comes from **Warangal** (4154). From **Halebid**, the Hoysala period is represented by several architectural pieces, including Vishnu and Lakshmi on flying Garuda (265) and Krishna playing the flute. A delicately executed bracket sculpture in the Late Chalukya style depicts a maiden dancing beneath a tree (50.190).

The bronze collection presents outstanding examples of the different styles.

The Pala period is indicated by a variety of Buddhist and Hindu figures; for example, standing Buddha from **Nalanda** (47.47), Padmapani (47.39), and the goddesses Prajnaparamita (47.34) and Hariti (47.50). There is a particularly fine Padmapani figure from **Sirpur** (68.148). Typical of the Hindu divinities are Balarama beneath the snake (47.36) and Kubera seated on a throne from **Nalanda** (47.46). Western Indian bronzes, mostly Jain icons from the 12th–15th centuries, include many small figures such as the enthroned Tirthankara surrounded by attendants from Akota (68.189).

Southern Indian sculptures from the 10th–12th-century Chola period comprise a large part of the bronze collection. Two magnificent dancing Shiva images are exhibited here, each with one foot uplifted, the four hands in different postures, the tassels and hair flying outwards and the head surrounded by haloes of flames (56.2/1, 57.16/1). More unusual is the small Shiva figure from Tiruvarangulam (55.40) with both legs bent but firmly placed on the ground. A further illustration of Chola dancing sculptures is provided by a delicately modelled Krishna dancing on the serpent demon; the youthful god holds up the tail (70.11). Among the other divinities are Shiva and Parvati together (47.109/1, 21), Parvati alone (47.109/2, 10) and standing Kali (59.204/2). Several small but gracefully poised figures depict Shaiva saints, such as Manikkavachakar (47.109/25, 57.16/3, 25).

Vijayanagara bronzes from the 14th–16th centuries are represented by Vishnu, Kubera, Parvati, smaller votive icons and figurative lamps. A standing royal devotee (57.16/2) is an unusual example of courtly portraiture. Later bronzes from Kerala are mostly diminutive; a seated Ganesha within an arch (66.87) is typical.

Among the bronzes from the northern Indian valleys of the Himalayas is a superb example from Kulu; this depicts a multiheaded goddess seated on Shiva and surrounded by an oval frame (64.102). Also of interest here are a set of 14th-century carved timber doors and a column from Katarmal.

Of the coins on display, perhaps the most interesting are the gold pieces from the Gupta era, many of which depict deities. Arms and armour, textiles, jades, metalwork, ivories and a substantial collection of manuscripts and miniature paintings are also exhibited.

Antiquities from Central Asia are assembled in a separate gallery. These demonstrate artistic connections between India and the Far East in the 4th–8th centuries. Fragments of wall paintings, silk hangings, stucco figures and wooden architectural pieces mostly depict deities of the Mahayana Buddhist pantheon. Particularly fine are the mandala of Avalokiteshvara from Tunhuang (Ch. XXVIII.006) painted on silk and the delicately toned mural fragments of Indra and Vairochana from Balawaste (Har.B, D).

Rashtrapati Bhavan

Two important sculptures are currently housed in this palace, now the residence of the President of India (for a description see Volume II). These are the 3rd-century-BC Maurya column capital, fashioned as a bull, from Rampurva; and the 5th-century standing Buddha from **Mathura**, one of the outstanding masterpieces of Gupta art. (The latter is almost identical to that exhibited in the Government Museum, **Mathura**.)

Crafts Museum

This is located in a compound of mudbrick structures that imitate the houses of different villages. The collection of craft objects is the finest in India. Many of the pieces are religious items or are related to rituals of domestic religious life. Metal and wooden figurines depict cult divinities of Hinduism in their different regional aspects or tribal deities unknown in Hinduism. Paintings on paper, cloth or even mud walls illustrate episodes from mythological stories of local significance: thus, the wall paintings of Gujarat and the rolled paper scrolls from Bengal. Among the ritual objects are spoons, ladles, fly-whisks and lamps.

PANDOH

Parashara Rishi Temple,
14th century and later

Spectacularly situated at a height of 4,250 m (14,000 ft) above the town of Pandoh, this small Hindu temple is built on the edge of a lake which has a floating circular island. Patronized by the rulers of **Mandi**, the temple was renovated many times; however, portions of the original wood-work are still visible. The roof has three tiers; the lower two are pyramidal, while the upper one is conical and covered with timber shingles. The sanctuary doorway has receding jambs and lintels, finely carved with miniature divinities in niches; the outermost jambs display entwined serpents. A wooden image of Parashara Rishi is worshipped in the sanctuary.

Grouped around the temple are the priest's house and rooms for pilgrims. These are built in the local timber-bonded style with gable roofs of slate.

PARASPORA

This site is identified with Parihasapura, the capital of Lalitaditya, the renowned 8th-century ruler of Kashmir. Among the remains of several ruined Buddhist struc-tures is the double-tiered basement of a large stupa; this is cruciform in plan with intermediate projections. Piles of rubble indicate a hemispherical mound above.

South of the stupa is a monastery which presents the usual plan of a rectangular court surrounded by small cells sheltered by a verandah. Further south is the base-ment of a square sanctuary with an ambulatory passageway set within a spa-cious enclosure.

PATIALA

Two Sikh gurudwaras commemorate the visit of the ninth Guru, Tej Bahadur, to

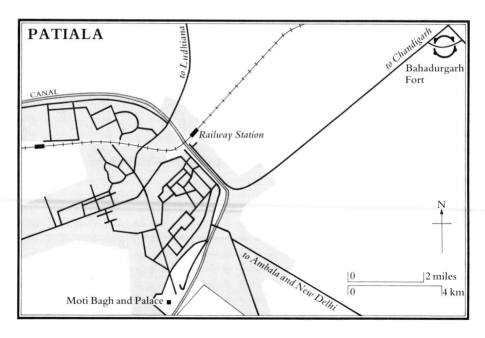

Patiala. These shrines were erected at the orders of the local rulers. One (Moti Bagh) is located within the town, while the other (Bahadur Bagh) is situated about 8 km (5 miles) outside the town to the north-east.

(For British monuments of the town see Volume II.)

Gurudwara Bahadur Bagh, 1837

A rectangle of high walls with subsidiary rooms contains this shrine within a court. Double-storey gateways employ Mughal features, such as multi-lobed arches, projecting balconies, chambers with curved roofs and octagonal pavilions. The shrine itself is a modest square building with arcades overhung by an eave. Upon the roof is a rectangular pavilion capped with a Bengali roof with curved ridge and cornices. Paintings adorned the walls inside.

Gurudwara Moti Bagh, 1862

This is a triple-storey shrine. In an inner chamber on the intermediate level the Adi Granth is displayed. Mughal arcades frame the doorway. Above is a single chamber with a Bengali roof.

PAYAR

Shiva Temple, 11th century

This Hindu temple is a typical example of the Kashmir style. A single chamber has four doorways surmounted by gabled pediments; the pyramidal roof is divided into two tiers. Classical influence is evident in the pilasters and cornices. Sculptures over the doorways are set within trilobed niches, especially Lakulisha (east), Bhairava (north), dancing Shiva and musicians (west) and triple-headed Shiva flanked by Bhairava and Devi (south). Above the linga within the sanctuary is a corbelled ceiling with flying figures.

PHIYANG

Founded in the 16th century, this Buddhist establishment of the Tibetan Kagyupa sect is one of the largest in Ladakh. Recent additions to the monastery include a residence for the head monk and a new entrance hall with a prayer wheel.

Dukhang, recently renovated

This enshrines a central image of Vairochana accompanied by Shakyamuni and teachers. The walls are painted with murals of Vajradhara and the five Buddhas.

Library

Among the sculptures exhibited here are stucco portraits of the lamas of the monastery, as well as a small group of Buddhist bronzes from Kashmir dating back to the 14th century and earlier. There is also a collection of 16th-century Chinese, Tibetan and Mongolian weapons and armour.

Guru Lhakhang, 16th century

This shrine is situated a short distance north of the main complex. The murals here indicate Indian stylistic influence; they are notable for their brilliant reds and blues. Among the Mahayana figures are Bodhisattvas, Taras and yoginis, guardians and saints. Of interest are the friezes illustrating episodes from the lives of various teachers; these resemble paintings on palm-leaf manuscripts.

RISHIKESH

Situated in the wooded upper valley of the Ganga river, Rishikesh is a haven for Hindus seeking meditation. Numerous gurus, holy men and pilgrims live in rest-houses in the town or retreat to the nearby hills. Among the establishments are the

Shivananda Ashram, Gita Bhavan and Swarga Ashram.

From Rishikesh begin the pilgrimage routes into the high Himalayas, particularly to such holy spots as **Badrinath**, **Kedarnath** and Gangotri; the last site is the nearest to the source of the Ganga.

SANGHOL

This site in the Punjab preserves traces of a Buddhist stupa and monastic complex. In 1985, portions of a stone railing were unearthed which appeared to have been carefully dismantled and buried. The style of the carving and the red sandstone material indicate that these posts and cross-bars were originally executed in **Mathura**, probably in the 2nd century, and then transported to distant Sanghol. Typical of the Kushana period are the finely modelled yakshas and female figures beneath trees, drinking wine, with children, holding toilet trays and playing musical instruments. A museum at the site will eventually house these antiquities (temporarily displayed in the National Museum, **New Delhi**).

SARAHAN

Sarahan is the former summer capital of the rulers of the Sutlej valley. The fort here consists of a large rectangular enclosure containing Hindu shrines, as well as apartments and stores. These are all constructed in the characteristic local technique of dry-stone masonry bonded with horizontal cedar logs.

Bhimakali Temple, 18th–19th century

This houses an important cult where human sacrifices were offered to Kali. It is the only temple in the region where brahmin priests officiate. The temple was renovated in the 1930s by the local ruler, who had the image of the goddess transferred from what is now the treasury (bhandar).

Raised high on a masonry tower, the temple itself is a two-storey timber structure. The upper floor serves as the sanctuary where a silver image of Kali is enshrined. The doors, also of silver, are embossed with mythological motifs. Timber panels completely enclose the balcony that surrounds the temple; these are carved with delicate floral patterns and geometric designs. Dormer windows in the roof are set into the gables; the ends of the ridges are fashioned as monster heads.

The treasury is a similar building, with carved doorways and balcony panels. Here are kept the musical instruments used in religious festivals, as well as banners and palanquins.

SASPOL

Cave temples at this site in the upper Indus valley preserve important Buddhist paintings. These are exceptional for their fluid linework and vivid reds and blues. The iconography is mostly restricted to deities of the Mahayana pantheon.

Cave 3, 13th–14th century

The paintings of this temple are in excellent condition. On the left wall are miniature Buddhas and eight Bodhisattvas, with an illustration of the paradise of Amitabha in the middle; to the right are other Bodhisattvas. In the middle of the rear wall is a large Shakyamuni figure accompanied by smaller goddesses. The right wall is dominated by three mandalas of Vairochana. At the top of the entrance wall are Bodhisattvas and three Mahakala figures.

SHEY

Until the 16th century, Shey was the residence of the rulers of Ladakh. On a hill overlooking the town stands an old summer palace and a Buddhist monastic establishment. A temple within the palace houses a large Buddha sculpture gilded with copper; this was erected by a 17th-century ruler. Higher up are the ruins of an ancient citadel.

At the foot of the hill is a rock carved with reliefs; these depict (left to right) Ratnasambhava, Akshobhya, Vairochana, Amitabha and Amoghasiddhi. A short distance away is a second temple, also with a colossal sculpture of Shakyamuni, dating from the 17th century. The walls are painted with saints and Shakyamuni between disciples; other walls are decorated with skulls or covered with mandalas of different deities. Another temple nearby also has paintings.

Hundreds of chortens of diverse forms and sizes dot the barren plains to the north; some have multi-tiered brass finials. Nearby is a collection of slabs sculpted in relief with Buddha and Bodhisattva figures; these date only from the 18th century.

SIMLA

(For British buildings in the town see Volume II.)

State Museum

Numerous damaged sculptures from sites throughout Himachal Pradesh are exhibited here. Among the more interesting are several 8th-century stone images from **Masrur** and **Bajaura**, and also some 11th-century miniature bronzes, such as the standing Vishnu figure (74.412).

SPITUK

Dominating the Indus valley, this Buddhist monastery of the Tibetan Gelugpa sect was originally founded in the 11th century; the present buildings date mostly from a later period. The complex, which includes courtyards and temples of various sizes, is laid out on different levels. In the main courtyard an annual dance festival takes place. Flights of steps passing by chortens lead to the highest 'Kali' shrine.

Dukhang, 16th–17th century

This two-storey hall is the largest in the complex; it is approached through a verandah with paintings of guardians and auspicious emblems. Within, two rows of long seats running the length of the hall frame a throne at the rear. Thangkas, sculptures of various Buddhist divinities and miniature silver chortens are displayed on the altar. To the left is a large painted image of Vajrabhairava; eleven-headed Avalokiteshvara appears on the right.

'Kali' Temple, 16th–17th century

Overlooking the complex near the crest of the rocks, this temple enshrines a large image of Vajrabhairava (often confused by Hindu devotees with Kali), together with sculptures of other fierce guardians.

SRINAGAR

That this was an important centre in the pre-Muslim era is indicated by the ruins of Buddhist and Hindu monuments on the hills overlooking the town. More substantial are the remains of stupas and a monastery at Pandrethan, 5 km (3 miles) south-east of the town. (For the other monuments of Srinagar see Volume II.)

Hariparbat

This low hill sacred to the goddess Durga lies between Srinagar and Nagin lake; it is surrounded by a rampart dating from the 16th century. On the north-western side stands the Chakradhara temple; the

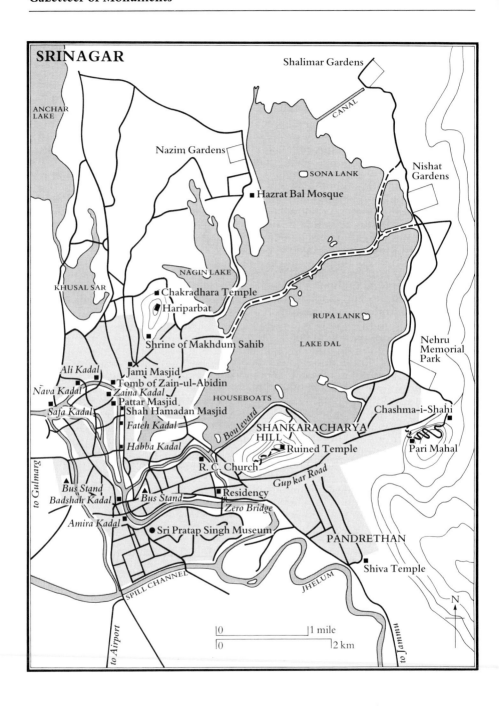

SRINAGAR

Shalimar Gardens

ANCHAR LAKE

CANAL

Nazim Gardens

SONA LANK

Nishat Gardens

Hazrat Bal Mosque

NAGIN LAKE

KHUSAL SAR

Chakradhara Temple

Hariparbat

RUPA LANK

Nehru Memorial Park

Shrine of Makhdum Sahib

LAKE DAL

Ali Kadal

Jami Masjid

Tomb of Zain-ul-Abidin

Nava Kadal

Zaina Kadal

Safa Kadal

Pattar Masjid

HOUSEBOATS

Shah Hamadan Masjid

Chashma-i-Shahi

Fateh Kadal

Boulevard

SHANKARACHARYA HILL

Habba Kadal

Ruined Temple

Pari Mahal

R. C. Church

Bus Stand

Badshah Kadal

Bus Stand

Gup kar Road

to Gulmarg

Residency

Zero Bridge

Amira Kadal

Sri Pratap Singh Museum

PANDRETHAN

Shiva Temple

SPILL CHANNEL

JHELUM

to Airport

to Jammu

N

|0 |1 mile

|0 |2 km

original sanctuary has been replaced by a mosque. Foundations of a 5th-century temple and a later enclosure wall are visible nearby.

Shankaracharya Hill

This hill is situated at the south end of Dal lake. On its summit is a ruined Hindu temple associated with Shankara, the 9th-century philosopher. Of the original structure, only the basement on a stepped plan can be made out. The temple replaces an earlier Buddhist monument tradition-ally believed to have been founded in the 3rd century BC by the son of Ashoka, the Maurya emperor.

Sri Pratap Singh Museum

Sculptures from various ruined monu-ments in the central valley of Kashmir are displayed here. The 3rd–4th-century Buddhist site of **Ushkur** is indicated by a series of terracotta heads. From **Harwan** come moulded terracotta plaques dating from the 4th–5th century. Pandrethan is represented by both Buddhist and Hindu sculptures. Images of Vishnu as Vaikun-tha riding on Garuda are executed in polished green stone; the finest examples come from Verinag (3080, 3082) and **Avantipur**.

Of the Buddhist metal sculptures on display, the earliest is a 5th-century copper image of standing Buddha; this is executed in a style related to the Gandhara region of north-western Pakistan. There is also a 10th–11th-century brass image of seated Lokeshvara (2986). The largest metal object is an oval frame (2661) for a Vishnu image, now lost. This 10th-century brass frame, which comes from Devsar, is inlaid with silver; in the sur-rounding medallions are miniature icons of Vishnu in his various incarnations.

The museum also houses a representa-tive selection of coins from Gandhara and the Kushana period.

PANDRETHAN

Shiva Temple, 12th century

Typical of the Kashmir style, this small Hindu structure preserves its double-tiered angled masonry roof. Porches with doorways framed by classical columns project on each side; above, trilobed openings are set within steep gables. The sanctuary enshrines a linga. The ceiling, with a design of rotated squares, is adorned with flying celestials around a central lotus.

TABO (map p. 134)

Overlooking the steep banks of the Spiti river at this site is one of the oldest Buddh-ist monasteries in the Lahul valley. Five halls arranged in a row and a number of chortens are contained with enclosure walls. Each hall is entered from the east through an open portico. Within, timber columns support flat roofs; woodwork is often elaborately carved. Wall paintings depict divinities of the Mahayana pantheon.

Sug Lhakhang, 11th century

This assembly hall is the most interesting building of the Tabo group in its lay-out, sculptural programme and painted ornamentation. At the western end of the hall, a sanctuary lit by an opening in the roof houses seated images of Amitabha attended by lesser deities. A large sculp-ture of seated four-armed Vairochana is placed in front of the sanctuary to face towards the entrance; this sculpture is partly obscured by a wooden altar. Pro-jecting from the lateral walls are seated stucco figures of guardians, goddesses, Tathagatas and Bodhisattvas; these have recently been restored. Beneath are paint-ings displaying influences from Kashmir and eastern India. These illustrate epi-sodes from the life of the Bodhisattva King Navsang and of Shakyamuni.

Serkhang, 16th century

Of the other temples at Tabo, this southernmost building has the most important murals. The walls are covered with paintings illustrating triple sets of Buddhist deities. Flanking the entrance (east) wall are guardian divinities in terrifying aspects.

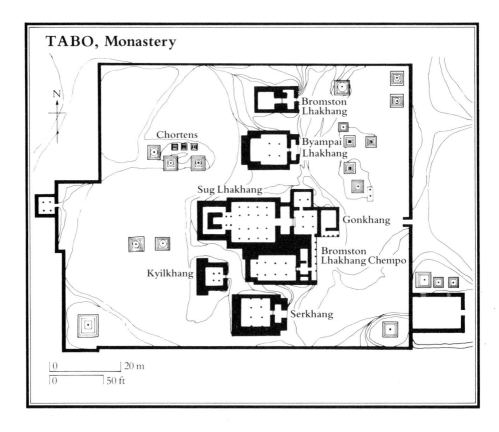

TABO, Monastery

Chortens

Bromston
Lhakhang

Byampai
Lhakhang

Sug Lhakhang

Gonkhang

Bromston
Lhakhang Chempo

Kyilkhang

Serkhang

0   20 m

0   50 ft

UDAIPUR

Markula Devi Temple,
13th–14th century and later

This modest Hindu temple in the Chenab valley is remarkable for the rich ornamentation of its wooden interior, which is datable to an early period. The temple is partly dug into the side of a steep hill.

Timber walls, columns and ceilings are completely covered with carvings; some were replaced after the temple was converted to Buddhist usage in the 16th century. Reliefs on the shrine doorway and walls include the Navagrahas seated in niches, river goddesses, guardians and epic themes. A large image of Vishnu as Trivikrama and a scene of the churning of the ocean are carved on to panels beside the balcony window. On the ceiling are Buddhist and Hindu divinities, as well as amorous couples (side panels), monster masks, stylized foliation and full lotus flowers (central panel). Two large guardian figures flank the sanctuary doorway. A metal image of Durga serves as the chief object of worship.

USHKUR

Stupa bases and other remains at this 3rd–4th-century Buddhist site in the Kashmir valley resemble those at contemporary sites in Gandhara (north-western Pakistan). Among the discoveries at Ushkur were delicately modelled terracotta heads, which may be compared with similar heads found at **Akhnur**. The Ushkur finds are exhibited in museums at **Chandigarh** and **Srinagar**.

CENTRAL INDIA

TEN

CENTRAL INDIA

Madhya Pradesh, eastern and central Uttar Pradesh

Introduction

More than two thousand years of religious activity are recorded in the monuments of central India, where both Buddhism and Jainism were first established in the 5th century BC. But central India was also subjected to repeated dynastic conflicts, culminating in the Muslim invasions from the late 12th century onwards. Architecturally the result is a profusion of abandoned monasteries, ruined temples and damaged sculptures. While only a few ancient shrines are still in use for worship, a pervasive sanctity is manifested throughout the region. Foremost among the Hindu pilgrimage centres are the holy cities of **Allahabad** and **Varanasi** on the Ganga river; **Mathura** and **Vrindavan** are on the bank of the Yamuna in the heartland of the Krishna cult.

Central India witnessed the birth of Buddhist, Jain and Hindu art; but the origins of these traditions have not been preserved. Excavators have uncovered evidence of occupation dating back to the 8th century BC at **Kausambi**, **Ujjain** and **Varanasi**. A number of other sites are linked with Buddha's life during the Magadha period: for example, **Piprahwa**, thought to be Kapilavastu, the capital of the Shakya clan into which Gautama was born; **Sarnath**, where Buddha delivered the First Sermon; **Sravasti**, where the Master stayed in nearby Jetavana grove; and **Kusinagara**, the setting of the Parinirvana.

Not until the Mauryas, in the 3rd century BC, were these Buddhist sites endowed with brick and stone constructions. Under the patronage of the emperor Ashoka and donors of the succeeding Shunga and Satavahana periods, these sites and others, such as **Bharhut** and **Sanchi**, became the settings for ensembles of impressive Buddhist monuments. The most venerated monuments were large-scale stupas, or hemispherical mounds, that enshrined relics of Buddha and his disciples. They were solid constructions, generally of brick and sometimes faced with stone; the more elaborate examples were surrounded by stone railings and gateways that imitated timber construction. Monastic brick structures that accommodated monks were symmetrically laid out, usually with small residential cells opening off a central square court surrounded by a verandah.

Sculptural remains from the Maurya era mark the beginnings of monumental Indian art. The series of polished sandstone columns associated with Ashoka are celebrated for their superbly carved animal capitals, as at **Sarnath**. Carvings assignable to the following periods, from the 2nd century BC to the 1st century AD, testify to the maturing of central Indian artistic traditions. The stone railings and gateways from stupas at **Bharhut** and **Sanchi** are carved with lively narrative scenes, attendant figures and diverse decorative themes. From this

Overleaf Varanasi, panorama of ghats

era date the first free-standing sculptures, mostly large images of yaksha folk divinities, from **Mathura**, **Sarnath** and **Vidisha**.

The first Buddhist and Jain cult images were fashioned in the 1st–2nd centuries, when central India was dominated by the invading Kushana rulers. These sculptures were influenced by earlier indigenous traditions, and also by contemporary developments in Gandhara (north-western Pakistan). **Mathura** and **Sarnath** were the two most important art centres in Kushana times. To the former site, which served also as the dynastic capital, belong a large variety of figures, as well as royal portraits, courtly scenes, attendant maidens and mythical beasts. There are, however, almost no structural remains other than traces of shrines at **Mat** and **Sonkh**.

Under the Gupta kings, who unified most of central India in the 4th–5th centuries, stone temple architecture was initiated. Two early small buildings at **Sanchi** and **Tigawa** are simple flat-roofed sanctuaries with entrance porches; the ruined temples at **Bhumara**, **Deogarh** and **Nachna** suggest more elaborate towered schemes with passageways and mandapas. The latter series preserves some fine sculptures; in particular, the wall panels depicting scenes from the mythology of Vishnu at **Deogarh**. Gupta brick structures are mostly ruined, as at **Ahichhatra**, **Pawaya** and **Bhitargaon**; the last example has terracotta plaques *in situ*. At various Buddhist sites, stupas and monasteries continued to be erected. The Dhamekh stupa at **Sarnath**, for instance, was faced with decorated stonework.

Other Gupta sculptures are the rock-cut images at **Badoh Pathari**, **Dhamnar** and **Udayagiri**, the most impressive of which is the magnificent tableau of Vishnu's Varaha incarnation at **Udayagiri** (Cave 5). Free-standing images at **Eran** are other important examples. The finest sculptures are the Buddhist and Jain images from **Mathura** and **Sarnath**; the

delicately modelled forms and the detached expressions of these figures are unsurpassed in Indian art. Almost no paintings of the period survive in this region, except a fragment in a rock-cut sanctuary at **Bagh**.

Few buildings are preserved from the 6th and 7th centuries, a period of political disintegration and invasions. By the beginning of the 8th century the Pratihara dynasty had become the dominant power in the region. Temples and sculptures from this period illustrate a continuation of Gupta stylistic traditions. (Examples are also found outside the region in both northern and western India.) Small-scale structures at **Amrol**, **Badoh Pathari**, **Batesara**, **Naresar** and **Terahi** are simple combinations of towered sanctuaries and entrance porches. The wall niches have pediments of arch-like motifs; similar motifs, sometimes combined into an overall mesh, cover the curved bands of the towers that rise over the sanctuaries; amalakas and pot finials characterize the summits. The columns are adorned with pot and foliage motifs; doorways are surrounded by miniature figures and foliate ornament.

More evolved schemes are presented in temples at **Gyaraspur** and **Mankheda**. At **Gwalior**, one of the capitals of the Pratiharas, the Teli ka Mandir is the largest of all of these temples; it is crowned with an unusual vaulted roof adorned with complicated designs. Fine examples of Pratihara sculptures are found at many of these sites and also at **Deogarh** and **Kanauj**.

At about the same time in the eastern zone of central India, the Somavamshi rulers were responsible for a distinctive series of brick buildings. These include Hindu temples at **Kharod**, **Rajim** and **Sirpur** as well as two Buddhist monasteries at the last site. Both stone and bronze sculptures of unusually fine workmanship were discovered at **Sirpur**.

After the decline of the Pratiharas in the 10th century, central India was divided into a number of independent dynasties which lasted until the disruptions caused by the Muslim invaders. Each of these kingdoms evolved a distinctive architectural and sculptural style. Temple building during this period achieved dramatic, large-scale compositions which were dominated by soaring towers rising over the sanctuaries. These superstructures were usually provided with clustered elements to create increasingly complex effects. Carvings covered most of the wall surfaces, as well as adorning the porches, balconies and interiors. These richly carved surfaces effectively integrated sculpture with architecture.

The Haihaya rulers in the eastern part of the region were responsible for temples at **Amarkantak** and **Chandrehi**. Fragments of a great Shiva temple at Gurgi have been removed to **Rewa**. An unusual circular sanctuary still stands at **Bheraghat**. In the northern zone, the Kacchapaghata kings patronized temples at **Gwalior**, **Kadwaha** and **Suhania**.

One of the Paramara rulers who controlled the western territory erected a magnificent monument at **Udayapur**; it still stands as one of the best-preserved temples of this period in central India. The vertical bands on its curved tower are characteristic of the Paramara style. The shrine at **Nemawar** is another impressive monument; the ambitious project at **Bhojpur** was never completed. (That the Paramara style was widely influential is shown by related temples in western India and the northern Deccan.)

In the temples at **Khajuraho**, the seat of the Chandella kings, the central Indian style reached the climax of its development. The superbly proportioned towers, rising above richly carved basements and walls, are among the finest in Indian architecture. The density and exuberance of figural sculptures are unsurpassed.

The last phase of religious monuments in central India coincided with the period of Muslim rule. The colossal rock-cut Tirthankara images at **Gwalior**, for example, testify to the popularity of Jainism during the 15th century. At **Vrindavan**, several unusual Hindu shrines from the 16th century indicate the influence of contemporary Muslim building styles and techniques. However, most of the sanctuaries at the important pilgrimage centres of **Ayodhya**, **Mathura**, **Varanasi** and **Ujjain** are no earlier than the 18th century. Though built in the typical central Indian style, temples here are usually small-scale, with abundant decoration but limited figural sculpture. Recent temple projects are usually in the revivalist manner, as at **Sarnath**, **Varanasi** and **Vrindavan**.

Opposite Sarnath, lion capital, 3rd century BC; Archaeological Museum

Above Sanchi, Stupa 2, 2nd century BC

Opposite Sanchi, Stupa 1, gateway, 1st century BC

Sarnath, Dhamekh Stupa, 5th–6th century

Above Tigawa, Temple, 5th century

Left Bhitargaon, Temple, 5th century

Opposite above Udayagiri, Cave 6, 5th century

Opposite below left Sirpur, Lakshmana Temple, 7th century

Opposite below right Gwalior, Teli ka Mandir, 8th century

Opposite Chandrehi, Temple, 10th century

Udayapur, Udayeshvara Temple, 11th century

Opposite above Vrindavan, Govindadeva Temple, 16th century

Opposite below Varanasi, Lakshmi Narayana Temple, 18th century

Khajuraho, Khandariya Mahadeo Temple, 11th century

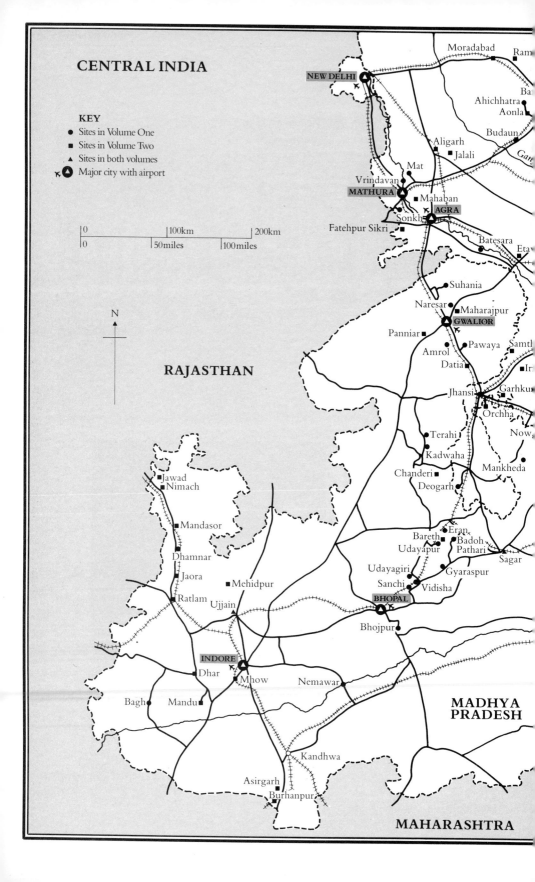

CENTRAL INDIA

KEY
- ● Sites in Volume One
- ■ Sites in Volume Two
- ▲ Sites in both volumes
- ⬟ Major city with airport

```
0          100km        200km
0     50miles     100miles
```

N

RAJASTHAN

MADHYA
PRADESH

MAHARASHTRA

Moradabad
Ram
Ahichhatra
Ba
Aonla
Budaun
NEW DELHI
Aligarh
Jalali
Mat
Gang
Vrindavan
MATHURA
Mahaban
AGRA
Sonkh
Fatehpur Sikri
Batesara
Eta
Suhania
Naresar
Maharajpur
GWALIOR
Panniar
Pawaya
Samtl
Amrol
Ir
Datia
Jhansi
Garhku
Orchha
Now
Terahi
Kadwaha
Mankheda
Chanderi
Deogarh
Jawad
Nimach
Bareth
Eran
Mandasor
Udayapur
Badoh
Pathari
Sagar
Dhamnar
Udayagiri
Gyaraspur
Jaora
Mehidpur
Sanchi
Vidisha
Ratlam
Ujjain
BHOPAL
Bhojpur
INDORE
Dhar
Mhow
Nemawar
Bagh
Mandu
Kandhwa
Asirgarh
Burhanpur

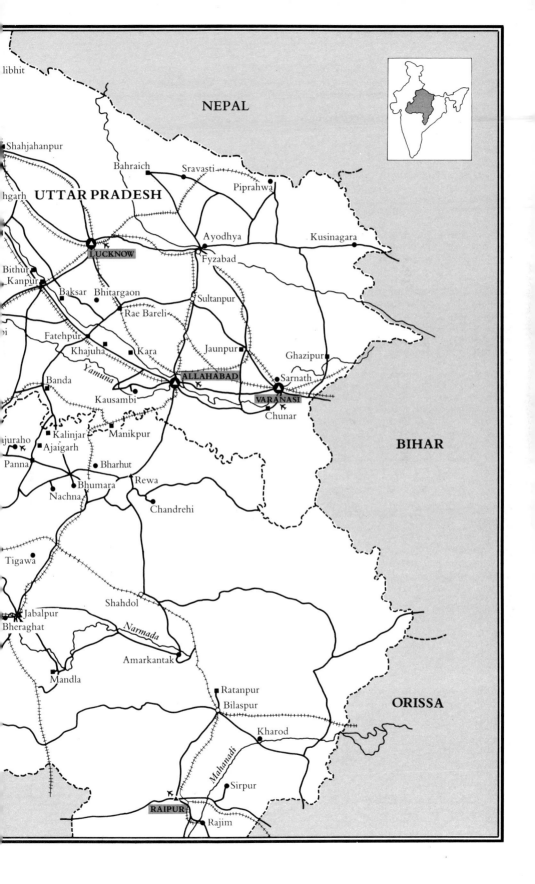

AHICHHATRA

Archaeological investigations at this ancient site have revealed evidence of occupation going back to the 3rd century BC. The brick defensive walls with buttresses which define the irregular space of the city date from the 1st century BC and are built over earlier earthen ramparts.

Outside the city zone are several mounds containing the buried remains of Gupta structures. Within the highest mound, a short distance to the west, a square multi-terraced building with brick walls has been unearthed. Associated artefacts dating from the 4th–5th centuries include stone and terracotta sculptures. (Many of these have been removed to the National Museum, **New Delhi**.)

ALLAHABAD

Known as Prayag, the Place of Sacrifice, Allahabad. is an important Hindu pilgrimage centre located at the confluence of the Ganga and Yamuna rivers. According to local belief, the mythical underground Sarasvati river also surfaces here, merging with the waters of the Ganga and Yamuna. Bathing in these three rivers is auspicious at all times, but every twelve years pilgrims come in vast numbers to India's greatest festival, the Kumbha Mela. Attracted to this event are innumerable gurus, who are accommodated in tents. The climax of the festival occurs when these holy men ride in procession on horses, camels and elephants towards the confluence.

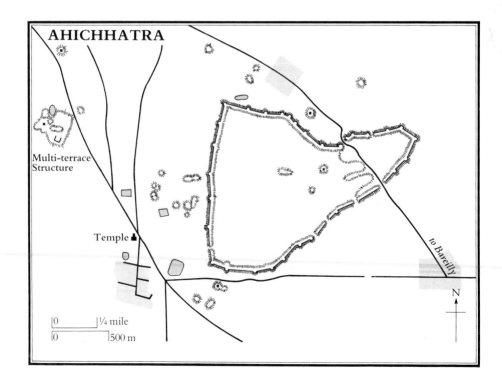

AHICHHATRA

Multi-terrace
Structure

Temple

to Bareilly

N

| 0 | 1/4 mile |
| 0 | 500 m |

Despite the undeniable antiquity of the site, almost no structures predating the Muslim period are preserved. (For the city and its monuments see Volume II.)

Ashoka's Column, 3rd century BC

This column was originally erected at **Kausambi** by the Maurya emperor Ashoka; in 1583, at the orders of Akbar, it was moved to its present position within the Mughal fort that overlooks the confluence. Edicts of the Maurya, Gupta and Mughal rulers are incised on to the polished sandstone shaft. No sculpture is preserved above the fluted capital.

Museum

This houses stone sculptures from different central and eastern Indian sites. Among the 2nd-century-BC pieces from **Kausambi** and **Bharhut** is a railing fragment depicting an unusual scene of acrobats (44). Many 1st–2nd-century sculptures from **Mathura** belong to the Kushana period. A standing Buddha figure, dated to AD 80, comes from **Kausambi** (69).

Gupta carvings are plentiful. These include a finely finished single-faced Shiva linga from Khoh (154) and a seated Karttikeya figure from **Bhumara** (153). There are several examples of the 9th–11th-century Pala style, including both Jain and Hindu sculptures from **Gaya**, such as the seated Tara image (241). From 11th-century **Khajuraho** come a number of sculptures, like Shiva seated with Parvati (291), as well as doorways richly carved with attendant deities, guardians and river goddesses. Particularly charming is a series of 12th-century bracket figures from Jamsoh depicting female dancers and musicians. Another interesting piece is a seated dog modelled in full relief.

Terracotta figurines include a large group from **Kausambi**. Several coins issued by the **Kausambi** rulers are seen in the coin cabinet.

Kausambi Museum, University of Allahabad

Among the excavated artefacts from **Kausambi** displayed here are pottery, terracotta figurines, coins, beads and bangles.

AMARKANTAK

This Hindu site at the source of the Narmada and Son rivers is a famous place of pilgrimage. Among the objects of veneration is a holy tank which is considered the head of the infant Narmada river; the water is believed to wash away all sins.

Only one temple, that known as Karan Mandir, is of interest. This consisted of three sanctuaries, evidently intended to be linked together by a common mandapa that was never completed. Assigned to the 10th-century Haihaya period, these sanctuaries each have a curved tower. The outer walls are divided into three registers; there are no sculptures except for the central niches. The doorways are devoid of figural carvings, but the jambs are decorated with simple scrollwork and lotus designs.

AMROL

Rameshvara Temple, 8th century

This small Hindu structure is a fine example from the Pratihara period. Over the sanctuary rises the curvilinear tower (partly collapsed and crowned with a later dome). The walls have niches surmounted by pediments with arch-like motifs that resemble those on the tower. Corner niches house images of the Dikpalas. Though partly damaged, the doorway preserves figures of amorous couples and delicately worked foliation.

AYODHYA

This city is identified with the mythical capital of Rama, the setting for many episodes in the Ramayana epic. As one of the holy cities of Hinduism it is a popular place of pilgrimage, and there are many dharmashalas within the town. Little remains of the ancient settlement, once the capital of the Kosala region, built on the right bank of the Gogra river. The many temples are mostly recent structures; some were later converted into mosques.

The temple of 'Hanuman's Fortress' is contained within a rectangle of massive walls, hence the name. Embossed silver doorways lead to images of Sita and Hanuman enshrined in the sanctuary. Other figures of Rama and Sita are worshipped in the temples of Kanak Bhavan and Kala Rama.

Of particular interest are the sites specifically associated with Rama. These include Rama Janam Bhumi (now Babri Mosque), believed to mark the god's birthplace; Janam Sthana, where Rama was brought up; and Lakshmana ghat, on the river, where Rama's brother is supposed to have ended his life after breaking a vow.

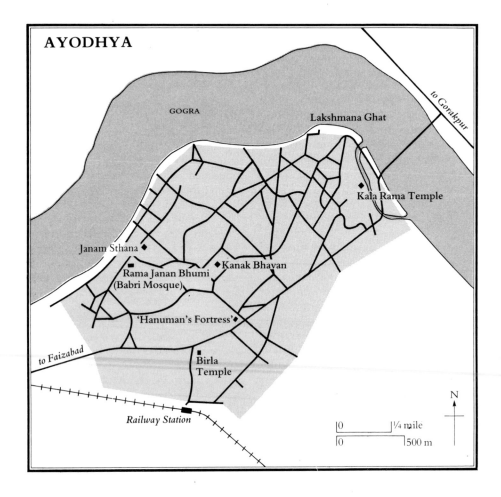

AYODHYA

GOGRA

Lakshmana Ghat

to Gorakpur

Kala Rama Temple

Janam Sthana

Rama Janan Bhumi (Babri Mosque)

Kanak Bhavan

'Hanuman's Fortress'

Birla Temple

to Faizabad

Railway Station

N

0 ¼ mile
0 500 m

BADOH PATHARI

Ruined Hindu and Jain shrines in these twin villages mostly belong to the Pratihara period; so does a free-standing column (khamba) erected in 869 by one of the Pratihara rulers. There are, however, some earlier sculptures dating from the 5th century. These include a set of figures of Virabhadra and the Matrikas cut into the walls of a cavern on a nearby hill.

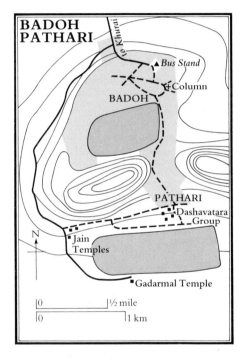

Gadarmal Temple, 9th century

This ruined but imposing Hindu temple has an unusually rectangular sanctuary above which rises a tall curved tower. Although much of the detail is damaged, vestiges of the rich ornamentation survive. These include delicately worked meshes of arch-like motifs that cover the basement, walls and tower. Some of the figural sculptures on the walls are still preserved, such as the torso of Surya in an arch-like frame on the east side. The doorway sculptures include interwoven snakes and amorous couples on the jambs, and friezes of fighting animals on the lintel. The adjoining porch is enclosed by a high balustrade punctuated with projecting elephant heads.

North of the temple stands part of a gateway with figural brackets above the columns. The surrounding shrines are ruined.

Dashavatara Group, 9th–10th century

Among the ruined temples of this Hindu complex are finely carved wall panels, door jambs and lintels. A 5th-century standing image of Varaha, now damaged, is set up in front.

BAGH

The Buddhist cave temples at this site are now mostly collapsed and destroyed. They belong to the 5th-century Gupta period and are related to contemporary monuments in the Deccan. Of the Bagh group, four caves (2, 4, 5 and 6) are important. These are similarly laid out, with a verandah, a large square columned hall with rows of small cells excavated into the side walls, and a sanctuary excavated in the rear wall, where a monolithic stupa is enshrined. The columns have decorated bases and capitals; the shafts are octagonal and sixteen-sided. Doorways and windows are surrounded by carved frames.

The Bagh caves were once adorned with a splendid series of murals comparable to those preserved at **Ajanta**. Unfortunately, the paintings at Bagh have mostly disintegrated; the only substantial fragment to have been preserved is in Cave 4. (Copies of the Bagh paintings are displayed in the Central Archaeological Museum, **Gwalior**.)

Cave 4, 5th century

This is the finest cave of the series. Its columns and brackets are adorned with animal carvings. Three ornate porticos are incorporated above the inner row of columns. The verandah doorway is decorated with guardian figures, river goddesses and bands of scrollwork and foliation.

The original paintwork survives only in patches; the largest segment is on the back wall of the verandah. This mural depicts a sequence of episodes: from left to right, a weeping princess being comforted by her companions; four seated persons absorbed in a religious discussion; monks performing the miracle of flying in the air; and dancers with musicians. Above are two grand processions with horses and elephants; floral and plant motifs appear elsewhere. The composition, drawing and colour of these murals testify to a sensuous and exuberant artistic tradition.

BATESARA

This Hindu site contains a number of dilapidated temples dating from the Pratihara period. These 8th–9th-century structures are generally small sanctuaries with curved towers. The towers are decorated with meshes of arch-like motifs. Projections on the front are usually large arched niches (empty); at the summit is an amalaka. Sculptures of different deities are occasionally preserved in niches on the outer walls. The doorways are surrounded by miniature figures, including river goddesses, amorous couples and flying warriors.

Mahadeva Temple, 8th century

In this example, which is the largest of the group, the sanctuary is enclosed within a passageway. The walls of the sanctuary have niches with sculptures of the Dik-palas and other deities surmounted by tall pediments of arch-like motifs. Similar motifs are used on the bands that run up the middle of the curved tower. A small image of Lakulisha is positioned on the front projection of the tower.

BHARHUT

Nothing is now visible of the celebrated 2nd-century-BC stupa at this Buddhist site other than a shallow circular depression in the ground. Bricks and sandstone fragments are strewn all around; portions of broken images are even fixed into the walls of a nearby modern Hanuman temple. The remains of the sandstone railing and gateways that surrounded the stupa have all been removed. They are mostly displayed in the Indian Museum, **Calcutta**, and the **Allahabad** Museum.

BHERAGHAT

Chaunsath Yogini Temple,
10th and 12th centuries

This unusual temple is located on top of a hill overlooking the Narmada river, barely 6 km (4 miles) from Tripuri, the site of the Haihaya capital. The temple consists of a circular colonnade with eighty-one peripheral shrines, 38 m (125 ft) in diameter. Among the numerous 10th-century images (mostly damaged) housed in these shrines are the sixty-four yoginis, the Matrikas and other goddesses. These are all inscribed with identifying labels.

The 12th-century Gauri Shankara shrine stands in the middle of the circular court. Several earlier panels have been placed inside the temple; these include Vishnu seated with Lakshmi, Shiva and Parvati riding on Nandi, and dancing Ganesha. The temple porch, with its curved roof, is a much later addition.

BHITARGAON

Temple, 5th century

This is the largest Hindu brick temple to survive from the Gupta period. Despite its extensive reconstruction, many original features are still visible. A square sanctuary with an entrance on the east and projections on the other three sides is roofed with a soaring pyramidal tower. The outer walls are elevated on a high plinth with terracotta panels regularly positioned between pilasters. Though mostly damaged, a few of these panels have identifiable figures of Shiva and Parvati seated together (south) and eight-armed Vishnu (west). A double cornice frames a frieze of ornamental plaques with aquatic monsters, miniature fighting figures and foliate panels. The arched niches of the tower also contain traces of terracotta panels.

BHOJPUR

This Hindu site is named after Bhoja (1018–85), a ruler of the Paramara dynasty, who was celebrated as an accomplished scholar. As well as the remains of an ambitious Shiva temple, there is also a later Jain shrine housing an image of Mahavira. Traces of an earthen embankment for a vast tank indicate the scale of hydraulic projects in the Paramara period.

Shiva Temple, 11th century

This colossal temple was never completed. The sanctuary preserves most of its outer walls, which have niches projecting outwards on ornamented brackets. The doorway jambs are fashioned from huge blocks on which figures, now damaged, were carved. Within, a polished stone linga is elevated on a massive pedestal more than 8 m (26 ft) high. Columns and brackets with carvings support the base of an incomplete corbelled dome.

North-east of the building is an earthen ramp, evidently used by elephants to lift massive blocks. Incompletely carved architectural pieces lie all around.

BHOPAL

(For the city and its monuments see Volume II.)

Birla Museum

Though most of the sculptures displayed here come from 9th–11th-century temple sites, such as Hinglajgarh and Ashapuri, there is at least one earlier 8th-century panel of Karttikeya from Varahkhedi (164). Belonging to Hinglajgarh are numerous damaged Shiva and yogini images. A standing Vishnu surrounded by miniature figures (151) and a dancing Ganesha (189) are both from Ashapuri.

State Museum

Sculptures in this collection have been assembled from central Indian sites dating from the 10th–12th centuries. Among the Hindu icons are panels showing Vishnu together with Shiva and Brahma from **Mankheda** (775), Shiva and Parvati seated together from Barhad (57) and, from Sarwantal, a multi-armed goddess (816). There is also a fine carving of an amorous couple from **Khajuraho** (842). The reclining mother and child from Gurgi (797) may represent the birth of a Jain saviour.

BHUMARA

Shiva Temple, 5th century

This restored Hindu temple is an important example of Gupta architecture; it consists of a small sanctuary elevated on a moulded terrace, with access steps on the east. While the walls of the sanctuary are plain, the doorway preserves delicately modelled figures of river goddesses and guardians, together with bands of foliation. Within is an exceptionally fine single-faced linga; the god wears an elaborate headdress.

Numerous sculptural fragments from this site have been removed to the **Allahabad** Museum and the Indian Museum, **Calcutta**.

CHANDREHI

This Hindu site preserves important monuments from the Haihaya period.

Temple, 10th century

This unusual structure has a sanctuary contained within a sixteen-sided tower, almost approximating a circle in plan. The heightened tower is curvilinear and is completely covered with a mesh of delicately worked arch-like motifs. At its summit is an amalaka and a pot finial. In contrast, the walls below are completely devoid of sculptures. Above the small porch at the front (west) is a projection with interlocking arched motifs. The interiors of the porch and sanctuary are roofed with corbelled domes.

Matha, 972

This is a rare example of a Hindu monastic building. With meditation chambers opening off a central court surrounded by a verandah, it resembles the layouts of earlier Buddhist monasteries. Carved doorways and bracket figures adorn the otherwise plain building.

DEOGARH

This site is celebrated for the well-preserved Gupta carvings on the Dashavatara temple. About 1 km (½ mile)

to the south-east, within a fort overlooking the Betwa river, is a group of Jain temples dating from the later Pratihara era.

Dashavatara Temple, 6th century

This ruined Hindu shrine consists of a square sanctuary raised on a moulded basement. The surrounding covered passageway and adjoining mandapa or porch have now vanished. The superbly carved wall panels and shrine doorway are among the masterpieces of Gupta art, particularly the sensuous modelling and subtle expressions of the figures. Decorated pilasters frame panels on three sides: these depict Vishnu on Garuda rescuing the elephant Gajendra (north), the penance of the sages Nara and Narayana seated beneath a tree (west) and Vishnu sleeping on the serpent with the five Pandava warriors and Draupadi beneath (south). The doorway (east) incorporates guardian figures and attendants (beneath), amorous couples (jambs), river goddesses (upper corners) and an image of Vishnu seated on the serpent (lintel). Only the lowest courses of the tower that rises over the sanctuary are preserved.

The basements of corner subsidiary shrines and several columns are elevated on a broad terrace. The sides of this terrace were ornamented with friezes depicting scenes from the Ramayana and Krishna legends. Most of these narrative panels have been removed to the Archaeological Museum and the National Museum, **New Delhi**.

Archaeological Museum

Damaged sculptures and broken architectural pieces from the site have been collected here. Among them are two 9th-century panels of the rescue of Gajendra and seated Nara and Narayana; these imitate compositions on the Dashavatara temple.

FORT

A group of Jain temples dating from the 9th–10th centuries is contained within a modern compound wall. Loose sculptures and carved columns of the same period are also incorporated into later structures. There is a small museum.

Temple 12, 862

The best preserved of the group, this temple is typical of the Pratihara style. A square sanctuary with a curved tower adjoins a mandapa on the west. The outer sanctuary walls have sculpture niches surmounted by tower-like pediments; in between are pierced stone windows with zigzag designs. Among the sculptures is a series of Jain yakshis (south). The tower is richly ornamented with horizontal elements; on the front (west) projection there are additional arched motifs and Jina figures. Columns with detailed carvings frame the entrance. The interior doorway is decorated with amorous couples, maidens and beasts; large guardian figures stand at either side.

Temple 15, early 9th century

This example has a moulded basement on a stepped plan; the wall panels depicting standing and seated Tirthankaras are mostly intact.

Sahu Jain Sangrahalaya

Among the finest of the 10th–11th-century Jain images assembled here are figures of Ambika seated with child (126, 136) and Chakreshvari displaying her weapons supported by kneeling Garuda (110, 142). There are also large sculptures of Tirthankaras. One panel has a dense composition of both seated and standing Jinas (98).

DHAMNAR

Rock-cut monuments at this hilly site belong to two distinct phases. More than fifty Buddhist cave temples date from the Gupta era; two are of particular interest. Monolithic votive stupas with tall cylindrical bases also belong to this early phase. The later Pratihara period is represented by a monolithic Vaishnava temple.

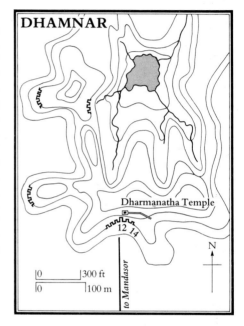

Cave 12, 4th–5th century

A flat-roofed monolithic chaitya hall with an apsidal end is contained within a columned structure. On three sides are small cells, some of which house Buddhist images. Left of the entrance is a chamber enshrining a stupa; other stupas are carved in relief on the porch.

Cave 14, 4th–5th century

In the middle of a rectangular court is a large monolithic stupa. Beyond the court is a flat-roofed rectangular sanctuary housing a large Buddha seated on a throne; this is surrounded by a passageway. Other similar figures are found carved on to the walls of the court and passageway.

Dharmanatha Temple, 8th–9th century

A narrow rock-cut passage leads to an excavated court in the middle of which stands this monolithic monument. The sanctuary has a curved tower covered with a mesh of arch-like motifs; at the summit is an amalaka. The porch is surmounted by a triangular pediment with arched motifs containing sculptures, now worn. Incorporated into the four corners of the hall are subsidiary towered forms; a pyramidal roof rises above. Seven smaller shrines are also excavated in the court.

ERAN

This fortified Hindu site surrounded on three sides by the meandering Bina river was occupied from the 2nd–1st centuries BC onwards. Among the excavated finds are terracotta figurines, beads, shells, semi-precious stones and coins. These artefacts are now exhibited in the Archaeological Museum, University of **Sagar**.

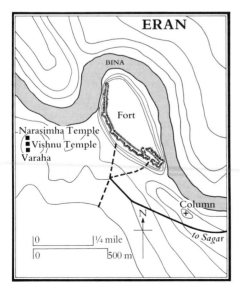

During the Gupta period the site attained some importance. Monuments from this era, now in a dilapidated condition, include a column with a royal inscription and several temples with large free-standing sculptures. One of these sculptures has been removed to **Sagar**.

Column, 484

This sandstone column is more than 13 m (42 ft) high. It has an inscription on its shaft dating to the reign of the ruler Buddhagupta. Above the fluted capital is a block with seated lions at the corners and a pair of back-to-back standing figures of Vishnu and Garuda. A wheel is positioned behind the heads of these figures.

Narasimha Temple, 5th century

Several columns and doorway fragments of this ruined structure still stand. A damaged Narasimha figure is set up within the sanctuary.

Varaha, 5th century

This large boar image is about 5 m (16 ft) long. It is completely covered with rows of miniature figures. The goddess Bhu is depicted above one of the tusks, now broken. An inscription of Buddhagupta is incised on to the animal's neck.

Vishnu Temple, 9th century

Several columns and a carved doorway are all that remain of this later structure. Within the sanctuary is an earlier 5th-century image of Vishnu of large proportions with a halo behind the head.

GWALIOR

The impressive fortress at Gwalior occupies an isolated sandstone outcrop that rises precipitously more than 100 m (330 ft) above the town. Almost 3 km (2 miles) from north to south and nowhere wider than 500 m (1,750 ft), this flat-topped hill is ringed with massive walls. The citadel is dominated by the palace of the 16th-century ruler Man Singh (see Volume II). Other earlier remains testify to the long history of the fortress.

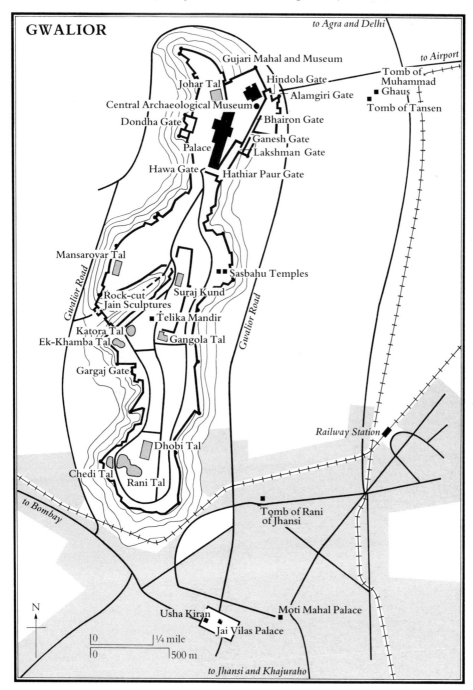

GWALIOR

to Agra and Delhi

to Airport

Gujari Mahal and Museum

Hindola Gate

Johar Tal

Alamgiri Gate

Central Archaeological Museum

Bhairon Gate

Dondha Gate

Ganesh Gate

Palace

Lakshman Gate

Hawa Gate

Hathiar Paur Gate

Tomb of Muhammad Ghaus

Tomb of Tansen

Mansarovar Tal

Gwalior Road

Sasbahu Temples

Rock-cut Jain Sculptures

Suraj Kund

Telika Mandir

Katora Tal

Ek-Khamba Tal

Gangola Tal

Gwalior Road

Gargaj Gate

Railway Station

Dhobi Tal

Chedi Tal

Rani Tal

to Bombay

Tomb of Rani of Jhansi

N

Usha Kiran

Moti Mahal Palace

Jai Vilas Palace

0 ¼ mile

0 500 m

to Jhansi and Khajuraho

In the middle of the 8th century, the Pratiharas shifted their capital from **Kanauj** to Gwalior; soon after, Yashovarman, one of their kings, constructed the temple now known as Teli ka Mandir. Under the succeeding 10th–11th-century Kacchapaghata rulers of Gwalior, the Sasbahu temples were erected. In the 15th century, numerous Jain images were cut into the steep sides of the plateau.

Teli ka Mandir, mid-8th century

This Hindu temple was the most ambitious architectural project of the Pratihara era. Despite its destruction, the monument has been carefully restored, though not always with all its carved detail intact.

The rectangular sanctuary is contained within a massive masonry tower; the wall niches (empty) have tall pediments of arch-like motifs. The sanctuary doorway preserves its carved ornamentation, especially figures of river goddesses (beneath), amorous couples, coiled serpents, foliation (jambs) and a flying Garuda (lintel). The tower, which is about 23 m (75 ft) high, has a vaulted roof with arched ends (restored). The projections in the middle of each side of the tower continue those of the walls beneath. On the sides, identical arched motifs of different sizes are superimposed in a succession of recessed planes to produce complicated designs.

Chaturbhuja Temple, 875

Constructed in a ravine, this dilapidated Hindu building consists of a small sanctuary with a curved tower, now rebuilt, that adjoins a small porch. Wall niches, columns and doorway preserve little of the original detail. The sanctuary enshrines a later image of Vishnu. The temple is contained within a later colonnade.

Sasbahu Temples, 1093

This pair of Hindu temples stands on a fortified bluff overlooking the town. The larger example has a sanctuary, missing its tower, adjoining a triple-storey mandapa with three projecting porches. The open design of the mandapa, which is roofed with a pyramid of masonry, is in striking contrast to the earlier Teli ka Mandir. Almost none of the original figural panels has survived, but many of the walls, niche pediments, doorways and ceilings preserve finely etched foliate decoration.

The smaller of the two temples is an open porch with balcony seating and a pyramidal roof. The designs on the basement are sharply cut, as are also the corbelled slabs forming the complex vaulted ceiling inside.

Rock-cut Jain Images, 7th–15th centuries

Most of these large figures are cut into the steep sides of the Urvahi valley on the western side of the plateau. A seated couple dates from the 7th century; other figures belonging to the 10th century include a reclining mother with child. The group is best known for twenty-two standing Tirthankaras; these bear six inscriptions dating from 1400 to 1453. One colossal figure, about 19 m (62 ft) high, is typical in its rigid posture and rounded modelling. The saviours stand in deep recesses, partly contained in niches with intermediate lintels.

Cut into the north-west and south-west sides of the plateau are other Jain images. Beneath the palace on the north-east side of the citadel are four caves; these are subdivided into cells and have seated Tirthankaras carved on to the walls. Cave 3 is the largest of the group; in Cave 4 is a reclining female figure.

Central Archaeological Museum

Hindu and Jain sculptures from various

nearby sites are displayed in this collection. Belonging to the Shunga period are several 1st-century-BC column capitals and railing fragments, mostly from **Vidisha**. The Gupta period is represented by a 5th-century fan-palm capital from **Pawaya**. An image of Surya or Vishnu (from the top of a column), and a fragmentary gateway lintel illustrating Vali's sacrifice (dance scene) and Trivikrama also come from **Pawaya**. Other contemporary pieces include damaged sculptures of the Matrikas. Lion capitals from **Udayagiri** (5) and **Vidisha** (6) are carved in imitation of Maurya models.

Sculptures from the 6th–7th centuries include a standing Shiva figure (62) and dancing Indrani (65), both from **Kota**. There are numerous images from the 9th–11th centuries, such as Balarama from Padhavalki, Karttikeya from **Suhania** (193), an elegantly posed dancing Shiva from **Ujjain** (81) and a delicately modelled maiden from **Gyaraspur** (87). From **Udayapur** comes an arched niche decorated with lotus ornament which frames a dancing Shiva figure (26.11). There are also miniature shrines, decorated pillars and other architectural fragments. Commemorative panels known as hero stones are carved with lively compositions.

Copies of the wall paintings in the Buddhist cave temples at **Bagh** are permanently displayed.

GYARASPUR

This ancient centre is best known for its Hindu and Jain remains belonging to the Pratihara era. They are dominated by the Maladevi temple, which is picturesquely situated on the slope of the hill overlooking the village from the south. About 1·6 km (1 mile) to the west, on the side of another hill, is a dilapidated Buddhist stupa dating from a slightly earlier period.

Stupa, 6th–7th century

This monument has a high vertical base

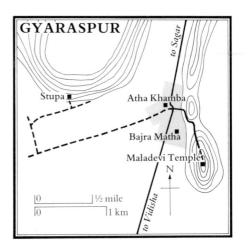

and a circular terrace for circumambulation. Remains of upright posts indicate a simple railing. Four seated Buddha images are placed against the stupa base.

Maladevi Temple, 9th century

This is an ornate and mature example of the Pratihara style. The temple is partly structural and partly rock-cut. The sanctuary, which is surrounded by a passageway, is roofed with a soaring curved tower. Tall pediments with meshes of arch-like motifs rise above the niches on the outer walls and within the passageway (empty); similar meshes decorate the tower. The porches that project from the mandapa have inclined seating slabs. Jain figures and a yakshi are installed within the temple, but a miniature image of a goddess carved on to the doorway lintel indicates the original Hindu dedication of the temple.

Atha Khamba ('Eight Columns'), 9th century

The remains of this large Hindu temple consist of eight columns, hence the name, and a doorway to a non-existent sanctuary. The columns and doorway are finely carved in the typical Pratihara style.

Bajra Matha, 10th century and later

The triple shrines of this temple are now occupied by Jain images; originally they were dedicated to Hindu images of Surya, Vishnu and Shiva. The towers rising over the sanctuaries are partly obscured by later additions. The evolved style of the temple is evident in the complicated designs that cover the bands of the curved tower. A profusion of carved motifs, now damaged, surrounds the doorway.

INDORE

(For the city and its monuments see Volume II.)

Central Museum

This collection is dominated by the large number of Jain and Hindu sculptures taken from the ruined 11th–12th-century temples at Hinglajgarh. These finely carved panels depict Harihara, Shiva and Parvati seated on Nandi (several examples), standing Parvati and a damaged Chamunda. Among the architectural fragments is a door frame complete with figures and ornamentation.

A 13th-century bronze of Shrutadevi, with attendants bearing fly-whisks, is also exhibited; this image comes from Ahurajpur.

JABALPUR

(For the city and its monuments see Volume II.)

Bara Jain Temple, 18th century

This temple enshrines a fine 12th-century image of Adinatha installed within the sanctuary. The seated figure of the saviour is surrounded by attendants, flying celestials and elephants.

Rani Durgavati Museum

Numerous 10th–11th-century sculptures from Hindu and Jain sites in the vicinity are exhibited in this collection. Among the finest are those from Tewar; these include two examples of Shiva seated with Parvati (47.310, 47.312).

KADWAHA

No fewer than eight 10th–11th-century Hindu temples belonging to the Kaccha-paghata period still stand at this site. Though partly ruined, these monuments are fine examples of the central Indian style.

The towers that rise over the small square sanctuaries are covered with arch-like motifs; amalakas are positioned at the summits. The outer walls are generally divided into two tiers of panels; the upper panels are sometimes surmounted by pediments or miniature projecting eaves at the central niches. Sculptures are preserved in only a few temples; these illustrate a wide range of divinities and attendant figures. Around the doorways are river goddesses, guardians and amorous couples; the thresholds have fighting animals and lotus motifs. The columns of the porches are generally adorned with pot and foliage motifs; brackets are fashioned as supporting dwarf-like figures.

The latest and largest temple at the site, known as the Murayat, dates from the end of the 11th century. While its layout maintains the simple scheme of earlier examples, the ornamentation of both the exterior and interior is the most elaborate of the series.

KANAUJ

Kanauj was once an important cultural centre as well as the capital of Harsha, the ruler of much of central India in the first half of the 7th century. (A description of this king and his court is given by the Chinese traveller Hiuen Tsang.) In the following centuries, Kanauj served as the capital for the Pratihara and Pala dynasties, and was overrun for a time by the Rashtrakutas of the Deccan. It was almost entirely destroyed by Muslim raids in the 13th century. (For the Islamic monuments in Kanauj see Volume II.)

East of the modern town, a series of mounds and segments of fortification walls indicate the ancient site. Excavations here have exposed the basements of Hindu temples and palaces. A Muslim sanctuary nearby is actually composed of two Hindu temples.

Archaeological Museum

Sculptures collected from the site are assembled here. From the 1st–2nd cen-

turies come pilasters and brackets carved in the Shunga style. Later Pratihara sculptures include a panel carved with figures of Tara and Ardhanarishvara on either side (79.251). There are also images of four of the Matrikas; Chamunda is depicted dancing on a prostrate figure.

J.N.Kapoor Collection

The two sculptures of outstanding quality for which this collection is celebrated are datable to the 9th century. They are among the finest examples of the Pratihara style, remarkable for the deep modelling of the figures and the unusually crowded compositions. One panel depicts the marriage of Shiva and Parvati, accompanied by various deities; the other shows Vishnu in his expanding form as Vishvarupa, surrounded by incarnations and flying figures.

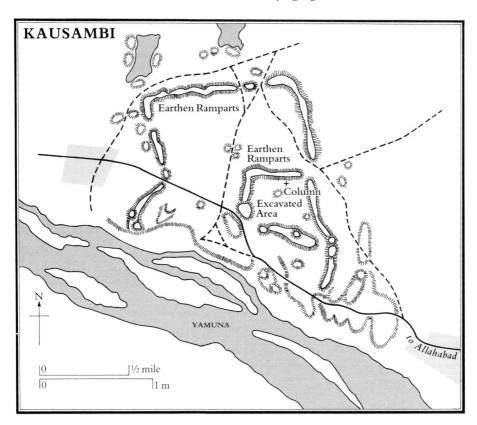

KAUSAMBI (map p. 165)

The remains of ancient Kausambi are identified with the mass of mounds at this site on the left bank of the Yamuna river. Kausambi was one of the earliest historical cities of central India. It was particularly connected with the life of Buddha, since through the efforts of its citizens the new religion was firmly established in the region.

A large part of the site is contained within an irregular area no less than 1·5 km (1 mile) on the north, south and east. The entire periphery is demarcated by ramparts with regularly spaced bastions; there was also a deep moat. The walls were originally of earth but were later surfaced with brickwork. Gates with guard rooms were positioned on all four sides. There are the remains of a stone altar, possibly used for fire sacrifices, which have been found outside the gateway on the east; the altar was laid out in the form of a large eagle.

The only standing feature at the site is the damaged shaft of a sandstone column, assignable to the era of the Maurya emperor Ashoka. Another column that once stood here was removed to the fort at **Allahabad** during the Mughal period.

Within the walled area, excavations have revealed evidence of continuous occupation from about the 8th century BC until the 6th century AD. Among the identifiable remains are a paved road, brick habitations, mud walls, wells, brick-lined tanks and pottery drains. At the south-western corner the remains of a large structure have been identified tentatively as a palace complex. There was also a large brick monastery with a stupa in the middle and chambers all around.

The artefacts that were recovered in the excavations include terracotta figurines of the 2nd-century-BC Shunga period, as well as seals, clay impressions, coins, bangles, beads and other ornaments. Many of these are now displayed in museums at **Allahabad**.

KHAJURAHO

In the early 9th century, the Chandellas emerged as one of the prominent dynasties of rulers in central India; Khajuraho appears to have served as their capital. The site was adorned with numerous tanks and Hindu and Jain temples, of which twenty-five still stand.

The Khajuraho monuments demonstrate a distinctive and coherent architectural evolution that marks the culmination of the central Indian style. The inventiveness of local architects is seen in the increasingly complex schemes of the building masses. The sculptures at Khajuraho are among the masterpieces of Indian art; they are applied to almost all parts of the temples. Other than numerous divinities enshrined in wall niches, there are attendants, semi-divine figures, guardians of the directions of space, graceful maidens in a variety of provocative postures, dancers, musicians and embracing couples. Many of these sculptural compositions vibrate with an unmistakable sensuality and warmth. There are also scenes of sexual activity, which possibly illustrate the tantric rites that accompanied temple worship. Ubiquitous are the rearing mythic beasts, usually rampant horned lions, with armed riders and attacking monsters.

The temples are described chronologically within each of three groups according to their layout. Unless otherwise stated they are all Hindu.

WESTERN GROUP

Chaunsath Yogini Temple,
late 9th century

This ruined structure is raised upon a high platform and consists of a rectangle of crudely constructed small square shrines. Each shrine has a tapering pyramidal roof. Of the original peripheral shrines, only thirty-five still stand; that in the middle

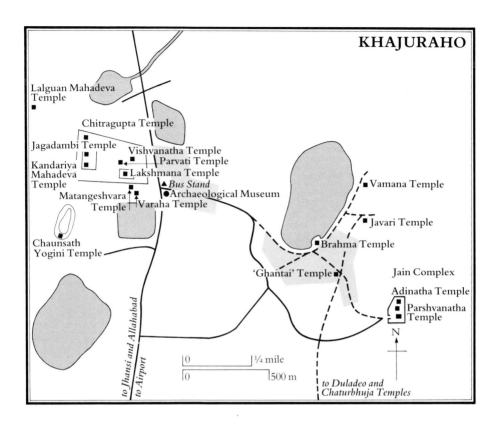

KHAJURAHO

Lalguan Mahadeva Temple

Chitragupta Temple

Jagadambi Temple
Kandariya Mahadeva Temple

Vishvanatha Temple
Parvati Temple
Lakshmana Temple
▲ *Bus Stand*
● *Archaeological Museum*
Matangeshvara Temple ┤ Varaha Temple

Vamana Temple

Javari Temple

Chaunsath Yogini Temple

Brahma Temple

'Ghantai' Temple

Jain Complex

Adinatha Temple
Parshvanatha Temple

N

to Jhansi and Allahabad
to Airport

|0 |¼ mile
|0 |500 m

to Duladeo and Chaturbhuja Temples

---

of the rear wall facing the entrance is enlarged. Three yogini images are enshrined here.

Lalguan Mahadeva Temple,
early 10th century

This ruined shrine is devoid of any carved decoration. Only part of the tapering tower still stands.

Varaha Temple, early 10th century

Elevated on a terrace, this rectangular pavilion is roofed with a stepped masonry pyramid. Within the sanctuary is an image of Varaha, the body of which is covered with miniature figures. Beneath the leg of the animal is a penitent naga figure. The lotus ceiling is carved in full relief.

Matangeshvara Temple,
early 10th century

Still in use for worship, this temple is partly obscured by modern steps on its front (east). Projecting from three sides of the sanctuary walls are deep balconies with angled seating and overhanging eaves; on the east is the entrance porch. Above rises the pyramid of horizontal elements that constitutes the roof; this is crowned with a number of successive amalakas. Above the porch is a seated lion. Enshrined within the sanctuary is a large polished stone linga.

Lakshmana Temple, 954

This is the earliest and most completely preserved of the mature Chandella temples. Raised on a high terrace, the principal temple is the focus of a complex that includes four subsidiary corner shrines. Access steps run up the middle of the east side.

The lively friezes carved on the terrace basement depict courtly subjects, including processions of horses, elephants, camels, warriors, battles, dancers and musicians. There are also sages with women, and ritualized sexual acts (the last on the south side).

The principal temple is elevated on a high basement with miniature niches. Of the sculptures positioned here, that of dancing Ganesha (south) is one of the finest. The sanctuary is surrounded by a passageway and adjoins a mandapa and porch, all aligned on an east–west axis. Additional smaller porches project outwards from the passageway and mandapa. Sloping balcony seating and angled eaves demarcate the porches. The succession of pyramidal roofs over the porch and mandapa reaches a climax in the clustered tower that rises over the sanctuary. This tower is composed of a number of identical superimposed elements that imitate the central shaft itself. Each of these elements is covered with arch-like motifs and capped by an amalaka and a pot finial. The pyramidal roofs of the mandapa and front porch have side projections with complex arched designs.

Two tiers of carved panels cover the exterior walls of the passageway. Here different divinities, attendant maidens, amorous couples and rearing beasts appear. Coupled figures in complicated sexual acts are reserved for the panels at the junction of the sanctuary and mandapa within.

The interior has columns with projecting figures at the capitals; the angled brackets, carved as maidens beneath trees, are among the masterpieces of Chandella art. Corbelled domes in receding planes are complicated compositions with multi-lobed and petalled motifs. The sanctuary doorway is covered with miniature figures, including Vishnu's incarnations and the Navagrahas. Inside the sanctuary is a triple-headed Vaikuntha image with boar and lion side heads. The sanctuary walls within the passageway are raised on a moulded basement; the niches house different Vaishnava icons.

The corner subsidiary shrines are smaller and simpler than the principal temple, but also incorporate carved panels and ornamented doorways. The towers have only a single curvilinear shaft.

Vishvanatha Temple, 1002

According to an inscribed slab placed in the porch, this temple was erected by the ruler, Dhangadeva. It is laid out in much the same manner as the Lakshmana temple and displays the mature evolution of the Chandella style. Only two subsidiary shrines (out of four) are intact; almost nothing of the original basement ornamentation on the terrace survives. The main shrine introduces subtle variations to the Lakshmana scheme: the basement has smaller niches, doubled in two tiers; sculptures in three rows adorn the walls; additional projections and miniature tower-like elements in the roof create a more complex three-dimensional effect. The elevation of the tower (best appreciated from the west) reveals a skilful manipulation of the building masses that soar upwards to the summit.

Of the numerous sculptures, depictions of sexual acts predominate. The ceiling panels have complicated patterns. A richly adorned doorway provides access to the sanctuary and its linga.

Immediately east of the temple is an open pavilion housing a large Nandi image. Unadorned sloping back-rests are raised on a basement with a frieze of elephants. The pavilion is roofed with a pyramid of horizontal elements.

Parvati Temple, late 10th century

This is located south-west of the Vishvanatha temple and is much restored. The

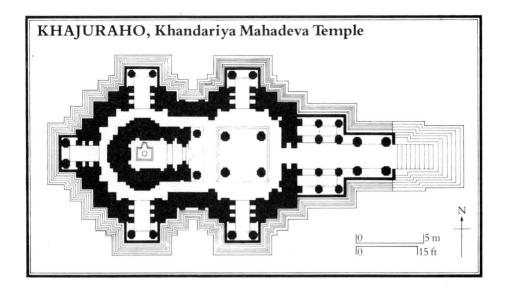

KHAJURAHO, Khandariya Mahadeva Temple

N

|0 |5 m
|0 |15 ft

carved doorway, however, retains some of its original decoration.

Chitragupta Temple,
early 11th century

Dedicated to Surya, this temple demonstrates several variant features when compared to the Lakshmana and Vishvanatha monuments. The outer walls of the passageway have no projecting balconies, only small niches; the walls are completely covered with sculptures in three tiers; the mandapa balconies are wide. The result is a longer and lower elevation. The tower over the sanctuary is much restored. Reliefs similar to those on the terrace of the Lakshmana temple are carved on to the basement. The sanctuary has a finely carved doorway with triple images of Surya.

Jagadambi Temple, mid-11th century

This follows the same scheme as the Chitragupta temple, but with an increased emphasis on the mandapa and its massive pyramidal roof. Sculpture panels present a fine range of deities, amorous couples and maidens. The sen-

suous modelling of the figures and their sinuous postures are typical of the fully developed Chandella style. Within, the ceiling panels are particularly fine. The shrine doorway is surrounded by densely carved couples, dancers, flying soldiers and beasts. Enshrined within the sanctuary is a later Parvati image.

Kandariya Mahadeva Temple,
mid-11th century

This temple is the climax of the Khajuraho series in terms of scale, overall composition and sculptural ornamentation. The schemes of the Lakshmana and Vishvanatha monuments are expanded and developed here; additional projections are carried up into the tower as a number of clustered elements. Although the resulting three-dimensional quality of the superstructure is visually complex, all of the elements are unified into a dramatic sweep upwards to the summit of the central tower, more than 30 m (98 ft) above the terrace.

The sculpture panels, arranged in three tiers on the outer walls, are celebrated for their depiction of ritualized sexual posures. Located at the junction of the sanctuary and mandapa within, these panels are surrounded by divinities, guardians, attendant women and other figures. Among the numerous deities are the Dikpalas, as well as ascetic and demonic aspects of Shiva. Maidens in a variety of poses, often twisting and turning in erotic allure, also appear. Sculptures continue on to the multi-tiered roof of the mandapa. Even the basement of the temple is provided with friezes that illustrate courtly themes. Niches in the basement house figures of goddesses carved almost in the round. The balcony seating has angled backs carved with stylized foliation.

Over the entrance to the porch is a finely executed multi-lobed arch rising from brackets which are fashioned as mythical beasts; flying figures are carved between the lobes. The corbelled ceilings, both vaulted and domed, are of exceptional delicacy. Niches in the sanctuary walls house diverse images of Shiva. Several brackets with maidens are preserved. An elaborately carved doorway leads to the sanctuary, where a linga is installed.

Shiva Temple, 11th century

This ruined monument stands on the terrace that links the Jagadambi and Kandariya Mahadeva temples. Only an isolated sanctuary doorway sheltered by a porch survives. Within the porch is a lionlike beast accompanied by a crouching female figure.

Archaeological Museum

A large number of 10th–11th-century sculptures and architectural fragments from the site is assembled in this collection; even the entrance to the museum is a temple doorway. Among the finest exhibits are the large dancing Ganesha figure (1130), a panel depicting two Tirthankaras (1635), a standing Surya figure surrounded by miniature attendants

(1262) and similarly crowded compositions with Harihara (558) and Varaha (861). Seated images of Buddha (450) and five-headed Shiva (1098) are also displayed.

Among the courtly themes are a hunting frieze (1318) and the votive portraits of a royal couple (2010). Brackets are carved with maidens and amorous couples (1317, 1342 and 2072, for example). The frieze illustrating the transportation and cutting of building blocks (1315) is unusual. Another panel depicts flying warriors (1821).

EASTERN GROUP

Brahma Temple, early 10th century

This simple square structure has a pyramidal roof divided into numerous horizontal mouldings. The temple is much restored.

Parshvanatha Temple,
mid-10th century

This is the largest Jain temple of the Chandella period. It is dominated by a curvilinear tower with numerous clustered elements, similar to the Lakshmana temple. The walls of the sanctuary and adjoining mandapa, however, are differently organized. Three rows of panels of decreasing size are set into shallow recesses and projections. Among the many well-preserved sculptures are numerous Vaishnava images and amorous couples in swaying postures.

The interior doorway is richly carved. Elephants and lions appear on the threshold; the jambs are adorned with river goddesses, attendants and guardian figures. The Jina figures on the lintel indicate the dedication of the temple.

'Ghantai' Temple, late 10th century

This fragmentary structure has columns with finely carved bells (ghantai) on chains, garlands and other motifs. A richly ornamented doorway, now damaged, still stands.

Vamana Temple, 11th century

This temple, which is of the fully evolved Chandella style, has a single tower without clustered elements. The tower rises in finely articulated bands that continue the projections of the walls beneath. These bands are covered with a mesh of arch-like motifs; at the summit are the usual amalaka and pot elements. Sculptures, many damaged, in two tiers cover the walls beneath. Within, a richly carved doorway leads to a sanctuary housing a Vamana image.

Javari Temple, late 11th century

This small temple consists of a towered sanctuary and double porch raised on a plain terrace. The tower is notable for its slender proportions. A particularly fine multi-lobed arch is preserved over the entrance.

Adinatha Temple, late 11th century

This simplified Jain temple has only a single shaft for the tower; it is covered with a mesh of arch-like motifs. Of the three bands of wall sculptures, the uppermost is reserved for flying celestials. The attached porch is a later addition.

SOUTHERN GROUP

Duladeo Temple, early 12th century

This is one of the last temples of the Chandella era. The projections of the sanctuary walls dominate the reconstructed tower, creating a star-like plan. Bands of sculpture on each projection are surmounted by two tiers of tower-like elements.

Chaturbhuja Temple, early 12th century

This is the finest temple of the southern group. It is similar to the Javari temple and is much restored. The sanctuary houses a large Shiva image, 2·7 m (9 ft) high.

KHAROD

Two brick Hindu temples from the 7th century are still preserved in this village, which is situated on the left bank of the upper Mahanadi river. The buildings are early examples of the brick style which flourished in the region. The better-preserved temple is the Indal Deul. This has finely worked basement mouldings, wall pilasters and tiers of ascending arch-like motifs on the tower. The sanctuary has pronounced projections, some of which are angled; these are carried up into the tower. The terracotta sculptures that once adorned the temple are badly eroded.

KUSINAGARA

This ancient capital is celebrated as the site where Buddha died, an event known in Buddhist texts as Parinirvana. Two extensive monasteries were established here, one associated with the Master's death, the other with his cremation. These flourished until the disappearance of Buddhism in the region in the 11th century.

The focus of the ruins is a stupa with a shrine in front, both standing on a platform. Excavations within the stupa have revealed precious stones and coins and also the buried remains of a 1st-century terracotta Buddhist figure. The shrine in front once housed a colossal sandstone image of Buddha lying in state, probably dating from the 5th-century Gupta era.

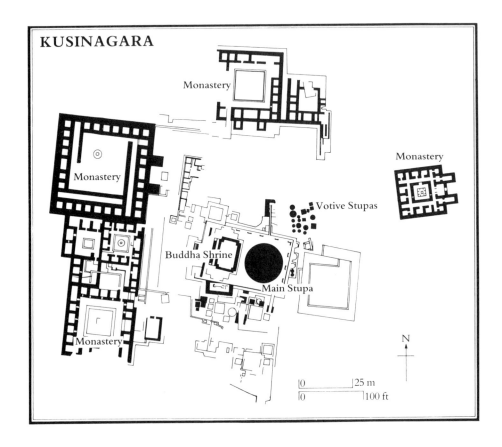

KUSINAGARA

Monastery

Monastery

Monastery

Votive Stupas

Buddha Shrine

Main Stupa

Monastery

Monastery

N

|0 |25 m
|0 |100 ft

Both stupa and shrine have been extensively rebuilt; the reclining image is completely reconstituted from original fragments and is covered with plaster. There are traces of numerous votive stupas and square monasteries in the vicinity. These date from the 1st–2nd century and were rebuilt many times.

About 1·5 km (1 mile) east of this complex is a large stupa, about 34 m (112 ft) in diameter; this is known as Ramabhar and is surrounded by subsidiary shrines. Bricks with composite sculptures were discovered in the excavations.

LUCKNOW

(For the city and its monuments see Volume II.)

State Museum

This large collection of stone sculptures includes many pieces from **Mathura**. 1st-century art from this site is represented by architectural fragments, such as columns, pillars and railings, a capital with palm leaves (J584) and votive Jain plaques carved with auspicious emblems (notably J250). One pillar is carved on both sides with scenes of music, dance, love and toilet (J535). But it is the impressive Bodhisattva figure (B12b), now headless and with a robe thrown over the shoulder, that is the outstanding example of **Mathura** art. 2nd- and 3rd-century sculptures from this site are mostly confined to the heads of Buddhist and Jain figures.

Gupta sculptures, mostly dating from the 5th century, include a seated Tirthankara figure with a decorated halo from **Mathura** (J118) and seated Buddha from Mankuwar (O70). There are numerous other Buddhist and Jain heads (notably G464). Hindu sculpture is represented by an interesting series of lingas, including a four-faced example from Kosam (H3) and a standing Vishnu figure from **Mathura** (H111). Within an arched niche from **Allahabad** is a head of Shiva (O74). From Garhwa come several narrative friezes, including the fight between Bhima and Jarasandha, an episode from the Mahabharata epic (488). The life-size effigy of a horse from Kairigarh (H219) is unusual.

8th- and 9th-century art in the Pratihara period is represented by a panel with standing Bodhisattvas from Pakhna (G219) and a double-sided panel with Lakshmi and Durga from Bhitari (55.201). To the 10th and 11th centuries belongs a large number of different images from a variety of sites; Buddhist deities of the Pala period are also exhibited. Among the more interesting figures are a standing Vishnu, carved almost in the round, from Seor (O199) and two perfectly preserved panels from Mahoba depicting seated Bodhisattvas (O224, O225). These last two figures are celebrated for their elegant postures, delicate modelling and serene expressions. Shiva and Parvati together (H11), reclining Vishnu from Umara (56.359) and Varaha covered with miniature figures from Dudhai (O84) are also fine sculptures. Numerous Pala votive stupas are also displayed.

MANKHEDA

Surya Temple, late 9th century

This is one of the best-preserved monuments of the Pratihara period. The Hindu temple is dominated by the tower, which has curved bands covered in meshes of arch-like motifs. Similar meshes adorn the elongated pediments over niches on the walls and even on the basement. A large amalaka crowns the tower. On the front (east) of the tower is a triangular projection composed of interlocking arched shapes, both large and small. In the central niche is a bust of Surya carrying lotus flowers; a fully carved rampant lion-like beast is positioned above. Other sculptures are preserved in the wall niches and also around the doorway, where river goddesses, amorous couples and fighting figures appear. An image of the sun deity is placed in the middle of the lintel.

MAT

This small village is situated 14 km (9 miles) north of **Mathura**, on the left bank of the Yamuna river. Here were discovered the remains of a structure dating from the 2nd century. Known locally as Tokra Tila, this shrine was laid out on a rectangular plan, with a circular sanctuary at one end. Among the sandstone figures that were unearthed in the ruins was a portrait sculpture of the Kushana ruler Kanishka, indicating that the shrine may have had a royal ceremonial purpose. (Sculptures from Mat are exhibited in the Government Museum, **Mathura**).

MATHURA

Mathura, on the right bank of the Yamuna river, is one of the seven holy cities of Hinduism; yet it was also once an important centre for Buddhists and Jains. Mathura played a significant role in the formation of the 1st–2nd-century Kushana empire, and was the capital of Kanishka and his successors. Mathura continued to be a town of some significance during Gupta times and later, but was eventually pillaged by the Muslims at the beginning of the 13th century. (For the Islamic and British monuments of the city see Volume II.)

Krishna was born in Mathura, and most of the stories associated with this god are believed to have taken place in the vicinity. In fact the whole region is

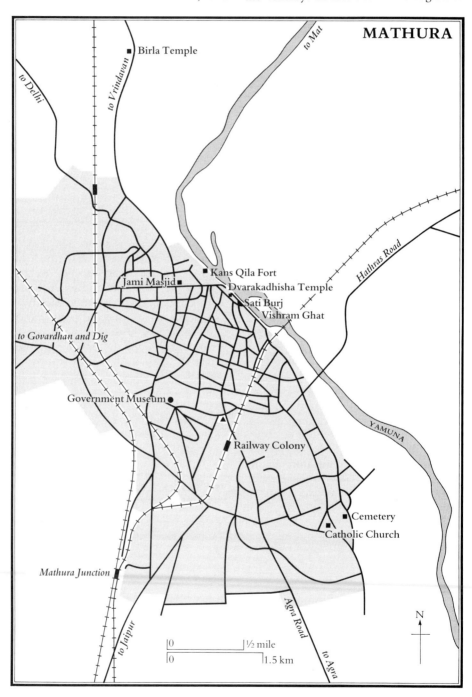

MATHURA

to Mat

to Vrindavan

to Delhi

Birla Temple

Hathras Road

Kans Qila Fort

Jami Masjid

Dvarakadhisha Temple

Sati Burj

Vishram Ghat

to Govardhan and Dig

YAMUNA

Government Museum

Railway Colony

Cemetery

Catholic Church

Mathura Junction

to Jaipur

Agra Road

to Agra

N

| 0 | ½ mile |
| 0 | 1.5 km |

dotted with localities commemorating different episodes in the Krishna story: for example, Gokul, where Vishnu first appeared as Krishna; Govardhan, where Krishna lifted up the mountain to shelter the herds from Indra's storm; and **Vrindavan**, 9 km (5½ miles) to the north, where the youthful god sported with the gopis. During the rainy season, large groups of devotees perform a pilgrimage circuit of these sites; theatrical troupes enact the scenes from the god's life.

Almost no monument of any antiquity is preserved at Mathura. The chief places of interest are the bathing ghats, particularly the Vishram Ghat (rebuilt in 1814), where Krishna rested after killing the tyrant Kamsa. The temples, notably the Dvarakadhisha, are mostly 19th-century reconstructions.

Archaeological investigations conducted in and around Mathura have recovered large quantities of sculptures and architectural fragments in the local red sandstone; pottery and terracotta votive objects have also been found, some dating back to the 6th century BC. While a large proportion of these materials are now housed in the Government Museum, important Mathura sculptures and artefacts appear in many collections (notably the Indian Museum, **Calcutta**, the State Museum, **Lucknow**, and the National Museum, **New Delhi**).

Despite the profusion of mounds within the city limits and in the immediate vicinity, archaeologists have not discovered any intact architectural remains. The fragments indicate the presence of Buddhist and Jain stupas and monasteries, mostly built of brick, dating from the 1st–6th centuries. In contrast, a short distance outside the city, at **Mat** and **Sonkh**, traces of Kushana structures have been found.

Sculptures from Mathura constitute one of the most significant early schools of Indian art. While its origins are to be sought in the preceding Maurya and Shunga periods (3rd–1st centuries BC), Mathura art was greatly stimulated by

influences introduced by the Kushana rulers. Under their patronage, the first images to represent the Buddha and Jain saviours were evolved. During the 4th–5th-century Gupta period, Mathura art reached its climax; some of the finest of all Buddhist sculptures in India were produced here at this time. Several Mathura images have been discovered at other sites, including **Sarnath** (Archaeological Museum), **Ahichhatra** and **Sanghol** (National Museum, **New Delhi**).

Government Museum

In this important collection there is a large number of Kushana and Gupta sandstone pieces found in and around Mathura. To the Shunga period belongs a 2nd-century-BC yaksha of impressive proportions, 2·65 m (9 ft) high, from Parkham (C1). Among the 1st-century pieces is a standing headless Buddha from Uspar (10.93).

Kushana sculptures form the nucleus of the collection. Among the numerous Buddhist and Jain figures are several standing Buddhas of the yaksha type (A63, 38.2798), a seated Buddha with a halo, flying celestials and attendants (A1) and also a partial image of a seated Tirthankara (B37). Of the many fragmentary sculptures, the heads of a Tirthankara (B78) and of Buddha (A27) are fine examples. Also belonging to the Kushana era are a portrait of Kanishka with foreign-styled tunic, sword and boots but now headless (12.213), and of a prince wearing a delicately worked costume (12.212). The first of these two royal statues comes from **Mat**. Some detached heads have pointed caps, which may indicate royal status (16.1252). Among the Hindu divinities is a seated Surya figure (12.269) and a crouching armless Kubera (C3). From **Sonkh** comes a frieze illustrating the court of a naga king (So.IV.36).

Also belonging to the Kushana period are numerous small railing posts. These are carved with maidens who stand on crouching figures or animals, clutching trees, holding pots, mirrors or flowers, or bearing offerings. One of the most attractive of these girls clutching a branch is carved as a curved bracket; this comes from **Sonkh** (So.IV.27). Several columns are carved with courtly narratives, such as the toilet scene on the column from Gurgaon (12.186). There are a large number of other architectural fragments, many adorned with undulating stalks and stylized lotus flowers (jamb 57.4447, in combination with narratives, for example). One fragment has a tree and squirrel carved on to the back (F2).

Numerous lions (O4, for instance) and other animals also date from the Kushana period. Of interest is a frieze from **Sonkh** depicting a figure emerging from an open-mouthed makara (So.IV.37), and another showing a makara swallowing a figure (M7).

Contemporary with these Kushana pieces are sculptures from Gandhara (north-western Pakistan) that were discovered at Mathura, demonstrating early contacts between these two distant centres. The largest Gandharan sculpture is a finely modelled female figure (F42), possibly Hariti.

Numerous Gupta sculptures are also exhibited. These include a finely carved Buddha head (49.3510) and also a large head of a Tirthankara (B61). The standing Buddha with the hand held in protection is typical (76.25). But it is the standing Buddha (A5) completely preserved with its ornamented halo that is the outstanding sculpture of this collection, and indeed one of the masterpieces of the Gupta period. The delicately modelled body cloaked with fluted robes and the subtle facial expression of detachment have never been surpassed in Indian art. Another fine example (A8), now headless, imitates the qualities of this great piece.

As for contemporary Hindu divinities, there are a fragment of Vishnu in his cosmic form (42.43.2939), a small bust of Ardhanarishvara (15.772) and a headless standing Vishnu figure (50.3532). Many architectural pieces, especially door jambs, also belong to the Gupta era. There are a few later images, including a 12th century group of the Matrikas (15.552), and a number of votive shrines.

Terracotta figurines dating from the 2nd–1st centuries BC are displayed separately. These include mother goddesses (66.2, for example) and a fragmentary nobleman wearing foreign dress (32.2556). Among the later examples from the Gupta period are a hermit cutting off his head (38.39.2792) and a courtesan with a jester (38.39.2795).

NACHNA

This Hindu site is known for both its Gupta temple and for later monuments that incorporate Gupta elements.

Parvati Temple, 5th century

Though this building is now ruined, the original scheme of a small square sanctuary surrounded on four sides by a passageway is clear. The sanctuary is raised up on a terrace the sides of which are adorned with cubic rock-like motifs. The doorway on the west is surrounded by finely carved guardians, river goddesses, amorous couples and bands of scrollwork. Pierced stone windows are positioned in the north and south walls, which are otherwise plain. No tower survives although one was probably intended. The guardian image placed in the sanctuary is not original.

Chaturmukha Mahadeva Temple, 9th century

This monument, which dates from the Pratihara period, is situated only a short distance north-west of the Parvati temple. The curved tower and its decoration of arch-like motifs are typical features of the later style. Carved panels, doorways and windows dating from the Gupta era are inset into the walls; these may be fragments from the dismantled Parvati temple. Within the sanctuary is an 8th-century quadruple-faced linga carved with remarkable vitality, especially the fierce open-mouthed face of the god (south).

Lying all around are loose fragments, including another multi-faced linga, as well as panels carved with Ramayana episodes.

Kumra Matha and Rupni ka Mandir, 15th century

These two later structures are notable for the Gupta doorways and columns incorporated into their brick structures.

NARESAR

Numerous 8th–9th-century Hindu temples dating from the early Pratihara period still stand at this remote site. The curved towers of these small sanctuaries are adorned with tiers of arch-like motifs; amalakas are positioned at the summits. On the fronts of the towers are projections with large circular frames containing sculptures, now worn. The walls have small niches with triangular pediments of arch-like motifs; the sculptures are generally damaged. The doorways are adorned with lotus ornament and miniature figures of river goddesses.

One of the temples is built on an unusual rectangular plan; the roof has a vaulted form. The wall niches housing figures of different divinities are relatively well preserved.

NEMAWAR

Siddheshvara Temple, early 12th century

This Hindu monument is the loftiest example of the Paramara style. The scheme familiar in the Udayeshvara temple at **Udayapur** is elaborated: the tower is heightened and there are nine tiers of miniature towered elements either side of the central tapering bands of mesh-like ornament. These tiers are clearly articulated, lending an almost rounded quality to the towered profile. Large arched niches are positioned at the base of the central bands.

Carved ornamentation is richly applied throughout the building; there are even niches with sculptures on the basement mouldings. Pierced stone windows in the mandapa resemble those in western Indian temples.

PAWAYA

Temple, 4th–5th century

This ruined Gupta structure consists of three brick terraces, the upper two of which are decorated with ornate pilasters. On the topmost terrace are the foundations of a later Hindu shrine. The stone sculptures discovered at this site have been mostly removed to the Central Archaeological Museum, **Gwalior**.

PIPRAHWA

This site is believed to be Kapilavastu, capital of the Shakya clan into which Buddha was born. Lumbini, the site linked with Gautama's birth, lies only 15 km (9½ miles) to the east, across the Nepalese border.

The remains of a Maurya stupa dating from the 3rd–2nd century BC have been discovered at Piprahwa. This construction of large bricks had a diameter of 35 m (115 ft), but was probably low in height; little is visible today. Excavation of the stupa has yielded a casket with an inscription (now in the Indian Museum, **Calcutta**); this indicated that the relics were of Buddha himself. Other artefacts include terracotta figurines, punch-marked silver coins, beads and pottery fragments. Traces of square brick monasteries have also been found in the vicinity.

RAIPUR

(For the city and its monuments see Volume II.)

Mahant Ghasidas Memorial Museum

Sculptures belonging to the 8th–9th centuries have been brought here from nearby sites. These include a stone image of Ganga from **Sirpur** (O560), as well as a number of architectural fragments. The collection is best known for a series of small Buddhist bronzes from **Sirpur**. These delicately modelled figures are mostly inlaid with silver. The finest are Avalokiteshvara (0016), Manjushri (3771) and Mayashri (3769).

RAJIM

An important group of Hindu temples is situated in the heart of the town on the right bank of the Mahanadi river. These temples are dominated by that dedicated to Rajivalochana; this is still in active worship and attracts large numbers of devotees. A short distance to the south is the Ramachandra temple. Despite modern additions and whitewashing, these buildings preserve many original sculptures. They date from the 8th century, a period when this part of central India was under the influence of the Somavamshi rulers.

Rajivalochana Temple, 8th century

This temple stands within an enclosure, entered on the west through a gateway. A characteristic feature is the tower that rises over the sanctuary and which has tiers of large arch-like motifs in the middle of each side, with an amalaka at the summit.

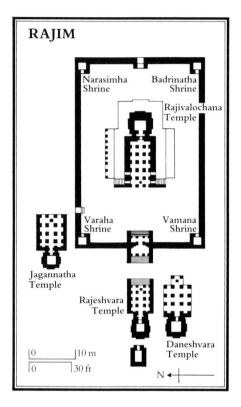

RAJIM

The mandapa doorways are richly carved with miniature guardian figures, amorous couples, serpents and foliation. An image of Vishnu worshipped as Ramachandra is enshrined within the sanctuary.

Sculpture panels depicting different aspects of Vishnu are scattered throughout the complex; the finest is Trivikrama and a penitent naga king (set into the north compound wall). The gateway also has a delicately carved doorway with unusual flying and falling figures.

Ramachandra Temple,
8th century and later

The original structure of this temple is mostly obscured by later additions. Even so, some of the columns within the mandapa preserve fine carvings of maidens beneath trees, and river goddesses. The fragmentary doorway jambs are encrusted with miniature figures.

REWA

The old city of Rewa is entered on the east through the Jhula Darwaza. This impos-ing gateway dates from the 10th–11th century; originally a free-standing monu-ment, it was brought from a ruined Hindu temple at Gurgi, about 19 km (12 miles) east of Rewa, and re-erected in the town. The sculptures on the columns and lintels illustrate the exuberant style of the Hai-haya period. The columns are adorned with dancing figures, alluring maidens

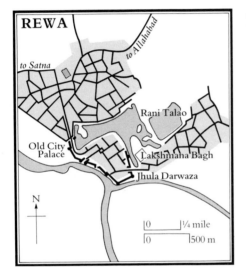

and rearing animals. The triple lintel has a cut-out lobed garland, as well as fringes of jewels and petals and mythical beasts with riders. Here too are narrative friezes depicting Shiva's wedding.

A colossal sculpture of Shiva with Parvati, displayed in the Lakshmana Bagh in the middle of the town, must have formed the principal cult image of a large temple, perhaps the same monument from which the gateway was taken.

(For the city palace see Volume II.)

SAGAR

(For the city fort see Volume II.)

Archaeological Museum, University of Sagar

Among the various Gupta sculptures col-lected here is a large 5th-century Varaha figure from **Eran**. Also displayed are architectural fragments and a number of 10th–11th-century panels carved with heroic figures.

SANCHI

The Buddhist establishment at this site is of outstanding significance for the num-ber and variety of its monuments, and also for the quality of its accompanying sculptures. Examples of almost all kinds of Buddhist structures are preserved at Sanchi, dating from the 3rd century BC to the 6th–7th centuries AD. The modern temple on the hill and the dharmashalas nearby indicate the recent revival of Bud-dhist interest in the site.

Sanchi has no known connection with Buddha, but stupas here enshrine relics of two of the Master's disciples, as well as those of later teachers. Inscriptions indi-cate that donors came from the nearby town of **Vidisha**.

Most of the monuments are located on the flat top of a hill. The plateau is sur-rounded by a stone wall which was added during the last phase of occupation in the 10th–11th century. Within this zone is located the majority of features, including the largest monument (Stupa 1) and a smaller copy (Stupa 3). Among the other edifices are the basements of smaller stupas, apsidal-ended shrines, structural temples and monasteries; there are also several free-standing columns. These features are laid out in three groups. An ancient path descends to the plain from the north-west corner of the plateau. Beneath the hill to the west is another monastery, the best preserved of the series, and a stupa. The Archaeological Museum is located a short distance away to the north-west.

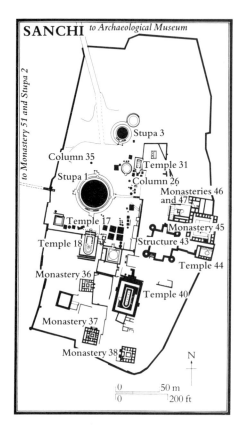

SANCHI *to Archaeological Museum*

to Monastery 51 and Stupa 2

Stupa 3
Column 35
Temple 31
Stupa 1
Column 26
Monasteries 46 and 47
Temple 17
Monastery 45
Temple 18
Structure 43
Temple 44
Monastery 36
Temple 40
Monastery 37
Monastery 38

N

0   50 m
0   200 ft

Archaeological Museum

Antiquities found at the site mostly belong to the Maurya and Gupta periods. From the earlier phase is a 3rd-century-BC capital (from Column 10) with four lions, the heads damaged, depicted back-to-back (2868). From Stupa 1 come two winged lions (2681, 2810) and the torsos of two yakshis clutching overhanging trees (2784, 2867). The later phase is represented by several 4th–5th-century images, such as a standing Balarama figure (A1102) and Padmapani (A100), both more than 2 m (6·6 ft) high, also Vishnu (61.533). A Vajrapani figure that once crowned Column 35 (2720) has an elaborate headdress and jewellery. A large seated Buddha figure (2771) is dated to the 6th century; the facial features are much worn. Several stone bowls and relic caskets from the stupas are displayed, as well as terracotta votive plaques and figurines.

MAIN TERRACE

Stupa I, 3rd–1st centuries BC and 5th century AD

The relatively complete preservation of this stupa, including the sculptures on its railings and gateways, makes it the finest example of monumental architecture and narrative art in the Shunga era.

The imposing stupa consists of a solid hemisphere 36·6 m (120 ft) in diameter; this is truncated at the top and crowned with a triple stone umbrella set within a square railing. A high circular terrace, approached by a double staircase (south side), is built against the base. A stone paved processional path at ground level is defined by an encircling balustrade. Access to this passageway is through four gateways.

The present stupa encases an earlier one of about half the dimensions, built of burnt bricks and ascribed to the 3rd century BC. A century later, the stupa was enlarged and faced with stone to produce the plan and form largely visible today. The unrelieved fabric of the stupa contrasts with the posts and railings of the encircling balustrade. These are carved with medallions displaying a variety of motifs, such as flowers, animals, birds, human figures and mythological beings. The balustrade is divided into four quadrants by L-shaped projections of the railing at the cardinal directions. These lead the devotee clockwise into the processional path. Throughout the balustrade, the reproduction of wood techniques in stone is remarkable.

The next embellishment was the four elaborately carved gateways, which were added during the 1st century BC. In their overall form, these gateways imitate techniques of wooden construction. Each gateway consists of two square posts crowned with a set of four lions, elephants or pot-bellied dwarfs. These support three architraves with scrolled ends to achieve an overall height of about 8·5 m (28 ft). Between the architraves are carved uprights and elephant- and horse-riders. Projecting from the tops of the posts and notched into the ends of the lowest architraves are brackets carved as graceful maidens clutching trees. The spaces

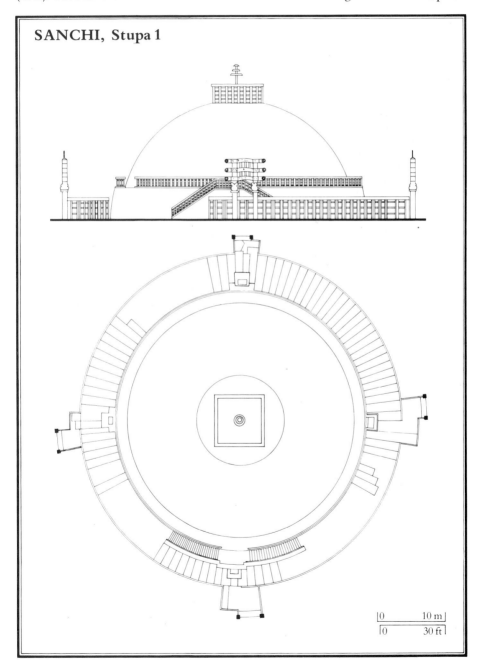

SANCHI, Stupa 1

|0   10 m|
|0   30 ft|

between the ends of the architraves are occupied by similar but smaller figures; on the scroll ends stand lions or elephants with riders. Crowning the whole compositions are wheels flanked by yakshis bearing fly-whisks and decorated tridents (symbolizing Buddha, the Dharma and the Sangha). All these elements are best preserved on the north gateway.

The posts and architraves are covered with sculptures. The varied compositions and liveliness of the figures are unsurpassed for their range of subject-matter. The most animated scenes illustrate episodes from Jataka legends. In the Chhaddanta Jataka, the Bodhisattva appears as an elephant (north gateway, uppermost architrave, inner face; south gateway, intermediate architrave, front face). In the Mahakapi Jataka, the Bodhisattva hero is a monkey (west gateway, right-hand post, front face), whereas in the Vessantara Jataka the Bodhisattva is a prince (north gateway, lowest architrave, both faces).

Though narrative episodes of Buddha's life also find a prominent place in these reliefs, the Master is never represented in human form; his presence is indicated only by emblems such as a riderless horse, an empty throne beneath the bodhi tree, footprints, a wheel or a trident. Referring to the life of the Master are scenes showing the dream of Maya (east gateway, left-hand post, inner face and uppermost architrave, front face), the temptation of Mara (west gateway, lowest architrave, inner face) and the sermon at **Sarnath** (west gateway, central architrave, front face). Particularly popular are illustrations of the miracles at **Sravasti** and Kapilavastu (**Piprahwa**) (north gateway, left-hand post, inner face). There is also a scene depicting the worship of the Buddha's headdress (south gateway, right-hand column, rear face).

Events in the subsequent history of Buddhism also appear, particularly the distribution of relics and the worship of the bodhi tree. Here are illustrated the wars waged for possession of Buddha's

SANCHI, Stupa 1, Gateways

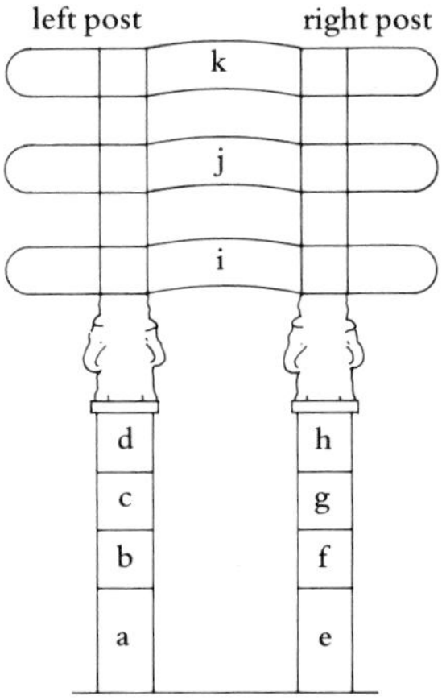

The lettering on the above drawing indicates the position of the carved panels on each of the four gateways, both front and back. The key to each gateway is below.

North Gateway: front face

a Scenes of pleasure; a royal procession
b Miracle of Sravasti
c Buddha in Jetavana grove
d Buddha teaching at Sravasti
e –
f Buddha preaching; miracle of Kapilavastu
g Buddha's drive; departure from the palace
h Buddha descends from heaven
i Vessantara Jataka; Vessantara gives away his elephant and leaves the city with his family (centre); the family journeys on foot (left, continuing on the rear face); Bodhisattva as the hermit
j–k Thrones, stupas and trees of the Manushi Buddhas

North Gateway: inside face of posts, rear face of architraves

a Guardian
b Buddha teaching; miracle at Kapilavastu
c Monkey offers honey to Buddha
d Dedication of a stupa
e Guardian
f Buddha at Rajgir

g Royal procession; Ajatashatru visits Buddha

h Indra visits Buddha

i Vessantara Jataka (continues from front face); arrival of the family in the forest (right); hermitage life and the gift of the children (centre); reunion of the family

j Sujata offers rice to Buddha; temptation of Mara

k Chhaddanta Jataka; elephants sporting in the forest; being shot by the hunter

East Gateway: front face

a Royal retinue of Bimbisara

b Buddha walking on the river

c Temple at Bodhgaya

d Buddha walking near the bodhi tree

e–h Heavens of the gods

i Ashoka visits the bodhi tree

j Buddha leaves Kapilavastu

k Stupas and trees of the Manushi Buddhas

East Gateway: inside face of posts, rear face of architraves

a and e Guardians

b Royal procession

c Dream of Maya

d Brahma entreats Buddha

f Conversion of Kashyapa

g Victory of Buddha over the serpent in the fire chapel

h Indra and Brahma visit Buddha

i Worship of the stupa

j Throne and tree being venerated

k Trees and thrones of the Manushi Buddhas

South Gateway: front face

(f–h in the Archaeological Museum)

a –

b Deities pay homage to Buddha's hair

c Ashoka and his retinue

d Worship of the wheel on a column

e –

f Merchants

g Buddha beneath the bodhi tree

h Buddha being worshipped by Muchalinda

i Dwarfs

j Ashoka visits the stupa

k Birth of Buddha

South Gateway: inside face of posts, rear face of architraves

(e–h in the Archaeological Museum)

a Buddha at Bodhgaya

b Offerings of Sujata

c Throne of Buddha

d Bodhi tree

e –

f Deities worship Buddha's hair

g Ashoka and queens in front of the bodhi tree

h Temple and the bodhi tree

i War over Buddha's relics

j Chhaddanta Jataka; elephant sporting in the pond; being shot by the hunter

k Stupas and trees of the Manushi Buddhas

West Gateway: front face

a –

b –

c–d Paradise of Indra (?)

e Lotus ornament

f–g Indra and the gods visit Buddha

h Mahakapi Jataka; the monkey acts as a bridge across which other monkeys escape; repentance of the king

i Elephants and devotees worship the stupa

j Sermon at Sarnath; bodhi trees

k Trees and stupas of the Manushi Buddhas

West Gateway: inside face of posts, rear face of architraves

a Guardian

b Buddha at Kapilavastu

c–d Enlightenment of Buddha; temptation of Mara

e –

f –

g Muchalinda in front of Buddha's throne

h Shyama Jataka; the dutiful son shot by the king; then restored to life by Indra

i Temptation of Buddha

j War over Buddha's relics

k Transport of Buddha's relics

relics (south gateway, lowest architrave, rear face; west gateway, intermediate architrave, rear face). Also depicted are the immediate predecessors of Gautama, the Manushi Buddhas; these appear symbolically as stupas or bodhi trees (upper architraves of all gateways). Among the scenes of a mundane character are various sports and pleasures, and also animals, both real and imagined. Among the delicately carved foliate designs are jewelled creeper motifs incorporating animals with riders (side panels of the posts).

The last accretion to the stupa took place during the 5th century, when four Buddha images were placed against the walls of the stupa, facing towards each entrance. The Master is depicted in the teaching posture, with an attendant on either side; the haloes behind the heads are finely carved.

Stupa 3, 2nd century BC–
1st century AD

This monument is clearly modelled on Stupa 1, but is smaller in dimension; there is only one gateway. The dome, extensively rebuilt, is more hemispherical. It is crowned with a single umbrella and was built together with its staircase not long after the reconstruction of Stupa 1. (Inscriptions record the same donor on both monuments.) The railing and carved gateway probably belong to the 1st century; these are similar in form and decoration to those of Stupa 1, though the workmanship is inferior. The importance of this monument lies in the fact that relics of two of Buddha's foremost disciples, Shariputra and Maudgalyayana, were enshrined within the solid dome. Fragments of bone, several beads and other precious objects were found inside the caskets.

Other Stupas, 2nd century BC–
7th century AD

The remains of other stupas in the vicinity are mostly confined to round or square basements. Stupa 4, datable to the 2nd century BC, exists only as a heap of loose stones. Stupa 5 had an image of Buddha (removed to the Archaeological Museum) on a moulded pedestal built against its southern side. Stupas 28 and 29 both have high square bases with mouldings characteristic of the Gupta era. The latter example contained a fragment of a highly polished vase of the 3rd century BC.

The group constituting Stupas 12–16 has square plinths and belongs to the 6th–7th century. Stupas 6 and 7 may be even later in date.

Columns, 3rd–2nd centuries BC
and 5th century AD

Of the free-standing columns only fragments remain. The stump of the most important example, Column 10, stands near the south gateway of Stupa 1. This was erected by Ashoka, who inscribed on it an edict warning Buddhist monks and nuns against creating schisms. The column was surmounted by a capital sculptured with four lions (Archaeological Museum, 2868).

The other columns variously belong to the 2nd century BC and the 5th century AD. One of the latter group, Column 26, was a poor imitation of Ashoka's example; Column 35 had as its capital a figure of Vajrapani (Archaeological Museum, 2720).

Temple 17, 5th century

This is the best-preserved temple at the site and an important example of early structural architecture during the Gupta era. The small plain building comprises a square sanctuary and an adjoining porch with four free-standing columns. The columns have petalled capitals, surmounted by blocks carved with seated double-headed lions. The doorway has foliate bands; no image is preserved in the sanctuary, which is roofed with flat slabs.

Temple 18, mostly 7th century

Built on the foundation of an earlier chaitya hall, this temple consists of an apse defined by circular walls and a columned nave with side aisles; these were all contained within a rectangle of walls. Several tall sandstone columns which still stand are decorated with part-circular incisions framing octagonal sections (a design familiar in cave architecture in the Deccan). In the 10th–11th century the floor level was raised and richly carved door jambs added. All vestiges of the small solid stupa which once stood in the middle of the apse have disappeared.

Temple 31, 5th and 11th centuries

This rectangular shrine is entered by steps on the south; it contains an image of a seated Buddha with an elaborately carved halo. To the early period belong the platform and pedestal of the sculpture. The rest of the structure, except the two Gupta columns standing in the middle, is much later.

EASTERN AREA

Building 43

The plan of this structure differs from any other at the site. A cruciform building of uncertain purpose has round bastions at the corners. Within are the fragmentary walls of a monastic establishment.

Temple 44, 10th–11th century

This is contemporary with Temple 45 and is now reduced to a plinth. An antechamber and rectangular hall are flanked by side chambers housing damaged Buddhist figures.

Monasteries 45–47, 7th and 10th–11th centuries

Only one example, Monastery 45, is of the standard courtyard plan; the others have several chambers.

Within Monastery 45 are the ruins of a towered temple mostly dating from the later period. A square sanctuary surmounted by a ruined hollow tower is surrounded by a passageway on three sides; traces of a columned hall are visible on the west. Damaged images of river goddesses, amorous couples, lions and lotus motifs adorn the doorway. In the sanctuary is a seated Buddha image with a richly decorated halo. Niches in the outer east and south walls of the sanctuary contain Bodhisattva figures. To the north and south of the temple are three chambers with a verandah.

SOUTHERN AREA

Temple 40, mostly 3rd–2nd centuries BC

This contains the remains of different periods, the earliest of which dates from the Maurya era and is probably contemporary with the first stage of Stupa 1. The original structure was an apsidal-ended chaitya hall built on a high stone platform. Much later a small shrine was constructed on the eastern side and the columns were re-erected.

Monasteries 36–38, 7th century

These three monastic establishments are built on the usual plan.

WESTERN SLOPE

Monastery 51, 7th century

This is the most impressive monastic establishment at Sanchi. It is comparatively well preserved and is entered on the east through two massive buttresses. The brick paved courtyard is separated from the verandah by regularly spaced column footings. A spacious chamber in the middle of the west side may have functioned as a chapel but was later converted into a passageway.

Stupa 2, 2nd century BC

This monument stands on an artificial terrace further down the hill from Monastery 51. Stupa 2 resembles Stupa 3 in size and shape, but there is no gateway nor any other external features. Of chief interest are the well-preserved balustrades with four L-shaped entrances that define the processional pathway. The posts of the balustrade are adorned with medallions decorated with both floral and plant designs and with real, mythical and composite animals, birds, fish, nagas, human figures, yakshas and kinnaras. Of the animals, the elephant and lion are the most common. Some of the horsemen are shown using stirrups (an early depiction of this feature). Throughout, the workmanship is crude but vigorous.

The monument is significant because it housed relics of several Buddhist teachers. These were contained in caskets buried deep within the solid mass.

SARNATH

10 km (6 miles) north of **Varanasi** is Sarnath and its deer park. At this site, Buddha preached his First Sermon, usually referred to as 'Turning the Wheel of the Law' (Dharmachakra). The significance of this event at Sarnath can hardly be over-estimated; the message revealed by Buddha on this occasion provided the basis for all future development of the religion. Here also the Master laid the foundations for the order of monks, the Sangha.

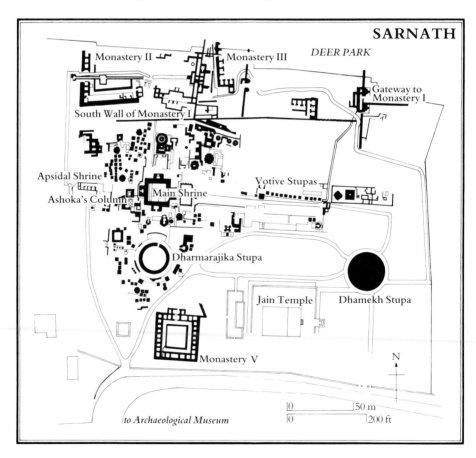

SARNATH

DEER PARK

Monastery II
Monastery III
Gateway to Monastery I
South Wall of Monastery I
Apsidal Shrine
Votive Stupas
Ashoka's Column
Main Shrine
Dharmarajika Stupa
Jain Temple
Dhamekh Stupa
Monastery V

N

0   50 m
0   200 ft

to Archaeological Museum

Owing to the sanctity of the site, Sarnath rapidly became one of the leading pilgrimage places of Buddhism. The remains here reveal a continuous occupation from the period of Ashoka in the 3rd century BC until the last days of the faith in northern India, in the 11th–12th centuries. The buildings excavated at this site are extensive and varied; except for the Dhamekh Stupa, however, they are mostly confined to the foundations of brick stupas, shrines and monasteries.

Numerous stone sculptures found at Sarnath testify to the importance of the site as an artistic centre. Many of them are now housed in the Archaeological Museum; other fine examples are in the Indian Museum, **Calcutta**, and the National Museum, **New Delhi**.

The archaeological zone is dominated by the Dhamekh Stupa, believed to mark the spot of Buddha's sermon. A short distance to the west are the remains of the Dharmarajika Stupa, the main shrine, Ashoka's column and an apsidal-ended shrine. They are surrounded by clusters of votive stupas. Both to the north and south are regularly laid-out monastic establishments. Between the Dhamekh and Dharmarajika monuments is a Jain temple erected in 1824; east of the Dhamekh is a modern Buddhist temple modelled on the Mahabodhi shrine at **Bodhgaya**; interior murals depict the life of the Master.

The monuments are described in sequence after entering the site at the south-east gate.

Monastery V, 5th century and later

This is typical of the series. A square court with a verandah is surrounded on four sides by small cells; there is an entrance portico on the north. Only parts of the brick foundations are preserved.

Dharmarajika Stupa,
3rd century BC and later

Attributed to Ashoka, this stupa has been extensively despoiled. In its core was found a green marble casket containing pieces of human bone, decayed pearls, gold leaf and other precious objects. The sanctity of the stupa is borne out by the six enlargements which it successively underwent, the last datable to the 12th century.

Main Shrine, 3rd century BC
and 5th century AD

This large Gupta structure consists of a central east-facing shrine with projecting smaller chambers on three sides. The base of the walls is relieved by moulded bricks. Delicately carved stone jambs are preserved at the doorways. No object of worship was discovered here, though probably a Buddhist image in teaching posture may have been intended for the central shrine. Within the south chamber, part of a monolithic sandstone railing dating from the Maurya period has been uncovered.

The shrine is surrounded by smaller stupas and shrines. To the east is a pathway lined with votive stupas leading towards the Dhamekh monument. On the south side of this pathway is a small brick basement with stepped sides and terracotta panels; this dates from the 5th century.

Ashoka's Column, 3rd century BC

Immediately west of the main shrine is the lower portion of a polished sandstone shaft. (The celebrated lion capital of this column is in the Archaeological Museum.) The column is inscribed with an edict threatening dissident monks with expulsion.

Apsidal Shrine

West of the column are the remains of an apsidal-ended chaitya hall covered by a later monastery.

Monasteries I–III, 2nd–12th centuries

North of the main shrine are the brick

remains of three monasteries. Each is of the standard type with small cells opening off a central courtyard.

Dhamekh Stupa,

mostly 5th–6th century

The most imposing of Sarnath's monuments, this cylindrical tower is more than 30 m (98 ft) high. It is a solid structure with a drum of stonework; the dilapidated upper part is of brick. Gupta designs are incised on to the high drum; these include luxuriant foliation with stalks, leaves and flowers, various geometric patterns, possibly derived from textiles, and occasional flowers with birds. Eight arched niches, now empty, are set in shallow projections.

While the foundation date of the stupa is unknown, excavations have revealed six successive enlargements, the last of which was in the 12th century. The standing Bodhisattva and teaching Buddha figures for which Sarnath is famous were found around this monument.

Archaeological Museum

This collection demonstrates the importance of Sarnath as an art centre for more than a millennium; almost all the sculptures displayed here were discovered at the site. From the 3rd century BC comes the most celebrated of all artefacts from Ashoka's reign, the lion capital (A1) that now serves as the emblem of modern India. This is superbly executed in polished sandstone and consists of a fluted bell-shaped lower portion and an upper circular portion with discs and animals (horse, lion, bull, elephant) in shallow relief. The capital is dominated by four magnificent lions; the eyes of the animals stare outwards, their mouths are open in expressions of fierce energy. The animals are fully modelled; the details of the hair and paws are rendered with remarkable clarity. Only fragments of the stone wheel that surmounted this capital have been recovered.

The Shunga period is represented by part of a 1st-century-BC railing with a capping stone (481–420). Buddhist emblems, such as the stupa, wheel and column, are contained within decorated medallions; flying celestials worship the stupa. Another example (528) testifies to the range of lotus ornamentation. A capital is carved on either side with a horse- and elephant-rider (537).

Two impressive life-size standing Bodhisattvas (349, 356) belong to the 1st–2nd-century Kushana period. The impact of the earlier yaksha tradition is evident in the solid forms and the flowing robes. One Bodhisattva has a stone parasol (348); this is delicately carved on its underside with lotus ornament and auspicious emblems.

A large number of Buddhist figures date from the 5th-century Gupta era. These are dominated by the masterpiece: the perfectly realized seated Buddha in teaching posture (340). The rounded modelling of the figure and its robes, the subtle facial expression of detachment and the finely etched lotus ornament on the halo are a consummate illustration of the Gupta style. Beneath, kneeling devotees, two deer and a wheel indicate the sermon at Sarnath. While other examples of the teaching Buddha are exhibited here, none can match this figure; but some standing Buddhas of the same period are comparable (especially 342 and 344). One example with lowered eyes and gently swaying posture is set within a part-oval frame (5512); yet another image, a partly damaged Bodhisattva, has flowing hair (252).

Several slabs and columns are carved with episodes from the Master's life, such as his birth, enlightenment, teaching and death (261, 262), or the miracle at **Sravasti** (260). Among the architectural fragments are columns, door jambs and lintels. One column displays finely carved pot and foliate motifs (284); another lintel is filled with deities, dancers and musicians, as well as episodes from one of the

Jataka stories (667). An unusual panel is carved with geese and a monster mask (698), and another with a rider on a vyala (4924).

10th–12th-century sculptures are often damaged. Two exceptions are the delicately carved Avalokiteshvara with lotuses (22) and Lokeshvara holding a bowl (67). There are also architectural fragments and temple models from this era. Later Hindu art at Sarnath is represented by the colossal, more than 3 m (10 ft) high, crudely fashioned image of Shiva spearing Andhaka (39).

Chaukhandi, 5th and 16th centuries

This monument is located about 500 m (1,750 ft) south of the main site. It consists of an octagonal tower built in 1588 to commemorate the visit of the Mughal emperor Humayun. The tower is elevated on a dilapidated brick structure, possibly a stupa with an octagonal base and three square terraces dating from no later than the Gupta period.

SIRPUR

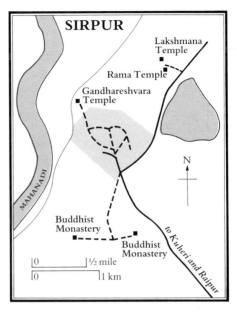

This site was of importance for both Buddhists and Hindus from the 6th century onwards; it also served as the capital for the Somavamshi rulers from the 7th century onwards. (This dynasty later extended its influence into neighbouring Orissa.) Vestiges of the ancient settlement are the mounds around the modern town, the comparatively well-preserved Lakshmana temple, the excavated remains of two Buddhist monasteries and the numerous fine bronzes (mostly removed to the museum in **Raipur**).

Lakshmana Temple, 7th century

This is the finest early Hindu brick temple still standing in central India. The building consists of a square sanctuary roofed with a curved tower. Almost all of the brick mouldings of the towers are preserved, including the large arched motifs in the central projections and the corner amalakas; the top is restored. The sanctuary walls have unusual blind doorways on three sides; these are raised on a moulded basement. Only portions of the mandapa walls are intact.

The sanctuary doorway is executed in stone. Bands of foliation and delicately modelled amorous couples adorn the jambs; a reclining Vishnu image (worn) is carved on to the lintel. Among the loose sculptures placed in the mandapa is a panel depicting a seated naga figure.

Rama Temple, 7th century

This ruined Hindu monument is situated some 50 m (165 ft) south-east of the Lakshmana temple, which it resembles in many respects. The outer walls of the Rama temple have unusual angled projections that form part of a star-shaped plan.

Buddhist Monasteries, 7th century

Two brick Buddhist establishments have been revealed by excavations. Both have central courts with verandahs surrounded by small cells, as well as side courts with subsidiary cells. In one example, the cells are grouped together to produce a layout that resembles a svastika. The main object of devotion in this monastery was a sculpture of Buddha seated on a throne flanked by Bodhisattva figures. In the other monastery, stone columns and doorway jambs have delicately applied ornament.

Archaeological Museum

Many Buddhist and Hindu sculptures as well as architectural fragments found at the site are assembled here.

SONKH

Naga Shrine, 1st–3rd centuries

Recent excavations at this site, 13 km (8 miles) south-west of **Mathura**, have revealed a ruined apsidal-ended sanctuary dating from the Kushana period. This appears to have been dedicated to a naga deity; it is one of the earliest-known Hindu shrines. The sculptures discovered in the ruins are now displayed in the Government Museum, **Mathura**.

SRAVASTI (map p. 191)

Sravasti was a prosperous city during the time of Buddha, who delivered many sermons in the nearby monastery at Jetavana. Here too the Master performed the famous miracle of walking in the air, an event frequently depicted in Buddhist art. After Buddha's death, Jetavana enjoyed the patronage of Ashoka, the Maurya emperor; the monastery continued to be of importance until about the 11th century.

Remains of the ancient city and the monastery have been discovered in the two villages of Maheth and Seth, about 500 m (1,750 ft) apart. Modern temples erected by Chinese and Burmese Buddhists, as well as a newly planted bodhi tree, testify to the renewed interest in the site.

MAHETH

Earthen ramparts define the area of Sravasti. This is about 2 km (1½ miles) long and follows a bend in the Achiravati river to the north. The ramparts are broken by gateways flanked by bastions. The ruins of two large structures are located within the city area. One structure, known as Kacchikuti, consists of a high plinth with a stepped plan upon which a shrine and two stupas were erected. The partly domed Shobhanatha temple is a later superimposition of the 12th century on an earlier plinth.

SETH

The remains of the monastery of Jetavana are located within an irregular enclosure. Excavations here have exposed the remains of numerous brick temples, stupas and monasteries dating from the 1st–10th centuries. The temples and monasteries are generally simple square constructions.

SUHANIA

Kokhanmatha Temple,
early 11th century

This Hindu temple was built by a Kirttiraja, one of the kings of the Kacchapaghata dynasty, and named after his queen. The ruined building stands on a lofty platform surrounded by subsidiary shrines. Notable for their size and sculptural wealth, the sanctuary and surrounding passageway are roofed with a tall tower (core still standing); the mandapa in front is only partly preserved.

TERAHI

'Shiva' Temple, 8th century

This Hindu temple is a well-preserved

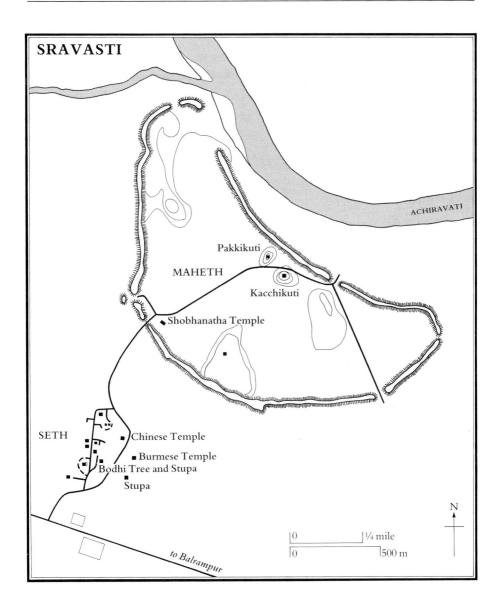

SRAVASTI

MAHETH

Pakkikuti

Kacchikuti

Shobhanatha Temple

ACHIRAVATI

SETH

Chinese Temple

Burmese Temple

Bodhi Tree and Stupa

Stupa

to Balrampur

N

| 0 | ¼ mile |
| 0 | 500 m |

example of the fully developed Pratihara style. The sanctuary walls have niches in the middle of each side sheltered by miniature eaves; the corner niches house sculptures of the Dikpalas. Above rises the curved tower, the central bands of which are covered with meshes of arch–like motifs; a large amalaka is positioned at the summit. The sanctuary doorway is sheltered by a small porch with columns decorated with pot and foliage motifs. The doorway is surrounded by miniature figures that include river goddesses, amorous couples and flying celestials; a figure of Vishnu on Garuda appears in the middle of the lintel. Despite this original Vaishnava dedication, a linga is now installed inside the sanctuary.

TIGAWA

Temple, late 5th century

Like Temple 17 at **Sanchi**, this well-preserved monument illustrates the first phase of structural temple architecture in the Gupta period. The small square sanctuary with a flat roof and the adjoining porch are plain except for the porch columns. These have pot and foliage capitals with seated lions carved on to the blocks above. The sanctuary doorway is adorned with sculptures of river goddesses elevated at either side of the opening.

UDAYAGIRI

6 km (4 miles) west of **Vidisha** is the sandstone ridge of Udayagiri with its series of rock-cut Gupta monuments. Of the twenty Hindu cave temples on this hill, half the number are merely niches of varying dimensions, some with large sculptures in high relief (Caves 5 and 13); the others, except one, are artificially excavated sanctuaries entered through small columned porches, now collapsed in most examples. Though badly eroded, the carved panels and doorways of these caves provide important evidence for the beginnings of monumental Hindu art.

Cave 1, early 5th century

A porch with four columns shelters the entrance to a reconstructed chamber. The columns have pot-like capitals with foliation at the corners. An image of Parshvanatha was placed within the sanctuary at a later date.

Cave 4, early 5th century

The small square sanctuary of this cave enshrines a single-faced Shiva linga. The doorway is surrounded by bands of foli-

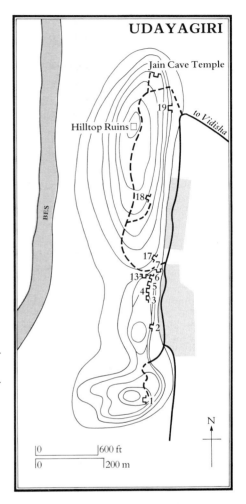

UDAYAGIRI

Jain Cave Temple

Hilltop Ruins

to Vidisha

BES

N

0   600 ft
0   200 m

ation, now worn. Guardians and pilasters, now damaged, are positioned at either side.

Cave 5, early 5th century

This large-scale sculpture is almost 4 m (13 ft) high. The composition depicts the rescue of the goddess Bhudevi by Varaha. One of the most impressive representations of this myth in Indian art, the panel is dominated by the majestic figure of the boar-headed god. The scene is sometimes interpreted as an allegory of the unification of northern India under the Gupta ruler Chandragupta II.

Varaha lifts up the goddess, who perches precariously on the lotus wreath beside the god's left shoulder. Rows of figures at the back depict sages and divinities, including Brahma and Agni (top row, left); on the right (top) are two male musicians. The formal postures and hierarchical arrangement of the figures are unique. (Persian influence has been suggested.) Beneath, two figures, one with a serpent hood, stand in water indicated by delicately incised wavy lines. The sides of the panel have images of Ganga and Yamuna, possibly emblems of the unified empire, with attendant figures.

Cave 6, c. 402

The doorway to this shrine has figures of river goddesses on either side. Guardians and images of Varaha and Durga, now worn, are carved on the flanking walls. Above is an inscription of Chandragupta II.

Cave 7, early 5th century

This cave is cut into a separate boulder with a ledge on top. The outlines of two fully modelled guardian figures flank an undecorated doorway.

Cave 13, early 5th century

This cave is located in a ravine that traverses the ridge. A relief panel, now worn, depicts Vishnu sleeping on the serpent.

Cave 17, early 5th century

The damaged doorway of this cave resembles that of Cave 6. On one side is a twelve-armed Durga figure, now eroded.

Cave 19, mid-5th century

The doorway of this shrine is adorned with bands of foliation and miniature figures; Ganga and Yamuna figures are raised up on one side. Over the lintel is a frieze of the gods and demons churning the ocean, now worn. Traces of guardian figures flank the doorway. Several columns with delicately incised ornamentation indicate that there was once a porch in front. Within the sanctuary are a later Nandi image and several lingas. Four massive columns have ornamented capitals.

Jain Cave Temple, early 5th century

There is an inscription of the Gupta ruler Kumaragupta here in association with a series of panels depicting seated Tirthankaras (damaged).

Hilltop ruins

These constitute the remains of a 5th-century structure, evidently a temple of large proportions.

UDAYAPUR

This town is noted for its well-preserved Hindu temple. 6 km (4 miles) to the east is the village of Bareth with its Muslim monuments (see Volume II).

Udayeshvara (Nilankantheshvara) Temple, 1080

This is the most impressive monument of the Paramara period. An inscription on the eastern porch proclaims the royal donor as Udayaditya. The temple is remarkable for its ambitious scale, rhythmic proportions and rich sculptural ornamentation; it may be compared with contemporary Chandella projects at **Khajuraho**.

The terrace on which the monument stands is located in the middle of the town at the highest point; the terrace is reached by a staircase flanked by large guardian figures. The temple itself consists of a towered sanctuary and a mandapa entered through three porches. Another mandapa and seven subsidiary shrines are also found on the terrace.

The sanctuary walls are built on a stepped plan that almost approaches a circle. Numerous sculpture panels, many now damaged, are raised on a high basement. Above rises the curved superstructure. This consists of seven tiers of miniature towers which continue the projections of the walls beneath but diminish in size as they ascend. Each miniature curved tower has arch-like motifs on the sides and an amalaka at the summit. A large amalaka of the same type crowns the central shaft. Characteristic of the Paramara style are the tapering vertical bands of mesh-like ornament in the middle of each side of the tower. These rise out of arched niches containing images of dancing Shiva. The trilobed niche on the front (east) face is enlarged and frames images of dancing Shiva (above) and a standing syncretic deity flanked by dancing goddesses (beneath). The foliation and scrollwork around these figures are naturalistically carved. The composition is capped by a monster head with protruding eyes; at either side are seated goddesses and the Matrikas.

The mandapa has a pyramidal roof with numerous amalakas in ascending and recessing tiers. The porches have angled balcony slabs and overhanging eaves. The doorways are elaborate compositions with foliate ornament and amorous couples; above are rows of goddesses. Within the mandapa, the columns are encrusted with niches, garlands and bells; projecting figures adorn the brackets. A linga is installed within the sanctuary.

UJJAIN

Ujjain is one of the seven sacred cities of Hinduism. It is built on the banks of the Shipra river and is much frequented as a pilgrimage centre. According to tradition, Shiva killed the demon Tripura at Ujjain. As at **Allahabad**, a Kumbha Mela is celebrated here every twelve years; the event attracts large numbers of pilgrims, who come to bathe in the river.

Ujjain was an important place in Maurya times and Ashoka was governor here during the reign of his father in the early 3rd century BC. The legendary ruler Vikramaditya, after whom the Hindu 'Vikram' era was named, held a famous court at Ujjain that was noted for its poets and scholars, including the celebrated Kalidasa. In the 4th–5th centuries the town was an important centre under the Gupta rulers; later it became the capital of the Paramara kings. Ujjain was sacked by the Muslims in 1235, but thereafter achieved a degree of prosperity, particularly in the 18th century under the rule of Jai Singh, who built an observatory here (see Volume II).

Excavations at a site about 6 km (4 miles) north of the town have revealed pottery and iron objects dating back to the 8th century BC. Structural activity is discernible from the 4th century BC onwards; this includes a brick-lined tank and canal. A dilapidated stupa dates from the first centuries of the Christian era. Cremated bones and skeletons, as well as coins, terracotta figurines, beads and semi-precious stones, were also discovered here. The rubble foundations of houses belong to the same period.

Mahakala Temple, 20th century

Despite its sanctity, this complex is a recent reconstruction in the traditional central Indian style. The curved superstructure, adorned with tower-like motifs on all sides, rises above projecting colonnaded porches. Mughal screens and pavilions are combined with marble colonnades that lead to the linga within the sanctuary.

Hara Siddhi Temple

The chief object of worship in this sanctuary is a rock in the middle of the court which is covered with turmeric paste; this is believed to represent the head of Vikramaditya that is offered to Durga at the Dasara festival.

VARANASI

Varanasi is a city of ritual and tradition filled with countless temples, shrines and sacred images. Dominated by a great bend in the Ganga river, which flows northwards here, the city crowds the steeply rising western bank. Traditionally known as Kashi, the City of Light, Varanasi is the supremely sacred place of Hinduism. For more than two and a half thousand years the river and shrines at Varanasi have attracted pious visitors and pilgrims from all over India.

In the 6th–5th centuries BC, Varanasi was celebrated as a holy place with many pools and groves near which sages had their retreats. The most famous seeker of this age, Buddha, also visited Varanasi. At the deer park at **Sarnath**, 10 km (6 miles) to the north, he delivered the sermon that marks the beginnings of Buddhism. Jain spiritual leaders were also associated with Varanasi: Parshvanatha is said to have been born here; Mahavira was a frequent visitor.

In subsequent times, Varanasi was under the control of the different kingdoms of central India. Only during the 11th century did it become the seat of a ruling dynasty, the Gahadavala kings. From the 12th century onwards the city was sacked several times by the Muslims, with a respite during the more liberal reign of the Mughal emperor Akbar in the second half of the 16th century. (For the Muslim and British monuments see Volume II.)

During these troubled times, Varanasi continued to be an important intellectual and religious centre. Hindu devotional movements flourished here, especially in the 15th century under Ramananda. One of India's greatest poets, Kabir, lived in the city. Here, Tulsi Das translated the Sanskrit Ramayana epic into Hindi.

No standing temples at Varanasi predate the 18th century. The innumerable examples that open off the crowded narrow lanes are mostly of the same type. They are mainly built in sandstone, sometimes covered with silver and gold plate. Invariably, these small shrines have pointed spires, often in clustered arrangements. Fluted columns, multi-lobed arches and stylized foliation display the influence of late Mughal practice; carved decoration and sculptural imagery, however, is traditionally Hindu.

Temple building continues into the present century. The recently completed Tulsidas sanctuary in the southern part of Varanasi and the Vishvanatha temple at the Benares Hindu University are important revivalist constructions.

WITHIN THE TOWN

Vishvanatha Temple, 1777

For more than a thousand years, Vishvanatha was the principal Shiva sanctuary at Varanasi, attesting to the god's presence in the city. The reconstruction of the temple on a large scale was undertaken in 1585; this consisted of a central sanctuary surrounded by eight chambers. But in less than a century the temple was dismantled at the command of the Mughal emperor Aurangzeb to provide material for a new mosque that was erected nearby.

The present structure dates only from the 18th century; its clustered pointed spires, gilded and decorated with flags, are typical of the last phase of the central Indian style. The columns, beams and walls are decorated with finely carved ornament. Within the temple (accessible to Hindus only) numerous lingas cluster around a central linga; subsidiary shrines in the courtyard contain yet other lingas and goddess images.

Behind the temple to the north is an open colonnade sheltering the Jnana Vapi, or Wisdom Well, the water of which is believed to be a liquid form of enlightening knowledge. (The adjacent mosque is named after this well.) At the west end of

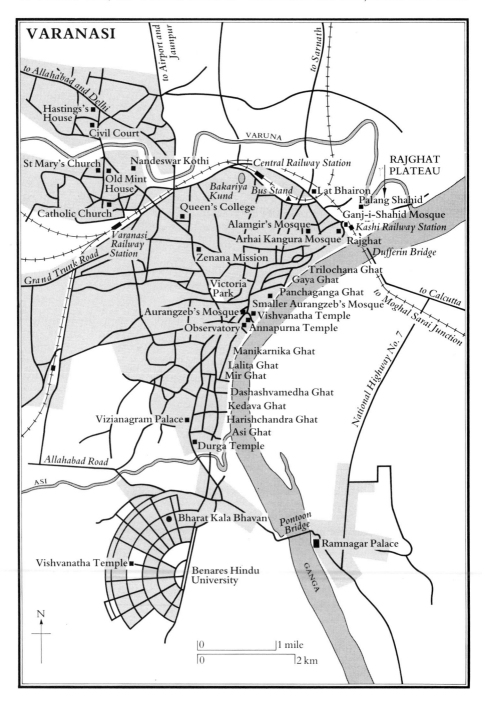

VARANASI

to Allahabad and Delhi

to Airport and Jaunpur

to Sarnath

Hastings's House

Civil Court

VARUNA

St Mary's Church

Nandeswar Kothi

Central Railway Station

RAJGHAT PLATEAU

Old Mint House

Bakariya Kund

Bus Stand

Lat Bhairon

Palang Shahid

Queen's College

Ganj-i-Shahid Mosque

Catholic Church

Alamgir's Mosque

Kashi Railway Station

Varanasi Railway Station

Arhai Kangura Mosque

Rajghat

Zenana Mission

Dufferin Bridge

Grand Trunk Road

Trilochana Ghat

Gaya Ghat

Victoria Park

Panchaganga Ghat

to Calcutta

Smaller Aurangzeb's Mosque

Aurangzeb's Mosque

Vishvanatha Temple

to Moghal Sarai Junction

Observatory

Annapurna Temple

Manikarnika Ghat

Lalita Ghat

Mir Ghat

Dashashvamedha Ghat

Kedava Ghat

National Highway No. 7

Vizianagram Palace

Harishchandra Ghat

Asi Ghat

Durga Temple

Allahabad Road

ASI

Bharat Kala Bhavan

Pontoon Bridge

Ramnagar Palace

Vishvanatha Temple

Benares Hindu University

GANGA

N

|0 |1 mile
|0 |2 km

the mosque, fragments of the earlier 16th-century Vishvanatha temple are visible.

Annapurna Temple, 18th century

Near to the Vishvanatha temple is this shrine dedicated to Kali; it is built in the typical Varanasi style.

Durga Temple, 19th century

Finely carved columns and wall ornamentation characterize this late temple set within a colonnaded court with a double-storey entrance.

RIVER FRONT

This demonstrates Varanasi's reputation as a sacred city. Along the Ganga are more than seventy stepped banks or ghats; in the early morning many of these are crowded with bathers. Immersion in the Ganga, a river believed to have fallen from heaven to earth, is the first act of pilgrimage at Varanasi. As the goddess and mother of life, Ganga is the prototype of all sacred water in India. It purifies the souls of the living and assures the liberation of the dead. The river is also a symbol of power; its waters are interpreted as the active energy of Shiva on earth.

Rajghat

In ancient times, the Ganga river was most easily forded at this point. Beyond the ghat is a plateau, bounded on the north and west by the Varuna river; the original centre of the city was located here.

Excavations at the Rajghat plateau have brought to light numerous artefacts dating from the 8th century BC; these include pottery, beads, glass and copper coins. The 1st–3rd centuries are particularly rich in terracotta seals, and from this era date the first brick structures. Other architectural evidence is available up to the 12th century. Also discovered at this site were 5th-century Gupta sculptures; these are now displayed in the Bharat Kala Bhavan.

At the north end of the plateau is the Adi Keshava temple. This commemorates the place where Vishnu first arrived when he was sent to Kashi by Shiva.

Rajghat to Trilochana Ghat

Most of these ghats have clay banks that front the river. At Trilochana there are several sacred lingas.

Panchaganga Ghat

This is the most magnificent ghat, with stone staircases leading down to the water. The ghat is dominated by Aurangzeb's mosque, built on the site of the destroyed Bindu Mahadeva temple. Early European visitors to Varanasi describe the enormous image of Vishnu adorned with jewels that was enshrined in this temple.

Yogis perform exercises and meditate in the numerous cubicles.

Rama and Lakshmana Ghats

These bathing places are associated with temples housing images of the Ramayana heroes. Nearby is the temple of Mangala Gauri, a popular goddess.

Manikarnika Ghat

Although this ghat is frequently linked with the adjacent cremation ground, its older and most important association is with a sacred well, originally a large lake. The water of this well is said to spring from a source independent of the Ganga. According to tradition, the well was dug out and filled with water by Vishnu as his first act of creation. The footprints of the god are displayed nearby. Two goddess temples dominate the ghat; a third temple has subsided into the water.

Lalita Ghat

This ghat is overlooked by a Nepalese temple, complete with tiers of sloping roofs supported on wooden struts and a brass finial.

Mir Ghat

Above this ghat is the temple of Vishalak-shi, one of the 108 'seats' of the goddess. Nearby is the well of dharma, surrounded by shrines and shaded by banyan trees. Here also is the Shiva temple where Yama received his jurisdiction over the fate of the dead. A new Vishvanatha temple is established nearby.

Dashashvamedha Ghat

This is the most popular ghat, drawing crowds of bathers each morning at dawn. Rows of priests sit on platforms beneath bamboo umbrellas administering to the needs of the devout. The ghat is celebrated as the site where Brahma performed the ten sacrifices for the king Divodasa. A small whitewashed shrine on the ghat shelters an image of Shitala.

Kedava Ghat

At this ghat is found the Kedareshvara linga, one of the most venerable temples in the southern part of the city. The red and white stripes of the temple walls indicate southern Indian management.

Harishchandra Ghat

This is the second cremation ground on the river front.

Asi Ghat

This southernmost ghat still preserves its clay bank. The focal point of worship here is the Shiva linga at the confluence of the Asi stream and the Ganga. Immediately north is Tulsi Ghat, which is named after the poet's house and temple.

BENARES HINDU UNIVERSITY

Bharat Kala Bhavan

This museum houses a representative collection of stone sculptures found at Varanasi and other sites. One of the earliest sculptures is a maiden bearing offerings from **Mathura** (170); this belongs to the 2nd-century Kushana period. Among the Gupta Buddhist images are a standing Buddha from Varanasi (148), a finely carved head from **Mathura** (21766) and a fragment of a stone head from **Sarnath** (642), all datable to the 5th century. To the same period belong several sculptures of Hindu divinities found at Varanasi, such as Krishna lifting the mountain (147), Krishna stealing the butter (180) and Karttikeya seated with the peacock (156), the last dating from the 6th century.

Later sculptures are represented by a standing Surya figure (179) and Shiva spearing Andhaka (172), both from Varanasi. Other carved panels include a depiction of the marriage of Shiva and Parvati surrounded by attendant figures (175), Varuna (20768), Vamana (21863) and Ganga (163), the last example from Etah.

Gupta terracotta figurines, including a 4th-century head of Shiva (1605), are also exhibited.

Vishvanatha Temple

This recently completed marble temple is an impressive construction in a revivalist style with curved towers derived from central and eastern Indian traditions. Subsidiary towered shrines cluster around the soaring superstructure of the principal sanctuary.

VIDISHA

The ancient centre of Vidisha is identified with the village of Besnagar, situated between the Betwa and Bes rivers about 3 km (2 miles) north of the modern town of Vidisha. The citizens of Vidisha are recorded as acting as patrons of the Buddhist monuments at **Sanchi**, 7 km (4½ miles) to the south-west. At **Udayagiri**, 6 km (4 miles) to the west, is a series of cave temples assigned to the Gupta era.

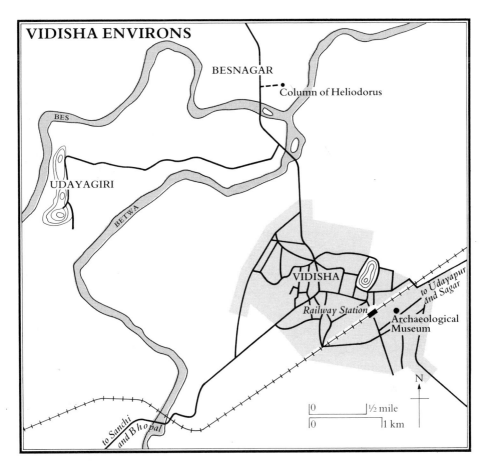

VIDISHA ENVIRONS

BESNAGAR
Column of Heliodorus

BES

UDAYAGIRI

BETWA

VIDISHA

Railway Station

to Udayapur and Sagar

Archaeological Museum

N

to Sanchi and Bhopal

| 0 | ½ mile |
| 0 | 1 km |

Archaeological Museum

Among the sculptures from the ancient site are standing yaksha figures; assignable to the 2nd century BC. One example is more than 3 m (10 ft) high. Later 10th–11th-century pieces are also on display, such as Vamana surrounded by attendant figures (10.IV) and seated Ambika (3.IV).

BESNAGAR

The extent of ancient Vidisha is indicated by large mounds. Architectural fragments and sculptures scattered over the area date back to the Maurya and Shunga periods.

A sandstone column stands beside the Bes river. According to an inscription on its shaft, it was erected in 113 BC by Heliodorus, the Greek ambassador of the ruler of Taxila (capital of Gandhara), in honour of the Hindu god Vasudeva. The fluted bell-shaped capital imitates earlier Maurya examples. Next to the column are the outlines of an elliptical structure.

VRINDAVAN

The pilgrimage town of Vrindavan is located 9 km (5½ miles) north of **Mathura**, on the right bank of the Yamuna river. Like other Hindu sites in the region, Vrindavan is closely linked with the Krishna legend. Here was located the

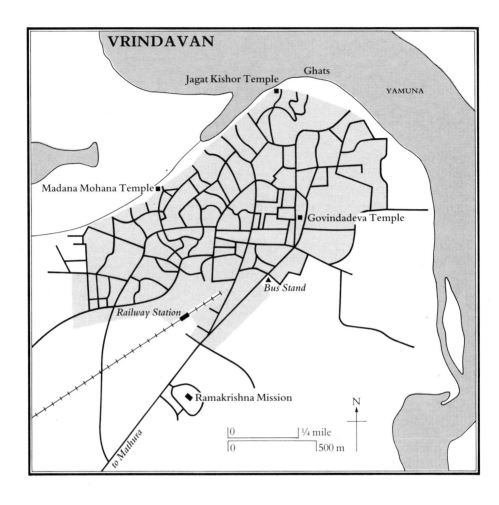

forest where Krishna as the youthful cowherd sported with the gopis.

Vrindavan preserves much of its traditional character and has several bathing ghats overlooked by temples. The town is the scene of an annual festival connected with the Krishna cult; numerous Vaishnava religious establishments are located here. Several later examples of temple architecture reflect the stylistic impact of Muslim practice, especially during the tolerant reign of the Mughal emperor

Akbar in the second half of the 16th century.

Govindadeva Temple, 1590

Only the large mandapa of this temple still stands; the towered sanctuary was destroyed on the orders of Aurangzeb. The mandapa is an open structure on a stepped plan. Its exterior has projecting porches and open balconies on two storeys; these are enlivened with elaborate brackets and overhanging eaves. The walls are notable for their sharply cut mouldings; nowhere is there any figural sculpture. True arches, pointed vaults and even a dome cover the interior space, exactly as in contemporary mosque architecture.

Jagat Kishor Temple, 16th century

The entrance to this temple is framed within a recessed arch above which is a stylized foliate design. Over the sanctuary rises an octagonal tapering tower. Its sides have vertical incisions and horizontal bands; an amalaka is positioned at the summit.

Madana Mohana Temple, 16th century

This resembles the Jagat Kishor temple in many respects. The octagonal tower here rises more than 20 m (66 ft) high. The outer surface, which curves gently, is divided into panels, each with a foliate medallion; there is no figural sculpture.

EASTERN INDIA

ELEVEN

EASTERN INDIA

Bihar, Orissa, West Bengal, Sikkim, Assam, Arunachal Pradesh, Tripura

Introduction

The earliest remains in eastern India belong to an era contemporary with Buddha in the middle of the 1st millennium BC. Fortifications, cave shelters and traces of a monastery at **Rajgir** are datable to the 6th–5th century BC. Rock-cut sanctuaries in the **Barabar** hills dating from the period of Ashoka, the 3rd-century-BC Maurya emperor, are clearly modelled on bamboo and thatch structures. Commemorative columns with carved animal capitals still stand at **Lauriya Nandangarh** and **Vaisali**; at **Dhauli** there are inscriptions and a monolithic elephant. Fragmentary timber remains at **Patna** are all that survive of Ashoka's capital, Patilaputra; a finely carved female figure was discovered here too.

Belonging to the succeeding Shunga period, in the 2nd–1st centuries BC, are pillars and railings from a dismantled shrine at **Bodhgaya**. Numerous terracotta plaques and figurines were found at various sites in Bengal, such as **Bangarh**, **Chandraketugarh** and **Tamluk**. In Orissa, the Chedi rulers were contemporary with the Shungas. **Sisupalgarh**, their capital, was laid out as a planned city with earthen ramparts. The Jain cave temples in the nearby hills of **Khandagiri** and **Udayagiri** testify to the vitality of sculptural traditions under the patronage of the Chedis.

Little is preserved from the first centuries of the Christian era other than isolated artefacts at various sites. From the 5th century onwards, parts of eastern India were brought within the realm of the Gupta rulers; as a result, artistic traditions here were closely linked with those of central India. The remains of an immense brick stupa have been revealed by excavators at **Lauriya Nandangarh**.

In the following centuries, eastern India was partly governed by a later dynasty of Gupta kings. To this era belongs a rare stone building, the unusual octagonal temple at **Mundesvari** dating from the 7th century. Though now ruined, the sculptural decoration of this monument indicates the survival of Gupta traditions. However, eastern Indian architecture consisted mostly of brick structures adorned with plaster and terracotta ornamentation. The great Mahabodhi sanctuary at **Bodhgaya** commemorates the spot where Buddha attained enlightenment. This temple preserves much of its original 7th-century form, suggesting the scale of brick building during this period; unfortunately, nothing survives of the original plaster coating. A contemporary brick monastery of large proportions has been discovered in the Buddhist establishment at **Antichak**. Other dilapidated Buddhist monuments are near **Jamui** and at **Sultanganj**. At **Rajgir**, the Maniyar Math is a small circular shrine once embellished with plaster sculptures. Contemporary Hindu art is represented by fragmentary stucco

Overleaf Ghurisa, view

reliefs on the ruined temple at **Aphsad**, as well as by rock-cut sculptures at **Jahangira**.

From the middle of the 8th century onwards, Bihar and Bengal were governed by kings of the powerful Pala and Sena dynasties. Until the end of the 11th century, these rulers patronized both Buddhist and Hindu shrines. **Nalanda** was the outstanding Pala Buddhist site, a celebrated university with numerous monasteries and shrines; it was also an artistic centre where stone and metal images were produced. Nearby **Kurkihar** and **Bodhgaya** are also known for their bronzes. (These Pala sculptures were of considerable importance in the spread of artistic traditions to the Himalayas and South-East Asia.) Substantial remains at **Lalitagiri**, **Ratnagiri** and **Udayagiri** indicate contemporary Buddhist architecture in Orissa.

This rich coastal zone had a complex dynastic history as successive rulers struggled for control. Stone shrines for Hindu cults were constructed by local kings as part of their policies of domination. The typical Orissan sanctuary was marked by a powerfully conceived tower (rekha deul); this had rounded shoulders and was capped by a large amalaka. The adjoining hall was generally roofed by a tiered pyramid of masonry (pida deul). Artists covered temple basements with animal friezes and foliate ornament; cult icons were installed in wall niches, where they were flanked by sculptures of attendant maidens and musicians; elaborate arched motifs embellished towers and roofs. The exuberant Orissan style was characterized by its soft modelling and an unmistakable sensuality.

The first stone temples in Orissa date only from the 7th–8th centuries. Those erected under the Shailodbhava rulers at **Bhubaneshwar** (Parashurameshvara temple) and **Simhanatha**, and under the Eastern Gangas at **Mukhalingam,** had towered sanctuaries which were attached to mandapas with sloping roofs. Even in this early phase, the sculptural treatment of walls and towers was elaborate. Under the succeeding Bhauma Kara dynasty, sacred architecture was further evolved at **Bhubaneshwar** (Vaital Deul).

From the middle of the 9th century onwards, during the Somavamshi period, Orissan architecture achieved a maturity of expression. (The Somavamshi rulers had already built extensively in the adjacent central Indian sites of **Rajim** and **Sirpur**.) 10th–11th-century structures at **Bhubaneshwar** (Gauri, Mukteshvara and Rajarani temples) and at **Chaurasi** were delicately ornamented buildings that fully integrated architecture and sculpture. The climax was reached in the monumentally conceived and richly adorned Lingaraja temple at **Bhubaneshwar**. Sculptures from this period are also preserved in shrines at **Hirapur** and **Khiching**. In Bengal, contemporary temples at **Bahulara** and **Barakar** were much influenced by these Orissan traditions.

The Eastern Gangas assumed control of central Orissa at the beginning of the 12th century. The ambitions of these rulers were fully realized in large-scale projects at **Puri** and **Konarak**. The **Puri** shrine is one of the chief pilgrimage places of Hindu India, in striking contrast to the colossal temple at **Konarak**, which is now abandoned. Despite the collapse of much of the latter monument, the surviving sculptures are unsurpassed for their profusion and delicacy of modelling. Other important temples dating from the Eastern Ganga period were constructed at **Bhubaneshwar** and **Ranipur Jharial**. Under the succeeding 14th–15th-century Gajapati rulers, halls and minor shrines were added to earlier projects.

The Muslim occupation of Bihar and Bengal in the 12th–13th centuries inevitably disrupted temple building activities. The 16th century, however, witnessed a revival of Hinduism in this region, due principally to the teachings of the saint Chaitanya. In the following centuries, small-scale brick shrines were erected at numerous sites, particularly in Bengal. Here, Muslim techniques, such as arches, vaults and domes, were integrated with hut-like forms. Temples at **Bansberia**, **Bishnupur**, **Ghurisa** and **Krishnanagar** are all typical examples of these indigenous schemes. Their façades were covered with terracotta plaques moulded with animated figures and decorative motifs. Other contemporary temples at **Barakar** and **Kabilaspur** indicate a dependence on Orissan practice. 18th–19th-century shrines at **Baranagar**, **Bishnupur** and **Kalna** continued the development of the indigenous brick style in Bengal; later examples in **Calcutta** and **Tarakeswar**, however, were sadly lacking in inspiration. The recent complex at Belur, on the outskirts of **Calcutta** is a largely revivalist structure, only partly regional in style.

In zones further east, particularly Assam and Tripura, local 17th- and 18th-century rulers were responsible for temple architecture in variant styles. Plaster-covered brick sanctuaries at **Gauhati**, **Sibsagar** and **Udaipur** have roof structures and towers influenced by traditions deriving from Bengal and also from neighbouring Burma.

Eastern India incorporates valleys of the Himalayas, as in Sikkim and Arunachal Pradesh, where Tibetan religious and cultural traditions still flourish. Monasteries at **Pemayangtse**, **Rumtek** and **Tawang** demonstrate the survival of Mahayana Buddhism in its Tibetan form. This distinctive architecture and art may be compared with that of similar establishments in the Ladakh, Zanskar and Spiti valleys of northern India. The revival of ancient Buddhist sites as places of pilgrimage, especially **Bodhgaya**, indicates that Buddhism in eastern India is once again a religious force. New shrines are also being constructed, as at **Dhauli**.

Above Barabar, Lomas Rishi Cave, 3rd century BC

Opposite Khandagiri and Udayagiri, Cave 3, 1st century BC

Lauriya Nandangarh, Column,
3rd century BC

Nalanda, Temple 3, 6th century

Bodhgaya, Mahabodhi Temple, 7th century

Konarak, Surya Temple, 13th century

Opposite above Mukhalingam, Madhukeshvara Temple, 8th century

Opposite below Bhubaneshwar, Mukteshvara Temple, 10th century

Above Bishnupur, Shyama Raya
Temple, 17th century

Below Baranagar, Gangeshvara
Temple, 18th century

Opposite above Sibsagar, Vishnu
Temple, 17th–18th century

Opposite below Udaipur, Temple,
17th–18th century

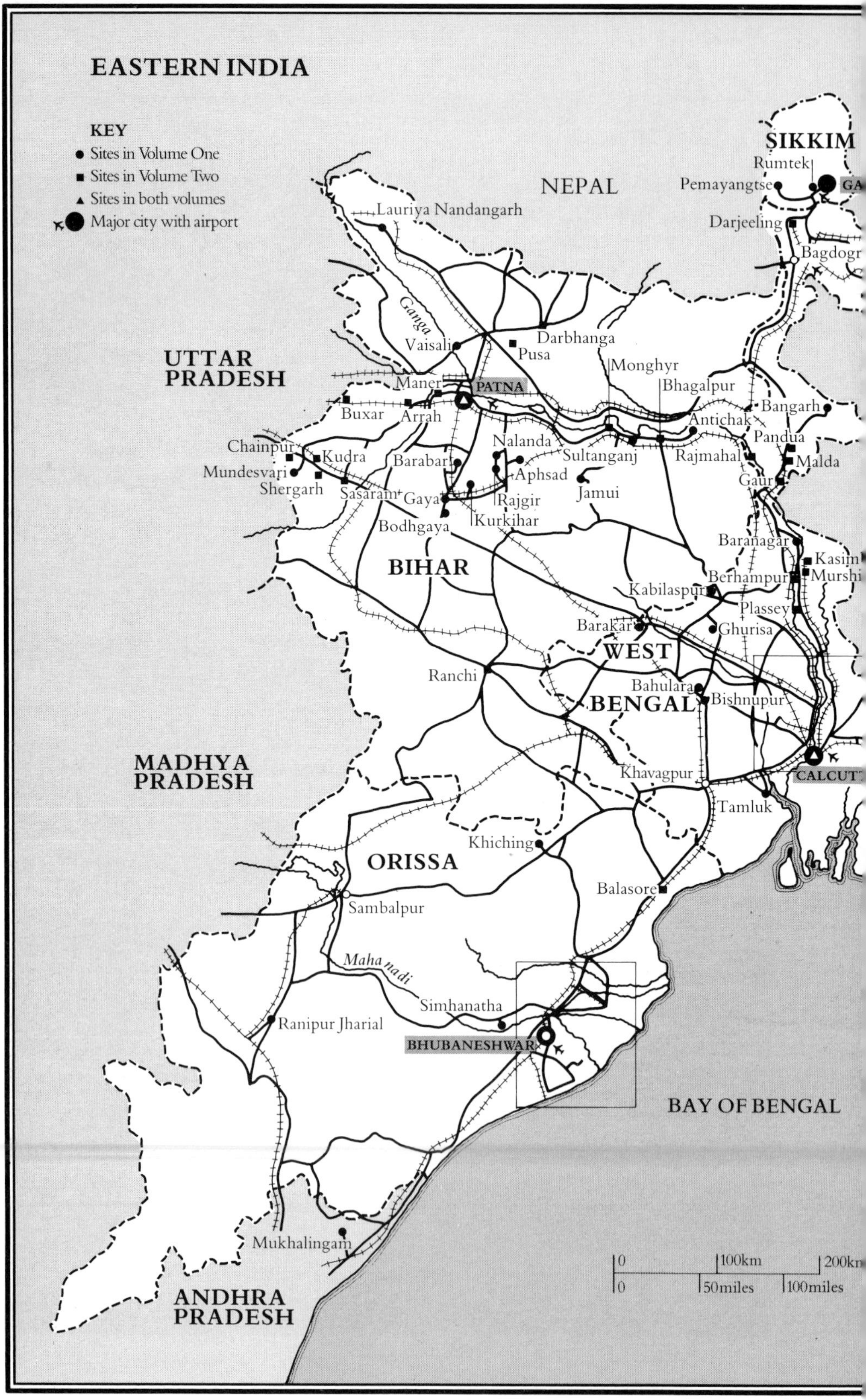

EASTERN INDIA

KEY
- Sites in Volume One
- Sites in Volume Two
- Sites in both volumes
- Major city with airport

NEPAL

SIKKIM

Rumtek
Pemayangtse
GA
Darjeeling
Bagdogr

Lauriya Nandangarh

UTTAR
PRADESH

Ganga
Vaisali
Darbhanga
Pusa
Monghyr
Bhagalpur
Bangarh
Maner
PATNA
Antichak
Pandua
Buxar
Arrah
Rajmahal
Malda
Chainpur
Nalanda
Gaur
Kudra
Sultanganj
Barabar
Mundesvari
Aphsad
Jamui
Shergarh
Sasaram
Gaya
Rajgir
Baranagar
Bodhgaya
Kurkihar
Kasim
Murshi
Kabilaspur
Berhampur

BIHAR

Plassey
Barakar
Ghurisa

WEST

Ranchi
Bahulara
Bishnupur

BENGAL

MADHYA
PRADESH
Khavagpur
CALCUT
Tamluk

ORISSA
Khiching
Balasore
Sambalpur

Maha nadi
Simhanatha
Ranipur Jharial
BHUBANESHWAR

BAY OF BENGAL

Mukhalingam

| 0 | | 100km | | 200km |
| 0 | | 50miles | | 100miles |

ANDHRA
PRADESH

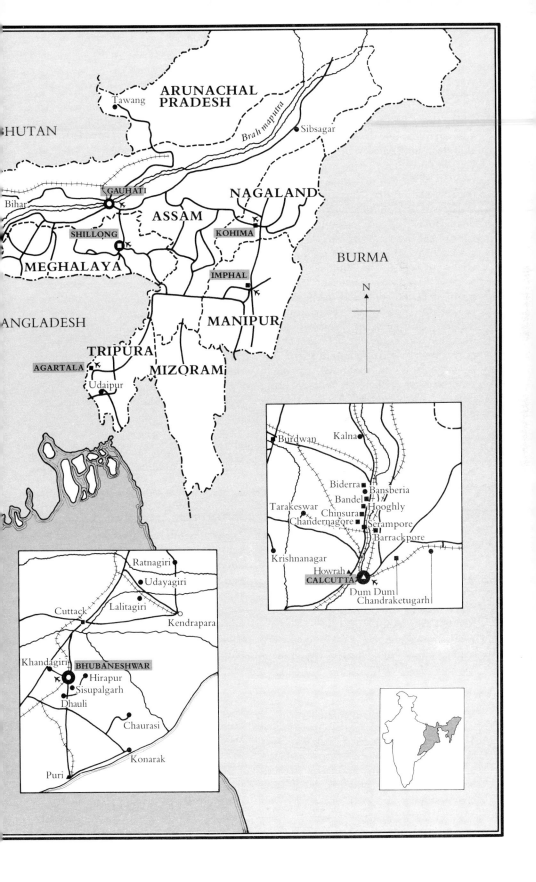

ANTICHAK

This site has been identified with Vikramashila, one of the most important Buddhist monasteries of eastern India. Excavations here have exposed the remains of various structures dating from the 8th–9th-century Pala period.

The site is dominated by a large but dilapidated brick edifice, about 110 m (360 ft) from north to south. This is laid out on a cruciform plan with two terraces, one above the other. The outer walls of the terraces have mouldings and terracotta plaques; in the middle of each side are projecting shrines for seated Buddha images. The upper central square block of masonry is possibly the base of a stupa, now missing. Surrounding this structure is a large court, bounded by small monastic cells, where stone and bronze images were discovered. A gateway complex with stone steps and balustrades is located in the middle of the north side.

Overlooking the Ganga river about 2 km (1½ miles) south-west of the site is Patharghat, where 5th-century Gupta reliefs are cut into the rock face. These include episodes from the Krishna story and Vishnu on Garuda.

APHSAD

The remains at this Hindu site are associated with the later Gupta rulers of Bihar. Most of the sculptures discovered here have been removed to the Indian Museum, **Calcutta**.

Varaha Sculpture, 7th century

This stone image of Vishnu's boar incarnation is now enshrined within a modern temple. The animal is covered with small figures; Bhudevi clutches the boar's tusk.

Vishnu Temple, 7th–8th century

The foundations of a large multi-terraced brick temple still survive. The basement was decorated with stucco reliefs, now almost entirely obliterated. Of particular interest was the series of panels depicting episodes from the Ramayana epic, among them Rama, Lakshmana and Sita with a forest sage, beneath a tree and in a boat.

BAHULARA

Shiva Temple, 11th century

This dilapidated Hindu brick structure demonstrates stylistic contacts between the traditions of Orissa and brick architecture in Bengal. The towered sanctuary of the temple is richly embellished with large arched motifs and other mouldings.

BANGARH

Excavations at this site have uncovered remains dating back to the 3rd-century-BC Maurya period. Terracotta figurines, drains, cesspits and a brick rampart wall belong to the 2nd–1st-century-BC Shunga era. Pottery from the succeeding Kushana and Gupta eras displays impressed decorative motifs. More substantial are the remains dating from the 9th–10th-century Pala period. These include a small but unique lotus-shaped tank, originally covered with a pillared canopy, as well as decorated bricks and stone carvings.

BANSBERIA

Two Hindu temples in different styles stand here; the later shrine is currently in use as a place of worship.

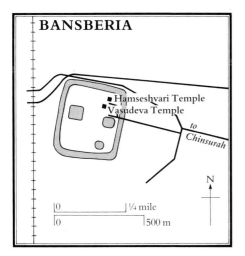

BANSBERIA

Hamseshvari Temple
Vasudeva Temple

to Chinsurah

N

|0 |¼ mile
|0 |500 m

Vasudeva Temple, 1679

This richly ornamented temple is built in the typical Bengal manner, with gently curved cornices. Verandahs on three sides provide access to the central domed chamber. Elevated on the curved vault of the roof is an octagonal pavilion with a pyramidal roof. The terracotta decoration on the east face is elaborate. Over the triple-arched entrance are miniature fighting figures, as well as repetitions of Krishna icons. Basement plaques have animated figures of gunmen in Portuguese costume travelling in boats (below) and scenes from the Krishna story (above). Krishna surrounded by dancing gopis appears in the terracotta roundels.

Hamseshvari Temple, 1814

This goddess temple has thirteen pinnacles symmetrically arranged on three levels. Unusually, these pinnacles have pointed domes covered with petalled motifs.

BARABAR

Some of the earliest examples of rock-cut architecture are found in the granite outcrops of the twin Barabar and Nagarjuni hills, where seven cave temples date from the 3rd-century-BC Maurya period. Inscriptions indicate that these caves served as retreats for Jain monks. Each cave consists of two small chambers cut into the rock parallel to the rock face, with entry through a side doorway. The circular and apsidal-ended plans of these chambers, many of which have vaulted roofs and sloping sides, reproduce the forms of thatched huts. The interiors are remarkable for their mirror-like polished surfaces. Two examples are of particular interest.

Sudama Cave, 261 BC

This unadorned chamber was dedicated by the emperor Ashoka himself. It consists of a circular vaulted chamber adjoining a rectangular mandapa.

Lomas Rishi Cave, 3rd century BC

An oval chamber with a dome-like roof is entered from a rectangular vaulted mandapa. The outer doorway is the most elaborate of the series. It imitates the elevation of a hut-like structure with sloping timber supports, curved eaves and a pot finial, all rendered in shallow relief. Within the curved architrave is a finely

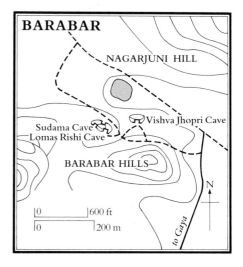

BARABAR

NAGARJUNI HILL

Vishva Jhopri Cave

Sudama Cave
Lomas Rishi Cave

BARABAR HILLS

N

to Gaya

|0 |600 ft
|0 |200 m

sculpted frieze of elephants; the animals proceed towards stupa-like emblems. When excavating the interior, workers encountered a flaw in the rock and so left the project unfinished.

BARAKAR

Siddheshvara Temple, 9th century

This early Hindu monument in the Orissan style consists of a towered sanctuary with plain walls except for niches, now empty, crowned with pediments. In contrast, the curved tower has miniature figures carved on almost all of the mouldings (especially the south face). At the summit is a large amalaka with seated figures and animals beneath. On the front (east) is a projection carved with a seated Lakulisha figure and the outlines of another image, possibly Shiva, beneath. The adjoining mandapa is a modern addition.

Ganesha, Durga and Panchanana Temples, 16th century

These almost identical Hindu monuments imitate the scheme of the earlier Siddheshvara temple. The sanctuary walls and towers are heightened; the mouldings are sharply cut, especially the pilasters around which snakes are coiled. Horizontal elements are repeated on the towers; animals project outwards. Above the walls are figurative friezes (missing on the Panchanana temple).

BARANAGAR

Char Bangla Group, 1760

Four hut-like Hindu temples face each other around a square court, in imitation of indigenous architectural practice. Each temple is roofed with a curved vault; access to the interior is through a triple-arched entrance. The principal façades are completely covered with terracotta plaques. Over the entrances are large representations of the Ramayana story, particularly the climactic battle between Rama and Ravana (north temple), sometimes with monkeys hurling rocks (west temple). Beneath the cornices, Vishnu's incarnations also appear (west temple). Basement friezes combine hunting scenes and courtly processions (beneath) with Ramayana episodes (above).

Bhavanishvara Temple, 1775

The sanctuary of this temple has an octagonal dome surrounded by a verandah. Each plastered façade is framed by columns and pilasters of Mughal design, with a curved cornice above. The vaulted roof has a dome-like tower, unusually decorated with inverted lotus petals.

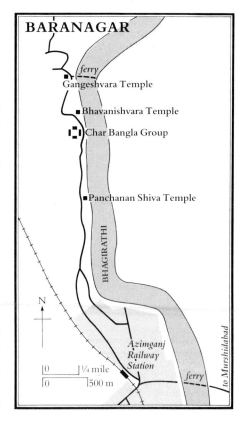

BARANAGAR

ferry
■ Gangeshvara Temple
■ Bhavanishvara Temple
■ Char Bangla Group
■ Panchanan Shiva Temple

BHAGIRATHI

N

Azimganj
Railway
Station

ferry

to Murshidabad

| 0 | ¼ mile
| 0 | 500 m

Gangeshvara Temple, 18th century

This brick structure reproduces the form of the double hut (jorbangla). The verandah and rectangular sanctuary are both vaulted; ridges and cornices are curved. On the front (west), the walls, columns and cornice are covered with terracotta plaques depicting miniature fighting figures (beneath the cornice), large mythical beasts (above the arches), episodes from the Krishna story (corner panels and upper part of basement) and courtly processions (lower part of basement). Numerous icons of Krishna playing the flute are found on the columns.

BHUBANESHWAR

While no monument at Bhubaneshwar predates the 7th century, remains at several sites in the vicinity, such as **Dhauli**, **Sisupalgarh** and the twin hills of **Khandagiri** and **Udayagiri**, testify to the antiquity of the region.

It was the rulers of the Shailodbhava and Bhauma Kara dynasties who first made Bhubaneshwar their capital in the 7th–8th centuries. Under their sponsorship, stone architecture in Orissa was initiated and developed (Parashurameshvara and Vaital Deul temples are the finest). Dating from the 9th–11th cen-

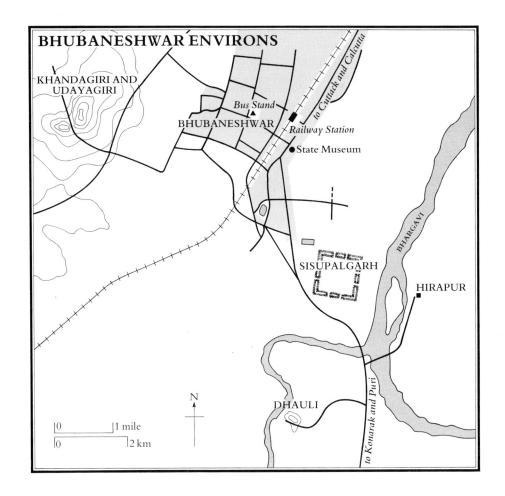

BHUBANESHWAR ENVIRONS

KHANDAGIRI AND UDAYAGIRI

to Cuttack and Calcutta

Bus Stand

BHUBANESHWAR

Railway Station

State Museum

BHARGAVI

SISUPALGARH

HIRAPUR

N

DHAULI

to Konarak and Puri

0   1 mile
0   2 km

turies, during the Somavamshi period, are several elaborate projects (Mukteshvara and Rajarani temples, for instance), as well as the largest complex at the capital (Lingaraja temple). The Eastern Gangas emerged as the dominant power at the beginning of the 12th century, but they constructed only a few temples here (Ananta Vasudeva is the principal example). Although there was less building activity under the Gajapatis in the 14th and 15th centuries, several earlier projects were extended.

The many sacred Hindu temples of Bhubaneshwar illustrate the complete evolution of the Orissan style. Temples generally incorporated two distinct elements. The towered sanctuary (rekha deul, in the local terminology) consisted of a curvilinear superstructure divided into horizontal bands which were ornamented with arch-like motifs. This tower was capped with an amalaka and a pot finial. Through the centuries the tower became higher and increasingly complex, with the addition of miniature replicas of itself at the corners. The other significant element was the square mandapa roofed with a pyramid of horizontal elements (pida deul). This does not appear in the earliest period, but became a prominent feature in later examples. It too is capped with an amalaka and a pot finial.

Sandstone sculpture is present in the earliest temples; indeed, some of the finest images of Hindu divinities belong to the 7th century. As the Orissan style evolved, the emphasis was increasingly focused on the principal cult icons in the wall niches. In the last phase, sculptural components became less prominent than the deeply cut architectural mouldings. Sculptures of divinities exemplify the Orissan style; they are fully modelled, gracefully posed and have sweetly detached facial expressions. Subsidiary figures, such as musicians, dancers, teachers, devotees, warriors and lovers, are more lively. Hardly any temple is without the seductively posed

maidens, as well as naga deities and lionlike beasts. Delicately incised patterns of lotus stalks, leaves, petals and scrollwork are ubiquitous.

The largest number of temples at Bhubaneshwar is grouped around Bindu Sagar, the tank in the middle of the ancient town; other examples are located to the north and east. The temples are dominated by the soaring tower of the Lingaraja complex, which is accessible to Hindus only.

The monuments are described in chronological order within the different groups.

State Museum

Stone sculptures displayed in the archaeological gallery have been brought from numerous sites throughout Orissa dating from the 7th–8th centuries onwards. Among the earliest Buddhist images are a large seated figure (damaged head) from Khadipada, also standing Avalokiteshvara (38) and Manjushri (24), both from Vajragiri. Of the Hindu icons, a series of chlorite Matrika sculptures from Dharmasala is noteworthy, especially a skeletal Chamunda figure (66). From Bhubaneshwar come sandstone panels, such as Shiva and Parvati seated in an intimate embrace and Ganesha (51). Sculptures of Ganga (690) and Yamuna (71) are other fine examples.

Exhibited separately is a remarkable group of 13th-century chlorite images depicting Ganesha and a complete set of the eight Dikpalas. These sculptures were found buried near the Rajarani temple at Bhubaneshwar and are in almost perfect condition. The delicate modelling and precision of detail are unsurpassed in the sculptural art of Orissa. Also belonging to this group are jamb fragments with ganas in deeply cut foliation.

Bronzes in this collection illustrate a local variation of the eastern Indian style, such as the 10th–11th-century Buddhist images from Banpur. Folk bronzes,

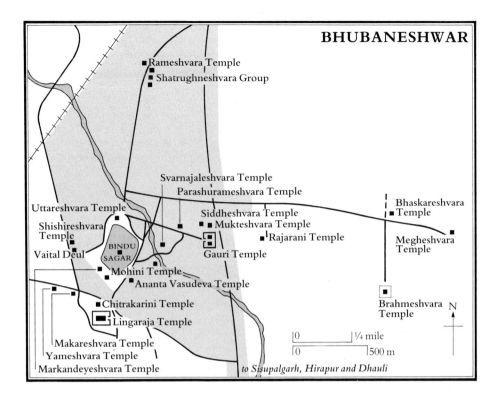

BHUBANESHWAR

palm-leaf manuscripts and temple hangings, many of which illustrate sacred themes, are also displayed.

NORTHERN GROUP

Shatrughneshvara Group,
early 7th century

Three similar but ruined temples of this group are known as Lakshmaneshvara, Bharateshvara and Shatrughneshvara. The overall scheme is best demonstrated by the southernmost Bharateshvara temple, where a small square sanctuary, entered from the west, has restored projecting niches on three sides. The curved tower which rises above is divided into horizontal elements, with a large amalaka at the summit. Arched motifs over the doorway have carvings of dancing Shiva

(above) and seated Ravana disturbing Shiva and Parvati (below). The doorway is damaged but an image of Shiva is preserved on the lintel.

Rameshvara Temple, 13th century

The rectangular mandapa of this temple is completely detached from the towered sanctuary. The mandapa has doorways on two sides; within is a small sanctuary. The roof consists of three sloping tiers. There is almost no carved ornamentation on the sanctuary walls or tower, except for projecting beasts above. Over the doorway are planetary divinities flanked by large ganas. Panels in the sanctuary walls depict Durga (north), Karttikeya (west) and Ganesha (south). Vyalas and amorous couples are seen in the recesses.

At the rear (west) of the temple is a large tank with stepped sides.

BINDU SAGAR GROUP

Parashurameshvara Temple,
mid-7th century

This is the earliest of the completely preserved temples at Bhubaneshwar. A square-towered sanctuary adjoins a rectangular mandapa with a sloping roof arranged in two tiers; this is a slightly later addition. The building is remarkable for its delicately carved figural sculpture and ornament.

The outer walls of the sanctuary have three projections on each side. The central projections house major icons, particularly Ganesha (south) and Karttikeya (east); these are surrounded by bands of miniature figures and lotus ornament. Above are pediments with tower-like mouldings. The empty side niches are raised on a moulded basement decorated with animals, beasts and birds; the niches are surmounted by pediments of arched motifs filled with images. The gently curved tower is divided into horizontal mouldings. On the central projections are large niches with arch-like forms, which contain figures of seated Lakulisha (east), Durga spearing the buffalo (north), Shiva begging for food from Parvati (south) and, on the front (west), seated Ravana (below) and dancing Shiva (above). The tower is capped by a large amalaka.

The mandapa is entered through two doorways adorned with figures of guardians, goddesses and amorous couples; Lakshmi adorns the lintel of the principal (west) entrance. Pierced stone windows decorated with dancers and musicians are located on the west. Above the walls are friezes of elephants, worship of the linga and other scenes. Divinities such as Shiva, Surya, Ardhanarishvara, Harihara, Yama, Varuna and the Matrikas appear in the niches. The interior columns are massive and plain. Over the sanctuary doorway is a frieze of planetary deities. Within the sanctuary, there is a linga on a circular pedestal.

Near the north-west corner of the temple is a sahasra linga, its surface engraved with multiple miniature lingas.

Svarnajaleshvara Temple,
late 7th century

This duplicates the towered sanctuary of the Parashurameshvara temple. The corner friezes (north and west sides) depicting episodes from the Ramayana are fragmentary; other sculptures are mostly damaged.

Uttareshvara Temple,
late 7th century

This temple consists of a sanctuary and rectangular mandapa of the Parashurameshvara type. The recent restoration has preserved little of the original carved decoration. To the south-west, a group of small shrines surrounds a rectangular tank.

Mohini Temple, late 8th century

Also related to the Parashurameshvara temple, this example has most of its carvings incomplete. A Durga image is installed in the sanctuary.

Vaital Deul, late 8th century

The form of this temple is almost unique in the Bhubaneshwar series. A rectangular sanctuary is roofed by a tower capped with a vaulted roof. The adjoining rectangular mandapa has miniature shrines built into the four corners and is roofed with a double tier of sloping slabs. Three sides of the sanctuary walls display niches elevated on a basement carved with luxuriant foliation. Within the niches are gracefully posed females and couples, with deities in the middle: Durga spearing the buffalo demon (north), Parvati (south) and Ardhanarishvara (west). All of these figures are framed by delicately etched bands of scrollwork; the panels above have animals and riders. The tower is divided for much of its height into horizontal elements, some adorned with friezes of miniature figures. On the short (north and south) ends are arch-like designs and medallions containing images. The surmounting arched ends of the roof are restored. On the long side of the vaulted roof are three pot finials on amalakas. The projection on the front (east) has figures of Surya (beneath) and dancing Shiva (above) framed in finely decorated arches; makaras and monster heads are carved at the apex.

The interior is unrelieved except for the sanctuary, which has sculpture panels set into the side walls. These depict Bhairava and the Matrikas (south), as well as a series of male deities that include a skeletal figure (north). The principal object of worship is a powerful sculpture of multi-armed Durga spearing Mahisha.

Shishireshvara Temple,
late 8th century

This building, in the same compound as the Vaital Deul, is now missing the upper portion of its tower. It generally follows the Parashurameshvara temple in form, but its decorative detail is closer in style to its neighbour. The carved ornamentation is finely executed. Among the sculptures are Ganesha and Lakulisha (south). A Nataraja panel is positioned on the front (east) of the tower.

Markandeyeshvara Temple,
late 8th century

This is a duplicate of the Shishireshvara temple. The sanctuary is relatively well preserved, but the mandapa is a modern replacement. Though much of the sculpture is damaged, a dancing Shiva within a large medallion survives on the front (east) of the tower. Over the sanctuary doorway appear the Navagrahas; images of Brahma, Agni and Varuna are carved on to the jambs.

Mukteshvara Temple, late 10th century

This is the most exquisitely ornamented temple of the Bhubaneshwar series. The monument marks a transition between the earlier group and the more fully evolved projects of the 11th–12th centuries.

The temple stands within a walled compound entered through a gateway to the west. There are smaller towered shrines all around; to the east is a rectangular tank. The gateway is remarkable for the heavy curved architrave created by corbelled slabs. This is carved on both sides with reclining maidens, foliation and human heads within medallions; monster heads project outwards at the ends.

The temple itself consists of a towered sanctuary and a square mandapa with a pyramidal roof. The sanctuary walls have projections and deep recesses; these are raised on a moulded basement with multi-faceted elements and foliate panels. The walls are embellished with maidens beneath foliation, snakes wrapped around part-circular pilasters and empty niches beneath tower-like pediments. The tower is adorned with curved bands created of narrow horizontal mouldings and meshed arch-like motifs. An amalaka and pot finial are positioned above. In the central projections, pairs of figures are depicted climbing on to large arched motifs capped by the heads of mythical beasts.

The exterior of the mandapa is distinguished by large pierced stone windows with geometric designs (north and south). These windows are surrounded by friezes of lotus stalks enlivened with playful monkeys. The pyramidal roof is divided into deeply cut horizontal mouldings and capped by a pot finial. Triangular projections in the middle of each side have lion-like beasts at the summits.

Above the sanctuary doorway within the mandapa are a Lakshmi icon and the Navagrahas. The ceiling is adorned with carvings of miniature warriors, flying figures and gods; various goddesses are carved inside the lobes of the central dome.

Gauri Temple, late 10th century

This small decorated sanctuary, which abuts a later mandapa, has affinities with the Mukteshvara temple with which it is contemporary. The walls have fully developed projections richly adorned with foliate and figurative carvings; the niches are empty. The incomplete tower is more rounded than the Mukteshvara example. The projections on each side are exuberantly decorated with ganas, maidens, foliate bands and tiers of arched motifs with monster heads above.

Siddheshvara Temple,
early 11th century

The mature Orissan style is anticipated in this example. The temple consists of a towered sanctuary and adjoining square mandapa with a pyramidal roof. Although all the elements are clearly articulated, there is little carved ornamentation. Sculptures of Ganesha (south) and Karttikeya (west) are still preserved in the niches.

Lingaraja Temple,
late 11th century, with additions

This temple is the climax of the Bhubaneshwar group; it is both the largest and most stylistically evolved building. The towered sanctuary, which rises about 36·5 m (120 ft) high, and the adjoining square mandapa with a pyramidal roof comprise the original scheme; two more mandapas were added at a later date. Numerous minor towered shrines stand within the enclosure, which is entered from the east through a gateway.

The sanctuary walls are divided into two storeys by a triple tier of mouldings with numerous projections and recesses. Each projection has a sculpted niche sur-

mounted by a pediment; rearing beasts are positioned in the recesses. The soaring superstructure integrates miniature towered motifs at the corners by emphasizing the horizontal recesses. In the middle of each side are foliated arched motifs with flanking figures surmounted by projecting lions. Beneath the large amalaka at the summit are crouching lions and seated deities. A pot finial draped in flags proclaims the presence of the god.

Also divided into storeys, the mandapa walls have numerous sculpted niches with amorous couples in the intervening recesses. The pyramid of deeply undercut mouldings above is separated into two tiers; large arch-like projections support crouching lion-like beasts. The circular roof is capped with an amalaka and a pot finial.

In the north-west corner of the Lingaraja compound is the 13th-century Parvati temple. This has many fine sculptures, such as female figures on the windows and snakes entwined around part-circular pilasters.

Ananta Vasudeva Temple, 1278

This is the only surviving Vaishnava shrine at Bhubaneshwar. Architecturally, it is similar to the Lingaraja temple but on a reduced scale. Four components of the plan are compactly grouped together to create a dramatic ascent to the tower that rises over the sanctuary. The building was profusely adorned, but many of the carvings are damaged. In general, the foliate ornament is more elaborate than that of the Lingaraja example, although the mouldings display smaller and simpler schemes. The sculpted figures resemble those of the contemporary Surya temple at **Konarak**. The corbelled interior is massive and unadorned.

Chitrakarini Temple, late 13th century

This temple consists of a sanctuary and mandapa only. It stands within a walled enclosure with four subsidiary towered shrines. The projections of the mandapa walls are extended and carried vertically up into the roof. Most of the sculptures are damaged, but there are erotic carvings on the window blocks and processions of camels over the north doorway.

Makareshvara Temple,
late 13th century

This building is another example of the later style, mostly devoid of sculpted ornamentation.

Yameshvara Temple, late 13th century

Resembling the Ananta Vasudeva temple in its structural features and rich ornamentation, this monument comprises a sanctuary and mandapa. These are richly carved with cornice mouldings and bands of foliation. Within the court in which the temple stands are the partly buried remains of several 7th-century temple towers.

EASTERN GROUP

Rajarani Temple, early 11th century

This is one of the finest examples of the mature Orissan style. The walls of the sanctuary project outwards so as to create a plan that almost approaches a circle. Raised on a deeply modelled basement decorated with delicately carved lotus ornament, each projection consists of two sculpted panels, one above the other; these are flanked by bands of delicate foliation. At the corners appear the Dikpalas: for example, Vayu and Varuna (north-west corner) and Indra and Agni (south-east corner). In between are amorous couples and alluring maidens, often clutching trees, with vyalas in the recesses. Miniature representations of temple towers are positioned beneath the central niches, now devoid of their carved panels.

At the edges and at intermediate points of the superstructure are vertical tiers of towered elements which repeat the overall towered form on a smaller scale, complete with capping amalaka. An incised mesh of arch-like motifs covers many of these features. In the middle of each side, two half-towers are superimposed. The whole composition is crowned by a large amalaka, with crouching figures beneath and a pot finial above.

In contrast to the sanctuary, the mandapa lacks any overall ornamentation. The roof has a pyramid of recessed eave-like elements with a pot finial at the summit. Projections on each side are surmounted by fierce lion-like beasts. Flanking the windows (north and south sides) and the doorway on the front (east) are part-circular pilasters with elephants and lions beneath. Coiled around the pilasters at either side of the doorway are naga deities holding garlands. Scrollwork with miniature guardians adorns the jambs; a Lakulisha figure appears on the lintel.

The corbelled interior of the temple is plain. No cult image is preserved in the sanctuary.

Brahmeshvara Temple, 1060

Set within a walled enclosure, this complex consists of a principal temple and four corner shrines. Where preserved, the ornamentation consists of foliation and scrollwork. Sculptures include guardian figures (corner panels), different forms of Shiva (double tiers of niches on the sanctuary walls), amorous couples (panels on the tower), maidens (blocks within the mandapa windows) and rearing beasts (recesses between the wall projections). Panels above the sanctuary niches and the south mandapa window unusually illustrate seated royal and saintly figures receiving homage. Additional tower-like profiles on the superstructure do not interrupt the overall square plan. Guardian figures and the Navagrahas adorn the outer doorway.

Bhaskareshvara Temple, 12th century

This temple consists of an unadorned sanctuary which is roofed with a simple pyramid of masonry capped by a large amalaka. The unusual interior is double-storeyed; doorways on four sides are provided at two levels, permitting devotees to look down on to the enshrined linga. This 3-m-high (10 ft) cult object is a reworked column, possibly dating from the 3rd-century-BC Maurya period. (Fragments of ancient Buddhist sandstone railings were found around the mound on which the temple is built.)

Meghesvara Temple, late 12th century

The tower over the sanctuary of this temple has numerous projections to create a rounded effect. The ornamentation bears a close resemblance to the earlier Brahmeshvara temple. Of the principal niches on three sides, only the east panel that depicts standing Karttikeya survives; most of the other sculptures are damaged.

BISHNUPUR

Capital of the Malla rulers of Bengal, Bishnupur preserves about thirty brick and stone Hindu temples dating from the 17th–18th centuries. The town is protected by strong lines of earthen ramparts and is surrounded by extensive tanks. Little remains of the fort, which is entered through stone gateways, or of the citadel housing the royal palace.

Rasa Mancha, early 17th century

This is the earliest structure at Bishnupur. It was built by the ruler Bir Hambir for the Rasa festival, in which images of Krishna and Radha are publicly displayed. A domed sanctuary is surrounded by four passageways with vaulted chambers. The exterior is dominated by a stepped masonry pyramid.

Shyama Raya Temple, 1643

In this temple a central domed chamber is approached through vaulted verandahs on four sides. An upper octagonal chamber is roofed by a pyramidal vault, now dilapidated; detached smaller towered chambers stand at the four corners (above). Each façade has a triple-arched entrance capped by a curved cornice. The terracotta sculptures include Ramayana panels, especially Rama, Ravana and archers, over the entrances, Krishna surrounded by gopis in roundels beside the entrance, and episodes from the Ramayana and Krishna stories on the basement friezes. Even the interior has terracotta friezes and roundels.

Keshta Raya Temple, 1655

This temple imitates the indigenous double hut (jorbangla) scheme. The exterior consists of two large vaulted chambers, each with curved ridges and cornices; above is a smaller square chamber with a pyramidal roof. In contrast, the interior has a central domed chamber surrounded by vaulted corridors and

**BISHNUPUR,
Shyama Raya Temple**

| 0 | 3 m |
| 0 | 16 ft |

N

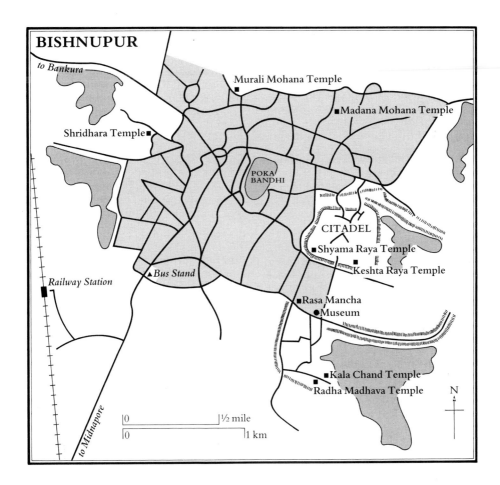

BISHNUPUR

to Bankura

Murali Mohana Temple

Madana Mohana Temple

Shridhara Temple

POKA BANDHI

CITADEL

Shyama Raya Temple

Keshta Raya Temple

Railway Station

Bus Stand

Rasa Mancha
Museum

Kala Chand Temple
Radha Madhava Temple

N

0   ½ mile
0   1 km

to Midnapore

verandahs. The terracotta ornamentation includes fighting figures from the Ramayana battle, as well as panels illustrating the Krishna story. Gunmen in boats, hunters fighting forest animals and courtly scenes are depicted on the basement friezes.

Kala Chand Temple, 1656

This stone construction is capped by a single curved tower with pronounced horizontal mouldings and a circular ribbed finial. The crudely carved sculptures covered with plaster are mostly of dancing figures and Ramayana scenes.

Murali Mohana Temple, 1665

In this example, a stone tower of the same type as at the Kala Chand temple is surrounded on four sides by an open verandah with partly fallen squat columns.

Madana Mohana Temple, 1694

Built of brick, this example repeats the scheme of the Kala Chand temple, but here the central tower has a dome. The principal façade is covered with panels, the outlines of which imitate the curvature of the cornice. Terracotta panels illustrate episodes from the Krishna story; there are also scenes taken from the Mahabharata epic, such as Krishna as the charioteer of Arjuna (panel over entrance). The basement friezes illustrate rows of geese (beneath) and cows (above). The temple stands in the middle of a compound where there is a subsidiary hut-shaped chamber.

Radha Madhava Temple, 1737

This is also a replica of the Kala Chand temple, but with the addition of pilastered elements on the principal façade.

Shridhara Temple, 19th century

This later temple has nine pinnacles on two levels; each pinnacle is a curved tower divided by horizontal mouldings. The sculptural decoration is executed in plaster. Among the figurative panels are Krishna and Radha together playing a single flute, dancing Shiva (above the arched entrance), Brahma and other gods. Dancers and musicians adorn the basement.

BODHGAYA

Marking the spot of Buddha's enlightenment, Bodhgaya is greatly revered by Buddhists, especially for the bodhi tree beneath which the Master sat in meditation. After the death of Buddha, Bodhgaya flourished as an important religious centre and numerous shrines, stupas and monasteries were erected. The site continued to attract pilgrims and was only abandoned in the 15th century.

The remains at Bodhgaya date from as early as the Maurya and Shunga eras, as well as from later Gupta and Pala periods. The site is dominated by the soaring tower of the Mahabodhi temple, which is built in front of the bodhi tree (only a remote descendant of the original). The temple is surrounded by a stone railing and innumerable votive stupas and several shrines. Today, Bodhgaya is once again

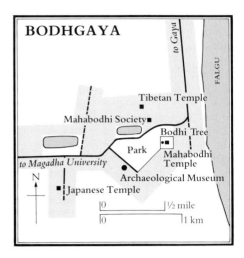

an important holy place, crowded with pilgrims from all over the Buddhist world. Modern shrines and rest-houses are to be found throughout the modern town.

During the Gupta and Pala periods, Bodhgaya was also an important artistic centre which produced stone and metal images. (Many of these are exhibited in the Archaeological Museum; others are in the **Gaya** Museum and the Indian Museum, **Calcutta**.)

Mahabodhi Complex, 7th century and later

This monument has a complex structural history. It probably assumed its present dimensions in the 7th century, when it was described by the Chinese visitor Hiuen Tsang. Renovations to the temple continued through the period of Muslim domination, from the 12th century onwards, the most recent being the extensive rebuilding at the end of the 19th century. While none of the original plaster decoration has survived, the present monument appears to preserve the overall form of the original building.

The temple is of outstanding interest, not only for its religious significance but also because it is the sole survivor of monumental brick traditions in eastern

India. The building is elevated on a broad terrace, the sides of which are divided by pilasters that frame niches with restored plaster sculptures. The temple itself consists of a large central sanctuary above which rises a lofty pyramidal tower more than 55 m (180 ft) high. This is divided into storeys by horizontal mouldings and arch-like motifs, and is capped by an amalaka and a tiered finial of umbrella-like motifs. Above the entrance (east) is a pyramidal projection. The shrine walls have regularly spaced pilasters between which restored sculptural panels are inserted. An earlier 6th-century standing Buddha figure is placed in a niche beside the main entrance. At the four corners of the terrace are subsidiary shrines; these 19th-century reconstructions reproduce on a smaller scale the features of the principal temple.

Beneath the bodhi tree at the rear (west) of the temple is a rectangular stone seat with palmettes and geese delicately carved on the sides. This seat may date back to the 3rd century BC. Set up around the temple are posts dating from the succeeding Shunga period. These once enclosed the bodhi tree in what was possibly the first stone sanctuary at the site. (These posts have been replaced by plaster copies; the sandstone originals are displayed in the Archaeological Museum.) The railing was extended several times. Posts from the later Gupta period are identified by elaborate foliate ornament and miniature figures, including amorous couples.

The Annapurna and Tara shrines within the compound probably belong to the 8th century. Despite extensive restoration, the pilastered walls and pyramidal towers of these shrines resemble those of the principal temple.

Stone stupas belonging to the Pala period are clustered around the temple. Each of these has a high basement, four seated Buddhist figures within decorated niches and a capping multi-tiered finial. Other sculpted slabs have been gathered within the compound of a nearby modern temple where the Bodhgaya mahant resides.

Archaeological Museum

Assembled here are the original Shunga posts and railings that surrounded the principal temple. These display carved panels and medallions with animal and lotus designs, as well as yakshis, amorous couples, winged horses and centaurs; there is even one depiction of Surya (1367). Both Buddhist and Hindu images belonging to different Pala sites are displayed. Of interest is the finely finished seated Buddha figure from Guneri (218); another similar sculpture from Bodhgaya is notable for its severe expression (1097). Among the 9th-century Pala bronzes are images from Fatehpur. Especially fine are a seated Bodhisattva figure (72) and a standing Vishnu with Lakshmi and Sarasvati (87).

CALCUTTA

No sacred buildings of any antiquity survive in Calcutta and its vicinity. Other than the sanctuary at Kalighat, after which the city was named, most of the Hindu temples and their cults are no earlier than the 19th century. (For the British monuments of Calcutta see Volume II.)

Kali Temple, rebuilt 1809

This famous shrine overlooking a tributary of the Hooghly river is the holiest in the city. It is here that the animal sacrifices associated with the worship of Kali take place. The building is of plastered brickwork; the roof has curved cornices in two tiers in the indigenous Bengal manner. There is no original decoration.

Dakshineshvara Temple, 1855

Ramakrishna, the famous teacher, first worked as a priest in this temple.

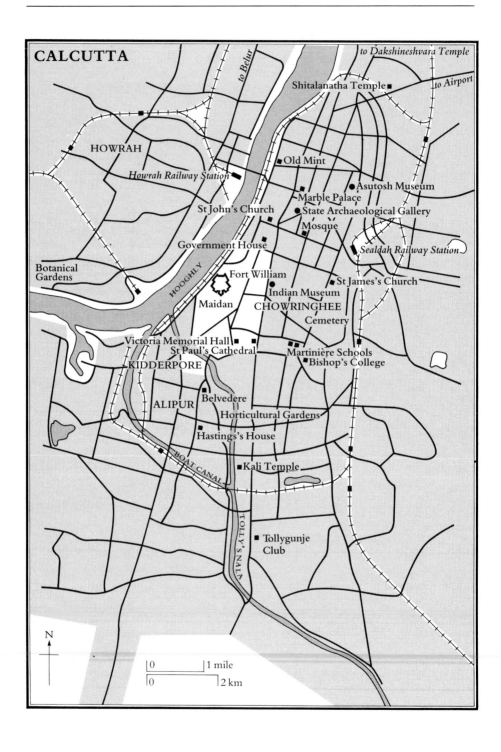

CALCUTTA

to Dakshineshvara Temple

to Belur

to Airport

Shitalanatha Temple

HOWRAH

Old Mint

Howrah Railway Station

Asutosh Museum

Marble Palace

St John's Church

State Archaeological Gallery

Mosque

Government House

Sealdah Railway Station

Botanical
Gardens

HOOGHLY

Fort William

St James's Church

Indian Museum

Maidan

CHOWRINGHEE

Cemetery

Victoria Memorial Hall

St Paul's Cathedral

Martinière Schools

KIDDERPORE

Bishop's College

ALIPUR

Belvedere

Horticultural Gardens

Hastings's House

BOAT CANAL

Kali Temple

TOLLY'S NALA

Tollygunje
Club

N

0   1 mile

0   2 km

Shitalanatha Temple, 1867

Founded and designed by the chief government jeweller, this Jain shrine and its formal garden present an astonishing blend of central Indian temple architecture with European Baroque features. The principal sanctuary has a clustered tower and is raised on a terrace; a verandah surrounds the temple on three sides. Tile mosaic, glass and gilt are everywhere employed to create glittering surfaces. In front is the garden with its pavilions, statuary and ornamental pools, all executed in the Italianate manner.

Ramakrishna Matha, 20th century

Ramakrishna, the famous Vaishnava saint, died in 1866. Soon after, a Hindu monastic order bearing his name was started by his followers, headed by Vivekananda. This has now become a worldwide mission.

The modern temple which serves as the headquarters of the mission is the largest in Bengal. It is situated at Belur, on the right bank of the Hooghly, about 5 km (3 miles) from the city centre. The temple is revivalist in style, blending traditional Bengal features, such as curved cornices and multiple dome-like towers and turrets, with Mughal columns, arches and balconies.

Indian Museum

Established in 1814, this was the first national museum of India. It houses a very large selection of antiquities and the archaeological section represents a fine collection of prehistoric and protohistoric materials. Here stone age tools and copper artefacts from all over India, as well as excavated finds from Harappa and Mohenjodaro (Pakistan), are displayed. Terracotta figurines from various sites dating from the 5th–2nd centuries BC are also shown. Among the terracottas from the later periods is a Gupta panel depicting Vishnu on the serpent.

It is, however, for the rich assemblage of stone and metal sculptures that the museum is best known. These come from many eastern Indian sites, as well as from other parts of the country. One of the most important early sculptures is the polished sandstone lion capital from Rampurva (6299). Though damaged, this 3rd-century-BC capital is an outstanding example of Maurya art. Another column capital is fashioned as a wish-fulfilling tree; this 2nd-century-BC Shunga sculpture comes from **Vidisha** (1795). Another impressive illustration of the Shunga style is the large standing Bodhisattva from **Sravasti** (Si:B), belonging to the 1st century BC.

The collection is famous for the extensive remains from the 2nd-century-BC Buddhist stupa at **Bharhut**. These posts, railings, capping stones and gateways, all fashioned in deep red sandstone, once surrounded a stupa. The remarkable precision of the carving and the liveliness of the figures, narrative scenes and decorative themes testify to the vitality of India's early artistic traditions.

Many of the **Bharhut** posts are carved with yakshis which protrude in part relief; they stand in attitudes of devotion upon ganas or clutch branches of trees. Here too are royal devotees, riders on horses and elephants, and even one example of a figure in foreign dress (A24798). Other carved panels depict Buddhist narratives, among them the dream of Maya (93); celestials celebrating Buddha's enlightenment, the worship of Buddha's throne and the bodhi tree (271–272); elephants paying homage to the bodhi tree, naga king worshipping the throne and adoration of the wheel (264–266); and stupa in worship (267).

Railing medallions display a variety of lotus designs, sometimes incorporating yaksha busts; other themes include Lakshmi bathed by elephants, scenes of everyday village life, deer, elephants and peacocks. Of particular interest are the illustrations of Jataka legends, complete with identifying labels: for instance, the Mahakapi Jataka, in which the Bodhisattva as a monkey carries his followers across the river (35), and the Ruru Jataka, in which the Bodhisattva as a stag rescues a merchant, who in turn saves the stag from being shot (129). These and other scenes are characterized by dense compositions, with figures and animals in a detailed landscape. As for the gateways, at least one example stands complete; its high posts support three horizontal architraves separated one from another by carved blocks.

Belonging to the later Kushana era are 2nd-century panels from **Mathura**. These include an amorous couple (A24250), a figure grappling with a lion (M17), a seated Buddha (A25024) and an unusual capital with four composite human and animal figures (M14). Railing posts are finely carved with maidens standing on crouching ganas (A24945–6). A seated Buddha from **Ahichhatra** (A25024) also belongs to the Kushana period.

The collection of 1st–3rd-century schist sculptures from the Gandhara region (north-western Pakistan) is the largest in India. Panels and friezes are carved with scenes from Buddha's life and the Jataka stories; seated and standing Buddhist images, isolated heads, divinities and devotees are also displayed. Outstanding examples include an impressive standing Maitreya figure from Mardan (A23192), a depiction of the miracle at **Sravasti** with Buddha seated inside a deeply cut architectural façade (A23434) and Buddha seated beneath the bodhi tree (A23462/4871), the last two pieces from Loriyan Tangai. Also from this site is a model votive stupa 1·45 m (5 ft) high; this is complete with a carved base, a hemisphere ornamented with lotus petals and a tier of diminishing umbrellas (412).

Contemporary Satavahana architectural fragments from stupas at **Amaravati** and **Nagarjunakonda** are displayed. These depict scenes from the life of the Master, such as the panel illustrating Buddha in heaven, Buddha's descent from heaven and Maya's dream.

To the 5th century belong many fine Gupta sculptures from **Sarnath**. These include standing Buddhist figures, one with a delicately worked halo (A25084), another without (A25102), a standing Padmapani figure (A25082) and a teaching Buddha (S49). Narrative scenes include the birth, enlightenment, teaching and death of the Master, all combined into a single panel (A25100). Architectural fragments with delicately incised lotus ornament, ganas and guardian figures come from the contemporary Hindu site of **Bhumara**.

Pala and Sena sites in Bihar and Bengal are represented by a large number of 9th–12th-century Buddhist and Hindu divinities. Among the outstanding examples of these styles are a four-faced linga in polished basalt (A25183), a naga couple beneath an outspread serpent hood (A25170), a standing Vishnu figure (A25195), Karttikeya (A25204) and seated Garuda (A25211). Among the female figures is Parvati standing within a frame (A25209), Durga vigorously slaying Mahisha (A24756) and an unusual reclining figure sometimes identified as Yashoda (A25212). To the same era and region belong many votive stupas and architectural fragments, including richly carved doorway frames and columns.

From central Indian sites of the 10th–11th centuries there is a selection of fine stone sculptures, especially from **Khajuraho**; thus, Varaha (862), and several bracket figures including a maiden writing on a slate (A25228) and another holding a child (A25230). Among the contemporary Buddhist pieces is a goddess from Satna (A25220). Sculptures from southern India include contemporary Hoysala pieces. A lintel depicting Krishna playing the flute, with foliated makaras at either side, comes from **Halebid** (A25238).

Contemporary sculptures from Orissa

include a panel with Shiva spearing Andhaka from **Puri** (A24127) and a seated Padmapani from **Ratnagiri** (A25224). From the 13th-century site of **Konarak** comes an unusual but damaged panel depicting the meeting of a temple committee (A24786). Other larger sculptures from various sites in Bihar and Orissa are seen on the verandah that surrounds the courtyard.

Among the outstanding examples of Pala bronzes are important images from **Nalanda**, such as Avalokiteshvara (A24294) and a standing Buddha (A24276). A standing Vishnu figure within a frame comes from Rangpur (A24354). Manasa is seated beneath a serpent hood holding a child (A24357).

South Indian bronzes are also represented, especially 11th–12th-century Buddhist images from **Nagapattinam**. Among the selection of finely modelled 11th–12th-century Chola bronzes are several dancing Shiva figures, as well as seated Shiva with an elaborate headdress (14200).

In the Art Gallery on the upper floor there is a substantial collection of Nepalese and Tibetan bronzes, as well as ivories, metalwork, woodwork and textiles from different regions. There is also a large repository of Indian coins, including many rare issues. Of the reliquaries, the most important is a vase from **Piprahwa**, which has an inscription datable to the 4th century BC.

Asutosh Museum, University of Calcutta

Some of the artefacts recovered in excavations at the Buddhist sites of Paharpur and Mahasthangarh (Bangladesh) and the full collections of antiquities recovered from **Bangarh** and **Chandraketugarh** are displayed here.

Among the sculptures assembled from various sites in West Bengal and Bangladesh is a well-preserved 8th-century Surya image from Kasipur (18).

The god stands in a chariot drawn by seven horses; a solar disc is positioned behind his head. Among the Pala pieces are several figures of standing Vishnu accompanied by Sarasvati and Lakshmi. From Orissa come two large panels carved with maidens. Belonging to the later period are numerous terracotta plaques from 17th–18th-century Hindu temples, as well as an unusual 19th-century wooden image of Krishna playing the flute carved in the round.

Also exhibited is a large collection of folk and tribal arts from Bengal. This includes terracotta figurines, paintings on paper, textiles and metal objects.

State Archaeological Gallery

Other than prehistoric antiquities, this museum houses a representative collection of sculptures from sites in West Bengal. Among the Pala images are the bust of Devi from Jagdal, a seated Buddha figure from Bareya and a delicately modelled Avalokiteshvara from Tapan. Later sculptures include a 19th-century relief panel of Krishna and the gopis from Jagadanandapur. Coins, scroll paintings and other examples of folk arts are also shown.

CHANDRAKETUGARH

Excavations at this site have recovered a rich collection of finds from different periods. Pottery dates from the 3rd century BC; figurines, terracottas, beads, ivory, steatite caskets and coins belong to the later Shunga and Kushana eras. Bricks and terracotta plaques with animal and human figures, the latter often portraying amorous couples, date from the 5th-century Gupta period. Also belonging to this era are the remains of a large polygonal structure with a central brick-lined pit, possibly the foundations of a sanctuary.

CHAURASI

Varahi Temple, late 10th century

This well-preserved example of the mature Orissan Hindu temple style has a rectangular towered sanctuary. The outer walls have projections carried up to the vaulted roof; in the central niche on the west wall is a finely carved Surya image. Much of the foliate and figurative ornamentation survives, including pierced stone windows in the adjoining mandapa and, at the entrance, snakes entwined around pilasters. A large image of the boar-headed goddess is enshrined within the sanctuary; she holds a skull in one hand.

DHAULI

8 km (5 miles) south of **Bhubaneshwar** is a rocky outcrop which overlooks an ancient battle site; here Ashoka, the 3rd-century-BC emperor, is believed to have been converted to Buddhism. This event is commemorated by a modern stupa built on the summit of the hill. Beneath the stupa is a traditionally styled Orissan temple dedicated to Shiva. At the base of the hill is a modern Japanese Buddhist temple.

Nearby is a boulder on which the edicts of this Maurya ruler are inscribed; these comprise the earliest historical records in Orissa. The upper part of the rock is sculpted naturalistically as the head, trunk and front legs of an elephant. This animal has been interpreted as a symbol of Buddha, whose religion Ashoka is known to have promoted in the region.

Shanti Stupa, 1970s

Erected by Japanese Buddhists, this concrete stupa commands extensive views over the surrounding countryside. The stupa copies early Deccan models, as exemplified by that at **Amaravati**. The hemisphere is raised on a high drum covered with carved panels, which illustrate scenes from the life of Buddha (above) and of Ashoka (beneath). Projecting shrines on four sides house large stone sculptures of the Master meditating (east), preaching (south) and dying (west); these are executed in the manner of the Gupta **Sarnath** style. At the top of the stupa is a box-like compartment defined by a high wall with railing motifs.

GAUHATI

The ancient importance of this town, which was the capital of the 16th–17th-century Koch rulers of western Assam, is seen in the fortifications and gateways which still stand within the town. There are several later Hindu brick temples; one dedicated to the Navagrahas is located on a low hill to the east. An important pilgrimage shrine is situated on the summit of Kamakhya hill, 3 km (2 miles) south-west of the town.

State Museum

The earliest objects exhibited here are stone and copper-plate inscriptions dating from the 5th–7th centuries. Among the sculptures from various sites in Assam are images of Vishnu from Barpeta (1486) and of Surya from Ambari; both date from the 11th–12th century and are influenced by Pala traditions. Terracotta plaques from Gauhati include an 11th-century depiction of a dancing maiden (3152). Various 18th-century moulded bricks similar to those from Bengal are also displayed, such as the figure of a warrior from Goalpara (3014.52).

KAMAKHYA HILL

Kamakhya Temple,
renovated 1565 and later

Commemorating the spot where a portion of Sati's dismembered body fell to

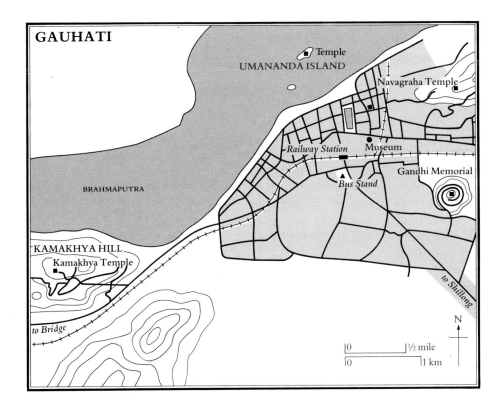

GAUHATI

Temple
UMANANDA ISLAND

Navagraha Temple

Railway Station   Museum

Gandhi Memorial

Bus Stand

BRAHMAPUTRA

KAMAKHYA HILL
Kamakhya Temple

to Shillong

to Bridge

N

| 0 | | ½ mile |
| 0 | | 1 km |

earth, this sanctuary enshrines a yoni of Devi. Of the original stone building renovated by the Koch ruler Nara Narayana only the moulded basement survives; the brick structure, including the tower, is recent.

The temple has a long low elevation divided into a sanctuary and three mandapas, each with a differently shaped roof. Octagonal and sixteen-sided dome-like towers rise over the sanctuary and adjoining mandapa. These towers are curved brick constructions, divided into horizontal layers by mouldings and capped by tiers of pot-like finials. One of the mandapas has a hut-like roof with curved cornices; the outermost apsidal-ended mandapa has a long low roof. Stone panels set into the unadorned brick walls of the sanctuary are carved with vigorously posed musicians and guardian figures.

GAYA

This town was closely associated with Buddhism, being merely 10 km (6 miles) north of **Bodhgaya**; but at least since the 10th century, Gaya has been an important Hindu religious centre. Pilgrims visit the temples of the town to relieve the souls of their ancestors by performing funeral rites. Offerings of special cakes and gifts are made to priests, who receive pilgrims on a spacious terrace shaded by a banyan tree.

Though no monument at Gaya predates the 18th century, many 9th–10th-century Pala sculptures are scattered about the town, and incorporated into later shrines and river ghats. Votive inscriptions are inserted into pavements and walls. Dharmashalas in the town accommodate the many pilgrims.

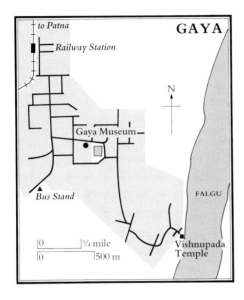

Vishnupada Temple, 1787

Erected by Ahalya Bhai, the widow of one of the **Indore** rulers, this temple consists of a towered sanctuary with multiple clustered elements and an adjoining columned mandapa roofed with a dome. In a subsidiary mandapa is an exposed rock carved with Vishnu's footprints (pada) set within a silver basin. This is the chief object of worship within the temple and, indeed, in the whole town. Only Hindus may enter the temple.

Gaya Museum

Pala stone sculptures from Gaya and nearby sites, in particular **Bodhgaya**, are exhibited here.

GHURISA

Raghunatha Temple, 1633

This early example of a Bengali hut-styled Hindu temple consists of a single domed chamber roofed with a pyramidal vault. Each wall is capped with a characteristic curved cornice. Terracotta sculptures on the principal façade depict Vishnu's incarnations, Lakshmi, Rama fighting Ravana (panels around the entrance), archers, erotic couples (panel over arched doorway) and fighting figures (corner panels).

Gopala Lakshmi Temple,
19th century

This Hindu temple has horizontal neo-classical mouldings instead of the more usual curved cornices; nine turrets on two levels create the pyramidal roof scheme. Plaster panels depict Vishnu on the lotus emerging from Brahma's navel (over the arched entrance) and Kali garlanded with skulls (side panel). The figures on the basement friezes are dressed in European clothes and hats.

HIRAPUR

Chaunsath Yogini Temple,
11th century

This unusual Hindu sanctuary consists of a small circular court defined by peripheral walls, with an entrance on the east and a reconstructed square pavilion in the middle. Small sculptures of yoginis are inserted into the nine niches on the outer face of the wall and almost continuously on the inner face. These goddesses are depicted in a variety of standing or dancing postures; they are identified by the weapons and emblems they hold, and by the animals, birds and even decapitated heads on which they stand. Though damaged, the delicate modelling and serene expressions of these figures are still evident. Crudely fashioned skeletal images flank the entrance. Immediately in front of the temple (east) is a rectangular platform.

Set up beside a small Shiva shrine nearby is a damaged chlorite panel depicting Krishna with attendant gopis.

JAMUI

3 km (2 miles) south of this town is the site of Indapaigarh; the extensive remains of a 7th-century Buddhist monastery with a stupa in the middle have been discovered here. The stone sculptures that were found, mostly depicting seated Buddha figures, are now housed in the Archaeological Museum at Jamui.

KABILASPUR

Dharmaraja Temple, 1643

This Hindu temple has a soaring curvilinear stone tower with shallow projections in the middle of each side and a pot finial above. Unusually, there is a complete absence of ornament.

KALNA

Numerous Hindu monuments from the 18th–19th centuries stand in this town, which was once an important centre for the local rulers of Burdwan. In the middle of Kalna is the palace compound, surrounded by walls with imposing neoclassical gateways.

Lalji Temple, 1739

This temple has twenty-five pinnacles arranged on three levels around a central structure. The domed sanctuary is flanked by vaulted chambers and entered through a porch with a curved roof. The front (south) façade is completely covered with terracotta plaques; over the arched entrances these illustrate Ramayana episodes.

Krishna Chandra Temple, 1752

Of the same type as the Lalji temple, this example has better-preserved terracotta

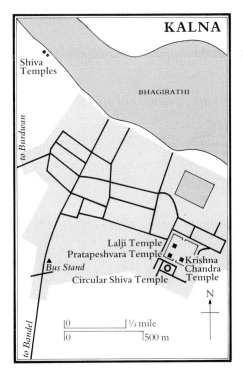

ornamentation. This includes two friezes of Krishna reliefs on the basement.

Shiva Temples, 1753

Each of this pair of identical temples has a double-vaulted roof with curved cornices. Terracotta plaques around the triple-arched entrances include figurative panels and scrollwork; courtly scenes are illustrated on the basement.

Shiva Temple, 1809

This unusual temple consists of 108 small shrines, each with a double-vaulted roof, arranged in two concentric rows.

Pratapeshvara Temple, 1849

This temple has a single square chamber above which rises a curved tower with horizontal mouldings. Each façade is richly embellished with delicately modelled terracotta plaques. The most frequently depicted themes are Ramayana episodes, Krishna with the gopis and musicians, dancers and attendant women.

KHANDAGIRI AND UDAYAGIRI

In the sandstone outcrops of the twin hills of Khandagiri and Udayagiri, 6 km (4 miles) west of **Bhubaneshwar**, is an important series of Jain cave temples. These are datable to the 1st century BC, a period when coastal Orissa was ruled by kings of the Chedi dynasty. The rock-cut sanctuaries provide the earliest evidence of artistic traditions in the region. The later reworking of several caves and the 19th-century temple here testify to the survival of Jainism in the region.

There are thirty-five excavated monuments on the two hills. Some are natural caverns, enlarged and suitably fashioned by artificial cutting; others are single cells only or have verandahs. Several larger examples consist of a number of cells grouped around an open court and sheltered by colonnades. Throughout, the caves are massive and austere. Columns have square or octagonal shafts and curved brackets. Doorways are framed by pilasters and headed with arches between which are figural friezes and railing reliefs.

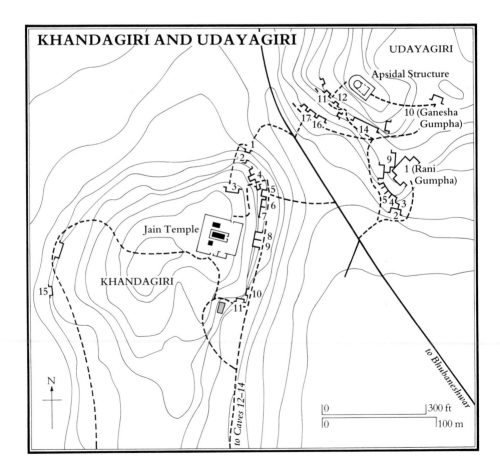

KHANDAGIRI

Caves 1 and 2, 1st century BC

The doorways that lead into the cells of these caves have pilasters and relief arches decorated with foliation. Between the arches there is a railing motif (Cave 1), or the representation of a vaulted roof form with pinnacles (Cave 2). The inner brackets are carved with a dancer, musician and devotee, as well as foliation. Guardian figures flank the verandah of Cave 1.

Cave 3, Ananta Gumpha,
1st century BC

The verandah of this cave has part-octagonal columns and curved brackets adorned with ganas and other figures. Above the four doorways, now partly collapsed, are arches in relief containing sculptural compositions: these represent (left to right) elephants, Surya in his chariot, Lakshmi bathed by elephants and worship of a sacred tree. The arches themselves are adorned with flowers, figures fighting with animals and birds; there are snakes with raised triple cobra hoods at either side. Between the arches are flying figures.

Caves 7 and 8, mostly 11th century

These adjoining caves were later converted into sanctuaries with figural carvings. Tirthankaras and associated goddesses are carved on to the rear and side walls.

Cave 9, 15th century

Remodelled in later times as a sanctuary, this cave contains twenty-four naked Tirthankara figures of crude workmanship. Three small chlorite panels are installed at the rear of the chamber. These 11th–12th-century sculptures depict Rishabhanatha surrounded by the Navagrahas.

Caves 10 and 11, 11th century

Three rock-cut shelters (collapsed in Cave 10) have images of Tirthankaras carved on to their rear walls. There are figures of Rishabhanatha and Neminatha in Cave 10.

Jain temple, 19th century

At the summit of Khandagiri, a temple in the traditional Orissan style is built upon the remains of an ancient terrace. During the festivals which are held here in February and August, some of the nearby caves may be closed.

UDAYAGIRI

Cave 1, Rani Gumpha,
1st century BC

This is the largest and most elaborate cave residence of the series. Numerous small cells excavated on two levels around three sides of a large court are sheltered by colonnades (collapsed, lower storey). The cell doorways are embellished with pilasters crowned by animals on the capitals. On the walls flanking the end pilasters are guardian figures, some in foreign dress (upper storey, right wing). The relief arches over the doorways have lotus ornament; they are connected by a railing frieze. On either side of the arches are carved panels. On the lower storey these represent pious couples and musicians and dancers (side wings), and scenes of nature with birds and animals (corner rooms). On the better-preserved upper storey there are episodes from an unidentified narrative: these depict (left to right) an attendant with a tray; elephants before a man with a club; an attendant woman; a fight between a man and a woman; the abduction of a woman; a riderless horse sheltered by a parasol; a hunter aiming at a winged deer; a hunter with a woman in a tree; and a seated woman with female attendants.

Caves 3, 4 and 5, 1st century BC

Elephants carved in relief flank the arch over the entrance to Cave 3. In the adjoining two-storey Cave 4 are sculptures of elephants, lions and pairs of winged animals on column brackets (upper storey). Cave 5, which is also two-storeyed, is linked with the upper cell of Cave 4. Here, figures are carved on the end pilasters. Above the doorways to the two cells are arches within which there is a depiction of a sacred tree surrounded by a railing.

Cave 9, 1st century BC

This complex of cells is arranged on two storeys. On the lower level, armed guardians (worn) are carved on to the end pilasters of the verandah. The doorways within are surmounted by relief arches, between which is a scene (damaged) with royal figures worshipping at a shrine. The cave is distinguished by its donative inscriptions of the Chedi rulers.

Cave 10, Ganesha Gumpha,
1st century BC

This is named after the image of Ganesha carved at a later date on to the rear wall of the right cell. In front of the cave are two detached monolithic elephants lifting branches with their trunks. The cave itself consists of two low-roofed cells with four doorways and a verandah. A guardian holding a spear is carved on to the left pilaster; the other pilasters have male or female figures. Each doorway is surmounted by relief arches between which are depictions of a fight, an abduction and an elopement (similar to the scenes in Cave 1).

Apsidal Structure, 1st century BC

The remains of this Jain edifice are located at the top of the hill. They consist of stone foundations and floor slabs of a circular chamber contained within an apsidal hall.

Post holes indicate a vanished wooden structure.

Cave 12, Bagh Gumpha,
1st century BC

The entrance to this cave is shaped into the semblance of the head of an open-mouthed tiger.

Cave 14, 1st century BC

The inscription on this rocky overhang gives information about one of the Chedi rulers.

KHICHING

This site was a flourishing Buddhist settlement in the 10th–11th-century Somavamshi era. Excavations here have partially exposed the remains of a square brick monastery, with cells on four sides of a court. There are also several later Hindu sanctuaries, but none preserves its original superstructure. One example has a central shrine surrounded by eight subsidiary chambers raised on a terrace.

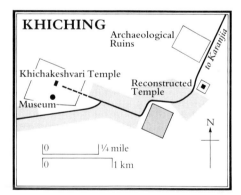

Khichakeshvari Temple,
modern reconstruction

This temple with a traditional Orissan tower incorporates several 9th–10th-century stone fragments. These include ornamental panels and figurative sculptures, such as naga deities, Ganga and Yamuna figures, dancing Ganesha and Durga. A ten-armed Chamunda image is enshrined within the sanctuary.

Museum

Stone Buddhist images and doorway fragments discovered in the excavations are assembled here; terracotta plaques are also on display. Sculptures from dismantled shrines at other sites have also been collected. These include a seated Buddha with a tree above the head, from Itamunda.

KONARAK

Though the great Surya sanctuary on the Bay of Bengal is now abandoned, thousands of pilgrims come to bathe here at the spring festival when the birth of the Hindu sun god is celebrated. For the remainder of the year the ruined monument stands in majestic solitude.

Surya Temple, 13th century

The climax of the Orissan series, this temple was constructed by the Eastern Ganga king Narasimha (*c.* 1238–64). This ruler seems to have taken a personal interest in the monument, which possibly served as a memorial to his successful campaign against the Muslim armies. Conceived as a colossal chariot of the sun god, drawn on twelve pairs of wheels by a team of seven horses, this is one of the most magnificent examples of Hindu sacred architecture. The temple is ruined and only partly reconstructed; even so, the sculpted terrace and walls (in coarsely grained khondalite) are among the masterpieces of Hindu art. (Numerous carved panels from the monument are housed in the Archaeological Museum; others have been removed to the Indian Museum, **Calcutta**, and the National Museum, **New Delhi**.)

The temple stands in a rectangular compound with gateways (roofless) on the east and south. In front (east) of the temple is a detached dance hall; south of

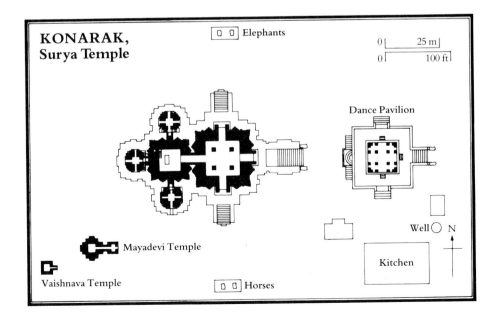

KONARAK, Surya Temple

Elephants

0 — 25 m
0 — 100 ft

Dance Pavilion

Mayadevi Temple

Vaishnava Temple

Well ○ N

Kitchen

Horses

this is the kitchen. In the south-west corner of the complex are two small shrines.

The sanctuary and mandapa of the main temple are raised on a broad terrace; this is reached by three flights of steps on the north, south and east. Twelve wheels, possibly symbolizing the twelve months, are carved against the sides of the terrace and also on both sides of the front (east) staircase. Positioned against the staircase are caparisoned galloping horses in full relief; one example is completely preserved on the south side. The sides of the terrace have continuous friezes at the bottom and top. Between these are two tiers of panels separated by deeply cut basement mouldings and multi-faceted pilasters fashioned like miniature shrines. The bottom frieze depicts elephants in their forest setting; the animals uproot trees and branches, give birth, fondle their mates and young ones and are captured by hunters. On the bottom and top friezes are marches and processions with elephants, horses and even camels; hunting of boar, deer and lions; and caravans, contests and duels. Lotus ornament and scrollwork cover many of the mouldings that surround the sculpted panels. Here are voluptuous maidens in alluring postures: they stand beneath a tree; clutch at branches; play on musical instruments; caress a child or pet bird; or attend to their toilet. Amorous couples in a variety of sexual embraces, seated princes, teachers with pupils, standing ascetics, hunters, warriors and soldiers also appear. Other recurring themes are rampant mythical beasts, as well as nagas and naginis, each with a human bust, a multi-hooded canopy and a serpent's tail. The chariot wheels are magnificently carved. The hubs and spokes have medallions with miniature deities, erotic and amorous figures, courtiers and hunters. Petalled friezes and scrollwork surround the medallions and cover the circular rims.

Little remains of the sanctuary and its tower other than the lower parts of the walls and the mouldings of their basement. The central niches house large green chlorite images of Surya standing in the chariot (south and west) or riding on a spirited horse (north). The precision of the carved details and the subtle facial expression of the god are particularly striking. Subsidiary figures include Aruna the charioteer, two armed attendants, a royal donor and a family priest beneath; goddesses dispelling darkness at the side; and flying celestials above. In front of these niches are porches reached by double flights of steps, and subsidiary shrines elevated on carved basements, each with three entrances (only the south shrine is partly preserved). Within the principal sanctuary (reached by a descending flight of steps on the west) is an ornate chlorite pedestal, which once supported the image of the presiding deity (vanished). The central niche of this pedestal is carved with a kneeling king, evidently the temple donor, conferring with priests.

The outer walls of the adjoining square mandapa are only incompletely preserved and have been much rebuilt. Large rearing beasts and amorous couples in two tiers are positioned in the niches and recesses. There are also portions of the high and elaborate basement. In the middle of three sides are impressive doorways (preserved fully only on the east, partly on the north), now blocked up. These are carved in chlorite with remarkable detail, especially the bands of foliation, scrollwork, entwined serpents and miniature amorous couples (on the jambs), as well as the seated Navagrahas, musicians and flying celestials (on the lintels). The pyramidal roof rises in three storeys, each with horizontal mouldings. The edges of these mouldings (projecting outwards from the middle of each side) are carved with friezes similar to those on the terrace beneath; upturned medallions at the corners and at other points are filled with miniature animals. In the two intermediate spaces between the storeys are large free-standing female dancers and

musicians; these figures are fully modelled and sensually posed. Multi-headed
images of Bhairava are positioned on the
east side. Crouching beasts surround the
immense amalaka that forms the capping
piece of the roof and which rises no less
than 38·4 m (126 ft) above the ground; no
finial is preserved.

Each of the three staircases leading up
to the mandapa is guarded by a pair of
animals: thus, rearing lions on crouching
elephants (east), richly decorated and
harnessed elephants (north) and richly
caparisoned stallions with armed
attendants (south). The animals from the
north and south staircases have been
installed on new pedestals a short distance
away from their original locations (facing
the staircases). In front of the east staircase
was a tall free-standing chlorite column
(now removed to the main gate of the
Jagannatha temple at **Puri**).

Of the square dance pavilion immediately east of the temple, only the terrace
and lower walls still stand. The terrace
on which the pavilion is elevated is
approached by flights of steps on four
sides. The front (east) steps are flanked by
fierce lion-like beasts rearing over kneeling elephants that firmly hold prostrate
figures in their trunks. The walls of the
terrace are almost completely covered
with sculptures. These are arranged in
three tiers, each panel surmounted by a
foliated arched motif; a miniature frieze
adorns the top. Many of the figures depicted here are connected with music,
such as male and female drummers and
other musicians, all in dance postures;
others are the familiar maidens and erotic
couples. Some panels in the corner pilasters depict the seated Dikpalas. Of interest are the large water spouts fashioned as
open-mouthed beasts. Similar sculptural
themes are found on the basement, walls
and piers of the pavilion itself. No roof or
superstructure is preserved. (A lotus panel
in the Archaeological Museum may have
formed the crowning piece of the ceiling.)

In the south-west corner of the compound is the ruined Mayadevi temple, of
which only the lower portions of the sanctuary and porch walls are preserved. Miniature figures are carved in the niches and
on the mouldings of the basement, which
is exuberantly decorated with scrollwork.
Maidens stand beneath branches; naginis
are coiled around part-circular pilasters.
Chlorite images of Surya, indicating the
original dedication of the temple, are
positioned in the exterior niches of the
sanctuary; the god rides on horseback
(north) or stands stiffly (south, now headless). On the north side are two spouts
fashioned as open-mouthed makaras.

South-west of the last temple is a
dilapidated brick shrine. Only the plan of
the sanctuary and porch can be made out.
Part of the stone sanctuary doorway with
river goddess carved on to the jambs still
stands.

Among the other subsidiary structures
is a kitchen, of which only the stone
column stumps are preserved. Several
other stone basements nearby indicate
pavilions for ceremonial occasions.

On the north and south edges of the
courtyard are pairs of large free-standing
animal sculptures: horses led by warriors
rear over fallen figures with shields on the
south side and elephants on the north side.
There are also several other overturned
and broken animal sculptures.

Archaeological Museum

All of the pieces exhibited here come from
the 13th-century Surya temple. These
include finely carved chlorite panels, such
as Varaha (220), Trivikrama (221), Agni
(171), Surya (210) and other deities; also a
scene depicting the royal patron with
various cult icons (174). Among the
khondalite images are Bhairava riding on
a dog (189), female musicians (75, 450), an
amorous couple (143) and several large
rearing beasts (84, 143). Architectural
fragments carved with friezes of animals,
birds and foliation are also displayed.

KRISHNANAGAR

Radha Vallabha Temple,
early 17th century

The central chamber of this Hindu brick temple is approached through a triple-arched entrance. Above the walls is a curved cornice; an upper chamber is capped with a pyramidal roof. The terracotta decoration is restricted to medallions, lotus ornament, scrollwork and fringes of leaves; this lack of figural imagery indicates the influence of Muslim traditions.

KURKIHAR

This ancient Buddhist site is marked by extensive mounds and an abundance of votive stupas. Numerous sculptural and architectural fragments are collected in the compound of a modern temple. The site is celebrated for the fine bronze figures dating from the 9th–11th-century Pala period. These have been removed to the **Patna** Museum.

LALITAGIRI

Two adjacent hills at this site preserve the remains of extensive Buddhist structures dating from the 9th–10th centuries. These are closely linked with contemporary remains at **Ratnagiri** and **Udayagiri**.

At the top of the Parabhadi hill is a terraced stone platform and a damaged sculpture of Padmapani. About 15 m (49 ft) below is a long terrace cut out of the hill, where there are remnants of a shrine with a gallery of life-size Bodhisattva figures. Similar but better-preserved sculptures are incorporated into the modern Hindu temple that is built over an earlier Buddhist sanctuary. Other images are housed in a small site museum.

Dilapidated structures, including brick mounds and the remains of an ancient monastery, still stand on the side and summit of nearby Landa hill. Near the top of this hill, Buddhist images and a finely carved doorway have been inserted into a modern structure.

LAURIYA NANDANGARH

The twin sites of Lauriya and Nandangarh are dotted with mounds, which represent the collapsed and overgrown remains of brick-faced earthen stupas. Excavations here have recovered figurines, coins, tablets and other artefacts dating from the 3rd century BC to the 6th–7th centuries AD.

Column, 3rd century BC

This polished sandstone column is typical of the Maurya series; its shaft is incised with seven edicts of the emperor Ashoka. A lion sits on top of the fluted bell-shaped capital.

Stupa, 4th–5th century

Only the stepped brick base and lower portion of the circular drum of this colossal structure, more than 150 m (490 ft) across, are preserved. The undecorated base rises in four receding terraces, each with angled projections, to create a complex polygonal plan. Three processional paths are provided at different levels. Within the dilapidated core is a small complete stupa 4 m (13 ft) high.

MUKHALINGAM

Though located in Andhra Pradesh, the Hindu temples at this site form part of the history of Orissan architecture. Mukhalingam was the first capital of the Eastern Ganga rulers, who were also the patrons of later temples at **Puri** and **Konarak**.

Madhukeshvara Temple,
8th century

This is one of the best-preserved examples of the early Orissan style. The temple consists of a sanctuary and a mandapa with subsidiary shrines built into the four corners. Between these shrines are sculpture panels set into niches with tower-like pediments. Among the numerous icons are finely carved images of dancing Shiva and Narasimha (south). The four shrines are roofed with curved towers with horizontal divisions; at the summits are amalakas. The large sanctuary tower is simplified in many of its details. The projection on the front (east) face has arch-like niches framing twin images of Shiva as the ascetic (above) and the dancer (below). The doorways (east and south) have their jambs carved with guardian figures, maidens and amorous couples, all set in luxuriant foliation. Over the east doorway are scenes of the Krishna story, as well as miniature friezes of battles with soldiers and elephants. The south doorway is surmounted by images of Shiva; the god dances with the skin of the elephant demons (above) or spears Andhaka (below).

The temple stands within a rectangular courtyard. Corner shrines imitate those of the mandapa; the detailed ornamentation of the towers is finely executed, particularly in the panels over the doorways. Against the north enclosure wall, a sculptured naga deity holds a pot for water to flow into a small basin. In the middle of the east side of the enclosure is a gateway; this has fine carvings on the door jambs, especially of ascetics. The gateway has a vaulted roof divided into horizontal tiers and is capped with three ribbed finials.

Bhimeshvara Temple, 8th century

This is almost identical to the Madhu-keshvara temple, with which it is contemporary, but is not so well preserved. Much of the original detail has been lost, except for the delicately worked doorways.

Someshvara Temple,
early 10th century

The curved tower of this single sanctuary is treated with narrow horizontal bands. The principal (west) doorway has panels of scrollwork with the Navagrahas and a seated Lakshmi figure over the entrance. Three niches on each side house an important series of images; thus (clockwise from the left jamb of the entrance), Yamuna, Shiva, Durga, Shiva, Harihara, Karttikeya, Ardhanarishvara, Lakulisha, Ganesha, Shiva and Ganga.

MUNDESVARI

Shiva Temple, 636

This unusual octagonal Hindu temple is built at the summit of a steep hill. The building is now dilapidated; parts of the outer walls still stand, but no tower has survived. The walls are elevated on a high basement embellished with garlands and bells; niches are capped with elaborate pediments. No sculptures are preserved (many have been removed to the **Patna** Museum). The pierced stone window in the middle of the east side and the doorways on the other three sides are surrounded by miniature figures of guardians, musicians and dancers set in bands of foliation. The octagonal interior is massive and unadorned, except for a quadruple-faced linga.

Lying all around are architectural fragments. Among these is a short column with deities carved at the base.

NALANDA

10 km (6 miles) north of **Rajgir** is the celebrated monastic establishment of Nalanda. This site was visited by both Buddha and Mahavira; Ashoka, the Maurya emperor, also came here to worship at the sanctuary of Shariputra, the disciple of Buddha. Despite such ancient traditions, however, no remains at this site are earlier than the 5th-century Gupta period. But by the 7th century Nalanda had become the outstanding centre of Mahayana Buddhist learning, a famous university with shrines and monasteries filled with scholars from many parts of Asia. The Chinese pilgrims Hiuen Tsang and I-Tsing studied at Nalanda and left accounts of the university and its intellectual life in the 7th century. During the long-lived Pala dynasty, Nalanda continued to be the principal Buddhist institution in eastern India. By the 12th–13th centuries, as Buddhism declined in the region and Muslim influence increased, Nalanda fell into disuse and was eventually abandoned.

The site has a planned layout with a row of nine Buddhist monasteries facing four temples. The brick foundations and lower walls of these structures, as well as of several others, are clearly exposed. The temples are solid square buildings on two levels, the central sanctuaries raised up and approached by steps. The outer elevations of both storeys have pilasters and niches containing stucco images. Temples 2 and 3 preserve sculptural portions on their walls. The monasteries are laid out according to a standard scheme. Each has a central rectangular court surrounded by a verandah off which open small cells. The cell in the middle of the rear (east) wall is enlarged so as to serve as a shrine. The entrance in the middle of the west side is flanked by two guard-rooms.

During the Pala period, Nalanda was one of the most important art centres in eastern India; numerous stone and metal images were produced here, as well as

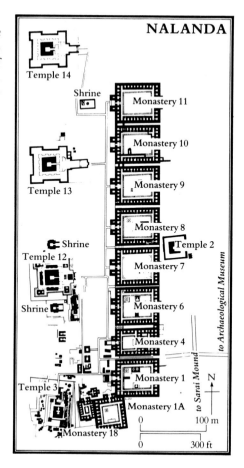

NALANDA

Temple 14
Shrine
Monastery 11
Monastery 10
Monastery 9
Monastery 8
Shrine
Temple 12
Temple 2
Monastery 7
Shrine
Monastery 6
Temple 13
Monastery 4
Monastery 1
Temple 3
Monastery 1A
Monastery 18
to Archaeological Museum
to Sarai Mound
N
0   100 m
0   300 ft

countless miniature votive plaques in terracotta. Many sculptures are displayed in the Archaeological Museum; others have been removed to the Indian Museum, **Calcutta**, the National Museum, **New Delhi**, and the **Patna** Museum.

Temple 2, 7th century

Only the basement of this structure still stands. This is of interest because of the numerous panels set between the decorated pilasters. The panels are carved with depictions of Rama, Sita and other divinities, as well as of maidens, dancers, musicians, fighters, amorous couples, birds, lions and mythic beasts.

Temple 3, 6th century and later

This ruined temple is the largest and highest structure at Nalanda, rising more than 31 m (100 ft) high. It consists of a central stupa elevated on a high basement that is approached by a flight of steps on the north; smaller stupas are built at the four corners. The temple stands in the middle of a court surrounded by small votive stupas. No less than seven renovations of the structure took place. The fifth phase is datable to the 6th-century Gupta period, while the last two phases belong to the 11th–12th centuries.

Subsidiary stupas, especially that on the north-east corner, give a good idea of the overall conception of the monument. Here, pilastered walls in three diminishing tiers support the octagonal base of the stupa. Set into the walls are plaster figures, especially standing Bodhisattvas (beneath) and seated Buddhas (arched niches above). Elsewhere, parts of the ornamented basement of the central stupa and its staircase are preserved; a standing Avalokiteshvara figure survives on the staircase wall.

Temple 12,
7th century and later

This temple represents two different phases of construction, a later building having been erected directly upon the ruins of an earlier one. The exterior was adorned with niches, a few of which are still preserved together with their stucco images. In front are votive stupas of different sizes.

Immediately north and south of the temple are brick shrines, each containing traces of Buddha figures in plaster-covered brickwork.

Sarai Mound, 7th century

Near the main entrance to the excavated area are the recently revealed remains of a brick temple with finely worked ornamentation. Of particular interest are the traces of paintings on the basement; these depict elephants, horses and seated maidens. They may be later in date than the temple itself.

Archaeological Museum

Almost all the sculptures exhibited here were discovered at the site. A fine seated naga deity (4) dates from the 7th century; most of the other examples are from the 8th–10th century Pala period. Among the many Buddhist and Jain sculptures in polished basalt are a standing Lokanatha figure (6) and Avalokiteshvara (16). In sandstone there is a panel of Avalokiteshvara with attendants (13102) and a seated Buddha (59). Miniature shrines and architectural fragments are also displayed, including friezes of gandharvas and kinnaras in foliation (10777, 10778).

Among the delicately modelled Pala bronzes are several fine standing Buddha images, their hands held out in protection (177, 10750), a seated Buddha figure (10752) and a standing Tara (11157). There are also miniature bronze stupas, as well as an intricately modelled frame for an image, now lost.

PATNA

As Patilaputra, ancient Patna was an important centre of the Magadha kingdom that flourished during Buddha's lifetime. In the 4th–5th centuries BC the town served as the capital of the Maurya rulers, and was even described by Megasthenes, a Greek envoy to India. Excavations within the modern town indicate continuous occupation up to the Gupta period. Among the artefacts discovered were pottery fragments, iron implements, terracotta figurines, coins and seals.

Investigations at two sites have revealed traces of Maurya timber structures. The wooden footings and floor of a columned reception hall were discovered at Kumrahar; here too there were traces of

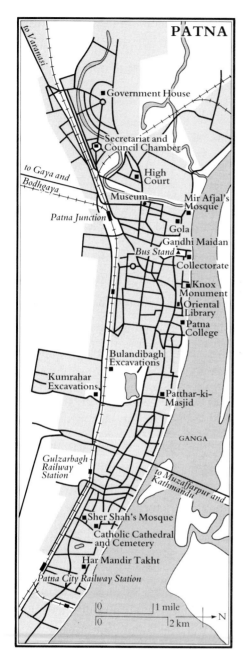

PATNA

to Varanasi

Government House

Secretariat and
Council Chamber

to Gaya and
Bodhgaya

High
Court

Museum

Mir Afjal's
Mosque

Patna Junction

Gola

Gandhi Maidan

Bus Stand

Collectorate

Knox
Monument

Oriental
Library

Patna
College

Bulandibagh
Excavations

Kumrahar
Excavations

Patthar-ki-
Masjid

GANGA

Gulzarbagh
Railway
Station

to Muzaffarpur and
Kathmandu

Sher Shah's Mosque

Catholic Cathedral
and Cemetery

Har Mandir Takht

Patna City Railway Station

0   1 mile

0   2 km   N

(For the city and its British monuments
see Volume II.)

Museum

This collection houses an important early
sculpture, the female attendant holding
a fly-whisk, found at Didarganj, a site
within modern Patna (134). This polished
sandstone figure is sometimes dated to the
3rd century BC. So too is the capital
decorated with Persian foliate ornament
(187).

Several heads of Jain saviours belong to
the 2nd–3rd-century Kushana period.
Contemporary sculptures from the Gandhara region (north-western Pakistan) are
also displayed. These include standing
Bodhisattvas, detached heads and narrative panels, such as that of Buddha's birth
(6335). Later art is represented by a jamb
fragment of a maiden holding a parrot
from Sakrigali (10346), as well as damaged figures and architectural pieces from
Mundesvari.

Pala sculpture in Bihar is represented
by 9th–11th-century Buddhist figures;
for example, standing Manjushri from
Bodhgaya (115), Avalokiteshvara from
Kurkihar (11086) and a seated Buddha
from Vishnupur (1681). Hindu sculptures
include a standing Vishnu figure (10609)
and dancing Ganesha (10611), both from
Eksari. Contemporary pieces from Orissa
are also displayed, especially a large standing Bodhisattva panel from **Udayagiri**
(6489) and a seated Tara (3745).

A set of remarkable Pala bronzes from
Kurkihar and **Nalanda** is also displayed.
Among the Buddhist sculptures from the
former site are many 9th-century standing and seated Buddhas and Bodhisattvas,
some with elaborate thrones and haloes,
others with crowns. (Among the finest
examples are 9588, 9591, 9593, 9597,
9636, 9723, 9788 and 9789.) These are all
delicately modelled and inlaid with silver.
From the 10th–12th centuries, also from
Kurkihar, are large Buddha figures
(9589, 9590), a seated Tara image (9795,

a monastic establishment and an apsidal
structure. At Bulandibagh, a unique
wooden passageway, more than 75 m
(246 ft) long, may have formed part of the
defence system.

9811) and Lokanatha (9786); there is even a Hindu deity, Balarama (9791). Several contemporary Buddhist figures from **Nalanda** are also shown (8639, 10542, for instance). Of interest are the miniature bronze stupas, complete with tiers of umbrellas.

Several 13th-century Buddha figures from **Nagapattinam** are among the bronzes from southern India.

PEMAYANGTSE

Supposedly the oldest monastic establishment in Sikkim, this complex is magnificently sited at the top of a long ridge with distant views of the Kanchenjunga range. The monastery is the headquarters of the Nyingmapa sect of Tibetan Buddhism and an important centre for Mahayana teachings. It is known through the region for its annual festival at which masked dances take place. A huge embroidered thangka is displayed on the last day of the ceremonies.

The complex consists of a main prayer hall surrounded by a school, a kitchen and residences. The architecture of the buildings is typical of the eastern Himalayas, with painted masonry walls overhung by steeply gabled roofs; the doorways and windows are surrounded by brightly coloured bands. Though the monastery dates back to 1705, if not earlier, the prayer hall has been extensively renovated in recent years. It is now freshly painted, the woodwork has been refashioned and the timber roof replaced with metal sheets. The prayer hall consists of a large chamber (dukhang) at the lower level, with smaller chambers above. The walls are covered with murals, some of which may be more than a century old, depicting the usual Mahayana divinities. The chief object of interest is a 4-m-high (13 ft) wooden model of the heavenly abode of Guru Rimpoche, one of the monastery's spiritual founders; this is housed in the attic chamber.

PURI

This is one of the holiest cities for Hindus, the principal centre for the cult of Jagannatha, another name for Krishna, whose temple is located here. Each June–July there is a festival in which images of Jagannatha, his brother (Balabhadra) and sister (Subhadra) are transported through the town in chariots. More than one hundred thousand pilgrims come to witness this event, the largest of its kind in India. Three chariots are specially constructed for the occasion. These convey the trio of deities from the principal temple along the main road to the Gundicha temple, where they reside for at least one week before being returned. The largest chariot is 14 m (46 ft) high and has sixteen carved wooden wheels. The superstructure, which is in the form of a curved temple tower, is created out of cloth draped over a wooden frame. Devotees from neighbouring villages are recruited to pull the chariots through the crowds. It is generally believed that anyone who touches or even views the effigy of Jagannatha will be freed from sin. The many stories of fanatics who deliberately throw themselves beneath the wheels of the chariot are probably responsible for the notoriety of the Jagannatha cult outside India. (Even the name of the deity has been anglicized into 'juggernaut' to designate any large heavy vehicle.)

In order to accommodate the great number of pilgrims, Puri is dotted with rest-houses and monasteries. Numerous holy men live here, and the city is always filled with students and pilgrims. An ancient pottery industry provides the ritual vessels required by devotees. Locally produced souvenir paintings record the triad of sacred images, as well as pictures of the temple and town. (For the British monuments of Puri see Volume II.)

The cult of Jagannatha has a complex history. In the early 12th century, the

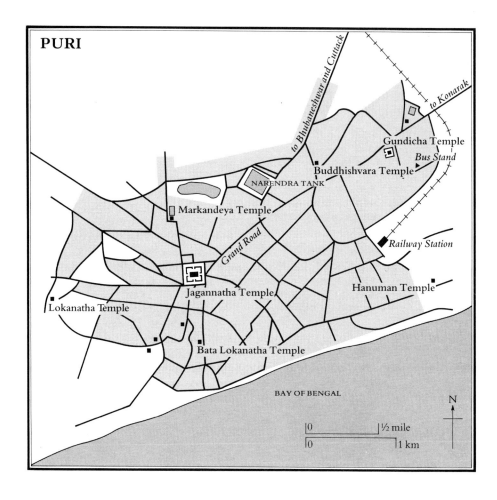

Eastern Ganga rulers annexed Orissa, choosing Puri on the coastal route as their new capital. Shortly after 1135, Ananta-varman Chodaganga founded a temple to Purushottama, an aspect of Vishnu. In the following century, Purushottama became the official state deity of the Eastern Ganga dynasty. Under the succeeding 15th-century Gajapati rulers, Purushottama was transformed into Jagannatha, the Universal Lord. This divinity was maintained through the centuries as a royal cult. Even today, the ruler of Puri is the servant of Jagannatha; at festival time he performs services for the god, such as the ritual sweeping of the chariots with a golden broom.

The image of Jagannatha is most unusual. The god has a flat face, large glowing eyes and a wide mouth; the body resembles a tapering tree trunk. This form indicates a non-Hindu, possibly tribal, origin. Originally, the image was linked with funerary rites; it served as a commemorative cult object for the royal founder and subsequent patrons of the temple. The wooden hieratic figures of Jagannatha, Balabhadra and Subhadra are renewed every few years in accordance with established ritual.

Jagannatha Temple,
12th century and later

Anantavarman Chodaganga obviously intended this to be the largest religious edifice within his kingdom. Modelled on the Lingaraja sanctuary at **Bhubaneshwar**, but on a grander scale, the monument is raised on a platform and consists of four structures surrounded by smaller shrines and two enclosure walls. (Only Hindus are permitted to enter.) The original temple consists of a towered sanctuary and a mandapa with a pyramidal roof; subsequent mandapas were added in the 13th and 15th centuries. The double enclosure wall dates from the Muslim period, when the temple had to be fortified.

Rising to a height of about 56·7 m (186 ft), the tower over the sanctuary is a powerful composition. It has bands in the middle of each side covered with 18th-century plaster illustrations of Vaishnava and Ramayana themes; these are flanked by miniature tower-like elements, one upon the other. The large amalaka capping piece has crouching figures and animals beneath; above is a pot finial, disc and flag, the last indicating the presence of the deity. Recently, the outer sanctuary walls have been cleaned of accumulated plaster layers to reveal a double series of sculpture niches. Each niche is surmounted by a tower-like pediment and separated one from the other by horizontal mouldings that reproduce those of the basement. The sculptures in the middle of each side are housed in two-storey shrines (13th-century additions); these depict Vamana (north), Narasimha (west) and Varaha (south). The deep recesses between the principal niches are occupied by large figures of fully modelled maidens.

The walls of the original mandapa are similar to those of the sanctuary, except for doorways in the middle of each side. The pyramidal roof has central projections with capping elements that reproduce the large example at the summit. The later mandapa additions, particularly the 15th-century structure (extreme east of the ensemble), maintain the highly elaborate wall treatment in which sculptural and architectural elements are integrated. Part-circular pilasters and horizontal mouldings divide the façade into numerous panels. Carvings display a distinctive royal iconography; the king is depicted enthroned, seated in a swing, standing, with female attendants in a boat, with a procession of soldiers, horses and elephants, carried in a palanquin and worshipping Durga. Images of Krishna, Rama, Shiva and the Dikpalas are included in the sculptural programme.

Within the compound is the 12th-century shrine of Lakshmi, the walls of which are covered with lotus ornament, miniature figures, coiled nagas and gracefully posed maidens. The windows, with their sculpted blocks, are surrounded by bands of scrollwork.

The main (east) gate of the complex has an elaborate doorway and a pyramidal roof capped with amalakas. In front is a multi-faceted column on a carved base with a figure of Aruna on top. This originally stood before the Surya temple at **Konarak**.

RAJGIR

This site still preserves the name of the ancient capital of the Magadha kingdom, Rajagriha. Buddha frequently visited this city, particularly during the reigns of Bimbisara and Ajatashatru (c. 543–459 BC), two early kings of the Magadha dynasty. From this centre the new religion spread throughout the region; after the death of the Master in the middle of the 5th century BC the first Buddhist Council was held here.

Rajgir is also sacred to the Jains. Mahavira, the last Tirthankara and a contemporary of Buddha, spent many rainy seasons here. Jain temples continue to be built in the vicinity.

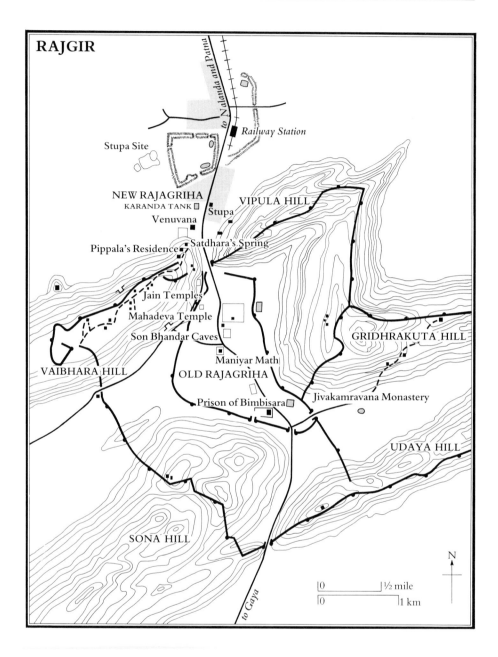

RAJGIR

to Nalanda and Patna

Railway Station

Stupa Site

NEW RAJAGRIHA

KARANDA TANK

Venuvana

Stupa

VIPULA HILL

Pippala's Residence

Satdhara's Spring

Jain Temples

Mahadeva Temple

Son Bhandar Caves

Maniyar Math

VAIBHARA HILL

OLD RAJAGRIHA

GRIDHRAKUTA HILL

Prison of Bimbisara

Jivakamravana Monastery

UDAYA HILL

SONA HILL

to Gaya

N

0   ½ mile
0   1 km

Situated in an extensive valley ringed by hills on all sides and entered through narrow passes, the original city is contained within a circuit of stone-faced earthen fortifications; gateways are located on the north and south. Another line of stone walls runs along the ridges of the surrounding hills. Beyond the valley to the north are the remains of the new city laid out by Ajatashatru. Both cities and the neighbouring hills are studded with localities identified with the life of Buddha. There are, however, only a few surviving monuments from this early era.

10 km (6 miles) further north are the remains of the Buddhist establishment at **Nalanda**.

OLD RAJAGRIHA

Excavations here have brought to light several structures; these include a square enclosure with stone walls identified as the prison of Bimbisara.

Gridhrakuta Hill

This was a favourite resort of Buddha; the two natural caves where the Master lived are reached by an ancient path. Higher up is a terrace with the remains of numerous brick and stone shrines of a later date.

Jivakamravana Monastery,
4th–3rd century BC

The remains of this Buddhist structure are located in the south-eastern corner of the valley. Recent excavations have revealed rubble foundations of four apsidal-ended halls and other long rooms. The plan of this complex does not conform to the usual monastic scheme; this may be due to its early date.

Son Bhandar Caves,
3rd century BC and later

The two rock-cut monuments may be compared with the contemporary sanctuaries in the **Barabar** hills, which also have side entrances and vaulted ceilings. The Jain images carved outside the lower cave possibly date from the 4th–5th century.

Maniyar Math, mostly 6th century

This Hindu shrine consists of a hollow cylindrical brick sanctuary set within an apsidal brick structure and is built over earlier stone buildings. The sanctuary, possibly dedicated to a naga deity, was enlarged several times. Niches were provided on its outer face to house stucco images of standing Vishnu, dancing Shiva and a graceful nagi figure, now mostly eroded.

NEW RAJAGRIHA

This site is partly occupied by the modern village of Rajgir; it is enclosed by walls laid out in an irregular square. In the southern wall there are the remains of a gateway. Excavations have yielded the remains of secular buildings. Outside the ramparts to the west is a large mound which marks a collapsed stupa. To the south is the Karanda tank and an excavated zone believed to be the site of Venuvana, the bamboo grove of Buddha. The foundations of nine brick stupas surrounded by a concrete floor have been discovered here.

VAIBHARA HILL

At the foot of this hill, south-west of New Rajagriha, are hot springs; the largest is known as Satdhara. Above the springs is a rectangular platform built of stone blocks, with small cells on all sides (note the later Muslim graves). Possibly a watchtower, this feature is generally known as Pippala's Residence. A rocky path leads to a group of natural caves in front of which the first Buddhist Council took place. At the summit of the hill are several modern Jain temples, which incorporate 8th-century architectural fragments and well-preserved sculptures. Another temple nearby is dedicated to Mahadeva. Several stone columns and brick walls from the 7th century are also found here.

RANIPUR JHARIAL

These two villages were flourishing Hindu sites in the 9th–13th centuries. They are situated on either side of a rocky outcrop where more than fifty temples

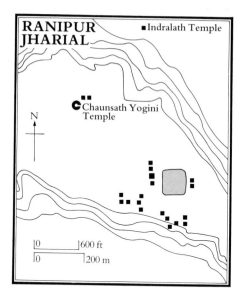

RANIPUR JHARIAL
■ Indralath Temple
C Chaunsath Yogini Temple
N
0 — 600 ft
0 — 200 m

motifs and amalakas are positioned above. The walls below have a moulded basement and projecting niches, now mostly empty.

RATNAGIRI

This remote site was once the principal centre of Buddhism in Orissa. It is closely linked with nearby establishments at **Lalitagiri** and **Udayagiri**. Like **Nalanda**, Ratnagiri was also an important university. Buddhism flourished here from about the 5th century until the 12th century, after which it steadily declined.

The monuments are located at the top of a mound. They consist of separate groups of stupas and monasteries connected by other smaller stupas and temples.

still stand. Most of these temples are small towered shrines devoid of any sculptural ornamentation. At the top of the outcrop is the circular Yogini temple; to the north, below the outcrop, is the brick temple known as Indralath.

Chaunsath Yogini Temple,
10th century

This temple is connected with the terrifying aspect of the cult of Shakti. Like the example at **Hirapur**, this crudely built sanctuary is circular in plan. Within the central court is a small square pavilion housing a three-headed image of Shiva. Damaged sculptures of different goddesses in dancing poses are set into the peripheral walls, where they are sheltered by a continuous colonnade. Two small towered thrones flank the entrance to the temple.

Indralath Temple, 10th century

This much restored brick structure is the only one to survive out of a group of six built in a row. The towered sanctuary has its outer walls regularly divided by mouldings into narrow storeys; arch-like

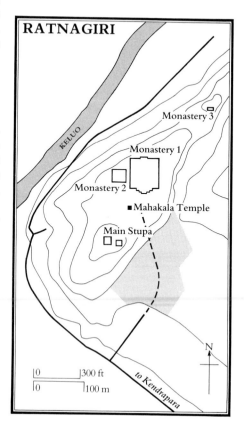

RATNAGIRI
KELUO
Monastery 3
Monastery 1
Monastery 2
■ Mahakala Temple
Main Stupa
N
to Kendrapara
0 — 300 ft
0 — 100 m

Excavations here have unearthed a large number of antiquities, including bronze images and stone sculptures of Buddhist deities. Several of these are exhibited in the State Museum, **Bhubaneshwar**, and the Indian Museum, **Calcutta**.

At the foot of the mound is a small village. A Buddhist sculpture has been set up in the school-yard here.

Main Stupa, 8th century and later

This is situated at the highest part of the mound. The circular brick basement has plaster-covered mouldings. The inner brick construction of the stupa drum is now exposed; the upper portion is in the form of a wheel with a central solid hub, twelve radiating spokes and an outer rim. The processional path and rectangular compound wall are later additions. Surrounding the monument are smaller stupas of varying dimensions and base forms, generally carved with seated Buddhist divinities. A large number of sculptures and stone and terracotta plaques are scattered in the debris.

Monastery 1, 7th–8th century and later

This is the best-preserved structure at the site. The monastery has a central square courtyard, paved in stone and surrounded by a colonnade from which small cells open. An entrance complex consists of two porches and a doorway, as well as steps leading to an upper level, now vanished. Within the court opposite the entrance is a large chamber serving as a shrine. While the brick structure preserves only the lower portions of the walls, stone facing exists within the entrance where images of Vajrapani and Padmapani have been placed in niches. The chlorite doorway perfectly preserves its delicate lotus ornament and scroll-work. Guardian figures are positioned beneath; Lakshmi is in the middle of the lintel. A large image of seated Buddha is displayed within the shrine.

Later rebuilding of the monastery is seen in the stone cladding of the peripheral walls, where a finely carved female Buddhist figure has been inserted (right side). The shrine walls were also refaced with stone and an antechamber with brick walls was added. Sculptures of Hariti and Panchika are housed here.

Monastery 2, 8th–9th century

Immediately west of Monastery 1, and separated from it by a narrow passage-way, is this similar example. Monastery 2, however, is smaller and has no upper storey. A unique feature of some cells is the provision of a raised floor and a carved stone window. In the stone paved shrine facing the entrance, a standing Buddha is flanked by smaller Bodhisattva images.

Temples, 9th–10th century

The lower portions of eight brick temples have been exposed in excavations here. Three temples stand side by side along the edge of the hill near the south-east corner of Monastery 1. In front of Monastery 2 are three further examples; these are surrounded by more than one hundred small stone stupas. One temple, now converted into a Hindu shrine, houses a standing image of Manjushri; another temple with a moulded basement contains three finely carved Bodhisattva images.

RUMTEK

Dharma Chakra Centre

Situated in one of the lower valleys of Sikkim, this monastery is now the head-quarters of the Kagyupa sect of Tibetan Buddhism. Though the monastery buildings are modern replacements of an earlier institution that was destroyed by an earth-quake, they are entirely traditional in style and ornamentation.

The principal building of the monastery is set in a large courtyard. The exterior is dominated by a verandah with carved columns and brackets; above rises an ascending tier of flat roofs, each capped with a brass finial. Within, a large meeting hall with seats for monks and an altar enshrining metal images is overlooked by upper chambers. Most of the architectural elements are vividly painted, especially the walls and ceilings; doorways and windows are also elaborately treated. The most common subjects are Buddhist divinities and fierce guardian figures of the Mahayana pantheon.

SIBSAGAR

This town was the capital of the 17th–18th-century Ahom kings of eastern Assam. These rulers and their wives were responsible for erecting Hindu temples in a distinctive regional style.

Overlooking the large tank in the middle of the town, the whitewashed brick temples at Sibsagar are dedicated to Shiva, Vishnu and Devi. Characteristic are the curved towers which have central curvilinear projections crowned with tiers of pot-like finials; similar but larger finials are positioned at the summits. There is no ornamentation. Adjoining mandapas have vaulted roofs and curved eaves, not unlike the traditional architecture of Bengal.

A variant scheme is found in the Vishnu temple. The walls of this building have shallow niches housing figurative panels; above are miniature turrets. The soaring tower on a circular plan is divided into small panels with medallions.

SIMHANATHA

This island in the middle of the Mahanadi river is reached either from Baideswar (south bank) or Baramba (north bank).

The Hindu temple located here is a well-known place of pilgrimage in the vicinity.

Simhanatha Temple, 8th century

This is a well-preserved example of the early Orissan style. The monument presents a scheme similar to the Parashurameshvara temple at **Bhubaneshwar**, with which it is almost contemporary. The towered sanctuary has triple niches on three sides which are raised on a moulded basement and surmounted by tower-like pediments. While the sculptures found in the niches are later insertions, those in the arched recesses above are original, especially Durga (north), Lakulisha (west), Shiva spearing Andhaka (south) and Shiva with Parvati (east, partly concealed by the mandapa roof). These panels are flanked by foliation and surmounted by smaller Shaiva icons. A frieze of fighting figures is carved at the base of the tower; other miniature figures cover the horizontal elements. The tower has the usual large capping amalaka and pot finial.

The mandapa is roofed with sloping slabs in three tiers. The walls have flat pilasters framing sculpture panels, and pierced stone windows filled with carved blocks. Throughout, lotus ornament is delicately applied; but other themes, such as pots, ganas and lotus medallions, also appear. On either side of the windows are the principal icons, which illustrate a mixed iconography; thus, Shiva and Agni (south) and Varaha and Narasimha (north). The doorway at the front (east) is flanked by river goddesses and Matrika figures. Continuous Ramayana reliefs are incised on to the lowest edge of the sloping roof.

Despite the dedicatory name of the temple, which refers to a form of Narasimha, the chief cult object within the sanctuary is a linga.

In the south-east corner of the temple compound stands the Somanatha shrine. This repeats on a smaller scale the design of the principal towered sanctuary.

SISUPALGARH

This fortified site is located 5 km (3 miles) south of **Bhubaneshwar**. It was first occupied in the 3rd century BC and soon after served as the capital of the Chedi kings. The site was abandoned in the 4th century.

The city is protected by extensive earthen ramparts, later partly faced with stone and brickwork. Visible from the main road, these walls form an immense square, almost 1 km ($\frac{1}{2}$ mile) across. There are two equally spaced entrances on each side. Excavations have exposed the remains of stone gateways, particularly on the west, where they were flanked by staircases and passageways. Much pottery was discovered inside the city, together with Roman and Indian coins from the 1st–2nd centuries. Dating from this later period are traces of brick houses facing on to regularly laid-out streets.

SULTANGANJ AND JAHANGIRA

The remains of extensive Buddhist monasteries and stupas have been discovered at Sultanganj. Traces of these are visible on the long mound near the local railway station. The finely modelled metal and stone Buddhist figures found here vary in date from the era of the later Gupta rulers in the 7th century to the 11th–12th-century later Pala period. Some of these sculptures are now exhibited in the **Patna** Museum.

Jahangira is about 2 km (1$\frac{1}{2}$ miles) north of the railway station, on the right bank of the Ganga river. This site is conspicuous for two great outcrops of granite. One is crowned with a mosque; the other, which stands in the middle of the water, has a linga at its summit. Large boulders on this rocky island are covered with carvings in bold relief. They date mostly from the 8th century and depict various aspects of

Shiva and Vishnu. One earlier relief shows Vishnu on the serpent.

TAMLUK

Once the ancient seaport of Tamralipta, this site is now located some distance inland. Among the terracotta objects found in abundance in the vicinity are plaques representing goddess figures; these have been dated to the 2nd-century-BC Shunga period. Pottery objects from the first two centuries of the Christian era suggest contacts with the Roman world. Occupation during the succeeding Kushana and Gupta eras is indicated by other terracotta finds. No structures have been discovered.

Tamralipta Museum and Research Centre

Pottery and other artefacts discovered at the site are displayed in this small collection.

TARAKESWAR

Tarakanatha Temple,
18th century and later

This is the most important Shaiva shrine in Bengal. Pilgrims visit the Hindu temple throughout the year, especially at Shivaratri (February–March) and Gajan (April). On these occasions, devotees offer pots filled with Ganga water that they have carried on poles from the river, more than 35 km (22 miles) away.

The temple walls are covered with terracotta plaques, now mostly obscured, above which rises a double tier of curved roofs. The adjoining mandapa is a modern structure.

TAWANG

This is one of the largest Buddhist establishments in the eastern Himalayas. The monastery's significance derives partly from its association with the sixth Dalai Lama, who was born in a nearby village, where his 'footprint' is revered even today. More than 250 lamas of the Tibetan Gelugpa sect reside at Tawang. The monastery is fortified and dramatically situated on a ridge about 3,050 m (10,000 ft) high.

The establishment dates back to the 17th century but has been much rebuilt. It consists of more than sixty buildings, with prayer halls, meeting halls and a library of large proportions. The principal shrine is an imposing stone structure in which painted thangkas, bronze images of deities of the Mahayana pantheon and a richly gilded seated Buddha, no less than 8 m (26 ft) high, are displayed. Of importance in the annual life of the monastery is the New Year's festival with its mask dances.

UDAIPUR

An interesting group of brick Hindu temples dating from the 17th century still stands at this site in Tripura. These structures are related to the brick traditions in Bengal, but they also display the influence of neighbouring Burma. The typical Udaipur temple consists of a square sanctuary and adjoining mandapa, both roofed with vaults with characteristically curved eaves. Rising over the sanctuary is a large hemispherical tower, rather like a Buddhist stupa in form but with an amalaka finial. The walls are unadorned, except for part-circular buttresses at the corners and horizontal mouldings in between.

UDAYAGIRI

As in the contemporary Buddhist sites of **Lalitagiri** and **Ratnagiri**, the hills here are dotted with traces of 9th–10th-century Buddhist structures, as well as numerous carved slabs. A well at the foot of the hills has an early inscription. Higher up are the remains of a shrine with a colossal image of seated Buddha.

The northern spur is covered with extensive remains of brick stupas around which carved panels of Bodhisattvas are placed. Near the top of the western spur is a gallery of rock-cut figures by the side of a cave with votive stupas in front.

Many loose sculptures have now been removed to the **Patna** Museum. These include a delicately carved door frame with Ganga and Yamuna figures on the jambs.

VAISALI

As the birthplace of Mahavira, this is a significant Jain site, but it is also linked with Buddhism, since it was the capital of the local Licchavi rulers during the lifetime of the Master. The remains include a standing column and the brick foundations of shrines, stupas and habitations.

Stupa, 5th century BC

Enlarged several times, this brick-lined earthen structure is believed to have been erected by the Licchavi kings over the relics of the Buddha.

Column, 3rd century BC

This is one of the best-preserved Maurya columns, but the shaft does not have the usual polished surface, nor is there any inscription. A single lion sits on the bell-shaped capital.

TWELVE

WESTERN INDIA

Gujarat, Rajasthan

Introduction

Substantial evidence of the earliest phase of Indian civilization is found in western India. The Harappan culture, named after Harappa (Pakistan), the site at which remains of this protohistoric culture were first discovered, flourished in the 3rd–2nd millennia in the Indus valley zone. At **Kalibangan** and at **Lothal**, there are many characteristic features of Harappan towns. Brick structures are regularly laid out on grid patterns with streets in between; drains and wells indicate a controlled use of water. Earthen embankments, possibly serving as fortifications, surround residential areas. Among the artefacts recovered from these sites are large painted earthenware jars, terracotta figurines and miniature stone seals with animal motifs and an undeciphered script.

Almost no monuments belonging to the early historic period are preserved in the western region. In contrast, the later centuries are exceptionally rich in temple architecture and art. The sacred mountains of the Jains in Gujarat and the memorials of the Hindu rulers in Rajasthan are testimonies to the survival of temple styles during the Muslim and Rajput eras.

The 3rd-century-BC rock-cut edicts at **Girnar** and the foundations of a stupa shrine at **Bairat** indicate the presence of Buddhism in western India during the reign of Ashoka, the Maurya emperor. That Buddhism survived in this region into later times is confirmed by terracotta images discovered at **Devnimori**. (The 4th-century stupa and monastery at this site are now flooded.) Under the 2nd–4th-century Kshatrapa rulers of **Junagadh**, monasteries for Buddhists and Jains were cut into the rock. The beginnings of stone structural architecture in Rajasthan date only from the 5th–6th centuries. The earliest examples are the ruined sanctuaries at **Mukundara** and **Kusuma**; these reveal the influence of Gupta traditions of central India. Terracotta plaques in a comparable Gupta-influenced style (exhibited in the museum at **Bikaner**) indicate that brick shrines must also have been built at this time.

In the 6th century, the Maitraka rulers of Gujarat sponsored the building of stone Hindu temples with distinctive features. Numerous small-scale projects survive in the Saurashtra peninsula. The earliest of these is the 6th-century temple at **Gop**, which has part of its towered sanctuary still standing. At **Bileshwar** the 7th-century temple has a pyramidal tower covered with arch-like motifs. Sculptures from the Maitraka period are mostly damaged; however, several finely modelled Hindu divinities and attendant maidens, in a style reminiscent of late Gupta traditions, come from **Roda** and **Samalaji**. 8th-century temples at the former site, where the largest early group of Hindu monuments in Gujarat still stands, are clearly linked to contemporary Pratihara architecture in central India.

Overleaf, Satrunjaya, panorama of Jain temples

Small square sanctuaries have curved towers covered with finely detailed arch-like motifs; amalakas and pot finials are positioned above. The outer walls have projections with small niches surmounted by pediments; doorways, columns and roofs are all elaborately decorated.

Under the Pratihara rulers and their successors, such as the Grahapatis, Chahamanas and Guhilas, temple architecture in Rajasthan continued to develop. Dating from the 8th and 9th centuries are examples at **Abaneri**, **Chitorgarh** and **Osian**; many important early structures still stand at this last site. Probably the finest 10th-century monument is that at **Badoli**; most of the delicately incised decoration and figural sculpture of this monument is intact. By the late 10th century at **Ahar**, **Eklingji** and **Nagda**, **Jagat** and **Kiradu**, the Pratihara style was fully evolved in its western Indian expression. Carved ornament covered much of the building surface, especially friezes of animals and stylized lotus designs on basements; panels of deities and attendant figures on walls; intricate meshes of arch-like motifs on towers; and pot and foliage motifs, looped snakes and other decorative themes on columns and doorways. Despite this sculptural exuberance, temples remained small-scale projects which were essentially combinations of sanctuaries, columned mandapas and porches. Wall projections and recesses, sometimes with pierced stone windows, and the clustered elements of towers and roofs exhibit considerable complexity.

At the beginning of the 11th century the Solankis emerged as the most powerful rulers in Gujarat and southern Rajasthan. Under the sponsorship of various kings and ministers of this dynasty, western Indian temple architecture developed distinctive characteristics. In the first group of Solanki monuments, such as the ruined shrine at **Modhera**, the Pratihara scheme is expanded. Sanctuaries with passage-ways adjoin columned mandapas with porches; additional detached mandapas are aligned on an axis with the central shrines. A rectangular tank is integrated into the overall layout. Throughout, the sculptural ornamentation of basement friezes, wall panels and column shafts is greatly increased. The most intricate workmanship adorns the supporting brackets and lintels, as well as the highly ornate ceiling compositions with corbelled domes and vaults.

In the 12th and 13th centuries, the Solanki style reached the climax of its development. Ruined monuments at **Ghumli**, **Girnar**, **Sejakpur**, **Sidhpur** and **Vadnagar** indicate the increased scale of architectural conception and the elaboration of carved decoration. (The celebrated Somanatha shrine at **Prabhas Patan** has been completely rebuilt in its original form.) One of the best preserved of the fully developed Solanki schemes is that at **Taranga**, where the temple displays a complicated towered form. For an illustration of the sculptural richness with which Solanki temples were embellished, the Jain monuments at **Abu** and **Kumbharia** are unsurpassed. Here, white marble surfaces are encrusted with intricate carvings; lintels and ceilings, in particular, are vehicles for dense and sharply modelled ornament. In these examples, and also that at **Bhadreshwar**, the principal sanctuaries stand in courts surrounded by subsidiary shrines and colonnades; entrance gateways consist of multi-storey porches.

That this developed style was not restricted to temple architecture is demonstrated by step-wells (vavs) at **Ghumli** and **Patan**; the example at **Patan**, though ruined, is unsurpassed for the grandeur of conception and the richness of carved detail. In Rajasthan, there are examples of related contemporary styles at **Bijolia**, **Jhalrapatan** and **Menal**. Temples at these sites were mostly patronized by the Chahamana rulers.

Jain monuments of western India continued to evolve stylistically even when the southern part of the region came under Muslim control from the 14th century onwards. While there continued to be an emphasis on complexity of architectural expression, few new features were introduced. Most of the sculpture loses its delicate quality; eventually it disappears altogether. Multi-storey sanctuaries and mandapas, and clustered towers with open balconies superimposed one upon the other, are characteristic features of these Jain temples. Typical examples are preserved on the holy mountains of **Girnar** and **Satrunjaya**, where numerous shrines crowd the rocky peaks. Other comparable temples are those at **Abhapur** and **Abu** and the slightly later sanctuaries at **Jaisalmer** and **Varkana**. The 15th-century **Ranakpur** monument is the masterpiece of the Jain series. The focus of this elaborate complex is a central towered sanctuary entered through four doorways. Throughout, the architectural elements are sumptuously decorated. Something of the same spatial richness is seen in contemporary vavs at **Adalaj** and **Ahmadabad**. That this ornate style also flourished in timber is demonstrated by a tradition of wooden domestic shrines (reconstructed examples are on display in museums at **Ahmadabad** and **Vadodara**).

Hindu sacred architecture during this period is illustrated by the main temple at the popular pilgrimage centre of **Dwarka** and the shrines of the Rajput rulers at **Chitorgarh**, **Eklingji** and **Udaipur**. Little of architectural interest survives at **Nathdwara** and **Pushkar**. Memorials (chhatris) of the Hindu Rajput rulers often imitated temple forms. At **Mandor**, for instance, chhatris illustrate the survival of western Indian temple styles into the 17th–19th centuries; the shrines at **Ahmadabad** and **Bikaner** also belong to this late period, by which time Mughal features had been thoroughly absorbed. Such Mughal influences have persisted even into the present century, as at **Deshnoke**.

Opposite Junagadh, 'Buddhist' Caves, 3rd–4th century

Right Gop, Temple, 6th century

Roda, Temple 5, 8th century

Osian, Harihara Temple 1, 8th century

Opposite above left Badoli Ghateshvara Temple, 10th century

Opposite above right Kiradu, Temple 3, 10th century

Opposite below Modhera, Surya Temple, 11th century

Left Chitorgarh, Jaya Stambha, 15th century

Below Ranakpur, Adinatha Temple, 15th century

Opposite Mandor, Chhatri, 17th–18th century

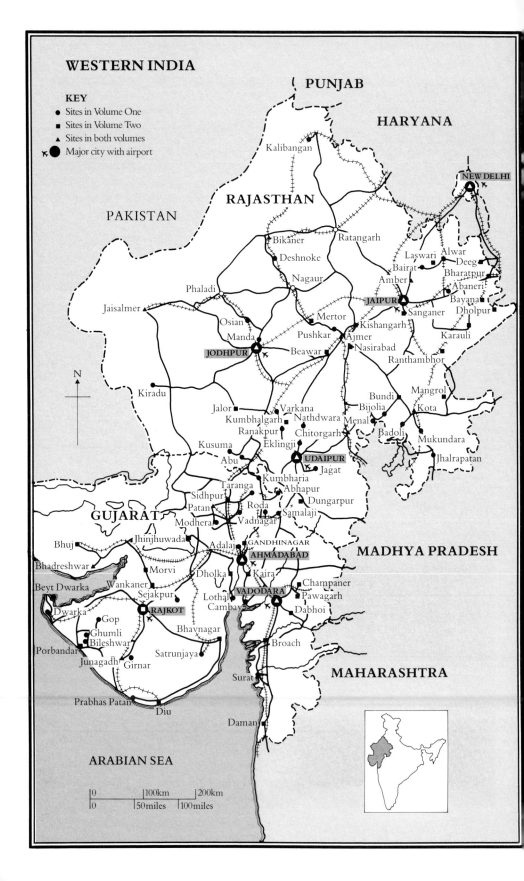

WESTERN INDIA

PUNJAB

HARYANA

KEY
● Sites in Volume One
■ Sites in Volume Two
▲ Sites in both volumes
✈● Major city with airport

RAJASTHAN

PAKISTAN

NEW DELHI

Kalibangan

Bikaner   Ratangarh
                              Laswari Alwar
Deshnoke   Deeg
                                       Bharatpur
        Nagaur   Bairat Abaneri
Phaladi   Amber   Bayana
                              JAIPUR   Dholpur
Jaisalmer   Mertor Sanganer Karauli
        Osian   Kishangarh
        Manda   Pushkar Ajmer
JODHPUR   Beawar   Nasirabad
                              Ranthambhor
Kiradu
                              Bundi   Mangrol
        Jalor   Varkana Bijolia Kota
        Kumbhalgarh Nathdwara Menal
        Ranakpur   Chitorgarh Badoli
        Kusuma Eklingji   Mukundara
        Abu   UDAIPUR
                         Jagat   Jhalrapatan
                Kumbharia
        Taranga   Abhapur
        Sidhpur   Roda   Dungarpur
        Patan   Samalaji
        Modhera Vadnagar
Bhuj   Jhinjhuwada Adalaj GANDHINAGAR
                    AHMADABAD   MADHYA PRADESH
Bhadreshwar   Morvi   Dholka   Champaner
Beyt Dwarka Wankaner Kaira   Pawagarh
        Sejakpur   VADODARA
Dwarka   RAJKOT   Lothal   Dabhoi
        Gop   Cambay
Ghumli   Bhavnagar
Bileshwar   Broach
Porbandar
Junagadh   Satrunjaya
        Girnar
                Surat   MAHARASHTRA

Prabhas Patan
        Diu

        Daman

GUJARAT

ARABIAN SEA

0   100km   200km
0   50miles 100miles

ABANERI

Harshat Mata Temple,
early 9th century

The terrace and portions of a Hindu sanctuary and columned mandapa are all that survive of this Pratihara temple. The terrace basement is complete in many of its details, including friezes of geometric ornament and miniature niches with sculptures of seated deities and amorous couples. Several mandapa columns and parts of the sanctuary walls still stand; the latter are adorned with scenes of dance, music, sport and love, now largely damaged. Architectural fragments, often with carvings, are scattered all around. (Numerous panels have been removed to the Archaeological Museum, **Amber**, and the Central Museum, **Jaipur**.)

Tank, 9th century and later

East of the temple is a deep tank. Carved panels contemporary with the temple are inserted into the sides.

ABHAPUR

Sarneshvara Temple, 12th century

Although this Hindu building is ruined, carved panels are preserved in two tiers on the lower parts of the sanctuary walls. Projecting balconies are richly carved with foliate and figurative designs; overhanging eaves are double-storeyed. The gateway leading into the temple compound still stands.

Lakhena Mandir, 16th century

This is a fine example of later Jain architecture. A columned mandapa with pierced stone screens adjoins a towered sanctuary. The superstructure is composed of a cluster of diminishing and overlapping curved turrets, each capped by an amalaka.

Triple-storey porches project outwards on three sides.

The carving is sharp and detailed, especially the frieze of animals on the basement, and the stone screens with foliate and geometric designs. The sanctuary doorway is surrounded by miniature seated Jina figures.

ABU

The rocky outcrops of the Abu plateau rise more than 1,000 m (3,300 ft) above the plain. The natural beauty of this hill station is enhanced by a group of Jain temples at Dilwara, one of the holy spots on the plateau. Dating from the Solanki period, these temples are among the most perfectly executed examples of the western Indian style. They are constructed entirely of marble and are encrusted with intricately carved detail. Abu is still an important Jain pilgrimage place; rest-houses and other facilities cluster around the Dilwara temples. (For Abu during the British period see Volume II.)

Abu also served as one of the headquarters of the local Paramara chiefs in the 12th–13th centuries. 4·8 km (3 miles) north-east of Dilwara, at Achalgarh, is a fort within which are two Jain temples, both much renovated. Overlooking a double tank are the equestrian statues of Rana Kumbha, the 15th-century ruler of **Chitorgarh**, and his son. Nearby is the popular temple of Achaleshvara, mostly a modern structure. An object of sanctity here is the toenail of Shiva deposited within a hole in the wall. A brass Nandi image in front of the temple is dated to 1408.

Another site of importance on the plateau is Guru Sikhar; at 1,772 m (5,760 ft) above sea level this is the highest peak at Abu. The cavernous weather-worn side of the summit has been transformed into a small shrine commemorating Data Brikha, a sage whose footprints are carved on a bench of rock within.

Another feature at Abu is a tank with a spout shaped like a cow's head (Gomukh), after which it is named. Close by is the brick temple of Vaishishtha, originally erected in the 14th century but much rebuilt since. In front of the temple is a cenotaph housing a brass figure of the last of the local Paramara chiefs.

DILWARA

Adinatha (Vimala Vasahi) Temple, 1032 and later

Founded by Vimala, a minister under the Solanki ruler Bhima I, this temple is one of the early examples of the Jain style in western India. The original structure consists of a sanctuary, an enclosed mandapa with two porches and an adjoining open mandapa; an outer mandapa with a central octagonal space was added in the 12th century. The temple is set within a rectangular court lined with a row of small shrines and a double colonnade, both later extensions. The enclosure wall is unadorned, in striking contrast to the exuberant decoration of the interior.

The wall niches of the sanctuary house Jina images. The doorway leading to the central chamber is elaborately decorated with guardian figures and seated Jinas. The principal Tirthankara within was installed during the restoration of 1322.

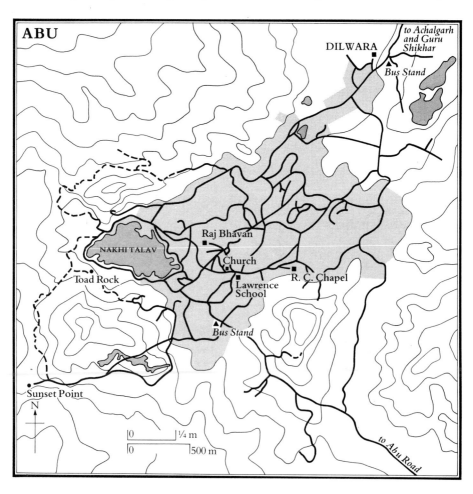

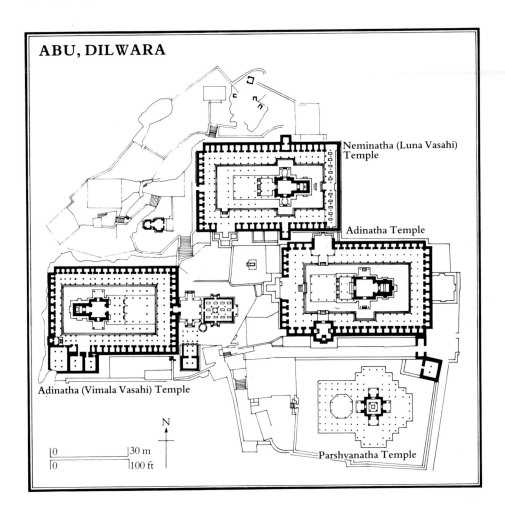

ABU, DILWARA

Neminatha (Luna Vasahi) Temple

Adinatha Temple

Adinatha (Vimala Vasahi) Temple

N

|0 |30 m
|0 |100 ft

Parshvanatha Temple

The chief glory of the architecture is its intricate decoration. Columns are covered with figures in niches, friezes of stylized ornament and scrollwork; brackets are fashioned as maidens. Connecting the columns flanking the central aisles of the outer mandapa are angled lintels covered with miniature figures. The corbelled domes and vaults of the ceilings have rows of dancers, musicians, soldiers, horses and elephants; these are arranged around multi-lobed medallions adorned with lotus designs. The variation in these ceiling compositions and the precision of the carving are remarkable. The large corbelled dome over the central bay of the open mandapa is more than 7 m (23 ft) in diameter; this incorporates sixteen brackets carved as seductively posed maidens; the central lotus is a cluster of pendant buds. The ceiling panels in the side aisles contain goddesses and other lively compositions, including Hindu subjects such as Narasimha and episodes from the Krishna story. In contrast, the Jina images within the shrines are stiff and repetitive.

Placed within the entrance porch is a sculpture of the temple patron, Vimala, seated on a horse. Immediately behind is a votive panel representing the holy mountain of **Satrunjaya**.

Neminatha (Luna Vasahi) Temple, 1230 and later

This monument was erected by two wealthy merchants, Vastupala and Teja-pala, and later extended. It imitates the Adinatha temple in all of its essential features, but the Neminatha temple is distinguished from its neighbour by the increased density of its carved ornamentation. This is visible on the columns and the angled lintels that emerge from open-mouthed makaras; doorways are framed by complex compositions of pilasters and pediments. The ceiling designs in the mandapas and colonnades attain unprecedented richness; that over the central bay of the open mandapa is the masterpiece of the series. Some panels are entirely devoted to cosmological themes; others depict scenes from the lives of the Jinas, with processions of soldiers, horsemen, elephants, dancers and musicians. Portrait sculptures of the donors and their wives have been placed in the entrance porch, which is enclosed by pierced stone screens with geometric patterns. Here too are sculptures of striding elephants in full relief.

Adinatha Temple, 14th century

This temple enshrines a massive brass Tirthankara image. While some of the columns and doorways are richly carved, other portions of the building are unfinished. The later style is evident in the unadorned exterior.

Parshvanatha Temple, 1459

Built in grey stone with its tower incompletely preserved, this temple is the tallest of the Dilwara group. The double-storey shrine housing quadruple Tirthankara images is entered through four doorways, each sheltered by a porch; the outer walls are covered with Jina figures. The shrine is contained within a columned mandapa embellished with ornate ceilings.

ADALAJ

Vav, 1502

The architectural features and wealth of carved ornamentation of this step-well, 19 km (12 miles) north of **Ahmadabad**, are stylistically related to contemporary temple traditions. The monument is not merely a utilitarian water structure; it once served as a Hindu sanctuary.

The octagonal well is approached by a long flight of steps. As the steps descend, columns and connecting beams create open structures of increasing complexity; the receding perspectives of columns and cross-beams are particularly striking. At ground level, two small structures with pyramidal roofs flank the entrance.

The carved decoration includes horses, foliate and pot motifs in niches, arabesques of lotus stalks and flowers, geometric medallions and bands of jewels and petals. Four-storey balconies overlooking the water are decorated with stylized foliate motifs. Wall niches incorporate miniature pilasters, eaves and roof-like pediments.

AHMADABAD

Few temples in Ahmadabad predate the 18th–19th centuries. They are both Hindu and Jain, and are built in a late variant of the western Indian style. Dating from the pre-Islamic period is one step-well; another example is contemporary with the city's Islamic monuments. (For the mosques and tombs of Ahmadabad see Volume II.)

Mata Bhavani's Vav, 11th century

This step-well is named after a small Hindu shrine set into the rear wall of the circular well. The water is approached by a long flight of steps above which rises a sequence of two-, three- and four-storey

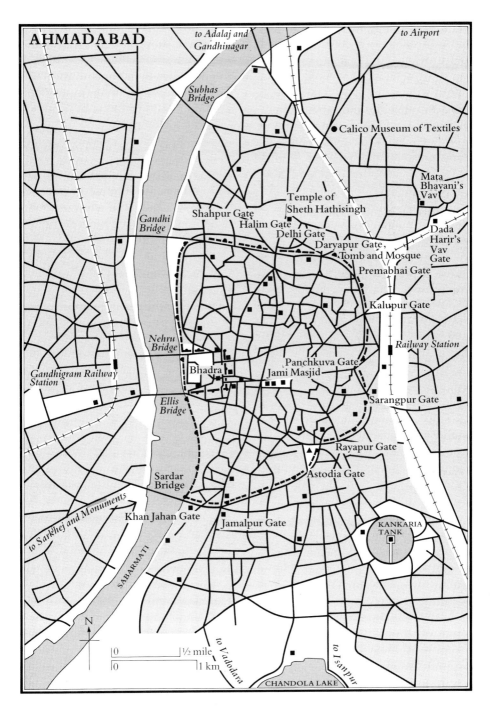

AHMADABAD

to Adalaj and
Gandhinagar

to Airport

Subhas
Bridge

● Calico Museum of Textiles

Mata
Bhavani's
Vav

Gandhi
Bridge

Shahpur Gate

Temple of
Sheth Hathisingh

Halim Gate

Delhi Gate

Dada
Harir's
Vav
Gate

Daryapur Gate,

Tomb and Mosque

Premabhai Gate

Kalupur Gate

Nehru
Bridge

Gandhigram Railway
Station

Bhadra

Panchkuva Gate

Jami Masjid

Railway Station

Ellis
Bridge

Sarangpur Gate

Rayapur Gate

Sardar
Bridge

Astodia Gate

to Sarkhej and Monuments

Khan Jahan Gate

Jamalpur Gate

KANKARIA
TANK

SABARMATI

N

0   ½ mile
0   1 km

to Vadodara

to Isanpur

CHANDOLA LAKE

open pavilions. The elaborate ornamentation of the columns, brackets and
beams, and the friezes of motifs and
niches set into the side walls are comparable to contemporary Solanki temple
architecture.

Dada Harir's Vav, 1499

This step-well, together with that at **Adalaj**, 19 km (12 miles) north of the city, is the finest example of the Muslim period in Gujarat. Modelled on the earlier Mata Bhavani vav, this example has an additional domed pavilion at the entrance. The decoration is intricately worked in a sharply cut style and there is a complete absence of figural themes. Birds in stylized scrollwork adorn the wall niches. Such motifs may be compared with those that appear in Islamic architecture.

Temple of Sheth Hathisingh, 1848

This is the most ornate Jain sanctuary in Ahmadabad. The temple stands in the middle of a rectangular court and is entered on the west through an elaborate gateway. The temple has three sanctuaries, each housing an image of Dharmanatha, which are approached through a sequence of enclosed and open mandapas. The trio of clustered spires rising over the sanctuaries contrast with the domes that roof the mandapas. Subsidiary shrines with spires similar to those of the temple line the peripheral court walls. Throughout, the decoration is sharply sculpted, but figures appear only at the brackets.

Calico Museum of Textiles

This museum is housed in a private mansion and is celebrated for the quality of its collection of textiles, some of which are closely related to religious art and architecture.

An important part of the display are the painted, dyed and embroidered cotton hangings known as pecchavais; these are used during the festivals of the Vallabha sect. (The chief icon of this sect is Shrinathji, a form of Krishna worshipped at **Nathdwara**.) Pecchavais sometimes depict Krishna playing the flute, surrounded by gopis and cows, or enshrined in the temple with devotees.

The Jain gallery incorporates several 18th–19th-century wooden shrines taken from private residences in Ahmadabad and **Patan**. Typical are the elaborate carvings, especially of brackets, doorways, windows and even dome-like ceilings. Other than stone and metal images of Tirthankaras, there are also manuscripts illustrating the lives of the Tirthankaras, and cosmographic and geographic treatises. Cotton hangings, or patas, are painted with meditational diagrams in a variety of geometric patterns. There are even depictions of the holy mountain of **Satrunjaya**, complete with rocky hills, ascending paths and temple compounds.

AJMER

(For the city and its monuments see Volume II.)

Rajputana Museum

Sculptures from nearby temple sites are exhibited here. Among those from the early Pratihara period is a fine head of a Buddha or Jina figure from Shergarh (43). The fully evolved 10th–11th-century style is demonstrated in two panels: Brahma and Vishnu on either side of the linga and the same deities seeking the linga's dimensions (27.374), both from Harshagiri. Another example from Kama, with Vishnu and Brahma beneath a quadruple-faced linga, is carved in high relief (26.15). A fine series of images from Baghera is also displayed, such as Varaha (358), Vishnu and Lakshmi on Garuda (22.352), and a well-preserved four-armed Vishnu on Garuda (17.1354). Also from Baghera is a door frame adorned with different forms of Vishnu (362). From Arthuna comes a sculpture of Varaha with a naga devotee (448).

One of the finest of the 13th–14th-century Jain sculptures is a seated Tirthankara figure with finely etched facial features; this piece comes from Tantobi (344).

BADOLI

Despite their dilapidated condition, the 10th-century Hindu temples at this site are among the finest examples from the Pratihara period in western India. (Loose sculptures from this site have been removed to the **Kota** Museum.)

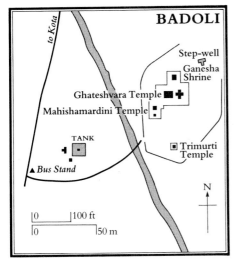

Ghateshvara Temple, 10th century

This is the best preserved of the Badoli group and, indeed, one of the finest temples in Rajasthan. The principal structure consists of a towered sanctuary adjoining a columned porch. The curvilinear tower is completely covered with delicately incised arch-like motifs; at the summit is an amalaka with a pot finial. Set into the walls beneath are elegantly posed sculptures, carved almost in the round; notably, dancing Shiva (west), Chamunda (north) and Shiva spearing Andhaka (south). Each panel is surmounted by an eave and a tower-like pediment. The sanctuary doorway displays another dancing Shiva image flanked by Brahma and Vishnu on the lintel, with guardians and river goddesses on the jambs beneath. The porch columns

have fully modelled maidens (damaged) carved on to the shafts. The ceiling panel has half-lotus medallions, multi-lobed motifs and miniature deities. The roof above incorporates niches with sculptures as well as diminutive towered forms at the corners.

Within the sanctuary is a square pedestal with five natural stones serving as lingas; the central stone resembles an inverted pot (ghata), hence the name of the temple deity.

Immediately to the east is a detached open mandapa, which was added almost a century later. It is laid out on a stepped plan with balcony seating between the peripheral columns; above is an angled eave. The roof is a pyramidal composition of numerous elements, each capped with an amalaka. The ceilings are richly sculpted with geometric and foliate designs.

Mahishamardini Temple, 10th century

This temple is located immediately south-west of the previous one. Its curved tower is completely covered with a finely etched mesh of arch-like motifs; the front (east) face is adorned with a triangular projection. Over the porch rises a small roof. In contrast to the upper portions, the walls are unadorned. A powerful image of Durga, her face now smashed, is housed within the sanctuary.

Trimurti Temple, 10th century

This dilapidated temple consists of a single towered sanctuary. The doorway, with sculpted bands, leads into the sanctuary, where there is a large triple-headed Shiva image, now defaced. Nearby, two columns from a ruined gateway have been delicately carved with maidens and worshippers, also with garlands and bells on chains.

BAIRAT

Stupa Shrine, 3rd century BC and later

The remains of the Buddhist shrine exposed at this site provide a unique example of Maurya architecture in western India. Only fragments of the stupa's foundation have survived, together with pieces of a stone umbrella and a pot finial. The main interest of the monument lies in the enclosing circular shrine, which is more than 8 m (26 ft) in diameter. This was constructed of plastered brickwork and wooden columns, now vanished, with a small entrance porch. At a later date, the shrine was contained within a rectangular compound.

BEYT DWARKA

A pilgrimage to **Dwarka** is considered incomplete without a visit to the Hindu temple on this island, just off the northwest tip of the Saurashtra peninsula. The temple, which dates only from the 19th century, is in the form of a large house with a series of shrines accommodating images of Krishna and his fifty-six consorts.

Excavations on the island have revealed evidence of occupation going back to the period of the Harappan culture in the 2nd millennium BC.

BHADRESHWAR

This seaport was an ancient town of some importance. A temple and two mosques date from the Solanki period. (For the Islamic monuments see Volume II.)

Jain Temple, 1248

The sanctuary and attached mandapa of this temple stand in a courtyard surrounded by small shrines. These subsidi-ary structures are capped by towers which reproduce on a smaller scale the clustered scheme rising over the principal sanctuary. The elaborate mouldings of the basements, the niches of the walls and the mesh of arch-like motifs covering the towers are all typical features of the evolved western Indian style. The complex is entered through a double-storey gateway; this is a later addition with Islamic arches, geometric ornament on the balconies and parapet, and domes above.

BIJOLIA (map p. 281)

The group of sacred monuments at this site comprises three Hindu temples, in addition to a tank known as Mandakini. The temples date from different periods; the oldest is typical of the 11th-century Solanki style. Inscriptions link the later temples with the rulers of the Chahamana dynasty.

Undeshvara Temple, 13th century

This temple is related to central Indian traditions as developed during the Paramara period. The outer walls of the sanctuary are divided into projecting and recessing planes, each with a moulded basement and a carved wall panel; niches are positioned in the central projection. Above rises the elegantly curved tower with characteristic bands of meshed motifs in the middle of each side; at the top of these bands are triple heads of Shiva. The bands are flanked by tiers of miniature towered motifs, each with a curved profile and an amalaka. The lower two registers of the towers are also provided with carved panels. Projecting from the adjoining mandapa are two porches.

Of interest is the sanctuary, the floor of which is set about 2·5 m (8 ft) below that of the mandapa. Water seeping into the sanctuary from the nearby tank submerges the enshrined linga.

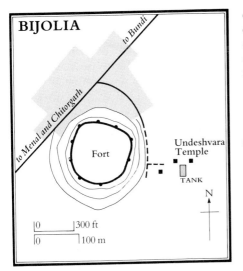

BIJOLIA

Fort

Undeshvara Temple

TANK

N

0 — 300 ft
0 — 100 m

to Bundi

to Menal and Chitorgarh

BIKANER

The Jain temples of this town are mostly 16th–17th-century constructions dedicated to the different Tirthankaras. Here, western Indian features are blended with Mughal columns, arches and decorative motifs. The Parshvanatha temple displays an unusual superimposition of chambers, one upon the other, each with projecting porches. Probably the finest example is the Neminatha temple, dated to 1536; this is characterized by a sequence of open mandapas with richly ornamented columns.

(For the palace and other monuments see Volume II.)

Ganga Golden Jubilee Museum

A group of Gupta terracottas belonging to the 4th–5th century is exhibited in this collection. Though damaged, these panels provide important evidence of early artistic traditions in Rajasthan. Those from Rangmahal illustrate divinities, such as Shiva with Parvati (2234) and Krishna holding up the mountain (229). Among the stone sculptures is a marble image of Sarasvati from Pallu (203); this

dates from the 11th century and is executed in the Solanki style. The finely carved goddess stands within a frame containing miniature figures. Sculptures from other sites are also displayed.

BILESHWAR

Shiva Temple, early 7th century

This important example of early Hindu temple architecture in Gujarat is the largest extant monument dating from the Maitraka period. It is contained within a later enclosure but still serves as a place of worship. The sanctuary has a multi-storey tower of a pyramidal design comparable to the earlier scheme presented at **Gop**. Large arch-like motifs are positioned in the middle of each side of the tower; similar but smaller motifs appear at the corners and at the summit. Plaster coating obscures much of the original decoration.

CHITORGARH

This impressive citadel rises about 150 m (490 ft) above the plain, where it occupies a narrow plateau almost 5 km (3 miles) long from north to south and no more than 1 km (½ mile) wide. It is protected by massive walls that encircle the plateau; seven gateways provide access. The main approach is by a winding road from the west.

The obvious strategic importance of Chitorgarh was responsible for its long and complex history. Archaeological investigation in the area has revealed Buddhist relics, some of which date back to the centuries before the Christian era. Later votive stupas have been discovered with images of the Master carved around the base. (These and other antiquities recovered from the site and its immediate vicinity are displayed in the small

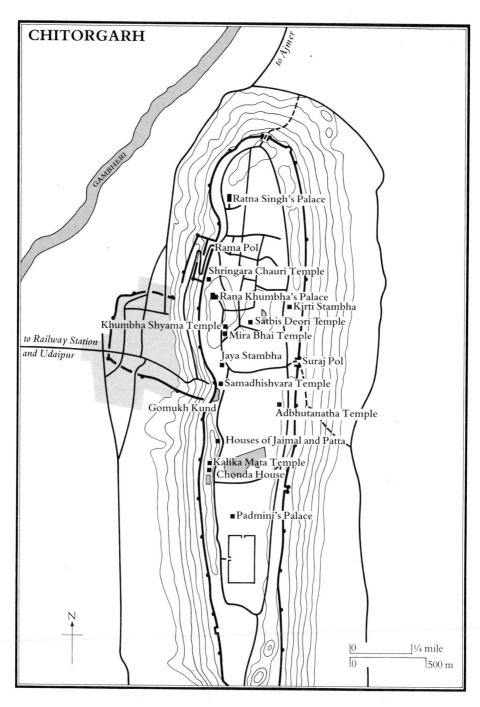

CHITORGARH

to Ajmer

GAMBHERI

■Ratna Singh's Palace

Rama Pol

Shringara Chauri Temple

■Rana Khumbha's Palace

■Kirti Stambha

Khumbha Shyama Temple■

■Satbis Deori Temple

to Railway Station
and Udaipur

■Mira Bhai Temple

Jaya Stambha

Suraj Pol

■Samadhishvara Temple

Gomukh Kund

■Adbhutanatha Temple

■Houses of Jaimal and Patta

■Kalika Mata Temple
Chonda House

■Padmini's Palace

N

| 0 | ¼ mile |
| 0 | 500 m |

museum within the Fateh Prakash palace.)

From the 7th century onwards, Chitorgarh was occupied by a succession of rulers, including the Moris and the Pratiharas, both of whom constructed stone temples. Thereafter, Chitorgarh was disputed by numerous dynasties. After the Muslim raids of the 12th and 13th centuries, the fort became the headquarters of the rulers of the Mewar state. The most celebrated of the many warrior kings who distinguished themselves in battles against the Muslims was Rana Kumbha (1433–68). The fort was sacked by Muslim armies three times. In 1567, after a long siege, Chitorgarh was abandoned and the capital was moved to **Udaipur**.

The gateways to the citadel and the palaces inside mostly belong to the period of Rana Kumbha (see Volume II). There are numerous Jain and Hindu temples, some in use for worship, others dilapidated. These date from a period spanning no less than eight centuries, demonstrating a continuous evolution of architectural styles. The fort also contains two commemorative towers that are unique in western India. Tanks and wells, essential in times of siege, are excavated deep into the rocky surface of the plateau.

The principal temples are described from north to south.

Shringara Chauri Temple, 1456

Dedicated to Shantinatha, this Jain temple has basement mouldings with intricately carved friezes of fighting warriors, maidens and musicians. Pierced screens with geometric motifs, and carved panels framed by pilasters, are set into the walls. Jain figures and those of river goddesses and yakshis adorn the sanctuary doorway.

Kirti Stambha (Tower of Fame), 13th century and later

This 24·5-m-high (80 ft) tower is actually a Jain monument dedicated to Adinatha. Large standing images of this naked Tirthankara are placed in four niches on the lowest storey; the same figure is repeated

some hundreds of times on the upper storeys. Within, a staircase around a square shaft ascends six levels to a small pavilion at the summit. This elegant structure, with a roof resting on twelve columns, is a 15th-century restoration. The multi-storey shaft of the tower has deeply cut mouldings typical of contemporary temple architecture.

Standing next to the tower is a ruined 14th-century temple. Its projecting walls are covered with sculptures; the restored tower above is of the clustered type. The interior is roofed with a corbelled ceiling with multi-lobed motifs and finely carved figures.

Satbis Deori (Twenty-seven Shrines), 15th century

This Jain temple stands within a walled compound surrounded by rows of small shrines, from which the name of the temple is derived. The entrance portal on the west has an angled lintel suspended between two columns. The temple itself is typical of the evolved western Indian style. Both sanctuary and mandapa have wall projections encrusted with sculptures; miniature niches with figures appear even on the basement. Over the sanctuary rises a tower with clustered elements; portions of the original decoration of arch-like motifs are still intact. The mandapa is roofed with a restored corbelled dome; the finely carved ceiling panels incorporate bracket figures. Pierced screens are inserted into the mandapa walls.

Kumbha Shyama Temple, 8th and 15th centuries

This Hindu temple may have once been dedicated to Varaha since an image of this deity is set into the rear wall of the sanctuary. Portions of the original 8th-century sanctuary still exist, such as the high basement, wall niches, and reused columns and ceiling panels. The 15th-century additions include a soaring tower with clustered elements at the base and a mandapa with an elaborate multi-tiered pyramidal roof.

Immediately south of this temple but within the same compound is another smaller temple. This is named after Mira Bhai, a 15th-century saintly princess of **Jodhpur** known for her poetic compositions. This memorial monument is typical of the later western Indian style, with its elegantly curved tower rising above the sanctuary. Enshrined within the sanctuary is an image of Krishna.

Jaya Stambha (Tower of Victory), 1448

This tower was erected by Rana Kumbha to commemorate his victory over the Muslim ruler of Delhi. Its exterior is clearly marked with nine storeys of openings and balconies; pierced stone screens are used at the lowest level. The dome at the summit is a modern addition. The interior staircase winds alternately through the central chamber and a surrounding gallery. The tower is dedicated to Vishnu, whose images, together with those of other Hindu divinities, cover the walls; each figure is identified with a label. There are even portraits of the architects (fifth storey).

Immediately beneath the tower is the Mahasti, where the early rulers of Chitorgarh and their wives were cremated. Entrance gateways into the enclosure are adorned with vigorous carvings.

Samadhishvara Temple, 11th and 15th centuries

This Hindu temple is located immediately south of the Jaya Stambha. As renovated in later times, the temple has a clustered tower decorated with arch-like motifs with an amalaka and pot finial above. The mandapa has projecting porches on three sides and a pyramidal roof. Most of the

sculptures are intact, especially the friezes of processions and hunting scenes, and even several Jain figures. The triple-faced Shiva image within the sanctuary, however, is modern.

Several smaller ruined Shaiva shrines nearby date from the 8th–9th century.

Below the Samadhishvara temple to the south, a long staircase descends to a sacred spring known as Gomukh Kund (Pool of the Cow's Head); this is overlooked by towered shrines.

Adbhutanatha Temple, 15th century

Though incompletely preserved, this Hindu temple is a fine example of the later western Indian style. Characteristic features are the wall sculptures and the clustered tower. The doorway is flanked by guardian figures and surrounded by decorated bands. A crudely carved triple-headed bust of Shiva is enshrined within the sanctuary.

Kalika Mata Temple, 8th century, rebuilt 1568

This Hindu shrine is partly rebuilt, particularly the sanctuary and corbelled domes over the mandapa. The original scheme was a sanctuary contained within a colonnade, creating a passageway on three sides and an open mandapa at the front (east). The outer walls have sculptures surmounted by tower-like pediments; these include images of Surya (central niches) and the Dikpalas (corner niches); there are also friezes of the gods and demons churning the ocean and dancing figures. The mandapa columns and projecting porches with seating are finely carved with pot and foliage motifs. The sanctuary doorway incorporates an image of Surya (lintel), thus indicating the original dedication of the temple. The ceiling panels within the mandapa are decorated with miniature divinities and flying celestials.

DESHNOKE

Temple of Karni Mata,
early 20th century

Erected by Ganga Singh, one of the rulers of **Jodhpur**, this Hindu shrine is dedicated to a 15th-century female saint who is revered as an incarnation of Durga. The interior is populated by hundreds of rats; as the sacred animals of the temple they are allowed to move freely.

The temple is built in a late Mughal style, mostly of marble. It is lavishly decorated, especially the delicately worked doorways, colonnades, pavilions and balconies. Petalled domes rise over the sanctuary.

DWARKA

Overlooking the Arabian Sea at the north-western tip of the Saurashtra peninsula, Dwarka is one of the holy cities of

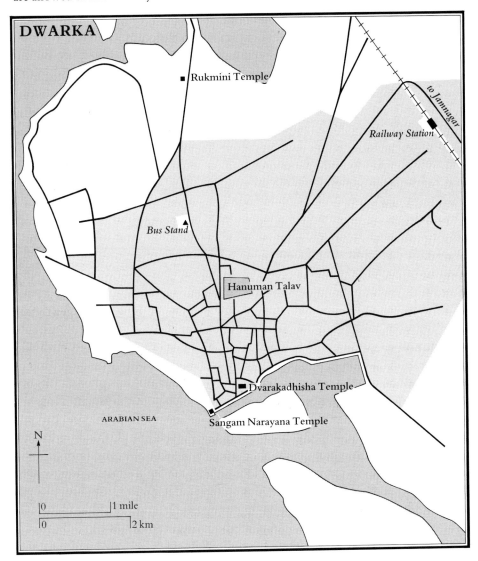

Hinduism. It is believed that Krishna settled here with his people after fleeing the wrath of Jarasandha at **Mathura**. Thousands of pilgrims visit the temples at Dwarka, especially on Krishna's birthday, Divali and Holi. Though parts of some temples belong to the Solanki period, most of the town's architecture dates only from the 19th century, when Dwarka was developed as a popular religious centre by the Gaekwar rulers. Among the numerous shrines and rest-houses, two temples, now much renovated, are of particular importance.

Rukmini Temple,
12th century and later

This small temple consists of a sanctuary on a stepped plan and a columned mandapa with later infill walls and a dome-like roof. The wall panels of the sanctuary are badly eroded. The superstructure has numerous turrets rising above the wall projections, where part of the original ornamentation survives. The high basement, balcony seating and mandapa columns are all finely carved; so too is the sanctuary doorway.

Dvarakadhisha Temple,
mostly 16th century

Though parts of the sanctuary walls of this temple date from the 12th century, the elaborate soaring tower that rises more than 50 m (165 ft) above is much later. This tower has seven open balconies, superimposed one upon the other in the middle of each side. Complex effects are achieved by the clustering of subsidiary towered elements. The multi-storey mandapa with richly modelled columns has a succession of open balconies on the exterior, each with seating and overhanging eaves.

EKLINGJI AND NAGDA

The Hindu sanctuary at Eklingji is built on the shore of a small lake ringed with hills. Enshrined within this temple is the guardian deity of the 15th-century **Udaipur** rulers. An earlier Lakulisha temple is located within the compound of the Eklingji complex; there are other temples of lesser interest found all around.

2 km (1½ miles) north of Eklingji is Nagda, where the twin Sasbahu temples are built on the edge of the water. Submerged within the lake are several later structures. Other 15th-century Jain sanctuaries are also situated in the vicinity.

EKLINGJI

Lakulisha Temple, 972

This large but simple structure consists of a sanctuary, a mandapa with pierced stone windows in the side projections, and a porch in front. The basement and wall niches are plain except for two niches, one inset with an inscribed slab, the other with an image of Sarasvati. The brick superstructures over the sanctuary and mandapa are badly eroded. The sanctuary enshrines a sculpture of seated Lakulisha; the doorway has a similar image carved on to the lintel, where it is surmounted by niches with various deities. Though the mandapa is square, the columns are laid out on an octagonal plan. Niches on the outer walls house different goddesses.

Ekalinga Temple, 15th century

Both the principal sanctuary and the two-storey mandapa on a stepped plan are built of marble. A clustered curved tower rises over the sanctuary; the mandapa is roofed with a pyramid of miniature architectural motifs. The interior is notable for an ornate silver doorway and screen; silver lamps add to the richness of the effect. Facing the principal four-faced Shiva image, which is carved out of black marble, is a small silver Nandi. Other Nandi icons are found within the courtyard. The underground pool in a corner has a small linga shrine.

NAGDA

Sasbahu Temples, late 10th century

These twin Vaishnava temples are raised on a common terrace to face east towards the tank. The temples are entered through a gateway with carved lintels and a central multi-lobed arch. The larger temple is surrounded by ten subsidiary shrines; the smaller one has only four shrines.

Both buildings follow the same basic scheme. Each consists of a sanctuary, a mandapa with projections and an open porch. The walls are plain, except for sculptures in two tiers on the principal projections: thus, Brahma, Shiva and Vishnu, surmounted respectively by Rama, Balarama and Parashurama. The brick towers, though ruined, have clusters of diminutive turrets. The mandapas and porches have sculptures and decorative motifs, in contrast with the unadorned sanctuary walls. Relief images comprise various deities, including the Dikpalas, amorous couples, maidens and narrative friezes, as well as scenes from the Ramayana. The columns are richly decorated; so is the octagonal ceiling, with eight female brackets in the smaller temple. The intricately carved stone windows in the mandapa of the smaller temple are replaced by porches in the larger temple.

GHUMLI

Picturesquely situated in a wooded valley, this site preserves ruins dating back to the Solanki period. There is also an unusual step-well.

Vikia Vav, early 12th century

This is one of the largest step-wells in Gujarat. As in other examples, it also served as a water sanctuary. A long staircase descends to the part-circular well. Constructed over the steps are pavilions of three, five and six storeys; another pavilion is located at the entrance. Each pavilion consists of richly carved columns, brackets and inclined balcony seating. The pyramidal roofs of the pavilions have partly collapsed.

Naulakha Temple, early 13th century

This ambitious Hindu temple is now mostly ruined. A sanctuary surrounded by a passageway with three projecting porches adjoins a two-storey open mandapa on a stepped plan. Though the tower and roof have fallen, the elaborate decoration of the basement, balcony seating, columns, brackets and beams is still visible. Portions of the sculptural friezes and wall panels are also preserved.

GOP

Temple, 6th century

This is one of the earliest Hindu temples in Gujarat and is a rare example dating from the Maitraka period. It is remotely situated in western Saurashtra, where it forms part of a series of monuments that dotted the Arabian Sea coastal region.

The temple is now much dilapidated. The sanctuary is raised on a high terrace, the sides of which are carved with basement mouldings and niches (traces of worn sculptures). It was once surrounded by a passageway, possibly with a mandapa at the front (east), but nothing has survived. Rising above the sanctuary is a pyramidal masonry roof with a capping amalaka. On each side of the roof are three large arch-like blind windows.

JAGAT

Ambika Mata Temple, 961

This small but elaborate Hindu temple dates from the Pratihara period. The building consists of a towered sanctuary, a mandapa with projections on two sides and a small porch on the front (west). The outer walls have figurative panels carved almost in the round; these are set in niches sheltered by miniature eaves. Within the niches are female deities, many of which are forms of Durga, as well as the Dik-palas, attendant maidens in seductive postures and rearing beasts. High up on the walls are seated musicians, sages and amorous couples. Rising above the sanctuary is the curvilinear tower, with diminutive towered motifs at the corners and in the middle of each side.

The mandapa has pierced stone windows on the north and south, flanked by carved panels similar to those on the sanctuary walls. Additional niches are positioned in the roof, which rises in a pyramidal formation in a number of eave-like tiers. The porch is sheltered by an angled eave. An elaborately carved doorway leads to the sanctuary, where a small Ambika image is enshrined. The ceiling panels of the mandapa and porch are carved with multi-lobed motifs and pendant medallions. Placed within the mandapa is a carved panel of dancing Ganesha.

In one of the nearby shrines is a skeletal figure of Chamunda. A detached entrance pavilion stands a short distance away.

JAIPUR AND AMBER

JAIPUR

Named after Sawai Jai Singh, the ruler who founded this town in 1727, Jaipur is a unique example of traditional Hindu town planning. The city is regularly laid-out in squares with straight streets; the central square is occupied by the palace complex with its celebrated observatory (see Volume II).

None of the temples of the town predates the 18th century. Overlooking the town from the nearby hills are shrines dedicated to Ganesha and Surya. These are partly constructed in a late Mughal style, but also have the more usual curved towers.

8 km (5 miles) south-east of the town is Galta, where there is a Shiva temple; the sacred pools nearby are fed by a natural spring. Amber is approximately the same distance to the north.

Central Museum

This houses a collection of 9th–10th-century sculptures from various sites in Rajasthan. Among the pieces from **Abaneri** are wall panels depicting Shiva and Parvati seated together with Ravana beneath (59.64) and a fine image of Durga slaying the demon (63.64). Four-headed Brahmani appears in a marble sculpture from Varmana (5.124). Also of note is a dancing Shiva, partly damaged, from Sambhar.

AMBER

This was an important Rajput capital until Jaipur was founded. Amber is picturesquely surrounded by rocky hills on which the Rajput palace and fort are built (see Volume II). The Hindu temples in the lower town mostly date from the 17th century; some are royal monuments. Fragments of earlier Pratihara structures are incorporated into later temples.

The temple of Jagat Shiromani and that dedicated to Narasimha have curved towers typical of the later western Indian style. The marble gateways in front of these temples are carved with miniature deities and animals. Several Jain temples are situated nearby.

600 m (1,950 ft) north-east of the town are the chhatris of the Amber rulers; these cenotaphs are in the form of domed pavilions.

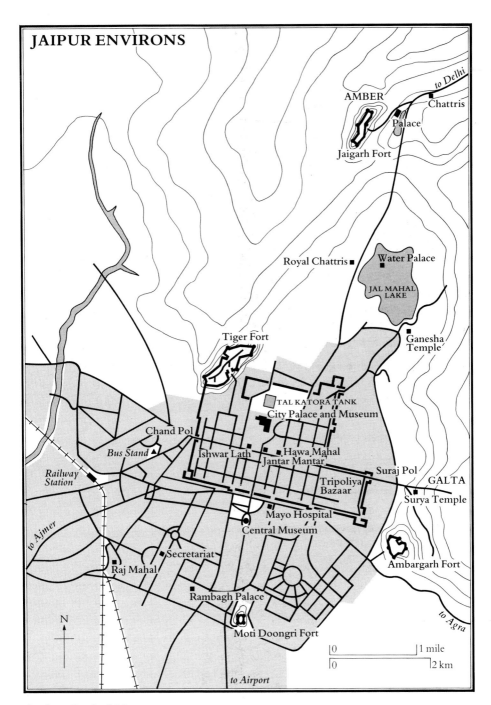

JAIPUR ENVIRONS

AMBER
to Delhi
Chattris
Palace
Jaigarh Fort

Royal Chattris
Water Palace
JAL MAHAL LAKE

Tiger Fort
Ganesha Temple

TAL KATORA TANK
City Palace and Museum

Chand Pol
Bus Stand
Ishwar Lath
Hawa Mahal
Jantar Mantar
Suraj Pol
GALTA
Railway Station
to Ajmer
Tripoliya Bazaar
Surya Temple

Mayo Hospital
Central Museum

Secretariat
Ambargarh Fort
Raj Mahal

Rambagh Palace
to Agra

N

Moti Doongri Fort

0   1 mile
0   2 km

to Airport

Archaeological Museum

In this small collection are 9th-century sculptures from **Abaneri**. These include a panel depicting Lakshmi flanked by Ganesha and Kubera (4.139), a column with an animal bracket supported on a

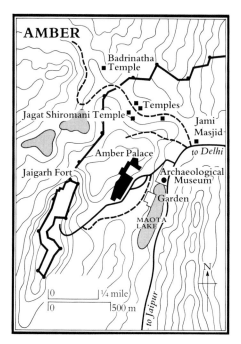

AMBER

Badrinatha Temple

Jagat Shiromani Temple

Temples

Jami Masjid

Amber Palace

to Delhi

Jaigarh Fort

Archaeological Museum

Garden

MAOTA LAKE

to Jaipur

0 ¼ mile
0 500 m

N

rearing mythical lion (9.149) and a seated lion carved in full relief (182.82). Also from **Abaneri**, but of a slightly later date, is a representation of a three-headed Skanda figure standing between two ornate pilasters (111.138).

JAISALMER

While the Rajput rulers of Jaisalmer were staunch Hindus, they permitted wealthy Jain merchants in the town, which was located on an important trade route, to act as temple patrons. A group of 15th–16th-century Jain sanctuaries is preserved in the fort above the town. Each temple is attached to one or more open columned mandapas that are roofed with a cluster of towers and surrounded by subsidiary shrines. The exteriors are mostly un-adorned, but the interior columns, brackets and walls are richly carved in the later western Indian manner. The presence of domes and parapets of merlons indicate Islamic influence.

(For the palace and fort see Volume II.)

Parshvanatha Temple, 1417

This has a fine gateway, an ornate porch, a series of columned mandapas and fifty-two subsidiary shrines surrounding the principal temple. Columns and ceilings recall the earlier Solanki style; so does the floral, animal and figural decoration. Brackets are elaborately carved as maidens and dancers.

Sambhavanatha Temple, 1431

Beneath this sanctuary, narrow tunnels lead to underground vaults where palm-leaf manuscripts are stored. Within the temple is a domed ceiling with brackets fashioned as dancing maidens.

Rishabhanatha Temple, 1479

The exterior of this shrine is embellished with more than six hundred images. In contrast, the interior is devoid of figural ornamentation.

Shantinatha Temple, 1480

Built on two storeys, both the sanctuary and attached mandapa are roofed with groups of clustered towers. There is little carved ornamentation on the exterior except for the pyramidal roof over the mandapa, which has elaborate seated lions on the sides.

Parshvanatha Temple, 1547

The walls of this temple are covered with a multitude of meditating Tirthankara images.

Ashtapadi ka Mandir, 16th century

Somewhat unusually, the sculptures of this Jain temple incorporate Hindu divini-ties such as the incarnations of Vishnu, Kali and Lakshmi. The frieze of dancers that runs around the walls is interrupted by vigorous dancing and fighting figures. Portraits of the temple donors mounted

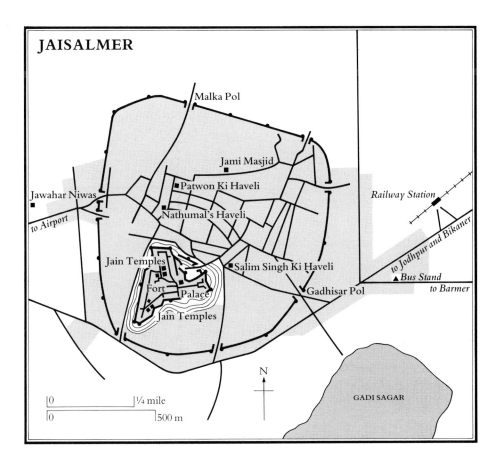

JAISALMER

Malka Pol

Jami Masjid

Patwon Ki Haveli

Jawahar Niwas

to Airport

Nathumal's Haveli

Railway Station

to Jodhpur and Bikaner

Jain Temples

Fort

Palace

Salim Singh Ki Haveli

Bus Stand

to Barmer

Jain Temples

Gadhisar Pol

N

0   ¼ mile

0   500 m

GADI SAGAR

on elephants are placed on one side of the court facing into the sanctuary.

JHALRAPATAN

Several fine Hindu temples of the 11th–12th centuries stand within this town, which also incorporates the ruined 7th–8th-century site of Chandravati, 1·5 km (1 mile) to the south, where dilapidated temples, fallen gateways and broken sculptures are preserved. Many of these overlook the left bank of the Chandrabhaga river; other architectural pieces from the site have been reused in later structures within the town. The loose sculptures that were discovered have been mostly removed to the Archaeological Museum, Jhalawar.

Surya Temple, late 11th century

This temple is closely linked with central Indian styles, especially in the treatment of the curved tower. This is adorned with miniature tower-like motifs, rising one above the other in the middle of each side; beneath these motifs are large arches containing figures and fully carved seated lions. Tiers of smaller tower-like motifs fill the intervening spaces. A large amalaka is positioned at the summit. The outer walls of the sanctuary are dominated by projections, which rhythmically expand outwards in the middle of each side.

Figural sculptures adorn each of the projections; similar figures are carved on to the shafts of the interior columns of the adjoining mandapa.

JODHPUR AND MANDOR

The Hindu temples in the Rajput city of Jodhpur mostly date from the 17th–18th centuries. They illustrate the later evolution of the western Indian style. 8 km (5 miles) north of the town is the royal commemorative site of Mandor.

(For the fort and the palace see Volume II.)

JODHPUR

Sardar Museum

Numerous 8th–10th-century sculptures and architectural fragments come from **Osian** and **Kiradu**. There are, however, several earlier pieces. Two pillars from Mandor have panels illustrating episodes from the Krishna story, such as kicking the cart, stealing butter, holding up the mountain (A15.26) and fighting the crane and the bull (A15.27). A later panel from the same site depicts a water wheel with camels pulling a cart (A15.25).

A fine schist image of a seated Vishnu from Didwana dates from the 10th-century Pratihara period (61.2010). An idea of the later 11th–12th-century Solanki style may be had from a detailed life-sized carving of Jivantaswami from Khimsar (116.2534).

MANDOR

Only a few remains at this site predate the 17th–18th centuries. The lower mouldings of an 8th-century Hindu temple, with large platforms added in later centuries, are preserved at the top of a nearby hill. A well with a 7th-century inscription and a panel of the Matrikas is carved into the rocky cliff near the railway station.

That Mandor was a site of royal significance in later times is demonstrated by the chhatris of the Jodhpur rulers. These cenotaphs were constructed in dark-red sandstone; their clustered towers imitate those of later western Indian temples. The adjoining open mandapas are of late Mughal inspiration, with double-curved eaves and ribbed domes.

A colonnade nearby shelters rock-cut images of fierce-looking local heroes and deities, all brightly painted.

JUNAGADH AND GIRNAR

The ancient centre of Junagadh is situated at the foot of the holy Girnar mountain, 3 km (2 miles) to the east.

JUNAGADH

This town was the capital of Gujarat in the 2nd–4th centuries under the Kshatrapa rulers. Several monastic complexes dating from this period were excavated into the rocks in Uparkot, the old citadel. These rock-cut monuments were associated with Buddhist or Jain communities. Nearby are two 11th-century step-wells, one of which is approached by a circular staircase.

(For the other monuments of the city see Volume II.)

Babapyara Caves, 2nd century

Numerous cells and columned verandahs opening off rock-cut courts comprise this Jain complex. One of the chambers is large and apsidal-ended.

'Buddhist' Caves, 3rd–4th century

This rock-cut complex may have been used by Buddhists, hence the name. The small square cells are arranged on two levels, connected by a winding staircase; they surround a number of excavated courts. Six richly carved columns on the lower level have garlands over pot-like mouldings at the bases; groups of figures, now worn, appear at the capitals. Bench seating is provided in many of the cells.

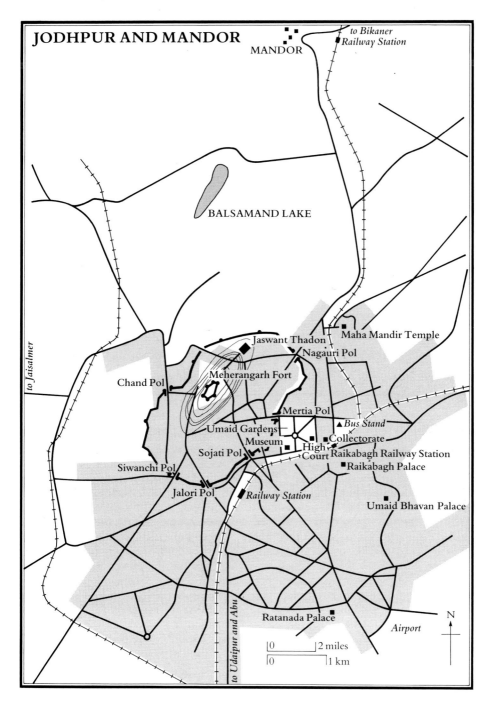

JODHPUR AND MANDOR

to Bikaner
Railway Station
MANDOR

BALSAMAND LAKE

to Jaisalmer

Jaswant Thadon
Maha Mandir Temple
Nagauri Pol
Meherangarh Fort
Chand Pol
Mertia Pol
▲ *Bus Stand*
Umaid Gardens
Museum
Collectorate
Sojati Pol
High
Court
Raikabagh Railway Station
Siwanchi Pol
Raikabagh Palace
Jalori Pol
Railway Station
Umaid Bhavan Palace

to Udaipur and Abu

Ratanada Palace
Airport
N

|0 |2 miles
|0 |1 km

Khapra Kodia Caves, 3rd–4th century This rock-cut complex is located about 300 m (1,050 ft) north of Uparkot. It contains five square cisterns approached by descending staircases, with colonnades and passageways on one side.

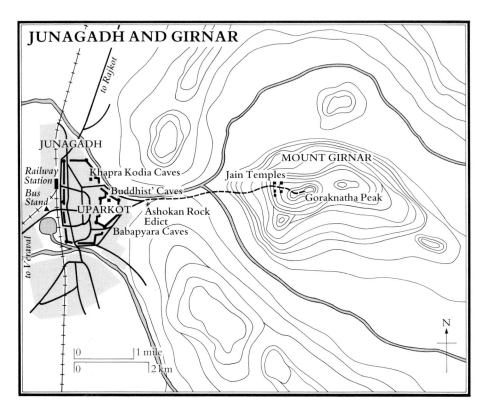

JUNAGADH AND GIRNAR

to Rajkot

JUNAGADH

Railway Station
Bus Stand

Khapra Kodia Caves

Buddhist' Caves

UPARKOT

Ashokan Rock Edict

Babapyara Caves

MOUNT GIRNAR

Jain Temples

Goraknatha Peak

to Veraval

0 — 1 mile
0 — 2 km

N

GIRNAR

Particularly sacred to the Jains is the Girnar mountain, which rises more than 900 m (3,000 ft) above the plain. That Girnar was an important religious centre from the 3rd century BC onwards is indicated by the inscriptions on a boulder beside the path at the foot of the hill. These record edicts of the Maurya emperor Ashoka, as well as proclamations of the later Kshatrapa and Gupta rulers. The boulder is now enclosed within a modern building.

The hill is actually the worn cone of an extinct volcano and it is almost completely surrounded by ridges. Gateways, shrines and tanks have been built at various points along the principal path that leads upwards to the central peak. On a rocky shelf at a height of about 650 m (2,100 ft) is a group of sixteen Jain sanctuaries; the largest is dedicated to Neminatha. These constitute a temple city, similar to but smaller than that at **Satrunjaya**. The monuments date from the Solanki period, as well as from later centuries. At the summit, on Goraknatha peak, is a dilapidated sanctuary dedicated to the goddess Ambika. Several Hindu shrines line the path.

Important festivals are held at Girnar, especially on the first full moon after the rainy season. On this occasion, pilgrims perform a ritual circumambulation of the mountain before climbing to worship at the different shrines. Since no accommodation is available on the peak, they must descend before nightfall.

Neminatha Temple, 1128 and later

This is one of the oldest monuments at Girnar. The principal temple stands in the middle of a rectangular court surrounded by a colonnade with seventy chambers.

The passageway around the sanctuary and the adjoining mandapa follow a stepped plan. Few of the original mouldings and sculptures have survived; the clustered tower is a later addition. The mandapa is roofed with a pyramid of miniature pot finials. The decoration displays the elaborate detail typical of the Solanki period, particularly the corbelled dome over the central bay. Most of the other portions of the temple are later replacements.

Mallinatha Temple, 1231 and later

Built by Vastupala and Tejapala, patrons of one of the **Abu** monuments, this temple has an unusual layout, with three sanctuaries opening off a single-columned mandapa. Though it has been much renovated, the building preserves portions of the original basement mouldings, wall niches and overhanging eaves; subsidiary clustered towers are positioned at the corners. The corbelled domes of the mandapa are typical of the Solanki style. Ceiling compositions here incorporate maidens and flying figures. Within the two side shrines are pedestals fashioned as representations of cosmic mountains and covered with miniature figures and shrines.

Temple of Samprati Raja, 1453

This sanctuary is possibly the finest of the later series, despite the renovation of the clustered tower. The projecting porches of the sanctuary and mandapa have pierced stone screens carved with geometric and foliate motifs.

Melak Vasahi Temple, 15th century

The corbelled domes and vaults of this temple are complex compositions with intricately carved foliate and geometric designs. One example even depicts Vishnu with flying figures. The outer walls of the sanctuary have sculptures, now damaged, arranged in two tiers.

KALIBANGAN

Together with **Lothal**, this is the most important prehistoric Harappan site in India. Kalibangan is situated less than 100 km (63 miles) south-east of Harappa (Pakistan), the site which has given its name to the civilization that flourished in the Indus valley in the 3rd–2nd millennia BC.

Evidence of the antecedents of the Harappan culture was discovered in two mounds at Kalibangan. At the smaller (western) mound, lower deposits are distinguished by red pottery that was poorer in quality and decoration than the overlying Harappan wares. The houses are of mud brick, but their orientation is at variance with that of the Harappan structures above. Built over these earlier deposits was a wide mud-brick wall, possibly defensive in purpose, which was probably erected by the Harappan people after their occupation of the site. Possibly this mound represented the citadel, as did the smaller western mound at the principal Harappan site of Mohenjodaro (Pakistan).

At the larger eastern mound, pre-Harappan and Harappan elements overlap, suggesting that peoples from both cultures may have lived side by side for a time. The artefacts found here include bronze implements, stone blades, faience and terracotta plaques. Among the numerous seals are those engraved with images of animals, such as the unicorn and the bull, together with an undeciphered script. The Harappan brick houses are laid out regularly on a grid.

KIRADU

Five dilapidated Hindu monuments at this site are representative of the western Indian style during the late Pratihara period. The typical Kiradu temple has a square sanctuary adjoining a small porch or columned mandapa. The sanctuary

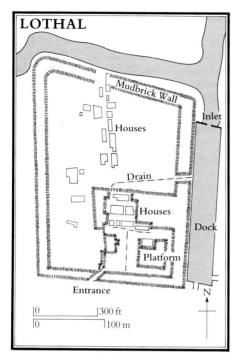

LOTHAL

Mudbrick Wall

Inlet

Houses

Drain

Houses

Dock

Platform

Entrance

N

| 0 | 300 ft |
| 0 | 100 m |

Within the settlement are the remains of houses, drains, channels and wells. Many of these features are aligned along a north–south road in the middle of the site. Other houses with drains are found in a clustered arrangement on slightly elevated ground in the middle of the southern part of the settlement. Streets appear to have been laid out on a regular grid pattern that divided the houses into blocks; this suggests a systematic plan. A raised platform is situated in the south-east corner.

Houses and Drains

In the earlier Harappan phase, both sun-dried and kiln-burnt brick were used. Houses were provided with fireplaces and bathrooms; in one house there was a brick platform into which jars containing beads were embedded. The paved drains from houses ended in large jars or were sometimes connected with covered public drains along the streets. One long drain was found connected with eight bathrooms at different points through subsidiary drains. Water was supplied by wells, both private and public.

Platform

The 4·5-m-high (15 ft) platform in the south-east corner of the settlement was built of sun-burnt bricks. It consisted of twelve square blocks, four on one side and three on the other, separated by narrow passageways. The platform has been interpreted as a kiln where plaques, sling balls and terracotta seal impressions were baked. But it might also have been a record room where sealed documents were stored or a warehouse for grain and other goods.

Dock

A unique feature at Lothal, known at no other Harappan site, is the brick-lined rectangular dock, which is 218 m by 37 m (715 ft by 121 ft). The dock was supplied

been discovered at this site. This civilization flourished in the Indus valley zone (Pakistan) in the 3rd–2nd millennia BC, but also reached the western coast of India by sea. Lothal is a comparatively large Harappan settlement which lies about 16 km (10 miles) from the sea.

The long habitation of Harappan peoples at Lothal has resulted in the accumulation of a mound 6·5 m (21 ft) high. Deposits here are divided into two uninterrupted phases spanning the period *c.* 2,200–1,700 BC. The first phase represents the mature Harappan culture, while the second marks its later, somewhat decadent continuation.

A broad mud-brick embankment, almost 20 m (66 ft) wide and sometimes faced with burnt brick, completely surrounds the settlement. This occupies a rectangular zone approximately 230 m by 170 m (750 ft by 557 ft), with an entrance on the south side. On the east, the embankment is flanked by a long rectangular tank, which may have served as a dock.

with a spill channel (south) and a 7-m-wide (23 ft) inlet channel (north), which connected it to a river on which boats could have travelled from the sea. Evidence of overseas trade is provided by the discovery of a seal from Bahrain, which depicts a double-headed dragon flanked by gazelles.

Cemetery

The cemetery at Lothal is situated immediately north-west of the settlement. Large funerary vessels were found here, indicating pit burials. Some of the graves had two skeletons.

Archaeological Museum

Artefacts of the Harappan culture discovered in the excavations are exhibited here. Typical are the inscribed steatite seals, stone weights, measuring instruments of shell, clay impressions of seals, terracotta plaques, ornaments of semi-precious stone, human and animal clay figurines, long stone blades and bronze implements. The pottery has paintings of animal motifs, such as deer, peacocks, birds and snakes. A copper figurine furnishes evidence of metal casting; metal hooks suggest a local fishing industry.

Finds belonging to the late Harappan phase include a goblet, a beaker and a perforated jar. The pottery is adorned with more limited animal themes, including bulls. There are stone blades made of jasper and agate.

MENAL

The temples at this Hindu site are built on the edge of a picturesque gorge with a waterfall. The main monument comprises the Mahanaleshvara temple, to which a monastery of the Pashupata sect is attached; there are also two groups of smaller shrines and an ornate well. All of

these features are contained within a fortified enclosure; this is entered through a two-storey gateway with carvings of Bhairava and Ganesha flanking the doorway. There is another temple, also with an adjoining monastery, on the opposite side of the gorge.

Though the earliest shrine dates back to the 9th-century Pratihara period, the principal monuments were sponsored by royal patrons of the Chahamana dynasty.

Mahanaleshvara Temple,
late 11th century

This is the best-preserved temple at the site and it is a fine example of the western Indian style. However, it also incorporates central Indian elements, such as the meshed bands in the middle of the tower and the tiers of miniature towered motifs that fill the spaces at either side. A large amalaka is positioned at the summit; the front is embellished with a seated lion. Guardian deities and Shaiva divinities are carved on to the wall panels, which project rhythmically outwards. The adjoining mandapa is dominated by projecting porches; the roof is a pyramid of masonry, arranged in tiers of ribbed motifs.

MODHERA

Surya Temple, 1027 and later

This first great achievement of the Solanki period is one of the finest Hindu temples in Gujarat. Despite its general dilapidation and partial reconstruction, the monumental conception and rich ornamentation of the temple are still apparent.

The sanctuary, two mandapas and a gateway to the complex are aligned with a tank to the east. The sanctuary and its adjoining mandapa are both laid out on a stepped plan; on the east is an entrance porch. The basement mouldings have

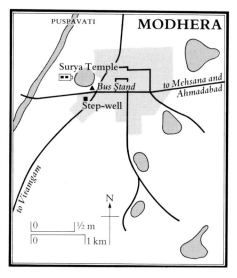

Surya (north). The tower, probably of the clustered type, has not survived. The outer walls of the porch have bands of scrollwork and figural panels beneath inclined seating slabs. The columns on the periphery and within the mandapa are richly ornamented. Beams and friezes support ceiling panels; the central corbelled dome is a reconstruction.

The detached mandapa, which is also laid out on a stepped plan, is slightly later than the temple itself. It has a large octagonal space in the middle, but the original corbelled dome is a replacement. Columns and brackets are adorned with miniature figures, foliation and scrollwork. Between the columns flanking the entrances on four sides are multi-lobed arches encrusted with figures.

Further east stand two columns, all that remains of the gateway at the top of the steps that lead down to the tank. The water is contained in an immense rectangle of masonry. Double flights of steps

friezes of elephants, horses and miniature figures. Wall panels are flanked by pilasters and capped with miniature eaves and pediments. Among the better-preserved images are Agni (south) and

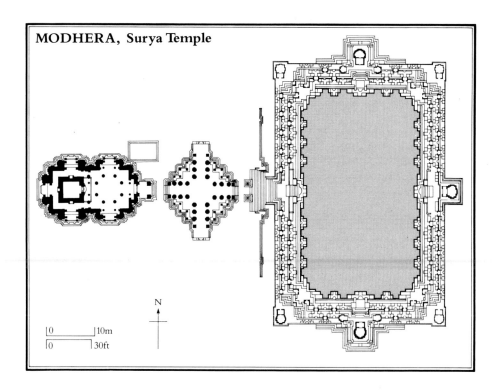

MODHERA, Surya Temple

on all sides create a richly patterned effect. Incorporated into these steps are miniature shrines with curved towers covered with arch-like motifs.

Vav, 11th century

To the west of the town is a circular well. This is approached by a flight of steps over which a small shrine is constructed.

MUKUNDARA

Temple, 5th century

This dilapidated Hindu structure is the only Gupta monument in Rajasthan. Portions of the columned mandapa in front of the sanctuary still stand on a low terrace. The simplicity of construction and the restrained ornamentation, particularly of the curved brackets and beams, are typical of the Gupta style.

NATHDWARA

Shrinathji Temple, 1691

This is the most important place of pilgrimage for the Hindu Vallabha sect. An image of Krishna brought to Nathdwara from **Mathura** in 1617 by the Rajput ruler of **Udaipur** is worshipped here. Carved out of black stone at some unknown date, the figure of Krishna holds one hand up as if to support the mountain.

In order to serve the needs of devotees, local artists have produced fine paintings on paper and cloth. These are known as pecchavais and depict the enshrined god being worshipped, or surrounded by cows and gopis in his forest setting. (There is a fine collection of pecchavais in the Calico Museum of Textiles, **Ahmadabad**.)

OSIAN

The 8th–9th-century temples at this site constitute the largest group of early Hindu and Jain monuments in Rajasthan. The typical Osian temple is raised on a terrace decorated with mouldings and miniature niches. The sanctuary walls have central projections with carved panels framed by pilasters and surmounted by tower-like pediments.

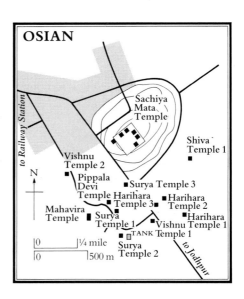

Above rises the curved tower covered with a mesh of arch-like motifs; an amalaka and pot finial are positioned at the summit. A small porch on the front has two or more columns. In later examples, the porch is expanded into an open columned mandapa, with balcony seating sheltered by an overhanging eave. Doorways are adorned with a variety of themes, including figures of river goddesses, coiled serpents and scrollwork.

The temples are clustered in several groups south and west of the town. Elevated on a hill to the north is another group with the Sachiya Mata temple, still in use for worship, at its core.

SOUTHERN GROUP

Harihara Temple 1, 8th century

Of this Hindu complex, the principal sanctuary and three out of four subsidiary shrines still stand. Much of the ornamentation is damaged, except for the exuberantly carved sanctuary doorway and the porch columns of the minor shrines.

Harihara Temple 2, 8th century

The principal shrine of this temple adjoins an open mandapa with a porch. Delicately carved foliate motifs adorn the terrace basement. Images preserved in the central wall niches include Narasimha (north), Harihara (east) and Trivikrama (south). The ceiling in front of the sanctuary is decorated with looped snakes.

Harihara Temple 3, early 9th century

The rectangular sanctuary of this temple has sculpture panels on the outer walls, with a frieze of narrative scenes taken from the Krishna story above. No superstructure has survived. The adjoining mandapa has an unusual vaulted ceiling in which curved slabs are supported on internal ribs. The columns are finely carved; figures of large river goddesses flank the sanctuary doorway. The ceiling is a highly elaborate dome-like composition with miniature figures, lotus ornament, scrollwork and serpent-like spokes.

WESTERN GROUP

Surya Temple 3, 8th century

This Hindu temple has a sanctuary with a curved tower adjoining an open mandapa. The double-height porch columns have bases and capitals carved with pot and foliage motifs. Set into the sanctuary walls are fine sculptures of Durga (north), Surya (east) and Ganesha (south).

Tank, 8th century

This dilapidated tank is contemporary with the early temples. The east face has projecting walls, gateways and a colonnade with carved columns and figural brackets. Within the colonnade are niches with angled eaves and ornamental pediments.

Pippala Devi Temple, early 9th century

The open mandapa of this Hindu temple is laid out on a stepped plan with balcony seating, which is partly preserved. At the north-east corner is an additional columned structure. The columns are finely decorated with pot and foliage capitals as well as figures, now damaged.

Vishnu Temple 2, late 9th century

An incomplete towered Hindu sanctuary adjoins a columned mandapa. Of interest is the figurative and foliate ornamentation on the balcony seating in the mandapa.

Mahavira Temple, mostly 11th century

The principal sanctuary of this Jain complex incorporates earlier 8th-century portions. For example, the outer walls of the principal shrine have sculpted niches with pediments typical of the earlier phase. Later features include the clustered tower rising over the sanctuary, the pyramidal roof of the mandapa, the pierced stone screens beneath and the corbelled domed ceilings. The subsidiary shrines are also later constructions. Sculpture panels on these shrines completely cover the walls; the porch columns and doorways are all richly decorated.

The ornate gateway nearby was erected in 1015; it comprises two elaborately carved columns covered with figures. The triangular architrave above the lintel frames a miniature shrine.

NORTHERN GROUP

Surya Temple 1, early 8th century

This shrine is incorporated into the compound of the Sachiya Mata temple. The projection on the front (west) of the tower has a large head, possibly of Surya, inside an arched niche. The interior columns are elaborately decorated. The sanctuary doorway is surrounded by amorous couples and other figures. The ceiling above the bay immediately in front is adorned with snakes looped around a lotus; the friezes beneath depict episodes from the Krishna story.

Sachiya Mata Temple,
11th–12th century

This Hindu complex was constructed in several phases. Dating from the 11th century are three subsidiary shrines notable for their fine sculptures. In the north shrine, for example, there are figures of Varaha (north), Trivikrama (west) and

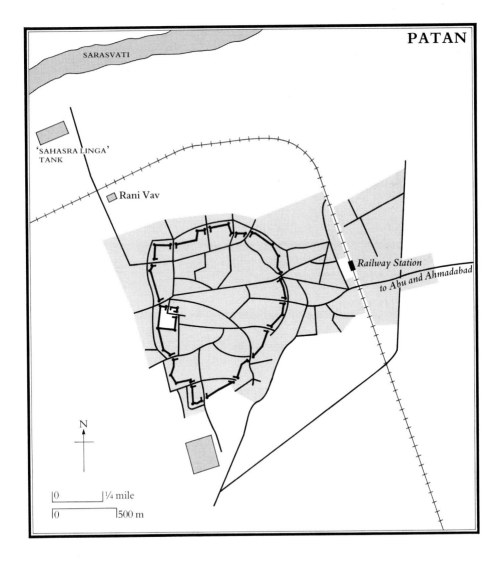

Vishnu with Lakshmi (east). A mesh of arch-like motifs completely covers the towers. The adjoining porches have balcony seating, overhanging eaves and pyramidal roofs. Within, domed ceilings are elaborate compositions with figurative friezes and brackets. The central shrine is dated to 1178. On the west face of the clustered tower is a triangular projection filled with sculptures. The damaged wall panels have elaborate pediments.

PATAN (map p. 303)

As Anahilvada, this town was the capital of Gujarat in the 11th–12th centuries under the Solanki rulers. Though the town was sacked several times by the Muslims at the end of the 12th century, it continued to maintain its importance as a cultural and artistic centre. It is known today for its fine textiles, produced in the characteristic ikat technique.

Little remains of ancient Anahilvada other than traces of fortifications, some impressive water structures and an immense tank. These are all located about 2 km (1½ miles) north-west of modern Patan. The temples within the town are no earlier than the 16th century. (For the later monuments see Volume II.)

Rani Vav (Queen's Well),
late 11th century

Only recently renovated to reveal its full glory, this is the most magnificent step-well of the Gujarat series. Its monumental conception and ornate architectural treatment suggest that it also served a ritual ceremonial purpose.

Multi-storey colonnades and retaining walls link a stepped tank to a deep circular well; the well is approached by a long flight of steps. Throughout, the ornamentation of the architectural elements is sumptuous. Columns, brackets and beams are encrusted with scrollwork, overflowing pots and foliate ornament;

wall panels within niches are carved with figures. Within the well itself, curving walls and multi-corbelled brackets are adorned with figures of divinities, exactly as in contemporary temple art. Hindu deities alternate with alluring maidens on the walls flanking the staircase. Characteristic are the clear carving and the vigorous postures of the figures.

'Sahasra (Thousand) Linga' Tank,
12th century

Near to the earthen embankment of this substantial reservoir are the remains of an unusual water shrine. This consists of an elevated podium and two rows of columns set into a water channel.

PRABHAS PATAN

This celebrated Hindu pilgrimage centre of Somanatha is situated on the shore of the Arabian Sea, 6 km (4 miles) east of Veraval. The chief focus is the great Shiva temple, now completely rebuilt in the traditional Solanki style. The new stone carvings on the monument testify to the continuity of artistic traditions in Gujarat up to the present day.

The holiness of this spot, which is considered to be the site of one of Shiva's Jyotirlingas, also extends to a nearby confluence of three rivers, where devotees come to bathe. Ruined gateways, other shrines and numerous wells and tanks are found in the vicinity.

Somanatha Temple,
modern reconstruction

Originally founded in the 10th century, the temple was subjected to successive demolitions followed by renovations; its proximity to the sea may also have contributed to its decay. The wealth of the temple's treasury attracted numerous raiders, the first of whom was Mahmud of Ghazni, who destroyed the sanctuary in

1026. During the Solanki period the temple was substantially reconstructed by the ruler Kumarapala (1143–72).

The architecture conforms to the scheme exemplified in the **Modhera** temple. A sanctuary surrounded by a passageway and an adjoining mandapa both have open porches on three sides. The basement and walls are covered with friezes and panels. The lofty tower over the sanctuary, which rises more than 50 m (165 ft) high, is of the clustered type; the mandapa is roofed with a stone pyramid. The principal entrance is flanked by balcony seating. Within, elaborately carved columns support corbelled domed ceilings.

Rudreshvara Temple, 11th century

This ruined temple is contemporary with the original Somanatha monument and is laid out on the same plan, though on a smaller scale. The sculptures on the walls, columns and doorways suggest the quality of the ornamentation of the first Somanatha sanctuary.

Archaeological Museum

Eroded sculptures and architectural fragments from the 11th-century Somanatha temple are displayed here.

PUSHKAR

11 km (7 miles) north-west of **Ajmer** is the sacred Hindu lake of Pushkar. This is lined with stone steps and shrines, the holiest of which is dedicated to Brahma. Devotees bathe in this lake, where it is believed that Brahma performed a sacrifice after killing a demon. The town is renowned for its popular cattle fair (November–December) at which numerous camels are sold.

RANAKPUR

This secluded wooded site is celebrated for its large-scale Jain monument. The complexity of the overall conception and the elaborate ornamentation of this temple reveal the full evolution of the western Indian style. Several other smaller shrines are also located here.

Adinatha Temple, 1439

The sanctuary is symmetrically planned around the central sanctuary of the Tirthankara. The complex is contained within a square enclosure more than 100 m (330 ft) on each side; this is raised up on a terrace with gateways in the middle of each side. The gateways consist of triple-storey open porches approached by steep flights of steps. Above the enclosure walls are rows of spires; these cap the subsidiary shrines that line the peripheries of the enclosure.

The main sanctuary has a clustered tower with projecting balconies, superimposed one upon the other in the middle of each side; secondary shrines in the four corners have simpler towers. The outer walls are provided with sharply cut basement and niche mouldings; figural panels are mostly restricted to depictions of the Jain saviours. The central chamber, which houses a quadruple image of Adinatha, is approached through four doorways.

The interior is unsurpassed for its spatial complexity. The columned mandapas adjoining the central shrine and the surrounding colonnades regularly open up to create large octagonal areas. These are double- or triple-storey, with balconies at the upper levels and elaborate corbelled domes above. Throughout, the decoration is detailed and precise. There are depictions of Jain saints, often in panels combining miniature figures in rows or concentric circles. Narrative scenes from the lives of the saviours and votive plaques representing sacred cities are also incorporated. Among the

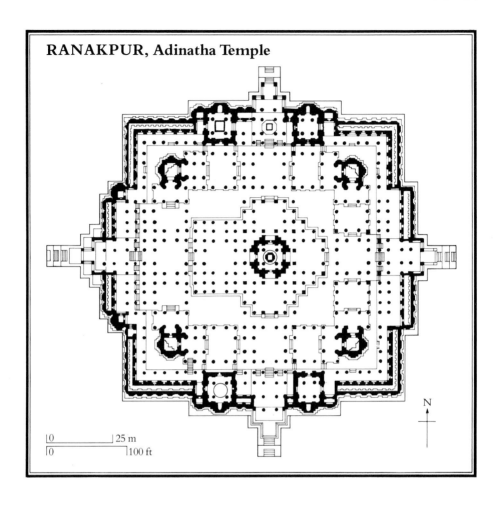

RANAKPUR, Adinatha Temple

0   25 m
0   100 ft

N

attendant figures are dancers, musicians and guardians. The columns and balconies are covered with stylized foliate motifs; over the central aisles the lintels are multi-lobed. The elaborate ceiling compositions incorporate multi-lobed motifs, medallions and great swirls of scrollwork.

Parshvanatha Temple,
mid-15th century

This sanctuary with a clustered tower adjoins a mandapa on a stepped plan. Much of the sculpture is intact, including Jain figures, attendant maidens and couples on the outer walls. The temple is remarkable for its pierced stone windows with ornate designs.

Surya Narayana Temple,
mid-15th century

The tower over the sanctuary of this Hindu temple almost approaches a circle in plan due to its numerous wall projections. Vertical bands of mesh-like ornament alternate with tiers of towered motifs. At the base of the tower are small projecting niches. The adjoining mandapa is unusually laid out on an octagonal plan with six projecting porches.

RODA

Five temples of the Maitraka period still stand at this site. These 8th-century structures comprise one of the earliest groups of Hindu monuments in Gujarat. Each temple consists of a small sanctuary entered through an elaborate doorway sheltered by a porch. The sanctuary walls are either plain or have projections adorned with niches and pediments. The curved towers are covered with meshes of arch-like motifs; amalakas are positioned at the summits. The front faces of the towers usually have triangular projections; this is sometimes a complex pyramidal composition (Temple 5). Carved detail is mostly restricted to the sanctuary doorways and porch columns; the most popular themes are pot and foliage motifs, scrollwork and miniature figures (the last in Temple 3). (Loose sculptures found at the site have been removed to the Museum and Picture Gallery, **Vadodara**.)

To the east of Temples 2 and 3 is a large tank with dilapidated sides and double flights of steps leading down to the water. Small shrines at the corners duplicate temple forms.

SAMALAJI AND DEVNIMORI

These twin sites, about 2 km ($1\frac{1}{2}$ miles) apart, are important for their Hindu and Buddhist antiquities. Samalaji is known throughout the region as a pilgrimage centre, attracting large numbers of tribal peoples at festival time.

SAMALAJI

Numerous blue schist sculptures of deities and attendant maidens dating from the 6th-century Maitraka period were found here. (Most of these are now exhibited in museums at **Bombay** and **Vadodara**.)

While one important monument dates from an earlier era, the main shrine still in use for worship is a 15th–16th-century construction. This has the slender clustered tower and pierced stone windows typical of the later phase. An image of Vishnu housed in the sanctuary probably dates from the 7th–8th century. Opposite is a small temple containing a fine 6th-century image of Shiva (identical to the one now in Bombay). Numerous other dilapidated shrines of different periods stand nearby. Of interest is a panel carved with Vishvarupa set up at a holy spot on the riverbank.

Harishchandrani Chauri Temple,
9th century

This is the oldest intact temple at Samalaji. A sanctuary adjoins an open porch with balcony seating. The clustered tower over the sanctuary still preserves its mesh of arch-like motifs. A short distance away is a gateway with two sculpted columns; these support a lintel fashioned as a double-curved arch which contains flying musicians (damaged).

DEVNIMORI

The brick remains of a 4th-century Buddhist stupa and monastery were

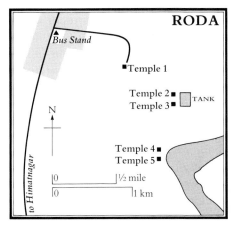

RODA

Bus Stand

Temple 1

Temple 2
Temple 3   TANK

N

Temple 4
Temple 5

to Himatnagar

0   ½ mile
0   1 km

discovered at this site. (Terracotta figures and decorative plaques recovered from the excavations are now displayed in the University Museum, **Vadodara**.) Unfortunately, the stupa and monastery are now submerged beneath the waters of an irrigation project.

SATRUNJAYA

This Jain temple city is the largest of its kind in India. According to local tradition, Adinatha, the first Tirthankara, visited the hill several times and the first temple was erected by his son Bharata. The Jains believe the hill to be particularly holy because Pundarika, the chief disciple of Adinatha, obtained enlightenment here.

Numerous temples occupy the twin summits of Satrunjaya hill, which rise about 600 m (2,000 ft) above the plain; the hill is approached from the town of Palitana, which lies 2 km (1½ miles) to the north. A sinuous line of temples and shrines crowns the two ridges, as well as filling the intermediate valley, creating a complex multi-spired silhouette. Most of these sanctuaries are grouped together in fortified enclosures or tuks. These are named after their founders, usually wealthy merchants, and have elaborate gateways and corner bastions. Each morning pilgrims ascend the hill, a climb of almost two hours, to pay reverence to the different Jain saviours and saints. Since no accommodation is provided they must return by nightfall; the city then lies empty and silent.

There is little evidence of building activity prior to the destruction by the Muslims in the 14th–15th centuries; most sanctuaries are no earlier than the 16th century. The relatively unadorned outer walls (no sculptures), the clustered elegant profiles of the towers and the double-storey porches are all characteristic of the final phase of western Indian temple architecture. Arches with petalled fringes, parapets of merlons and fluted domes indicate the impact of contemporary Islamic architecture.

NORTH RIDGE

A number of tuks occupy this part of the Satrunjaya hill. The largest is the Khartaravasi Tuk, which is situated on the highest point of the north ridge.

Adinatha Temple,
16th century and later

This temple is the central monument of the Khartaravasi Tuk. Quadruple Tirthankara images housed in the sanctuary are approached through four entrance porches; another three porches provide access into the adjoining columned mandapa. Over the sanctuary rises the slender curvilinear tower. Built into the outer corners of the temple at ground level are colonnades roofed with fluted domes. Brackets within the colonnades are fashioned as dancers and musicians.

Nandishvara Dvipa, 16th century

Unusual in its layout, this temple is the principal monument of the Tuk of Sheth Hemabhai Vakatachand. The walls of the temple consist almost entirely of perforated stone screens. Inside, forming a large cross of five squares, are fifty-three altars; each is a miniature spire with compartments on four sides for Jina images.

INTERMEDIATE VALLEY

The lowest point between the ridges is occupied by two tuks. The one known as Motisah is the largest at Satrunjaya and is substantially fortified.

Vallabhai Temple, 19th century

This temple has a finely clustered spire rising above the sanctuary. Double-storey porches are crowned by fluted domes.

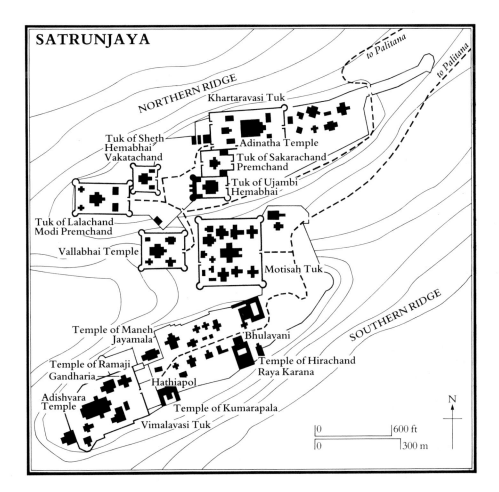

SATRUNJAYA

to Palitana

to Palitana

NORTHERN RIDGE

Khartaravasi Tuk

Tuk of Sheth
Hemabhai
Vakatachand

Adinatha Temple

Tuk of Sakarachand
Premchand

Tuk of Ujambi
Hemabhai

Tuk of Lalachand
Modi Premchand

Vallabhai Temple

Motisah Tuk

SOUTHERN RIDGE

Temple of Maneh
Jayamala

Bhulavani

Temple of Ramaji
Gandharia

Temple of Hirachand
Raya Karana

Hathiapol

Adishvara
Temple

Temple of Kumarapala

Vimalavasi Tuk

N

| 0 | 600 ft
| 0 | 300 m

Motisah Temple, 1836

This monument was constructed by a merchant family from Bombay. Its double-storey porches are similar to the entrance gateway.

SOUTH RIDGE

The Vimalavasi Tuk occupies most of the south ridge. It consists of an ascending street lined on both sides with temples, of which there are almost sixty, leading to the Adinatha temple at the summit.

Adishvara Temple,
mostly 16th century

Dominating the south ridge and, indeed, the whole of Satrunjaya, this imposing temple is similar in layout to the Adinatha temple on the north ridge. This example has a double-storey mandapa and there are no colonnades at ground level. The colossal image of Rishabhanatha enshrined within the temple has eyes of crystal and a crown and jewels of gold. The tower rising above is one of the most complicated of the series, with a profusion of miniature towered elements at the base.

Temple of Ramaji Gandharia,
16th century

This temple houses quadruple Tirthankara images approached through four double-storey porches.

Bhulavani (Labyrinth),
mostly 18th century

This intriguing structure is divided into small crypt-like chambers, each roofed with a dome. The central shrine has an unusual opening in the floor through which an image in a sunken storey can be viewed.

Hathiapol (Elephant Gate),
19th century

This gate is named after the elephants fashioned in low relief on the walls at either side.

SEJAKPUR

Navalakha Temple, 12th century

Though partly ruined, this is one of the finest Hindu temples of the Solanki period. The sanctuary and mandapa are both laid out on stepped plans, with the sanctuary walls rhythmically expanding outwards. The high basement with multi-faceted mouldings includes a frieze of elephants. Wall panels are framed by pilasters with pediments above; one of the finest is the figure of dancing Shiva (west). The complicated profile of the superstructure is achieved through multiple tower-like motifs, each covered with a mesh of arched motifs and capped with an amalaka. The projecting porches of the large mandapa have inclined balcony seating overhung by angled eaves. Above rises the pyramidal mass of the roof. Columns, brackets and ceilings are exuberantly carved throughout.

SIDHPUR

The holy Sarasvati river and the sacred Bindu lake attract numerous Hindu pilgrims to this town. While the site is known for its Solanki remains, several later sanctuaries are also of interest.

Rudra Mahalaya Temple, 12th century

Constructed by the Solanki ruler Jayasimha (1094–1143), this was a magnificent multi-storey Shiva sanctuary with eleven subsidiary shrines. The mutilated fragments of the edifice reveal the remains of several of these shrines, as well as two porches and four columns of the principal temple. The ambitious scale of the project and its sumptuous ornamentation are still evident in these surviving portions.

Incorporated into the adjoining mosque are several columns, ceilings and even a clustered tower from the original complex.

A short distance to the north is a well-preserved gateway with two high columns. Double brackets support an eave and an elaborate architrave fashioned as a triangular pediment. Makaras project outwards from the ends of the architrave. Throughout, the carving, now damaged, is exceptional for its deep cutting and exuberant detail.

TARANGA

Ajitanatha Temple, 1166

This Jain temple is one of the best-preserved Solanki projects; it is attributed to the ruler Kumarapala (1143–72). Despite later additions and modern white-washing, the building maintains most of its original features.

The temple is an integrated composition combining a sanctuary and a columned mandapa with three porches; the porch in the front (east) is enlarged. The outer walls are divided into two tiers of sculpture panels; these are framed in niches with elaborate tower-like pediments adorned with the Dikpalas, dancing maidens and seated goddesses with attendants. The figures are carved in full relief and are characterized by lively poses and sharply cut faces and costumes. Beneath, the basement is decorated with medallions and miniature niches. The porch columns have multi-faceted shafts.

The superstructure is one of the most complicated of the Solanki series. The clustered tower over the sanctuary has numerous miniature towered motifs crowding the base, each a replica of the central curved shaft. This is covered with a mesh of arch-like motifs and crowned with an amalaka and a pot finial. Over the mandapa, the pyramidal roof has numerous finials rhythmically arranged in tiers; miniature towers reproduce the tower over the sanctuary.

The interior has finely carved ceiling panels. The one over the octagon in the middle of the mandapa is a corbelled dome with friezes of petals and lobed motifs; the sixteen brackets are fashioned as dancing maidens.

UDAIPUR AND AHAR

The Rajput capital of Udaipur is celebrated for its picturesque palaces, pavilions and gateways, many overlooking Pichola lake. In the middle of the town is the Jagannatha temple erected by Jagat Singh I, the Rajput king, in 1652. The building possesses a fine porch; enshrined within the towered sanctuary is a large bronze image of Garuda. Nearby is another smaller temple dedicated to Radha and Krishna. (For the fort and the palace see Volume II.)

3 km (2 miles) east of Udaipur is the royal cremation site of Ahar.

Pratap Museum

Sculptures from **Jagat** and **Nagda** are assembled here; these include a group of Matrikas, some with children, from the former site (122). A large 6th-century head of Shiva, with delicately carved headdress and earrings (facial features recut), comes from Kalyanpur (62). There is also a black schist image of Kubera from Ranimalia Barsi (117A).

AHAR

The chhatris at this site serve as memorials for the Rajput rulers of Udaipur. These pavilions are carved with decoration that resembles the nearby 15th-century temples. The most notable is the chhatri of Amar Singh (died 1621), which has a quadruple-faced image in the middle; friezes on the basement depict the immolation of the king's wives.

There are also two tanks. The earlier one has a central pavilion sheltering a multi-faced linga, now worn. Inserted into the sides of the later tank are several 10th-century images of Brahma and Surya.

Temple of Mira Bhai, 10th century

The rhythmically projecting walls of this temple are elevated on a high basement with deep mouldings and an almost continuous band of sculptures. Above rises the clustered form of the tower.

Adinatha Temple, 11th century

Only the original walls of the sanctuary and adjoining mandapa of this Jain temple are preserved; the tower is renovated. The high basement and the richly carved wall niches are typical of the evolved western Indian style.

Mahavira Temples, 15th century

Several sanctuaries in this group of shrines are crowned with diminutive towered motifs that cluster around the central shafts.

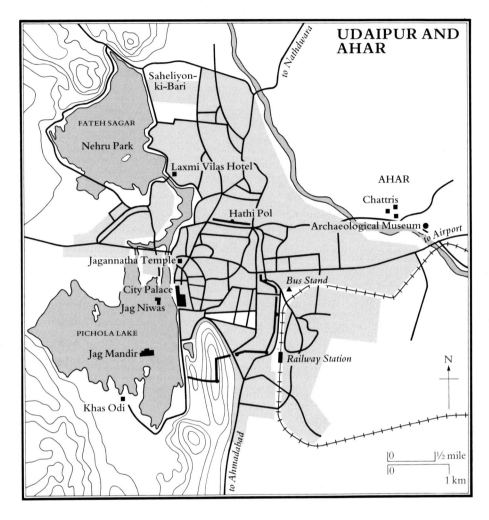

The map shows **UDAIPUR AND AHAR** with labelled locations including: to Nathdwara, Saheliyon-ki-Bari, FATEH SAGAR, Nehru Park, Laxmi Vilas Hotel, Hathi Pol, AHAR, Chattris, Archaeological Museum, to Airport, Jagannatha Temple, Bus Stand, City Palace, Jag Niwas, PICHOLA LAKE, Jag Mandir, Railway Station, Khas Odi, to Ahmadabad, N, 0 ½ mile, 0 1 km.

Archaeological Museum

The pottery sherds, terracotta toys and a large earthenware grain-storage pot displayed here all date from the 1st millennium BC. These antiquities were discovered in nearby excavations. Among the later pieces are several 10th-century sculptures, including a fine Surya image.

VADNAGAR

Adinatha Temple, 10th century and later

Due to extensive renovation, this Solanki Jain monument preserves only fragments of its original form. The sanctuary walls are clearly articulated by mouldings with niches in the middle of each side. The clustered tower is a later century reconstruction; the adjoining mandapa and surrounding subsidiary shrines are additions.

Gateways, 12th century

These two gateways were associated with a large temple, comparable with that at **Sidhpur**, of which nothing now survives. Each gateway consists of two circular columns covered with carvings of figures in niches, friezes of elephants and stylized foliation. Angled brackets are fashioned as maidens and beasts. Between the columns is a multi-lobed arch encrusted with miniature figures rising from makara heads. The columns support an overhanging eave and a pyramidal architrave containing deities seated in niches, possibly Shiva and Ganesha, now worn.

VADODARA

(For the city and its monuments see Volume II.)

Museum and Picture Gallery

Hindu sculptures from various sites in Gujarat are displayed in this collection. 6th-century blue schist figures from **Samalaji** indicate the influence of Gupta traditions of central India. The finest of these Samalaji carvings are a delicately modelled Shiva with Nandi (2.544), standing Ganesha (2.537) and several gracefully posed maidens holding children or with attendants. From **Roda** come a number of 8th-century sculptures. Also of interest is the skeletal Bhairava figure from Ladol (2.20), dating from the 11th century.

Bronze figurines from Akota are an important part of the collection; these are mostly Jain images and are datable to the 6th–8th centuries. Standing Rishabhanatha (AR.580), seated Ambika (AR.548) and a female devotee holding a fly-whisk (AR.547) are among the finest.

Also exhibited is a typical example of wooden architecture taken from a dismantled 19th-century Jain temple. Its columns, brackets and corbelled dome-like ceiling are all covered with elaborate carvings.

Museums, Maharaja Sayajirao University

Two collections are of importance. The Department of Museology houses a well-preserved series of 9th-century marble sculptures from Vadaval. These include Shiva with a musical instrument, Virabhadra and a complete set of Matrikas, such as Indrani, Varahi and Brahmani. The figures are characterized by smooth modelling and occasional dance-like postures.

In the Department of Archaeology, 4th-century finds from the excavated Buddhist monuments at **Devnimori** are displayed. These provide a unique record of Buddhist traditions in Gujarat during the Kshatrapa period. Terracotta Buddha figures and numerous decorative plaques come from the large stupa at this site; an inscribed relic casket mentions the royal patron.

VARKANA

Parshvanatha Temple, 15th century

This is a typical well-preserved example of the later Jain style in western India. The sanctuary walls are elevated on an elegantly moulded basement that rhythmically projects outwards. Deeply carved figures in animated postures are placed above. The pyramidal tower incorporates miniature towered motifs, each with a curved profile and an amalaka. The same features dominate the large central shaft.

The mandapa walls are less adorned, but present a regular succession of changing planes. Equally complex is the pyramidal roof with its clearly articulated elements. Within the mandapa are intricately carved ceiling panels.

In front of the mandapa is a two-storey porch with decorated columns and angled lintels. The upper level is surrounded by ornamented balcony slabs. The interior ceiling has brackets fashioned as flying celestials; concentric circular bands of stylized foliation have a pendant geometric design in the middle.

THE DECCAN

THIRTEEN

THE DECCAN

Maharashtra, northern Andhra Pradesh, northern Karnataka, Goa

Introduction

The beginnings of monumental architecture and art in the Deccan are unusually well preserved, due to the early adoption of rock-cut techniques. Sanctuaries and monasteries belonging to the Satavahana period are dated from the 2nd century BC to the 2nd century AD. These monuments are excavated into the basalt outcrops of the western Deccan at numerous Buddhist sites, especially **Ajanta** (Caves 9 and 10), **Bedsa**, **Bhaja**, **Junnar**, **Karli** and **Pitalkhora**. These cave temples provide important evidence of timber origins; their rock-cut forms clearly imitate wooden vaults, horseshoe-shaped arches and openings, posts and railings, and columns with pot bases and capitals.

The principal architectural form was the apsidal-ended chaitya hall. This was divided into three aisles; at the end of the central nave, which was roofed with a curved vault, was a monolithic votive stupa. The finest example at **Karli** has its column capitals carved with animals and figures. Unusual circular chaitya halls are preserved at **Guntupalle** and **Junnar** (Tulja Lena). The more evolved arched motifs and decorative reliefs on the façades of chaitya halls at **Junnar** (Bhuta Lena), **Kanheri** (Cave 3) and **Nasik** indicate that these belong to the later phase of the Satavahana–Kshatrapa transition in the 1st–2nd centuries AD. Rock-cut monasteries consisted of a number of small plain cells opening off a columned mandapa or verandah. Occasionally, as at

Bhaja and **Pitalkhora**, there were figural reliefs.

In the 2nd–4th centuries, the eastern Deccan was governed by a succession of Satavahana and Ikshvaku rulers. Monuments from this period testify to the beginnings of structural traditions. At **Ter** there is a rare example of an apsidal-ended brick sanctuary, originally Buddhist; the brick monastery at **Sankaram** is dilapidated. Other important Buddhist monuments of the eastern Deccan are now dismantled (the great stupa at **Amaravati**) or flooded (the shrines and monasteries at **Nagarjunakonda**). Surviving limestone sculptures from these sites demonstrate the vitality of Buddhist art, especially in the representations of stupa forms, fully modelled Buddha images and animated narrative scenes.

The 5th–6th centuries in the western Deccan witnessed a revival of rock-cut traditions. Under the Vakatakas, **Ajanta** was provided with a superb series of chaitya halls (Caves 19 and 26) and monastic sanctuaries (especially Caves 1, 2, 16 and 17), the latter with Buddha shrines set into the rear walls. Figural sculptures included a new repertory of Buddhist divinities, goddesses, guardians and attendants, as well as an exuberant ornamentation. The wall paintings at Ajanta are remarkable for their range of subjects, especially the depictions of Jataka stories; the colours and virtuosity

Overleaf, Badami, panorama

of linework are unsurpassed. Only slightly later are the cave temples at **Aurangabad**, some of which (Caves 3 and 7) have fine sculptures. Related to these monuments are the 6th–8th-century excavations at **Ellora**, the latest in the Buddhist series. Cave 10 (Vishvakarma) at this site is the last great chaitya hall.

Hindu cults gained wide popularity during this period. From the 6th century onwards, Shaiva and Vaishnava cave temples were excavated at numerous western Deccan sites under the patronage of the Kalachuri and Early Chalukya rulers. One of the earliest examples is the magnificent cave at **Elephanta**. Its interior is dominated by large-scale figural compositions, which are impressive visualizations of the Shaiva pantheon. Related monuments are the nearby cave at **Jogeshwari (Bombay)** and the Dhumar Lena (Cave 29) at **Ellora**. Other contemporary Hindu and Jain sanctuaries were excavated at the Early Chalukya sites of **Aihole** and **Badami**. These caves have elaborately decorated columns and finely modelled sculptures. In the eastern Deccan, comparable but later Hindu cave temples survive at **Bhairavakonda** and **Undavalli**.

By the 7th century, constructed temple architecture was firmly established in the Deccan. Early Chalukya buildings at **Aihole**, **Badami**, **Mahakuta** and **Satyavolu** comprise the largest group of Hindu temples in the Deccan at this time. Their unusual variety of forms demonstrates a diversity of influences from different regions: the curved towers, niches with pediments and highly decorated doorways and columns are of central and western Indian origin, while the deeply moulded basements, pilastered walls, parapets of roof elements and multi-storey towers are closely related to contemporary Pallava architecture in southern India. At **Pattadakal** and **Alampur** in the 8th century, the Early Chalukya temple reached the climax of its evolution in both its central Indian

(**Alampur**) and southern Indian (**Pattadakal**) expression. The later evolution of the Chalukya style in the eastern Deccan is illustrated by temples at **Biccavolu** and **Samalkot**.

Under the Rashtrakuta rulers in the 8th–9th centuries, there was yet another resurgence of rock-cut architecture. The artistic activities of this dynasty were mainly concentrated at **Ellora**, where the Hindu caves were dominated by the monolithic Kailasa temple (Cave 16). This ambitious rock-cut monument has an entrance gateway, a court, a principal temple with a columned mandapa, a detached Nandi pavilion, a surrounding colonnade and a series of subsidiary shrines, all laid out in imitation of a structural complex, not unlike the Early Chalukya schemes (as at **Pattadakal**). The doorways, columns and brackets were elaborately decorated; figural sculptures were sometimes dramatic large-scale compositions. The final phase of rock-cut art is the group of Jain excavations at **Ellora**. The temples at **Kukkunur** and **Pattadakal** are comparable structural projects of the Rashtrakutas.

Temple architecture in the 10th–13th centuries is represented by a large number of examples. Built in a variety of closely related styles, temples were linked with central and western Indian traditions (Paramara and Solanki temples) and also with southern Indian practice (temples of the Nolambas, Western Gangas and Hoysalas). The typical Deccan building of this period had one or more towered sanctuaries opening off a columned mandapa with porches; complicated plans were achieved with numerous stepped projections. The plinth mouldings, wall pilasters and columns were all sharply cut; carved figures generally adorned the brackets and corbelled ceilings.

Temples in the northern Deccan were erected under the patronage of the Yadavas. At **Ambarnath, Anwa, Balsane, Kolhapur, Ratanvadi** and **Sinnar**, sanctuaries had curved towers covered with meshes of arch-like motifs. Late Chalukya temples of the south-western Deccan, such as those at **Dambal Ittagi**, **Kukkunur**, **Kuruvatti** and **Lakkundi**, are among the most ornate of the period. Under the Kakatiyas of the eastern Deccan, temples were built at **Hanamkonda** and **Warangal** and at **Palampet** and **Ghanpur**. Late Chalukya and Kakatiya buildings have multi-storey towers; column brackets and doorways are often adorned with fully modelled or cut-out sculptures.

At the same time, variant styles were evolved on the peripheries of the Deccan. At **Simhachalam** on the eastern coast, there were artistic contacts with neighbouring Orissa. In the western zone, several Kadamba temples survive, as at **Degamve** (and architectural fragments in Archaeological Museum, **Old Goa**).

The Muslim invasions at the end of the 13th century considerably disrupted building traditions. In the following centuries, temples continued to be built in the Vijayanagara territories to the south of the Krishna river. This newly founded empire rapidly became the dominant cultural force. Deccan architecture under Vijayanagara in the 15th–16th centuries was at first dependent on previous developments in southern India. The early phase of the new style is preserved in temples at the capital **Vijayanagara**, and at lesser sites such as **Tadpatri**. Important

religious centres at **Ahobilam** and **Srisailam** were provided with large-scale temple complexes. The typical evolved Vijayanagara temple was set in a vast rectangular compound entered through gateways with soaring brick towers (gopuras). Shrines had extensive mandapas and colonnades in which granite columns were decorated with considerable delicacy, frequently with animal motifs. At the capital, surviving palaces, pavilions, watchtowers, bath-houses and stables provide important evidence of contemporary courtly architecture (see Volume II). An idea of temple architecture sponsored by independent Nayakas in the region is given by the temples at **Ikkeri**.

In later times, the northern Deccan once again witnessed the emergence of indigenous artistic traditions. Under the Marathas in the 17th–18th centuries, temple architecture proliferated. The pilgrimage centres of **Nasik** and **Pandharpur** were provided with innumerable shrines built in a distinctive regional style. The example at **Mahuli**, with its multi-niched tower capped by a bulbous dome, is typical. In contrast, the sanctuary at **Trimbak** recalls earlier Yadava projects.

Meanwhile, temple architecture in Goa incorporated features of the Christian Baroque style. Sanctuaries at **Mardol** and **Ponda** have domed superstructures, bell-towers and other church-like characteristics.

Opposite Bhaja, Cave 12, 2nd century BC

Above Karli, Cave 8, 1st century

Opposite Ajanta, Cave 19, 5th century

Below Ter, Trivikrama Temple, 2nd–3rd century

Above Badami, Malegitti Shivalaya, 7th century

Below Alampur, Vira and Vishva Brahma Temples, 7th–8th centuries

Opposite above Ellora, Cave 16 (Kailasa), 8th century

Opposite below Ambarnath, Ambaranatha Temple, 11th century

Left Dambal, Dodda Basappa
Temple, 12th century

Below Warangal, ruined Svayambhu,
Temple, gateways, 12th–13th century

Opposite above Vijayanagara, Vitthala
Temple, 16th century

Opposite below Ikkeri, Aghoreshvara
Temple, 16th century

Nasik, Narayana Temple, 18th century

Mardol, Mahalasa Narayanai Temple, 18th century

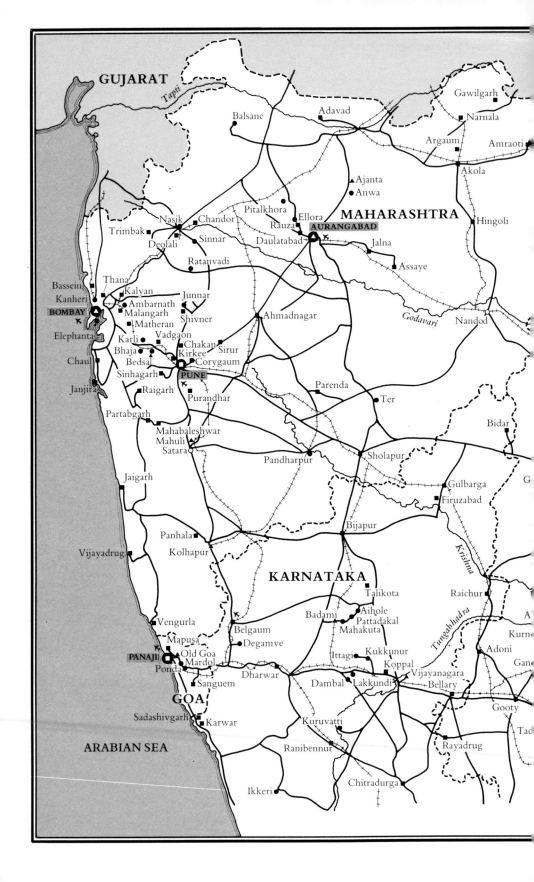

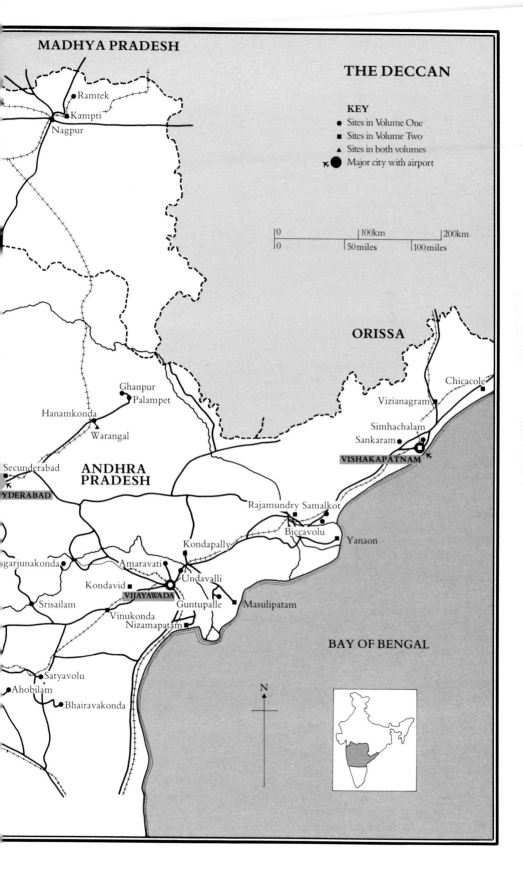

MADHYA PRADESH

THE DECCAN

KEY
● Sites in Volume One
■ Sites in Volume Two
▲ Sites in both volumes
✈● Major city with airport

0   100km   200km
0   50miles   100miles

ORISSA

Ramtek
Kampti
Nagpur

Chicacole
Vizianagram
Ghanpur
Palampet
Simhachalam
Hanamkonda
Sankaram
VISHAKAPATNAM
Warangal
Secunderabad
ANDHRA
PRADESH
YDERABAD
Rajamundry Samalkot
Biccavolu
Kondapally
Yanaon
garjunakonda
Amaravati
Undavalli
Kondavid
VIJAYAWADA
Srisailam
Guntupalle
Masulipatam
Vinukonda
Nizamapatam
BAY OF BENGAL
Satyavolu
Ahobilam
Bhairavakonda

N

AHOBILAM

This Hindu pilgrimage site is celebrated as the chief place of worship of Narasimha, to whom all of the temples and shrines are dedicated. According to local belief, it was at Ahobilam that Narasimha emerged out of the pillar to destroy the demon Hiranyakashipu.

The town, lower Ahobilam, is dominated by one great sacred complex; about 8 km (5 miles) to the east, set in a picturesquely wooded ravine, is a second complex, upper Ahobilam. The region is dotted with numerous sanctuaries and natural caverns.

While temple construction at the site was initiated by the local Reddi rulers in the 14th century, it was only under the patronage of the Vijayanagara kings in the 15th–16th centuries that the temples reached their present form. The sanctuaries were plundered by the Muslims in 1578, but they were renovated in later times. Today, Ahobilam is the seat of a well-known Vaishnava matha.

LOWER AHOBILAM

Narasimha Temple, mid-16th century

The principal shrine is approached through a large open mandapa with projections on three sides. Together with a minor shrine and several subsidiary structures, this temple is contained within a rectangle of walls, with a towered gopura on the east. A second circuit of walls, also with a gateway, surrounds the complex. Beyond this is a stepped tank and a smaller temple in a compound.

The architecture is typical of the evolved Vijayanagara style. The inner gopura, which is the better preserved of the two, has its outer walls adorned with elongated pilasters. The successive storeys of the steeply rising pyramidal tower and also the vaulted capping form with arched ends have been renovated recently.

Within the courtyard, the columned mandapa has granite piers fashioned as elaborate colonnettes; the columns of the central aisles have carvings of divinities, musicians and devotees; those on the periphery display rearing animals with riders. Processions of elephants and horses are carved on to the basement.

UPPER AHOBILAM

Narasimha Temple,
15th–16th centuries

The main focus of worship in this temple is a natural cavern which is reached after passing through a columned mandapa surrounded by a verandah. The temple, together with a number of free-standing mandapas, a lamp-column and several subsidiary structures, stands in the middle of a paved court. This is entered in the middle of the east and west sides through towered gopuras. Outside the complex to the west is a detached mandapa and a large stepped tank.

The architectural treatment is typical of the early Vijayanagara style. Column shafts have figural panels, while the peripheral piers are fashioned as rearing animals; the pilastered walls are covered with small figures of divinities, saints and maidens, as well as scenes of hunting.

AIHOLE

This site preserves a large number of Hindu and Jain temples belonging to both the Early and Late Chalukya periods, as well as to the intervening Rashtrakuta era, a period spanning the 6th–12th centuries. That the town was an important commercial centre is suggested by inscriptions mentioning the 'Ayyavole 500 Guild' of merchants.

Together with the temples at the nearby Early Chalukya sites of **Badami**,

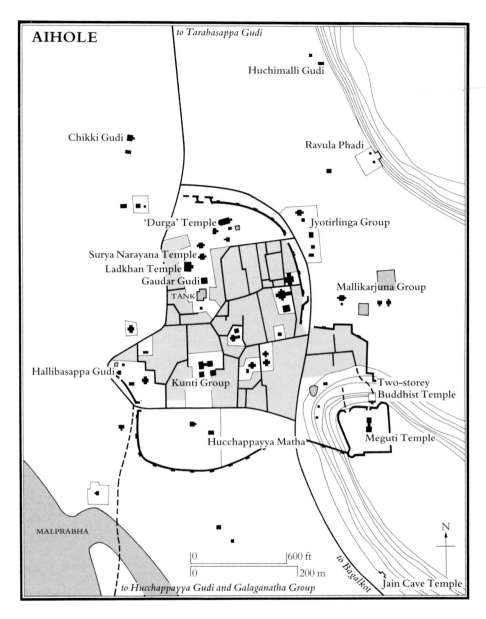

AIHOLE

to Tarabasappa Gudi

Huchimalli Gudi

Chikki Gudi

Ravula Phadi

'Durga' Temple

Jyotirlinga Group

Surya Narayana Temple
Ladkhan Temple
Gaudar Gudi

TANK

Mallikarjuna Group

Hallibasappa Gudi

Kunti Group

Two-storey
Buddhist Temple

Meguti Temple

Hucchappayya Matha

MALPRABHA

N

0   600 ft

0   200 m

to Bagalkot

Jain Cave Temple

to Hucchappayya Gudi and Galaganatha Group

Mahakuta and **Pattadakal**, those at Aihole display an unusual diversity of forms in which architectural influences from different regions were absorbed. Curved towers adorned with arch-like motifs and elaborately carved doorways are typical of central and western Indian practice, while pilastered walls with inserted carved panels are related to southern Indian traditions. Typical Deccan features are the inclined balcony slabs overhung by angled eaves, the sloping roof slabs and the elaborately carved columns and ceiling panels.

Rashtrakuta and Late Chalukya temples dating from the 9th–12th centuries are often combinations of two or more shrines, mostly devoted to Jain divinities.

Their outer walls are plain except for slender pilasters; the superstructures are generally pyramidal with horizontal mouldings. The open porches and mandapas have carved or lathe-turned columns; balcony seating is overhung by steeply sloping roof slabs.

The site is dominated by a fortified hill to the south-east. On the flat top of the hill is the Meguti temple; other monuments, both structural and rock-cut, dot the northern flank of the hill. The town itself is enclosed in a circle by walls with regularly spaced bastions and gateways. Both inside and outside these walls are temples belonging to different periods; some buildings incorporate two or more phases of construction. A cave temple is cut into the side of a rocky outcrop to the north of the town. (Confusingly, many monuments are known by the names of local inhabitants.)

ON THE HILL

Two-storey Buddhist Temple,
6th century

This partly rock-cut temple is arranged on two levels, each with a verandah in front. A ceiling panel in the upper porch depicts a seated Buddha figure. The doorways are surrounded by delicate relief carvings.

Meguti Temple, 634

This north-facing Jain temple bears an inscription of the Early Chalukya ruler Pulakeshin II; it is thus one of the earliest dated temples in India. Its outer elevation is clearly divided into plinth, pilastered wall surface and parapet, all with regular projections and recesses. The chamber rising over the sanctuary is a later addition; so too are the porch and mandapa extensions.

An impressive Jina figure is seated within the sanctuary. A sculpture of a Jain yakshi has been removed to the Archaeological Museum, **Badami**.

WITHIN THE TOWN

'Durga' Temple, late 7th century

This is the largest and most elaborate Hindu temple at Aihole. Despite its name, which refers to a fort not a goddess, the temple may have originally been dedicated to a Surya.

The apsidal-ended plan imitates the chaitya halls of earlier Buddhist architecture. The temple is elevated on a high plinth and is surrounded by an open colonnade. It consists of a semicircular sanctuary, an ambulatory passageway, a columned mandapa with three aisles and a porch with balcony seating. A fragmentary tower rises over the sanctuary.

The sculptures are among the finest of the Early Chalukya series. At the entrance, the outer columns are carved with amorous couples and guardian figures. The porch columns are adorned with medallions, garlands and jewels; the ceiling panels are carved with serpent and lotus motifs. The mandapa doorway is an elaborate composition, with river goddesses and guardians beneath at either side. In the outer colonnade, the pierced stone windows and carved wall panels are framed by pilasters and pediments; the basement has friezes of ganas and foliation. Different deities are depicted in the niches: these are (in clockwise sequence) Shiva with Nandi, Narasimha, Vishnu with Garuda, Varaha, Durga and Harihara. Only traces of the ceiling sculptures survive. (Two well-preserved ceiling panels have been removed to the National Museum, **New Delhi**.)

The interior is plain and partly restored. No image is preserved on the circular pedestal within the sanctuary.

Immediately south of the temple is a small gateway; several later shrines stand nearby.

Surya Narayana Temple, 7th century

A Hindu sanctuary with a partly preserved curved tower adjoins a rec-

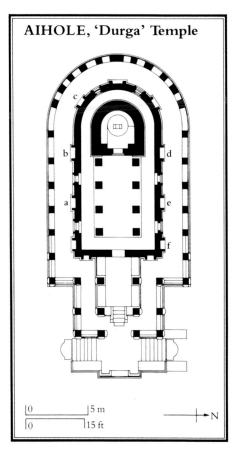

AIHOLE, 'Durga' Temple

| 0 | 5 m |
| 0 | 15 ft |

→N

Key to Sculpture Panels:

a   Shiva with Nandi
b   Narasimha
c   Vishnu with Garuda
d   Varaha
e   Durga
f   Harihara

tangular mandapa and projecting porch. The doorway has delicately incised lotus ornament; a later image of Surya is placed within the sanctuary.

Ladkhan Temple, 7th–8th century

This stone Hindu structure is built in obvious imitation of timber models. A spacious columned mandapa is roofed with sloping stone slabs in two tiers; log-like strips cover the joints. A small sanctuary is positioned against the rear (west) wall (an arrangement familiar from the cave temples at **Badami**). Large perforated stone screens on three sides light the interior. River goddesses and couples embracing beneath trees are carved on to the porch columns; the sloping balcony slabs are embellished with pot and knot motifs.

Rising over the middle of the mandapa is a second smaller sanctuary; this has damaged carvings of Vishnu, Surya and Ardhanarishvara on the outer walls.

Gaudar Gudi, 7th century

This Hindu temple has a simple rectangular layout that incorporates an open columned mandapa and a small sanctuary. The roof has sloping slabs on four sides. Inclined balcony slabs are carved with a frieze of pots. The wall niches with triangular pediments are empty, but the doorway preserves its carved ornamentation.

Chakra Gudi, 7th century

This small sanctuary has a curved tower capped with an amalaka.

Kunti Group, 7th–9th centuries

Four Hindu temples dating from different periods are built close together. They consist of partly open mandapas with sloping roofs and overhanging eaves; small sanctuaries are positioned against the rear walls.

The south-east temple is the earliest. It is entered from the north side, where the columns are carved with amorous figures. Slightly later is the east-facing north-west temple. Within this example are three finely carved ceiling panels depicting Shiva with Parvati, Vishnu on the serpent and Brahma on the lotus. Guardians flank the sanctuary doorway. Belonging to the same period is the free-standing gateway with yali brackets linking the two southern temples.

The two remaining structures are assigned to the later Rashtrakuta era. The north-east temple has massive columns with foliate and figural ornamentation.

Hucchappayya Matha, late 7th century

Fine Hindu sculptures enliven this otherwise simple structure. The columns flanking the east entrance are embellished with embracing couples; the interior has ceiling panels of Shiva on Nandi, Vishnu on the serpent and Brahma on the goose.

Hallibasappa Gudi, 9th–10th century

This Rashtrakuta temple has large figures of Ganga and Yamuna flanking the entrance doorway.

NORTH AND EAST OF THE TOWN

Chikki Gudi, 7th century

The sanctuary, surrounding passageway and columned mandapa of this Hindu temple are all contained within a rectangle of walls; a porch adjoins the mandapa to the east. The roof is sloping on four sides; the ceiling slabs have elaborate lotus medallions flanked by panels of Shiva (dancing, spearing the demon) and Vishnu (sleeping on the serpent, Trivikrama). The exterior is plain except for pierced stone screens which light the passageway.

Huchimalli Gudi, early 7th century

Within this rectangular structure is a Hindu sanctuary surrounded by a passageway and a columned mandapa; a porch protrudes from the front (west). The tower over the sanctuary is built in the curved form. The ceiling panel within the

porch depicts Karttikeya riding on a peacock; the interior ceiling panels have lotus designs.

Ravula Phadi, late 6th century

This Hindu cave temple consists of two side chambers (incomplete on the south) and a sanctuary (east) enshrining a linga which opens off a common mandapa. The finely modelled sculptures include ten-armed Shiva dancing with Parvati, Ganesha and the Matrikas (three sides of the north chamber), Ardhanarishvara, Harihara and Shiva with Ganga (mandapa) and Varaha and Durga (sanctuary antechamber). The ceiling is delicately incised with foliate designs that incorporate figures and makaras around a central lotus. Unusual guardian figures in tunics, now worn, flank the entrance.

Outside the entrance are three small temples, their sanctuaries entered through columned porches. A broken fluted stone column stands on an axis with the cave entrance.

Mallikarjuna Group, 7th and 11th centuries

The decorated columns and doorways of the main Hindu temple of this group are typical of the early period; the outer walls and tower with horizontal mouldings are later. The 7th-century gateway nearby is decorated with makaras and auspicious emblems.

Tarabasappa Gudi, late 7th century

This small temple combines a towered sanctuary with a rectangular mandapa and an open columned porch. The sanctuary doorway is finely carved.

SOUTH OF THE TOWN

Jain Cave Temple, late 6th century

Though this rock-cut monument is incomplete, figures of Parshvanatha, Bahubali and Mahavira were sculpted on to the walls. The ceiling is delicately carved with foliate scrollwork and makaras.

Hucchappayya Gudi, late 7th century

The square sanctuary, rectangular mandapa and porch of this Hindu temple form a simple tripartite scheme. Over the sanctuary rises a curved tower. The porch columns have couples and guardians carved in full relief; the ceiling panels depict Shiva dancing. The sanctuary doorway is flanked by guardian figures. (Ceiling panels from the mandapa have been removed to the Prince of Wales Museum of Western India, **Bombay**.)

Galaganatha Group, 9th–10th century

These Hindu shrines belong to the Rashtrakuta period. They are entered through a gateway, the lintel of which is carved with makaras and looped garlands. The doorway within the principal shrine is carved in imitation of earlier designs.

AJANTA

With their remarkably well-preserved sculptures and paintings, the cave temples at Ajanta provide the most complete illustration of early Buddhist traditions in India. The monuments demonstrate the iconographic and stylistic sources for much of Central Asian and Far Eastern Buddhist art.

The beauty of the site is incomparable. The cave temples are cut into the rocky sides of a dramatic crescent-shaped gorge at the head of which is a natural pool fed by a waterfall. Thirty artificial excavations in basalt, not all of which were completed, span a period of about six centuries. They are clearly divided into two groups, coinciding with the Hinayana and Mahayana phases of Buddhist art.

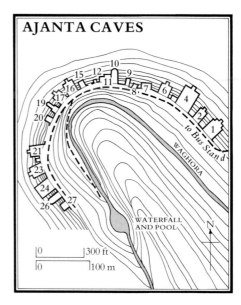

AJANTA CAVES

Among the earlier monuments are Caves 9 and 10, both chaitya halls, and also several monasteries (Caves 8, 12, 13 and 15A); these date from the 2nd–1st centuries BC. After a period of more than six centuries, excavations were once again revived, during the Vakataka era, especially during the reign of the ruler, Harishena (460–78). From this period date two more chaitya halls (Caves 19 and 26) and a number of monasteries (Caves 1, 2, 16 and 17, for example).

The later caves at Ajanta are fine examples of rock-cut chaitya halls and monasteries. They contain an impressive array of sculptures: principal votive images, accessory figures, narrative episodes and an elaborate repertory of decorative motifs. The soft modelling of the figures and the delicacy of the carving indicate the influences of central Indian Gupta traditions.

The series of paintings, mostly belonging to the later caves, is unparalleled in the history of Indian art, both for the wide range of subjects illustrated and the assured mastery of the medium. Buddhist divinities and incidents from the life of the Master are shown many times. More

335

vibrant are the episodes from the Jataka legends. These consist of large-scale crowded compositions depicting life in the court, town, hermitage or forest, with princes, consorts, attendants, musicians and servants. Never again did Indian mural painting exhibit such virtuosity and freedom. The dense compositions have overlapping figures to suggest receding perspectives. Colours are harmoniously blended, with ochres, browns and greens predominating; the linework is sinuous and sensitive.

Cave I, late 5th century

This is one of the finest monasteries. A verandah with cells and porches at either end has three doorways leading into the hall. Twenty columns arranged in a square surround an open space within the hall. Small cells open off on three sides; in the middle of the rear wall is an antechamber leading to the principal shrine.

The sculptural embellishment is elaborate throughout: column shafts have medallions adorned with scrollwork and flutings with jewelled motifs; compressed ribbed fruit motifs serve as the capitals. The brackets have flying couples flanking figurative compositions, such as scenes from the life of Buddha and animals. Above the verandah are figurative friezes; these include the sick man, old man, corpse and saintly man encountered by the prince Siddhartha (over the left porch). Doorways are embellished with naga deities, musicians and amorous couples; maidens beneath trees are positioned above at either side.

The devotional focus of the monastery is a large seated Buddha in preaching attitude carved in high relief within the sanctuary. On either side is a Bodhisattva attendant and a flying figure holding a garland. The pedestal on which the Master sits has a wheel, deer and monks; these indicate the first sermon at **Sarnath**.

The interior murals are among the greatest at Ajanta. Graciously posed Bodhisattvas with elaborate headdresses flank the antechamber doorway; Padmapani (left) and Avalokiteshvara (right) are accompanied by attendants, divine musicians and flying figures. Further to the right, another Bodhisattva is offered a tray of flowers by a king. The side walls of the antechamber record incidents from the Master's life: the assault and temptation of Mara (left) and the miracle of **Sravasti**, when the Master multiplied himself (right).

Jataka scenes occupy most of the hall walls. Left of the main doorway is the Shibi Jataka, where the Bodhisattva as a king rescues a pigeon from a hawk. The next panel possibly depicts the conversion of Nanda, who had to abandon his wife Sundari. The palace scene which forms the theme of the end panel comes from the Samkhapala Jataka; this is continued beyond the corner on to the left wall. Here, the Bodhisattva as a serpent king listens to the sermon of an ascetic; to the right, his wounded snake-body is dragged by hunters; beneath is Alara, the householder who delivers the king by offering his oxen as ransom.

The remainder of the left wall is occupied by Mahajanaka Jataka. On the extreme right is the shipwreck of the king Mahajanaka; on the extreme left the queen and her attendants tempt the prince with worldly pleasures. Next, the king comes out of a city gate to meet an ascetic in a rocky shelter; later he announces his decision to renounce the world; finally he leaves his capital on horseback.

Beside the Bodhisattva guarding the right side of the doorway in the middle of the rear wall are episodes from the Champeyya Jataka. The serpent king, Champeyya, is captured and made to perform by a snake-charmer; Champeyya's wife begs the ruler of **Varanasi** to release her husband; in the final deliverance scene both kings are seated with ladies and attendants.

To the right of the outer doorway, foreigners with peaked caps and beards

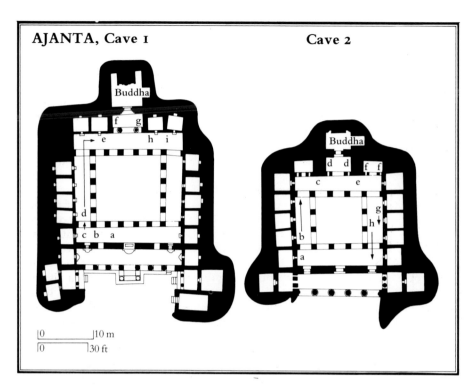

AJANTA, Cave I

Buddha

f g

e h i

d

c b a

0 _____ 10 m

0 _____ 30 ft

Cave 2

Buddha

d d f f

c e

g

h

b

a

Key to Paintings in Cave I:

a Shibi Jataka
b Conversion of Nanda (?)
c Samkhapala Jataka
d Mahajanaka Jataka
e Padmapani
f Assault and temptation of Mara
g Miracle of Sravasti
h Avalokiteshvara
i Champeyya Jataka

Key to Paintings in Cave 2:

a Hamsa Jataka
b Birth of Buddha
c Seated Buddha
d Seated Buddha
e Bodhisattva
f Female devotees
g Vidhurapandita Jataka
h Conversion of Purna and sea voyage

respectfully offer gifts to a seated ruler; this may portray the Vakataka king Harishena. The ceiling is covered with small panels filled with a rich repertory of floral and vegetal motifs, ganas, embracing couples, drinking figures, elephants and geese.

Cave 2, late 5th century

This monastery repeats the basic scheme of Cave 1; the sculptural ornamentation is

also similar but more profuse. There are several additional sculpted images. At either end of the verandah, small shrines contain a seated naga king with yaksha attendants (left) and Hariti with a child on her lap (right). Subsidiary shrines in the rear wall of the hall house Panchika and Hariti (right) and corpulent yakshas with attendants (left).

The cave is remarkable for its painted ceiling. As in Cave 1, there are numerous compartments filled with a variety of designs and also large medallions with delicate bands of lotus ornament, scroll-work and geometric patterns.

Miniature seated Buddhas are painted on to the side walls of the shrine and antechamber, and even in the hall (left side); these are later additions. Buddha and Bodhisattva figures flank the door-ways to the antechamber and sanctuary. Nativity episodes, such as the dream of Maya, the interpretation by priests and the birth of Gautama, are painted on to the left wall of the hall.

Several Jatakas cover the hall walls. In the Hamsa Jataka the Bodhisattva as a goose is captured, then released at the order of a royal couple to whom he delivers a final sermon (left wall). A large portion of the right wall is devoted to the Vidhurapandita Jataka, especially the courtly scene with the princess Indrati in a swing, Punnaka's proposal of marriage, the game of dice in which Punnaka defeats the king Vidhurapandita (Bodhisattva) and the final happy union. Beneath is the conversion of Purna and the rescue of Purna's brother from shipwreck.

Processions of gracefully posed female devotees carrying offerings adorn the walls of the two subsidiary shrines. Seated Buddhas cover the walls of the main central shrine.

Cave 4, late 5th century

This is the largest monastery at Ajanta, planned on an ambitious scale but never completed. The verandah, with eight octagonal columns, has a cell at either end. Three doorways lead into the hall, where part of the ceiling has collapsed. The central doorway is embellished with guardians, couples, flying figures and maidens clutching trees (jambs), and also Buddhas and ganas with garlands (lintel). To the right of the doorway a panel depicts Avalokiteshvara surrounded by worshippers suffering torments; on the left is the miracle at **Sravasti**.

Only a few of the hall columns are richly decorated; the others resemble those of the verandah. On three sides several cells are incomplete. The shrine has the usual arrangement of a central teaching Buddha with Bodhisattva attendants; the antechamber is provided with additional large standing Buddhas, two unfinished. Traces of paintings survive.

Cave 6, late 5th century

This monastery is excavated on two levels. The lower hall has sixteen octagonal columns arranged in four rows without any large central space. The shrine doorway has an ornamental arch springing from open-mouthed makaras. Within the shrine is a seated Buddha accompanied by standing Buddhas. Among the mural fragments on the ante-chamber walls are the temptation of Mara (right) and the miracle at **Sravasti** (left).

A flight of steps leads to the upper level; this is more conventional in its arrangement of columns. Additional shrines are at either end of the verandah and the front aisle of the hall. Sculpted Buddha figures are in the verandah shrines, as well as on the walls of the hall, antechamber and shrine.

Cave 7, late 5th century

This monastery has no hall but only two small porticos, each supported in front by heavy octagonal columns with fluted cushion-like capitals. These support an overhanging eave relieved by ornamental horseshoe-shaped windows. Small cells are positioned at a higher level at either end. The shrine in the middle of the rear wall houses a seated and a standing Buddha. Both walls of the antechamber are carved with the miracle at **Sravasti**.

Cave 9, 1st century BC

Unusually rectangular in plan, this chaitya hall is divided into three aisles by plain octagonal columns. The central nave is roofed with a curved vault; the timber ribs have vanished. The devotional focus is a monolithic hemispherical stupa raised on a high drum and crowned with an inverted stepped pyramid.

The outer elevation is dominated by a large horseshoe-shaped window, complete with ribs in imitation of timber construction. Beneath, a doorway and two windows are surmounted by arches in relief, similar to those at the top of the façade. Buddha figures on the façade and side walls were added later.

Traces of paintings within the hall survive in two layers, the earlier being contemporary with the excavation. Left of the doorway, the heads of two ascetics are superimposed over an earlier composition in which a naga deity and attendants are seated in a rocky shelter. On the left wall (extreme left end) is a procession of devotees walking towards a stupa and monastery, also dating from the earlier phase. The remnant of another older mural survives in a thin strip above the left colonnade; higher up are later Buddha figures.

Cave 10, 2nd century BC

This is among the first excavations at the site and is one of the most impressive early Buddhist chaitya halls. The apsidal-ended interior is divided into three aisles by plain octagonal columns. The side aisles have half-vaults with rock-cut ribs; the raised vault over the central nave is missing its timber ribs. The votive stupa has a double-storey drum. Much of the wooden façade has fallen away.

As in Cave 9, there is evidence of two phases of paintings, one executed over the other; the earlier style is characterized by a continuous frieze. Substantial fragments are preserved on the left wall, particularly the visit and worship of a bodhi tree and stupa by a royal figure accompanied by soldiers, dancers, musicians and women. On the right wall there are two Jatakas.

The composition begins with a king shooting an arrow toward Sama, the Bodhisattva, who holds a pitcher on his shoulder. The remainder of this story is told in the following episodes: the penitent king, the sorrowing parents of Sama, the restoration of Sama to life and, finally, the reconciliation of the king and Sama. The remainder of this wall is occupied by the Chhaddanta Jataka, in which the Bodhisattva assumed the form of a royal elephant. The main incidents here are Chhaddanta's pleasurable life in the Himalayas, the queen of **Varanasi** directing that he be killed, his tusks being cut off to satisfy the queen, who subsequently swoons, and, as a concluding episode, the royal couple approaching a chaitya hall.

Traces of later paintings survive on the columns and aisle ceilings; later Buddha figures are often superimposed upon earlier decorative motifs. The cave also preserves a number of painted and carved inscriptions.

Cave 11, 5th century

This monastery is clumsily executed and partly incomplete. The high plinth and parapet of the exterior are decorated with a railing pattern; the verandah columns and doorway were once painted with decorative motifs. Four columns with pot-like capitals stand within the hall. The shrine, with no antechamber, has a Buddha image carved against an unfinished stupa.

The verandah roof is covered with painted motifs, including foliations, birds and animals. Large Bodhisattva figures with attendants are carved on either side of the verandah doorway.

Caves 12 and 13, 2nd century BC

These monasteries are possibly the earliest excavations of the series. Their façades have completely collapsed to expose their interior square halls; there were no columns. Cells on three sides are provided with rock-cut beds. The cell doorways in Cave 12 are capped by arched motifs, complete with internal ribs; these are connected by friezes of railing motifs. Holes in the sills and lintels indicate door hinges.

Cave 14, 5th century

Planned on a large scale, this late monastery was never finished. The decoration of the verandah columns, now reconstructed, differs from other examples; the doorway leading into the partially excavated hall is adorned with attendants and maidens clutching branches.

Cave 15, 5th century

The verandah of this monastery has mostly fallen. Above the doorway is a stupa sheltered by a canopy of serpent hoods. Buddha images appear in the shrine and on the rear wall of the hall.

Cave 15A, 1st century BC

This monastery, which is comparable to Caves 12 and 13, is reached by a descending flight of steps near Cave 15. Only portions of the front wall survive.

Beyond the cave is a doorway flanked by elephants in relief and a delicately modelled seated naga deity; this leads to Cave 16.

Cave 16, late 5th century

This is one of the finest monasteries at Ajanta. It is provided with a donative inscription datable to the reign of Harishena.

Most of the hall columns have plain octagonal shafts. The ceiling of the front aisle is carved in imitation of wooden beams, with the ends supported by ganas, musicians and flying couples. There is no antechamber leading to the shrine, which has narrow side aisles (later additions); the front columns are richly adorned. Within, a passageway surrounds an image of teaching Buddha seated on a lion throne.

Only portions of the cave were painted. Within the hall on the left wall is an illustration of the conversion of Nanda. Scenes depict Nanda's wife fainting, Nanda's efforts to practise self-control and his journey to heaven in the company of Buddha.

On the rear wall of the hall (left and right of the shrine) there is the miracle of **Sravasti** and a fragment of an elephant procession. Here also (right wall of the hall) incidents from the life of the Master appear; for instance, Buddha begging, Bimbisara's visit, Gautama's first meditation, Gautama at school, and (at the extreme right) the sleeping figure of Maya and a royal couple in a circular pavilion.

Two Jataka stories are depicted on the front wall of the hall (left side). In the Hasti Jataka, Bodhisattva appears as an elephant who throws himself off a precipice to provide food for hungry travellers. Episodes from the Maha Ummagga Jataka illustrate the story of Mahosadha in which the wise Bodhisattva settled disputes over the motherhood of a child and the ownership of a chariot.

Cave 17, late 5th century

Like the previous monastery, this also dates from the period of Harishena. While it resembles Cave 16 in many respects, the triad of Buddha and Bodhisattva figures in the shrine is approached through an antechamber. The ornamentation of the shrine doorway, with its Buddha figures, female guardians, river goddesses, scrollwork and lotus petals, is elaborate.

Cave 17 preserves the greatest number of murals, among which are many outstanding compositions. Over the doorway in the verandah is a row of eight seated Buddhas above amorous couples. The panel to the left is much damaged; this shows Indra flying through the clouds accompanied by his troupe of celestial apsaras and musicians. The next scene (at the left) depicts a princely couple seated within a pavilion drinking wine, then

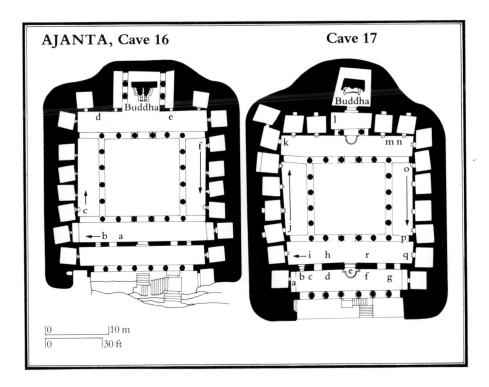

AJANTA, Cave 16 / Cave 17

Buddha

d · e

f

c

b · a

Buddha

k · l · m · n

o

j

i · h · r · q

a · b · c · d · e · f · g

p

[0 _____ [10 m
[0 _____ [30 ft

Key to Paintings in Cave 16:

a Hasti Jataka
b Maha Ummagga Jataka
c Conversion of Nanda
d Buddha teaching and elephant procession
e Miracle of Sravasti
f Early life of Buddha

Key to Paintings in Cave 17:

a Wheel of Life
b Prince distributing alms
c Princely couple
d Indra with consorts
e Seated Buddhas
f Celestial maidens
g Buddha subdues the elephant
h Chhaddanta Jataka
i Mahakapi Jataka
j Vessantara Jataka
k Sutasoma Jataka
l Buddha teaching
m Matiposaka Jataka
n Sama Jataka
o Story of Simhala
p Princess with maids
q Ruru Jataka
r Nigrodhamriga Jataka

proceeding towards a city gate and finally distributing alms to a large assembly. An unusual Wheel of Life composition is painted on the left side wall of the verandah.

To the right of the verandah doorway are celestial maidens. One of these has her eyes cast to one side; her jewelled necklace swings with her movement. Further to the right, a panel depicts Buddha subduing the furious elephant sent by Devadatta to crush him.

The ceiling of the verandah has a central multi-lobed medallion surrounded by delicate foliation. Similar motifs are found in the ceilings of the interior.

The paintings on the walls of the hall mostly illustrate Jataka legends. Immediately to the left of the main entrance (front wall) is the Chhaddanta Jataka, from which the following episodes are taken: a royal elephant sporting in a lotus pond, a hunter aiming his arrow at the elephant, the hunter proceeding towards the capital and, finally, the queen fainting at the sight of the tusks.

Further right is the Mahakapi Jataka, in which the Bodhisattva appears as a monkey. Depicted here are the king on horseback with his retinue shooting arrows at the monkeys, the monkeys escaping over the stretched body of the Bodhisattva and the monkey preaching to the king.

The entire left wall is covered with scenes from the Vessantara Jataka. Despite the poor state of preservation several episodes can be identified: these include the farewell of the prince Vessantara, his drive with his family in a chariot, his life in the hermitage, his gift of his children to a brahmin in a forest hermitage, the redeeming of the children and, finally, the return of the family to the capital.

Left of the antechamber doorway (rear wall) are several episodes from another Jataka, in which the Bodhisattva as the lioness Sutasoma cured a prince of cannibalism. The scenes show the education of the prince, the cutting and cooking of human flesh, the appeal to the prince to give up cannibalism and, finally, his banishment to the forest.

To the right of the antechamber doorway are four Jataka stories. The scenes of an elephant refusing food and later bathing with other elephants come from the Matiposaka Jataka; those showing a youth carrying his blind parents in slings suspended from bamboo rods derive from the Sama Jataka.

The right wall is mostly devoted to the story of Simhala's conquest of Sri Lanka. This begins (bottom right end) with the shipwreck of Simhala and his merchants, who are cast ashore on the island of ogresses. Simhala accepts the aid of Bodhisattva, born here as a horse; Simhala kneels before the horse in gratitude. One of the ogresses marries a king and then devours him; Simhala leads an expedition against the demonic forces and a battle ensues. Finally, Simhala is crowned king of the island in the presence of the benevolent horse. The pilaster beyond this concluding scene contains the celebrated depiction of a princess with maids and a female dwarf.

Returning to the front wall (left of the verandah doorway), there are a number of forest scenes in which a king and his retinue appear, possibly taken from the Ruru Jataka, in which the Bodhisattva assumes the form of a deer. The remainder of this portion of the wall contains the Nigrodhamriga Jataka, in which the Bodhisattva as a deer offers himself for slaughter to the palace cook to save a pregnant doe.

Paintings also adorn the antechamber walls; on the left wall Buddha is shown (top to bottom) preaching, descending from heaven accompanied by Indra and addressing an assembly.

Cave 19, late 5th century

This is one of the most perfectly executed rock-cut chaitya halls. The exterior has an elegant portico with fluted columns that shelter the entrance. The columns of the flanking walls are covered with ornate foliation, scrollwork and jewelled bands; between these are numerous standing and seated Buddhas. Similar figures, which are later carvings, appear on the side walls. The façade is dominated by a large horseshoe-arched window flanked by corpulent yakshas with elaborate headdresses; behind these yakshas are Buddha figures carved in delicate relief. Side chapels flank the court in front; these have columns with luxuriantly carved pot and foliage capitals. On the left wall is a delicately carved but fully modelled naga couple seated on a rock.

Equally elaborate is the treatment of the interior. Here, seated Buddha figures as well as riders, flying couples, hermits and musicians adorn the column capitals; the panels above depict Buddhas surrounded by bands of scrollwork. Rock-cut ribs are cut out of the vault; the side aisles have flat roofs. An innovation is the introduction of a Buddha image on the front of the votive stupa; the Master stands in a niche beneath an arch that springs from open-mouthed makaras. The tier of umbrellas with supporting figures that rises above the stupa is monolithic. The ceiling paintings include floral motifs, figures and animals.

Cave 20, late 5th century

In this small monastery the antechamber protrudes into the hall; there are no columns. The verandah columns and bracket figures are delicately carved (like those of Caves 1 and 2); the roof has rock-cut beams.

Caves 21 and 23, late 5th century

These two monasteries are almost identical in plan and in dimensions. Although partly incomplete, many columns in the verandah and halls are richly ornamented. Above the side shrines of the verandah are Hariti and attendants (right) and a court of a naga king (left).

Caves 26 and 27, late 5th century

The chaitya hall (Cave 26) is larger than Cave 19 but is somewhat similar in its arrangement and decorative scheme. A columned verandah, partly collapsed, extends across the façade, with columned chambers at both ends. The court in front has subsidiary shrines, cells and verandahs. An extension of the landing to the left leads to a partly collapsed wing (Cave 27).

The interior of the chaitya hall is enlivened with carved Buddha figures.

The focal stupa has an image of the Master seated in a pavilion. There are two narrative scenes (left aisle). One shows the temptation of Mara, in which Buddha is assaulted by elephants, demonic forces and dancing maidens. The other composition represents the Parinirvana, with a 7-m-long (23 ft) figure of Buddha reclining on a couch; the eyes are closed as in undisturbed sleep. Disciples beneath mourn the decease of the Master.

(For monuments in the nearby village of Ajanta see Volume II.)

ALAMPUR

This site overlooks the Tungahbhadra river near its confluence with the Krishna river. (Much of this riverine landscape is now submerged beneath the waters of the **Srisailam** dam.) Nine Early Chalukya Hindu temples dating from the 7th–8th centuries are situated here; although they are known collectively as the Nava Brahma, all of the shrines are dedicated to Shiva.

With the exception of the Taraka Brahma, the temples conform to a standard scheme. An east-facing sanctuary surrounded by a passageway and a columned mandapa divided into three aisles are contained within a rectangle of walls. Rising over the sanctuary is a curved tower derived from central and western Indian models. This is divided into tiers and adorned with arch-like motifs; a large amalaka is positioned at the summit. The outer walls are regularly divided into projecting niches.

Alampur continued to be an important site in later times, as is indicated by fortifications and gateways in the town and by the Papanasi group of temples, which has been dismantled and re-erected about 4 km (2½ miles) to the south-east.

The temples are described from north to south.

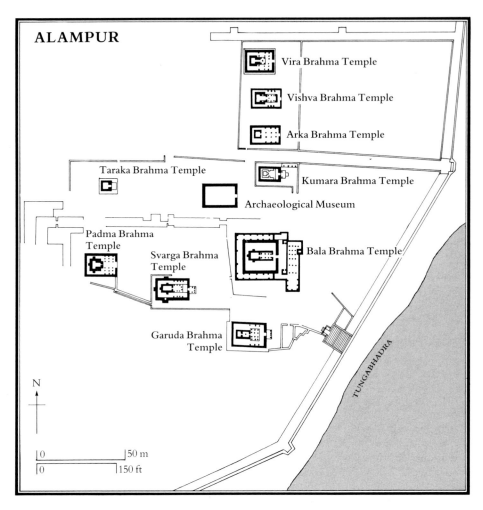

ALAMPUR

Vira Brahma Temple

Vishva Brahma Temple

Arka Brahma Temple

Taraka Brahma Temple

Kumara Brahma Temple

Archaeological Museum

Padma Brahma Temple

Bala Brahma Temple

Svarga Brahma Temple

Garuda Brahma Temple

TUNGABHADRA

N

0   50 m
0   150 ft

Vira Brahma Temple, 7th century

The outer walls of this temple have niches framed by pairs of pilasters, with triangular pediments of arch-like motifs above. While no sculptures are preserved in the niches, flying figures embellish the top of the walls. The superstructure has pronounced central projections as well as an extension on the front.

Vishva Brahma Temple,
early 8th century

The architectural elements in this temple are elaborately treated. Niches are capped by pediments with increasingly complex designs; intermediate niches and windows also have pediments. Small basement blocks beneath are carved with ganas, musicians, dancers, monster masks and foliated birds. The interior columns are elongated; some have seated lions at the base, fluted shafts and ribbed pot-like capitals. The beams are incised with scrollwork. Triple niches appear in the passageway.

Arka Brahma Temple, late 7th century

Little of the original ornamentation is preserved in this partly ruined temple.

Kumara Brahma Temple, 7th century

This is possibly the earliest temple of the series. The outer walls are plain, except for perforated stone screens that light the passageway. The internal columns and beams are decorated with foliation and miniature figures.

Bala Brahma Temple, late 7th century

This temple is currently in use for worship; the outer walls are partly concealed by an outer colonnade, where sculptures of the Matrikas have been placed.

Garuda Brahma Temple,
early 8th century

This temple is of the same type as the Vishva Brahma but is almost devoid of carved decoration. The sanctuary doorway has bands of foliation, a flying Garuda figure and flanking guardian figures.

Svarga Brahma Temple, 689

In this temple the front (east) porch has six columns, each with a fluted shaft and a base and capital embellished with a pot and foliage motif. Additional porches with similar columns shelter the windows on three sides of the passageway. The temple is notable for its elaborate sculptures. The principal images include a complete series of the Dikpalas (corner niches). Among the Shaiva icons are the god appearing out of the linga, shooting arrows at the Tripura demon, dancing and seated in the teaching posture beneath a tree (east wall). Accessory images include amorous couples, flying figures at the top of walls and guardians on the columns. The tower has additional mouldings; the large front projection has an arched niche framing a dancing Shiva image.

Padma Brahma Temple, 8th century

This is probably the latest in the series. The temple has complicated niche forms on the outer walls and within the passageway. The tower is incomplete; there is no entrance porch.

Taraka Brahma Temple,
late 7th century

This is the only temple with Deccan and southern Indian elements such as a pilastered wall and a stepped superstructure with a vault-like projection; there is a damaged dancing Shiva image on the arched end of the projection.

Archaeological Museum

Almost all the sculptures of this collection come from the site and its immediate vicinity. Dating from the 7th–8th-century Early Chalukya era are Durga images (40, 45) and ceiling panels carved with dancing Shiva (5) and a coiled serpent (9). Probably the finest sculpture is a dancing Shiva, superbly modelled in basalt (19). A slab for libations is carved with a squatting female figure with a lotus head (52). There are numerous decorated columns and beams.

Several other pieces belong to the 11th–12th-century Late Chalukya period. These include a polished basalt Nandi ridden by Shiva and Parvati (51).

Papanasi Group, 10th–11th century

The small temples of this group belong to the period of the Rashtrakuta–Late Chalukya transition. Most examples have pyramidal multi-tiered towers; one has an unusual apsidal-ended roof. There is little exterior decoration; within, the columns have figurative and foliate panels on the shafts. A fine Durga image is preserved in one temple; in another is a ceiling panel carved with Vishnu's incarnations.

AMARAVATI

Almost nothing is preserved of the great Buddhist stupa at this site other than a

dilapidated earthen mound and a surrounding circular pathway defined by
upright slabs. The stupa, which was once
the largest in the eastern Deccan, was
founded in the 3rd–2nd centuries BC and
enlarged in the 1st–4th centuries AD
under both Satavahana and Ikshvaku
patronage.

The monument is celebrated for the
finely carved capping pieces and the posts
and railings. Most of these have been
removed from the site: the largest collection is displayed in the Government
Museum, **Madras**. Together with sculptures from **Nagarjunakonda**, the art of
Amaravati is of outstanding importance
for the development of the Buddha figure;
an accompanying narrative tradition was
devoted to illustrating the life of the
Master.

The site continues to be of religious
significance; the Amareshvara temple is a
popular place of pilgrimage for Hindus.

Archaeological Museum

Broken panels, posts, railings and sculptures found at the site are assembled in this
collection. Depicted on the slabs are
seated Buddhas, representations of stupas
(31, 32, 182) and pot and lotus motifs (57,
65). A post carved with symbolic scenes
from the life of the Buddha, particularly
the episodes from the end of the Master's
life, and a small yakshi figure, date from
the 2nd century BC (506); a 3rd-century-
AD cross-bar has a medallion illustrating
the presentation of Buddha's son Rahula
(181). Among the free-standing images is
a 3rd-century Buddha with delicately
modelled drapery (80).

Antiquities from other contemporary
Buddhist sites, such as Gummadidurru
and Alluru, are also displayed. These include relic caskets, coins, beads and terracotta figurines, in addition to limestone
sculptures and stupa slabs. An example of
the last category depicts a stupa in worship with Buddha seated within the gateway (D15).

Amareshvara Temple,
late 10th century

This Hindu monument is assigned to the
period of the Late Chalukya rule of
the eastern Deccan. The exterior of the
temple has regularly spaced pilasters, but
there are no carved panels. The central
sanctuary supports an upper chamber;
above this rises the triple-storey tower
with a later roof. The temple stands
within a courtyard with a gateway in the
northern wall.

AMBARNATH

Ambaranatha Temple, 1060

This fine example of Yadava architecture
is closely related to other Hindu temples
in the Deccan, as at **Sinnar**, as well as to
contemporary examples in central and
western India. The monument is partly
ruined. It consists of a mandapa with three
porches and an adjoining sanctuary; both
expand outwards in a number of stepped
projections. The walls have moulded
basements, sculpture panels and cornices;
the niches and porches are provided with
angled eaves. Over the sanctuary rises the
curved tower, which is surrounded by a
cluster of miniature elements that repeat
the central towered shaft; these continue
the projections of the walls beneath. In the
middle of each side is a band of meshed
arch-like motifs. The mandapa is roofed
with a pyramid of recessed capping
elements.

Most of the sculptures on the outer
walls are damaged, but graceful female
figures survive in the recesses. The wall
projections on the south preserve images
of dancing Shiva, Harihara, Brahma and
Bhairava.

ANWA

Vaishnava Temple, 12th century

Although it is now ruined, this Hindu
temple was one of the most ambitious

Yadava projects in the northern Deccan. In its overall form and decoration, the temple is related to contemporary traditions of western India.

The temple consists of a sanctuary, a closed columned mandapa and an open mandapa with three porch extensions. Despite the loss of the upper portions of the building, the basement preserves its deeply cut mouldings; the balcony walls of the open mandapa and porches are relieved by flat pilasters with stylized lotus ornament. The walls of the mandapa and sanctuary are divided into projections that rhythmically expand outwards; niches for principal icons occur in the middle of each side.

The interior doorways are embellished with rows of miniature divinities; the columns have figural panels covering the shafts. A multi-lobed corbelled dome survives within the mandapa.

AURANGABAD

An important series of rock-cut Buddhist monuments overlooks the town from a range of hills situated 3 km (2 miles) to the north. They are arranged in two main groups (Caves 1–5 and Caves 6–9) separated by about 1·3 km (¾ mile). The caves may be compared with slightly earlier examples at **Ajanta**. Other than one early example (Cave 4), the Aurangabad caves are assigned to the successive Vakataka and Kalachuri periods.

(For the city and its later monuments see Volume II.)

Cave 1, late 5th century

Only the portico and verandah of this cave are complete. The richly carved columns have multi-faceted shafts; the brackets are fashioned as maidens beneath trees. The doorways are surrounded by river goddesses and miniature couples. On the walls of the verandah are three later panels depicting Buddha with Padmapani and Vajrapani. Outside to the left is a

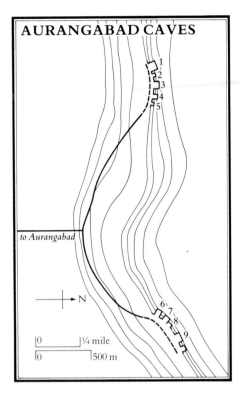

AURANGABAD CAVES

to Aurangabad

N

0   ¼ mile
0   500 m

relief of seven Buddhas, all in preaching attitude, flanked by Bodhisattvas.

Cave 2, 6th century

This excavation consists of a square sanctuary surrounded by a passageway, with a porch in front. The columns are delicately incised with medallions which contain amorous couples and scrollwork. Large Avalokiteshvara figures flank the sanctuary doorway; inside is a large seated Buddha in teaching posture. The side walls of the sanctuary are covered with panels of Buddhas in gestures of contemplation or preaching.

Cave 3, 5th century

This the largest cave of the first group. It consists of a columned verandah with end chambers, a columned hall with a central portico and cells at either side and an antechamber leading to a sanctuary at the rear. Twelve columns in the hall have multi-faceted shafts, medallions with seated couples and pot and foliage capitals. Bands of scrollwork, foliation and jewelled garlands embellish these elements. Friezes on the 'beams' above illustrate Jataka scenes.

The sanctuary is entered through an elaborate doorway. The interior presents a splendid tableau of kneeling devotees, some with folded hands, others with floral offerings; they gaze fervently towards the saviour, Buddha, who sits in preaching attitude attended by bejewelled Bodhisattvas.

Cave 4, 1st century BC

This unusually rectangular chaitya hall containing a monolithic stupa is only partly preserved. The ceiling has finely carved ribs.

Between Caves 4 and 5 is a rock-cut image of Buddha seated on a lion throne.

Cave 5, 6th century

This excavation resembles Cave 2 but the façade is now missing. At a later date this cave was appropriated by Jains, who repainted the image of Buddha as a Tirthankara.

Cave 6, 6th century

This temple has no hall; the sanctuary is entered directly from the verandah and interior porch. In the surrounding passageway are small shrines; those at the rear corners have Buddha images. Finely carved Bodhisattva figures with attendants and flying celestials appear at either side of the sanctuary doorway. Within is a teaching Buddha accompanied by a congregation of kneeling devotees, a later version of the more impressive arrangement in Cave 3. Traces of a painted ceiling survive in the verandah.

Cave 7, 6th century

This is the finest cave of the second group; in many respects it is similar to Cave 6. Columned shrines at either end of the verandah house images of Panchika and Hariti (right) and a panel of six goddesses together with Padmapani and Shakyamuni (left). The passage doorway is flanked by bold figures; that on the left represents Avalokiteshvara surrounded by scenes of rescue. Goddesses with attendants and dwarfs adorn the sanctuary doorway. In the rear wall is the usual large preaching Buddha. The side walls have seated Buddhas accompanied by Lokeshvara and Tara (right) and a female dancer with female musicians (left).

Cave 9, 6th century

This has three unfinished sanctuaries and porches opening off a common verandah. Among the numerous Buddhist and female divinities is a Parinirvana scene, now damaged, as in Cave 26 at **Ajanta**.

BADAMI

This Hindu site has been identified as Vatapi, capital of the Early Chalukya rulers in the 6th–8th centuries. The town is spectacularly situated at the foot of a rugged outcrop of red sandstone that surrounds an artificial lake on three sides; steps lead down to the water on the west. Overlooking the town are two later forts (see Volume II).

The sides of the south fort have four rock-cut shrines; these are related to similar monuments at **Ellora**. Structural temples of a slightly later date on the opposite north fort dominate the site. At the eastern end of the tank is the Bhutanatha complex; images are sculpted on to boulders nearby. A single early monument is almost completely concealed by houses in the town; several Late Chalukya temples also stand within the town.

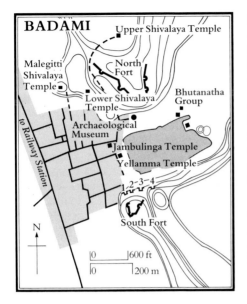

The temples at Badami provide important evidence of the formative stages of southern Indian architecture. Stylistic contacts with the Pallavas of **Kanchipuram** are attested by inscriptions at the site. Examples of the later evolution of Early Chalukya architecture are at the nearby sites of **Aihole**, **Mahakuta** and **Pattadakal**.

SOUTH FORT

Cave 1, late 6th century

This is probably the earliest of the rock-cut series. The cave temple consists of a small square sanctuary containing a linga excavated into the rear wall of a large columned mandapa. The mandapa is divided by raised floor bands and 'beams' into aisles; it is approached through a triple entrance from a long outer porch. The column shafts are incised with jewel and garland motifs as well as miniature medallions containing figures and foliation; the capitals are often fluted.

Large sculpture panels at either end of the porch depict Harihara accompanied by Lakshmi, Garuda, Parvati and Nandi

(left) and Shiva with Nandi (right). Among the ceiling panels in the porch are a coiled naga deity as well as depictions of Shiva and Parvati and flying couples. Brackets are adorned with rearing beasts.

Outside the porch on the right is a small shrine housing images of Durga, Karttikeya and Ganesha. A vigorous representation of sixteen-armed dancing Shiva is carved on to the adjacent rock face; a guardian stands opposite. Flanking the access steps is a frieze of ganas.

Cave 2, late 6th century

This Vaishnava sanctuary is similar in layout and ornamentation to Cave 1. Panels at either end of the porch depict Varaha (left) and Trivikrama (right), both with friezes of ganas beneath. The brackets are fashioned as figures emerging out of open-mouthed makaras. The elaborate ceiling panels include a wheel of radiating fish surrounded by foliation and also a composition incorporating svastika motifs and flying couples. Graciously posed guardians flank the porch entrance.

Cave 3, 578

According to its dedicatory inscription, this monument was excavated during the reign of the Early Chalukya ruler Pulakeshin I. The large scale of the temple, which otherwise follows the basic scheme of Caves 1 and 2, and the elaborate sculptural ornamentation make this the finest of the series; indeed, this rock-cut monument is one of the most remarkable in the Deccan. Throughout, the carving of the deep-red sandstone is exceptional. The columns have a variety of multi-faceted and fluted designs. Medallions on the shafts contain amorous couples and delicately incised lotus ornament. The brackets are elaborately treated, especially those of the outer row, which are fashioned as embracing couples or maidens beneath trees; rearing beasts support the overhang of the eave. Carved on to the inner face of this eave is Garuda flanked by flying figures. On either side there are faint traces of paintings. (Copies made some time ago indicate courtly scenes with royal figures.)

Major figural compositions in high relief are carved at either end of the porch: to the left are Vishnu on the coiled serpent (end panel), Varaha and standing Vishnu (side panels); to the right, Narasimha (end panel), Harihara and Trivikrama (side panels). The last deity is set within a crowded scene with Vamana and other accessory figures. High up on the walls are friezes illustrating epic stories; these include the ocean-churning scene and Krishna vanquishing demons. The ceiling is carved with medallions in which divinities are surrounded by smaller figures. The central medallion depicts Vishnu flanked by Lakshmi and Garuda; among the other principal deities are Karttikeya (left panel), Shiva, Indra and Varuna (right panels).

The ceiling within the mandapa is embellished with flying figures of the Dikpalas with Brahma in the middle. The sanctuary doorway is framed by pilasters with temple-like motifs above. No votive image is preserved inside.

Cave 4, 6th century and later

Although this Jain temple is the latest in the excavated series, it is smaller in scale and less elaborate. Both seated and standing Tirthankara figures adorn the walls; their full modelling distinguishes them from later carved insertions of small standing Jinas.

NORTH FORT

A long staircase passing through a gateway with reused sculpted slabs leads through a deep gorge up to the temples on the north fort.

Archaeological Museum

Among the sculptures in this small collection is a 7th-century Jain goddess from **Aihole**; the figure is seated beneath a tree and accompanied by attendants. Two 8th-century panels of Shiva showing the god spearing the demon and riding in a chariot shooting arrows are from **Pattadakal**. A squatting female divinity has an unusual lotus head.

Upper Shivalaya, early 7th century

This is possibly the first of the Early Chalukya structural projects. The temple is partly ruined; most of the columned mandapa has now fallen. The sanctuary has a pyramidal tower capped with a square roof. The basement preserves friezes of ganas as well as scenes from the Krishna legend (south side). Between the central wall pilasters are depictions of Narasimha (north), Krishna lifting the mountain (south) and Krishna subduing the serpent (west). Evidently, this was originally a Vaishnava temple.

Lower Shivalaya, 7th century

Of this temple, only the sanctuary with its empty oval-shaped pedestal and the tower capped by an octagonal domed roof still stand.

Malegitti Shivalaya, late 7th century

This temple is dramatically elevated on a boulder. The building combines a sanctuary, a square columned mandapa and an entrance porch into a harmonious composition. Above the sanctuary walls rises a multi-storey superstructure capped by an octagonal domed roof. The walls of the mandapa have pierced stone windows with makaras and garlands above. Between the windows are delicately modelled sculptures of Vishnu (north) and Shiva (south). Guardian figures (east) flank the entrance porch.

EAST END OF THE TANK

Bhutanatha Group,
late 7th and 11th centuries

The small shrines of this group are typical of the Late Chalukya period; they have unadorned exteriors and pyramidal towers with narrow horizontal mouldings. The principal shrine overlooking the water consists of an Early Chalukya towered sanctuary and adjoining mandapa, partly contained within later additions.

Caverns

To the rear of the Bhutanatha group are boulders with natural openings and carved images. These include a Jina figure seated on a throne and also Vishnu sleeping on Ananta attended by Lakshmi.

WITHIN THE TOWN

Jambulinga Temple, 699

This temple has three sanctuaries opening off a columned mandapa, which is approached through a large porch. The shrines were originally dedicated to Shiva, Vishnu and Brahma but are now empty. While the exterior is of little interest (there is a later brick tower), the interior preserves a series of fine ceiling panels. These depict Shiva and Parvati, Vishnu, Brahma, a coiled naga, a wheel with fish spokes and svastikas with flying couples.

Yellamma Temple, 11th century

This is the finest of the Late Chalukya temples in the town. The walls are divided into narrow projections framed by elongated slender pilasters; secondary pilasters are capped with miniature roof forms. Above rises a multi-storey stepped superstructure.

BALSANE

The Hindu temples at this site illustrate the Yadava Deccan style of the 11th–12th centuries; this is related to contemporary traditions in central and western India.

Temple, 12th century

Three shrines dedicated to Shiva, Vishnu and possibly Parvati open off a common mandapa, entered through a porch on the east. The temple exterior is dominated by repeated wall projections on deeply cut basement mouldings. The principal cult images in the niches at the corners of the three shrines are mostly damaged. Only the tower over one of the sanctuaries partly stands; this continues the projections of the walls beneath. The interior has columns with multi-faceted shafts and stylized decoration; the corbelled dome above has two rings of lobed motifs. The doorways are surrounded by bands of miniature divinities and female attendants.

BEDSA

This small group of early Buddhist excavations is located about 9 km (5½ miles) south-east of **Bhaja**. It contains a well-preserved chaitya hall and monastery. The monuments are assigned to the Satavahana period.

Cave 7, 1st century

This apsidal-ended chaitya hall is reached through a long narrow passageway cut into the hill. The front verandah is dominated by four large columns with octagonal shafts, pot-like bases and inverted bell-like capitals; on top are paired animals ridden by couples. The main doorway is flanked by pierced stone windows. Above is a large arch complete with timber-like ribs. The side walls are embellished with multi-storey reliefs with arched windows and railings. In contrast to the richly embellished exterior, the interior is plain. The three aisles are separated by octagonal columns leaning slightly inwards. An unadorned hemispherical stupa is located at the rear. The timber ribs of the vault over the central aisle have disappeared.

Cave 11, 1st century

This dwelling consists of a verandah with subsidiary cells and an apsidal-ended vaulted hall. Nine small cells are excavated into the side walls. Above the doorways are arched motifs linked together by railings in shallow relief.

BHAIRAVAKONDA

Eight small rock-cut shrines at this Hindu site date from the 7th–8th century, during which period the Kondavidu chiefs controlled much of the eastern Deccan. The seated lions at the column bases and the large figures with clubs guarding the entrances are executed in a style resembling the contemporary Pallava traditions of southern India. Lingas are housed within the shrines and there are also small images of Shiva and other divinities.

BHAJA

The monuments at this site, 6 km (4 miles) south of **Karli**, are among the earliest examples of Buddhist art in the Deccan; they date from the Satavahana period. There are more than twenty rock-cut monasteries; most have a verandah and hall with small cells provided with benches. Two exceptional examples have circular cells. Most of the monasteries are associated with cisterns. One excavation has fourteen rock-cut stupas bearing the names of religious teachers.

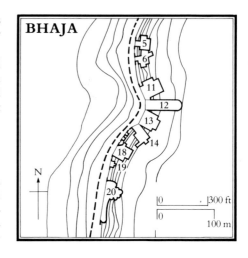

BHAJA

N

300 ft

100 m

Cave 12, 2nd century BC

This is possibly the earliest apsidal-ended chaitya hall of the rock-cut series in the western Deccan. Throughout, the dependence on timber practice is obvious. The hall is divided into three aisles by octagonal columns that slope inwards slightly. The roof is a curved vault into which teak beams were once set. A monolithic stupa, unadorned and hemispherical in shape, provides the devotional focus. Socket holes indicate that a wooden façade was inserted into the horseshoe-shaped opening; the timbers have now vanished.

Representations of multi-storey structures with arched ends are carved on to the rock face around the arched opening; standing figures appear in one of these structures.

Cave 19, 2nd century BC

This irregularly shaped monastery has a verandah with cells at either end; the two doors leading into the interior are flanked by guardian figures; there is also a pierced stone window. The verandah roof has an unusual half-vault complete with timber-like ribbing. Supporting columns have part-octagonal shafts.

On either side of the doorway leading to the cell at the right end of the verandah are sculptural compositions; these are among the earliest examples of figural art in India. The left panel depicts a royal personage, or the god Surya, attended by two women driving a chariot through the air; the four horses pulling the chariot trample a demonic figure. The corresponding panel on the right represents a majestic person, possibly Indra, riding a mighty elephant in the company of an attendant carrying a banner and spear; below the elephant are dancers and a man with a horse-headed woman.

The interior of the cave has a bench and four side cells. The doorways are framed by horseshoe-arched motifs with intermediate railings in relief.

BICCAVOLU

The Hindu temples at this site date from the 9th–10th centuries, a period in which the Eastern Chalukyas were the dominant force in the eastern Deccan. The most important monuments are three temples that stand side by side, dedicated to Rajarajeshvara (south), Golingeshvara (middle) and Chandrashekhara (north). They seem to have been built at the same time, but the Golingeshvara temple is the largest and most richly decorated. Characteristic features are the moulded plinths, the pilastered walls with regular projections, the parapets of miniature roof forms and the multi-storey superstructures crowned with square roofs (restored). Sculptures of Ganesha, Karttikeya and Durga are common; additional images of Vishnu, Surya, Brahma and the Dikpalas appear on the Golingeshvara temple. Panels are set into niches on the walls and towers; the niches in the middle are surmounted by makaras with foliated tails. Fine sculptures of Durga and Virabhadra are placed in the mandapa of the Golingeshvara temple.

BOMBAY

The expansion of modern Bombay has meant that several ancient sites, such as **Jogeshwari** and **Parel**, have been incorporated into the built-up area. **Kanheri** is situated 42 km (26 miles) north of the city, while **Elephanta** island is located in Bombay harbour.

(For the British monuments of the city see Volume II.)

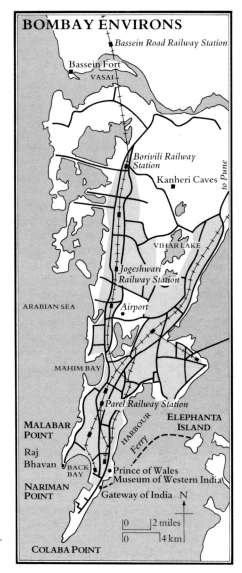

BOMBAY ENVIRONS

Bassein Road Railway Station
Bassein Fort
VASAI
Borivili Railway Station
Kanheri Caves
to Pune
VIHAR LAKE
Jogeshwari Railway Station
ARABIAN SEA
Airport
MAHIM BAY
Parel Railway Station
MALABAR POINT
HARBOUR
ELEPHANTA ISLAND
Ferry
Raj Bhavan
BACK BAY
NARIMAN POINT
Prince of Wales Museum of Western India
Gateway of India N
0   2 miles
0   4 km
COLABA POINT

Prince of Wales Museum of Western India

The prehistoric antiquities assembled here include pottery, jewellery, terracotta figurines and seals from Mohenjodaro (Pakistan). These are typical artefacts of the Harappan culture, which flourished in the 3rd–2nd millennia BC.

Among the earliest stone pieces are several 2nd-century-BC fragments from **Pitalkhora**, such as the yaksha guardian (66.58). Dating from the 2nd–3rd centuries are the sandstone heads from **Mathura**, as well as schist figures and architectural fragments from Gandhara (north-western Pakistan), especially seated Buddhas, standing Bodhisattvas and narrative scenes. Contemporary Deccan Buddhist sites are represented by limestone panels from **Amaravati**.

4th–5th-century Buddhist terracottas from Mirpur Khas (southern Pakistan) illustrate the spread of the Gupta style. These include a delicately modelled seated Buddha (58) and a number of ornamented bricks. Other terracotta heads come from the northern Indian site of **Akhnur**. Belonging to the same period is a seated gana with curly hair from Khoh (61.1).

From the 6th-century cave temple at **Elephanta** come broken images of Brahma (152) and Durga (80). There is a plaster copy of the impressive image of Shiva in his multiple form (90); the original is housed in a temple in the Bombay suburb of Parel (see below). A smaller figure of standing Shiva also comes from Parel (81.6/1).

Among the finest sculptures are three 7th-century sandstone ceiling panels from **Aihole**. These depict Vishnu reclining on the serpent (82), Brahma surrounded by ascetics in clouds (83) and Shiva seated with Parvati (89). These diverse compositions testify to the vitality of Early Chalukya traditions. A well-preserved panel from **Samalaji** showing standing Shiva and attendants delicately carved against a background of rocks (577) and

an image of Varuna and consort seated on a makara (75) also belong to the 7th century.

Other examples of western Indian sculpture are a large anthropomorphic form of Garuda (99) and a reclining Vishnu (106), both from Dohad and dating from the 11th century, a contemporary marble bust of multi-headed Vishnu (95), a slightly later standing Tirthankara from Veraval (117) and a series of panels depicting donors.

Other Deccan sculptures are assigned to the Late Chalukya period. Typical examples are the 12th-century yakshis, each seated within a highly ornate frame. A Durga image from Thana (65.25) and an image of Harihara from Purandhar (71) belong to the same era.

There is a representative collection of bronzes. This includes a 9th-century Western Ganga image from **Shravana Belgola** depicting Bahubali, his legs and arms entwined with foliation (105). Among the western Indian bronzes are a miniature 6th-century figure from Vala (122), a standing 9th-century Tirthankara within a frame of miniature figures (42) and a 10th-century Vishnu figure with attendants, also within a frame (28.5574).

Southern Indian bronzes include an 8th-century Pallava standing Vishnu from Nallur (123), a 10th-century Buddha from **Nagapattinam** (67.4) and a 13th-century Bhudevi image (125). Belonging to the 11th-century Pala period of eastern Indian art is a fine example of a standing Vishnu (68.2).

Also housed in this collection is a superb 8th-century ivory from Kashmir; this represents a miniature seated Buddha with attendant figures. Several 17th–18th-century Christian ivories from Goa are displayed, especially the finely modelled figures of the infant Jesus.

Of later carved woodwork from Gujarat, the reserve collection contains a domestic shrine with intricately carved columns and brackets. The dome-like ceiling has friezes of animals and Tirthankara figures; there is a central lotus medallion.

The museum also has a large collection of Buddhist material from Nepal and Tibet. Among the gilded bronze items are miniature figures of Mahayana divinities; these mostly date from the 16th–17th centuries. One of the finest figures is a standing Maitreya from Nepal assigned to the 12th century (67.39). Bronze ritual instruments, painted cloth thangkas from Tibet and narrative scrolls from Nepal are also on display.

Dr Bhau Daji Lad Museum

A dilapidated sculpture of an elephant removed from **Elephanta** island stands within the garden of this institution.

JOGESHWARI

Shiva Cave Temple, 6th century

This large rock-cut Hindu monument, about 30 km (19 miles) north of the city's centre, is now badly eroded. Though it is slightly earlier than the excavated shrine on **Elephanta** island, it is also assigned to the Kalachuri era.

The shrine is approached by two long flights of steps on the east and west which are deeply cut into the rock. These lead to a square columned mandapa, in the middle of which is a sanctuary with four doorways. The verandah on the north side has windows and doorways in the rear wall; in front is an incompletely excavated court.

Only traces of the original sculptures survive. The east doorway to the mandapa is flanked by guardians; the lintel above has a Nataraja figure and a scene of Shiva and Parvati playing dice.

PAREL

Mahadeva Temple, 20th century

This modern shrine is of unusual interest because of the 3·5-m-high (11½ ft) image of Shiva that is worshipped there. The 6th-century stone sculpture was accidentally discovered in 1931. It represents the god in cosmic form, expanding through multiple figures that extend upwards and outwards. Ganas with musical instruments squat at ground level.

DAMBAL

Dodda Basappa (Great Nandi) Temple, 12th century

This Late Chalukya Hindu monument has an unusual plan, with numerous angled projections that almost approach a circle; this plan is related to those of the Hoysala temples of southern India. Finely executed elongated pilasters, some terminated by tower-like motifs, adorn the walls. Above the sanctuary rises a multi-storey superstructure which continues the angled projections of the walls beneath; the capping roof form is star-like in plan. The interior columns of the sanctuary and adjoining mandapa are characteristically polished and lathe-turned; a fully cut-out lintel is positioned above the sanctuary doorway. The mandapa doorways are surrounded by bands of stylized foliation with miniature figures beneath.

The attached mandapa at the eastern end of the temple houses an unusually large polished stone image of Nandi (after which the temple is named).

Someshvara Temple, 11th–12th century

This smaller building is located near the Dodda Basappa temple; it is less elaborate in design.

DEGAMVE

Kamala Narayana Temple,
late 12th century

This is a rare example of the temple style that was patronized by rulers of the Kadamba dynasty in the western Deccan. The triple shrines of this Hindu temple are contained within a rectangle of walls relieved only by perforated stone windows. The front (east) façade is a long verandah overhung by a sloping eave. The columns here and within the long mandapa are adorned with carved panels; so too are the door frames. The central shrine houses an image of Vishnu; those at either side are for Lakshmi and Kamala. The towers above have not been preserved.

ELEPHANTA

This island is about one hour's journey by boat from Bombay. The island was named after a stone elephant discovered here by the Portuguese. (This damaged piece now stands in the garden of the Dr Bhau Daji Lad Museum, **Bombay**.) The celebrated Hindu cave temple on the island is excavated into a cliff high above the water; it is approached by a long flight of steps. The temple was probably excavated during the Kalachuri period; it may even have been a royal monument.

Shiva Temple, 6th century

The principal shrine is flanked by two excavated courts and is entered through openings on the east, north and west. The stepped plan of the interior is symmetrically laid out (similar to Cave 29 at **Ellora**). The scheme combines two axial approaches, one from the east entrance towards the sanctuary and the other from the north entrance towards the great triple-headed bust of Shiva. The columns

have squat tapering shafts and fluted cushion-like capitals; brackets above support 'beams' that articulate east–west aisles. To the west, the square sanctuary is detached from the walls and is entered through four doorways, each flanked by a pair of large guardian figures. Inside the sanctuary, a monolithic linga is set into a pedestal.

Large-scale figural panels, now damaged, are deeply recessed into the walls. These depictions of Shiva's different aspects are among the great masterpieces of Hindu sculpture. The north entrance, which serves today as the principal doorway, is flanked by images of Shiva as Lakulisha (left) and Nataraja (right). These figures indicate the inward and outward manifestations of the god's energy. At the east entrance there are twin images of Shiva and Parvati seated in their mountain home gambling at dice (left) and undisturbed by Ravana, who attempts to shake their mountain home (right). Panels showing Shiva impaling the demon Andhaka (left) and the marriage of Shiva with Parvati (right) are positioned at the west entrance. These compositions contrast violence and anger with peace and happiness.

Even more impressive are the three panels of the south wall. To the left, Shiva and Parvati are joined together in a composite androgynous figure; to the right, Shiva assists in the descent of the goddess Ganga, observed by Parvati. These subtle male–female, husband–wife relationships are embodied in the immense triple-headed Shiva image which dominates the interior. The god emerges only partly from the mountain, his fourth head turned unseen into the rock. The two side profiles contrast a feminine aspect (proper left) with a fierce masculine aspect (proper right); the central head is immobile, introspective and serene.

Outside the temple to the east and west are small courts. On the south side of the east court is a porch with side chambers. Images of Karttikeya, Ganesha and the

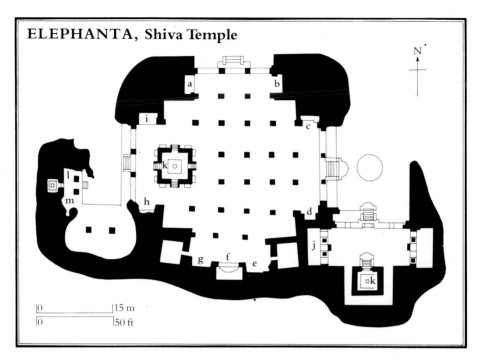

ELEPHANTA, Shiva Temple

Key to Sculpture Panels:

a   Lakulisha
b   Nataraja
c   Shiva and Parvati on Kailasa
d   Shiva and Parvati playing dice
e   Ardhanarishvara
f   Triple-headed Shiva
g   Shiva receiving Ganga
h   Marriage of Shiva and Parvati
i   Shiva spearing Andhaka
j   Matrikas with Karttikeya and Ganesha
k   Linga Shrine
l   Shiva as the Yogi
m   Nataraja

Matrikas, now damaged, are carved inside the right (west) chamber. The porch leads to a sanctuary that houses a monolithic linga. Opening off the west court is another smaller sanctuary approached through a porch. This porch has unfinished images of Shiva as the yogi and the dancer. The adjacent cistern is rock-cut.

ELLORA

This site is celebrated for its three successive groups of Buddhist, Hindu and Jain cave temples. These extend for more than 2 km (1½ miles) in an approximate north–south line along the west face of a basalt escarpment. The monuments at Ellora represent the last phase in the evolution of rock-cut architecture in the western Deccan; they are remarkable for the large-scale sculptural compositions and the range of iconographic schemes. Though the Hindu group represents the height of artistic development at the site, the Buddhist and Jain caves are also of interest.

The southernmost group comprises twelve Buddhist excavations; these belong to the period of Early Chalukya control of the Deccan in the 7th and early 8th centuries. The figural sculptures illustrate the Mahayana Buddhist pantheon.

Overlapping chronologically with this group are seventeen Hindu caves in the middle of the site. These date from the 7th to the 9th centuries, a period spanning both the Early Chalukya and Rashtrakuta periods. The earliest of the Hindu group (Caves 19, 20 and 21) reflect the influence of the Buddhist monuments but with the substitution of Hindu images. Later examples (Cave 15) evolve unique plans with complex iconographic programmes. The monolithic Kailasa temple (Cave 16) represents the climax at Ellora, both artistically and technically. The ambitious scale of this monument and its superbly executed sculptures are unsurpassed.

Five Jain excavations at the northern extremity of the site date from the 9th-century Rashtrakuta period. With one exception (Cave 32) these are modest but lavishly decorated schemes.

BUDDHIST GROUP

Cave 1, 7th century

There are four cells each in the south and east walls of this plain monastery. There is no verandah and nor are there any columns or side chambers.

Cave 2, 7th century

The verandah of this cave is elevated on a basement carved with a frieze of ganas. Four columns once supported a roof. The recess at the right end of the verandah houses images of Panchika with Hariti. Guardians flank the entrance, next to which there is a profusion of Buddha figures and other divinities, such as Lakshmi on the right door jamb.

Within the square hall a central space is defined by partly fluted columns with cushion capitals; in the side aisles the capitals display pot and foliage motifs.

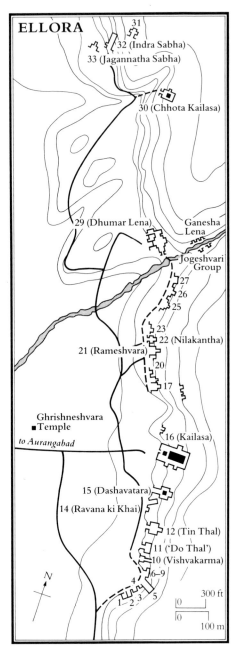

ELLORA

31
32 (Indra Sabha)
33 (Jagannatha Sabha)
30 (Chhota Kailasa)
29 (Dhumar Lena)
Ganesha Lena
Jogeshvari Group
27
26
25
23
22 (Nilakantha)
21 (Rameshvara)
20
17
Ghrishneshvara Temple
to Aurangabad
16 (Kailasa)
15 (Dashavatara)
14 (Ravana ki Khai)
12 (Tin Thal)
11 ('Do Thal')
10 (Vishvakarma)
6–9
4
1 2 3 5
N
300 ft
0
0
100 m

Depicted on each of the lateral walls are five seated Buddhas flanked by Bodhisattvas and flying celestials. A similar but larger Buddha is in the sanctuary in the middle of the rear wall. Side porches lead from the sanctuary to small cells. The right porch is carved with a relief depicting the miracle at **Sravasti**.

Cave 3, 7th century

This monastic excavation has the usual image of Buddha (unfinished) in the shrine. Pot and foliage capitals adorn the hall columns.

Cave 4, 7th century

This two-storey excavation is largely ruined. At the lower level, the plain hall has a columned aisle at the rear leading to a shrine where a figure of seated Buddha is accompanied by attendants. A smaller shrine with similar figures is located on the upper level.

Cave 5, 7th century

This large cave is entered at a higher level. It consists of a long spacious hall divided into three aisles; two benches are carved out of the floor. Porches in the middle of the side walls are flanked by small cells. The shrine in the rear wall houses the usual Buddhist figures. Several columns are delicately carved with medallions and other motifs surrounded by exuberant foliage; the remaining columns resemble those of Cave 2.

Cave 6, 7th century

This has a rectangular columned hall off which smaller halls open, each with two cells. The columns have large pot and foliage capitals. At the rear of the central hall is a columned antechamber leading to a small shrine. The walls of the antechamber are covered with Bodhisattva figures and goddesses; the latter include Tara and Mahamayuri. The shrine doorway is guarded by large Bodhisattvas; river goddesses appear on the pilasters. Within, a seated Buddha is flanked by multiple smaller Buddha figures, attendants and devotees on the side walls.

Cave 7, 7th century

There are twelve unfinished cells in this monastic excavation. The central hall has four central columns. Multiple attendant Bodhisattvas accompany the seated Buddha figure in the shrine.

Cave 8, 7th century

Instead of being recessed, the shrine of this monastery projects into the hall, where it is provided with a processional passageway on three sides (as in several examples at **Aurangabad**). The passageway has three cells on the left, an incomplete columned gallery at the rear and two columns in front. The front hall is reached through a smaller columned space with a subsidiary shrine. Sculptures include the usual Buddhist figures; on the outside wall is a scene depicting Panchika and Hariti.

Cave 9, 7th century

This is approached through the hall of Cave 6 and a small columned hall. The cave consists of an open terrace with a balcony; a shrine houses Buddhist divinities. The highly embellished façade has, among other motifs and deities, an unusual scene of the goddess Tara guarding the snake, sword and elephant (left) and fire and shipwreck (right).

Cave 10 (Vishvakarma), 7th century

This is the last noteworthy chaitya hall of the Deccan cave temple series; it has come to be named after the mythical architect of the gods.

The hall is positioned at one end of an excavated court entered through a doorway. A portico on three sides is raised on a basement carved with animals. Beyond are cells arranged in two storeys. The columns have partly fluted shafts, pot and foliage capitals and plain brackets. A long frieze depicting a hunting scene appears above. At the rear end of the court, an upper gallery has a parapet wall embellished with amorous couples and scrollwork.

The main verandah was intended to have subsidiary shrines at either end; the one to the left is incomplete. The antechamber walls to the right are covered with reliefs of Buddha and goddesses; there is a figure of Lokeshvara in the shrine.

The hall itself is entered through three doorways at the rear of the verandah. Access to an upper gallery is provided by steps cut into the left side of the verandah. The façade behind this upper gallery consists of a doorway flanked by Buddhist figures; side niches contain Bodhisattva images with female attendants. Both niches are capped with pyramidal compositions of arch-like motifs. The composition over the doorway is larger and contains a horseshoe-shaped window between arched motifs. Flying celestial figures, naga deities with coiled bodies and scrollwork adorn this scheme. Suspended over the façade is a ceiling rendered with 'beams'.

The upper gallery doorway leads to an internal gallery with a parapet wall (over the front bays of the hall). The inner face of the parapet is sculpted with amorous couples and maidens. The spacious apsidal-ended hall is divided into three aisles by elongated octagonal columns; the central two columns of the front row have pot and foliage capitals. Above the columns are a frieze of ganas, as well as preaching Buddhas flanked by Bodhisattvas. Curved ribs demarcate the vault of the ceiling.

A large teaching Buddha is carved on to the front of the votive stupa. The Master is seated within a frame adorned with flying attendants; Bodhisattvas stand at either side. The stupa is raised on a tall drum with a central frieze of Buddha figures and a multi-tiered finial above.

Cave 11 ('Do Thal'), 8th century

Together with Cave 12, these last two Buddhist monuments each have three storeys. (Cave 11 is known erroneously as 'Two-Storeyed' because its ground floor was once buried.) Both monuments are entered through spacious excavated courts reached by passages cut through the front walls.

The lowest level has two cells and a central sanctuary; a Buddha image in teaching posture is positioned at the rear of the verandah. A flight of steps at the north end of the verandah ascends to the intermediate level; this consists of five excavations of which the first is incomplete and the last is a cell with a rock-cut bed. The remaining excavations have sanctuaries housing Buddha images attended by Bodhisattvas. The uppermost level has a porch leading to a long columned hall; in the middle of the rear wall is a Buddha shrine, while to the left is a second sanctuary. The images of Durga and Ganesha carved on to the rear wall indicate that this cave was later appropriated by Hindus.

Cave 12 (Tin Thal), 8th century

The lowest floor of this temple consists of a long hall with three rows of columns; small cells, some with stone beds, open off the side walls. An antechamber leading to the Buddha shrine is recessed into the rear wall. Steps from the south-west corner of the hall ascend to the intermediate level, which is similarly organized.

The spacious uppermost level consists of a verandah, a hall with four rows of columns and an antechamber and shrine. Carved on to each of the side walls of the hall are five large Bodhisattvas; these are seated on thrones and flanked by attendants. Rows of seven Buddhas with flying figures above are placed on both sides of the antechamber entrance. The Buddhas on the left are in meditation posture, while those on the right touch

ELLORA, Cave 15 (Dashavatara)

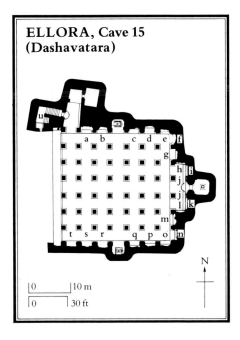

N

| 0 | 10 m |
| 0 | 30 ft |

Key to Sculpture Panels:

a   Shiva spearing Andhaka
b   Nataraja
c   Shiva and Parvati playing dice
d   Marriage of Shiva and Parvati
e   Ravana disturbing Shiva and Parvati
f   Shiva rescuing Markandeya
g   Shiva receiving Ganga
h   Ganesha
i   Parvati and musicians
j   Guardians
k   Lakshmi with elephants
l   Karttikeya
m   Shiva appearing out of the Linga
n   Shiva riding in the chariot
o   Krishna holding up Govardhana mountain
p   Vishnu sleeping on Shesha
q   Vishnu on Garuda
r   Varaha
s   Trivikrama
t   Narasimha
u   Ganesha, Shiva and Parvati, Surya, Durga, Ardhanarishvara, Kali, etc.

the earth. Within the antechamber are twelve goddesses seated on double-petalled lotus flowers held by nagas.

HINDU GROUP

Cave 14 (Ravana ki khai),
early 7th century

This single-storey excavation is the last of the earlier series at the site. A small sanctuary surrounded by a passageway adjoins a square columned mandapa and a verandah. Large guardians and river goddesses flank the sanctuary doorway; there is an image of Durga, now broken, inside. Columns have pot and foliage capitals and rectangular brackets. Figural panels carved on to the side walls include: (left wall, front to back) Durga, Lakshmi bathed by elephants, Vishnu as Varaha, seated Vishnu with Shri and Bhu, and Vishnu with single consort; (right wall, front to back) Durga, Shiva and Parvati playing dice, dancing Shiva, Ravana disturbing Shiva and Parvati, and Shiva spearing Andhaka.

Cave 15 (Dashavatara),
mid-8th century

Begun as a Buddhist monastery, this cave has an open court with a free-standing monolithic mandapa in the middle and a two-storey excavated temple at the rear. The layout of the temple, with its columned aisles and its carved figures, is closely related to Buddhist excavations (Caves 11 and 12). An inscription records a donation of the Rashtrakuta king Danti-durga (ruled c. 730–55).

The free-standing mandapa has pilastered walls with shallow niches and pierced windows overhung by an eave. The entrance doorway is flanked by river goddesses; other female figures are carved on to the walls. On the roof there are reclining lions.

A flight of steps to the left of the

entrance ascends to a spacious mandapa on the upper floor; this was later modified for Hindu usage. The columns have profuse pot and foliage motifs carved on to the shafts. Shrines are recessed into the middle of three sides; the side at the rear which houses a linga is approached through a porch flanked by guardians.

Large sculptural panels, now worn, occupy the spaces between the wall columns. These illustrate a wide range of mythological subjects: (in clockwise sequence, from the front of the left wall) Shiva spearing Andhaka, Nataraja, Shiva and Parvati playing dice, marriage of Shiva and Parvati, and Ravana disturbing Shiva and Parvati; (rear wall, left side) Shiva emerging out of the linga to rescue Markandeya, and Shiva with Parvati assisting in the descent of Ganga; (antechamber walls) Ganesha, Parvati with musicians, Lakshmi bathed by elephants, and standing Karttikeya; (rear wall, right side) Shiva emerging out of the linga, and Shiva in a chariot; (right wall) Krishna, Vishnu sleeping on the serpent, Vishnu on flying Garuda, Vishnu as Varaha, Trivikrama with one leg upraised, and Narasimha destroying Hiranyakashipu.

Cave 16 (Kailasa),
mid-8th century and later

This complex with its central monolithic temple represents the climax of the rock-cut phase of Indian architecture. This was a royal monument patronized first by Krishna I (ruled c. 756–73), and then by successive kings of the Rashtrakuta dynasty.

From the exterior, the temple is obscured by a screen wall, in the middle of which is a two-storey gateway with an upper gallery overhung by an eave. Flanking walls have shallow pilasters that frame figures, including those of the Dikpalas and river goddesses. The interior of the gateway is flanked by columned porches, and carved panels of Durga (right) and Ganesha (left). The inner face

of the enclosure wall also has figures, such as Durga on the lion and Shiva in the chariot.

At the entrance of the spacious court which surrounds the temple there is a free-standing Nandi pavilion. A panel depicting Lakshmi seated in a lotus pond being bathed by elephants faces the entrance. Monolithic columns, 17 m (56 ft) high, stand at either side; these have elaborate mouldings decorated with lotus friezes, garlands and sculpture niches. Two three-dimensional elephants, their trunks broken, stand nearby.

Cave 16 (Main Temple),
mid-8th century

While this monolithic temple is influenced by structural traditions, especially Early Chalukya architecture such as at **Pattadakal**, it is an advance on all previous schemes.

The west-facing temple is raised on a solid lower storey. At the upper level, which is reached by staircases, is a sixteen-columned mandapa with three porches; at the rear (east) an antechamber leads to the sanctuary. The sanctuary is surrounded by five small shrines that stand on an open terrace. Bridges connect the temple with the Nandi pavilion and, in turn, with the upper storey of the gateway.

Elephants gathering lotus flowers in their trunks are deeply sculpted into the lower storey; the animals appear to support the high basement. The walls are rhythmically divided by slender pilasters that frame carved panels or pierced stone windows; a parapet of miniature roof forms is positioned above. On the Nandi pavilion, the brackets are more elaborate; the corner pilasters with ganas at the top are almost free-standing. The wall niches here are framed by pediments with arch-like motifs. The porches have intricately decorated columns overhung by curved eaves; the balconies are decorated with pot motifs and foliate friezes.

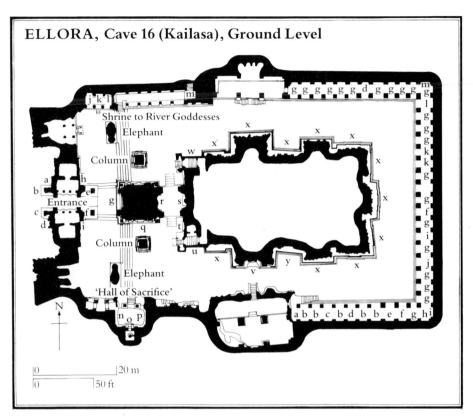

ELLORA, Cave 16 (Kailasa), Ground Level

Key to Sculpture Panels:

a Dikpalas
b Ganga
c Yamuna
d Dikpalas
e Ganesha
f Durga
g Lakshmi
h Shiva in the chariot
i Durga on the lion
j Sarasvati
k Ganga
l Yamuna
m Lakshmi with elephants
n Durga, Chamunda and Kali
o Ganesha and the Matrikas
p Female attendants
q Narasimha
r Shiva dancing with elephant king
s Dakshinamurti

t Brahma
u Ramayana
v Ravana disturbing Shiva and Parvati
w Mahabharata and Krishna story
x Elephants
y Shiva

Key to Sculpture Panels in Outer Corridor:

a Lakshmi
b Vishnu
c Varaha
d Vamana
e Narasimha
f Brahma
g Shiva, often with Parvati and/or Nandi
h Ardhanarishvara
i Bhairava
j Nataraja
k Shiva appearing out of the Linga
l Virabhadra
m Shiva rescuing Markandeya

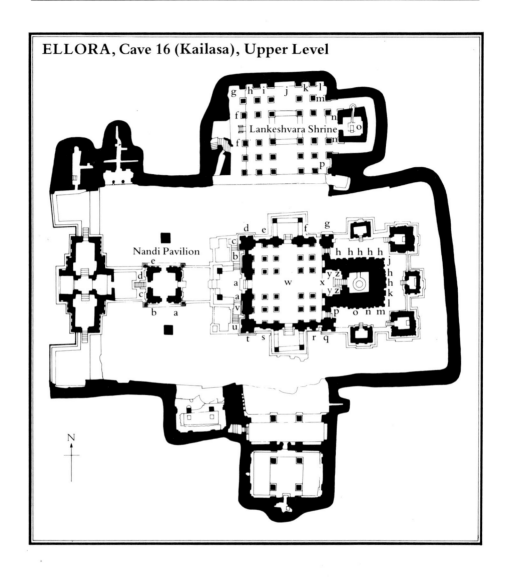

ELLORA, Cave 16 (Kailasa), Upper Level

Key to Sculpture Panels on Main Shrine:

a Guardian
b Shiva receiving Ganga
c Shiva
d Shiva with Nandi
e Durga
f Shiva spearing Andhaka
g Vishnu rescuing Gajendra
h Shiva
i Ardhanarishvara
j Nataraja

k Parvati
l Shiva with Nandi
m Nataraja
n Shiva
o Vishnu
p Shiva and Parvati
q Narasimha
r Vali and Sugriva fighting
s Jatayu attacking Ravana
t Lakulisha

u Brahma
v Shiva appearing out of the Linga
w Nataraja (ceiling panel)
x Uma (?), Brahma and Vishnu (ceiling
   panel)
y Shiva and Parvati
z River goddesses

Key to Sculpture Panels on Nandi Pavilion and Lankeshvara Shrine:

a Shiva (?), Agni (?) and Brahma (?)
b Couple
c Shiva

d Couple
e Vishnu
f Guardians
g Surya
h Varaha
i Parvati
j Shiva with Vishnu and Brahma
k Narasimha
l Ganesha
m Shiva and Parvati
n River goddesses
o Triple-faced Shiva
p Shiva and Parvati

The pyramidal mass of the tower over the sanctuary rises 32·6 m (107 ft) above the level of the court. The superstructure is divided into three receding storeys, each with carved panels, pilastered walls and a parapet; the roof is an octagonal dome. The projection on the front face, over the antechamber, has a vaulted form; within its arched end is a seated image of Shiva surrounded by ganas and jewelled garlands. Subsidiary corner shrines have similar but smaller towered superstructures. The mandapa roof is flat; in the middle is a large lotus with four striding lions carved in full relief. Lions also adorn the roof of the pavilion.

Throughout, the sculptural scheme is elaborate. At the lower level, the staircases leading up to the mandapa are flanked by walls covered with narrative friezes. On the north side, these depict episodes from the Mahabharata epic (above) and Krishna's birth and youthful exploits (beneath); the battle scenes with monkey armies on the south side illustrate episodes from the Ramayana. Large-scale panels adorn the lower storey; they show Shiva dancing with the skin of the elephant demon, the same god as Dakshinamurti (both beneath the bridge linking the mandapa with the Nandi pavilion) and Ravana disturbing Shiva and Parvati seated in their mountain home

(middle of south side). The upper storey has figures carved on to the projections. On the mandapa walls there are Shiva spearing Andhaka (north), Shiva appearing out of the linga (west) and Jatayu attacking Ravana (south). The outer walls of the sanctuary have Shaiva images set into highly ornate niches; pairs of pilasters support foliated makaras alternating with arched motifs that frame miniature temple towers. Attendant maidens and amorous couples also appear.

The mandapa is entered through a doorway flanked by pairs of guardians with attendants. To the left is a panel depicting Shiva in the scene of the descent of Ganga; on the right, Shiva emerges out of the linga. The decorated columns within the mandapa support a ceiling carved with a dancing Shiva image. Further depictions of Shiva and Parvati are displayed within the antechamber. The sanctuary doorway is highly ornamented, with river goddesses at either side. Within is a linga on a circular pedestal.

Fragmentary murals survive on the porch ceilings. Among the subjects here are flying figures and dwarfs amid clouds, a deity riding a mythical beast and battle scenes with elephants, horses and infantry (west porch). A dancing Shiva image is painted on to the mandapa ceiling.

Cave 16 (Side Shrines),
8th–9th centuries

Porticos and shrines are cut into the vertical walls that form the sides of the court. To the left of the entrance gateway is a shrine housing images of Sarasvati, Ganga and Yamuna. These river goddesses stand in niches framed by arches issuing from open-mouthed makaras.

To the right of this shrine is the Lankeshvara temple; this is reached by a staircase at the end of the colonnaded portico. An image of Lakshmi is carved on to the wall of the staircase landing. The temple itself has a columned mandapa with balcony seating on two sides, partly overlooking the court; the sanctuary at the rear is surrounded by a passageway. A seated Nandi image is set into a recess in the west wall. The columns have jewelled bands and large pot and foliage motifs with cushion-shaped or fluted capitals. The balcony slabs are adorned with amorous couples between pilasters. Large panels on the side walls depict Ganesha, Narasimha, the trio of Brahma, Shiva and Vishnu, and Parvati, Varaha and Surya (left wall). River goddesses and guardians flank the sanctuary doorway; within, a linga stands in front of a triple-headed bust of Shiva which is sculpted on to the rear wall.

The remainder of the north wall, all of the rear (east) wall and part of the south wall bordering the court have a continuous portico. Sculptures here illustrate the principal aspects of Shiva and Vishnu.

On the south side of the court is a small shrine sometimes identified as a hall of sacrifice. The interior has almost three-dimensional sculptures of seated Durga, Chamunda and Kali, the last in front of an emaciated prostrate body (right wall), the seven Matrikas with Ganesha, and Parvati (rear wall) and female attendants (left wall).

To the left (west) is a three-storey temple. The lower level is entered through a doorway flanked by female guardians and attendants. An adjacent staircase leads to the upper level.

Other smaller mandapas and shrines are excavated at different levels into the side walls of the court.

Cave 17, late 6th century

This cave is entered through a projecting porch, mostly collapsed, set in a small court. This leads to a columned mandapa and a sanctuary enshrining a linga surrounded by a passageway. The columns of the central aisle have female bracket figures. Among the deities represented in the wall panels are Ganesha (left) and Durga and Vishnu (right); there is also an unusual image of Brahma outside the court (left wall).

Cave 21 (Rameshvara), late 6th century

A court with a monolithic Nandi on a plinth in the middle and side shrines leads to a verandah, also provided with side shrines. A linga sanctuary opens directly off the verandah.

The cave is celebrated for the sensuous beauty of its fully modelled sculptures. Female figures adorn the brackets of the outer columns of the verandah; amorous couples in panels are carved on to the balcony wall. On the left of the verandah is a gracefully posed figure of Ganga; Yamuna appears in the corresponding position on the right. Figural panels in the verandah include Karttikeya, the marriage of Shiva and Parvati in the presence of the gods, Durga (left end shrine), Shiva and Parvati disturbed by Ravana, Shiva and Parvati playing dice with Nandi beneath (rear wall), dancing Shiva, the seven Matrikas with Ganesha and Virabhadra, and skeletal Kala and Kali (right end shrine). Large guardians flank the sanctuary doorway.

Cave 22 (Nilakantha), 8th century

This cave is distinguished for its free-standing Nandi pavilion, now damaged, and separate shrine for the Matrikas.

Cave 26, late 6th century

A verandah with end shrines adjoins a sanctuary surrounded by a passageway. The columns are finely finished with fluted shafts and cushion–like capitals.

Cave 29 (Dhumar Lena),
late 6th century

In overall conception this cave is influenced by the example at **Elephanta**. Access to the columned interior is from three sides; there is a court on the west. Seated lions guard the steps to the three entrances. The columns of the spacious mandapa have part-fluted shafts and cushion-like capitals. Towards the rear wall is a detached square sanctuary with four doorways, each with a pair of tall guardian figures with female attendants. A monolithic linga is enshrined within.

Large-scale wall panels at either end of the outer aisles on three sides depict Shiva impaling Andhaka, the divine couple disturbed by Ravana (west), Shiva dancing, Lakulisha (north), the marriage of Shiva and Parvati in the presence of the gods and the couple playing dice (south). River goddesses are positioned outside the north and south entrances.

Ganesha Lena and Jogeshvari Groups,
9th century

These two groups of small shrines are the latest in the Hindu series. They are situated in a ravine about 90 m (300 ft) above Cave 28. The last cave in the Ganesha Lena group preserves traces of paintings on the ceilings; these depict Shiva appearing out of the linga and the churning of the ocean scene.

JAIN GROUP

Cave 30 (Chhota Kailasa),
early 9th century

This is a small-scale but incomplete replica of Cave 16, with a temple standing in the middle of a court. This monolith consists of a columned mandapa entered through a porch; balcony seating is adorned with friezes of pots, pilasters and elephants. Carved ornamentation is mostly restricted to Jain saints and goddesses; twenty-two seated Tirthankaras are located in the mandapa; the columns here have their shafts decorated with foliation and garlands. An image of Mahavira seated on a lion throne is enshrined within the sanctuary at the rear of the mandapa.

Cave 32 (Indra Sabha), early 9th century

This is the finest of the Jain series. A simple gateway leads into an open court in the middle of which stands a monolithic shrine; this has a pyramidal superstructure capped with an octagonal roof. Miniature Jina figures adorn the arched niches of the roof projections. A free-standing elephant and column are also positioned here. The sides of the court are adorned with lion and elephant friezes as well as Tirthankaras.

A double-storey temple is excavated into the rear side of the court. The lower level is an unfinished mandapa with incomplete cells. The columned mandapa of the upper level is more complete, with niches on three sides and in the sanctuary in the middle of the rear wall. Among the carved figures are repeated images, often damaged, of Ambika with a child seated on her lap, a lion beneath and a spreading tree above; other panels depict Mahavira, Gommateshvara and Parshvanatha. Exuberant foliate and garland motifs are carved on to the fluted shafts and capitals of the columns. Fragmentary paintings on the ceiling of the upper mandapa show couples and maidens flying through the clouds.

Cave 33 (Jagannatha Sabha), 9th century

Five independent shrines, each with a columned mandapa and sanctuary, are irregularly disposed on two levels. Little original sculpture is preserved.

Ghrishneshvara Temple, 18th century

This finely finished structural temple, dedicated to Shiva, is situated in the nearby village. It is a typical example of later architecture during the Maratha period.

(For the tombs at Khuldabad, 6 km (4 miles) away, see Volume II, under Rauza.)

GUNTUPALLE

This hill site overlooking a ravine has a number of early Buddhist antiquities, both structural and rock-cut, which mostly date from the 2nd–1st-century-BC Satavahana period.

A circular brick structure occupies a commanding position. This contains an unadorned hemispherical stupa surrounded by a passageway; part of the limestone cladding of the stupa is intact. Several standing Buddha images assignable to a later era are placed here. In front of the circular shrine are more than thirty stupas of varying sizes. The ruins of a columned hall and an apsidal-ended shrine are situated nearby. All of these structures are built on a terrace approached by a long flight of steps.

Two groups of rock-cut shrines are excavated at different levels; these are in a poor state of preservation. The chaitya hall is the chief monument; it has an unusual circular plan and a dome-like ceiling with a network of rock-cut ribs in imitation of wooden rafters. The entrance is framed by a horseshoe-shaped arch.

HANAMKONDA AND WARANGAL

These twin cities – only 6 km (4 miles) apart – preserve important remains of fortifications and Hindu temples dating from the 12th–13th centuries. During this period both sites served successively as capitals of the Kakatiya rulers and were the most important political and artistic centres of the eastern Deccan. At various times from the 14th century onwards the cities were incorporated into the Vijayanagara and Muslim kingdoms.

HANAMKONDA

Shiva ('Thousand Pillared') Temple, 1163

This impressive example of Deccan architecture was erected by the Kakatiya king Rudradeva. The main temple is built of grey-green basalt and is finely worked. Three shrines dedicated to Shiva, Vishnu and Surya lead off a columned mandapa, which is partly open on the south as a porch. The outer walls rise upon a deeply moulded basement; no sculptures remain in the wall niches, which are headed by tower-like pediments. The superstructures over the shrines have fallen. The balcony seating of the porch is sheltered by an angled eave.

The mandapa interior is enlivened by columns with sharply cut and multi-faceted shafts; the capitals are adorned with bands of jewels and petals. The central ceiling panel is an elaborate composition with monster masks and scroll-work surrounding an image of Nataraja. The doorways have cut-out lintels, with deities in the middle flanked by makaras and scrollwork; attendant figures are positioned beneath.

The plinth of the mandapa extends southwards. A magnificent polished Nandi is placed here. Yet further south is another columned mandapa, less finely worked and now dilapidated; it is constructed entirely of granite. Its many columns are responsible for the name by which the temple is best known.

In the gateway to the east is an upright basalt slab covered with an inscription. This contains information about the royal patron and his military victories.

WARANGAL

This unique circular city dates from the 12th century, when it was founded by Ganapatideva, a prominent Kakatiya ruler. Warangal was partly destroyed by the Muslims, but was occupied by them in later times. (For monuments of the Islamic period see Volume II.)

The city is defined by two concentric circles of fortifications. The outer circuit is an earthen rampart protected by a moat. Four arched stone gateways of the Muslim era are positioned at the cardinal points. The inner circuit is entirely of stone. The four gateways in these walls have large double-bent entrances; door frames and yali balustrades are typical features of the Kakatiya period.

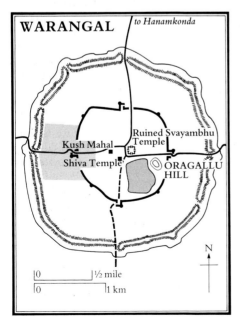

The four roads of the city converge on a ruined temple in the middle. This was once dedicated to Shiva, under the name Svayambhu. It is now merely a colossal pile of rubble and overturned slabs. Four free-standing portals leading into the temple still stand, remarkably untouched. These each have double posts supporting a lintel, the ends of which are carried on angled brackets. While the decoration of these portals is typical of the Kakatiya style, with sharply cut tower-like motifs, looped garlands and birds, the form of the portals is familiar from the gateways of early Buddhist architecture (such as those at **Sanchi**). The temple was once surrounded by an enclosure wall, part of which has been cleared recently to reveal the foundations of several small linga shrines.

Near to the south portal of the Svayambhu temple is another smaller but better-preserved shrine, also dedicated to Shiva. This 14th-century structure consists of a mandapa with three porches; the tower is a later addition. Stored within the compound is the top portion of a colossal linga that was discovered in the ruins of the Svayambhu temple.

The modern town now occupies the western part of the circular city. To the south-east is a tank overlooked by a granite hill known as 'One Stone' (Oragallu), from which the name of Warangal is derived. At the summit of the hill is a small Shiva shrine and an octagonal pavilion. Several other smaller shrines are dotted around the site.

HYDERABAD

(For the city and its monuments see Volume II.)

State Museum

Limestone Buddhist antiquities from the 1st–4th centuries are exhibited in this collection. They illustrate the artistic traditions of the Satavahana and Ikshvaku periods in the eastern Deccan. Prominent among the sites represented is **Amaravati**, from where several slabs carved with lotus medallions and pot and foliage motifs come. There are reliefs of stupas, such as that sheltered by a tree-like parasol from Chandavaram. Among the Buddha figures is a white marble one from Uppugunduru with an elegantly modelled robe (5388). Copies of paintings from the Buddhist caves at **Ajanta** are exhibited in an upstairs gallery.

Rashtrakuta art of the 8th–9th centuries is represented by a strident Durga figure slaying the demon (7579). Later 11th–12th-century sculpture is represented by a group of Jinas, such as seated Mahavira in polished basalt from Dilsukhnagar. An unusual altar block carved with a lotus and signs of the zodiac, a seated Ganesha and a ceiling slab depicting Varaha (1338) are all from Patancheruvu. Also displayed is a selection of Kakatiya sculptures, including two columns depicting Ramayana episodes from Katangur, a toilet scene from **Warangal** (3340A) and a panel with a depiction of ritual suicide from Nalgonda (8871). In the garden, part of a columned mandapa from **Ghanpur** has been re-erected; this incorporates a ceiling slab carved with Vishnu on the serpent, dancing Shiva and other figures.

A series of Shaiva divinities and saints from Motupalli is exhibited separately; these span the Chola and Vijayanagara eras. The group from the 9th–10th-century site of Bapatla is the finest, especially the image of Ambika (P.5313). There are also Jain bronzes from the eastern Deccan, as well as bronze bells and copper-plate grants, and a collection of Roman coins discovered in the eastern Deccan.

Srisailam Pavilion

Erected within the grounds of the State Department of Archaeology, this museum houses a collection of excavated antiquities and stone sculptures from sites recently submerged by the **Srisailam** dam. Animated stucco fragments from Gollathagudi are dated to the 4th–5th century. Among the later Kakatiya stone pieces are finely carved female busts from **Ghanpur**. In the entrance hall stands an intricately carved temple doorway.

IKKERI

This town, situated 3 km (2 miles) south of Sagar, was the seat of a local dynasty of Nayakas who achieved independence during the Vijayanagara era. The distinctive temple style suggests links with earlier Deccan traditions.

Aghoreshvara Temple, 16th century

This is the largest and finest of the Ikkeri Hindu temples. A sanctuary surrounded by a passageway adjoins a spacious mandapa. The plain outer walls of the sanctuary are framed by a deeply moulded basement and cornice; niches surmounted by tower-like elements are positioned in the middle of each side. Above rises the multi-storey pyramidal tower; this is capped by a domed roof and pot finial. Friezes of shallow pilasters with towered motifs adorn the mandapa walls, which are overhung by steeply angled eaves. Elephants flank the steps ascending to the principal doorway.

The interior columns are ornately treated, some with rearing animals in the typical Vijayanagara manner. Other Vijayanagara columns with carved panels appear in the detached Nandi pavilion and subsidiary shrine. The merlon-like parapets of these smaller structures indicate the influence of Islamic architecture.

ITTAGI

Among the numerous Hindu antiquities at this site is a gateway with a sculpted lintel dating from the Early Chalukya era. A fine Late Chalukya monument overlooks a large tank.

Mahadeva Temple, 1112

As in the temples at nearby **Kukkunur** and **Lakkundi**, this temple consists of a towered sanctuary, an inner enclosed mandapa and an outer open mandapa with three porches. Throughout, the delicacy of the ornamentation is remarkable. The outer walls are divided into pilastered projections; these expand outwards in the middle of each side of the sanctuary and mandapa, where niches, now empty, with tower-like pediments are positioned. The parapet has deeply cut arch-like motifs surrounded by foliation and monster masks; these are repeated in diminishing tiers on the multi-storey pyramidal superstructure that rises over the sanctuary.

Lathe-turned and multi-faceted columns are used in the porches and within the mandapas. The doorways are delicately carved with miniature figures; over the entrance to the sanctuary the lintel is sculpted with a dancing Shiva figure flanked by makaras, all set in elaborate scrollwork. The ceiling panels have corbelled domes with ribs and intricate lotus designs.

JUNNAR (map p. 372)

This town is dominated by a fortified hill on which there is a temple dedicated to Bhavani as well as a monument commemorating the birthplace of Shivaji, the 17th-century Maratha leader. More than fifty Buddhist cave temples from an early period are excavated into the eastern side of the hill; similar cave temples, numbering more than one hundred, are cut into the sides of the other hills that surround the town. Most of these rock-cut monuments are unadorned monasteries with small cells for accommodation. They are assigned to the era of the Satavahana and Kshatrapa domination of the western Deccan, a period spanning the 2nd–1st century BC to the 3rd century AD.

TULJA LENA GROUP

These cave temples are located 2 km (1½ miles) west of the town. One of the excavations (Cave 3) is an unusual circular chaitya hall. This has twelve tall octagonal pillars surrounding a plain hemispherical stupa; the roof is fashioned as a rock-cut dome-like ceiling.

BHUTA LENA GROUP

Three groups of caves are excavated into the sides of Manmodi hill, about 1·5 km (1 mile) south of the town. The chaitya hall (Cave 40), which is the largest monument of this group, has a well-preserved façade. Above the entrance is a horseshoe-shaped arch containing petal-like compartments; these are filled with reliefs of Lakshmi, elephants and devotees. Flanking the finial of the arch are a winged animal-headed figure (left) and a naga deity (right) as well as two stupas; the whole is framed by a sequence of arched façades. The interior of the hall is unadorned and only partly complete.

GANESHA LENA GROUP

The monuments of this group are located on Lenyadri hill, 4 km (2½ miles) north of the town. The spacious monastery (Cave 7) has a verandah with doorways and windows. Nineteen small cells open off the hall; in one of these a later Ganesha image has been placed. The octagonal

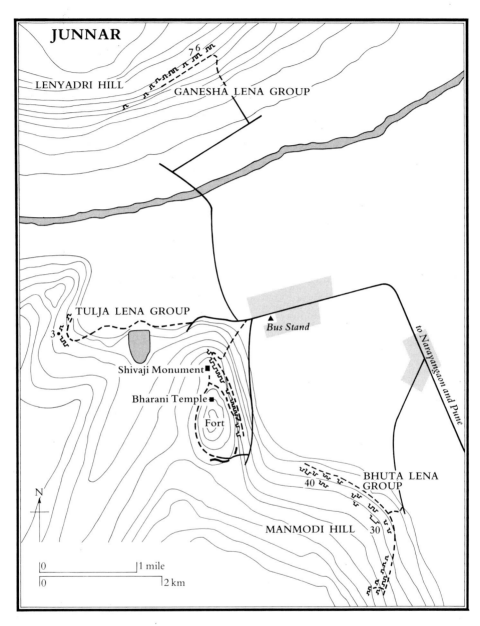

columns of the verandah have bell-like capitals and seated animals. Similar columns appear in the adjacent chaitya hall (Cave 6). The vaulted interior of this hall has rock-cut ribs; the devotional focus is a hemispherical stupa raised on a plain drum. The blind chaitya arch of the main façade is a unique feature.

KANHERI

More than one hundred Buddhist rock-cut monuments dot this picturesquely wooded site, about 42 km (26 miles) north of the centre of **Bombay**. Kanheri was occupied by a substantial and wealthy

religious community from the Satavahana period in the 1st century to as late
as the 11th century. Its situation on
the western coast and its accessibility to
thriving ports ensured its continued
prosperity.

The caves are generally small and consist of a verandah and hall with a cistern
nearby. An unusual feature is the group of
small commemorative stupas, both rock-
cut and brick built, exposed on a terrace to
the north-east of the site.

A few caves preserve a profusion of
carved figures, mostly of Buddha standing or seated in the teaching posture;
accompanying images include Bodhisattvas, female divinities and naga deities.

The style of these carvings is attributable
to the later Vakataka era. The sculptures
of Cave 90 include an Avalokiteshvara
figure standing between two female
deities; in the surrounding miniature
scenes the Bodhisattva is shown deliver-
ing his devotees from the eight great
perils. The image of Avalokiteshvara in
Cave 41 has four arms and eleven heads.

Cave 3, 2nd century and later

This chaitya hall is the most impressive
monument at Kanheri; in many of its
features it is a copy of the one at **Karli**.
The exterior is dominated by a rock-cut
wall, partly restored; this is flanked by

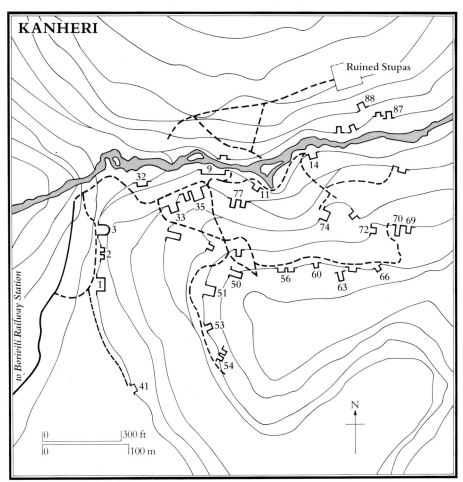

KANHERI

Ruined Stupas

N

0   300 ft
0   100 m

to Borivili Railway Station

columns with sculpted bases and capitals. The façade of the hall has three doors between which two donor couples have been carved on each side; the window above is a semicircular opening devoid of ornamentation. The side walls of the verandah are occupied by large reliefs of standing Buddha; these are additions of the 5th–6th century. The apsidal-ended hall is divided into three aisles by octagonal columns; several of these have pot-like bases and bell-like capitals surmounted by animal riders, worship of stupa, footprints under the bodhi tree and other motifs. The vaulted roof of the nave was originally provided with wooden ribs. The hemispherical stupa at the rear of the hall is unadorned.

Large structural stupas have been found outside the hall; one of them yielded two urns containing relics and an inscription dated 495.

Cave 11, 6th century

This monastic excavation has a verandah with eight octagonal columns and a small shrine at one end with three doors and two windows in the rear wall. The hall has columned aisles on three sides and a number of small cells; the shrine in the rear wall houses Buddha images. On the floor of the hall are two low benches (similar to those in Cave 5 at **Ellora**).

KARLI (map p. 375)

This Buddhist site is 6 km (4 miles north of **Bhaja**. The antiquities include rock-cut monasteries, a few cisterns and, at a height of about 110 m (360 ft) above the valley, the celebrated chaitya hall. This hall is assigned to the brief period of Kshatrapa rule in the western Deccan during the 1st century. Two excavations of lesser interest date from the late 5th century.

Cave 8, 1st century

This is the largest and most completely preserved chaitya hall of the early Buddhist series in the western Deccan. It is approached through an excavated court. On the left side stands a high monolithic column with a capital of four lions. A modern Hindu shrine protrudes into the court on the right; this may be built over the remains of another monolithic column.

The façade of the hall is dominated by a large horseshoe-shaped window, complete with ribs. Panels depicting six stately pairs of donors are positioned between the three doorways, each of which is capped by an arched motif. The Buddha images here are later insertions of about the 5th century. The side walls display the foreparts of three elephants; these animals support reliefs of multistorey vaulted buildings with arched windows and railings.

The interior is divided into three aisles. The magnificently carved columns mostly have octagonal shafts with pot-like bases and fluted capitals. Carved upon the capitals are pairs of seated elephants ridden by embracing couples. The impressive vault of the nave has teak ribs set into the rock. The monolithic stupa serving as the devotional focus has a double circular drum with railing friezes, a hemispherical dome and an inverted stepped finial. The whole composition is capped by a remarkable wooden umbrella, the underside of which is carved with delicate patterns.

KOLHAPUR

Within this town are several Hindu and Jain temples belonging to the Yadava period. Shrines and lamp-columns crowd the bathing ghats on the Panchaganga river.

(For the later monuments of the city see Volume II.)

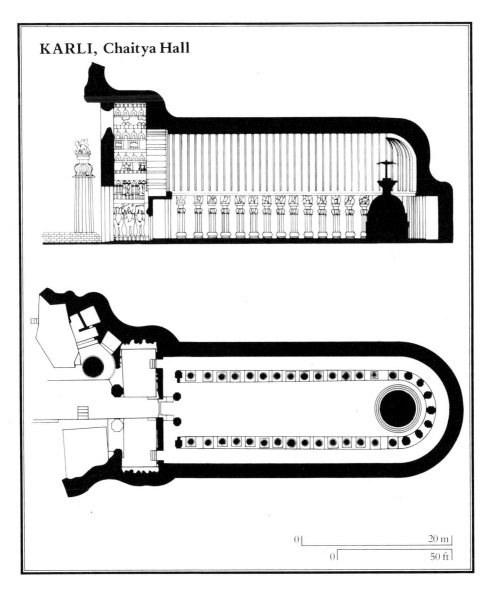

KARLI, Chaitya Hall

0 [—————— 20 m]
0 [—————— 50 ft]

Amba Bhai Temple, 10th century
and later

Although it is much rebuilt, this large
Hindu temple preserves portions of the
original structure. The entrance hall is
laid out on a stepped plan with a deeply
recessed basement and eave mouldings;
the sculptures are set into small niches.
The doorways are flanked by pilasters
and pierced stone screens. The steeply
pyramidal tower dates from only the 18th
century.

In front of the subsidiary Sheshagiri
shrine is a columned mandapa with a
magnificently carved ceiling. This is
divided into eight panels, which depict
the Dikpalas with standing Vishnu in the
middle. The exuberance of the detail is a
remarkable illustration of Late Chalukya
art.

BRAHMAPURI

This mound in the western part of the city overlooks the right bank of the Panchaganga river. Excavations here have exposed brick remains assignable to the Satavahana period. Among the artefacts discovered were miniature bronze figures, including the Hellenistic god Poseidon, and an elephant with riders. These are now displayed in the Kolhapur Museum.

KUKKUNUR

Two temples at this Hindu site mark the transition between the Rashtrakuta style and the more pervasive Late Chalukya idiom that spread throughout the southwestern Deccan in the 11th century.

Navalinga Complex, late 9th century

This cluster of nine shrines, each with a multi-storey square tower, is built around three interconnecting columned mandapas. Despite the presence of votive lingas, the shrines were originally dedicated to female divinities. Together with other temples, some ruined, and a tank, the nine shrines stand in the middle of a large courtyard. Two entrance gateways date from the later Vijayanagara period.

The niches of the unadorned pilastered walls are headed by makaras with foliated tails and parapets of miniature roof forms. The lintels over the shrine entrances are elaborately carved with cut-out makaras, looped garlands and flying figures (especially in front of the western shrine). The columns have lathe-turned or multi-faceted shafts and capitals.

Kalleshvara Temple, 10th century

This temple anticipates the Late Chalukya style, as exemplified in the nearby monuments at **Lakkundi** and **Ittagi**. The square sanctuary of this shrine has a triple-storey tower with a front projection; this

adjoins an antechamber and enclosed mandapa. The walls are adorned with temple-like reliefs of different designs. The capitals of the lathe-turned columns within the mandapa are intricately worked. Two rectangular shrines dedicated to Ganesha and Durga face the four central mandapa columns.

KURUVATTI

Mallikarjuna Temple, late 10th century

This is a typical small-scale Hindu temple of the Late Chalukya period. A sanctuary and mandapa with three porches have slender wall pilasters; these frame niches capped by tower-like motifs. Over the sanctuary rises the multi-storey square superstructure; this is capped by a part-domed roof with a projection on the front. The columns of the interior and the porches are lathe-turned and multi-faceted. The lintel in front of the sanctuary doorway is carved with figures of Brahma, Shiva and Vishnu; these divinities stand within a highly ornate arch flanked by makaras with flowing foliated tails. The mandapa doorway has bands of foliation with miniature figures beneath.

The inclined bracket figures on the porch columns are outstanding examples of Late Chalukya art. The fully modelled female dancers and the intricate foliage backgrounds are delicately carved.

Facing towards the mandapa doorway is a large Nandi sculpture.

LAKKUNDI

No fewer than seventeen Hindu and Jain temples from the 11th–12th centuries stand within this town; all are built in the typical Late Chalukya style. The temples are entirely constructed of schist, and are elaborately treated with sharply cut

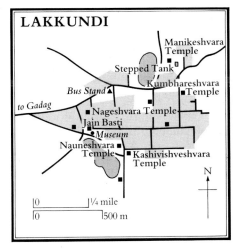

LAKKUNDI

Manikeshvara Temple
Stepped Tank
Kumbhareshvara Temple
Bus Stand
to Gadag
Nageshvara Temple
Jain Basti
Museum
Nauneshvara Temple
Kashivishveshvara Temple
N

|0 |¼ mile
|0 |500 m

details. The basements have deep mouldings, while the walls are generally provided with elongated pilasters; niches are capped with different tower-like designs in shallow relief. The superstructures are multi-storeyed and pyramidal. The mandapas and porches have lathe-turned or multi-faceted columns, which support beams and corbelled ceilings covered with finely carved detail. The doorways are richly encrusted, sometimes with figures and foliate motifs set in pierced screens. Most of the temples have open porches with balcony seating overhung by steeply angled eaves.

On the outskirts of the town to the north-east is a stepped masonry tank; a two-storey colonnade here serves as a bridge.

Jain Basti, late 11th century

This is the largest and most prominent temple at Lakkundi. The sanctuary walls rhythmically expand outwards in a number of shallow projections which are repeated in the parapet of miniature vaulted roof forms above. The pyramidal tower has five storeys and is capped with a square roof. Both an enclosed and an open mandapa adjoin the sanctuary; the latter is greatly enlarged by projections on three sides.

Kashivishveshvara Temple,
12th century

Despite its incomplete condition, this Hindu temple is one of the finest of the Lakkundi series. The two sanctuaries which face each other are linked by an open porch, now mostly collapsed. Only the tower of the western sanctuary is partly standing.

Throughout, the sharply carved details are typical of the evolved Late Chalukya style. The basement is adorned with friezes of elephants and lotus petals. The walls have pairs of pilasters capped either with makaras with flowing foliated tails or with temple-like reliefs of different designs. On the most prominent projections are niches with miniature eaves and curved tower-like forms (in contrast to the stepped pyramidal superstructure of the temple itself). Carvings of maidens and attendants appear between the pilasters. The doorways are surrounded by bands of stylized foliation with attendant figures beneath.

MAHAKUTA

This sacred Hindu complex dating from the Early Chalukya era is still a place of worship. Two temples and a number of shrines are grouped around a rectangular tank that is fed by a natural spring. Standing within the tank is a small pavilion sheltering a four-faced Shiva linga. The complex is enclosed within recently renovated high walls entered through a gateway on the north-east. Outside the enclosure to the south-east is another gateway with unusual skeletal figures of Chamunda and Bhairava; this leads to the Bananti shrine. (A fallen sandstone column with a ribbed capital, found outside the enclosure, was removed some time ago to the Archaeological Museum, Bijapur; carved on to its fluted shaft is an inscription recording a royal grant in 601.) To the east of the complex stands a

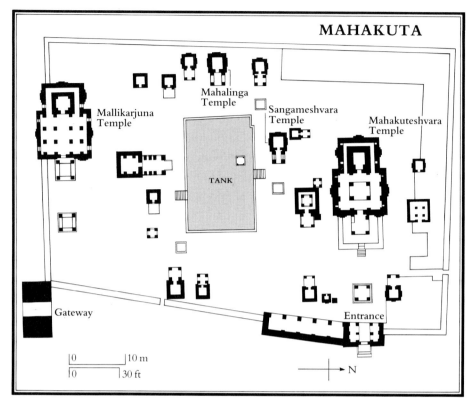

MAHAKUTA

Mahalinga Temple

Mallikarjuna Temple

Sangameshvara Temple

Mahakuteshvara Temple

TANK

Gateway

Entrance

| 0 | | 10 m |
| 0 | | 30 ft |

N

pair of abandoned temples dating from the 10th century.

The larger of the Mahakuta temples represents an intermediate phase of development between the earlier examples at **Badami** and the later projects at **Pattadakal**; both these Early Chalukya sites are only a short distance away. At the head of a ravine, about 2 km ($1\frac{1}{2}$ miles) to the south-west of the Mahakuta complex, is the temple dedicated to Naganatha.

Mahakuteshvara Temple,
late 7th century

This temple consists of a sanctuary housing a Shiva linga surrounded by a passageway; this is approached through a columned mandapa divided into three aisles and an entrance porch, partly concealed by modern additions. Further east is a detached Nandi pavilion. The outer walls have pilastered projections and

pierced stone windows. Above the sanctuary rises a multi-storey tower capped by an octagonal domed roof. Carved friezes of epic subjects and foliate panels appear on the basement; images of Ardhanarishvara (north), Shiva (south and west) and guardians (east) are framed by wall pilasters.

Mallikarjuna Temple, late 7th century

Although this is a slightly later copy of the Mahakuteshvara temple, there are certain small differences: the roof slabs over the side aisles are sloping, a Vishnu image is placed on the south wall and unusual guardian figures are carved on to the porch columns. There are three ceiling panels inside the mandapa; these are a nine-panelled composition with lotuses and flying couples, Brahma with four guardians, and Shiva and Parvati on Nandi.

Sangameshvara and Mahalinga Temples, 7th century

These small sanctuaries with adjoining entrance porches have curved towers adorned with arch-like motifs and capped with amalakas. Sculpture panels in the wall niches depict Harihara (north), Ardhanarishvara or Narasimha (west) and Lakulisha or Varaha (south).

Naganatha Temple, 7th century

This abandoned temple may be compared with similar examples at **Aihole**. The sanctuary surrounded by a passageway and the adjoining columned mandapa are contained within a rectangle of walls. Pierced stone windows light the interior. The porch extending to the east has columns carved with couples beneath trees. The ceiling panels, now damaged, depict Vishnu, Brahma surrounded by the Dikpalas, and Shiva and Parvati on Nandi.

MAHULI

At the confluence of the Krishna and Yenna rivers, 4·8 km (3 miles) east of Satara, is a group of 18th–19th-century Hindu temples built in the typical Maratha style. The largest sanctuary, which is dedicated to Vishveshvara Mahadeva, was completed in 1735. The nearby cenotaphs are for the royal family of Satara.

The temples are characterized by towers crowned with fluted dome-like elements. Miniature versions of these elements cluster around the main shafts of the towers, which are divided into niches and are almost circular in plan. The adjoining mandapas are mostly double-storeyed. The upper levels are late Mughal in style with shallow pilasters and multi-lobed arches; the lower levels have temple-like columns. The detached Nandi pavilions also have towered superstructures. Stone columns with protruding lamps stand in front of some of the temples.

MARDOL (map p. 390)

As at **Ponda**, 7 km (4½ miles) to the south, the Hindu temples at Mardol are typical of the unique Goa style.

Mahalasa Narayani Temple, 18th century

The temple courtyard is reached through a triple-arched neo-classical doorway. Immediately in front are a lamp-column and a bell-tower. The brass lamp-column has twenty-one tiers; at the base is a tortoise, above which four yalis prance outwards. The bell-tower is a six-storey octagonal building with neo-classical pilasters and cornices; at the summit is a small dome.

The temple itself preserves examples of wooden construction and carving. The rectangular mandapa has projecting porches on three sides; the outer walls have friezes of carved figures as well as balustraded openings. Above rises the gabled timber roof in two tiers covered with metal sheets. In contrast, the sanctuary walls are of masonry, with neo-classical basement and wall pilasters but Islamic arched niches. Over the sanctuary is an octagonal tower capped by a dome; this is now contained within a metal cupola with a pot finial.

The mandapa interior has finely carved wooden columns; the elaborate capitals support brackets with lotus designs. Peripheral walls have raised seating areas. The doorways to the antechamber and sanctuary are of silver; among the finely embossed figures is Lakshmi on the lintel with peacocks at either side.

To the south of the main temple is a smaller neo-classical shrine housing Vaishnava divinities; an octagonal tower rises over the sanctuary. At the rear (west) of the court is a colonnade with shrines and a tank with stepped sides.

Mangesha Temple, 18th century

Less than 1 km (½ mile) north of the town a long avenue leads from the main road to the temple. In front of the courtyard is a tank overlooked by a tower; ramps beneath descend to the water.

A six-storey bell-tower stands within the temple court. This has neo-classical elements and is capped with a small dome. The main temple is entered on the east through a part-octagonal porch roofed with an unusual dome. The outer walls are raised on a high neo-classical basement; the windows have renovated trefoil openings. On the north and south, entrance porches are reached by balustraded staircases and roofed by fluted domes with ribbed finials. The sanctuary, which is part-octagonal in plan, has an octagonal tower with a pierced parapet and ribbed finials above.

The arcaded nave of the mandapa is adorned with glass chandeliers hanging from a flat wooden ceiling with geometric designs. The silver doorways are embossed with foliate motifs; there are also large guardian figures. The side niches house sculptures of Ganesha (left) and Shiva (right). Within the sanctuary, a pot for libations is suspended over the linga; a metal mask of Shiva is encased in the rear wall.

NAGARJUNAKONDA

This was the most extensive early Buddhist settlement in the eastern Deccan. The ancient site occupied an area of about 23 sq km (9 sq miles) in a valley bounded on the west by the Krishna river. During the 3rd–4th centuries, when Nagarjunakonda was the capital of the Ikshvaku rulers, a large number of monasteries and shrines was erected to serve the needs of different Buddhist sects. Inscriptions name many of these religious communities as well as those who acted as building patrons and donors.

Though most of the excavated remains were submerged beneath the waters of Nagarjuna Sagar, a few monuments have been reconstructed on a hilltop that is now an island in the middle of the reservoir; a museum is also located here. Other reconstructions of excavated ruins are situated on the hill above the east bank.

Monastic architecture at Nagarjunakonda is characterized by elaborate and symmetrical planning. Votive stupas were usually combined with halls (circular, apsidal-ended or rectangular) and residential structures (cells arranged in three or four wings around a court). The stupas had concentric infill walls of brick or rubble; their exteriors were coated with plaster or limestone slabs. The halls and monasteries had limestone columns set into brick or rubble walls; of these, only the lower portions were preserved, including pavement slabs and access steps. Hindu shrines were also discovered at the site.

Limestone panels and friezes have been discovered in many structures at the site; together with those from **Amaravati**, they constitute the most important Buddhist sculptures of the eastern Deccan. Nagarjunakonda's art is distinguished by its animated carving with vigorously posed figures.

ISLAND

The hilltop, which is now an island, is accessible by ferry from Vijayapuri. On the island there are fortifications and several ruined civic structures that date from about the 16th century. The reconstructed Buddhist monuments are assigned to the Ikshvaku period.

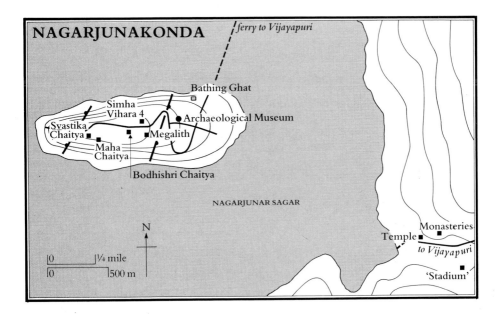

NAGARJUNAKONDA

ferry to Vijayapuri

Bathing Ghat

Simha Vihara 4

Svastika Chaitya

Archaeological Museum

Megalith

Maha Chaitya

Bodhishri Chaitya

NAGARJUNAR SAGAR

N

Monasteries

Temple

to Vijayapuri

0 — ¼ mile
0 — 500 m

'Stadium'

Megalith, 1st millennium BC?

This provides evidence of the early occupation of the site. A stone circle encloses a heap of stones; beneath this is a simple burial pit which once contained four skulls.

Simha Vihara 4, 3rd–4th century

This complex consists of a stupa built on a high platform accompanied by double chaitya halls, one enshrining a stupa, the other a Buddha image.

Bodhishri Chaitya, 3rd–4th century

This is a simple hemispherical stupa raised on a cylindrical drum, entirely cased in limestone slabs. The stupa is contained within an apsidal-ended structure.

Maha Chaitya, 3rd–4th century

With a diameter of about 27·5 m (90 ft), this large stupa has radiating masonry walls; projections with columns are positioned at the four cardinal directions. The stupa once contained a reliquary with a tooth relic. Nearby is an apsidal-ended shrine.

Svastika Chaitya, 3rd–4th century

The brick walls within this stupa are arranged in the shape of a svastika.

Bathing Ghat, 3rd–4th century

This was originally located on the bank of the Krishna river. Its steps are entirely constructed of finely finished limestone slabs.

Archaeological Museum

The 3rd–4th-century Ikshvaku limestone sculptures discovered in the excavations here constitute the majority of the exhibits. Among the capping panels are several examples with representations of stupas in the company of flying celestials and seated Buddhas (34, for instance). Other slabs depict incidents from the life of the Master: for example, leaving the palace, the gods carrying Siddhartha's crown and the report of the departure

(50); protection of Buddha by Mucha-linda, Buddha receiving alms and the first sermon (52). Another double-sided panel shows courtly couples, elephants and ganas (129).

Long friezes are divided into panels; these illustrate episodes from the Mandhatu Jataka (24), the conversion of Nanda (interspersed with amorous couples) (3) and scenes from the life of the Master, such as the renunciation, the departure from the palace, the assault of Mara, the enlightenment and preaching (separated by medallions). Columns are adorned with lively courtly scenes and dancing ganas. There are only a few free-standing sculptures. One headless Buddha with delicately modelled robes (39), is typical of the Ikshvaku style; another example (8) is more than 3 m (10 ft) high.

There are also 16th-century sculptures, such as seated Narasimha (75).

EAST BANK

Temple, 3rd–4th century

This comprises a rectangular sanctuary and columned hall. A subsidiary square shrine near to the entrance yielded the lower half of a sculpted female deity.

Monasteries, 4th century

These typical examples of the evolved Nagarjunakonda monastery include additional features such as a refectory, store and bath. The principal residence consists of four wings of cells around a court within which there is a rectangular Buddha shrine. Another residence, possibly a convent, has two wings of cells approached through a narrow passage-way. On the south side is an open space enclosed by walls; this contains three circular chambers in a row. The associated stupa has six radial walls.

The adjacent structure is similar except

that it has double chaitya halls, one containing a stupa with eight radial walls, the other a Buddha image.

'Stadium', 4th century

This monument was probably intended for musical and dramatic performances and perhaps also for athletic contests. Tiered galleries provided seating around a rectangular court.

NASIK

Nasik is one of the holy cities of Hinduism and a celebrated pilgrimage centre in the northern Deccan. Here, it is believed, Rama spent part of his exile, together with Lakshmana and Sita. 8 km (5 miles) south-west of the town is a range of hills with a series of important rock-cut Buddhist monuments known as Pandu Lena.

The town lies on both sides of the Godavari river, the banks of which are dotted with temples, shrines, memorials and bathing ghats. The river is considered to be as sacred as the Ganga, especially at its source at **Trimbak**, 29 km (18 miles) upstream. Every twelve years the Kumbha Mela at Nasik attracts large numbers of pilgrims anxious to purify themselves by bathing in the river.

Despite the antiquity of the site, most of the shrines date from no earlier than the 18th-century Maratha period. Temple architecture displays the influence of Muslim practice, especially in the use of dome-like roofs, but there are also more traditional curved spires.

Narayana Temple, 1756

This temple is built on the steeply rising west bank of the river and is reached by a long flight of steps. Three black stone images of Vishnu with consorts are enshrined within the sanctuary.

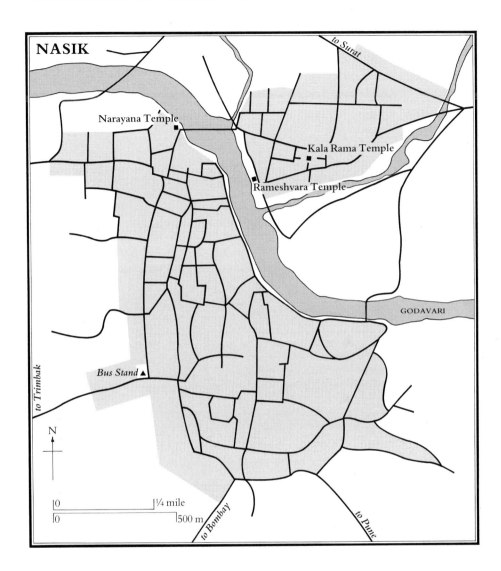

NASIK

Narayana Temple

Kala Rama Temple

Rameshvara Temple

GODAVARI

to Trimbak

to Surat

Bus Stand ▲

N

0 .... ¼ mile
0 .... 500 m

to Bombay

to Pune

Rameshvara Temple, 18th century

Near to this temple is the pool where Rama is believed to have performed funerary rites in memory of his father. The temple, which houses a linga, stands in the middle of an enclosure. The roof over the adjoining mandapa is adorned with grotesque figures and animals. In the middle of the west enclosure wall is a pavilion with a large bell of Portuguese workmanship.

Kala Rama Temple, 1782

This temple is surrounded by colonnades and columned mandapas; images of Rama, Lakshmana and Sita are housed within the sanctuary. The curved tower is about 25 m (83 ft) high.

PANDU LENA

Twenty-four monastic establishments constitute this group of rock-cut Buddh-

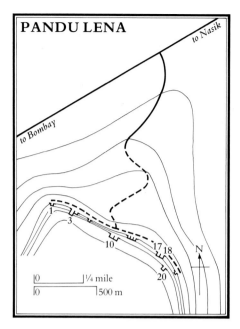

PANDU LENA

to Nasik

to Bombay

1
3
10
17 18
20
N

0 — ¼ mile
0 — 500 m

ist monuments. They are accompanied by a large number of donative inscriptions belonging to the Satavahana and Kshatrapa periods, dating from the 1st century BC to the 3rd century AD. Later Buddha images assignable to the Vakataka era have been added to many of the caves.

Cave 3, 2nd century

This is one of the largest and most elaborate monasteries at the site. The octagonal columns of the verandah have pot-like bases and bell-like capitals which support pairs of seated animals with riders; imitation rafters and railings adorn the ceiling. The doorway is framed by a relief representation of a decorated wooden gateway with curved architraves; guardian figures are positioned at either side. The balcony walls have ganas which appear to support railing reliefs, now worn.

Nineteen small cells, each with a rock-cut bed, open off the large hall. The rear wall is carved with a stupa in relief; this is flanked by female devotees.

Cave 10, 2nd century

This is similar to the previous example except that there is no balcony, nor any carved reliefs framing the doorway. A later Buddha figure was cut into the stupa panel in the rear wall of the hall.

Cave 18, 1st century BC

The exterior of the chaitya hall has finely carved details. The entrance is framed by a horseshoe-shaped arch containing ribs and shallow reliefs of auspicious emblems and animals; a guardian figure stands on the left of the doorway. Above is a similarly shaped but larger window, complete with internal timber-like ribs. This forms part of an elaborate façade with railings, columns, stupas, cornices and arched windows, all in shallow relief. The interior is plain except for the pot-like column bases; the wooden ribs of the vaulted ceiling have vanished. The focal stupa has a high drum crowned with a railing; the finial is an inverted stepped pyramid.

Caves 17 and 20, 2nd–3rd centuries

The chaitya hall (Cave 18) is flanked by these two monasteries, which were apparently linked to it by access staircases, preserved only on the left. Both these excavations were enlarged in the 6th century, when Buddha images were added to the shrines. The pot-like bases and capitals of the columns, however, are original features.

OLD GOA

(For the Christian monuments see Volume II.)

Archaeological Museum

The disused Convent of St Francis of Assisi houses a collection of sculptures and commemorative stones dating from the era before the Portuguese conquest. Most of these belong to the 12th–13th centuries, a period when Goa came under the rule of the Kadamba dynasty.

Among the sculptural and architectural fragments is an image of Vishnu standing within a frame adorned with miniature incarnations. Numerous hero stones are exhibited, some with vigorous naval battles; these suggest the importance of maritime trade for the Kadamba rulers. One example shows a royal figure sitting inside a palace with sun and moon emblems above. Other commemorative panels depict heroes on horseback.

PALAMPET AND GHANPUR

Several Hindu temples in the Kakatiya style are preserved at Palampet; the best known, which is dedicated to Ramappa, was erected by a general of the king Ganapatideva. A large tank nearby also belongs to the same period. Other examples of Kakatiya temples stand at Ghanpur, 6 km (4 miles) to the north-west.

PALAMPET

Ramappa Temple, 1213

The sanctuary and antechamber adjoin an open mandapa laid out on a stepped plan. The reddish sandstone exterior has a sharply moulded basement with a miniature frieze of elephants; slender wall pilasters frame multiple niches, now empty, in the middle of each side. A projecting eave continues around the building. The front porch is contained within high balcony walls adorned with pilasters and stylized lotus ornament. The brick tower is multi-storeyed, with miniature pilastered walls and parapets; the roof is square. A typical Deccan feature is the vaulted projection on the front face of the tower.

The polished basalt columns of the mandapa have sharply modelled capitals. The peripheral columns are distinguished by their angled brackets, which are carved as rearing mythic beasts or as female dancers and musicians beneath trees. These figures are the masterpieces of Kakatiya art, notable for their delicate carving, sensuous postures and elongated bodies and heads. A finely modelled Nandi is placed within the mandapa. The ceiling panels are elaborate compositions; that over the central bay incorporates miniature figures within rotated and ascending squares.

A detached Nandi pavilion and a columned mandapa also stand within the walled compound; several ruined shrines are located nearby.

GHANPUR

Two partly ruined 13th-century temples and an open columned mandapa are surrounded by eighteen minor shrines. As at Palampet, the basements of these structures have sharply cut mouldings; the columns have prominent brackets and are overhung by angled eaves. Where preserved, the towers have multiplied elements capped with hemispherical roofs. In the principal temple, the doorways are surrounded by carved figures, now damaged. (Other sculptures have been removed to museums in **Hyderabad**.)

PANDHARPUR

This is one of the most popular Hindu pilgrimage centres of the northern Deccan; it is of particular importance for the Varkari sect. The town lies on the west bank of the Bhima river and is crowded with temples, shrines, monasteries, bathing ghats and shaded banks. The religious focus is the Vithoba temple in the middle of the town. This mostly dates from the 18th-century Maratha period.

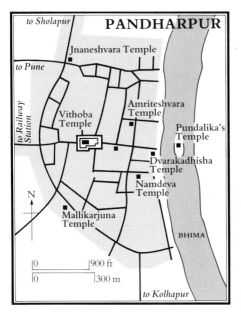

PANDHARPUR

to Sholapur

Jnaneshvara Temple

to Pune

to Railway Station

Vithoba Temple

Amriteshvara Temple

Pundalika's Temple

Dvarakadhisha Temple

Namdeva Temple

Mallikarjuna Temple

BHIMA

N

|0 _____ 900 ft
|0 _____ 300 m

to Kolhapur

umns with lotus bases and stylized foliate motifs are derived from Mughal architecture.

Pundalika's Temple, 18th century

About 500 m (1,750 ft) east of the Vithoba temple is a funerary shrine in the middle of the river bed; this commemorates the spot where Pundalika, a devotee of Vithoba, spent the last years of his life. A brick and plaster spire with a brass finial rises over the sanctuary.

Vishnupada Temple, 18th century

This temple is also situated in the middle of the river but is reached by a causeway. It is notable for the funerary rites performed by pilgrims. Within the sanctuary are three boulders on which footprints revered as those of Vishnu have been carved.

Vithoba Temple, 17th century and later

This complex faces eastwards towards the most important bathing ghat. While portions of the temple date from as early as the 12th–13th century, the building was extensively renewed in later times. The image of Vithoba, an aspect of Vishnu depicted with two hands placed on the waist, is probably older than the temple itself. To save it from Muslim sacrilege this image was often removed; it is even supposed to have been brought to **Vijayanagara**.

The sanctuary is preceded by two columned mandapas, in which embossed silver plates cover many of the columns and doorways. The open columned mandapa is an earlier structure. The courtyard immediately east of the temple is surrounded by a colonnade; in the middle stand several altars and a small pavilion for Garuda. The complex is contained within a rectangle of walls.

The architecture is typical of the later Deccan style in the use of dome-like forms and decorative motifs. A curved tower with niches rises over the sanctuary. The multi-lobed arches, fluted col-

PATTADAKAL

This royal commemorative Hindu site served as a setting for the coronation ceremonies of the Early Chalukya rulers. Seven temples, grouped closely together and surrounded by numerous minor shrines and plinths, face eastwards towards the Malprabha river. A temple dedicated to Papanatha is situated on the south side of the village; about 500 m (1,750 ft) to the west is a later Jain monument.

The Pattadakal temples provide a striking illustration of the coexistence of different building styles and artistic traditions derived from different regions of India. The large scale of the architecture, the complex elevational and spatial treatments and the rich ornamentation represent the climax of the Early Chalukya phase. The contemporary Virupaksha and Mallikarjuna temples are the largest of the series initiated at nearby **Badami** and continued at **Mahakuta** and **Aihole**.

The temples are described from north to south.

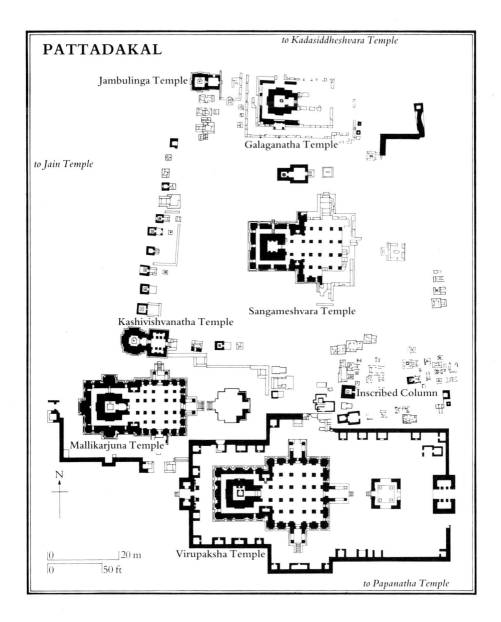

PATTADAKAL

to Kadasiddheshvara Temple

Jambulinga Temple

Galaganatha Temple

to Jain Temple

Sangameshvara Temple

Kashivishvanatha Temple

Inscribed Column

Mallikarjuna Temple

N

Virupaksha Temple

0 ⎯⎯⎯⎯ 20 m
0 ⎯⎯⎯⎯ 50 ft

to Papanatha Temple

Kadasiddheshvara and Jambulinga Temples, 8th century

These two small shrines have curved towers adorned with horseshoe-shaped and ribbed elements, in the typical central and western Indian style. The sculptures, now worn, on the outer walls of the sanctuaries are framed by pilasters. On the front (east) faces of the towers are panels carved with Nataraja images. The sanctuaries adjoin small mandapas.

Galaganatha Temple, 8th century

This temple is closely related to contemporary monuments at **Alampur**. The most striking feature is the well-preserved curved tower with horizontal tiers covered with horseshoe-arched motifs;

amalakas are positioned at the edges and at the summit. Of the three porches that once sheltered the pierced stone windows, only that on the south still stands; it shelters a carved panel depicting Shiva killing Andhaka. Damaged river goddesses and an icon of dancing Shiva adorn the sanctuary doorway.

Sangameshvara Temple,
early 8th century

Founded by the Early Chalukya ruler Vijayaditya, this temple was never completed. The finely proportioned building demonstrates the essential features of the southern Indian style: a deeply moulded basement, walls divided into projections and recesses by pairs of pilasters, a parapet of miniature roof forms and a multi-storey tower with a square roof. Most of the sculpture panels are incomplete; the intermediate perforated stone windows have geometric designs.

Kashivishvanatha Temple,
late 8th century

Protruding into the Mallikarjuna temple courtyard, this building is a later example of the central and western Indian styles. The wall projections have pediments of arch-like motifs. Similar motifs adorn the tower, especially the central band, which consists entirely of a mesh of these motifs. A dancing Shiva image is positioned on the front (east) face.

Virupaksha and Mallikarjuna Temples, c. 745

These neighbouring, almost identical, temples were erected by two queens of Vikramaditya II to commemorate the victory of the Early Chalukyas over the Pallavas at **Kanchipuram**. In plan, the temples consist of sanctuaries housing Shiva lingas surrounded on three sides by passageways; these adjoin columned mandapas, each divided into five aisles and entered through three porches. East of the temples are open pavilions sheltering large images of Nandi. Enclosure walls with minor shrines and gateways contain the temples and pavilions in rectangular paved courtyards (incomplete in the Mallikarjuna complex). The diagonal arrangement by which the two enclosures interlock is unique. The Virupaksha courtyard has a gateway on the east.

Deriving from the Sangameshvara scheme, these temples demonstrate a remarkable stylistic evolution in the increase of scale and elevational complexity. Plinths, pilastered walls, sculpture niches, open porches, parapets and multi-storey pyramidal towers are combined in slightly different ways in the two temples. For example, in the Virupaksha temple the wall projections are flanked by double pairs of pilasters, while in the Mallikarjuna temple these are increased to triple sets; the Virupaksha has a square roof, while the Mallikarjuna has a hemispherical roof. Both towers have horseshoe-shaped frontal projections framing images of dancing Shiva.

The vitality of Early Chalukya art is amply displayed in the sculptures. The outer walls have numerous figurative panels, many depicting Shiva and Vishnu in their different forms. On the Virupaksha temple, some of the finest panels are Shiva appearing out of the linga, Vishnu as Trivikrama (either side of east porch), dancing Shiva (east end of south wall), Bhairava (middle of south wall of sanctuary) and Vishnu with Durga beneath (middle of north wall of sanctuary). Figural panels are less well preserved on the Mallikarjuna temple but there is a robust Nataraja on the west wall of the sanctuary. Perforated stone windows are delicately carved with foliate motifs. Both panels and windows are surmounted by arch-like pediments filled with figures or makaras with foliated tails. Divinities, embracing couples and guardians with clubs, now worn, are carved on to the porch columns and on panels beside the doorways. On the Virupaksha temple, for instance, there are pot-bellied attendants (east doorway), Ravana subdued by Shiva (south porch column) and Vishnu on Garuda (north porch column).

The interior columns have bands of narrative friezes, which include illustrations of epic scenes, scrollwork and lotus ornament. Peripheral columns are adorned with amorous couples. Over the central aisle the raised ceiling panels have naga deities, dancing Shiva icons and scenes of Lakshmi bathed by elephants. Other panels in the porch ceilings of the Virupaksha temple depict Shiva with sages (north), Surya in his chariot (east) and Brahma (south). The doorways are elaborate compositions with river goddesses and attendants beneath at either side and makaras with foliated tails raised on pilasters above. Guardians with clubs are carved on the adjacent columns. A remarkable three-dimensional sculpture of Durga is placed in the minor north shrine of the Virupaksha temple mandapa. The sanctuaries house polished black stone lingas. The shallow projections with decorated pediments in the passageways have empty niches.

The large Nandi images within the open pavilions are naturalistically carved; the animals are ceremonially decked with garlands and bells. The circular columns have projecting brackets and delicately applied foliate decoration.

Papanatha Temple, 8th century

The two interconnecting columned mandapas of this temple lead to the sanctuary surrounded by a narrow passageway. There is a single entrance porch; the Nandi image sitting immediately inside the doorway is misplaced. Three blind porches at the western end of the temple shelter pierced stone windows and carved panels, now damaged.

Elements derived from different architectural traditions are combined in the elevation. The tower over the sanctuary resembles those of the Kadasiddheshvara and Jambulinga temples, which are central and western Indian in origin. The parapet of roof forms and the makaras with foliated tails on the pilasters that flank niches and doorways are typical of southern Indian practice.

The basement preserves traces of fighting elephants and lions (east porch). Epic friezes in the niches of the outer walls illustrate scenes from the Mahabharata and Ramayana; processions of monkeys appear on the south wall. Porch columns have fully modelled couples, maidens and guardians; similar figures adorn the peripheral columns of the interior mandapas. In the middle of the outer mandapa there are niches housing images of Durga (north) and Ganesha (south). The columns have brackets decorated with monster heads and foliation; the brackets are fashioned as open-mouthed makaras disgorging lions. The raised ceiling panels over the central aisles in both mandapas have carved compositions; the finest are Nataraja and the coiled naga deity of the inner mandapa. The doorways to the mandapas and sanctuary are the most ornate of the Pattadakal series.

Jain Temple, 9th–10th century

This Rashtrakuta monument has slender pilasters on the outer walls but no sculptures. The stepped tower is capped with a square roof. Large elephants, carved in full relief, are placed in the mandapa; the doorway here is framed by makaras with unusually elaborate tails.

PITALKHORA

The Buddhist cave temples at this site date from the early Satavahana period. They are excavated into the side of a secluded ravine. Most of these rock-cut monuments are monasteries in which cells open off a central hall or verandah; many cave fronts have collapsed. Two monuments are of particular interest.

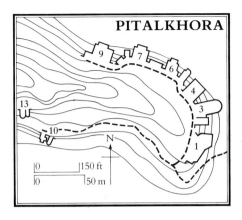

Cave 3, 2nd–1st century BC

This chaitya hall is conceived and executed on a large scale; it shares a common court with the adjacent monastery (Cave 4). The exterior appears unadorned, due to the collapse of the façade. The usual apsidal-ended interior is divided into a nave and two aisles by octagonal columns which incline inwards slightly. The half-vaults of the side aisles have rock-cut ribs; the timber rafters and beams set into the central nave are missing. The focal stupa has a monolithic base, but the structural drum has disintegrated. Painted fragments indicate that the hall was in use until the late 5th century.

Cave 4, 2nd–1st century BC

The basement of the monolithic outer walls of this monastery is sculpted with elephants and attendant figures. The doorway is flanked by guardians in foreign dress holding spears and shields; two elephants above once framed a Lakshmi image, now missing. From this doorway a covered flight of steps ascends to the monastery itself. This is now open, due to the loss of the front wall; the upper part of the façade, which is badly weathered, has traces of ornamental horseshoe-shaped arches. The columns of the interior hall have mostly crumbled. The doorways to the cells are framed by arched motifs, railings and pilasters with decorated capitals, all carved in shallow relief. Six cells have vaulted ceilings with rock-cut beams and rafters.

PONDA

Together with the temples at **Mardol**, 7 km (4½ miles) to the north, the shrine at Ponda is among the finest examples of Hindu architecture in Goa. The influence of contemporary church design is unmistakable.

(For the other monuments in Ponda see Volume II.)

Shanti Durga Temple, 1738

This temple is picturesquely set in a forested surrounding, 2.5 km (1½ miles) west of the town. It was erected by a minister of one of the Maratha rulers of the western Deccan to enshrine the goddess of peace.

Outside the temple there is a tank at a lower level surrounded by a balustraded wall. The gateway, which is modern, leads into a rectangular court. In front of

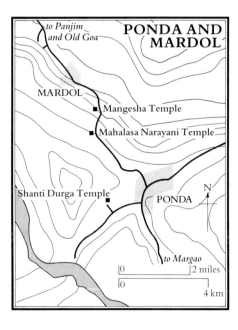

the temple is an octagonal five-storey bell-tower. This has neo-classical pilasters and cornices; at the top is a small dome.

The temple itself consists of a sanctuary and a surrounding passageway; this adjoins a rectangular mandapa with an entry porch. A secondary shrine abuts the structure on the north. Neo-classical basement and pilaster details adorn the walls. The mandapa has a gabled roof; over the sanctuary rises an octagonal tower capped by a dome.

The interior has glass chandeliers hanging from a wooden ceiling with carved designs. Silver screens with elaborately embossed doorways separate the mandapa and antechamber from the sanctuary. A small silver image of the goddess is enshrined beneath a dome-like canopy.

RAMTEK

This town is dominated by a steep hill to the east. At the summit is a fort with massive walls and gateways, within which are several small Hindu shrines. Other shrines are grouped around Ambala lake, at the foot of the hill. While most of these structures belong to the 18th-century Maratha era, several of the shrines date back to the 5th century, when the town served as the capital of the Vakataka rulers.

The early shrines are constructed of deep-red sandstone and consist of simple small sanctuaries with detached open mandapas, later enclosed by infill walls. Columns and balcony slabs are decorated with delicate foliage ornament. The large

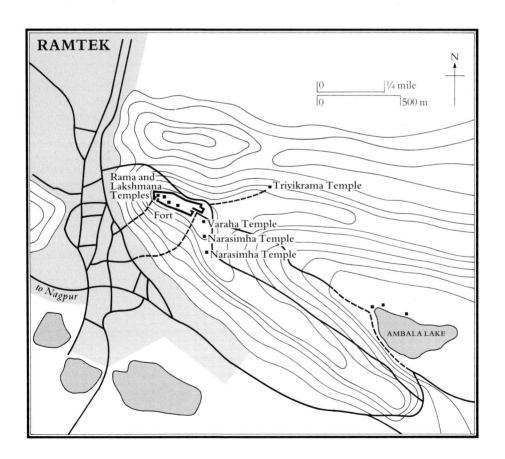

images of Narasimha, Varaha and Trivikrama that are worshipped in these shrines indicate the ancient Vaishnava association of the site. The hill is considered particularly holy to Rama and three shrines of more recent date are dedicated to Rama and Lakshmana.

RATANVADI

Amriteshvara Temple, 13th century

This Hindu temple is a later variant of the northern Deccan style. While the well-preserved tower rising over the sanctuary is closely related to other examples, such as at **Sinnar**, the outer walls of the sanctuary and adjoining mandapa are influenced by Kakatiya and Late Chalukya traditions. The horizontal lines of the elevation are emphasized by sharply cut mouldings; sculpture niches are contained in small wall niches.

SAMALKOT

Bhimeshvara Temple,
early 10th century

This Hindu temple is assigned to the period of the Eastern Chalukyas. It is unusually arranged on two levels; rising above the roof is the double-storey tower with a dome-like roof. The exterior is devoid of any sculpture, the walls between the pilasters being quite plain. The interior columns have finely worked double capitals; the shafts are occasionally adorned with figural motifs. The temple stands within a courtyard, with entrances on the north and south. The gateways have pilastered walls but there are no towers.

SANKARAM (map p. 393)

Two hills near the village of Sankaram preserve the dilapidated remains of Buddhist monuments dating from the 3rd–5th centuries. The eastern hill is dominated by the basement and lower portions of a stupa; this is surrounded by smaller stupas. Almost all of these are partially rock-cut and finished with brickwork and plaster. Immediately to the east is a brick-built monastery. This consists of a rectangular court surrounded by small cells; in the middle is an apsidal-ended shrine. Rock-cut sanctuaries are located in the sides of the hill; four of these contain reliefs of Buddha. The cave with a monolithic votive stupa has sixteen columns. Images of Ganesha and Bhairava carved on to the sides of another cave indicate that the site was used in later times for Hindu worship.

The western hill has numerous rock-cut stupas in tiers; these are dominated by the outlines of a large monolithic stupa.

SATYAVOLU

Two monuments at this Hindu site date from the Early Chalukya era. The 7th-century Bhimalingeshvara temple is a small plain structure with a curved tower rising over the sanctuary. Above the porch is a large horseshoe-shaped projection containing a dancing Shiva image. The adjacent 8th-century Ramalingeshvara temple has a more elaborate tower, also with a front projection, comparable to the examples at **Alampur**. Sculpture panels adorn three sides of the sanctuary walls.

Nearby is a diminutive apsidal-ended shrine with a vaulted roof.

SIMHACHALAM

Varaha Narasimha Temple,
mostly 13th century

This sacred Hindu complex is situated in the coastal region of the eastern Deccan. In 1268 it was completely reconstructed

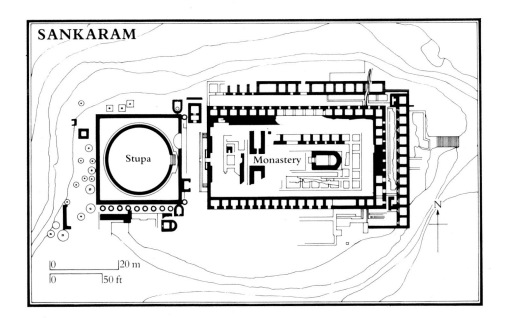

SANKARAM

Stupa

Monastery

N

0 ———— 20 m
0 ———— 50 ft

by a military commander of Narasimha, the Eastern Ganga ruler responsible for the great Surya temple at **Konarak**. As a result, the temple's architecture is a mixture of Orissan and Deccan features.

The sanctuary is picturesquely secluded in the wooded Kailasa hills, about 16 km (10 miles) north of Vishakapatnam. The hills are noted for their natural springs and there are several beside the flight of steps that ascends to the temple. The growth of nearby Vishakapatnam has ensured the continuity of worship in this shrine, which is one of the most popular in the region. According to one tradition, the temple was originally Shaiva but after the visit of Ramanuja at the end of the 11th century it was converted into a Vaishnava shrine. This story is borne out by the principal votive image, which is encased within a linga-like form composed of sandalwood paste.

The temple is set within a double enclosure wall with a modest gateway on the west. A tall flag-pole stands immediately in front of the entrance porch to a columned mandapa. This mandapa leads into the inner enclosure, where the main temple is situated. The principal sanctuary and its adjoining mandapa are surrounded by a colonnade into which three small shrines are incorporated; that in the north-east corner is fashioned as a chariot. A large columned mandapa used for the marriage ceremonies of deities is located in the north-west corner of the outer enclosure. Nearby, in the middle of the north wall, is another gateway.

Throughout, the basements, pilastered walls, columns, brackets and multi-storey pyramidal towers are adorned with delicately cut mouldings as well as friezes of mythical beasts and jewelled garlands. Attendant figures are carved on to pilasters, which are separated by panels of scrollwork extending the full height of the walls. In the central niches of the outer sanctuary walls are fully modelled figures of Varaha (north), Narasimha (east) and Trivikrama (south); these are essentially Orissan in style. The mandapa windows are filled with decorated pilasters, also in the Orissan manner. Both the wall niches and windows are headed with decorated multi-lobed arches which frame miniature deities.

A chariot-like shrine in the colonnade of the inner enclosure has large wheels carved out of the basement; prancing horses flank the access steps. The columns of the open mandapa in the outer court are embellished with delicately cut garlands and foliate panels.

SINNAR

Gondeshvara Temple, 11th century

This monument was erected under the patronage of the Yadava rulers of the northern Deccan; it is one of the largest and best-preserved temples in the region.

The principal temple and its facing Nandi pavilion are elevated on a plinth; the four corner shrines are dedicated to Surya, Vishnu, Parvati and Ganesha. A hall with three porches adjoins a towered sanctuary. Projections on the exterior create a rhythmic elevation. The basement has sharply cut mouldings, including an animal frieze at the bottom. The walls are adorned with sculptures, but the principal niches are now empty. The tower rising over the sanctuary continues the projections of the walls beneath. Miniature tower-like elements flank a central band covered with a mesh of arch-like motifs; this last feature indicates a stylistic relationship with Paramara temples of central India. In contrast, the pyramid of masonry that roofs the hall, the porch columns with their bracket figures (many missing) and the richly carved balcony slabs are reminiscent of Solanki architecture in western India.

The interior columns are embellished with sculptures; a corbelled dome is positioned over the middle of the hall.

SRISAILAM

This is one of the most important Hindu pilgrimage centres in the Deccan. At the annual Shivaratri festival (February–March), thousands of devotees come to bathe and to worship at the Shiva temple here. The site overlooks a deep wooded gorge, through which the Krishna river flows and which is now filled with the waters of a new hydro-electric project.

Mallikarjuna Temple, 14th–16th centuries

This temple is contained within a rectangle of high walls with Vijayanagara-styled gopuras on four sides. Within the enclosure stand the principal temple together with smaller shrines and columned mandapas. The temple itself is an unadorned 14th-century structure with a pyramidal tower rising over the sanctuary. The adjoining mandapa with three porches is dated to 1405. Most of the subsidiary structures belong to the 15th–16th centuries. The small shrine immediately north of the entrance porch of the temple houses a sahasra linga; a serpent encircles the base.

Numerous and varied panels are carved on to the outer face of the enclosure walls, which are dated to 1456. The lowest course is ornamented with a procession of elephants, some uprooting trees. The second course is devoted to equestrian and hunting scenes, while the panels on the third and fourth courses depict processions of soldiers, dancing girls, musicians, sages, pilgrims and mythical beasts. A host of scenes represent Shiva in his many forms: as the wandering ascetic, as the hunter fighting Arjuna, as the slayer of the buffalo demon and as the rescuer of Markandeya. Near to the east gateway is a large panel of a seated king, possibly a portrait of Krishnadeva Raya, who visited the temple in 1514. Further south, a miniature shrine houses a standing Shiva image.

Uma Maheshvara Temple, 16th century

This ornate Vijayanagara temple is located on a bend in the river, about 3 km (2 miles) north-west of the Mallikarjuna complex.

TADPATRI

Two Hindu temples here were erected under the patronage of local governors during the Vijayanagara era. One complex overlooks the Penner river, which flows past the town to the north; the other complex is located within the town itself.

Ramalingeshvara Temple,
early 16th century

This complex has large unfinished gopuras on the north and south; the gopura on the west is more modest in scale but is better preserved. Two temples stand within the rectangular court. The one on the north houses a linga which is set in a pedestal filled with water; this is perpetually fed by a small spring. The adjoining mandapa is entered through

TADPATRI

PENNER

Ramalingeshvara Temple

to Railway Station and Anantapur

Venkataramana Temple

N

Bus Stand

0   ¼ mile

0   500 m

two porches. The temple on the south has two sanctuaries, enshrining images of Parvati (east) and Rama with Lakshmana and Sita (north); both sanctuaries open off a common mandapa. Pilastered walls are raised on delicately modelled basements. The towers are multi-storeyed and pyramidal, with hemispherical roofs. The piers of the porches and open mandapa are fashioned as rearing animals and donor portraits. The ceiling of the mandapa has deeply cut pendant lotus designs.

The incomplete gopuras are unusually elaborate; they illustrate an exuberant variation of the Vijayanagara style. The architectural elements include double basements, pilastered walls, niches framed by multi-lobed arches or surmounted by tower-like pediments, and pilasters standing in pots. All of these are encrusted with friezes of jewels and petals, scrollwork and miniature animals and birds. Among the figural themes are divinities, donors, guardians, sages, riders on rearing animals, and maidens clutching foliage. The resulting sculptural density is unparalleled.

Venkataramana Temple,
mid-16th century

This complex is slightly later in date. The rectangular court with a peripheral colonnade has a soaring gopura in the middle of the east side; a small doorway also provides access on the north. The principal shrine, which houses an image of Vishnu, adjoins a closed mandapa with two porches. To the east is an open mandapa with a central space defined by raised floor slabs and by rows of columns; at its eastern end is a stone chariot. A circular shrine and a goddess temple, the latter with its own columned mandapa, are situated immediately north-west of the principal temple.

Throughout, the architecture is grandly conceived and delicately executed. The outer walls of the principal temple and the enclosed mandapa are raised on a delicately modelled basement. The walls have sculptures positioned between pilasters which illustrate episodes from the Krishna and Ramayana legends. The lintels over the doorways to the enclosed mandapa are also carved with Ramayana scenes: thus, the heroes with sages (east), Sita's ordeal by fire in the presence of the gods (south) and Rama's final enthronement (north). Above is a multi-storey pyramidal tower (with later plaster sculptures) with a hemispherical roof. The columns of the porches and the open mandapas are fashioned as rearing beasts with riders; life-size, almost three-dimensional figures of female devotees adorn the mandapa columns. Traces of paintings are preserved on the ceilings. The double-curved eaves are enlivened with miniature musicians and playful monkeys.

The chariot that houses an image of Garuda is treated as a miniature temple, complete with pilastered walls and a restored storeyed tower. The four stone wheels are decorated with lotus ornament.

Although it is partly ruined, the towered gopura is an impressive structure. Its upper brick storeys rise in a steep pyramid. Sculptures are preserved on the stone basement and walls. A ceremonial swing and a tall lamp-column stand in front (east) of the gateway.

TER

This Satavahana site preserves the remains of several 2nd–3rd-century Buddhist antiquities. These include a stupa with internal brick walls, limestone slabs carved in a style reminiscent of **Amaravati** and terracotta and ivory figurines.

Trivikrama Temple, 2nd–3rd century

This rare apsidal-ended shrine indicates the structural origins of a building type otherwise familiar only from rock-cut examples. Originally a Buddhist founda-

tion, the shrine was later converted to Hindu usage. It is entirely built of brick without internal columns; the roof consists of a curved vault. Externally, the walls are relieved by shallow pilasters. Over the entrance doorway is a large horseshoe-shaped arch motif that frames a later image of Hanuman. The black stone image of Trivikrama placed in the sanctuary is Early Chalukya in style.

TRIMBAK

This Hindu pilgrimage site, 29 km (18 miles) west of **Nasik**, derives its sanctity from a tank fed by natural springs; known as Gangasagar, this tank is considered to be the source of the Godavari river. Numerous shrines and ponds dot the town, which is enclosed by a semicircle of hills. The fort above dates from the Maratha period (see Volume II).

Trimbukeshvara Temple, 18th century

This Shiva sanctuary is the principal focus of worship for pious visitors. The temple, which stands in the middle of a paved court, is dominated by the tower which rises over the sanctuary; this is of the clustered type that imitates earlier Yadava projects in the region, as at **Sinnar**. The outer walls have projections, each adorned with basement mouldings and figural carvings. These projections are carried up into the tower, where they become miniature replicas of the central curved shaft. Several tiers of these towered elements cluster around the central shaft, which is capped with a large ribbed motif and a pot finial. The mandapa is roofed with a pyramid of masonry.

UNDAVALLI

The Hindu cave temples at this site are assigned to the period of the 7th–8th-century Kondavidu chiefs in this part of the Deccan. The rock-cut sanctuaries are architecturally massive and unrelieved.

The most impressive temple consists of four storeys, one recessed above the other, separated by overhanging eaves. Large lions and seated ganas serve as parapet elements above the second level. The four connected columned mandapas at this level each have a shrine. Among the images sculpted on to the walls and columns are panels of Vishnu on Ananta and Vishnu on Garuda.

Nearby are several crudely cut monolithic temple models as well as other excavated mandapas and shrines.

VIJAYANAGARA

Vijayanagara, the City of Victory, was the largest and most powerful Hindu capital in the Deccan between the 14th and 16th centuries. Under the patronage of the newly established dynasty, the religious centre at Hampi on the

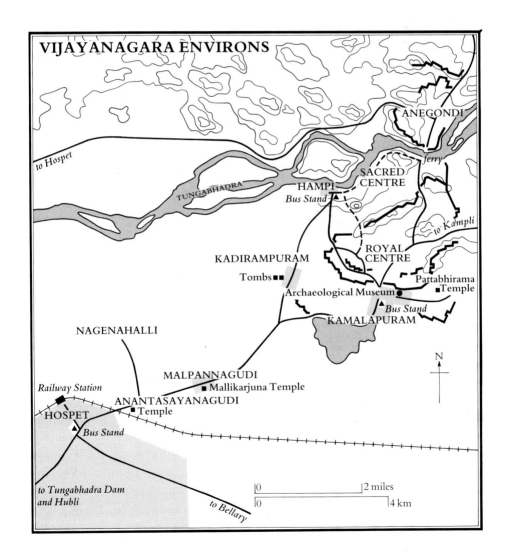

Tungabhadra river was transformed into a fortified and magnificently appointed capital. Kings sponsored a variety of cults and numerous temples were erected here. The capital became the setting for a wealthy, cultured and cosmopolitan society where Muslims and Europeans were welcomed; some of these visitors have left accounts of life in the city, including descriptions of the spectacular Mahanavami festival. Among the greatest Vijayanagara rulers were Deva Raya I (1422–46) and the successive kings Krishnadeva Raya and Achyutadeva Raya (1509–42).

For more than two hundred years the Vijayanagara rulers struggled with the sultans of the Muslim kingdoms in the north for supremacy in the Deccan. In 1565 the Vijayanagara army experienced a catastrophic defeat. Thereafter, the capital was abandoned and ultimately destroyed.

Vijayanagara occupies a spectacular setting. To the north the granite landscape is dominated by a gorge through which the Tungabhadra river flows; to the south and west there is an extensive plain. This terrain offered natural protection for the capital, but it was also imbued with mythological significance. The river and nearby hills were associated with episodes from the Ramayana epic. According to local belief, this was Kishkindha, the abode of the monkey chiefs, where Rama met Hanuman and Sugriva, and where the campaign to Sri Lanka was planned.

The Vijayanagara site incorporates a number of distinct zones. On the south bank of the Tungabhadra river are the temples and small shrines of the sacred centre; these are grouped around the village of Hampi. An irrigated valley to the south, through which ancient canals still run, separates this from the fortified urban core. This is enclosed by a ring of massive fortifications defining an elliptical zone about 4 km (2½ miles) along its axis. Within the urban core there is abundant evidence of habitations, temples, gateways, tanks and wells.

At the south-western end of the urban core a cluster of enclosures contained by high granite walls constitutes the royal centre of the capital. Within and around these enclosures are palaces, temples, ceremonial platforms, columned halls, stables, treasuries, storehouses, watch-towers, tanks and wells.

In the plains extending south and west beyond the urban core are the city's suburbs. Fragmentary fortifications indicate a system of concentric protective walls. Gateways are located along the roads leading into the urban core; other monuments are preserved at Kamalapuram, Kadirampuram and Hospet, the last town more than 10 km (6 miles) south-west of the royal centre. Anegondi on the opposite bank of the river is still reached by coracle.

SACRED CENTRE

Hemakuta Hill, 10th–14th centuries

Small temples are built on a sloping shelf of granite that overlooks the village of Hampi from the south. These date from a period when the site was celebrated as a holy spot dedicated to the worship of Shiva. The hill was fortified in the 14th century; gateways were built on the north and south and tanks excavated into the rock. A later 16th-century towered entrance, still incomplete, provides access to the complex from the east.

The temples illustrate pre-Vijayanagara styles. The larger examples each have three shrines opening off a common mandapa, part of which serves as an open porch. The shrines are roofed with granite pyramidal roofs.

Virupaksha (Pampapati) Temple, 13th–17th centuries

The cults of Pampa, an indigenous goddess, and of her consort Virupaksha (also known as Pampapati), an aspect of Shiva,

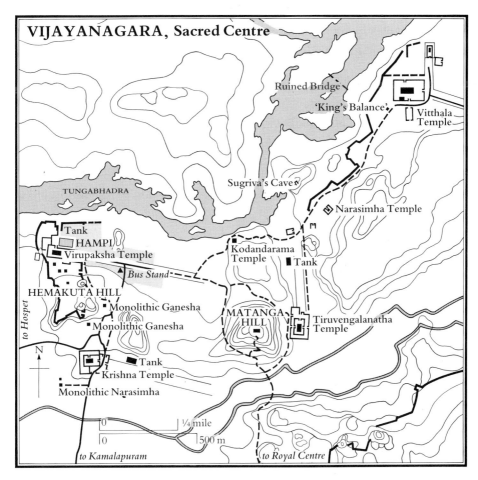

VIJAYANAGARA, Sacred Centre

Ruined Bridge

'King's Balance'

Vitthala Temple

Sugriva's Cave

TUNGABHADRA

Narasimha Temple

Tank

HAMPI

Virupaksha Temple

Kodandarama Temple

Tank

Bus Stand

HEMAKUTA HILL

Monolithic Ganesha

MATANGA HILL

Tiruvengalanatha Temple

Monolithic Ganesha

to Hospet

N

Tank

Krishna Temple

Monolithic Narasimha

0   ¼ mile

0   500 m

to Kamalapuram

to Royal Centre

appear to have existed at the site before the establishment of the capital. These cults survived the destruction of the city; today, this is the only sacred complex at Vijayanagara still in use for worship. Annual chariot festivals held here to commemorate the betrothal and marriage of Virupaksha and Pampa are attended by thousands of pilgrims. Clustered around the walled enclosure of the complex are the modern houses of the village of Hampi.

The complex consists of two courts, each entered through a towered gopura. The largest gateway (on the east) was erected by Krishnadeva Raya and rises about 52 m (170 ft) high. Each level of its multi-storey brick tower has pilastered walls and sculptures flanking an open window.

The outer court contains several small shrines. In the south-west corner is a large columned mandapa; running along one side is a water channel.

The inner court is completely surrounded by a colonnade; in the middle is the principal temple, which is approached through a mandapa with columns finely carved as rearing animals. The scenes painted on to the ceiling depict aspects of Shiva and also the Dikpalas and a procession with the sage Vidyaranya. The outer walls of the sanctuary have reliefs illustrating Shaiva themes. A brass image of Nandi faces the linga within the sanctuary.

Two pre-Vijayanagara shrines dedicated to Pampa and Bhuvaneshvari are built into the north colonnade. Their highly ornate doorways, column forms and ceiling panels, all carved in schist, are typical of the Late Chalukya style.

The towered gopura on the north side of the court was renovated in the 17th century. This gateway leads to a large tank with stepped sides. Facing eastwards towards the tank are several small shrines assigned to the pre-Vijayanagara period. Another gateway on the north provides access to the river.

Extending eastwards from the east gopura is a colonnaded street about 1 km ($\frac{1}{2}$ mile) long. The residences here were probably those of courtiers who attended the religious festivals. A pavilion at the end of the street houses a monolithic image of Nandi, now defaced.

Monolithic Ganesha Images

South-east of Hemakuta hill is a plain shrine built around a boulder which is carved with a large Ganesha image. Unusually elongated columns are used in the porch. Further to the south, an open pavilion shelters a slightly smaller Ganesha.

Krishna Temple, 1513

South of Hemakuta hill is the Krishna temple complex erected by Krishnadeva Raya to commemorate his successful military campaign in Orissa. The temple is ruined: the monumental gateways have partly collapsed and the colonnaded street and tank to the east are mostly overgrown.

A double series of enclosure walls contains the principal shrine. This is provided with two mandapas that lead to the narrow passageway that surrounds the sanctuary. Friezes are carved on to the passageway walls but no image is preserved in the sanctuary. A triple-storey tower crowned with a restored hemispherical roof rises above.

Fragmentary plaster reliefs survive on the tower of the east gopura. These depict military scenes with warriors, horses and elephants. The multi-domed structure in the south court of the temple may have served as a granary (note the holes in the domes).

Monolithic Narasimha Image, 1528

This colossal rock-cut sculpture of Narasimha seated beneath a multi-headed serpent is 6·7 m (22 ft) high. The image was a donation of Krishnadeva Raya. Nearby is a small structure housing an unusually large linga.

Matanga Hill and Kodandarama Temple

East of Hampi is Matanga hill, the most prominent outcrop within the city. The view from the summit gives the best possible idea of the layout of Vijayanagara. The hill is named after the sage who protected Sugriva and Hanuman after they were expelled by Vali. In spite of such Ramayana associations, the 15th-century temple built at the summit is dedicated to Virabhadra.

Immediately north of Matanga, on the bank of the Tungabhadra river, is the Kodandarama temple, which marks the spot where Rama crowned Sugriva. The temple houses a large image of Rama.

Tiruvengalanatha ('Achyuta Raya's') Temple, 16th century

Built at the order of a prominent military commander of Achyutadeva Raya, this sacred complex is commonly named after the ruler himself. The layout follows the standard scheme of the mature Vijayanagara temple, but in addition there are two walled rectangular enclosures, one within the other. Most of the towered gopuras, columned mandapas and colonnades are ruined. Even so, some sculptures are well preserved, especially the column carvings in the mandapa to the west of the main (north) gopura.

A chariot street lined with colonnades proceeds northwards towards the river. A large tank is located to the west of the street.

Narasimha Temple, 14th century

This east-facing temple is the only Vaishnava shrine at the site dating from the earlier period; in style it resembles the shrines on Hemakuta hill. It is overlooked by a two-storey open gateway.

Sugriva's Cave and Bridge

In front of the Narasimha temple is a natural cavern marked with painted stripes. This marks the spot where Sugriva is supposed to have hidden the jewels dropped by Sita after she was abducted by Ravana. The pool nearby is also associated with Sita.

Standing in the river are granite pylons, all that remains of a footbridge. A large columned mandapa stands on the riverbank facing the bridge.

Vitthala Temple, 16th century

Even in its ruined state this temple is one of the outstanding achievements of the Vijayanagara period. Although its foundation date is unknown, there are inscriptions of Krishnadeva Raya. According to tradition, the temple was built to enshrine an image brought from **Pandharpur**.

The complex comprises an impressive ensemble of structures set within a rectangular court. The principal shrine has a low elevation with unadorned pilastered walls; the modest brick tower over the sanctuary is capped with a hemispherical roof. In front of the sanctuary is an enclosed mandapa with finely carved columns; much of the ceiling here has now collapsed. Two doorways lead into the dark narrow passageway that surrounds the sanctuary. While the outer walls of the sanctuary are embellished with reliefs, no cult image is preserved.

The glory of the temple is its open mandapa, which is laid out on a stepped plan and can be entered from three sides. Massive granite piers are fashioned with remarkable virtuosity into clusters of colonnettes. (The tones emitted by these colonnettes when tapped have been interpreted by some as musical notes of an ancient scale.) Peripheral piers are fashioned as rearing animals and riders. Composite brackets support beams with huge spans; ceilings, fully preserved in the side aisles, are decorated with foliage and geometric designs. The deeply overhanging eave is double-curved; lotus designs are incised on to the corners, where there are stone rings for stone chains. The moulded basement is adorned with friezes of lions, elephants and horses, the last accompanied by foreign attendants. Elephant balustrades flank the access steps.

Immediately in front (east) of the temple is the celebrated stone chariot housing an image of Garuda. Reproducing in granite the form of a real chariot used in temple festivals, it is fashioned like a miniature shrine but with wheels; the delicacy of the carved ornament, especially the lotus designs on the wheels, is exceptional. The detached open mandapas standing within the court have unusually slender columns.

Three gopuras give access to the temple precinct. Although partly ruined, their granite walls are elaborately carved. Among the sculptures are maidens clutching foliage (jambs within the doorways). Multi-storey brick towers rise above.

Running eastwards from the principal (east) gateway is a street almost 1 km ($\frac{1}{2}$ mile) long lined with colonnades, now partly collapsed. To the north is a large tank with stepped sides and a small pavilion in the middle. Another shorter colonnaded street runs northwards from the main gate. This leads to another temple, also of impressive proportions, with Ramayana reliefs adorning the gateway. A double-storey rest-house nearby is provided with kitchen facilities.

Beside the path that follows the river (south-west of the complex) is an unusual feature known as the 'king's balance'. This was used for rulers to weigh themselves against food, less commonly against gold and jewels, that was then distributed to brahmins.

ROYAL CENTRE

(For the structures in this zone associated with the ceremonial, administrative and military functions of the Vijayanagara rulers, see Volume II.)

Ramachandra Temple, 15th century

Known popularly as Hazara Rama, this Hindu temple in a rectangular compound lies at the core of the royal centre, on the boundary between the zones of royal performance (west) and royal residence (east).

The cult of Rama was of particular significance for the Vijayanagara rulers and this temple functioned as a state chapel; its royal character is clearly expressed in the vivid reliefs carved on to the outer face of the enclosure walls. These depict the processions of elephants, horses, militia and dancing girls of the Mahanavami festival. Unadorned gateways lead into the rectangular court. On the inner faces of the enclosure walls (east and north sides) are friezes depicting scenes from the Ramayana epic.

In the middle of the compound stands the principal temple, dedicated to Rama. The outer walls have delicately modelled basement and pilastered niches; a partly restored multi-storey brick tower rises above. Wall panels illustrating the Ramayana epic run around the mandapa and

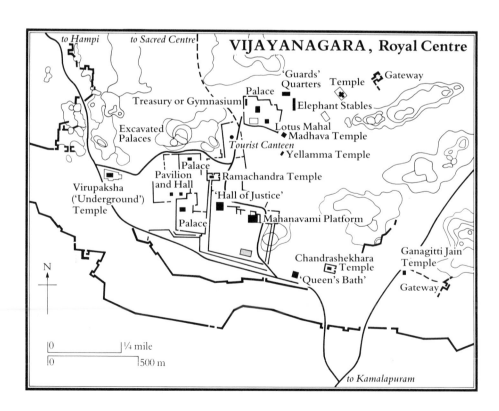

antechamber in three tiers. The episode in which the golden deer is killed and the battle scenes between Rama and Ravana are positioned on the east wall of the mandapa; scenes showing Hanuman receiving Rama's ring and then bringing the ring to Sita are depicted on the antechamber walls.

An open columned mandapa (built in two phases) leads into an inner enclosed mandapa with four polished basalt columns. These are adorned with incarnations and other aspects of Vishnu set in elaborate frames. The sanctuary is now empty.

A smaller double-shrined temple stands immediately to the north-west. This too has finely carved mouldings and sculpture panels showing a continuation of the Ramayana and also Krishna scenes. This temple possibly housed images of Narasimha and Krishna.

Outside the complex to the east are a ruined Garuda shrine and a fallen lamp-column.

Virupaksha ('Underground') Temple, 14th–16th centuries

Dedicated to the guardian deity of the Vijayanagara rulers, this temple served as a private chapel for the king's household. The complex presents a bewildering assemblage of sanctuaries, colonnades, courts and gates; at the core is an early shrine, partly concealed by additions. A later towered gateway stands incomplete in front of the principal (east) entrance. (The surrounding earthen walls have given this temple its 'underground' name.)

EAST OF THE ROYAL CENTRE

Ganagitti Jain Temple, 1385

This is a typical early Vijayanagara structure. The double shrines, now both empty, plain walls, columns with double

capitals and pyramidal stepped towers are comparable with the early shrines on Hemakuta hill. A tall lamp-column stands in front of the temple and has an inscription on its shaft.

Raghunatha Temple, 16th century

This complex is built on Malyavanta hill, a site closely linked with the Ramayana story. Two shrines and a columned mandapa are set within high walls (note the aquatic emblems carved on to the granite blocks). The court is entered through two towered gopuras, which blend with the rocky setting. The sanctuary of the principal shrine is built around a large boulder which protrudes through the roof; this is carved with images of Rama and Sita.

Outside the complex to the west is a small Shiva sanctuary. A crevice nearby has its sides carved with rows of lingas and Nandis.

SUBURBAN CENTRES

Anegondi

This town has a longer history than the capital, having been a fortified settlement in pre-Vijayanagara times. The streets and houses are encircled by walls. Temples and a 17th-century example of civic architecture, now serving as the town hall, survive. Numerous 14th–15th-century shrines are built above the bathing ghat to the south-east. Outside the town to the south is a dilapidated two-storey structure with reused earlier columns; traces of Vijayanagara paintings survive on the ceiling.

To the west of the town is a large rocky outcrop ringed by fortifications. Within this citadel are the remains of military barracks, granaries, wells, tanks and palaces. Elaborate gateways are flanked by circular bastions.

Kamalapuram

A ruined temple stands within this fort in the middle of the town. Immediately to the south-west is a large tank with massive dam walls.

1 km ($\frac{1}{2}$ mile) north-east of Kamalapuram is the Pattabhirama temple, an impressive 16th-century complex. The principal shrine stands within an unusually large rectangular court. Its long elevation has a mandapa with slender columns. The towered gopura is almost completely preserved.

Archaeological Museum

Situated on the outskirts of Kamalapuram, this museum houses sculptures collected from all over the site. There are many images of Bhairava and Durga, and also a royal couple, now headless (607.1639), a sleeping Vishnu figure, now damaged, with attendant goddesses (1611) and a striding Hanuman (674).

Memorial stones are exhibited and also several slabs carved with nagis (622).

A large-scale model of the site occupies the central court.

Malpannagudi

Facing on to the main road of this village is the 16th-century Mallikarjuna temple with a towered gopura. South-west of the village is a well-preserved octagonal well with finely constructed Islamic arches.

Anantasayanagudi

The village of Anantasayanagudi, immediately north-east of Hospet, is named after its 16th-century temple. This monument has an unusual brick tower, with double apsidal ends, more than 24 m (79 ft) high. The long pedestal in the rectangular sanctuary was intended to support a reclining image of Vishnu. The sanctuary is approached through a mandapa with elongated columns.

SOUTHERN INDIA

FOURTEEN

SOUTHERN INDIA

Southern Andhra Pradesh, southern Karnataka, Tamil Nadu, Kerala

Introduction

Only isolated remains, such as the 1st-century-BC linga at **Gudimallam**, suggest the antiquity of religious and artistic traditions in southern India. The beginnings of architecture and sculpture in this region are no earlier than the Pallava period. The first monuments are the 7th-century cave temples at **Mamallapuram, Mandagappattu** and **Tiruchirapalli**. These are simple combinations of columned mandapas and shrines excavated into granite. Later cave temples at **Mamallapuram** have large-scale sculptural compositions with naturalistically modelled figures and animals.

Cave temples continued to be excavated in the 8th century under the patronage of the Pandyas. Examples at **Namakkal, Tiruchirapalli** and **Tirupparankunram** are massive and simple, relieved only by carved Hindu icons executed in a vigorous style. At **Sittannavasal** there are Jain saints as well as traces of mural paintings.

The next phase in the evolution of southern Indian architecture is represented by the 'rathas' at **Mamallapuram**. These 7th-century monoliths illustrate a variety of square, rectangular and apsidal-ended schemes. Elevations present sequences of moulded basements, wall projections with pilasters, overhanging eaves and parapets of miniature roof forms. The diminishing storeys of the superstructures repeat these wall treat-

ments; roof forms are hemispherical, octagonal or vaulted. Sculptures are confined to wall niches, which are framed by pilasters with makara pediments.

Almost all of these elements appear in the structural projects initiated during the reign of the Pallava ruler Rajasimhavarma (*c.* 700–728). The 'Shore' temple at **Mamallapuram** has twin pyramidal towers of slender proportions. At **Kanchipuram**, the Kailasanatha temple is a fully realized complex; its towered sanctuary and columned mandapa stand within a rectangular courtyard surrounded by subsidiary shrines. The carved images depict a large range of Hindu divinities. In the later Vaikuntha Perumal temple in the same city, royal scenes are also incorporated.

Later Pallava monuments of the 8th–9th centuries at **Panamalai, Tiruttani** and **Uttaramerur** are relatively modest structures with few innovations. The contemporary monolithic shrine at **Kalugumalai** imitates Pallava models.

From the 9th to the 13th centuries, artistic production in southern India was dominated by that sponsored by the Chola rulers. The heart of the Chola territory was the Cauvery river valley, where temples were built at many sites. 9th–10th-century examples at **Kilaiyur, Kumbakonam, Narttamalai, Punjai** and **Srinivasanallur** are small towered sanctuaries with hemispherical roofs.

Finely modelled figures are placed in the niches of the pilastered walls. A variant on this early Chola style is seen in the small shrine at **Kodumbalur**.

At **Thanjavur** and **Gangaikonda-cholapuram**, two capitals founded by the successive rulers Rajaraja I and Rajendra I (*c.* 985–1044), Chola architecture achieved its most monumental expression. These sanctuaries are surmounted by steeply rising pyramidal towers with crowning dome-like roofs. Sculptures of exceptional quality adorn the walls; paintings inside the **Thanjavur** monument are the main evidence for a Chola pictorial tradition. Gateways (gopuras) in the enclosures have squat pyramidal towers capped by vaulted roofs with arched ends (preserved at **Thanjavur**).

Temple architecture during the late Chola period was generally reduced in scale. Projects at **Darasuram** and **Tribhuvanam** testify to the refinement of architectural design in the 12th–13th centuries. The monumental gopuras at **Chidambaram** and **Tiruvarur** date from this period. They have granite basements and pilastered walls, with massive towered pyramids of brick and plaster.

Bronze sculptures of this era are the finest in southern India. Comparable to stone carvings, Chola bronzes are delicately modelled and gracefully posed, especially those depicting Shiva in his many aspects (there are examples in museums at **Madras**, **Pudukkottai** and **Thanjavur**). The Buddhist bronze figures at Kadri (**Mangalore**) are unique; other examples have been discovered at **Nagapattinam**.

Contemporary with early Chola projects were the distinctive styles that evolved in the northern part of the region. The temples erected in the 9th–10th centuries during the Nolamba and Western Ganga periods were closely linked with contemporary developments in the Deccan, especially the monuments of the Rashtrakutas and Late Chalukyas. At **Aralaguppe**, **Hemavati** and **Nandi**,

Nolamba temples have unadorned pilastered walls and stepped towers. Perforated windows and ceilings are elaborately treated. Jain temples in a closely related style are assigned to the Western Ganga period, as at **Kambadahalli** and **Shravana Belgola**. The latter site is dominated by the enormous monolith of Gommateshvara, which was imitated in later centuries at **Karkal**.

Artistic traditions in this zone reached their height in the 12th–13th centuries. Temples erected during the reigns of the Hoysala kings have complicated plans with numerous angled projections. Carved surfaces are executed with remarkable precision, usually in chlorite. The basements have figural and animal friezes, while intricately carved panels cover the walls. The interiors are enlivened by lathe-turned or multi-faceted columns; corbelled ceilings are elaborate dome-like compositions.

Among the large number of Hoysala monuments are temples at **Belur**, **Dodda Gaddavahalli**, **Halebid**, **Harnahalli** and **Somnathpur**. The last example has pyramidal towers preserved over the triple sanctuaries. The shrine dating from the 14th century at **Sringeri** is executed in a variation of the Hoysala style.

Architectural traditions in southern India were abruptly interrupted by Muslim raids at the end of the 13th century. Though the Muslim presence in this region was only temporary, it was not until the 15th century that monumental temple building was once again resumed. Early Vijayanagara temples, as at **Penukonda**, are modest structures influenced by late Chola practice.

By the 16th century almost all of southern India was incorporated into the Vijayanagara empire. Temple architecture throughout the entire region (and also in the southern part of the Deccan, where the capital was situated) continued the traditions of the late Chola period but on a grander scale. The characteristic feature of the Vijayanagara period was the

Opposite above Kanchipuram,
Kailasanatha Temple, 8th Century

Opposite below Kalugumalai,
Vattuvan Kovil, 8th–9th century

Above Narttamalai, Vijayalaya
Cholishvara Temple, 9th century

Right Gangaikondacholapuram,
Brihadeshvara Temple,
11th century

Above Chidambaram, Nataraja Temple, gopura, 13th century

Opposite Nandi, Bhoganandishvara Temple, 9th century

Above Somnathpur, Keshava Temple, 13th century

Opposite Madurai, Minakshi Sundareshvara Temple, gopura, 17th century

Opposite Srirangam, Ranganatha Temple, mandapa, 16th century

Above Trichur, Vadakkunatha Temple, 12th century and later

Below Mudabidri, Chandranatha Basti, 15th century and later

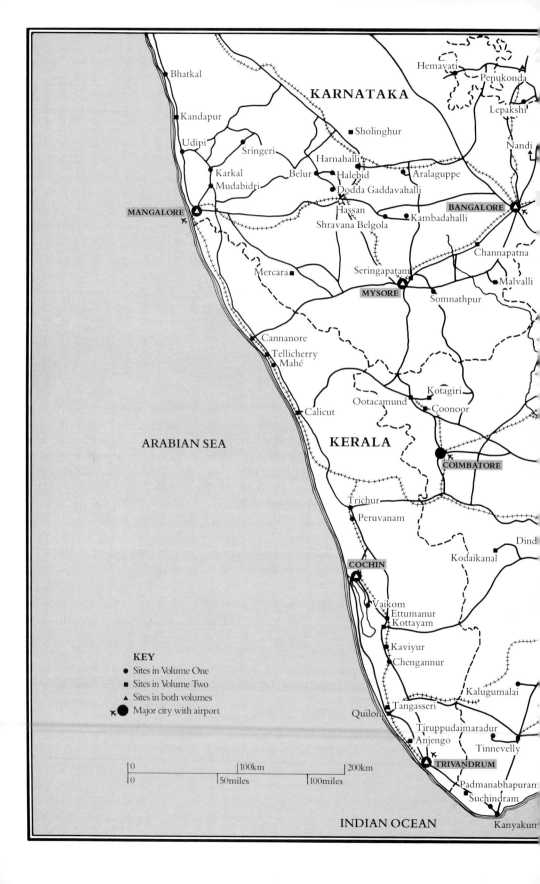

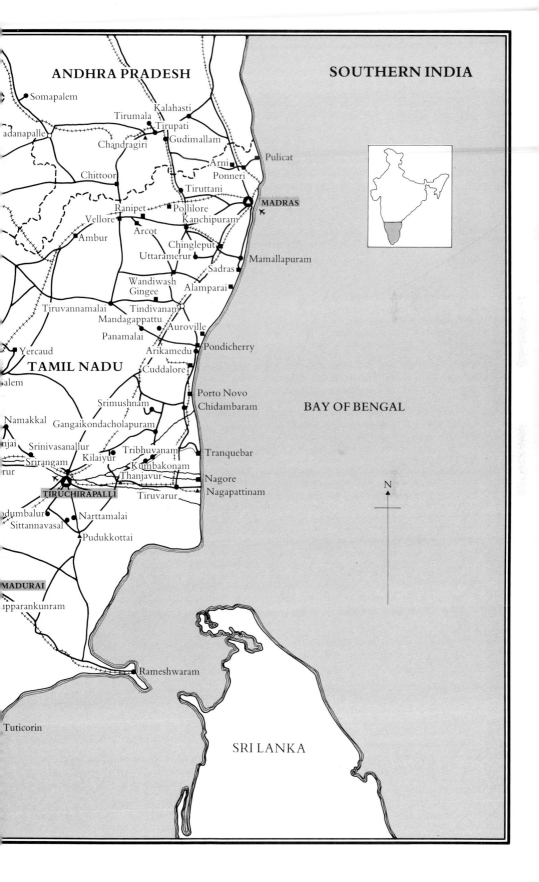

ARALAGUPPE

Kalleshvara Temple, late 9th century

This modest Hindu temple is typical of the Nolamba style. The exterior is unadorned except for pilastered walls and carved stone windows. The inner mandapa contains nine ceiling panels; these depict the Dikpalas, with a dancing Shiva figure in the middle, all carved in high relief. Fully modelled bracket figures carry garlands.

Chennakeshava Temple, 13th century

This later Hoysala monument has fine examples of column carvings and corbelled domes within the mandapa. Sculptures are positioned between pilasters on the outer walls. Richly carved friezes on the basement, though worn, illustrate scenes from the Krishna story.

ARIKAMEDU

This ancient site is located on the eastern bank of a lagoon formed by the Ariyankuppam river, about 3 km (2 miles) south of Pondicherry. Excavations here have revealed traces of an Indo-Roman port that flourished in the 1st–2nd centuries. The architectural remains include the brick remains of structures, possibly warehouses, and a courtyard with two small tanks.

Roman artefacts were discovered in abundance, particularly pottery fragments of two-handled amphorae, gems, lamps and glass moulds. Local pottery is represented by grey and red wares, usually with simple incised designs. Stray coins from the Chola period and fragments of Chinese celadon wares indicate that the site continued to be occupied into the 11th–12th centuries. (These finds are now exhibited in the Pondicherry Museum.)

BANGALORE

(For the town and its monuments see Volume II.)

Government Museum

This contains a collection of sculptures brought from different sites in Karnataka. Early Satavahana art is illustrated by limestone pillars carved with courtly scenes; these come from the 2nd–3rd-century Buddhist site of Sannathi. The later Western Ganga period is represented by a series of Matrikas from Begur; a fine sculpture of Durga from Avani (32) is in the Nolamba style. 12th-century Hoysala images include Krishna playing the flute (7) and standing Surya (9), both from **Halebid**. Among the sculptures from the Late Chalukya and Kakatiya periods are two brackets from Telsang; these are fashioned as smoothly modelled female musicians. Commemorative panels depicting battles, with war animals and warriors, belong to the Vijayanagara period.

BELUR

Chennakeshava Temple, 1117

This Hindu temple is one of the early masterpieces of the Hoysala period. It was erected by the ruler Vishnuvardhana to commemorate his victory over the Chola armies. The monument stands in the middle of a courtyard surrounded by subsidiary shrines and columned mandapas. The entrance gopura is on the east; its soaring tower was added during the later Vijayanagara era.

Entirely built of grey-green chlorite, the temple itself consists of a sanctuary with minor shrines on three sides and a columned mandapa partly open as a porch. Multiple projections, some set at an angle, create a complicated star-shaped plan. The sanctuary and mandapa are raised on a terrace that repeats the stepped outlines of the main building.

The mandapa is reached by double flights of steps on three sides; these are flanked by free-standing miniature shrines. The doorways are highly elaborate compositions that incorporate guardian figures and prancing vyalas (below), large makaras with profusely foliated tails (side pilasters) and icons of Vishnu (lintels). The mandapa is enclosed by pierced stone screens that were added in the early 13th century; these are set between lathe-turned columns. The screens have complex geometric designs adorned with miniature figures. The basement beneath has friezes of elephants, meandering lotus stalks, figures, garlands, couples and musicians all carved with remarkable precision.

Beneath the overhanging eave, angled brackets carved as maidens are supported on the column capitals. These bracket figures are among the finest examples of Hoysala art. Maidens beneath intricately worked trees and foliage are posed in an unusual variety of dance movements; they are sensuously modelled and have sweet facial expressions. Particularly notable are the huntress and the maiden dressing herself (north side) and the maidens plaiting hair, gazing into a mirror and holding a parrot (south side). Label inscriptions identify the individual artists.

The outer sanctuary walls are covered with architectural and sculptural elements, with the former predominating. The basements of the projecting shrines have successive friezes of elephants, lions and horses. Wall panels are positioned beneath elaborate pediments or miniature roof forms. Most of the figural carvings depict aspects of Vishnu, particularly the incarnations and the god seated with Lakshmi. The tower intended for the sanctuary has vanished.

The highly polished columns within the mandapa are both multi-faceted and lathe-turned. Bracket figures, similar to those on the exterior, are positioned above. The ceilings of rotated squares with corbelled domes incorporate lotus ornament and scrollwork; friezes of miniature figures include the Dikpalas. The sanctuary doorway is protected by large guardian figures with richly jewelled costumes. The lintel is adorned with elaborate makaras at either end; Vishnu and Lakshmi are seated in the middle. The temple is dedicated to the Shrivaishnava god Vijaya Narayana, whose image is enshrined within the sanctuary.

To the south of the temple is the shrine of Kappe Chennigaraye. This is contemporary with the main temple and is built in the same ornate style. In the passageway that surrounds the sanctuary are carved panels of Vishnu, Durga and Ganesha. Large guardian figures flank the sanctuary doorway.

Immediately to the west is the Vahana hall, dating from the 13th century. In the north-west corner of the enclosure is the Andal temple, a 12th-century monument. Sculptures here depict maidens and divinities beneath trees.

BHATKAL

Temples at this town on the western coast illustrate the impact of indigenous traditions on stone architecture.

Ketapai Narayana Temple,
17th century

This small rectangular Hindu structure has a sloping stone-tiled roof. The stone railings between the peripheral columns create a screen wall. The entrance steps are flanked by typical Vijayanagara animal balustrades; the doorway is protected by guardian figures. The interior columns have carved panels. The ceiling consists of rotated squares with a central medallion surrounded by friezes of miniature figures. A stone lamp-column stands in front of the temple.

Chandranatha Basti, 17th–18th century

This Jain complex is located a short distance north of the town. It consists of two buildings linked by a long porch. The western structure has a sloping stone-tiled roof in two tiers; this shelters the mandapa, which has internal stone screens, and a shrine. The eastern structure is a double-storey gateway. A tall lamp-column stands in front.

CHENGANNUR

Narasimha Temple,
mostly 18th century

Although this is an important early Hindu foundation in southern Kerala, dating back to the 14th century, the temple itself, especially its wooden portions, is much later. The small west-facing square sanctuary surrounded by a corridor is roofed with a simple pyramidal gable. Elevated on an earlier stone basement, the timber walls are carved with friezes of miniature animals and scenes from the Ramayana and Krishna legends. Large guardian figures flank the two doorways. The interior corridor is lit by intricately worked wooden screens.

CHIDAMBARAM

As the holy spot of Nataraja, the form of Shiva as the cosmic dancer, Chidambaram has been an important Hindu centre since at least the 9th century. The legend regarding the foundation of the temple refers to a dance competition between Shiva and Kali in which the god was the victor. The golden pavilion within the complex which commemorates this event is known as Chit Sabha or Chit Ambalam (Chidambaram).

Nataraja was a favoured divinity of the Chola kings, who built one of their palaces near to the temple. At the end of the

10th century, the sanctuary is said to have been covered in gold by the Chola ruler Parantaka I; Rajaraja I, builder of the **Thanjavur** monument, was himself a devotee. Later kings of the Vijayanagara and Nayaka dynasties were also patrons of Nataraja. Today, the temple is entirely owned and managed by a local clan of brahmins.

Nataraja Temple,
12th–13th century and later

Unlike other large-scale sacred complexes in southern India, a large portion of this temple is comparatively early; most of the structures date from the late Chola era.

The temple occupies an area of about 22 hectares (55 acres) in the middle of the town. The nearest streets are wide thoroughfares that run parallel to the outer walls of the complex; the temple chariot is pulled along these streets during festival times.

Four enclosure walls incorporate the sacred precinct. The outermost wall is a 17th-century Nayaka addition; gateways in the middle of each side are flanked by porticos but there are no towers. From each of these gateways, passageways flanked by low walls lead to towered gopuras in the third enclosure wall. This wall defines an irregular paved court that is partly surrounded by a two-storey colonnade. The most prominent feature here is the Shivaganga tank; this has steps and a colonnaded gallery on four sides. East of the tank is a large columned hall known as the Raja Sabha. A temple dedicated to Shivakumasundari occupies an extension of the enclosure on the north-west. This extension forms a distinct unit with a surrounding colonnade and entrance gateway. To the north is the Subrahmanya temple. Near the south gopura a Nandi image is placed in a pavilion; two platforms nearby have unusually high and elaborate basements. In front of the east gopura are several rows of tall thin columns with fluted and slightly tapering shafts.

CHIDAMBARAM, Nataraja Temple

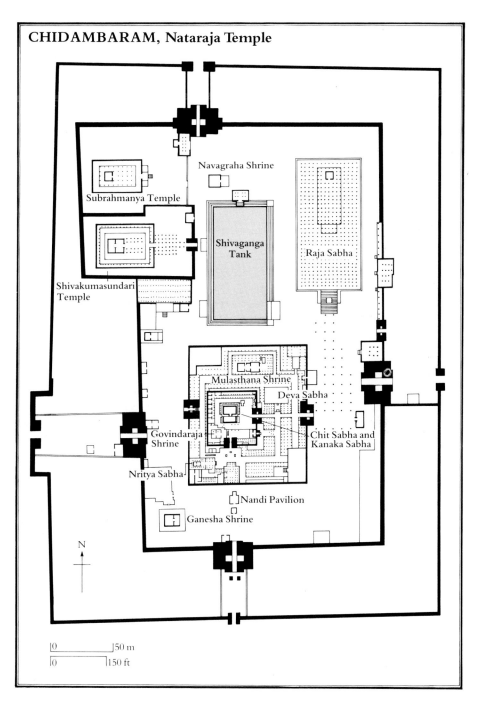

Navagraha Shrine

Subrahmanya Temple

Shivaganga Tank

Raja Sabha

Shivakumasundari Temple

Mulasthana Shrine

Deva Sabha

Govindaraja Shrine

Chit Sabha and Kanaka Sabha

Nritya Sabha

Nandi Pavilion

Ganesha Shrine

N

0   50 m
0   150 ft

The second enclosure wall is pierced on the east and west by gateways without towers. The court within has been extensively rebuilt in recent years and is now almost entirely occupied by colonnades with passageways between; many structures here serve as stores and a kitchen. Original features include the Deva Sabha, where processional images are kept, the Mulasthana with its Devi shrine (north) and the hall known as the Nritya Sabha (south).

The innermost enclosure is entered through two gateways on the east (the one with a tower is recent) and a single gateway on the south. In the middle of this enclosure is the south-facing shrine (Chit Sabha) and attached hall (Kanaka Sabha) that form the devotional focus for the complex. These are wooden pavilions raised on a common masonry basement. Their gabled roofs, which are entirely sheathed in copper, have unusual curved profiles. Two forms of Shiva are enshrined here: the image of Nataraja and the Akasha (space) linga, the latter fashioned in crystal. The Govindaraja shrine with its reclining Vishnu image is a 16th-century Vijayanagara structure; most of the colonnade on three sides and the subsidiary chambers are modern.

One of the earliest buildings within the complex is the 12th-century Shivakamasundari temple. The surrounding colonnade is elevated on a basement adorned with figures of dancers and musicians as well as friezes of yalis and horses. The columns are carved with medallions typical of the late Chola era. The paintings on the ceilings date from the 17th century.

The carvings on the basement and columns of the Raja Sabha are similar. Large elephants also appear on the basement (east and west). The interior of this hall is partly roofed with curved vaults; these later additions imitate the timber roofs of the Chit Sabha. Within the hall is a dais to which the temple deity is brought on festival occasions. An extension on the south side, with sculpted piers and overhanging eaves, dates from the Vijayanagara era.

The finely executed Nritya Sabha of the second enclosure is an early-13th-century structure. This hall is elevated on a double basement adorned with rows of dancers, ganas and yalis; wheels with prancing horses are carved on to the sides (they are partly concealed). The columns are delicately ornamented with miniature façades. A wall niche housing a Bhikshatanamurti image is framed by fluted pilasters.

The Subrahmanya temple was erected in the second half of the 13th century. While the sanctuary and its surrounding passageway are plain, the adjoining hall is elaborately treated. The columns are covered with tiers of miniature façades; figural panels adorn the brackets. Access steps are flanked by balustrades with yalis and elephants carved in full relief. Double brick vaults roof the hall; paintings here depict scenes from the Skanda Purana. The image of Subrahmanya enshrined within the sanctuary is about 2·4 m (8 ft) high.

The monumental gopuras in the third enclosure wall are impressive examples of the later Chola style; they are also the largest and most elaborate gateways in southern India prior to the Vijayanagara era. The four gopuras conform to a standard scheme. The walls are divided into two storeys, each with moulded basements, pilastered niches and overhanging eaves. The upper storey is expanded with the addition of pilasters standing in pots and pierced stone windows. Over the walls are brick parapets with plaster sculptures and miniature roof forms. Above rise the pyramidal brick towers, divided into diminishing storeys with sculptured walls and parapets, all ornamented with plaster. Projections in the middle of each side have openings at each level. The towers are capped with elongated vaulted roofs, with arched ends and pot finials.

Large sculptures in the upper wall niches depict the full range of Shaiva deities. Among the finest figures are Bhikshatanamurti (north gateway), Dakshinamurti (south gateway) and Shiva, as the ascetic with a trident and dancing on the demon (east gateway).

Other divinities also appear, especially on the lower storey, such as Subrahmanya (west gateway), Durga, Sarasvati (north gateway) and the Navagrahas (south gateway), as well as sages, guardians and attendants. Throughout, the architectural elements are adorned with delicately incised foliage and scrollwork.

The wall pilasters within the high passageways are covered with figural sculptures illustrating the different dance movements; explanatory labels are provided for each of the 108 postures in the east and west gateways. Wall niches house portrait sculptures of donors; an image of Krishnadeva Raya, the **Vijayanagara** ruler, was a later insertion (north gateway). Ceiling panels are adorned with dancers and musicians (east gateway).

DODDA GADDAVAHALLI

Lakshmidevi Temple, 1113

This is an early example of the Hoysala style. Unlike the ornate temple at **Belur**, with which it is roughly contemporary, this Hindu monument is almost completely devoid of external sculpture. In this respect, it is closely related to Late Chalukya architecture in the Deccan.

The temple, which stands in the middle of a large court, consists of four shrines opening off a common mandapa. Here are housed images of Mahalakshmi (east), Bhutanatha (west), Bhairava (south) and Kali, originally Vishnu (north). Other smaller shrines are positioned in the corners of the enclosure.

The outer walls of the temple are plain except for pilasters containing niches, now empty, surmounted by tower-like pediments. The towers are pyramidal sequences of eave-like mouldings capped with multi-faceted square roofs and pot finials. Prancing vyalas are positioned on the front projections of each tower. The doorways are flanked by fierce-looking guardians. The sixteen columns within the mandapa are ornately fashioned.

ETTUMANUR

Mahadeva Temple, 16th century and later

This large circular Hindu shrine is typical of the Kerala series. A square sanctuary enshrining a linga is contained within a circular columned mandapa. Both sanctuary and mandapa are roofed with a conical timber structure covered with metal tiles which rises smoothly to a brass pot finial at the apex. The roof overhangs an open wooden screen that admits light to the circular passageway surrounding the mandapa. This screen is carved with friezes of animals and Ramayana and Krishna scenes. Similar carvings are seen within the circular passageway, where angled brackets are carved as deities and other figures. The three doorways are flanked by wooden guardian figures, dancers and musicians. Stone balustrades at the steps are also adorned with sculptures, such as Nataraja (west).

Standing in front (west) of the temple is a detached open square pavilion with a pyramidal roof. The wooden ceiling within the mandapa is divided into twenty-five panels, each depicting a different divinity.

The temple is contained within a rectangular enclosure defined by colonnades with sloping roofs. The entrance on the west is marked by a double tier of gabled roofs with tiles. On the walls of the inner porch of this gateway are large painted compositions dating from the middle of the 17th century. They include an animated depiction of multi-armed Shiva dancing on a dwarf within a circular frame. Among the crowd of attendant figures are Krishna and Brahma (left). In another composition Vishnu is shown reclining on Shesha.

GANGAIKONDACHOLAPURAM

This Hindu site was established as a capital by the Chola ruler Rajendra I (1012–44) after his successful military expedition through eastern India to the Ganga river. Other than the magnificent Brihadeshvara temple, however, only a few remains indicate that this was once a capital. 1·5 km (1 mile) north-west of the temple, brick debris indicates the ruins of the royal palace; several dilapidated tanks can also be seen in the vicinity.

Brihadishvara Temple
mid-11th century

This temple is one of the outstanding monuments of the Chola period; it was erected by Rajendra to rival the temple constructed by his predecessor at **Thanjavur**. While the Gangaikonda-cholapuram monument resembles that at **Thanjavur** in most of its essential features, there are significant innovations; it was also spared restoration during the Nayaka era.

The temple stands in the middle of a rectangular enclosure entered from the east through a gateway, now dilapidated. The temple itself consists of a square sanctuary surrounded by a passageway; this adjoins a transept with access stairs on the north and south. Extending eastwards is the partly restored long columned mandapa.

As at **Thanjavur**, the double pilastered walls of the sanctuary are elevated on a moulded basement with lions and scroll-work beneath and yalis and makaras aligned on the topmost moulding. Both storeys are overhung by curved eaves. The pilastered projections house fully modelled sculptures. Those in the central niches, on both storeys, depict Dak-shinamurti (south), Vishnu (west) and Brahma (north). The flanking niches mostly house Shaiva images, such as the splendid figure of the god dancing on the

dwarf (west end of south wall) and the composition that depicts the god bestowing a wreath on the saint Chandesha, sometimes identified with the temple patron (north end of east wall). The walls are otherwise covered with miniature figures carved on to blocks.

The nine-storey tower is slightly concave in profile. The roof forms of the parapet are emphasized, but the capping dome-like roof is reduced in size (compared with that of the **Thanjavur** temple). Numerous sculptures, some restored, are carved on to the walls beneath the parapets.

The transept is entered through doorways protected by large guardian figures. Only the two-storey walls at the western end of the mandapa are preserved; sculpture panels here represent Lakshmi (south) and Sarasvati (north). The principal entrance at the eastern end of the mandapa is reached by two flights of steps, also with protective figures.

A massive linga on a circular pedestal is enshrined within the sanctuary. The columns of the mandapa are unadorned. Several fine bronze images are displayed here; these include Shiva with Uma, Subrahmanya and Devi. A stone altar carved with a lotus on the top has the Navagrahas carved on to the sides.

Two subsidiary shrines within the enclosure are dedicated to Kailasanatha; these were erected by two queens of Rajendra. They are almost identical in form; the sanctuaries have small towers with hemispherical roofs (the plasterwork is later). Fine sculptures are preserved on the pilastered walls. In front of the temples stand detached columned mandapas, one of which has mostly collapsed. Another small structure in the south-west corner of the enclosure houses a Ganesha image. A large Nandi sculpture constructed of blocks is placed in front (east) of the principal temple. North of the Nandi is a circular well; its entrance is contained within a small structure fashioned as a seated lion.

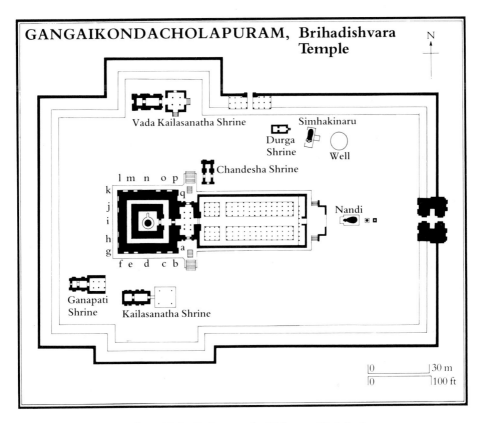

GANGAIKONDACHOLAPURAM, Brihadishvara Temple

N

Vada Kailasanatha Shrine

Simhakinaru

Durga Shrine

Well

Chandesha Shrine

l m n o p

k
j
i
h
g

q

Nandi

f e d c b

a

Ganapati Shrine

Kailasanatha Shrine

0   30 m
0   100 ft

Key to Sculpture Panels on Main Shrine:

a Shiva holding the skull

b Ganapati

c Ardhanarishvara

d Dakshinamurti

e Harihara

f Nataraja

g Shiva receiving Ganga

h Shiva appearing out of the Linga

i Vishnu and Lakshmi

j Subrahmanya

k Vishnu

l Shiva

m Durga

n Brahma

o Bhairava

p Shiva

q Shiva bestowing a wreath on Chandesha

GUDIMALLAM

Parashurameshvara Temple,
9th century and later

This Hindu monument is celebrated for the well-preserved linga that is venerated within the sanctuary. This cult object is almost 1·5 m (5 ft) high and dates back to the 1st century BC. The linga is dis-

tinguished by the figure of Shiva carved on to its shaft; it is one of the earliest representations of this divinity in Indian art.

The temple itself belongs to two phases. The apsidal-ended sanctuary with an adjoining antechamber is a Pallava foundation dating from the 9th century. So too is a small goddess shrine in the courtyard. The mandapa and colonnade

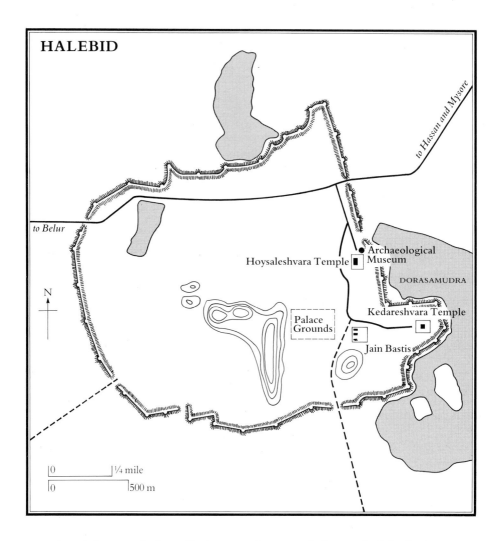

HALEBID

to Hassan and Mysore

to Belur

Hoysaleshvara Temple ■ ● Archaeological
Museum

DORASAMUDRA

N

Kedareshvara Temple

Palace
Grounds

Jain Bastis

0   ¼ mile
0   500 m

extensions belong to the later Chola era, while the outer gateway in the enclosure walls and the outer mandapa are typical of the Vijayanagara period. Over the sanctuary, the apsidal-ended tower is a recent replacement.

HALEBID

This site is identified with Dorasamudra, the capital of the Hoysala rulers in the 12th century. Numerous remains are scattered over the site. These include the outlines of earthen ramparts and several tanks; the largest tank (east end of the fort) gave its name to the capital. The most important Hindu temple here is the Hoysaleshvara, dedicated to Shiva. Though work on this monument was initiated in about 1121 by an officer of the ruler Vishnuvardhana, the temple was not completed until the period of Narasimha I (c. 1142–73). Several other Hoysala temples still stand within the ancient zone.

Hoysaleshvara Temple,
mid-12th century

Both architecturally and artistically, this monument represents the climax of the

Hoysala style. It is the largest of the series, comparable in many of its features to the earlier temple at **Belur**.

Two identical temples are linked to form a complex with two sanctuaries and two mandapas. Each sanctuary consists of a central chamber off which open three smaller chambers; subsidiary shrines project from the outer walls on three sides. Attached to each sanctuary is a large columned mandapa laid out on a stepped plan; the two mandapas are linked to form a spacious interior. They are only partly enclosed; open porches with balcony seating are found at the peripheries. In front (east) of each mandapa is a detached pavilion for a Nandi image.

The twin temples and their Nandi pavilions are raised on a high plinth that repeats the complicated outline of the building itself. The chlorite basement of the walls of the sanctuaries and mandapas is decorated with friezes. These depict successive rows of elephants, lions, horses, scrollwork, epic scenes, makaras and geese with foliated tails. The precision of the carving and the vitality of the compositions are unsurpassed. Among the illustrations of epic subjects are scenes from the Ramayana, such as Rama killing the golden deer, and Rama and Sita riding in procession. Mahabharata episodes include battle scenes and the death of Bhishma on a bed of arrows. The Krishna legend is recognized by the profusion of Krishna figures with gopis or fighting with demons. There are also scenes of courtly life and hunting expeditions.

Sculpture panels set at different angles constitute the outer walls. Various divinities in animated poses are depicted beneath luxuriant scrollwork or foliage; they wear richly decorated costumes and headdresses. Among the finest panels are Brahma seated on the goose, Shiva dancing with the flayed skin of the elephant demon, the same deity dancing on the dwarf, Ravana shaking the mountain, Krishna holding up the mountain, Krishna playing the flute and Vishnu in his many incarnations. These diverse figures are attended by maidens, dancers and musicians. Above the panels are pilasters and an overhanging eave with a petalled fringe. No towers survive over the sanctuaries.

The doorways to the columned mandapas are approached by flights of steps flanked by free-standing miniature shrines. (The pyramidal towers of these shrines suggest the forms of the superstructures that were never completed.) At either side of the doorways are large guardians in swaying postures, exuberantly decorated with jewels and tassels. The lintels are carved with dancing Shiva icons set in foliated frames with open-mouthed makaras at the ends. Pierced stone screens with geometric designs are set between the peripheral columns and overhung by a projecting eave.

Both lathe-turned columns and those with multi-faceted shafts and capitals are used within the mandapas. Brackets on the central columns are fashioned as dancing maidens and musicians carved almost in the round. The corbelled ceilings have friezes of miniature figures, especially Shiva surrounded by the Dikpalas, as well as lotus motifs and monster masks. The sanctuary doorways are protected by guardian figures. Polished lingas elevated on pedestals are found within the shrines.

Detached from the temples are open pavilions with finely executed lathe-turned columns. The southern pavilion houses a large seated Nandi image; the animal is adorned with bells and jewels.

Archaeological Museum

In the grounds of the temple is a large collection of sculptures gathered from all over the site. Large and detailed panels depict a seated Ganesha, a dancing Shiva and other figures.

Kedareshvara Temple,
early 13th century

This smaller temple is typical of the later Hoysala style. The shrine has a star-like plan with a moulded basement and a continuous series of sculpture panels (less finely carved than those of the Hoysaleshvara temple); there is no superstructure. Pierced stone screens are used in the mandapa.

Jain Bastis, 12th century

In contrast with the other temples, these small examples are almost completely unadorned. The exteriors have basement mouldings and pilastered walls; the only sculptures are the striding elephants at the steps. The interior columns are elongated and lathe-turned; the ceilings are decorated with friezes of miniature figures.

HARNAHALLI

Lakshmi Narasimha Temple, 1234

This Hindu temple is a well-preserved example of the mature Hoysala style. Much of the sculptural ornamentation in chlorite may be compared with the carvings of the **Halebid** monument, with which this temple is almost contemporary.

A single sanctuary with projecting subsidiary shrines on three sides adjoins a mandapa laid out on a stepped plan. The mandapa is only partly enclosed; stone screens on the periphery are pierced to admit light. The temple is raised on a plinth with steps on three sides flanked by miniature shrines.

Throughout, the basement and walls are completely encrusted with carved friezes and panels. Above the overhanging eave that continues around the building rises the pyramidal tower. This consists of diminishing storeys of ornamented elements with a dome-like roof at the summit.

The internal columns have lathe-turned shafts. The ceiling compositions are elaborately carved with lobed motifs, pendant buds and miniature figures.

HEMAVATI

This site served as the capital of the Nolamba rulers in the 9th–10th centuries. The Hindu monuments erected here testify to a distinctive temple style that was closely related to contemporary Rashtrakuta and Late Chalukya traditions of the Deccan. Though sculptures from this site have been removed (mostly to the Government Museum, **Madras**), some still remain.

Doddeshvara Temple, late 10th century

This modest structure has a plain exterior with regularly spaced pilasters. The only features of interest are the perforated stone windows, which are carved with standing deities, including a gracefully posed Ganga figure (east) as well as foliate designs. The superstructure was never built. The internal columns have panels carved with figures and looped garlands. A finely decorated doorway leads to the linga enshrined in the sanctuary.

Siddheshvara Temple,
late 10th century

This temple is similarly laid out to the preceding one, but has been substantially reconstructed. Some of the original columns with carved panels are preserved in the mandapas in front of the sanctuary. Among the detached sculptures housed here is an impressive seated Bhairava; this has been placed in the sanctuary.

Virupaksha Temple, late 10th century

This temple preserves a finely carved doorway with figures entwined in scrollwork. The columns are also decorated.

KALAHASTI

This town is picturesquely situated on the right bank of the Svarnamukhi river, at the foot of the Kailasa hills. The celebrated Shiva temple at Kalahasti benefited greatly from the patronage of the **Vijayanagara** emperors; Achyutadeva Raya was even crowned here in 1529. The temple maintained its importance in later times; today it is one of the principal Hindu pilgrimage towns of the region.

While the bathing ghats and the shrines on the hills attract a steady flow of devotees, religious life is mainly focused on the Kalahastishvara temple. This complex enshrines the Vayu (air) linga, one of the five elemental emblems of Shiva in southern India. The town was also the home of Kannappar, a well-known Shaiva saint; a small sanctuary in which he is worshipped is located at the summit of the hill immediately above the temple.

Kalahasti is also known for the production of kalamkaris, the highly coloured

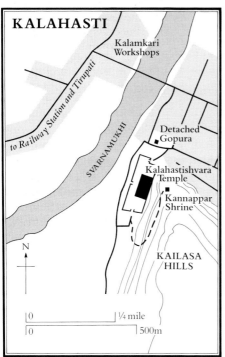

KALAHASTI

Kalamkari Workshops

to Railway Station and Tirupati

SVARNAMUKHI

Detached Gopura

Kalahastishvara Temple

Kannappar Shrine

N

KAILASA HILLS

| 0 | ¼ mile |
| 0 | 500m |

painted cotton hangings that illustrate different deities and mythological subjects.

Kalahastishvara Temple,
16th–17th centuries

The town is dominated by an impressive gopura which faces towards the river. This detached structure was erected in 1516 by the emperor Krishnadeva Raya. The granite basement and walls are adorned with finely finished pilasters, some in pots, and niches, now empty. The steeply pyramidal tower rises about 36·5 m (120 ft) high. Sculptures (modern cement renditions) and architectural elements are arranged in six diminishing storeys; the vaulted roof has arched ends with exuberant plasterwork, including monster masks at the summits.

Smaller gateways with later towers define a pathway that leads to the outer enclosure of the temple. This enclosure surrounds the main temple on three sides. On the east is the rocky side of the hill; the river ghat is on the west, reached through another gopura. Columned mandapas, pavilions, lamp-columns and other structures crowd the enclosure. The columned mandapa at the south-west corner is raised on a high basement with finely carved friezes; the piers with animal carvings are typical of the Vijayanagara style. A path ascends the hill from the gopura on the south.

The temple itself is contained within a rectangle of high walls with a single towered entrance on the south. Within the temple there are four shrines facing different directions; these date from the early Vijayanagara period. The shrine opening to the west houses the elongated linga that is the chief object of worship; a brass covered lamp-column stands in front. The other shrines are dedicated to Jnanaprasumbha (east), Dakshinamurti (south) and Ganesha (north).

Subsidiary shrines are contained within a 17th-century colonnade which is laid out as a vast rectangle with a corridor on four sides. Typical of the Nayaka style are the massive piers fashioned as riders on animals or as fantastic beasts; projecting brackets terminate in pendant buds. Among the bronze sculptures displayed within the colonnade are processional images of dancing Shiva and a series of sixty-three Shaiva saints (north side). A large stone sculpture of Kannappar as a hunter is placed in the west colonnade.

KALUGUMALAI

Vattuvan Kovil, 8th–9th century

This incompletely excavated monolithic temple is a rare example of the early Pandya style. Only the pyramidal tower and octagonal dome were finished. Among the many fine sculptures with which this was adorned are friezes of ganas beneath the eaves and fully modelled Nandis at the corners; in the middle of each side are gracefully posed seated Hindu images of Shiva with Uma (east), Dakshinamurti (south), Narasimha (west) and Brahma (north). Arch-like motifs are embellished with delicately incised foliage and jewelled garlands.

A steep cliff rises behind the rock out of which the temple was hewn. This is carved with rows of Jain figures; next to these is Ambika flanked by a lion and a dancer. A crowned figure, possibly of a king, kneels in front of a Tirthankara who is depicted larger than life-size; another Tirthankara is seated on a lion-throne surrounded by attendants.

KAMBADAHALLI

The monuments at this site form an ensemble of two coordinated groups of shrines within the same compound; this is entered on the north through a small gateway. Dating from the 10th-century Western Ganga period, the shrines are among the most important examples of Jain temple architecture in southern India; they are stylistically linked with contemporary Chola monuments. Characteristic features are the clearly articulated basement mouldings, pilastered walls and stepped towers crowned with square or dome-like forms.

The triple-shrined Panchakuta Basti houses images of Adinatha (south), Neminatha (east) and Shantinatha (west). The double-shrined Shantinatha Basti incorporates a later porch. Among the many sculptures are a finely modelled seated Jina figure and several standing guardians. The ceiling of the Shantinatha shrine is carved in high relief with the Dikpalas around a seated Tirthankara.

Outside the compound to the north is a lofty stone column with a seated pot-bellied yaksha on the top.

KANCHIPURAM

One of the holy cities of Hinduism, Kanchipuram is known throughout the country as a vibrant religious and cultural centre. The temples house different Hindu sects and Buddhism and Jainism also flourished here at one time. The city had a political significance since it served as the capital for the Pallava rulers in the 7th–9th centuries; it continued to maintain its importance during the succeeding Chola, Vijayanagara and Nayaka periods.

Important examples of Hindu temple architecture spanning almost a thousand years are preserved at Kanchipuram. These are distributed in three distinct zones: the Shaiva sanctuaries are clustered in a suburb to the north; the most significant Vaishnava establishment is found at the extreme east of the town; at Tiruparuttikunram, across the river to the south, there is a Jain group. Among the important Pallava monuments are the Kailasanatha and Vaikuntha Perumal temples. The larger complexes, especially

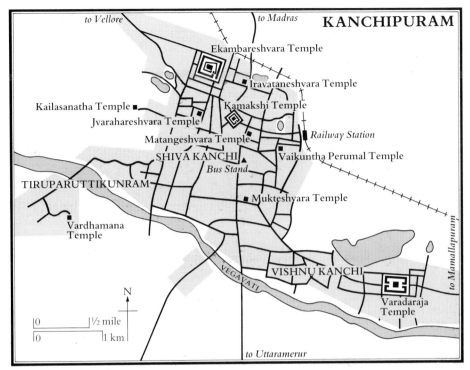

those dedicated to Kamakshi, Ekamba-reshvara and Varadaraja, were originally Chola foundations, but they were sub-stantially expanded under the patronage of the Vijayanagara and Nayaka rulers. (In many of these temples, entry is restric-ted to Hindus only.)

SHIVA KANCHI

Kailasanatha Temple, early 8th century

This is the finest structural project of the reign of the Pallava ruler Rajasimha (*c.* 700–728). The temple is almost entirely constructed of sandstone and it is integrated into a coherent complex. The sanctuary stands within a rectangular enclosure lined with small shrines. Gate-ways are positioned on three sides; the one on the east is enlarged.

The principal sanctuary houses a multi-faceted Shiva linga; a Somaskanda panel is carved on to the rear wall. The sanctuary is entirely surrounded by a narrow pass-ageway. The outer walls have projecting shrines at the corners and in the middle of each side. The walls are raised on a moulded basement that is relieved by friezes of ganas and foliage. The shrines are framed by pilasters with rearing yalis at the bases. Above rise the ascending storeys of the pyramidal superstructure; these repeat the wall scheme below but on a diminishing scale. The capping roof form is hemispherical (it was renovated in later times).

A large variety of Shaiva images adorns the outer walls; these include Shiva appearing out of the linga flanked by Vishnu and Brahma (south) and Shiva in the chariot shooting arrows flanked by Durga and Bhairavi (north). The sculp-tures are framed by pilasters that support makaras with foliated tails.

East of the sanctuary stands a columned mandapa, originally a detached structure. Guardian figures appear on the outer walls. Further east is the Mahendra-varmeshvara shrine added by the son of

435

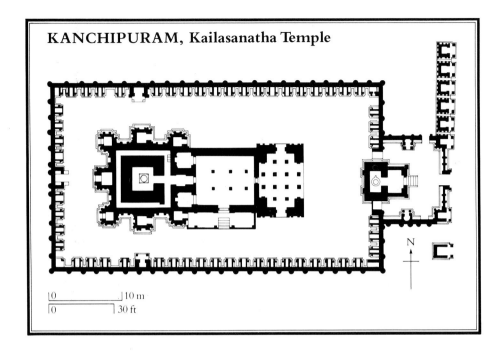

KANCHIPURAM, Kailasanatha Temple

0 _____ 10 m

0 _____ 30 ft

Rajasimha. This oblong structure is surmounted by a large vaulted roof with arched ends. In the middle of the outer walls are depictions of Bhikshatanamurti (south), Shiva with Uma (west) and dancing Shiva (north). A polished linga is enshrined within.

The peripheral shrines all have dome-like roofs, with three-dimensional sculptures of Nandis and lions in between. Images of Shiva as well as those of other divinities are carved in relief within the shrines; these sculptures are mostly eroded and overlaid with plaster and later colourwork. The inner walls of the shrines were once painted. Fragmentary scenes of Shiva with Uma and Skanda, and of Shiva accompanied by Vishnu and Brahma are preserved in the shrines along the north wall.

Externally, the enclosure walls are relieved by pilasters. Additional minor shrines flank the eastern extension of the enclosure. Facing the temple is a seated Nandi.

Iravataneshvara Temple,
early 8th century

This small building is contemporary with the Kailasanatha temple. A square sanctuary with a pyramidal tower is crowned with a large square roof. The sculptures in the middle of each side depict Shiva as the yogi (north), dancing Shiva (west) and Dakshinamurti (south); makaras with foliated tails are carved above. Attendant deities and guardians are positioned at either side.

Matangeshvara and Mukteshvara Temples, mid-8th century

These separate temples are alike in many respects. Both have small square sanctuaries with pyramidal towers capped by dome-like roofs, these adjoin columned mandapas open to the west. Columns with seated lions at the base flank the entrances to the mandapas.

Vaikuntha Perumal Temple,
late 8th century

The ruler Nandivarma II (*c.* 731–96) was directly responsible for this temple, one of the finest Pallava achievements. The principal structure consists of three sanctuaries, one above the other on three ascending levels; these adjoin a columned mandapa which opens to the west. The temple is surrounded by a colonnade. The entrance hall is an addition of the later Vijayanagara period.

Externally, the temple has pilastered walls surmounted by eaves and parapets; an octagonal roof is positioned at the summit. On the lowest level, deities sculpted on projections and recesses are mainly restricted to images of Vishnu and his incarnations. Doorways lead into the double passageway that surrounds the sanctuary, now empty. Vaishnava sculptures also appear on the second level (reduced in plan).

The panels carved on to the rear walls of the surrounding colonnade illustrate historical events pertaining to the genealogy of the Pallava dynasty. These include coronation scenes, receptions and battles, now worn. The columns have seated lions at the bases.

The outer walls of the enclosure have pilasters adorned with rearing yalis. The pyramidal composition of temple elevation is clearly evident from outside.

Jvarahareshvara Temple, 12th century

This is the only Chola structure at Kanchipuram that has not been incorporated into a later complex. The temple has an unusually elliptical sanctuary which adjoins a rectangular antechamber, columned mandapa and porch on the east. The outer walls are raised on a finely modelled plinth; pilasters standing in pots, pairs of pilasters framing niches, now empty, and pierced stone windows ornament the walls. The plaster-decorated brick tower crowned with an elliptical domed roof is a recent renovation.

In front of the temple is an altar and a small Nandi pavilion. The complex is surrounded by an enclosure wall with a later gateway on the east.

Ekambareshvara Temple, mostly
16th–17th centuries

This is the principal Shaiva sanctuary at Kanchipuram and also the largest religious edifice in the vicinity, easily recognized by the soaring gopuras that dominate the city's skyline.

A lofty pavilion is built in the middle of the street that leads up to the south gateway of the complex. The gopura that provides the focus for this street rises no less than 58·5 m (192 ft) high. This impressive structure was erected in 1509 by the Vijayanagara emperor Krishnadeva Raya. The pyramidal tower has eight diminishing storeys in plaster-covered brickwork (there are no sculptures). The vaulted roof has arched ends surmounted by monster masks with bulging eyes; pot finials adorn the ridge.

Two smaller gopuras on the south and west lead into the inner enclosure of the complex. That on the south is elaborately decorated in the typical late Vijayanagara style. In front of the entrance to this gateway is an extensive columned mandapa. This has two raised areas inside, partly divided into chambers. A tank with stepped sides is to the east.

The principal temple faces east. It is preceded by a long columned mandapa into which earlier shrines, altars, pavilions and even lamp-columns have been incorporated. On the north side is a large stepped tank filled with fish. On entering the temple itself, which is contained within a rectangle of enclosure walls, an impressive corridor is reached. This surrounds the principal shrine on four sides, presenting a continuous sequence of receding piers. These piers have animal and lotus brackets projecting outwards in the characteristic Nayaka manner. Within the main shrine, which is entered directly from the east, is a large linga. This represents the Prithvi (earth) linga worshipped by Kamakshi; this goddess is frequently depicted throughout the temple clutching Shiva's emblem.

Smaller multi-faceted lingas are displayed within the surrounding colonnades; a sahasra linga is placed in the shrine at the north-east corner. Another shrine nearby houses a large metal Nataraja icon. Yet other shrines at the rear (west) are preceded by mandapas with finely carved columns, some with rearing yalis. Here also is a small courtyard in the middle of which is a sacred mango tree. The spreading branches overhang a raised walkway for worshippers.

Kamakshi Temple,
mostly 16th–17th centuries

Four towered gopuras of modest proportions provide access into the temple enclosure. The gateways belong to the Vijayanagara period, though their pyramidal towers are modern. That on the east is the most elaborately decorated; Ganesha (right) and Subrahmanya (left) are among the carved panels set into the outer walls.

An ornate columned mandapa stands inside the enclosure, to the north of the main temple. Friezes of deities are carved on to the mandapa basement; column shafts, attached pilasters and brackets are all covered with ornate sculptures. The raised dais in the middle is supported on a tortoise base. West of the temple is a sunken tank with stepped sides.

The temple itself comprises a cluster of small shrines and columned spaces contained within another rectangle of walls. The principal shrine of the goddess is identified by a gilded tower that rises above.

Outside the temple compound but near to its north-east corner is a small abandoned Shiva temple. This dilapidated Chola structure has a hemispherical roof with arched motifs.

VISHNU KANCHI

Vardhamana Temple,
12th century and later

As the principal Vaishnava temple at Kanchipuram, this complex with its four enclosures has a long history spanning the Chola and Vijayanagara periods. According to local legend, the temple commemorates the site where Brahma performed a fire sacrifice (yajna) to invoke the presence of Vishnu. This ritual was carried out on an altar raised upon a high square platform. The layout of the innermost enclosure of the temple conforms to this description of the altar.

Two high towered gopuras on the east and west lead into a spacious rectangular compound; another smaller gopura (west) provides access to the inner enclosures. These gateways have soaring towers divided into diminishing storeys with vaulted roofs at the top. The outer western gopura is an earlier construction; its squat proportions resemble the 12th–13th-century projects of the Chola era. The eastern gopura, with its steep eight-storey pyramid of masonry, is characteristic of the 16th-century Vijayanagara period. (It can be compared with the principal gopura of the Ekambareshvara temple.)

To the left of the outer (west) gopura is a large mandapa dating from the late Vijayanagara period. Ninety-six columns are elaborately carved with figures and scenes depicting the full range of Vaishnava iconography. The peripheral columns and those flanking the central aisle are fashioned as large warriors and huntsmen on rearing horses, Kama on the swan and Rati on the parrot. The three-dimensional carving is remarkable for its vitality and fluency. Among the subsidiary subjects depicted on the column shafts are saints, amorous couples and jesters. A dais in the middle of the mandapa is raised on a tortoise base; the surrounding piers have clustered colonnettes. The peripheral columns are sheltered by a double-curved eave with stone chains for lamps hanging from the corners. Ramayana episodes are sculpted on to the moulded basement.

Behind the mandapa to the north is a tank with a small pavilion in the middle; there is another tank at the extreme eastern end of the enclosure. Two pavilions with elongated columns are aligned with the entrance into the third enclosure. Portraits of royal patrons and donors are carved on to the column bases of these pavilions. Other shrines, pavilions and altars are located nearby.

The intermediate enclosure is mostly occupied with columned mandapas and subsidiary structures dating from the 13th–14th centuries. The mandapa immediately in front of the entrance on the west has Chola columns. The shrine dedicated to Anantalvar is a small Chola structure with simply moulded basement and pilastered walls; the tower has a hemispherical roof. The shrine to Perundevi Tayar (south-west corner), chief consort of Varadaraja, is a Vijayanagara structure. This has sharply cut capitals and brackets, pilasters standing in ornamental pots and delicately ornamented eaves.

The innermost enclosure is mostly occupied by a colonnade lining the perimeter walls. The Andal shrine in the north-west corner has elaborately carved columns depicting Vaishnava icons.

A small 11th-century gateway and a flight of steps lead to the raised structure which contains the principal sanctuary. This enshrines bronze images of Vishnu flanked by his consorts; guardian figures protect the main doorway. The rectangular tower that rises above has been renovated recently. The sanctuary is surrounded by a passageway with subsidiary shrines. Vijayanagara paintings are preserved on the peripheral walls; these depict the presiding divinities of different Vaishnava centres as well as saints and holy men.

TIRUPARUTTIKUNRAM

Vardhamana Temple,
12th century and later

At the heart of this Jain complex are two double shrines, each with part-circular plans. The exteriors have been much renovated. The temples are built in the late Chola style, with small towers capped by hemispherical roofs. They are preceded by a long columned mandapa, the ceiling of which is covered with paintings dating from the 17th century. These murals illustrate scenes from the lives of Rishabhanatha and Neminatha as well as episodes from the Krishna legend. The paintings consist of long friezes with painted labels.

Immediately north of the complex is a 9th-century Pallava temple dedicated to Chandraprabha. The early date is indicated by the rearing yalis on the wall pilasters and the square tower with a renovated domed roof.

KANYAKUMARI

The rocky promontory at the southernmost tip of the Indian subcontinent is one of the holy places of Hinduism; it is particularly associated with the goddess Kumari. Here the waters of the Bay of Bengal and the Arabian Sea merge with the Indian Ocean; here too the sun rises from and sinks into the water. Pilgrims come to bathe in a rocky pool near a temple to Kumari. A memorial to Vivekananda, founder of the Ramakrishna order, is built in a revivalist manner on a small island. Another significant monument is the memorial to Mahatma Gandhi.

KARKAL

This religious centre, only 15 km (9½ miles) north of **Mudabidri**, is known for its many Jain temples and a monolithic

Gommateshvara statue. These are mostly 15th–16th-century foundations; the Gommateshvara image is obviously modelled on the earlier example at **Shravana Belgola**.

Gommateshvara Image, 1432

This 13-m-high (42 ft) image was installed by a local ruler at the summit of a rocky hill. It stands in the open, surrounded only by a low stone railing. The head has elongated ears and half-opened eyes; the expression is serene. Set up in front of the statue is a granite pillar with a figure of Brahma seated within a miniature pavilion at the top.

Chaturmukha Basti, 1587

This is named after the four black stone figures of the Tirthankaras. The temple has gabled roofs with stone tiles, which are supported on rows of external columns that obscure the façade. There is no superstructure.

KAVIYUR

Cave Temple, 8th century

This small rock-cut shrine dedicated to Shiva is the best-preserved early monument in Kerala. A small chamber with a monolithic linga is approached through a columned verandah. Figures carved on to the verandah walls depict a chieftain, a bearded sage, seated Ganesha and guardian figures.

Mahadeva Temple,
11th and 18th centuries

About 1 km (½ mile) west of the cave temple is this fine example of later temple architecture in Kerala. A wide flight of steps leads to an entrance porch with two gabled roofs from which the outer court is entered. Yet another gateway provides access into the inner enclosure in which the temple is situated. Between the two gateways is a tall brass column; its capital supports a small Nandi image.

The temple consists of a square linga shrine within a circular columned mandapa; the outer narrow passageway is entered on two sides. While the sanctuary walls are of masonry, the walls of the circular mandapa and passageway are mostly of timber. These walls are adorned with vigorously carved figures that are typical of the later Kerala style. Shaiva and Vaishnava divinities appear together with fierce guardians. Set into the walls are wooden screens decorated with stylized lotus designs. The temple has a conical roof covered with smooth metal sheets.

A square columned mandapa with a pyramidal roof stands outside the temple enclosure. The ceiling is divided into nine panels and carved with different deities; miniature dancers and musicians adorn the supporting brackets. Beams have friezes of battle scenes and episodes from the Ramayana epic.

KILAIYUR

Agastyeshvara and Cholishvara Temples, late 9th century

The twin Hindu temples at this site were erected by local rulers subordinate to the early Cholas. The larger of the two is known as Agastyeshvara. This simple structure consists of a sanctuary enshrining a linga, and two adjoining mandapas, the outer of which is a later addition. Niches in the middle of the sanctuary walls are framed by double pairs of pilasters and contain finely carved panels of Subrahmanya (east), Shiva (south) and Brahma (north). Rows of yalis adorn the basement. Above rises the double-storey tower, which is crowned with a square roof. Large Nandi images and additional figures are positioned beneath the roof.

The adjacent Cholishvara temple repeats this essential scheme except that the roof is hemispherical. The panels in the wall niches, however, depict seated divinities.

KODUMBALUR

Muvarkovil, 9th century

This Hindu complex was constructed by local rulers who were feudatories of the Cholas. The temples are built in a variant of the early Chola style. Only two of three original west-facing shrines still stand. The elevations of these small structures are clearly articulated: the moulded basements are adorned with friezes of yalis; the pilastered walls have niches housing Shaiva icons in the middle of three sides; the superstructures are capped with square roof forms with pot finials. The sculptures inserted into the superstructure are particularly fine; for example, the depiction of Shiva dancing (south side of southern shrine).

A moulded stone basement extends in front of the three temples. This was probably intended for temporary constructions at festival times.

KUMBAKONAM AND DARASURAM

Kumbakonam was an important centre during the Chola period and in later times. There are fifteen temples in the town devoted both to Shiva and Vishnu. While some of these temples were originally Chola foundations, they were substantially extended under the patronage of the Vijayanagara and Nayaka rulers. The Airavateshvara temple in the suburb of Darasuram, about 2 km (1½ miles) south-west of Kumbakonam's centre, is one of the finest late Chola monuments. Another temple dating from the same era is at **Tribhuvanam**, 6 km (4 miles) to the north-east.

KUMBAKONAM

Nageshvara Temple, 886 and later

The pilastered walls of the sanctuary and adjoining columned mandapa are raised on a basement carved with lotus petals (beneath) and miniature epic scenes (above). Sculptures of Dakshinamurti (south), Ardhanarishvara (west) and Brahma (south) occupy the central panels of the sanctuary walls; attendant maidens are positioned in the side niches. Durga (north) and sages (south) appear on the walls of the mandapa. These figures are among the finest of the Chola period, unsurpassed for their graceful postures, delicate modelling and sweetly detached expressions. Rising over the sanctuary is a pyramidal tower which is crowned with a renovated hemispherical roof.

The temple stands in a courtyard entered through gateways with squat brick towers that are typical of the later Chola period. A Nataraja shrine within the complex has large wheels, with miniature figures as spokes, and richly bridled prancing horses carved on to the basement.

Sarangapani Temple, 13th and 17th centuries

This is the largest Vaishnava temple in Kumbakonam. The temple is entered through a lofty gopura that rises in ten diminishing storeys to a height of about 45 m (147 ft). The storeys are completely covered with sculptures; openings in the middle of each side are flanked by guardian figures.

On entering the court there is a hundred-pillared mandapa belonging to the Nayaka period. A second gopura of lesser height leads directly to the extensive columned mandapa of the next court. On the right (north) is a small Lakshmi shrine with a vaulted roof.

The principal shrine which stands within the innermost court is a late Chola

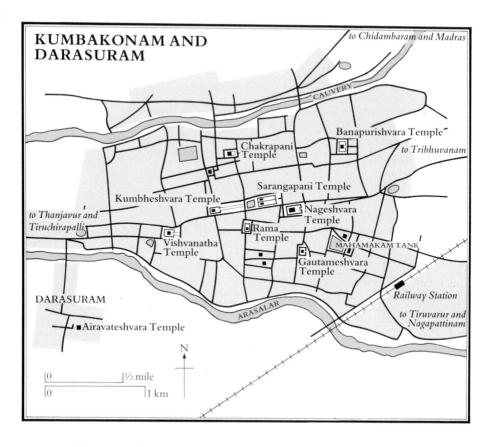

KUMBAKONAM AND
DARASURAM

to Chidambaram and Madras

CAUVERY

Banapurishvara Temple

Chakrapani
Temple

to Tribhuvanam

Sarangapani Temple

Kumbheshvara Temple

*to Thanjavur and
Tiruchirapalli*

Nageshvara
Temple

Rama
Temple

Vishvanatha
Temple

MAHAMAKAM TANK

Gautameshvara
Temple

DARASURAM

Railway Station

*to Tiruvarur and
Nagapattinam*

ARASALAR

Airavateshvara Temple

N

0 — ½ mile
0 — 1 km

structure; it is partly obscured by a later colonnade that is built right up to its walls. The temple is conceived as a chariot, with horses and elephants carved in full relief on the basement; a pair of wheels is decorated with dancing girls and musicians. The shrine walls are elaborately treated but the niches are empty; figures of saints are sculpted directly on to the walls. On either side of the main entrance is a stone trough supported on figures and lions with a spout at one end. A tower with a vaulted roof rises over the rectangular shrine.

Rama Temple, 16th–17th centuries

The gopura of this temple is another example of Nayaka construction. After passing through the doorway a spacious columned mandapa is reached. This has fine carvings typical of the Vijayanagara style. The peripheral piers and those that line the central aisles are adorned with riders on rearing horses and yalis, fully modelled maidens, courtiers and sages.

The outer walls of the shrine are divided into pilastered projections with niches into which small planes are inserted. Above rises the pyramidal tower with pronounced projections in the middle of each side.

Kumbheshvara Temple,
mostly 17th century

This is the largest Shaiva temple in Kumbakonam; it is a typical example of the Nayaka style. The principal gopura is approached by a long colonnaded corridor. The temple is remarkable for the variety of its silver conveyances (vahanas) for transporting images at festival times.

Mahamakam Tank, 17th century

This rectangular reservoir is a popular place of pilgrimage, especially at the important festival of Kumbhareshvara which takes place here every twelve years. The waters of all the sacred rivers of India are believed to unite in this tank, which is surrounded by steps with four shrines on each side. Each shrine is a small pavilion with a dome-like roof in brick. One example has a finely carved ceiling.

DARASURAM

Airavateshvara Temple,
mid-12th century

This temple is one of the finest architectural projects of the late Chola period; it was a royal foundation of Rajaraja II (1146–72).

The complex is entered through two gateways, the outer of which is now dilapidated. A smaller inner gateway leads into a rectangular court surrounded by a colonnade; in the middle stands the principal temple. This consists of a sanctuary aligned with an antechamber and two mandapas, one enclosed, the other partly open and extended on the south.

The outer walls of the sanctuary and enclosed mandapa are elevated on a basement, the lowest mouldings of which have rows of yalis and panels of dancing ganas. The uppermost register of the basement has miniature friezes depicting the stories of various Shaiva saints: for example, the legend of Chandesha, who had his legs cut off rather than be interrupted in his devotions (south) and the deliverance of a child from the jaws of a crocodile by the intervention of Sundara (north). The elongated spout emerging from the north side of the sanctuary basement is supported on a standing gana and a rearing yali.

Full-height pilasters divide the walls into projections, while secondary pilasters frame sculpture niches or stand in pots in the recesses. The carved black basalt panels in the central niches depict Shiva as Dakshinamurti (south, partly hidden), Shiva appearing out of the linga (west) and Brahma (north), all with attendant devotees and divinities. Similar panels on the walls of the inner mandapa are of Ganesha (south) and Durga (north). Over the eave that shelters the walls is an extended parapet with pilastered walls capped by large roof forms. Three diminishing storeys that repeat the parapet scheme create the pyramidal roof; this is capped by a domed roof (with later plaster decoration).

Steps flanked by curved balustrades provide access to the antechamber. The walls here, and also those of the adjacent inner mandapa, have pilastered niches filled with figures of different aspects of Shiva. A small shrine attached to the south wall houses an unusual scene of the god subduing Narasimha. The outer mandapa is approached on the south by two flights of steps with balustrades fashioned as striding elephants. Carved on to the adjacent basements are prancing horses pulling wheels; these are carved in high relief to suggest the chariot of Shiva. As driver of the chariot, Brahma appears in the middle niche on the south side.

The peripheral columns, which are overhung by the double-curved eave, have seated yalis at the bases. Internal columns have medallions of scrollwork containing dancers and musicians carved on to the shafts. Other columns are covered with reliefs of temple façades containing miniature divinities and attendants. A detailed account of the legend of Skanda is depicted on some of the column panels. Lotus medallions and groups of musicians are carved on to the flat ceilings.

Pairs of large guardian figures protect the doorways leading from the outer mandapa to the sanctuary. Within the inner mandapa, diverse images are placed in the wall niches; for example, three-headed Ardhanarishvara, Ganesha, eight-armed Durga and six-headed Kumara (the last is left of the sanctuary doorway). A linga is enshrined within.

Adjoining the inner mandapa on the north is the Chandikeshvara shrine; this small building is capped with a dome-like roof. The colonnade surrounding the court is expanded at the corners to create projecting mandapas. Access steps are flanked by balustrades carved in vivid relief with yalis, some with riders (northeast corner), others fighting lions (northwest corner). The columns are decorated with colonnettes and yalis. A small museum in the north-east corner of the enclosure houses some recently discovered sculptures.

The gateway to the enclosure is partly open as a porch. Above rises a superstructure with the characteristic vaulted roof with plaster sculptures. Immediately outside (to the east) of the gateway is a Nandi shrine with its own columned mandapa. Two small altars with flights of steps are located further to the east.

Daivanayaki Amman Temple, mid-12th century

This goddess temple, surrounded by its own enclosure wall, is positioned immediately north of the Airavateshvara monument. The outer walls are raised on a basement adorned with friezes of ganas and yalis; pilasters have rearing beasts. Most of the niches, which are interspersed with pierced stone windows, are empty. The tower over the sanctuary is elaborate (with later painted plasterwork); there are sculptures here. The roof is unusually cruciform in shape; its arched ends are adorned with flame motifs and monster masks.

LEPAKSHI

Virabhadra Temple, mid-16th century

This Hindu complex was erected under the patronage of two brothers who were governors of the region under the **Vijayanagara** emperor Achyutadeva Raya. The temple preserves important examples of Vijayanagara sculptures and paintings.

Built on an uneven granite outcrop, the temple is surrounded by two approximately rectangular enclosure walls. In the outer enclosure, which is entered on three sides (only the north gateway is open), there are colonnades and many inscriptions. The inner enclosure contains an unfinished columned mandapa in the south-west corner. The finely detailed piers are carved with rearing animals, guardians, sages and deities. A nearby arched gateway leads to a rock-cut cistern on the western side of the enclosure. A boulder on the east side of the mandapa has been fashioned as a coiled serpent; the multi-hooded head rears up to shelter a polished granite linga.

The principal temple is entered on the north through two gopuras with unfinished brick towers. The inner gateway leads directly to an open mandapa. From here, steps ascend to the temple interior, which consists of an enclosed and unlit mandapa off which open a number of small shrines. The principal cult deity is housed in a sanctuary facing north; another shrine, dedicated to Maheshvara and Uma, is partly excavated into a boulder on the east.

Externally, the temple is plain except for the basement mouldings. Pyramidal brick towers with domed roofs rise over the principal sanctuary and the Vishnu shrine. The open mandapa has its columns elaborately carved with a variety of divinities, attendant maidens, dancers and musicians. Large divinities appear on the columns of the central bays; for example, Nataraja and Bhikshatanamurti. Brackets with pendant lotus buds support decorated beams. The outer columns are sheltered by a double-curved eave. Narrative reliefs on the south wall depict a procession of elephants and various Shaiva legends, especially the story of

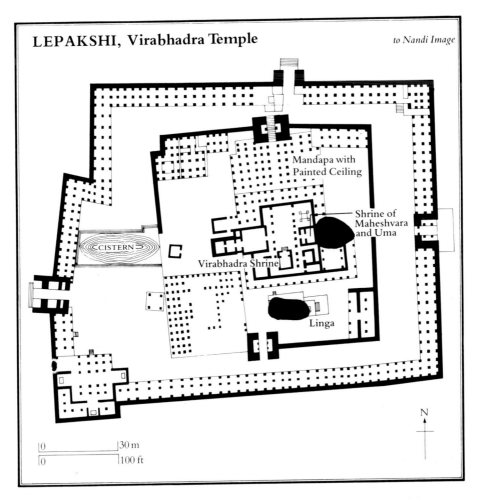

LEPAKSHI, Virabhadra Temple · *to Nandi Image*

Mandapa with Painted Ceiling

Shrine of Maheshvara and Uma

CISTERN

Virabhadra Shrine

Linga

N

0   30 m
0   100 ft

Arjuna's penance to obtain the bow of Shiva.

However, it is for its vividly coloured murals that this mandapa is celebrated; these constitute the principal examples of Vijayanagara paintings. The long friezes adorning the ceiling depict popular legends from the Puranas and the Mahabharata and Ramayana epics. There are also portraits of the donor brothers, processions of maids in attendance on Shiva and Parvati (east corridors) and the boar hunt of Shiva (west corridor). The elegant linework, vibrant colours (mostly browns and ochres) and details of costumes and facial types are of outstanding interest.

The murals on the ceiling of the inner mandapa are difficult to see. Over the central bay is a large icon of Virabhadra together with the temple donors; elsewhere, there are other aspects of Shiva. The columns here are also carved with deities and guardians. Enshrined within the principal sanctuary is a fierce life-size image of Virabhadra decked with skulls and carrying weapons.

Nandi Image, 16th century

East of the town is a large Nandi image which has been sculpted out of a granite boulder. The bull is adorned with garlands and bells.

MADRAS

Numerous Hindu temples have been incorporated into the ever-expanding suburbs of Madras; some of these predate the foundation of the city. The two largest complexes, those dedicated to Kapaleshvara and Parthasarathi, are of paramount importance for worshippers of Shiva and Vishnu respectively. They are typical examples of southern Indian temple styles after the 17th century.

(For the British monuments of the city see Volume II.)

Kapaleshvara Temple,
17th century and later

This is the largest and most important Shaiva complex in Madras. The original foundation was destroyed by the Portuguese in 1566 and fragments from this earlier structure were incorporated into the bishop's house at St Thomé, overlooking the sea. The present temple is located a short distance inland. It is dedicated to Shiva in the form of a peacock (mayil), after which the surrounding district of Mayilapur (Mylapore) was named.

The complex is entered on the east through a high gopura (with renovated coloured plaster sculptures on the tower). Depictions of Shiva in his various forms are carved into the scrollwork that adorns the doorway jambs. Within the enclosure, the principal shrines, which house an image of Subrahmanya and a large Shiva linga, face west. In front of the doorways to these shrines are brass lamp-columns, altars and pavilions. A smaller shrine to the goddess opens to the north of the linga sanctuary. A small gopura on the west side of the enclosure leads to a vast tank.

Parthasarathi Temple,
17th century and later

This celebrated Vaishnava sanctuary is located within the suburb of Triplicane.

The temple has two enclosures, which are entered through gopuras on both the east and west sides. Within the east enclosure are the twin shrines of Krishna and Rukmini (access is restricted to Hindus only). Outside the east gopura is a large tank.

Government Museum

This important collection of antiquities from sites in southern India and the Deccan is exhibited in three separate buildings: the Archaeological section, the Art Gallery and the Bronze Gallery.

Stone sculptures are displayed in the Archaeological Section. Early examples from the Deccan illustrate the beginnings of Buddhist artistic traditions. From Jaggayyapeta come several fragments, including the depiction of a royal figure (10). From Goli there is a long frieze illustrating scenes from the Vessantara Jataka. Both of these limestone sculptures date from the 2nd–3rd centuries.

However, it is for the large number of damaged limestone panels, posts and railings from the dismantled stupa at **Amaravati** that this collection is best known. The substantial remains of this major Buddhist monument testify to the vitality of early artistic traditions in the Deccan.

Several of the **Amaravati** fragments date from the 2nd century BC. These include a representation of a multi-storey tree shrine with flying celestials (IB.18), a column with a fluted capital with seated elephants above and a panel carved with a yaksha and a youth (IB.11). The remainder of the pieces mostly belong to the 2nd–3rd centuries. Numerous panels and railings are adorned with lotus flowers, pots sprouting abundant foliage, yakshas bearing garlands and other themes. Medallions are often filled with crowded narrative scenes; the lively compositions and delicate sculpturing of the figures are still evident despite the decomposition of the limestone. Among the episodes depicting the life of the Buddha

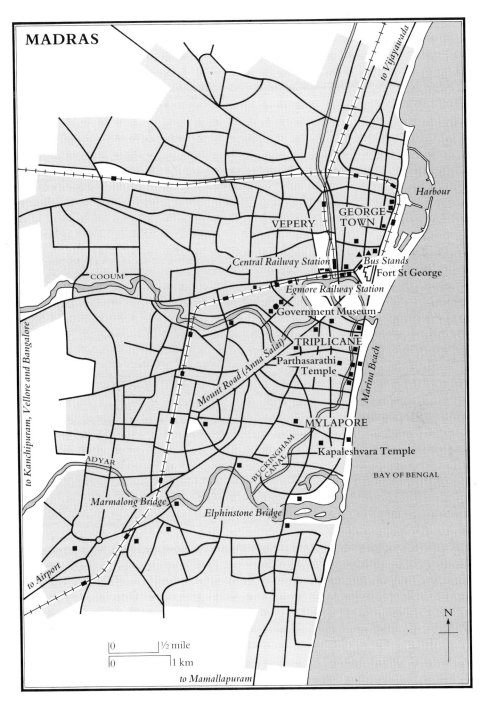

are the Master subduing the elephant (IIIA.15), a courtly scene (IIIB.23) and the bowl of the Buddha uplifted by devotees (IIIA.6). Jataka stories are also illustrated, such as that in which the Bodhisattva appears as a white elephant. On the railings, long friezes illustrate the birth of Rahula and other scenes of Buddha's life (IIIA.12), and the temptation of Buddha and his enlightenment (IIIA.8). Lotus medallions and garlands are highly elaborate (IIIC.21 and IIIE.6, for example). Representations of the stupa itself include a magnificent relief in which the monument is surrounded by a railing and flanked by columns with wheels on top; flying celestials crowd in on either side and there are scenes from Buddha's life above (IVC.1). Another panel shows a stupa wreathed in snakes and attended by nagas (IVA.17). There are also some rare free-standing Buddha figures wearing elegant finely fluted robes (IVF.6–7, for instance).

Hindu images from the later periods of southern India date from the 8th century onwards. The 10th-century sculptures from **Kodumbalur** depicting Shiva and the goddess (604.53, 605.53), both elegantly poised and delicately modelled, are fine examples of the early Chola style. Contemporary sculptures belonging to the Nolamba era include part of a ceiling panel from **Hemavati** (104.38) and Shiva and Parvati seated together within an elliptical frame from **Penukonda** (65.37). The Hoysala style is represented by an ornate doorway. A sage leaning on a staff from **Tadpatri** (2546) and a figure of Durga standing on the buffalo head (1284.59) belong to the Vijayanagara era.

There are many architectural fragments and memorial stones; the latter illustrate the exploits of heroes. A group of Jain images is displayed separately.

The collection of southern Indian bronzes is the largest in the country. Some of the finest Chola examples are exhibited in the Art Gallery. The magnificent 11th-century Nataraja from Tiruvengadu is displayed here. The dance posture of the figure is perfectly realized; the headdress with snakes and flames is delicately depicted. No less impressive are the seated images of Shiva and Parvati from **Kilaiyur** and the large standing figures of

Rama, Lakshmana and Sita from Vadakkuppanaiyur. Paintings shown here date from later centuries; they occasionally illustrate religious themes.

The other metal images are exhibited in the Bronze Gallery. Hindu figures from the 9th-century Pallava period are small but delicately worked, such as the dancing Shiva from Kuram (53.38) and the seated Shiva from Kilapuddanur. The 11th–12th-century Chola era is represented by numerous seated and dancing images of Shiva, some quite large and detailed. The masterpiece of the series is Ardhanarishvara from Tiruvengadu (447.60). This figure presents a harmonious blending of male and female physiognomies and dress. Among the icons of the goddess there is Maheshvari with a flame-like headdress from Velankanni (267). An unusual example from the Pandya period is the dancing Shiva figure from Poruppumettupatti (92.48).

Later Chola bronzes include a 13th-century Parvati from Kodaikkadu (47-4.36), as well as depictions of Vishnu, Rama and Krishna. To the later Vijayanagara era belong a finely worked image of Shiva as Bhikshatanamurti from Tirukkalar (241) and Krishna dancing on the serpent from Nilappadi (123). Among the smaller images of Shaiva saints is Manikkavachakar (339).

Most of the Buddhist bronzes come from **Nagapattinam** and are assigned to the Chola period and later. One of the finest is an enthroned Buddha seated beneath a tree with diminutive naga attendants on either side. Other examples are standing Buddha (241), four-armed Maitreya (46) and Avalokiteshvara (47), the last within a frame. Several Jain icons are also on display.

MADURAI

Although this was the capital of the 7th–13th-century Pandya rulers, there are no surviving monuments from this period.

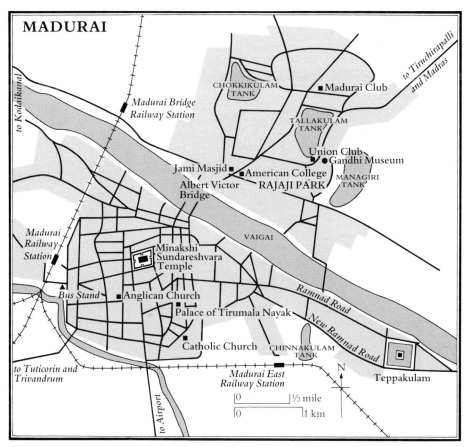

MADURAI

CHOKKIKULAM TANK

Madurai Bridge Railway Station

Madurai Club

to Tiruchirapalli and Madras

to Kodaikanal

TALLAKULAM TANK

Union Club

Gandhi Museum

Jami Masjid

American College

Albert Victor Bridge

RAJAJI PARK

MANAGIRI TANK

Madurai Railway Station

Minakshi Sundareshvara Temple

VAIGAI

Bus Stand

Anglican Church

Palace of Tirumala Nayak

Ramnad Road

Catholic Church

CHINNAKULAM TANK

New Ramnad Road

to Tuticorin and Trivandrum

Madurai East Railway Station

Teppakulam

to Airport

N

0   ½ mile
0   1 km

After the raid of Malik Kafur in 1310, Madurai became the headquarters of a small Muslim state, but this did not last beyond 1364, when it was absorbed into the new Hindu empire established by the kings of **Vijayanagara**. However, the local governors, known as Nayakas, quickly asserted their independence. By the middle of the 16th century Madurai was virtually an independent kingdom, and continued to be so until the coming of the British. Of the many powerful Nayaka rulers, Tirumala (1623–60) was one of the most prominent. The temple at Madurai was largely constructed under his patronage, but he also sponsored other projects and his portraits are found in temples throughout southern India.

Madurai is dominated by the great Minakshi Sundareshvara complex, which stands in the middle of the town. It is surrounded by broad thoroughfares for the annual chariot festivals. Less than 1 km (¼ mile) to the south-east is the impressive palace of the Nayaka rulers (see Volume II). At the extreme eastern end of the town, about 3 km (2 miles) from the main temple, is a large rectangular tank.

Religious life at Madurai focuses on the cult of Minakshi, a local fertility goddess. The ceremonial marriage of this deity to the god Sundareshvara is the most important festival of the town.

Minakshi Sundareshvara Temple,
mostly 17th century

The temple is contained within a vast rectangle of high enclosure walls entered

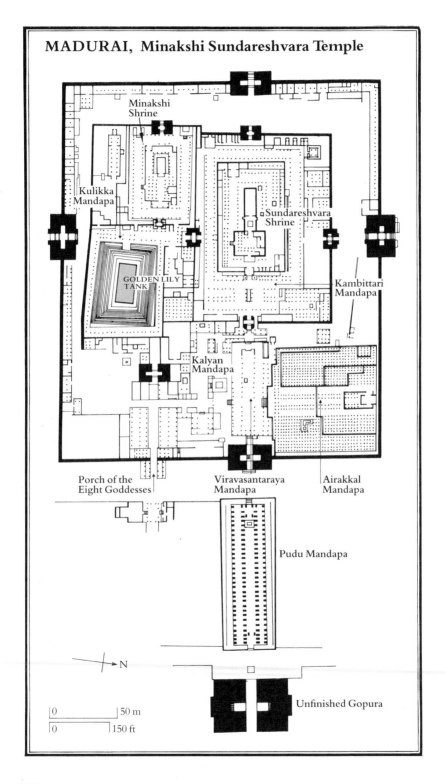

MADURAI, Minakshi Sundareshvara Temple

Minakshi
Shrine

Kulikka
Mandapa

GOLDEN LILY
TANK

Sundareshvara
Shrine

Kambittari
Mandapa

Kalyan
Mandapa

Porch of the
Eight Goddesses

Viravasantaraya
Mandapa

Airakkal
Mandapa

Pudu Mandapa

N

0   50 m
0   150 ft

Unfinished Gopura

in the middle of each side through towering gopuras. Within the enclosure is a complex of colonnades, columned mandapas, tanks, stores, shrines and, at the core, the two temples of Shiva as Sundareshvara and Devi as Minakshi.

The gopuras at Madurai are among the most elaborately adorned in southern India. They are exceptional for their elongated proportions and curved profiles which achieve a dramatic sweep upwards; that on the south reaches about 60 m (196 ft) high. As is usual with these structures, the lower portions, consisting of a moulded basement and pilastered wall, are constructed of granite. The towers are of brick and plaster with openings and porticos at each level to admit light to the hollow chambers. They are completely covered with figures of divinities, celestial beings, monster masks, guardians and animal mounts which inhabit the diminishing storeys of the towers. Above are the vaulted roofs with arched ends and rows of pot finials. All of these elements are encrusted with plaster decoration and painted in vivid colours (recently restored).

Visitors usually enter the temple through the porch of the eight goddesses (south of the east gateway), which projects beyond the enclosure wall. A doorway flanked by images of Ganesha and Subrahmanya leads into a columned mandapa used for shops, stores and stables. At the far end of this mandapa is a doorway surrounded by a brass frame covered with small oil-lamps. Another towered gateway located here is on an axis with the Minakshi shrine further west.

Continuing westwards towards the Minakshi shrine, the courtyard of the Pottamari Kulam is reached. This contains the rectangular Golden Lily tank with stepped sides; a brass lamp-column stands in the middle. The walls of the surrounding colonnade are decorated with murals representing the sixty-four miracles which Shiva is said to have performed in and around Madurai. The long friezes are notable for their vividly drawn figures and distinctive brown and ochre colouring. The ceilings are painted with large medallions. On the western side of the tank, the columns of the kulikka Mandapa are finely carved with yalis and figures of the five Pandava brothers.

A doorway in the west wall of the colonnade leads to the Minakshi temple. This stands in its own enclosure, within which are several subsidiary shrines. The 'bed chamber' on the north is where the image of Sundareshvara is brought each night.

Passing northwards out of the colonnade around the tank, another rectangular enclosure is entered. It also has towered gateways in the middle of each side, but these do not reach the heights of the outer gateways. This enclosure is almost entirely colonnaded and surrounds on four sides the innermost enclosure, which contains the temple of Sundareshvara. In the middle of the east side (second enclosure) is the Kambittari Mandapa, a hall erected at the end of the 19th century. Columns here are carved with considerable virtuosity with images of Shiva dancing, Kali and Virabhadra; these figures have numerous limbs and elaborate jewels.

East of this mandapa (in the outermost enclosure) is the Viravasantaraya Mandapa, in which an image of Nandi is placed. To the south of this is the Kalyan Mandapa, where images of Minakshi and Sundareshvara are brought at the festival that celebrates their marriage. In the north-west corner of the enclosure is the extensive Airakkal Mandapa, which now serves as a museum. Fine bronzes, especially of dancing Shiva, are displayed in the central pavilion (north); there are also stone sculptures and ivory fragments. Here too is a small, possibly earlier, linga sanctuary. There are almost exactly one thousand elaborately decorated columns in this mandapa. The piers have attached colonnettes, while numerous divinities, female musicians and attendant figures are carved in full relief on to the shafts. Brackets with pendant buds project outwards from seated yalis.

Outside the complex, in front of the east gopura, is the Pudu Mandapa. This long hall has piers carved with magnificent yalis and portrait sculptures of the Nayaka rulers and their ministers (middle of the central aisle). Projecting brackets are carried on seated yalis. Within the mandapa there is a small pavilion fashioned of polished black granite (western end).

Beyond the mandapa to the east stands the lowest storey of Tirumala's unfinished gopura; this is more than twice the dimensions of other examples at Madurai. The door jambs, which are more than 15 m (49 ft) high, are finely carved with scrollwork.

Teppakulam

This large rectangular tank is surrounded by a balustrade with three flights of steps on each side. In the middle of the reservoir is a square island on which a small whitewashed towered temple stands among palms and flowering trees; pavilions are positioned at the four corners. Each year, images of Minakshi and Sundareshvara are placed in a raft lit by oil-lamps and floated on the water. This festival, which was originated by Tirumala, still takes place on the anniversary of this ruler's birthday.

MAMALLAPURAM

As the port of the Pallava rulers of **Kanchipuram**, this site was of particular importance in the 7th–8th centuries. Most of the Hindu monuments date from this period; they are particularly associated with two Pallava rulers, Mamalla (c. 630–68) and Rajasimha (c. 700–728).

The rock-cut and monolithic temples at Mamallapuram are the earliest examples of monumental architecture in southern India; structural projects too are the first in the region. Sculptures at the site, including several large-scale compositions, are the finest of the Pallava period.

Most of the cave temples are excavated into the sides of a granite hill only a short distance from the sea; here also is the celebrated frieze of Arjuna's penance. A group of five monolithic temples, known as 'Pancha Rathas', is located south of this outcrop. Dramatically overlooking the Bay of Bengal is the 'Shore' temple. A few other monuments are further away to the north and west.

HILL AREA

The monuments are described from north to south.

Kotikal Mandapa, early 7th century

This may be the earliest monument at the site. It comprises a crudely excavated shrine opening off a small verandah. Female guardians with relaxed postures flank the entrance to the shrine; no image is preserved within.

Trimurti Cave Temple,
early 8th century

Three shrines are arranged here in a row. Each is flanked by pilasters, between which stand guardians; an eave and a parapet of ornamental roof forms are fashioned into the rock face above. Carved on to the rear walls of the shrines are Brahma (left), Vishnu (middle) and Shiva (right), attended by kneeling devotees; a polished stone linga is placed before the Shiva image. Beyond the shrine to the right is a niche with Durga standing on the buffalo head; the goddess is framed by a foliated arch springing from makaras.

Varaha Cave Temple, late 7th century

The columns of this rock-cut mandapa have lion bases; a parapet of roof forms is

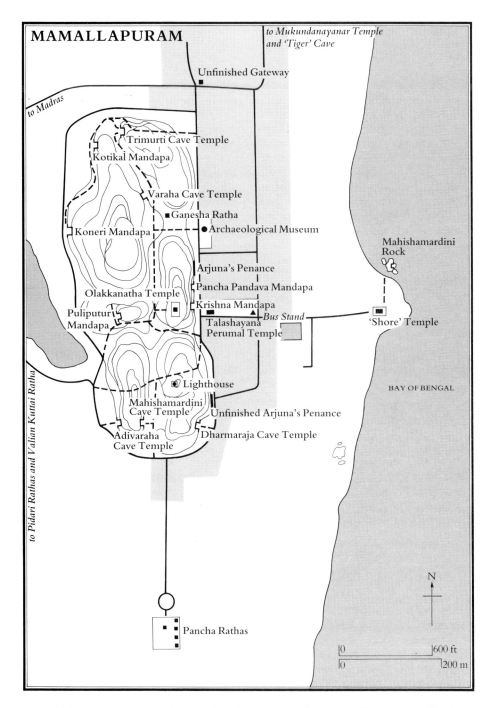

MAMALLAPURAM

to Mukundanayanar Temple
and 'Tiger' Cave

to Madras

Unfinished Gateway

Trimurti Cave Temple

Kotikal Mandapa

Varaha Cave Temple

Ganesha Ratha

Koneri Mandapa

Archaeological Museum

Mahishamardini
Rock

Arjuna's Penance

Pancha Pandava Mandapa

Olakkanatha Temple

Krishna Mandapa

Puliputur
Mandapa

Bus Stand

Talashayana
Perumal Temple

'Shore' Temple

BAY OF BENGAL

Lighthouse

Mahishamardini
Cave Temple

Unfinished Arjuna's Penance

Adivaraha
Cave Temple

Dharmaraja Cave Temple

to Pidari Rathas and Valian Kuttai Ratha

N

Pancha Rathas

0   600 ft
0   200 m

carved above the eaves. In the middle of
the rear wall is a projecting shrine, now
empty, flanked by guardian figures.

Large-scale compositions are sculpted on
to the walls: at the sides, Varaha lifting up
Bhudevi (left) and Trivikrama (right); on

453

the rear wall, Lakshmi (left) and Durga (right).

Ganesha Ratha, late 7th century

This well-finished monolithic monument consists of a rectangular sanctuary with a verandah, which has columns with seated lions at the base, and a sanctuary in which an image of Ganesha was recently installed. Above the pilastered walls, framing guardians on either side of the verandah, rise the parapet and the upper storey; this is capped with a large vaulted roof complete with arched ends and pot and trident finials.

Archaeological Museum

Granite sculptures and architectural fragments found in and around the site have been assembled here.

Arjuna's Penance, mid-7th century

This is one of the most remarkable sculptural compositions in Indian art. Throughout, the relief carving is of the highest quality. The naturalism of the delicately modelled figures and animals and the vitality of the overall composition have never been surpassed.

Two large boulders with a narrow cleft in between are covered with flying gods, goddesses and semi-divine beings, as well as with elephants and other animals. These all converge on the cleft, which is filled with a slab sculpted with a naga and nagi, their hands held in adoration. (Originally, water flowed over these figures from a tank behind the cleft into a basin beneath.) On the left side of the cleft Arjuna stands on one foot deeply engaged in penance. To his right is four-armed Shiva holding the magic weapon which Arjuna hopes to win. Beneath these figures is a hermitage shrine of Vishnu in front of which sit sages, two deer and a lion; disciples beneath engage in austerities. At the bottom right side of the cleft is

the story of the cat who performed penance, thus tricking a group of rats.

This scene has also been interpreted as an illustration of the penance of Bhagiratha. This sage persuaded Shiva to receive the Ganga in his matted locks. The cleft with its naga figures, over which water once flowed, is thus considered to represent the descent of the celestial river.

Immediately to the right of the boulders is a group of monkeys carved almost in the round. A short distance to the left (in front of the modern lighthouse) is another boulder with an incomplete, possibly earlier, version of the same scene.

Pancha Pandava Mandapa, mid-7th century

Only six columns with lion bases were completed of this large cave temple.

Krishna Mandapa, mid-7th century and later

This columned mandapa shelters a large composition carved on to a boulder; it depicts the scene of Krishna protecting the herds and gopis by lifting up Govardhana mountain. As in the scene of Arjuna's penance, the fluid modelling of the figures and animals is remarkable.

Dharmaraja Cave Temple, early 7th century

This early monument consists of three empty sanctuaries excavated into the rear wall of an open mandapa. Throughout, the architectural elements are unadorned; guardian figures flanking the doorway to the central shrine have been chiselled away.

Mahishamardini Cave Temple, mid-7th century

This consists of a long verandah with three shrines, the central one of which has a projecting porch. The columns are slender and fluted; the parapet above is only blocked out. The sculpture panels at either end of the verandah are among the masterpieces of Pallava art: they show Vishnu sleeping on the serpent in the presence of the gods (left) and Durga on the lion approaching the buffalo-headed demon (right). The latter panel is unusually dynamic in its composition.

Olakkanatha Temple, early 8th century

This free-standing structure is built on the summit of the hill. Pairs of pilasters on the walls frame worn Shiva images. No ceiling or superstructure survives.

Adivaraha Cave Temple, mid-7th century

This temple, which is partly obscured by a modern structure, consists of a verandah with a shrine excavated into the rear wall. The two columns have seated lions at the base. A parapet with a row of miniature roof forms is carved above. The doorway to the sanctuary, which projects into the verandah, is flanked by guardian figures; an image of Varaha is enshrined within. The sculpture panels on the verandah walls depict both royal and mythological figures. On either side of the sanctuary are rulers with queens; inscriptions identify these as portraits of two of the early Pallava kings. The end panels of the verandah depict Lakshmi bathed by elephants (left) and Durga standing on the head of the demon (right).

'PANCHA RATHAS'

These temple-like monoliths were never completed and may have served only as models of different building types. In this respect, they have been compared to mobile shrines or chariots (rathas). Without any historical basis they have been named after Draupadi and the Pandava brothers. It is most likely that

they were excavated in the 7th century during the reign of Mamalla.

Draupadi Ratha, 7th century

Together with the Arjuna ratha, this small temple is elevated on a plinth carved with elephants and lions. The monument is recognized by its hut-like roof with curved ridges. Female guardians between pilasters flank the doorway (west side); a makara arch is positioned above. On the three other sides are standing images of Durga; a similar representation of the goddess standing on the buffalo head is carved on to the rear wall of the shrine. In front is a free-standing lion.

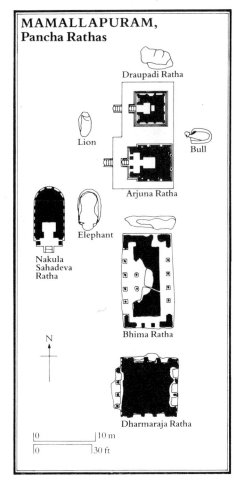

MAMALLAPURAM, Pancha Rathas

Draupadi Ratha

Lion

Bull

Arjuna Ratha

Elephant

Nakula Sahadeva Ratha

Bhima Ratha

N

Dharmaraja Ratha

| 0 | 10 m |
| 0 | 30 ft |

Arjuna Ratha, 7th century

This is a smaller version of the Dharma-raja ratha. Elegant pilasters frame sculptures of guardians, couples and, in the middle of each side, deities such as Shiva leaning on Nandi (south), Indra on the elephant (east) and Vishnu with Garuda (north). The wall is overhung by an eave with a parapet of roof forms above. The upper storey repeats this scheme on a smaller scale; the roof is an octagonal dome.

Projecting from the front (west) of the temple is a porch (with replacement columns) leading into a verandah and empty sanctuary. East of the temple is a finely sculpted Nandi.

Bhima Ratha, 7th century

The lower portions of this temple are incomplete except for the columns with seated lions on the front (west) and the finely modelled eaves and parapet. The building is dominated by its large vaulted roof with arched ends.

Dharmaraja Ratha, 7th century

This is the tallest and most elaborate temple of the group, being a triple-storey version of the Arjuna scheme. Columns with lion bases flank the entrance porch that leads to the unfinished sanctuary. Sculptures framed by pilasters are positioned in end panels on each side: Ardhanarishvara and Brahma (east), Shiva and the royal patron Mamalla (south), Shiva (west) and Brahma and Harihara (north).

The second level consists of a passageway around a square shrine. This is also provided with sculptures of Shiva, guardians and attendants. Devotees are carved on to the walls of the second storey, as are figures of Chandra and Surya (middle of north and east sides). At this uppermost level is a chamber entered on the west with carvings of a Somaskanda group accompanied by Brahma and Vishnu on the rear wall.

Nakula Sahadeva Ratha, 7th century

Characterized by its apsidal end, this temple stands to the west, detached from the others. The crowning roof is also apsidal-ended; its arched end faces north. Nearby is a free-standing monolithic elephant.

ON THE COAST

'Shore' Temple, early 8th century

Together with the Kailasanatha temple at **Kanchipuram**, this is the first significant structural temple of the Pallava period; it dates from the period of Rajasimha. Despite its general erosion, this is an impressive monument with elegantly proportioned towers. The temple is approached from the west through a number of ruined courts with Nandi images placed on the walls. Here there are basements of altars, one with decorated sides, and other structures. A small boulder nearby is carved with an image of Durga's lion; the goddess is seated on the hind leg of the animal.

The temple itself is a complex of three shrines. The original sanctuary was a small chamber built to shelter an image of Vishnu sleeping on Ananta that was carved on to a granite boulder. To the east, a sanctuary facing the ocean houses a multi-faceted polished basalt linga with worn images of a Somaskanda group on the rear wall. An open passageway surrounds the sanctuary. Another smaller sanctuary facing west, similarly provided with Shaiva icons, abuts the Vishnu shrine.

Pilasters with worn lion bases adorn the outer walls; these are sheltered by an eave and parapet. Above the two Shiva shrines rise the steeply pyramidal superstructures; these repeat the wall schemes in diminishing storeys. The towers are capped by octagonal domes.

Along the coast, to the north and south of the temple, are several rocks carved with Durga images.

WEST OF THE SITE

Three small monolithic temples, the twin Pidari rathas and the Valian Kuttai ratha, date from the late 7th century. These square temples each have two storeys with square or domed roofs.

NORTH OF THE SITE

Unfinished Gateway, 16th century

This unfinished gopura dates from the Vijayanagara period.

Mukundanayanar Temple,
early 8th century

This small structural temple imitates the forms of the simpler rathas.

'Tiger' Cave, early 8th century

This unusual rock-cut monument is located 4 km (2½ miles) to the north, near the village of Saluvankuppam. A boulder fashioned into a small portico, possibly for processional images, is surrounded by fierce yali ('tiger') heads; two elephant heads are positioned to the left.

Atiranachanda Mandapa,
early 7th century

Nearby is another early example of an unadorned cave temple, with a Soma-skanda group carved on to the rear wall.

MANDAGAPPATTU

Cave Temple, beginning 7th century

This Hindu temple is one of the earliest Pallava shrines, comparable with examples at **Mamallapuram** and **Tiruchirapalli**. An inscription links the temple with the ruler Mahendravarman I (c. 580–630); although it indicates that Brahma, Shiva and Vishnu were worshipped here, no

images are preserved. The part-octagonal columns of the mandapa are massive and plain. Guardian figures with clubs are carved into recesses at either side of the façade.

MANGALORE

(For the city and its British monuments see Volume II.)

Manjunatha Temple,
10th century and later

This important Hindu shrine is located at Kadri, 3 km (2 miles) north of the city's centre. Facing west, the original square shrine is enclosed by a later colonnade with screen walls and a tiled roof. The

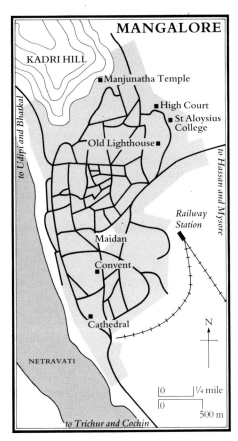

457

pyramidal tower, possibly also a later addition, has ascending storeys with pilastered walls and pronounced cornices.

The temple houses the rituals of the Natha Pantha cult; these focus on the irregular stone which serves as a linga within the sanctuary. But this cult also reveres Buddhist deities. Metal sculptures of Buddhist figures in this temple are the finest and largest in southern India. The bronze image of Lokeshvara, which is 1·6 m (5 ft) high, is dated to 968. This four-faced figure with six arms is seated within an elaborate frame; smaller guardians are positioned at either side. The other sculptures, which are of teaching Buddha and Manjushri, belong to the 11th century. The exceptional quality of the latter figure is evident in the delicately modelled face and headdress.

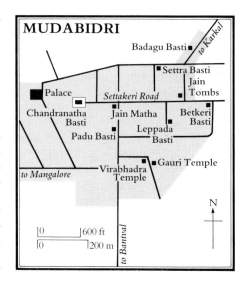

MUDABIDRI

This town in the Kannara region has no fewer than twenty Jain foundations (bastis); there are similar temples at **Karkal**, 15 km (9½ miles) to the north. The sloping roofs of these buildings are typical features of the coastal style. Many fine sculptures, both in stone and metal, dating from the 11th–13th centuries, are kept in these bastis.

Chandranatha Basti, 1429 and later

This complex dominates the principal street of the town. The temple consists of a sanctuary preceded by a sequence of three columned mandapas surrounded by a colonnade; a fourth mandapa, dedicated to Bhairavadevi, is a free-standing structure with projecting sides. Each mandapa is roofed with sloping tiers, the uppermost covered with copper sheets; above the sanctuary is a triple-gabled roof. Stone columns are carved with foliation and miniature figures, particularly in the detached mandapa.

Standing in front of the temple is a 16·5-m-high (54 ft) monolithic column. Animals and figures adorn the double capital; a pot finial is placed above.

Jain Matha

The library of this institution houses a significant collection of illustrated manuscripts. Those that date from the 12th–13th-century Hoysala period are painted in bright colours on to unusually large palm leaves. Metal images of Tirthankaras are also displayed here.

Tombs

These unique stone memorials of Jain priests are solid towered constructions with three, five or seven storeys of sloping roofs.

Palace, 17th century

The local Chetiar rulers were also Jains. Their palace, though unimposing from the outside, is set in spacious grounds. It is decorated with wood carving of exceptional workmanship. The columns and screens are adorned with divinities, attendant figures, animals, birds and foliate motifs. The walls were originally painted, but nothing has survived.

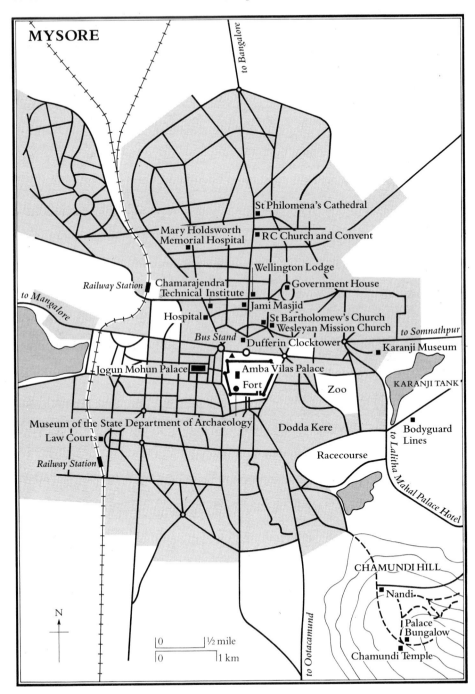

MYSORE (map p. 459)

(For the city and its monuments see Volume II.)

Museum of the State Department of Archaeology

This collection is accommodated within the grounds of the palace. Among the fine bronzes are 12th-century images of dancing Shiva and Shiva seated with Parvati from Kudalur. There is also a seated Tirthankara surrounded by miniature figures.

CHAMUNDI HILL

The granite hill, 3 km (2 miles) to the south-east, that overlooks Mysore is named after the goddess who is enshrined in a temple built near the summit. Chamundi was the guardian divinity of the ruling Wadiyar family, who founded the shrine.

Beside the road that ascends the hill is a colossal Nandi image hewn out of a single boulder in 1659. The seated animal is decked with ceremonial bells and garlands.

Chamundi Temple,
17th century and later

This Hindu complex is entered through two gopuras. The outer gateway has a steep pyramidal tower, which is a modern addition on earlier stone walls. The doors, which are of embossed silver, have panels depicting different goddesses. The shrine itself is a modest structure; it is approached through a small mandapa. Metal cladding covers the doorways that lead to the sanctuary where the richly attired goddess is enthroned. The sanctuary's tower is modern.

NAGAPATTINAM

Although this was once the most important Buddhist centre on the Coromandel coast, no ancient monuments have survived. Records of foreign writers indicate a thriving port town with numerous temples, one of which was erected specifically for the Chinese Buddhist community. A multi-storey brick tower with tiers of angled roofs was still standing in the middle of the 19th century. (For the British monuments see Volume II.)

Nagapattinam is also known for the fine bronze figures and miniature stupas that were discovered in the excavations here; these 13th-century images are displayed in various collections, particularly the Government Museum, **Madras**.

Kayarohana and Tyagaraja Temples,
11th century

These typical Chola Hindu structures have clearly moulded basements and pilastered walls; sculptures are preserved only in the niches of the Kayarohana shrine.

NAMAKKAL

Important examples of Pandya sculptures are preserved in temples cut into the eastern and western sides of a granite outcrop at this Hindu site. On the south-eastern side of the hill is a large tank and a monolithic statue of Narasimha.

Narasimha Cave Temple,
8th century and later

A towerless 17th-century gateway and subsidiary structures lead to the excavated chamber that forms the focus of this complex. Carved on to the rear walls are figures of seated Narasimha accompanied by Surya and Chandra (centre), eight-armed Narasimha savagely attacking Hiranyakashipu (left) and Varaha (right).

Vishnu seated on Ananta, accompanied by Shiva, Brahma and other figures (left), and Trivikrama with his leg kicked up high (right) are carved on to the side walls. The vigorous postures and rounded modelling of the figures are typical features of the Pandya style.

Anantashayi Cave Temple, 8th century

The Vaishnava images carved on to the walls of this smaller sanctuary are similar but more static than those in the Narasimha temple. The interior is dominated by the large figure of Vishnu reclining on Ananta.

NANDI

The granite hill that is named after Shiva's bull rises to about 600 m (2,000 ft) above the plain. Under Tipu Sultan in the 18th century, the hill was transformed into a fortified citadel (see Volume II). At the foot of the hill is Nandi village. The temple here is an important example of the Nolamba style; it is harmoniously blended with Vijayanagara extensions.

Bhoganandishvara Temple, 9th and 16th centuries

The Hindu complex is entered on the east through a Vijayanagara gopura without a tower. The colonnaded enclosure is only reached after passing through a smaller second gateway. Immediately in front is a large columned mandapa with Vijayanagara piers; some have fully modelled attendant maidens holding lotus flowers (central aisle). Within the mandapa are the Nandi pavilions and the front (east) façades of two Shiva shrines dedicated to Bhoganandishvara (north) and Arunachaleshvara (south).

The earlier architectural style of the twin shrines is clearly evident at the rear (west) of the enclosure. Plain pilastered walls are unadorned except for pierced stone windows; these are adorned with figures of dancing Shiva (south side of Arunachaleshvara), Durga standing on the buffalo head (north side of Bhoganandishvara) or dancers in scrollwork. The parapets appear to be supported on miniature gana figures. The multi-storey pyramidal towers are complete with pilastered walls, eaves and parapets. Black stone sculptures of Shiva and Nandi are placed on to the uppermost storey of the Bhoganandishvara shrine; the roof is octagonal.

Columns with carved panels on the shafts enliven the interiors. The Bhoganandishvara shrine has a finely finished ceiling panel of Shiva and Parvati surrounded by the Dikpalas. Large polished black stone lingas are housed within the two sanctuaries.

Between the shrines is the smaller Uma Maheshvara sanctuary; behind this is a screen wall that links the two shrines. The Uma Maheshvara sanctuary is approached through a Vijayanagara pavilion; basalt columns, brackets and ceilings are all intricately carved with miniature figures, birds, animals and foliage. The outer walls are covered with a continuous procession of gods and sages who are witnesses of the wedding of Shiva and Parvati. Similar friezes adorn the walls of the two goddess shrines set into the colonnade at the rear (west) of the enclosure.

A doorway on the north side of the enclosure leads to a smaller colonnaded court with two open pavilions that were used at festival times. Another doorway provides access to a stepped tank surrounded by colonnades.

NARTTAMALAI

Vijayalaya Cholishvara Temple, mid-9th century

Although this Shiva temple was named after the founder of the Chola dynasty, it was erected by a local ruler during the late

Pallava period. Its style anticipates the early Chola projects.

Unusually, the temple has a circular sanctuary contained within square outer walls; the columned mandapa is rectangular. The outer elevation consists of pilastered walls surmounted by an eave and a parapet; above rises the double-storey tower with a hemispherical roof. No wall sculptures are preserved other than the guardian figures that flank the entrance on the west; deities and Nandi images are positioned beneath the roof. (Loose sculptures from this temple are now displayed in the Government Museum, **Pudukkottai**.)

The temple once formed part of a complex with eight subsidiary shrines facing it; six of these still stand.

Kadambavaneshvara Temple, *c.* 1007

This dates from the period of the Chola ruler Rajaraja I. The small temple is built close to the rocky cliff; its northern face is the rock itself. This is a fine small-scale Chola temple. The pilastered walls support the eave and a frieze of yalis. Over the sanctuary rises a simple hemispherical roof with large arched niches in the middle of each side.

Cave Temples, 9th century

Several small sanctuaries are excavated into a cliff immediately to the west of the Vijayalaya Cholishvara temple. The Vaishnava example is notable for the twelve identical standing figures of Vishnu, each wearing a tall crown with a flame-like emblem.

The terrace built in front of this cave temple has a moulded basement and numerous loose sculptures.

PANAMALAI

Talagirishvara Temple,
early 8th century

This Hindu temple, built on top of a hill, is an early example of Pallava structural architecture. The walls of the sanctuary are laid out on a square plan, with shrine projections in the middle of each side. The regularly spaced pilasters have rearing lions at the bases. A pyramidal superstructure with vaulted roofs over the projecting shrines rises over the sanctuary; the roof is hemispherical. A Somaskanda panel is carved on to the rear wall of the sanctuary, where there is also a multi-faceted linga. Smaller lingas on circular pedestals are placed in the outer shrines, which were once adorned with paintings. A mural fragment in the northern shrine depicts Shiva dancing attended by Parvati. The adjoining mandapa to the east is a later addition of the Vijayanagara period.

Beneath the hill to the south-west is a cave temple with an eight-armed image of Durga.

PENUKONDA

This site was an important fortress during the Vijayanagara era; it also served for a time as a royal residence after the sack of **Vijayanagara** in 1565. The site is dominated by a steep hill; columned structures and gateways line a pathway leading to the summit. Beneath the hill on the east, massive walls and gateways define a fortified zone; here are grouped several courtly structures, small temples and a large tank.

(For the courtly structures and nearby Islamic monuments see Volume II.)

Parshvanatha Temple, 15th century

Of little interest architecturally, this Jain temple enshrines a sculpture of remark-

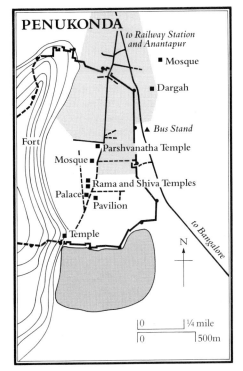

PENUKONDA

to Railway Station
and Anantapur

■ Mosque

■ Dargah

▲ Bus Stand

Fort

Mosque ■ ┊ ■ Parshvanatha Temple

Palace ■ ┊ ■ Rama and Shiva Temples

┊ Pavilion

■ Temple

to Bangalore

N

|0 |¼ mile
|0 |500m

PERUVANAM

Shiva Temple, 12th century

Two Hindu shrines within this complex in Kerala are of interest because of their stylistic links with contemporary Chola traditions.

The Madattilappan shrine consists of a square structure surrounded by two passageways converted internally into a circular linga chamber. A small mandapa approached by a flight of steps on the west adjoins the passageway. The exterior pilastered walls are elevated on a deeply modelled basement; secondary pilasters are capped with large arched motifs. Over the eaves rises the parapet with ornamental roof forms. The superstructure is sheltered by a double tier of gabled roofs covered with tiles and extended over the mandapa. The roof, which is coated with metal sheets, is octagonal; arched dormer windows are positioned on each side.

The Irattayappa shrine is circular in plan with openings on three sides. A conical roof with a pot finial shelters the square sanctuary, which is positioned in the middle of a columned mandapa. Although the main entrance is on the west, another entrance on the east leads to the Parvati image installed behind the sanctuary. Carved wooden brackets are used inside the mandapa.

able quality; this dates from the 11th century and is executed in the Late Chalukya style. It depicts the naked figure of Parshvanatha standing in front of an undulating serpent.

Rama and Shiva Temples, 15th century

These two granite Hindu temples, which stand next to each other within a compound, are typical of the early Vijayanagara style, which was much influenced by Chola traditions. They have long low elevations with deeply moulded basements and regularly positioned wall pilasters. Carved on to the walls are divinities and epic episodes, many of which illustrate scenes from the Ramayana epic. The sanctuaries are surrounded by internal passageways. The towers have domed roofs. Attached to the Rama temple is a later mandapa, in front of which is a finely finished column.

PUDUKKOTTAI

(For the town and its monuments see Volume II.)

Government Museum

The Archaeology Section displays sculptures found at nearby temple sites. These include 9th-century stone images from **Narttamalai**, especially a series of Matrikas, and Shiva as Dakshinamurti. There are other fine sculptures from

Kodumbalur. The earliest bronzes are several 10th-century pieces found within the town itself. Bronzes from the Chola and later periods illustrate a wide range of divinities. Copies of the murals at **Sittannavasal** are also exhibited.

PUNJAI

Naltunai Ishvara Temple,
mid-10th century

This Hindu temple presents the standard Chola arrangement of sanctuary, antechamber and columned mandapa. The walls are rhythmically divided by pilasters with large capitals; secondary pilasters frame niches with pediments above. The sculptures placed in the niches here are among the finest of the period; their fully modelled forms resemble contemporary bronzes. Set into the sanctuary walls are images of Dakshinamurti flanked by sages (south), Shiva appearing out of the linga (west) and Brahma (north). Ganesha and Agastya (south), Durga (north) and guardians on either side of the entrance (east) appear on the mandapa walls. Miniature panels depicting unidentified narrative scenes are carved on to the basement. Most of the upper part of the temple is a later replacement.

RAMESHWARAM

This sacred Hindu island, which is connected to the mainland by a causeway, is believed to be the place where Rama worshipped Shiva after crossing over from Sri Lanka. Having killed Ravana, Rama wished to purify himself by making offerings to the linga. This emblem is the chief object of worship in the Ramalingeshvara shrine. 2 km (1½ miles) to the north is Gandhamadana hill, which is crowned by

a small temple enshrining the footprint of Rama. At the extreme south-eastern end of the island is the bathing spot known as Dhanushkodi, where Rama is supposed to have bathed.

The Rameshwaram complex is built in the northern part of the island at a point where the land rises gently, overlooking a lake. Although it was founded during the Chola period, the temple belongs mostly to the Nayaka period. In the 17th–18th centuries it benefited greatly from the endowments made by the Sethupathi rulers of nearby Ramnad.

Ramalingeshvara Temple,
mostly 17th–18th century

This complex is contained within a vast rectangle of high walls, with towered gopuras in the middle of three sides. The east gopura is positioned in the wall of the intermediate enclosure; two entrances in the peripheral walls on this side, one leading to the principal sanctuary, the other to the Devi shrine, are approached through columned mandapas. The towers of these gopuras are constructed of stone; those on the east and west were completed comparatively recently. Their diminishing storeys rise in a pyramidal mass to the crowning vaulted roof.

The gateways lead to a spacious corridor, which surrounds the intermediate enclosure on four sides, and also to a large tank and several subsidiary shrines. The colonnade is exceptional for its great length: 205 m (671 ft) on the north and south sides. The receding perspective of piers is a characteristic feature of the temple. These piers are raised on a moulded basement; their shafts are adorned with scrollwork and lotus designs (covered with plaster). Large pendant lotus brackets rest on crouching yalis. Traces of painted medallions with figures are preserved on the ceilings. The colonnade on the west side is interrupted by the Chokkattam corridor, which leads from the outer gopura to the second enclosure wall. The

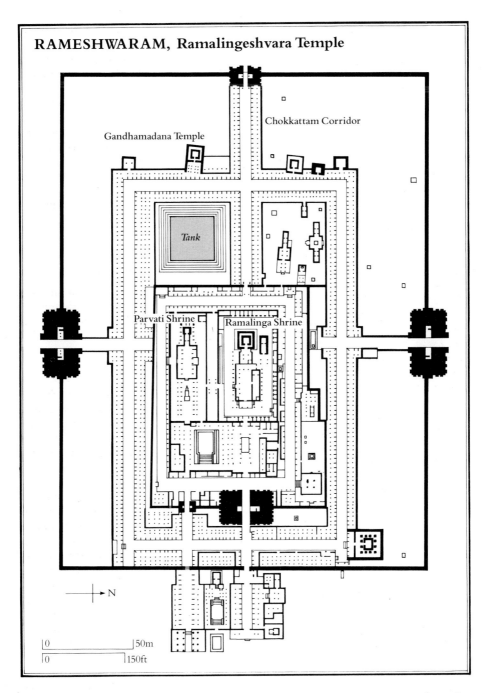

RAMESHWARAM, Ramalingeshvara Temple

Chokkattam Corridor

Gandhamadana Temple

Tank

Parvati Shrine

Ramalinga Shrine

N

0   50m

0   150ft

piers in this corridor are carved with rearing animals, warriors, maidens and other figures.

On the west side of the outer enclosure are several earlier shrines dating from the 12th century; some of these are built into the later colonnade. These small structures have simply moulded basements,

465

pilastered walls with traces of sculptures in the niches, and single- or double-storey towers crowned by hemispherical roofs.

Two gateways on the east lead to the colonnaded corridor of the intermediate enclosure. Two more entrances provide access into the innermost zone, where the principal shrines are located. Preceding these are a columned mandapa, a tank, a pavilion sheltering a large Nandi image, and several subsidiary sanctuaries. Both the shrines are surrounded by enclosure walls; the one on the north houses the linga worshipped by Rama and the one on the south is for the goddess Parvati.

Portrait sculptures of the Nayaka rulers and their ministers are carved on to the columns in front (east) of the Ramalinga shrine; attendant maidens adorn the columns in front of the Devi shrine.

SHRAVANA BELGOLA

This is one of the most celebrated Jain religious sites in southern India. It is dominated by the colossal monolithic image of Gommateshvara. The site was established in the 9th–10th century during the era of the Western Gangas; it particularly benefited from the patronage of Chamundaraya, an important general. Many temples dating from the 12th century were associated with Gangaraja, commander of the Hoysala army. The site continued to be developed in later centuries during the Vijayanagara and Wadiyar periods. Today it is still a significant pilgrimage spot. In 1981, on the thousandth anniversary of the Gommateshvara monolith, a great commemorative festival took place. The statue was ritually bathed with milk, water, coconut milk and solutions of sugar and rice, sandalwood paste, turmeric, vermilion and flower petals.

The monuments and temples at Shravana Belgola are located on two granite hills and in the village that lies between. On Vindhyagiri, the hill that rises 143 m (470 ft) above the plain south of the village, shrines line the steps that ascend to the summit, where the monolith is situated. Most of the monuments and inscriptions on Chandragiri, to the north, are grouped within an enclosure.

VINDHYAGIRI

The shrines are described in ascending order.

Odegal Basti, 12th century

This triple-shrined temple houses images of Adinatha (south), Neminatha (east) and Shantinatha (west). The exterior is severely plain, except for angled struts that support the basement.

Brahmadeva Mandapa, 10th century

This small pavilion shelters a column that is intricately carved with scrollwork. An inscription of Chamundaraya has been partly effaced by a later epigraph.

Akhanda Bagilu, 12th century

This gateway is located at the entrance to the last flight of steps leading up to the Gommateshvara compound. The lintel over the doorway is adorned with Lakshmi and two elephants within an ornate makara frame.

A boulder to one side is carved with rows of miniature Jina figures.

Siddhara Basti, 12th century

This small shrine houses an image of a Jain saint. Inscribed memorial pillars stand at either side of the entrance. The tops of the pillars are fashioned as miniature temple towers.

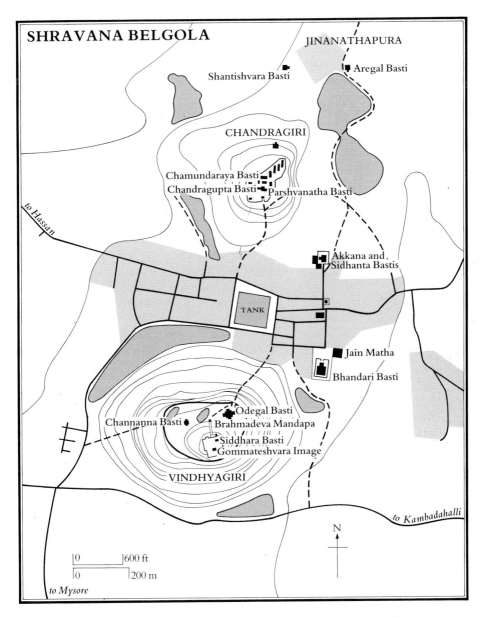

SHRAVANA BELGOLA

JINANATHAPURA

Shantishvara Basti

Aregal Basti

CHANDRAGIRI

Chamundaraya Basti
Chandragupta Basti — Parshvanatha Basti

to Hassan

Akkana and Sidhanta Bastis

TANK

Jain Matha

Bhandari Basti

Odegal Basti
Channanna Basti — Brahmadeva Mandapa
Siddhara Basti
Gommateshvara Image

VINDHYAGIRI

to Kambadahalli

N

0 ⊢ 600 ft
0 ⊢ 200 m

to Mysore

Gommateshvara Image, 981

This monolithic sculpture represents Bahubali, the son of the first Tirthankara. After defeating his brother Bharata in battle, Bahubali renounced the world and sought enlightenment.

At 17·7 m (58 ft) high, this is the largest free-standing sculpture in India. The naked saint stands immobile, his glance fixed steadfastly ahead; creepers wind around his legs and arms. The proportions of the figure are unusual, especially the extended shoulders and elongated arms; the modelling of the anatomy is uniformly smooth. The facial features are finely carved, as are also the coils of the hair. Snakes and ant-hills are carved on to the rock beneath, where inscriptions record the donations of Chamundaraya, the original sponsor, and subsequent donors.

The monolith is surrounded by a compound wall with a colonnade that was added in the 12th century; forty-three Tirthankara images are housed here. Intricately carved ceiling panels depict the Dikpalas; in the middle is Indra holding the pot which is to be used to anoint Gommateshvara.

Channanna Basti, *c.* 1673

This small temple consists of an unadorned shrine and open mandapa. A tall lamp-column with a miniature pavilion at the top stands in front of it.

WITHIN THE TOWN

Jain Matha, 18th–19th centuries

Formerly the residence of the head guru of Shravana Belgola, this building consists of a number of shrines arranged around a courtyard. Here is displayed an important collection of Jain bronze figures from the Western Ganga period, and a number of later images with highly elaborate frames. A remarkable series of brightly painted murals, mostly dating from the 18th–19th centuries, is also preserved within the matha. These animated narratives illustrate the past and present births of Parshvanatha: in particular, the story of Marubhuta and his wicked brother Kamatha and incidents from the legend of prince Nagakumara. There is even an animated depiction of the annual fair at the site.

Bhandari Basti, *c.* 1159 and later

This temple enshrines twenty-four Tirthankara images; these are arranged in a row on a long pedestal within the spacious sanctuary. The parapet and tower are later

additions. In front of the temple stands a stone column with a small pavilion on top.

CHANDRAGIRI

Beneath the summit of this hill is an irregular enclosure, which contains temples, open mandapas, inscriptions and sculptures dating from both the Western Ganga and the Hoysala periods. The temples are characterized by their plain exteriors, relieved only by regularly positioned pilasters and elaborate parapets. Multi-storey superstructures rise over the sanctuaries of some of the temples. A natural cavern and a pond are situated on the side of the hill. Two other temples are located at Jinanathapura, about 300 m (975 ft) to the north.

Chamundaraya Basti, late 10th century

Named after the patron of the Gommateshvara image, this is the largest temple of the group. An image of Neminatha is housed in the sanctuary. The hollow tower, capped by an octagonal dome, also serves as a shrine, with its image of Parshvanatha. Miniature sculptures adorn the parapet elements.

Chandragupta Basti, 12th century

This small shrine has finely carved stone screens with miniature panels depicting incidents from the lives of the saint Bhadrabahu and his disciple King Chandragupta. A mandapa links the shrine to the Kattale Basti.

Parshvanatha Basti, 12th century

The exterior of this temple can be recognized by its elongated pilasters. The sanctuary houses a fully modelled 5-m-high (16½ ft) image of Parshvanatha. The 17th-century lamp-column which stands in front has a miniature pavilion elevated on the double capital.

Shantishvara Basti, late 12th century

This temple is located on the outskirts of Jinanathapura. It is the only temple at the site to display the ornate sculptural treatment of the Hoysala style. Though dilapidated, the basement and wall panels preserve Jina figures and attendant maidens. Scrollwork between the pilasters and miniature tower-like pediments over the sculptures are typical features. The mandapa is adorned with corbelled ceiling compositions. A Jina figure seated on a throne is enshrined within the sanctuary.

SITTANNAVASAL

Cave Temple, 8th century

Although this rock-cut Jain sanctuary is associated with the period of the Pandyas, its layout and columned forms resemble earlier Pallava monuments. Images of Parshvanatha (right) and a Tirthankara (left) are carved on to the walls at either end of the verandah; within the sanctuary are other Jina images. Despite the unadorned architectural elements, there are traces of wall paintings with vibrant reds and greens. The composition on the ceiling is of a lake with lotus flowers, geese and fish. A mural fragment on the pilasters depicts a king wearing a crown accompanied by his queen and two female dancers.

SOMAPALEM

Chennakeshava Temple, 16th century

This Vijayanagara Hindu temple is entered through a gateway with an incomplete pyramidal brick tower. Sculptures of courtly donors are carved on to columns in the mandapa to the right. In front of the gateway is a lamp-column 18 m (59 ft) high; its shaft is incised with an undulating stalk and delicate scrollwork.

The interior of the temple is ornate. The pavilion in the south-west corner of the enclosure has columns, brackets and doorways encrusted with miniature figures, rearing animals and scrollwork; these are all carved in delicate relief. The mandapa that precedes the principal Vishnu shrine is overhung by a double-curved eave with a brick and plaster parapet above (the sculptures are missing). The columns are carved with numerous divinities; the brackets have pendant buds. Traces of paintings, comparable with those at **Lepakshi**, are preserved on the ceiling. Courtly and fighting figures illustrate episodes from the Ramayana epic. Painted medallions and friezes on the beams incorporate animal and foliate motifs.

SOMNATHPUR

Keshava Temple, 1268

This is one of the most completely preserved Hindu temples of the Hoysala period. It was erected by Somanatha, a Hoysala general during the reign of Narasimha III. The triple-sanctuaried shrine stands in the middle of a rectangular court. A colonnade is built into the enclosure walls. On the east is a gateway with an open portico and lathe-turned columns; an inscribed slab here records the original donation of Somanatha.

The three shrines of the temple are laid out on star-like plans that approximate circles. The shrines open off a columned mandapa, which extends eastwards as a screened porch. The shrines and mandapa are elevated on a plinth that repeats the complex outlines of the plan. Carved elephants project from the plinth, which is deeply cut but otherwise plain.

Carved chlorite is used throughout. Processions of elephants, horses and riders, scrollwork, mythological scenes, makaras and geese adorn the basements of

SOMNATHPUR, Keshava Temple

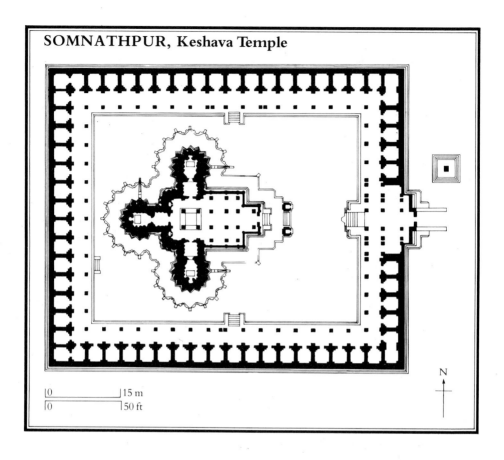

0   15 m

0   50 ft

N

the sanctuaries. The walls above consist entirely of figural panels set at different angles. As at **Belur** and **Halebid**, a large range of divinities appears. Most of the figures are of Vishnu, his incarnations and his consorts. Of particular interest are Vishnu and Lakshmi on Garuda, Indra and Shachi on the elephant, and dancing Vishnu and Ganesha. The figures are richly encrusted with tassels and jewels and sometimes they wear elaborate crowns. The frames in which they stand are decorated with scrollwork or over-hanging trees; labels beneath identify the artists.

Above the panels are pilasters support-ing tower-like pediments of different designs. An angled eave with a petalled fringe projects above. Over the sanctu-aries rise the pyramidal towers, almost ·

circular in plan, with vaulted projections on the front. Each of the diminishing storeys of these towers consists of numerous pot motifs and flattened roof forms; foliated arch-like niches house miniature seated deities. Dome-like roofs are positioned at the summits.

The mandapa basement introduces additional friezes of temple façades and towers, and amorous couples on flattened pilasters. Pierced screens set between col-umns are sheltered by angled eaves; above is an ornamented parapet.

Columns with lathe-turned or multi-faceted shafts enliven the interior. The wall niches have tower-like pediments. The corbelled ceilings are complicated dome-like compositions with lobed motifs, pendant buds and looped bands. Life-size images of Krishna playing the flute (south shrine) and Janardhana (north shrine) are fully modelled and richly jewelled. Krishna is surrounded by attendants, gopis and herds. (The Vishnu image in the west shrine is a replacement.)

Panchalinga Temple, 1268

Although it is contemporary with the Keshava temple, this ruined granite building is completely different in style. It served as a memorial monument to Somanatha and his family.

The five sanctuaries, each housing a linga, stand in a row. There is no carved decoration; unadorned pilastered walls support pyramidal towers with dome-like roofs.

SRIMUSHNAM

Nityeshvara Temple,
10th–11th century

This Hindu temple is a typical example from the middle Chola period: a small square sanctuary with a later tower adjoins an enclosed mandapa. Set into the outer walls are finely executed panels, such as Brahma (north), Shiva appearing out of the linga (west) and Dakshinamurti flanked by rishis (south).

Bhu Varaha Temple, 16th century

This early complex of the Nayakas of **Thanjavur** is comparable to later projects in the wealth and quality of its carvings. The complex is entered through two gopuras; that on the west is the larger and more impressive. Granite basements and walls are articulated by pilastered projections and niches, now empty; the overhanging eave is decorated. Above rise the six diminishing storeys of the pyramidal tower; the plaster sculptures are mostly later replacements.

Within the enclosure walls, two mandapas precede the main shrine. These are distinguished by the ornate treatment of the column shafts, which are covered with figurative panels. Corner piers have clusters of colonnettes; those in between are embellished with vigorous depictions of riders on prancing beasts. Fully modelled portraits of Nayaka nobles are carved on to the columns of the central aisles. The ceilings are adorned with delicately incised lotus medallions.

The walls of the shrine itself are raised on a decorated basement. No sculptures are preserved in the pilastered walls. A small tower (with later plasterwork) with a square roof rises over the sanctuary.

SRINGERI

This important Shaiva centre is picturesquely situated on the upper Tunga river. The celebrated matha here is believed to have been founded by Shankara, the 9th-century Hindu philosopher. The site benefited from the direct patronage of the early **Vijayanagara** rulers in the 14th century.

Vidyashankara Temple,
mid-14th century

This temple dates from the early Vijayanagara period. It is unusual in its layout: both the sanctuary with its surrounding passageway and the attached mandapa are provided with numerous wall projections in the typical Hoysala style; the result is a plan with almost rounded ends. The outer walls have continuous basement mouldings and regularly positioned pilasters framing small sculptures. The tower which rises above is virtually circular in plan. A multi-faceted dome-like roof and a pot finial are positioned above; on the front (east) is a projection with a vaulted roof.

Elephant balustrades flank the entrance steps to both mandapa and passageway; guardian figures with clubs protect the doorways. The interior columns are carved with rearing beasts and riders; the brackets are fashioned as projecting figures.

SRINIVASANALLUR

Koranganatha Temple, *c.* 927

In this fine example of a small-scale Hindu temple of the middle Chola period the towered sanctuary is attached to a small mandapa. The basement has friezes of animated yalis and makaras. The wall pilasters frame deeply cut images of Dakshinamurti discoursing with sages (centre niche, south), Bhikshatanamurti (south), Brahma with devotees (centre niche, north) and attendant maidens (west). The elegant postures of the figures, which are often turned at a slight angle to the wall, and the delicate modelling are remarkable. The pediments over the central niches are carved in considerable detail with foliated makaras and miniature figures. The pyramidal tower, which contains an upper sanctuary, is capped by a square roof. Foliate decoration is incised around the doorway on the east.

SUCHINDRAM

The Hindu temple here is one of the holiest in southern India, being situated only 6 km (4 miles) from **Kanyakumari**, the southernmost point of the peninsula. The temple, originally a foundation of the Pandya period, was greatly expanded in the 17th century under the patronage of Tirumala, the Nayaka ruler of **Madurai**. In later times, the temple served as the royal sanctuary of the Travancore rulers.

Shiva Temple, mostly 17th century

The temple is contained within a rectangular enclosure, approached on the east through the soaring tower of the principal gopura. Parallel to the enclosure walls are four broad streets used for chariot festivals. A street leading down to the river extends eastwards from the gateway. Immediately north of the temple is a large tank with a small pavilion in the middle.

A long colonnade with columns carved with donor figures and attendant maidens precedes the main entrance to the temple. Sculptures of Shiva and Parvati on Nandi, Ganesha and Subrahmanya are placed over the main façade of the colonnade. The gopura, which was completed only in the 19th century, rises in a soaring pyramid of seven diminishing storeys. Together with the vaulted roof and its arched ends, these are completely covered with plaster figures. The passageway within the gateway is flanked by demonic figures and smaller panels of Shiva dancing (north) and Trivikrama (east). The upper chambers within the tower have 19th-century paintings depicting events from the Ramayana epic and local legends.

On entering the enclosure, the first structure is a small square pavilion. The figures on the corner columns of this pavilion, such as Manmatha, Rati, Arjuna and Karna, are fashioned almost in the round and are among the finest examples of Nayaka art. South of this mandapa begins the broad colonnade which surrounds the principal shrine. The massive piers are adorned with carvings of women, donors and a host of subsidiary figures. Large brackets and crouching yalis above support a flat ceiling. Small shrines and stores are also incorporated into the colonnade.

The Alankara Mandapa on the north has its piers fashioned as rearing yalis or as clusters of colonnettes with multiple brackets. Nearby, to the east, is the Chitra

Sabha, a columned mandapa with sculptures of Shaiva divinities and saints. A monolithic altar inside has elephants and serpents carved on to its side; the mirror in the shrine is believed to represent the formless aspect of Shiva.

A particularly large Nandi image in plaster-covered masonry faces the Chemparakaman Mandapa. Both Shaiva and Vaishnava figures adorn the columns of this long hall; the ceiling is painted with floral designs. Friezes on the outer walls illustrate episodes from the Ramayana and Krishna legends. At the end of the mandapa is a cluster of shrines housing accessory divinities such as Durga, Ganapati and Vishnu. Processional images are stored in a chamber to the north; to the west, a small chamber displays important bronze sculptures of Shiva and Uma. Most of these structures and their divinities date from the 12th century onwards.

The principal sanctuary, which enshrines a linga, is a modest 9th-century temple; of the same date is the Vishnu shrine to the south. Both these buildings have moulded basements and pilastered walls; no sculptures are preserved in the niches.

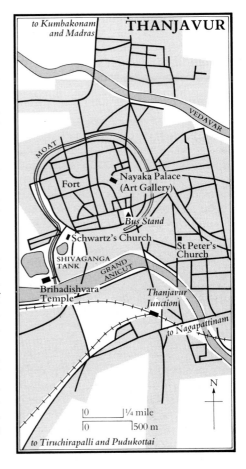

THANJAVUR

This Hindu site attained prominence under the 9th–12th-century Chola rulers, who established one of their capitals here. The town maintained its importance in later times and was a Nayaka stronghold in the 16th–17th centuries. The circular fort surrounded by a moat dates from the 18th-century Maratha period. Within the fort stands the palace of the Nayakas (see Volume II); the celebrated Brihadishvara temple is situated to the south-west.

Brihadishvara Temple, *c.* 1010

Monumental in concept, design and execution, this temple is the greatest architectural achievement of the Chola era. It was a royal foundation inaugurated by Rajaraja I (*c.* 985–1012), who personally donated the gilded pot finial at the summit of the tower.

The temple stands in the middle of a large rectangular court partly occupied by other smaller shrines; it is entered on the east through two gateways. The square sanctuary, which is surrounded by a narrow passageway, adjoins an antechamber and a long columned mandapa on the east, approached through an open porch. The double-storey pilastered walls of the sanctuary are raised on a high basement. This is adorned with yalis and makaras (top moulding) and covered with inscriptions relating the origins, construction and endowments of the temple (lower mouldings). A seated gana supports a spout emerging from the sanctuary basement (north). In the middle of each side of the walls is a doorway flanked by guardian figures with clubs. The wall projections have niches occupied by fully modelled images, mostly of Shiva. Among the finest figures are Bhikshatanamurti (east end of south wall), dancing Shiva (west end of south wall), Harihara (south end of west wall) and Ardhanarishvara (west end of north wall). Other divinities are carved in the semicircular niche tops. Attendant figures flank the pilasters in pots that stand in the recesses.

The steeply pyramidal stone tower rises to a height of about 66 m (217 ft). Thirteen diminishing storeys, each with pilastered walls, an eave and parapet, ascend dramatically to the octagonal dome-like roof. Rajaraja's pot finial is still in place at the apex. The projection on the front (east) is partly obscured by later additions.

The walls of the antechamber are triple-storeyed, with doorways on the north and south sides. The access steps are flanked by balustrades with curved tops and miniature figural panels on the sides. The long mandapa that extends eastwards is only partly completed; the sculptures in the wall niches are mostly unfinished. The entrance porch with an overhanging eave is an addition of the Nayaka period; the peripheral columns are fashioned as rearing beasts. The mandapa doorway in the porch is guarded by large figures with clubs.

In the middle of the sanctuary is a colossal linga 3·66 m (12 ft) high, which is elevated on a circular pedestal. The surrounding passageway is divided into chambers; sculptures here include a large dancing Shiva image (north wall). Paintings also adorn the walls and ceiling, but these are only partly visible, being overlaid by later Nayaka murals. Among the Chola fragments are delicately coloured scenes of Shiva seated on a lion-skin with dancers and musicians, a royal visit to the temple at **Chidambaram** (west wall) and Shiva riding in a chariot drawn by Brahma (north wall). Carved on to the basement of the upper passageway walls is a series of 108 miniature dancers in different postures.

A short distance to the east of the temple is a tall lamp-column and a monolithic Nandi image sheltered by a 16th-century pavilion. The pavilion has slender columns with carvings of devotees on the shafts. Among the subsidiary buildings is the Chandeshvara shrine, which faces southwards towards the main temple. The sanctuary of this small building is crowned with an octagonal roof; the basement and wall details imitate those of the main temple but on a smaller scale.

Another shrine north-west of the main temple is dedicated to Subrahmanya. This finely finished monument dates from the 17th century. It has delicately carved basement mouldings and wall pilasters. The parapet and tower are executed in plaster-covered brickwork. A mandapa in the north-east corner of the enclosure belongs to the same era.

A treasury, museum and library are also included within the courtyard. Lining the enclosure walls is a colonnade with shrines for images of the Dikpalas. The two gateways on the east date from the Chola period. These impressive rectangular structures are dominated by pyramidal towers with vaulted roofs (the outer gateway is higher); sculptures are preserved on the upper storeys. Enormous guardian figures protect the east entrance to the inner gateway. Small carvings on the basement beneath illustrate Shaiva legends, such as the marriage of Shiva and Parvati, and Shiva protecting Markandeya.

Art Gallery

This collection is housed within one of the palace halls. It is famous for its Chola sculptures, especially the bronzes that have been collected from various sites in the vicinity.

Granite sculptures of the 10th century include a damaged but delicately modelled Ardhanarishvara (53), standing Shiva with elaborate headdress from Sendalai (40), Shiva as Dakshinamurti seated beneath a tree (100) and Brahma (16). A seated Buddha from Pattisvaram (18) testifies to the later development of Buddhism in southern India. Among the many 12th-century sculptures is an interesting series from **Darasuram**. This includes an image of Shiva with begging-bowl, fly-whisk and dog (64), attended by the wives of the ascetics and by ganas (58–69). Other sculptures are Shiva as the hunter (28) and a remarkable dancing image of Shiva triumphantly holding up the skin of the elephant demon (19).

The Chola bronzes are among the finest in India. Depictions of Shiva in his various aspects predominate. As the archer (with bow and arrow missing), the god is delicately poised with a slight tilt in his posture (19–21). With Parvati, Shiva is shown standing (34–35), sometimes gently taking the hand of the goddess (88–91) or seated with the miniature figure of Skanda (112, for instance). The masterpiece of the collection shows Shiva, leaning slightly with one arm outstretched, with Parvati (86–87). The refined modelling of these figures, the meticulous detailing of the costumes and snake headdress of the god, and the subtle facial expressions are unsurpassed. Shiva as naked Bhikshatanamurti, accompanied by a jumping dog (92), and an eight-armed Bhairava figure (93) are other fine figures. Many of these examples date from the 11th century and come from Tiruvengadu.

There are several splendid images of Shiva dancing with one foot upraised and the hair and tassels flying outwards; the god is surrounded by a halo of flames. The finest examples are the 11th-century bronzes from Tiruvelvikudi (110) and Jambavanodai, the unusual figure from Kiranur without any flying hair (71) and example from Vedavanyam.

Among the more subtly modelled standing images of Parvati are examples from Tiruvelvikudi (111), **Kilaiyur** (72) and Voimedu (27). The Vijayanagara style is represented by a seated Parvati image (97) and by Kali with her hair standing on end (109).

Several Vaishnava figures are also fine pieces. These include dancing baby Krishna (47) and standing Vishnu (54), both from Peruntottam, and Vishnu seated with Lakshmi (50–51). There are numerous depictions of saints and devotees: for example, Sundara from **Kilaiyur** (99) and Pattinattar and Kannappar from Tiruvengadu (173).

TIRUCHIRAPALLI AND SRIRANGAM

Dominated by a granite rock rising steeply more than 83 m (270 ft) above the Cauvery river, Tiruchirapalli has been an important Hindu centre since Chola times. However, apart from two shrines excavated into the sides of the rock, there are almost no remains dating from earlier than the 17th century. At the summit of the rock is a recent Ganesha temple; there is a Shiva sanctuary lower down. (For the other monuments of the town see Volume II.)

On Srirangam island in the Cauvery river, 3 km (2 miles) north of the town, are the Ranganatha and Jambukeshvara complexes, which are the most important Hindu sanctuaries in the vicinity.

TIRUCHIRAPALLI

Upper Cave Temple, early 7th century

This temple is located at the top of the second flight of steps. It is contemporary with cave temples at **Mamallapuram** and **Mandagappattu**, having been executed during the reign of the Pallava ruler Mahendravarman I (c. 580–630). The exterior of the columned mandapa,

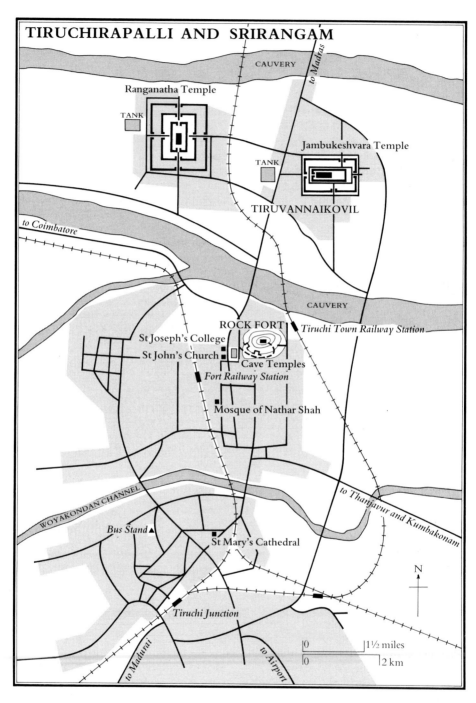

TIRUCHIRAPALLI AND SRIRANGAM

CAUVERY

to Madras

Ranganatha Temple

TANK

Jambukeshvara Temple

TANK

TIRUVANNAIKOVIL

to Coimbatore

CAUVERY

ROCK FORT | *Tiruchi Town Railway Station*

St Joseph's College

St John's Church

Cave Temples

Fort Railway Station

Mosque of Nathar Shah

WOYAKONDAN CHANNEL

to Thanjavur and Kumbakonam

Bus Stand

St Mary's Cathedral

N

Tiruchi Junction

to Madurai

to Airport

| 0 | 1½ miles |
| 0 | 2 km |

which is entered on the side, is unadorned except for scrollwork medallions incised on to the column shafts. The doorway to the small shrine (right wall) is flanked by guardian figures with clubs. Carved on to the left wall of the mandapa is a panel depicting Shiva receiving the goddess Ganga in his hair.

Lower Cave Temple, 8th century

This temple belongs to the Pandya era. It consists of a columned mandapa with two side shrines with carvings of Shiva and Vishnu on the rear walls. Other deities appear in the niches on the rear wall of the mandapa thus: Ganesha, Subrahmanya, Brahma (centre), Surya and Durga. This full range of divinities is typical of Pandya art. The columns are massive and unadorned.

SRIRANGAM

This long island in the middle of the Cauvery river, considered the Ganga of southern India, is particularly holy; here the great Vaishnava complex dedicated to Ranganatha is located. About 2 km (1½ miles) to the east, in the village of Tiruvannaikovil, is the Jambukeshvara temple, which is a Shaiva sanctuary. Several minor shrines and tanks are scattered over the island and there are numerous bathing ghats.

Ranganatha Temple,
mostly 13th–17th centuries

This is one of the largest and most complete sacred complexes in southern India. It was founded during the Chola period but received its first substantial additions under the patronage of the 13th-century rulers of the Pandya and Hoysala dynasties. In the early 14th century the temple was sacked twice by the Muslim invaders. Systematic expansion took place in the 16th–17th centuries under the sponsorship of the Vijayanagara and Nayaka rulers; construction on the outer gateways continues even today.

The temple is laid out in a series of seven concentric rectangular enclosures defined by high walls. The overall area contained within these walls is 63 hectares (155½ acres). Gopuras in the middle of four sides are aligned along roads that proceed axially towards the innermost zone. The outer three enclosures are occupied by houses; the majority of the town's population lives here. The broad roads separating these outer enclosures are used for chariot festivals. The roads running northwards and southwards are lined with shops; beyond the complex these roads lead to the river.

The gopuras increase in size from the innermost enclosure outwards. The outer gateway on the south, which was completed to a height of 72 m (236 ft) only in 1987, is one of the largest in southern India. Mostly dating from the 16th–17th centuries, the gateways follow a standard scheme. They have brick and plaster pyramidal towers with projecting porches in the middle of each diminishing storey. The walls and the vaulted roofs with arched ends and pot finials are completely covered with vividly coloured plaster figures and decoration. The finest gopura is on the east (fourth enclosure wall); it is a superbly proportioned structure with double projections in the middle of each side and a slightly concave profile.

Buildings of architectural interest are located in the fourth enclosure. On the south side is the impressive Rangavilasa Mandapa, which has elongated columns covered with a diversity of carvings. Immediately to the west of this is the small Veugopala shrine. This was erected during the period of the Nayaka expansion of Srirangam in the late 16th century. The finely finished shrine is built in a late Chola style; it has a delicately moulded framed by pilasters and miniature eaves. Fully modelled maidens holding musical instruments, mirrors, a parrot or branches of a tree are carved on to the walls. The sanctuary is crowned with a whitewashed hemispherical roof. Paintings within the porch, probably dating from the 17th century, depict Krishna

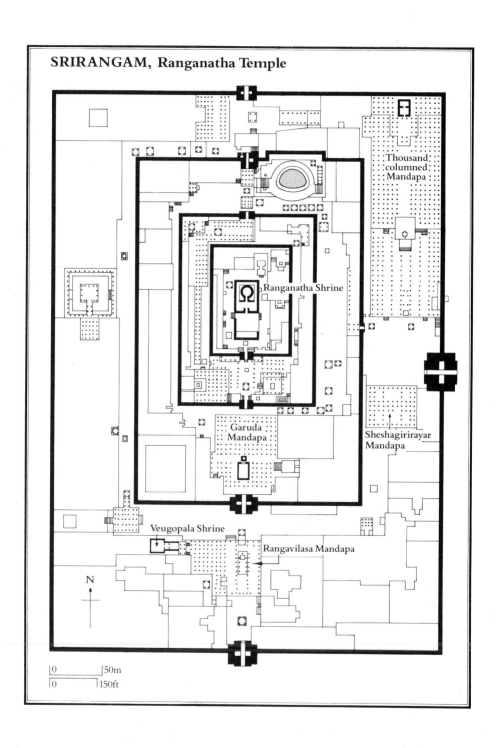

SRIRANGAM, Ranganatha Temple

Thousand columned Mandapa

Ranganatha Shrine

Garuda Mandapa

Sheshagirirayar Mandapa

Veugopala Shrine

Rangavilasa Mandapa

N

0   50m

0   150ft

playing the flute surrounded by gopis.

The north-eastern part of the fourth enclosure is occupied by an expansive mandapa with carved columns. A small pavilion inside stores the processional images used at festival times. To the south (in front of the east gopura) is the 16th-century Sheshagirirayar Mandapa. The peripheral piers of this structure are fashioned as mythical beasts or rearing horses with riders and attendant warriors. The animation and virtuosity of the almost three-dimensional carvings are unsurpassed; the weapons, bridles and costumes are all rendered in remarkable detail. Together with the similarly fashioned piers at **Vellore**, these are the outstanding examples of sculptural art during the Vijayanagara period. Within the mandapa, the columns have attached colonnettes as well as a host of figural motifs.

Also in the fourth enclosure is a small museum in which stone and bronze sculptures, as well as several interesting ivory plaques, are exhibited. Most of these date from the Nayaka period.

On the south side of the third enclosure (between the two gateways) is the Garuda Mandapa. Its columns have characteristic Nayaka sculptures of attendant maidens, courtly donors and a host of accessory themes. A small shrine within the mandapa houses an image of Garuda.

The innermost sanctuary (inaccessible to non-Hindus) is a modest part-circular structure, but the tower is capped with a gilded hemispherical dome. The arched projection on the front has a figure of Vishnu standing within a highly decorated frame covered with gold leaf. In the corridor surrounding the sanctuary (second enclosure) are paintings that date from the late Nayaka period. These depict local legends as well as episodes from the Vishnu Purana. At the end of one frieze is a portrait of a Nayaka patron of **Madurai** together with his queens in a courtly setting.

Jambukeshvara Temple,
mostly 17th century

With its four concentric enclosures, this is a smaller complex than the Ranganatha temple. It also is a fine example of Nayaka architecture. The seven towered gopuras are large-scale constructions, magnificently proportioned and elaborately decorated. The west gopura of the outermost enclosure leads directly into a columned mandapa. On the right (south) is a tank fed by a spring; the corresponding space on the left (north) is occupied by a thousand-columned mandapa with decorated piers incised with scrollwork. Extended brackets with pendant lotus buds are supported on large seated yalis; maidens are carved in high relief on the end columns.

At the heart of the complex is a small sanctuary housing the Ap (water) linga; this is immersed in a basin continually fed by a natural spring.

TIRUMALA

This Hindu pilgrimage is celebrated for the popular cult of Venkateshvara, an aspect of Vishnu, whose shrine is located here. This deity benefited from the direct patronage of the **Vijayanagara** rulers, who established their later capital at Chandragiri, 11 km (7 miles) to the south-west. (See Volume II.)

Venkateshvara's sanctuary is picturesquely located in seven wooded hills (Venkatachalam), about 700 m (2,300 ft) above the plain. A long flight of covered steps and a road connect the temple with the town of **Tirupati**, 11 km (7 miles) to the south-east. Pilgrims from all parts of India frequent Tirumala, offering substantial contributions in gold and silver, jewellery and other valuables. The temple is reputed to be the wealthiest in India, with no less than ten thousand daily visitors; it finances the many rest-houses of the pilgrimage town which has grown up around the temple.

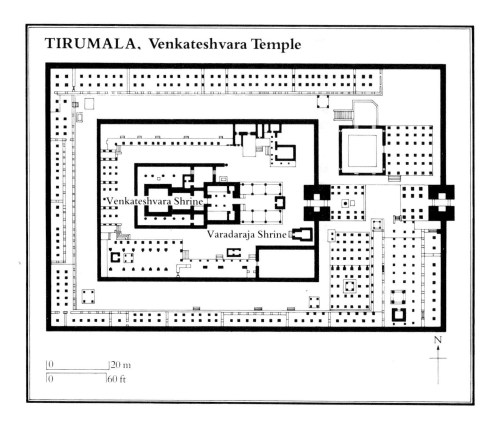

TIRUMALA, Venkateshvara Temple

Venkateshvara Shrine

Varadaraja Shrine

0   20 m

0   60 ft

N

Venkateshvara Temple,
10th century and later

This temple has been recently renovated
to provide facilities for the large numbers
of devotees who visit the shrine daily. The
complex is entered through a single
towered gopura on the east side. This is
possibly a Vijayanagara foundation but
has been much rebuilt, especially the
upper portions. Immediately inside the
gateway is a columned portico in which
are displayed life-size portrait sculptures
of the royal patrons. These include copper
images of Krishnadeva Raya and his two
queens (right) and stone images of
Achyutadeva Raya and his queen (left).
Left of the gateway are two columned
mandapas, each with a small shrine. One
has finely carved piers, some with warriors on rearing horses, in the typical
Vijayanagara style. There are numerous

reliefs, including depictions of Narasimha
and Krishna. To the right of the gateway
is a later construction which abuts a well.
Colonnades and stores occupy much of
the outer enclosure. A portico has columns
carved with reliefs, including attendant
maidens and embracing couples. The
lofty flag-column and altar in the middle
of the enclosure are embossed with gold
sheets. The gateway leading into the inner
enclosure is possibly a Chola foundation;
the tower above is much later, with
recently restored sculptures. The gateway
has sheets of embossed silver covering the
jambs and lintels.
Within the inner enclosure, the
principal temple stands to the west. To
the south is a small 14th-century shrine
housing an image of Varadaraja. A
kitchen, colonnades, stores and several
minor shrines line the peripheral walls of
the court.

The sanctuary itself is a modest structure dating from the 9th–10th century. A later tower capped by a domed roof covered with gold sheets rises over the sanctuary. The adjoining mandapa has columns with piers and carvings; gold sheets cover the overhanging eave. Within the sanctuary, the object of worship is a standing image of Vishnu; the dress, garlands and high crown of the god are all encrusted with jewels and precious metals. On either side are images of Shridevi and Bhudevi.

Some distance away from the main complex is a large rectangular tank with stepped sides; a columned pavilion in the middle has a small towered superstructure.

Museum

This displays a collection of stone, metal and wooden images, copper-plate inscriptions and paintings; many of these date from the Vijayanagara era. There are also votive figurines, lamps, musical instruments and arms.

TIRUPATI

Of the many temples at this Hindu pilgrimage centre, the Govindaraja complex in the middle of the town is the largest. North of the town rise the red bluffs of the Venkata hills, where the celebrated sanctuary of **Tirumala** is located, 11 km (7 miles) to the north-west.

Govindaraja Temple,
mostly 16th–17th centuries

This temple is invisible from the surrounding streets. Unusually, the complex consists of a sequence of three enclosures, each entered through a gopura aligned along an east–west street. Beyond the temple to the east is a square tank with a small pavilion in the middle.

The first gopura is an impressive structure. The lower stone walls are typical of the Nayaka style, with a high double basement with wall pilasters, some in pots; the concrete tower is modern. The seven storeys have a typical vaulted roof. Within the first enclosure are two pavilions used for the festivals at which the deities are put in swings. The columns of one of these pavilions are adorned with finely carved scrollwork issuing out of makaras.

The second gopura is smaller; its lower portions are assigned to the Vijayanagara period. Within the gateway, carved panels depict episodes from the Krishna story and the Ramayana epic. Columned mandapas and minor shrines crowd the second enclosure. The first shrine on the left (south) is dedicated to the tortoise incarnation of Vishnu. Within an adjacent mandapa are stored processional palanquins and large gilded images of Garuda and Hanuman.

The third gopura is even earlier; its simple basement and unadorned walls are typical of the 14th–15th century. Within the third enclosure are the two principal sanctuaries. These enshrine images of Vishnu reclining on the serpent (north) and Krishna standing with the bow (south). Another minor shrine has an icon of Lakshmi, identified with the poetess Andal. The doorway to the Vishnu shrine is covered with embossed brass sheets; the sanctuary is approached through a long antechamber where metal processional images are displayed. The architecture of these shrines indicates a 9th–10th-century date; the mandapa and roof are later. The mandapa in the southern part of this enclosure is typical of the later Vijayanagara style. The piers have large animal brackets. In the middle of the mandapa is a pavilion with exquisitely worked basalt piers and an eave on curved ribs. The shrine within this mandapa houses images of Vishnu and consorts.

Kapaleshvara Tirtha

This sacred spot is located at the foot of the hills, about 2 km (1½ miles) north of the town. The tirtha consists of an artificial pond surrounded by colonnades; during the rainy season the pond is fed by a natural waterfall. Within the upper colonnade on the right (east) is a sanctuary partly built into a rocky ledge. A linga sheltered by a brass naga is worshipped as Kapaleshvara.

Shri Venkateshvara Art Museum

This museum houses an exhibition of photographs, models, diagrams and small metal objects. These are arranged to explain the principles of Vaishnava artistic traditions, architecture and rituals.

TIRUPPARANKUNRAM

Although the temple at this Hindu site is a late Nayaka structure, a group of rock-cut shrines in the vicinity belongs to the earlier Pandya era. These 8th-century monuments are of interest because of the range of Hindu divinities carved on to the walls. Their massive and unadorned architecture is comparable to that of the cave temples at **Mandagappattu** and **Tiruchirapalli**.

Subrahmanya Cave Temple, 773

This temple has a shrine dedicated to Durga in which the goddess is flanked by figures of Ganesha and Subrahmanya; lateral shrines are devoted to Shiva and Vishnu. The outer wall of the shrine is adorned with a Natesha composition in two panels, with Shiva dancing on the dwarf (right) and Parvati, Nandi, musicians and ganas (left).

TIRUPPUDAIMARADUR

Narumbunatha Temple,
mostly 16th century

This Hindu temple was enlarged during the Vijayanagara period, when the gopura on the east was added. Within the hollow tower of this gateway are chambers on each of the five ascending storeys. The plaster walls of these chambers preserve paintings from the late Vijayanagara era. The colours of the murals are brilliant, with red predominating; the linework is generally heavily applied in black paint. The paintings illustrate both mythological and courtly subjects; there are also animated scenes of reception and battle. Of particular interest are the depictions of an Arab ship carrying horses (second chamber) and the marriage of Minakshi to Sundareshvara (third chamber).

TIRUTTANI

Virattaneshvara Temple, 9th century

This small Hindu temple with an apsidal-ended sanctuary enshrining a linga dates from the late Pallava period. The vaulted roof, also on an apsidal-ended plan, has an arched projection adorned with the figures of a Somaskanda group. The sanctuary is entered through an antechamber and later porch. The niches preserve sculptures of Ganesha (south) and Durga (north) on the antechamber walls; Dakshinamurti, Vishnu and Brahma are depicted on the curved sanctuary walls. Grouped within the mandapa are loose sculptures of the Matrikas, Shiva, Ganesha and Surya.

TIRUVANNAMALAI

This town is known for its Shiva temple, one of the largest in southern India. A great Hindu festival takes place here in November–December, accompanied by a popular cattle fair. On the night of the tenth day, a huge bonfire is lit on the summit of the rocky hill above the town. This fire burns for many days and is visible from a great distance. Devotees prostrate themselves at the sight of the

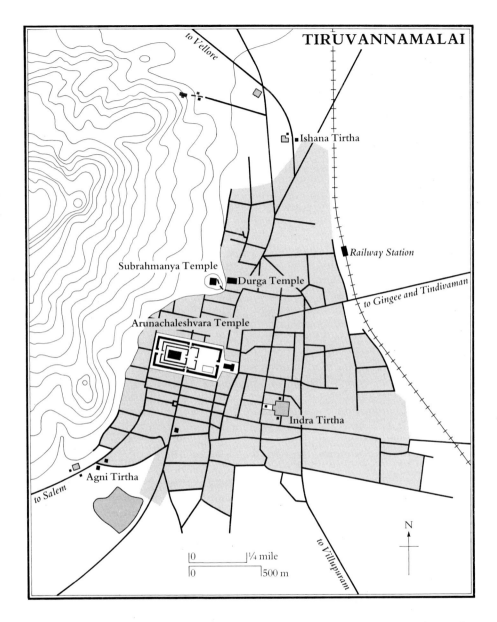

TIRUVANNAMALAI

to Vellore

Ishana Tirtha

Railway Station

to Gingee and Tindivaman

Subrahmanya Temple

Durga Temple

Arunachaleshvara Temple

Indra Tirtha

Agni Tirtha

to Salem

to Villupuram

N

|0 |¼ mile
|0 |500 m

flames, which are considered to be the manifestation of Shiva's fiery linga.

Other smaller shrines within the town are dedicated to Durga and Subrahmanya. Tanks or tirthas are associated with three of the directional guardian divinities: Agni, Indra and Ishana. Float festivals regularly take place here. The ashram of the celebrated guru Ramana Maharishi,

who died in 1950, is located on the outskirts of the town.

Arunachaleshvara Temple,
mostly 16th–17th centuries

This complex is remarkable for the clarity of its layout. Three sets of walls define concentric rectangular enclosures, with the eastern portion of each expanded to form large courts. The complex is entered from the east; in front of the principal gateway there are two adjoining colonnades with central walkways. One colonnade has a corbelled timber ceiling supported on curved brackets; the other has a painted stone ceiling.

Of the four gopuras in the outermost enclosure walls, those on the east and north are the largest. The former is an immense structure rising no less than 66 m (217 ft) high. The lower portions of the gopuras date from the late Vijayanagara period but the towers are later; some are still being renovated. The ornamentation of the lower granite elements is highly elaborate, with decorated basements, pilasters and eaves. Finely carved panels are inserted into the outer walls of the eastern gopura: for example, Shiva as Bhikshatanamurti (middle of north side) and Shiva dancing with the skin of the elephant (south corner). Ten diminishing brick and plaster storeys rise above to create the soaring pyramidal mass of the tower. This is capped by a vaulted roof with arched ends. Within this gopura, and also that on the north, doorway jambs and wall pilasters are covered with figures of Shiva, dancers and maidens clutching branches of scrollwork. Related themes illustrating Shaiva subjects are carved on to the ceilings; there are even traces of paintings in the east gopura.

Passing through the east gopura, the outermost of the three courts is reached. Immediately on the right (north) is an immense thousand-columned mandapa belonging to the Vijayanagara period. Piers have typical yalis with riders; there is a raised dais in the middle. On the west side of the mandapa is a linga chamber, its roof now partly obscured by the raised floor of the hall. On the south of the court is a small but ornate shrine dedicated to Subrahmanya. The intricate carving of the columns and outer walls is typical of

the later Vijayanagara style. South of this shrine is a large stepped tank.

Four smaller gopuras with less decorated walls date mostly from the 14th century; the plaster carvings on the towers, which have been recently renovated, lead into the intermediate court. Here there is another stepped tank and also a large columned mandapa with an open porch facing south.

Access to the innermost enclosure is provided by a single gateway on the east; this is a modest unadorned structure, probably dating from the 11th-century Chola period. The two principal shrines of the complex are located within this enclosure. The one dedicated to Shiva is situated on an axis with the gateway. The principal sanctuary is a Chola structure, approached through a long antechamber. Stone images set into the outer sanctuary walls include Dakshinamurti (south), Shiva appearing out of the linga (west) and Brahma (north); a linga is enshrined within. This sanctuary is bounded on four sides by extensive corridors. These date from the 17th-century Nayaka period and have characteristic perspectives of receding piers overhung by projecting brackets. The corridor leading up to the sanctuary doorway is adorned with brass and glass lamps; an ornate brass frame demarcates the doorway. Stone lingas and metal images, particularly of Shaiva saints, are housed in the surrounding colonnades. Two small but delicately decorated shrines dedicated to Ganesha (left) and Subrahmanya (right) flank the outer porch. A brass lamp-column and a Nandi image are positioned in front.

The goddess shrine is set back to the right (north). The almost three-dimensional carvings on the interior piers are fine examples of the Nayaka style, which illustrate different aspects of the goddess. Other smaller shrines, dating back to the 12th–13th centuries, are preserved nearby.

TIRUVARUR

The temple at this Hindu site is one of the largest in southern India. The Soma-skanda form of Shiva enshrined here, together with Nataraja at **Chidambaram**, was the most honoured deity of the Chola rulers. The earliest Tamil saints, such as Appar and Jnana-sambandha, glorified the Tiruvarur divinity.

Tyagaraja Temple, 13th–17th centuries

Originally a Chola foundation, this temple complex reveals a pattern of growth over several centuries, culminating in the Nayaka additions of the 17th century.

At the heart of the complex are the east-facing shrines of Vanmikanatha and Tyagaraja. Other shrines, including two goddess sanctuaries, and columned mandapas occupy three concentric rectangular enclosures; these are connected by gopuras distributed along an east–west axis.

The earliest structure is the Vanmikanatha shrine, which in its original 10th-century form was a square sanctuary preceded by an antechamber. Pilastered walls with carved panels, overlaid by thick plaster, are elevated on a moulded basement. The pyramidal tower is crowned with a square roof; most of the plaster decoration is later. The adjacent Tyagaraja shrine is a 13th-century rebuilding of an earlier structure, with

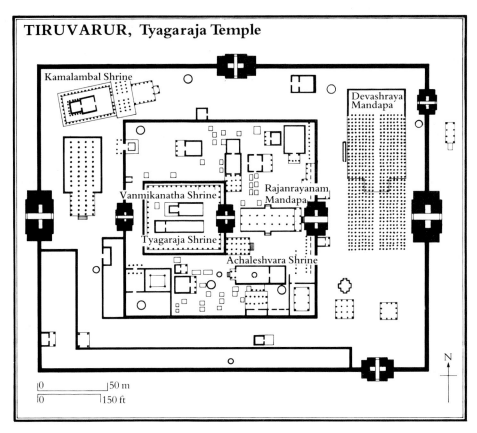

TIRUVARUR, Tyagaraja Temple

Kamalambal Shrine

Devashraya Mandapa

Vanmikanatha Shrine

Rajanrayanam Mandapa

Tyagaraja Shrine

Achaleshvara Shrine

0   50 m
0   150 ft

N

typical late Chola features, such as yalis on the basement, pilastered niches with semicircular pediments and a tower dominated by a large hemispherical roof. The sculptures in the middle of the sanctuary walls depict Dakshinamurti (south), Vishnu (west) and Brahma (north). Enshrined here is the principal divinity of the temple, Shiva, together with Uma and Skanda. The columned mandapa linking both shrines is also a 13th-century construction. The two shrines stand in the middle of a courtyard surrounded by a colonnade in which several fine bronze images are displayed.

Another early building is the 10th-century Achaleshvara shrine in the second enclosure. This west-facing temple conforms to the standard early Chola scheme, with a simple basement, pilastered walls and pyramidal tower crowned with a hemispherical roof. The finely modelled sculptures in the wall niches include Dakshinamurti (south), Shiva appearing out of the linga (east) and Brahma (north) in the central projections of the sanctuary. Elaborate plaster decoration and figurative sculpture adorn the tower. The columned mandapa is a 12th-century addition.

Almost all the other shrines have been completely rebuilt. Some are as late as the 17th century; the north-facing Nilotpalambal shrine of the second enclosure is earlier in parts. The Kamalambal shrine in the third (outer) enclosure is a complete temple with its own towered gateway and lamp-column. Its long sanctuary, unusually oriented north-east, is surrounded by a colonnade.

Of the various columned mandapas, the Rajanrayanam Mandapa is the oldest. It is situated in the second enclosure between the two gopuras. The seated yalis at the bases of the peripheral columns are typical of the 13th century; the central part of the ceiling was raised in the Vijayanagara era. The largest mandapa of the complex is the Devashraya Mandapa; this occupies the north-east corner.

Several columns have friezes of miniature façades in the typical Chola style; composite columns from the later era are also found here. Paintings on the ceiling depict the exploits of the mythical king Muchukunda, who brought the image of Tyagaraja down from heaven. On the south side of the mandapa is an unusual group of plain columns unattached to any structure; these may have supported temporary shelters during festival times.

The gopuras, especially the east gateways to the second and third enclosures, are monumental structures, among the most impressive of the late Chola period. Typical features are the high basement (panels of rearing yalis), the double-storey pilastered walls with sculptures (particularly Durga, Surya and dancing Shiva) and the pyramidal multi-storey tower with an elongated vaulted roof. The northern and western gateways of the third enclosure are additions of the Vijayanagara and the Nayaka periods.

Immediately outside the complex, to the east, is a small shrine with a porch. Wheels are carved in high relief on to the basement. The figure beneath one of these wheels refers to a legend in which a prince was crushed to death but restored to life by Shiva. Beyond the outermost western gateway is the immense Kamalaya tank. On an island in the middle of the water is a temple with a small gopura.

TRIBHUVANAM

This fine example of a late Chola Hindu temple is located 6 km (4 miles) north-east of **Kumbakonam**.

Kampahareshvara Temple,
early 13th century

This is the last large-scale towered sanctuary of the Chola era; it was a foundation of Kulottunga III (1178–1218).

The temple is contained within two enclosures: the outer one is entered on the east and west through gopuras; the inner one, which is surrounded by a colonnade, has a single gopura on the east. The temple itself, which stands in the middle of the courtyard, has a sanctuary and columned mandapa separated by a transept from two large mandapas on the east. Steps on the north and south provide access to the transept; another flight approaches the outermost mandapa from the south.

The pilastered walls are elevated on a basement carved with friezes of yalis; miniature panels illustrate scenes from the Ramayana epic. The outer walls have full-height pilasters with circular shafts defining projections; secondary pilasters flank sculpture niches while others stand in pots in the recesses. Only a few original carved panels are preserved; Durga standing on the buffalo head (middle of north side) is one of the finest. The painted icons are recent. Above the walls is a parapet with large roof forms. The steeply pyramidal tower consists of five diminishing storeys, each repeating on a diminishing scale the form beneath; the crowning roof is hemispherical. Throughout, the plaster decoration, which has been renovated, is highly ornate.

Pilastered niches in the mandapa walls are mostly empty, but the semicircular pediments are filled with reliefs. Stone windows have perforated designs. Warrior figures and large yalis are carved on to the curved balustrades that flank the access steps to the transept. The basement of the projecting porch on the south side of the outer mandapa is adorned with dancing figures and attendant maidens. Many of the mandapa columns are covered with architectural friezes; the peripheral columns have attached pilasters and emphasized upper capitals.

North of the main temple stands a small Chandeshvara shrine with a hemispherical roof. Other subsidiary shrines are located in the spacious outer court. The one dedicated to the goddess has a rectangular vaulted roof, with figures of Devi carved on to the outer walls. These shrines and the gopuras may be compared with the principal temple, with which they are contemporary. Many of the sculptures on the walls of the gateways are intact.

TRICHUR

Vadakkunnatha Temple,
12th century and later

This is one of the largest Hindu complexes in Kerala. The temple preserves different types of shrines as well as fine examples of carved woodwork and mural painting.

The nucleus of the complex is a rectangular court surrounded by a colonnade in the middle of which are three west-facing shrines. The two northern shrines, dedicated to Vadakkunnatha and Shankara Narayana, are circular structures, which contain square sanctuaries surrounded by passageways. The third, southernmost shrine is dedicated to Rama; this consists of a sanctuary and passageway laid out on a square plan with an attached columned mandapa. To the west of each shrine is an open pavilion. South of the Vadakkunnatha shrine is a row of seven altars for the Matrikas. A smaller shrine of Ganesha is interposed between the two northern shrines.

In the two circular shrines, simple basement mouldings support masonry pilastered walls and niches. The conical timber roofs are covered with metal sheets; pot finials are positioned above. The Shankara Narayana shrine has two tiers of sloping roofs. In the Rama shrine the masonry walls have pilastered projections; secondary pilasters frame niches, now empty, with pediments. Over the walls rises the parapet with its miniature roof motifs. The walls of the superstructure are similarly treated. Two tiers of overhanging angled roofs shelter the

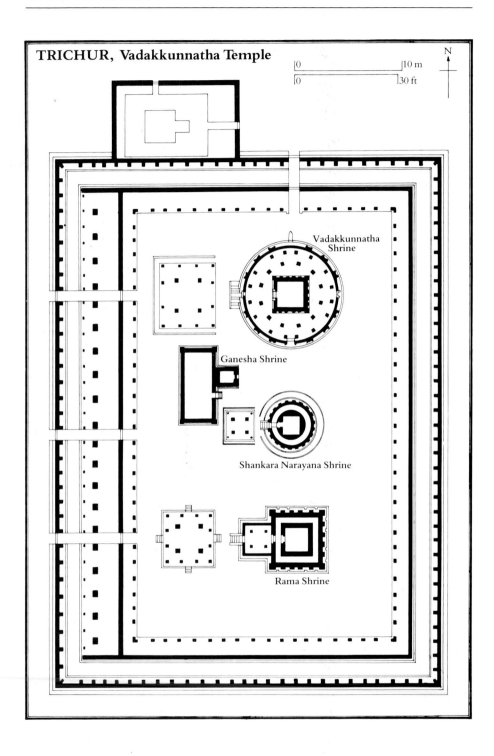

TRICHUR, Vadakkunnatha Temple

0 — 10 m
0 — 30 ft

N

Vadakkunnatha Shrine

Ganesha Shrine

Shankara Narayana Shrine

Rama Shrine

walls; arched dormer windows project from the upper roof.

The shrine walls are richly painted and the timber screen walls and brackets have ornate carvings. Most of this work dates from no earlier than the 18th century. The finest paintings are on the curved passage-way walls of the Shankara Narayana shrine; these depict two large composi-tions of Nataraja, and Vishnu reclining on Ananta, as well as scenes from the Mahabharata epic.

Smaller shrines housing lesser deities are located in the outer court; the one dedicated to Shasta is apsidal-ended. In the north-west corner of the outer court is the Kuttambalam pavilion used for per-formances of music and drama. This con-struction has an overhanging pyramidal roof with three pot finials on the ridge. An interior portico has lathe-turned wooden columns; the ceiling is exuberantly carved with figural brackets and friezes of lotus ornament.

A stone wall with gateways on four sides surrounds both courts. The gate-ways have pilastered masonry walls and triple tiers of gabled roofs.

Archaeological Museum

This houses a collection of stone, metal and wooden sculptures from the immedi-ate vicinity. Two demonic guardian fig-ures in bronze date from the 17th century. There is also a fine assemblage of brass lamps, many in the shape of birds and animals.

TRIVANDRUM

(For the city and its civic monuments see Volume II.)

Padmanabha Temple,

mostly 18th century

Much of this Hindu complex was reconstructed during the period of

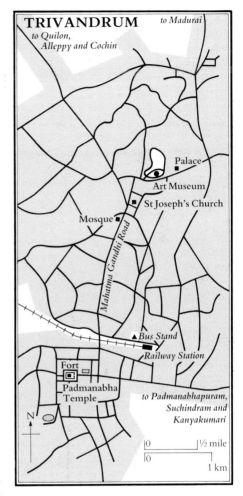

Martandavarma, the ruler of Travancore. At the heart of the complex is a shrine built in the typical Kerala style. The outer walls, which are covered with murals, are sheltered by a double tier of gabled roofs. Three doorways in the rectangular sanc-tuary reveal the face, navel and feet of a large reclining Vishnu image; murals adorn the outer walls. Subsidiary shrines to Krishna, Narasimha and Garuda are also located here. An entrance gateway on the north follows the traditional Kerala pattern with its multi-tiered gable roof.

Other buildings of the complex are more influenced by contemporary Naya-ka traditions. The soaring tower of the east gopura, with its seven ascending storeys capped with a vaulted roof, is exceptionally broad. The colonnade surrounding the shrine and the extensive columned mandapa are both elaborately treated.

Art Museum

This collection has fine metal images from the Kerala region. These include an interesting 9th-century bronze Vishnu with inlaid crystal eyes.

Dating from the 17th–18th century are a silver image of Shasta and bronze figures of Vishnu and Garuda. Among the other metal objects are brass lamps fashioned as miniature female figures.

Numerous wooden sculptures from the same period are also exhibited. These include Indra, Narasimha and other deities, as well as bracket figures such as Durga on the buffalo.

UDIPI

This important Hindu pilgrimage centre in the Kannara region commemorates the birthplace of Madhava, the 12th-century saint. Prominent among the religious establishments here is the Krishna temple. This has a large tank, the Madhava Sarovar, in the middle of which is a small pavilion. There is also a Jain foundation built in the traditional coastal style with overhanging roofs supported on external columns.

UTTARAMERUR

Two Hindu temples at this site date from the period of the Pallava ruler Dantivarman (c. 796–817); not only are they the finest examples of the late Pallava style but they also anticipate later developments during the Chola era.

Sundaravarda Perumal Temple, c. 805

This temple consists of three sanctuaries, one superimposed on the other, each with projecting subsidiary shrines on three sides. Steps from the attached columned mandapa ascend to the upper storeys. Three forms of Vishnu, standing, seated and reclining, are enshrined in the sanctuaries; other aspects of this divinity are housed in the subsidiary shrines.

The moulded basement of the outer walls is unadorned except for yalis and makaras at the corners. Balustrades flanking the steps to the subsidiary shrines are carved with panels, such as Lakshmi (south). The walls are plain except for flat pilasters and shallow niches. Above the overhanging eaves rises the brick and plaster parapet, which has pronounced roof forms over the projecting shrines. The multi-storey tower has a hemispherical roof. Much of the plaster ornamentation of the tower is later.

Kailasanatha Temple,
early 9th century and later

Only the lower part of this sanctuary, which resembles the Sundaravarda Perumal temple, belongs to the Pallava period. The attached mandapa and upper multi-storey tower are mostly 11th-century restorations. Columns within the mandapa have decorated shafts and fluted capitals.

VAIKOM

Shiva Temple, 16th century and later

This large Hindu temple consists of a simple square sanctuary contained within an elliptical columned mandapa. The outer masonry walls are raised on a moulded basement; a squatting gana figure supports the protruding spout (north). Brightly coloured murals occupy the spaces between the pilastered doorways and windows. Dating from the 18th century, these paintings depict dancing Shiva with attendants, Parvati with Ganesha, Garuda supporting Vishnu and his consorts, and other divinities; guardian figures flank the doorways. The murals are sheltered by an overhanging metal roof, which rises in a smooth cone towards the pot finial.

In front of the temple is a detached columned mandapa with a pyramidal roof. Both temple and mandapa are set within a rectangular courtyard. The entrance is a 19th-century portico with a gabled tiled roof; in front of the gateway are elaborate brass lampstands.

VELLORE

The large and substantial fort surrounded by a moat in the middle of this city was the headquarters of Chinna Bomma, a local governor during the Vijayanagara era. Within the fort stands a Hindu complex;

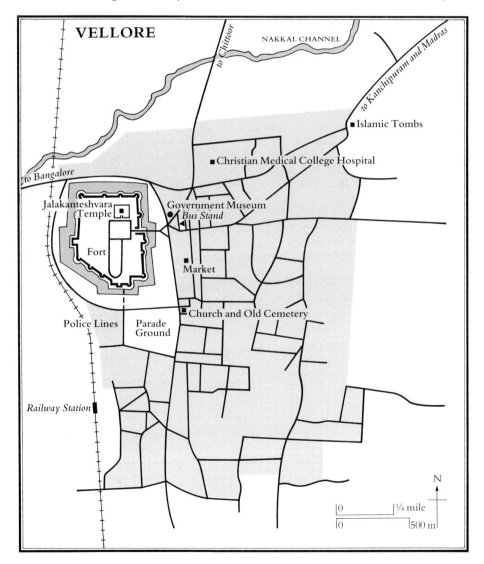

its towering gopura is clearly visible above the walls.

(For the fort and British monuments see Volume II.)

Jalakanteshvara Temple, 16th century

This temple has recently been re-established as a place of worship. Not only is the complex an important example of the Vijayanagara style but almost all of its parts belong to the same period.

The complex is contained within a rectangle of high walls, entered on the south by an imposing gopura. The two lower storeys of this gateway are adorned with mouldings, delicate and ornate pilasters, some standing in pots, and niches, now empty. Above rise the six diminishing storeys of the recently renovated plaster and brick pyramidal tower. Openings in the middle of each side are flanked by guardian figures. The arched ends of the roof are decorated with makaras and monster masks.

Passing through the gateway, the outer enclosure is reached. Immediately to the left is a free-standing columned mandapa, which contains the magnificent carvings for which the temple is famous; the sculptures here are among the finest of the Vijayanagara period, equalled only by those at **Srirangam**. The outer piers are fashioned as rearing lion-like monsters, yalis and richly bridled horses, all with riders; accessory themes include warriors, hunters and other mythical beasts. The vitality of these powerful compositions and the virtuosity of the carving, almost in the round, are unsurpassed. Panels of warriors separated by ganas adorn the basement. The interior columns have panels with miniature figures; other columns are treated as piers with attached colonnettes. The ceilings are elaborately treated; the central panel is carved as a fruit surrounded by parrots hanging upside down.

Another mandapa is located at the south-east corner; colonnades with carved panels on the columns follow the outer walls and detached sculptures are displayed here. A smaller gopura of the standard type, also on the south, leads into the inner enclosure. Within this stands the main temple, a modest building in the typical Vijayanagara manner; the towers, however, are modern renovations. The temple consists of a linga shrine (west) and a Nataraja shrine (north), both opening off a common mandapa. Large guardian figures flank the inner doorway of the principal shrine. A lamp-column and Nandi images are set in front of a pierced stone window in the east wall of the mandapa. Colonnades along the peripheral walls house images of Shaiva saints (south) and Ganesha (west). A fire altar is located on the north; in the north-west corner is a small goddess shrine.

GLOSSARY OF
ARCHITECTURAL TERMS

amalaka, circular ribbed motif (derived from a gourd) at the summit of a temple tower or at the ends of the 'storeys' of a tower

antechamber, chamber preceding the sanctuary

apsidal, part-circular plan, as in the apse of a church

arch-like motif, generally horseshoe-shaped, this motif appears in an enlarged form as an opening in a **chaitya hall** and as a **blind window** in a temple tower; smaller but similar motifs form parts of complicated **pediment** and towered designs

architrave, horizontal beam-like element on free-standing gateways

ashram, rest-house

bagh, garden

bagilu, gateway

bangla, hut with a curved thatch roof in Bengal; imitated in brick temples

basement, lower part of walls, usually adorned with decorated mouldings

basti, Jain temple

bhandara, treasury

bhumi, 'earth'; refers to a horizontal moulding of a **shikhara**

blind arch, blind doorway, blind window, ornamental arch, doorway or window forming part of a wall or tower

bracket, transitional element between a column and beam; imitated in **pilasters**

buttress, wall support

capital, upper part of a column or **pilaster** shaft

cave temple, rock-cut sanctuary or monastery

cenotaph, funerary monument, usually takes the form of an open pavilion with a dome or of a replica of a temple

chaitya hall, Buddhist hall with an **apsidal** end, mostly divided into a central nave and side aisles by two rows of columns, with a votive **stupa** at the end

char bangla, four hut-like temples in Bengal

chaumukha, Jain sanctuary with quadruple votive images approached through four doorways

chhatri, see **cenotaph**

chlorite, soft greenish stone that hardens on exposure permitting intricate carving

chokhang, Tibetan Buddhist prayer hall

chorten, memorial **stupa** in a Tibetan Buddhist religious complex

circumambulation, clockwise movement around a **stupa** or temple **sanctuary** constituting an act of worship; in architecture this movement requires a paved pathway or enclosed passageway

classical, style of Graeco-Roman architecture

corbel, corbelled, projecting horizontal block or stone course that supports a vertical structure or covers an opening

cornice, horizontal band at the top of a wall

cupola, small dome

curvilinear, curved profile, generally of a tower

darwaza, gateway

dharmashala, rest-house for visiting pilgrims

dome-like, hemispherical forms in temple architecture generally created by **corbelled** stone courses

dormer window, blind window in the roof or tower

dukhang, Tibetan Buddhist prayer hall

dvipa, lamp-column, generally of stone or brass-covered wood

eave, overhang that shelters a porch or verandah

epigraph, inscription incised on to the stone blocks of a building

faience, coloured tilework

finial, emblem at the summit of a **stupa**, tower or dome, also at the end of a **parapet**; generally takes the form of a tier of umbrella-like motifs or a pot

foliate, foliation, ornamental design derived from foliage

frieze, horizontal band of figures or decorative designs

gable, end of an angled roof

garbhagriha, 'womb-chamber'; name of a temple **sanctuary**

ghat, sacred bathing place, often demarcated by steps, platforms and small shrines

gompa, Tibetan Buddhist monastery

gopura, towered gateway in southern Indian temple architecture, developed into monumental high-rising structures

gudi, name of a temple in Karnataka

gumpha, cave temple

gurudwara, Sikh religious complex, generally with a temple and rest-house

Hellenistic, style of ancient Greek architecture

hero stone, commemorative panel on which the exploits of a hero are recorded and sometimes illustrated

icon, principal votive image in a temple

jamb, vertical side slab of a doorway

jorbangla, double hut-like temple in Bengal

kalasha, pot-like finial

kalyan mandapa, columned hall used for the symbolic marriage ceremony between the temple deity and his consort

keystone, central wedge-shaped block in a masonry arch

khamba, column

khondalite, crudely grained basalt

kovil, Tamil term for a temple

kund, well or pool

kuttambalam, hall in a Kerala temple where dance and music are performed

lath, column

lathe-turned, column with circular shaft decorated with incisions indicating that the column was placed on a lathe and then carved

lena, cave, usually refers to a rock-cut sanctuary

lhakhang, Tibetan Buddhist assembly hall

lintel, horizontal beam over doorway, often adorned with a miniature image of the deity worshipped in the sanctuary

mahasti, memorial cemetery

mandala, geometric diagram symbolizing the structure of the cosmos, often used to regulate temple plans

mandapa, columned hall preceding the sanctuary in a Jain or Hindu temple; sometimes also an independent structure; used for congregational worship and performances of music and dance

mandir, temple

mani, wall with inscribed stones at Tibetan Buddhist sites

matha, Hindu or Jain monastery

medallion, circle or part-circle framing a figure or decorative motif on a wall or tower

merlon, parapet element shaped like a battlement, usually with a pointed top

meshed motif, continuous design of **arch-like** motifs

multi-lobed, multiple concave profile of an arch or circle

neo-classical, 18th–19th-century revival of ancient Roman and Greek styles

niche, wall recess containing a sculpted image or emblem, mostly framed by a pair of **pilasters**

oedgal, buttress

494

parapet, wall extending above the roof; often elaborately treated with ornamental roof forms

pediment, mouldings, often in a triangular formation above an opening or **niche**

pendant, hanging, generally refers to a motif depicted upside down

pida deul, hall with a pyramidal roof in an Orissan temple

pier, a short wall or masonry mass sculpted into different elements

pilaster, ornamental small column, complete with **capital** and **bracket**, usually forming part of the wall construction

pinnacle, protruding roof element

pol, gateway

porch, covered entrance to a shrine or hall, generally open and with columns

pot and foliage motif, decorative motif at the base of columns and **pilasters**

ratha, temple chariot; sometimes also refers to a temple model

rekha deul, sanctuary and curved tower of an Orissan temple

revivalist, recent temple style that imitates earlier practice

roundel, circular design

sabha, columned hall

samadhi, funerary memorial, like a temple but enshrining an image of the deceased

sanctuary, chamber housing the principal votive image or emblem of the temple deity

sangrahalaya, rest-house for Jain pilgrims

schist, grey or green finely grained stone in north-western Pakistan

scrollwork, stylized design derived from foliage

shala, barrel-vaulted roof form, often appearing in ornamental form in **pediment** and **parapet** designs

shikhara, curved temple tower

stambha, free-standing column, often with lamps or banners

steatite, finely grained grey mineral

stucco, plaster

stupa, hemispherical funerary mound, generally of earth faced with stone or brick; principal votive monument in a Buddhist religious complex

superstructure, tower rising over a sanctuary or gateway, roof above a hall

sutradhara, chief architect

talar, **tank**

tank, reservoir bounded by a dam wall; in temple architecture a masonry-lined body of water, often with stepped sides

teppakulam, Tamil term for a large **tank**

terracotta, burnt clay

thangka, cloth painted with a Tibetan Buddhist deity; gigantic thangkas are displayed at festival times

threshold, doorstep

tirtha, holy spot, also a sacred **tank**

torana, gateway with two posts linked by **architraves**

trilobed, with three concave profiles

tuk, fortified enclosure containing Jain shrines

turret, spire or protruding roof element

vav, step-well

verandah, enlarged porch in front of a hall

vihara, Buddhist monastery with cells opening off a central court

vimana, towered sanctuary

voussoir, wedge-shaped block in a masonry arch

GLOSSARY OF INDIAN NAMES

(B)	Buddhist	(J)	Jain
(d)	dynastic	(r)	royal or military
(H)	Hindu	(S)	Sikh

Abhinavagupta (H), 11th-century **Shaiva** philosopher

Achaleshvara (H), Lord of the Hill; title of **Shiva**

Acharya (J, H), religious teacher

Achyutadeva Raya (r), 16th-century **Vijayanagara** emperor

Adbhutanatha (H), Wondrous Lord; name of **Shiva**

Adi Buddha (B), Primordial **Buddha** from which all other forms are manifested

Adi Granth (S), the holy book of the Sikhs

Adi Keshava (H), name of **Vishnu**

Adinatha, Adishvara (J), the first of the twenty-four **Tirthankaras**, distinguished by his bull mount

Adivaraha (H), Primordial Boar; epithet of **Vishnu** in his **Varaha** incarnation

Agama (H), text giving rules for temple rituals

Agastya (H), legendary sage who brought the **Vedas** to South India

Agastyeshvara (H), name of **Shiva**, worshipped at Kilaiyur

Aghoreshvara (H), Non-fearful Lord; terrifying form of **Shiva**

Agni (H), Vedic fire divinity, intermediary between gods and men through his form as the sacrificial fire; guardian of the south-east

Ahalya (H), a woman liberated by **Rama** in the **Ramayana**

Ahmad Shahi (d), 15th–16th-century Muslim rulers of Gujarat

Ahom (d), 17th–18th-century dynasty of eastern Assam

Airavateshvara (H), Lord of the Heavenly Elephant; name of **Shiva** worshipped at Darasuram

Ajatashatru (r), 5th-century-BC **Magadha** ruler

Ajitanatha (J), the second of the twenty-four **Tirthankaras**, distinguished by his elephant mount

Akbar (r), 16th-century **Mughal** emperor

Akshobhya (B), Imperturbable; **Buddha** who symbolizes the desire for enlightenment, presides over the eastern paradise

Alara (B), hero of the **Samkhapala Jataka**

Alvar (H), Tamil **Vaishnava** saint

Amaranatha, Amareshvara (H), Lord of the Gods; name of a **linga** worshipped at Amarnath

Amba, Amba Bhai (H), Mother; form of **Devi**, name of **Durga**

Ambaranatha (H), Lord of the Sky; name of **Shiva**

Ambika (J), Mother; goddess associated with **Neminatha**, distinguished by her lion mount and a child that she holds

Amitabha (B), Immeasurable Glory; **Buddha** who presides over the western paradise

Amman (H), Mother; Tamil goddess or consort of a god

Amoghasiddhi (B), Infallible Power; **Buddha** who presides over the northern paradise

amrita (H), ambrosia, the beverage of immortality

Amriteshvara (H), Lord of Ambrosia; name of **Shiva**

Ananda (B), disciple of **Buddha**

Ananta (H), multi-hooded serpent associated with **Vishnu**

Anantalvar (H), a **Vaishnava** saint

Anantashayana, Anantashayi (H), **Vishnu** sleeping on **Ananta** in the cosmic ocean

Anantavarman Chodaganga (r), 12th-century **Eastern Ganga** ruler

Andal (H), worshipper of **Vishnu**; also name of a poetess

Andhaka (H), demon killed by **Shiva**

Annamalaiyar (H), name of **Shiva**

Annapurna (H), Filled with Food; epithet of **Parvati**

Appar (H), a Tamil **Shaiva** saint

apsaras (B, J, H), celestial nymph or dancer

Ardhanarishvara (H), Lord Who is Half-Woman; **Shiva** represented as half-male and half-female

Arjan (S), fifth Sikh **Guru**, completed the **Adi Granth**

Arjuna (H), important hero in the **Mahabharata** to whom **Krishna** delivered the **Bhagavad Gita**

Aruna (H), Red; charioteer of **Surya**, personification of dawn

Arunachaleshvara (H), Lord of the Eastern Mountain; name of **Shiva** worshipped at Tiruvannamalai

Aryan (d), people who invaded India in the 2nd millennium BC; their religious beliefs are preserved in the **Vedas**

Ashoka (r), 3rd-century-BC **Maurya** ruler

Asita (B), sage who predicts that **Gautama** will become a **Chakravartin**

Asita (H), Black; name of **Bhairava**

atman (H), 'self' or spirit; the philosophical concept of soul

Aurangzeb (r), 17th-century **Mughal** emperor

Avalokiteshvara (B), Lord Who Looks Down; **Bodhisattva** whose special attribute is compassion

Avantishvara, Avantisvamin (H), Lord of Avanti; name of **Shiva**

Avantivarman (r), 9th-century **Utpala** ruler

Avatara (H), Descent; incarnation of a divinity, usually refers to **Vishnu**

Ayanar, Ayappar (H), deity popular in Kerala, considered son of **Shiva** and **Mohini**

Baba Atal (S), son of the sixth Sikh **Guru**

Badrinatha (H), name of **Vishnu** worshipped at Badrinath

Bahubali (J), son of **Adinatha**, sometimes regarded as a **Tirthankara**; recognized by the creepers winding around his limbs

Balabhadra, Balarama (H), elder brother of **Krishna**, also considered an incarnation of **Vishnu**

Bhadrabahu (J), A Jain saint

Bhagavad Gita (H), Song of the Lord; section of the **Mahabharata** in which **Krishna** preaches a sermon to **Arjuna** explaining the Hindu ways of knowledge, duty and devotion

Bhagiratha (H), a king who performed austerities to induce **Ganga** to descend to earth

Bhairava (H), Terrible; name of a fearful aspect of **Shiva**

Bhairavadevi, Bhairavi (J, H), consort of **Bhairava**

bhakti (H), adoration of a particular god or goddess

Bharata (H), half-brother of **Rama**

Bharata (J), brother of **Bahubali**

Bharateshvara (H), form of **Shiva**

Bhaskareshvara (H), epithet of **Surya** or **Shiva**

Bhauma Kara (d), 8th–9th-century dynasty in Orissa

Bhavani (H), name of **Parvati**

Bhavani Sen (r), 20th-century ruler of Mandi

Bhavanishvara (H), Lord of **Parvati**; name of **Shiva**

Bhikshatanamurti (H), **Shiva** in the form of the wandering beggar

Bhima (H), mighty **Pandava** hero of the **Mahabharata**

Bhima (r), 11th-century **Solanki** ruler

Bhimakali (H), epithet of **Kali**

Bhimalingeshvara, Bhimeshvara (H), name of **Shiva**

Bhishma (H), a hero in the **Mahabharata**

Bhoganandishvara (H), name of **Shiva** worshipped at Nandi

Bhoja (r), 11th-century **Paramara** ruler

Bhu, Bhudevi, Bhumidevi (H), Earth; goddess usually associated with **Vishnu**, rescued by **Varaha**

Bhutanatha (H), Lord of Spirits; epithet of **Shiva**

Bhuvaneshvari (H), Ruler of the World; name of **Parvati**

Bimbisara (r), 6th-century-BC **Magadha** ruler

Binda Mahadeva (H), name of **Shiva**

Bir Hambir (r), 17th-century **Malla** ruler

Birla, modern family of industrialists; sponsors of Hindu temples in New Delhi, Hyderabad and other cities

bodhi (B), the tree beneath which **Buddha** attained enlightenment

Bodhisattva (B), Enlightened One; saintly or compassionate being destined to become **Buddha**

Brahma (H), the Creator; god recognized by his four heads

Brahmadeva (J), four-faced **yaksha**, an obvious borrowing from the Hindu **Brahma**

Brahmanas (H), ancient ritual texts

Brahmani (H), consort of **Brahma**

Brahmeshvara (H), name of **Shiva**

brahmin (J, H), uppermost class of society, to which all Hindu and Jain priests belong

Brihadishvara (H), Great Lord; epithet of **Shiva**

Brihatsamhita (H), early astronomical text

Buddha (B), Enlightened One; founder of Buddhism who is worshipped as the supreme being; in developed **Mahayana** theology there are five directional **Buddhas**: **Akshobhya** (east), **Ratnasambhava** (south), **Amitabha** (west), **Amoghasiddhi** (north) and **Vairochana** (centre)

Buddha (H), a delusory incarnation of **Vishnu**

Buddhagupta (r), 5th-century **Gupta** king

Burdwan Rajas (d), 18th–19th-century rulers of Bengal

Chahamana (d), 10th–12th-century dynasty of Rajasthan

Chaitanya (H), 16th-century **Vaishnava** teacher responsible for the revival of **Krishna** worship

chakra (H), disc weapon associated with **Vishnu**; energy node located along the spine

Chakradhara, Chakrapani (H), epithet of **Vishnu**

Chakravartin (B, J, H), Wheel-Turner; epithet of a world sovereign

Chakreshvari (J), **yakshi** associated with

Adinatha, distinguished by her many weapons, especially the disc

Chalukya (d), see **Early Chalukya, Eastern Chalukya** and **Late Chalukya**

Champeyya (B), serpent king of a **Jataka** story

Chamunda, Chamundi (H), emanation of **Durga**, usually refers to a terrifying form of the goddess

Chamundaraya (r), 10th-century **Western Ganga** military commander

Chandella (d), 9th–11th-century dynasty of central India

Chandesha, Chandeshvara, Chandikeshvara (H), devotee of **Shiva**

Chandra (H), Moon; one of the planetary deities

Chandragupta (r), early-5th-century **Gupta** ruler

Chandranatha, Chandraprabha (J), seventh of the twenty-four **Tirthankaras**, distinguished by his crescent moon emblem

Chandrashekhara (H), Moon-Crested; name of **Shiva**

Channa (B), charioteer of **Gautama**

Chaturbhuja (H), Four-Armed; name of **Shiva**

Chaturmukha (H), Four-Faced; epithet of **Brahma** or of **Shiva**

Chaunsath Yogini (H), Sixty-four **Yoginis**

Chedi (d), 2nd-century-BC-1st-century-AD dynasty of Orissa

Chennakeshava (H), Beautiful God; name of **Vishnu** worshipped at Belur

Chera (d), 12th–14th-century dynasty of Kerala

Chetiar (d), 17th–19th-century dynasty of Kannara

Chhaddanta (B), elephant hero of a **Jataka** story

Chinna Bomma (r), 16th-century **Vijayanagara** governor

Chintala Venkataramana (H), **Venkataramana** of the Tamarind Tree; form of **Vishnu** worshipped at Tadpatri

chintamani (J, H), gem which has the power to grant all desires

Chitragupta (H), name of **Surya** worshipped at Khajuraho

Chitrakarini (H), name of a **Shaiva** goddess

Chola (d), 9th–13th-century dynasty of southern India

Cholishvara (H), epithet of **Shiva** named after the **Chola** dynasty

Daivanayaki (H), name of **Parvati** worshipped at Darasuram

dakini (B), sorceress

Dakshinamurti (H), manifestation of **Shiva** as the master of universal knowledge and the teacher of **Yoga**

Dakshineshvara (H), Lord of the South; name of **Shiva**

Dalai Lama (B), spiritual leader of Tibetan Buddhism

Dantidurga (r), 8th-century **Rashtrakuta** ruler

Dantivarman (r), 8th–9th-century **Pallava** ruler

darshana (J, H), auspicious viewing of the temple deity

Dasara (H), ten-day festival (September–October) during which **Durga** is worshipped and the **Ramayana** story is related or publicly enacted

Dasharatha (H), king of Ayodhya and father of **Rama** in the **Ramayana**

Dashashvamedha (H), Ten Horse Sacrifices; name of a bathing ghat at Varanasi

Dashavatara (H), Ten Incarnations; **Vishnu** as **Matsya**, **Kurma**, **Varaha**, **Narasimha**, **Vamana**, **Parashurama**, **Rama**, **Balarama** or **Krishna**, **Buddha** and **Kalki**

Data Brikha (J), name of a Jain sage

Dattatreya (H), teacher of the gods, also an emanation of **Vishnu**

deva (B, J, H), god

Deva Raya (r), 15th-century **Vijayanagara** ruler

Devadatta (B), cousin of **Buddha**

Devaki (H), mother of **Krishna**

Devi (H), Goddess; usually refers to **Parvati**

Dhangadeva (r), 10th-century ruler of the **Chandella** dynasty

Dharma (B), law of Buddhism

dharma (H), traditional law or duty

Dharmachakra (B), Wheel of Law; refers to the first sermon of **Buddha** at Sarnath

Dharmanatha (J), fifteenth **Tirthankara**

Dharmapala (B), protector of Buddhism, usually a terrifying guardian

Dharmaraja (H), epithet of **Yama**; also eldest of the **Pandava** brothers in the **Mahabharata**

Digambara (J), one of the two main Jain sects, in which the monks go naked

Dikpala (H), guardian of the directions; mostly appear in a group of eight: **Indra** (east), **Agni** (south-east), **Yama** (south), **Nirriti** (south-west), **Varuna** (west), **Vayu** (north-west), **Kubera** (north) and **Ishana** (north-east)

Divali (H), festival of lights (September–October), usually marks the end of the rainy season

Divodasa (H), mythical king for whom **Brahma** performs sacrifices

Doddeshvara (H), title of **Shiva** worshipped at Hemavati

Dogra (d), 17th–19th-century rulers of Jammu

Draupadi (H), common wife of the five **Pandava** brothers in the **Mahabharata**

Duladeo (H), name of a **Shiva** worshipped at Khajuraho

Durga (H), principal goddess of the **Shakti** cult; riding on her lion or tiger and armed with the weapons of all the gods, she destroys demons, especially **Mahisha**

Durga Puja (H), name of the **Dasara** festival

Dvarakadhisha (H), name of **Krishna** worshipped at Dwarka

dvarapala (B, J, H), **yaksha** who guards the temple doorway

Early Chalukya (d), 6th–8th-century dynasty of the Deccan

Eastern Chalukya (d), 9th–10th-century dynasty of the eastern Deccan

Eastern Ganga (d), 8th–14th-century dynasty of Orissa

Ekalinga (H), Unique **Linga**; name of **Shiva** worshipped at Eklingji

Ekambareshvara (H), Lord of the Mango Tree; name of **Shiva** worshipped at Kanchipuram

Gaekwar (d), 18th–19th-century rulers of Vadodara

Gahadavala (d), 10th–12th-century rulers of Varanasi

Gajan (H), **Shaiva** festival

Gajapati (d), 14th–16th-century dynasty of Orissa

Gajendra (H), elephant king rescued by **Vishnu**

Galaganatha (H), name of **Shiva**

gana (H), dwarf attendants of **Shiva**

Ganapati, Ganesha (J, H), Lord of the **Ganas**; popular elephant-headed deity who removes obstacles and who is invoked at the beginning of all enterprises; the son of **Parvati**

Ganapatideva (r), 13th-century **Kakatiya** ruler

Gandhamadana (H), mountain home of **Kubera** and the **yakshas**; renowned for its healing herbs

gandharva (B, H), semi-divine being, often depicted flying; also a celestial musician

Ganga (H), goddess personifying the Ganga river

Ganga Singh (r), 20th-century ruler of Jodhpur

Gangadhara (H), name of **Shiva** when bearing the weight of **Ganga**'s descent to earth

Gangaraja (r), 12th-century **Hoysala** commander

Gangeshvara (H), Lord of **Ganga**; name of **Shiva**

Garuda (H), mythical eagle mount of **Vishnu**

Gauri (H), Fair One; epithet of **Parvati**

Gaurishankara (H), **Shiva** with **Parvati**

Gautama (B), family name of **Buddha**

Gelugpa (B), Yellow Cap Tibetan sect

Ghateshvara (H), name of a **Shiva linga** at Badoli

Ghrishneshvara (H), name of **Shiva** worshipped at Ellora

Gita Govinda (H), poetic version of the **Krishnalila** composed by **Jayadeva**

Golingeshvara (H), name of **Shiva** worshipped at Biccavolu

Gommateshvara (J), name of **Bahubali**

Gondeshvara (H), name of **Shiva**

Gopala, Govinda (H), Cowherd; epithet of **Krishna**

gopi (H), milkmaid companions of **Krishna**

Gorkhnath (J), name of a sage

Govardhana (H), name of a mountain lifted by **Krishna**

Govindaraja, Govindadeva (H), Lord of the Cowherds; name of **Krishna**

Grahapati (d), 11th–12th-century dynasty of Rajasthan

Guhila (d), 11th–12th-century dynasty of Rajasthan

Gupta (d), 3rd–5th-century dynasty of central India; see also **Late Gupta**

Guru (S), title of a Sikh religious leader

guru (H), sage, teacher

Guru Rimpoche (B), leader of the Tibetan Buddhist monastery at Pemayangtse

Haihaya (d), 8th–10th-century dynasty of central India

Hamseshvari (H), **Sarasvati** who rides on a swan

Hanuman (H), popular monkey hero of the **Ramayana**; devotee of **Rama**

Hara, Hara Siddhi (H), name of **Shiva**

Hari (H), name of **Vishnu**

Harihara (H), **Vishnu–Shiva**; combination of the two cult divinities into one figure

Harishchandra (H), a mythical sage

Harishena (r), 5th-century **Vakataka** ruler

Hariti (B), goddess of prosperity and patroness of children, sometimes appears as the consort of **Kubera**

Harsha (r), 7th-century ruler of central India

Harshat Mata (H), name of **Shakti**

Hayagriva (B), Horse-Necked; fierce form of **Avalokiteshvara**

Hayagriva (H), form of **Vishnu** as patron of knowledge

Hema (H), sage who obtained a book from **Rama**

Hevajra (B), emanation of **Akshobhya**

Hidimba Devi (H), Wrathful Goddess; name of **Durga** worshipped at Manali

Hinayana (B), Lesser Vehicle; term created by **Mahayana** theologians referring to the original Buddhist doctrine

Hiranyakashipu (H), demon king killed by **Narasimha**

Holi (H), spring festival (February–March), sometimes associated with **Krishna**

Hoysala (d), 11th–14th-century dynasty of southern India

Hoysaleshvara (H), name of **Shiva** worshipped at Halebid

Humayun (r), 16th-century **Mughal** emperor

Huna (d), 6th–7th-century dynasty of northern and central India

Ikshvaku (d), 2nd–4th-century dynasty of the eastern Deccan

Indra (B, J, H), king of the gods, lord of the heavens; guardian of the eastern direction

Indrani (H), consort of **Indra**, one of the **Matrikas**

Irattayappar (H), same as **Ayappar**

Iravataneshvara (H), name of **Shiva** worshipped at Kanchipuram

Ishana (H), one of the **Dikpalas**, guardian of the north-east

Ishvara (H), Lord; epithet of **Shiva**

Jagadambi (H), Mother of the World; epithet of **Parvati**

Jagannatha (H), Lord of the World; particularly refers to the form of **Krishna** worshipped at Puri

Jagat Kishor (H), name of **Krishna**

Jagat Shiromani (H), name of **Krishna** worshipped at Bijolia

Jagat Singh (r), 17th-century **Rajput** ruler of Udaipur

Jalakanteshvara (H), title of **Shiva** worshipped at Vellore

Jambhala (B), god of riches, chief of the **yakshas**

Jambudvipa (J, H), Continent of the Rose-Apple Tree; name of earth

Jambukeshvara, Jambulinga (J), name of **Shiva** as lord of the earth on which the distinctive jambu tree grows

Janaka (H), father of **Sita** in the **Ramayana**

Janardhana (H), name of **Vishnu**

Jarasandha (H), demon who attacked **Krishna**

Jataka (B), Birth Story; narrative of one of the former lives of **Buddha**

Jatayu (H), vulture ally of **Rama**, killed by **Ravana** in the **Ramayana**

Javari (H), name of **Vishnu** worshipped at Khajuraho

Jayadeva (H), poet who composed the **Gita Govinda** in the 13th century

Jayasimha (r), 12th-century **Solanki** ruler

Jina (J), Victor; spiritual conqueror or **Tirthankara**, after which Jainism is named

Jivakamrava (J), name of a **Jina**

Jivantaswami (J), a minor Jain deity

Jnanaprasumbha (H), name of **Parvati**

Jnanasambandha (H), a **Shaiva** saint

Jvarahareshvara (H), Lord Who Cures Fever; name of **Shiva** worshipped at Kanchipuram

Jyeshtha (H), goddess of misfortune, also a form of **Shakti**

Jyotirlinga (H), luminous energy of **Shiva** manifested at twelve sites, including Kedarnath, Prabhas Patan, Srisailam, Ujjain and Varanasi

Kabir (H), 16th-century poet who lived at Varanasi

Kacchapaghata (d), 10th–11th-century dynasty of central India

Kadamba (d), 11th–13th-century dynasty of the western Deccan

Kadambavaneshvara (H), name of **Shiva** who resides in the forest of the kadamba trees

Kadasiddheshvara (H), name of **Shiva**

Kagyupa (B), Red Cap Tibetan sect

Kaikeyi (H), stepmother of **Rama** in the **Ramayana**

Kailasa (H), mountain home of **Shiva**

Kailasanatha (H), Lord of **Kailasa**; title of **Shiva**

Kakatiya (d), 11th–14th-century dynasty of the eastern Deccan

Kala (H), Time; epithet of **Yama**

Kala Chand (H), Black Moon; epithet of **Krishna**

Kalachuri (d), 5th–6th-century dynasty of the western Deccan

Kalahastishvara (H), name of **Shiva** worshipped at Kalahasti

kalamkari (H), painted cotton hanging

Kali (H), Black; terrifying aspect of the goddess **Durga**, recognized by her withered body and skull necklace

Kalidasa (H), 4th–5th-century Sanskrit poet and dramatist

Kalika Devi, Kalika Mata (H), name of **Kali**

Kaliya (H), serpent subdued by **Krishna**

Kalki (H), future incarnation of **Vishnu**, appears on a horse

Kalleshvara (H), name of **Shiva**

Kama (H), Desire; god of love

Kamakhya (H), title of **Parvati** worshipped at Gauhati

Kamakshi (H), Wanton-Eyed; name of **Parvati**

Kamala, Kamalambal (H), name of **Devi**

Kamatha (J), evil king in the story of **Marubhuta**

Kampahareshvara (H), name of **Shiva** worshipped at Tribhuvanam

Kamsa (H), a wicked king killed by **Krishna**

Kandariya Mahadeva (H), name of a **Shiva** temple at Khajuraho

Kanishka (r), 1st–2nd-century **Kushana** ruler

Kannappar (H), a **Shaiva** saint, hunter devotee of **Shiva**

Kanyakumari (H), Virgin; epithet of **Parvati**

Kapaleshvara (H), Lord of the Skull; title of the terrifying aspect of **Shiva**

Karkota (d), 7th–9th-century dynasty of Kashmir

karma (B, J, H), the present consequences of past lives

Karna (H), a hero of the **Mahabharata**

Karni Mata (H), female saint worshipped as an incarnation of **Durga** at Deshnoke

Karttikeya (H), warrior son of the Pleiades (Krittika) or of **Shiva** and **Parvati**; also known as **Kumara**, **Skanda** and **Subrahmanya**

Kashivishvanatha, Kashivishveshvara (H), Lord **Vishvanatha** at Kashi (Varanasi); title of **Shiva**

Kashyapa (B), disciple of **Buddha**

Kayarohana (H), name of **Shiva** worshipped at Nagapattinam

Kedareshvara (H), great **linga** of **Shiva** worshipped at Kedarnath

Keshava (H), Long-Haired; name of **Krishna**

Keshta Raya (H), name of **Vishnu**

Khichakeshvari (H), name of goddess worshipped at Khiching

kinnara (B, H), celestial musician with part-bird body

kirttimukha (J, H), lion-like monster mask

Kirttiraja (r), 11th-century **Kaccha-paghata** ruler

Koch (d), 15th–17th-century dynasty of Assam

Kodandarama (H), **Rama** carrying the Bow

Kokhanmatha (r), queen of one of the **Kacchapaghata** rulers

Kondavidu (d), 7th–8th-century dynasty of the eastern Deccan

Koranganatha (H), name of **Shiva**

Krishna (H), incarnation of **Vishnu**; also the popular cult divinity who appears in various forms as the mischievous but beloved child, the pastoral cowherd (**Gopala**, **Govinda**) dallying with the **gopis** and the charioteer of **Arjuna** in the **Mahabharata** epic, where he propounds the **Bhagavad Gita** to **Arjuna**

Krishna (r), 8th-century **Rashtrakuta** ruler

Krishnadeva Raya (r), 16th-century **Vijayanagara** emperor

Krishnalila (H), story of **Krishna**

Kshatrapa (d), 2nd–4th-century dynasty of western India and the Deccan

kshatriya (J, H), second highest class of society, to which warriors and nobles belong

Kubera (B, J, H), chief of the **yakshas**, pot-bellied keeper of the treasures of the earth, guardian of the northern direction

Kulottunga (r), 12th–13th-century **Chola** ruler

Kumara (H), Youthful God; name of **Karttikeya** or **Skanda**

Kumarapala (r), 12th-century **Solanki** ruler

Kumari (H), Virgin; epithet of **Durga**

Kumbha Mela (H), river festival, especially that at Allahabad

Kumbhakarna (H), giant brother of **Ravana** in the **Ramayana**

Kumbhareshvara (H), name of **Shiva** worshipped at Kumbakonam

Kundalini (B, H), **Tantric** goddess who awakens the **chakras** of the spine

Kurma (H), Tortoise; second incarnation of **Vishnu**

Kushana (d), 1st–3rd-century dynasty of central and eastern India

Kushmandini (J), name of a **yakshi**

Lakshana Devi (H), Auspicious Goddess; epithet of **Durga**

Lakshmana (H), younger brother of **Rama** in the **Ramayana**

Lakshmaneshvara (H), name of **Shiva**

Lakshmi (B, J, H), popular goddess responsible for wealth and good fortune, usually associated with the lotus, sometimes bathed by elephants

Lakshmidevi (H), name of **Lakshmi**

Lakulisha (H), Lord with the Club; founder of the **Pashupata** sect, believed to be an incarnation of **Shiva**

Lalguan (H), name of **Shiva** worshipped at Khajuraho

Lalita (H), Playful; name of **Parvati** or **Lakshmi**

Lalitaditya (r), 8th-century **Karkota** ruler

Lalji (H), name of **Krishna** worshipped at Kalna

lama (B), head monk of a Tibetan Buddhist monastery

Lankeshvara (H), name of **Shiva** worshipped at Ellora

Late Chalukya (d), 10th–12th-century dynasty of the Deccan

Late Gupta (d), 6th–8th-century dynasty of eastern India

Licchavi (d), 6th–5th-century-BC dynasty of eastern India

linga (H), **Shiva** as the phallic emblem, usually mounted on a **yoni** pedestal as the principal object of worship

Lingaraja (H), title of **Shiva** worshipped at Bhubaneshwar

Lokanatha, Lokeshvara (B), Lord of the World; name of **Avalokiteshvara**

Madana Mohana (H), Infatuated by Love; epithet of **Krishna**

Madattilappan (H), name of **Shiva** worshipped at Peruvanam

Madhava (H), name of **Vishnu**; also a 12th-century teacher and philosopher who founded a **Vaishnava** sect

Madhukeshvara (H), name of **Shiva** worshipped at Mukhalingam

Magadha (d), 6th–4th-century-BC dynasty of eastern India

Mahabharata (H), Story of the Great Bharatas; in this celebrated epic the central event is the climactic battle between the **Pandavas** and Kauravas

Mahabodhi (B), Great Enlightenment of **Buddha**

Mahadeva (H), Great Lord; epithet of **Shiva**

Mahadevi (H), Great Goddess; epithet of **Parvati**

Mahajanaka (B), royal hero of a **Jataka** story

Mahakala (B), fierce guardian divinity

Mahakala (H), **Shiva** as Lord of Time

Mahakapi (B), monkey hero of a **Jataka** story

Mahakuteshvara (H), name of **Shiva** worshipped at Mahakuta

Mahalakshmi (H), Great **Lakshmi**

Mahalasa Narayani (H), form of **Lakshmi** worshipped at Mardol

Mahalinga (H), Great **Linga**

Mahamayuri (B), consort of **Amoghasiddhi**

Mahanaleshvara (H), name of **Shiva** worshipped at Menal

Mahanavami (H), ninth day of the **Dasara** festival

mahant (B, H), head of a monastery

Mahapurusha (J, H), Cosmic Man displaying all of creation

Mahavira (J), Great Hero; last of the twenty-four **Tirthankaras**, teacher contemporary with **Buddha**, alleged founder of Jainism

Mahayana (B), Great Vehicle; this school of Buddhism stresses the saviour role of the **Bodhisattva** in aiding all beings to achieve salvation

Mahendravarman (r), 6th–7th-century **Pallava** ruler

Mahendravarmeshvara (H), epithet of **Shiva** named after **Mahendravarman**

Mahesha, Maheshvara (H), Great Lord; epithet of **Shiva**

Maheshvari (H), consort of **Shiva**, one of the **Matrikas**

Mahisha (H), buffalo demon killed by **Durga**

Mahishamardini, Mahishasuramardini (H), Slayer of the Buffalo Demon; epithet of **Durga**

Mahmud (r), 11th-century Muslim commander from Ghazni in Afghanistan

Mahosadha (B), wise hero of a **Jataka** story

Maitraka (d), 6th–8th-century dynasty of western India

Maitreya (B), Benevolent; as a **Bodhisattva** he awaits his rebirth as the next mortal **Buddha**; as **Buddha** of the future he presides over earthly paradise

makara (H), aquatic monster

Makareshvara (H), name of **Shiva**

Mala Devi (H), name of a goddess worshipped at Gyaraspur

Maladevi (H), name of **Devi**

Malik Kafur (r), 14th-century commander of the Muslim king of Delhi

Malla (d), 17th–18th-century dynasty of Bengal

Mallikarjuna (H), name of **Shiva** worshipped at Srisailam

Mallinatha (J), nineteenth of the twenty-four **Tirthankaras**, distinguished by the emblem of a water pot

Mamalla (r), 7th-century **Pallava** ruler

Man Singh (r), 16th-century **Rajput** ruler of Gwalior

Manasa (H), snake goddess, destroyer of poison; form of **Shakti**

Mandakini (H), name of river **Ganga**

mandala (B, J, H), magical diagram reproducing the structure of the universe; orders deities into pantheons

Mandhatu (B), royal hero of a **Jataka** story

Mangala (H), Mars; the planetary divinity

Mangala Gauri (H), name of **Parvati**

Mangesha (H), name of **Shiva** worshipped at Mardol

Manikantheshvara (H), name of **Shiva**

Manikarnika (H), Jewelled Earring (of **Shiva**); a sacred pool in Varanasi

Manikkavachakar (H), a **Shaiva** saint

Manimaheshvara (H), name of **Shiva**

Manjunatha (H), name of **Shiva** worshipped at Mangalore

Manjushri (B), **Bodhisattva** whose special duty is to stimulate understanding, sometimes holds the sword with which to destroy falsehood

Manmatha (H), name of **Kama**

mantra (B, J, H), magical verbal formula, often the name of a deity

Manushi Buddha (B), mortal **Buddha**; name of a series of earthly saviours

Mara (B), Tempter; together with his armies and daughters, tried to disturb the meditation of **Buddha**

Maratha (d), 16th–18th-century dynasty of the Deccan

Markandeya (H), youthful devotee of **Shiva** who was rescued from **Yama** while worshipping the **linga**

Markandeyeshvara (H), name of **Shiva**

Markula Devi (H), name of **Kali** worshipped at Udaipur

Martandavarma (r), 18th-century ruler of Kerala

Marubhuta (J), previous birth of **Parshvanatha**

Mata (H), Mother, popular goddess; sometimes identified with **Parvati**

Matangeshvara (H), name of **Shiva**

Matrika (H), Mother; often appears in multiple forms as **Brahmani, Chamunda, Indrani, Maheshvari** and **Varahi**

Matsya (H), Fish; first incarnation of **Vishnu**

Maudgalyayana (B), disciple of **Buddha**

Maurya (d), 4th–2nd-century-BC dynasty of central, eastern and western India

Maya, Mayashri (B), mother of **Buddha**

Mayadevi (H), name of **Devi**

Megheshvara (H), name of **Shiva**

Meru (J, H), axial mountain supporting the heavens

Minakshi (H), Fish-eyed; name of **Parvati** worshipped at Madurai

Mira Bhai (H), 15th-century Rajput princess who became a saintly devotee of **Krishna**

Mohini (H), female incarnation of **Vishnu**

moksha (J, H), enlightenment; literally 'release'

Mori (d), 7th–8th-century dynasty of Rajasthan

Mrityunjaya (H), Conqueror of Death; epithet of **Shiva**

Muchakunda (H), mythical king connected with the legend of **Tyagaraja**

Muchalinda (B), serpent who protected **Buddha** from **Mara**

mudra (B, J, H), symbolic hand gesture

Mughal (d), 16th–18th-century empire of northern, central, eastern and western India, as well as parts of the Deccan

mukhalinga (H), **linga** with one or more faces of divinities

Mukteshvara (H), name of **Shiva**

Mukunda (H), name of **Vishnu**

Mukundanayanar (H), a **Vaishnava** saint

Munishvara (B, H), Tamil folk deity depicted as an ascetic

Murali Mohana (H), Flute-Playing Seducer; epithet of **Krishna**

naga (B, H), snake deity; associated with fertility and protection

Nagakumara (J), royal hero of a Jain legend

Naganatha, Nageshvara (H), name of **Shiva**

nagi, nagini (B, H), female snake deity

Nakula (H), one of the **Pandava** brothers in the **Mahabharata**

Nalagiri (B), elephant sent by **Devadatta** to trample **Buddha**

Naltunai Ishvara (H), name of **Shiva** worshipped at Punjai

Nambunatha (H), name of **Shiva**

Namgyal (d), 16th–19th-century dynasty of Ladakh

Nanak (S), first Sikh **Guru**

Nanda (B), cousin of **Buddha** who was converted by him

Nanda (H), foster-father of **Krishna**

Nandi (H), bull mount of **Shiva**

Nandishvara (H), a form of **Shiva**

Nandivarma (r), 8th-century **Pallava** ruler

Nara (H), name of a sage

Narasimha (H), incarnation of **Vishnu** as a man–lion to destroy **Hiranyakashipu**

Narasimha (r), 13th-century **Eastern Ganga** ruler; two 12th–13th-century **Hoysala** rulers

Narayana (H), epithet of **Vishnu**; sometimes appears in the form of a sage

Nataraja, Natesha (H), Lord or King of Dance; epithet of **Shiva**

Natha Pantha (H), name of a cult at Kadri (Mangalore)

Nava Brahma (H), Nine **Brahmas**

Nava Durga (H), Nine **Durgas**

Navagraha (H), Nine Planetary Deities; these include **Surya, Chandra, Mangala** and **Rahu**

Navaratri (H), Nine Nights; name of the **Dasara** festival

Navsang (B), royal hero who was a **Bodhisattva**

Nayaka (d), 16th–18th-century governors, then independent rulers at Ikkeri in the Deccan and at Gingee, Madurai and Thanjavur in southern India

Nayanar (H), **Shaiva** saint

Neminatha (J), twenty-second of the twenty-four **Tirthankaras**, distinguished by his conch emblem

Nigrodhamriga (B), deer hero of a **Jataka** story

Nilakantha, Nilakantheshvara (H), Blue-Throated; epithet of **Shiva** after he drank the poison produced at the churning of the cosmic ocean

Nilotpalambal (H), name of **Bhumidevi**

Nirriti (H), one of the **Dikpalas**, guardian of the south-west

nirvana (B), enlightenment; literally 'extinguished'

Nityeshvara (H), name of **Shiva**

Nolamba (d), 9th–11th-century dynasty of southern India

Nyingmapa (B), name of a Tibetan Buddhist sect

Olakkanatha (H), name of **Shiva**

pada (B, H), foot, mostly refers to a footprint

padma (B, J, H), lotus flower

Padmanabha (H), epithet of **Vishnu** in his emanation as **Anantashayana**

Padmapani (B), epithet of **Avalokiteshvara**, who is distinguished by the lotus flower that he holds

Padmaprabha (J), sixth of the twenty-four **Tirthankaras**, distinguished by the lotus emblem

padmasana (B, J, H), Lotus Seat; posture of meditating figures

Pahari (d), 16th–19th-century dynasties of the Himalayan valleys in northern India

Pala (d), 7th–12th-century dynasty of eastern India

Pallava (d), 6th–9th-century dynasty of southern India

Pampa (H), name of **Devi** worshipped at Hampi (Vijayanagara)

Pampapati (H), Lord of **Pampa**, name of **Virupaksha**

Pancha Pandava (H), Five **Pandavas**

Panchalinga (H), Five **Lingas**

Panchanana (H), Five-Faced; an epithet of **Shiva**

Panchika (B), epithet of **Kubera**

Pandava (H), lineage of Pandu; often refers to the five heroes of the **Mahabharata**: see **Arjuna, Bhima, Dharmaraja, Nakula** and **Sahadeva**

Pandya (d), 7th–13th-century dynasty of southern India

Pannaka (B), prince who beats **Vidhurapandita** in a **Jataka** story

Papanasana (H), Destroyer of Sin; name of **Shiva**

Papanatha (H), title of **Shiva** worshipped at Pattadakal

Paramara (d), 10th–12th-century dynasty of central and part of western India

Parantaka (r), 10th-century **Chola** ruler

Parashara Rishi (H), sage worshipped at Pandoh

Parashurama (H), Rama with the Axe; incarnation of **Vishnu**

Parashurameshvara (H), name of **Shiva**

Parinirvana (B), Great **Nirvana**; the death of **Buddha**

Parshvanatha (J), the second last of the twenty-four **Tirthankaras**, distinguished by the multi-headed serpent which rears over his head; believed also to be a historical figure whose teachings influenced those of **Mahavira**

Parthasarathi (H), name of **Vishnu** worshipped at Triplicaine (Madras)

Parvati (H), Daughter of the Mountain; gracious and peaceful consort of **Shiva**, also known as **Gauri** and **Uma**; mother of **Ganesha** and **Skanda**

Pashupata (H), name of a **Shaiva** sect

Pashupati (H), Lord of Animals; epithet of **Shiva**

pata (J, H), painted hanging in scroll

Pattabhirama (H), Crowned **Rama**

Pattinattar (H), a **Shaiva** saint

pecchavai (H), votive painting of **Shrinathji**

Perumal (H), God; usually refers to **Vishnu**

Perundevi Tayar (H), consort of **Vishnu**, same as **Lakshmi**

Pippala Devi (H), local goddess worshipped at Osian

pradakshina (B, J, H), rite of circumambulation in a clockwise direction

Prajnaparamita (B), goddess personifying total wisdom who embodies the qualities of the **Bodhisattva**

prana (B, H), breath, the control of which is the aim of **Yoga**

Pratapeshvara (H), title of **Shiva**

Pratihara (d), 8th–11th-century rulers of northern and central India

puja (J, H), rite of temple worship

Pulakeshin (r), two 6th–7th-century **Early Chalukya** rulers

Pundalika (H), devotee of **Vithoba**

Pundarika (J), devotee of **Adinatha**

Punnaka (B), **yaksha** general in the **Vidhurapandita Jataka**

Purana (H), Old; sacred texts which are compilations of traditional lore, including myths, legends and ritual practices

Purna (B), convert of **Buddha**

Purushottama (H), title of **Vishnu**

Putana (H), ogress killed by **Krishna**

Radha (H), **Krishna**'s favourite consort

Raghunatha (H), name of **Rama**

Rahu (H), deity representing the planetary node believed to cause the solar eclipse

Rahula (B), son of **Buddha**

Rajagopala (H), name of **Krishna**

Rajaraja (r), 10th–11th-century **Chola** ruler

Rajarajeshvara, Rajeshvara (H), Lord of Kings; name of **Shiva**

Rajasimha (r), 8th-century **Pallava** ruler

Rajendra (r), 11th-century **Chola** ruler

Rajivalochana (H), Lotus-Eyed; epithet of **Rama**

Rajput (d), dynasties of western and central India from the 14th–20th centuries

Rama (H), incarnation of **Vishnu** and hero of the **Ramayana**, embodiment of the perfect son, husband and king

Ramachandra (H), name of **Rama**

Ramakrishna (H), 19th-century Hindu teacher and philosopher

Ramalinga, Ramalingeshvara, Rameshvara (H), name of **Shiva**, especially the **linga** worshipped by **Rama** at Rameshwaram

Ramana Maharishi (H), a **Shaiva** saint who lived at Tiruvannamalai

Ramananda (H), a **Vaishnava** teacher

Ramanuja (H), a **Vaishnava** philosopher and teacher

Ramappa (H), name of the **Shiva** temple at Palampet

Ramayana (H), story of **Rama** composed by **Valmiki**, one of the two great Hindu epics; the chief characters are Rama, his brother **Lakshmana** and his wife, **Sita**, who were exiled from Ayodhya; Sita was abducted by **Ravana**. Rama, aided by the monkey heroes **Sugriva** and **Hanuman**, rescued Sita and slayed Ravana

Rana Kumbha (r), 15th-century **Rajput** ruler of Chitorgarh

Ranbir Singh (r), 19th-century **Dogra** ruler

Ranganatha (H), name of **Vishnu** shown reclining on **Ananta**

Rasa (H), festival celebrating **Krishna** and **Radha**

Rashtrakuta (d), 7th–10th-century dynasty of the Deccan

Rathor (d), **Rajput** rulers of Jodhpur and Bikaner

Rati (H), wife of **Kama**

Ratnasambhava (B), Jewel-Born; **Buddha** presiding over the southern paradise

Ravana (H), demon king of Sri Lanka; disturbs **Shiva** and **Parvati**; is slain by **Rama** in the climactic battle of the **Ramayana** epic

Reddi (d), 14th–16th-century rulers of the eastern Deccan

Rig Veda (H), oldest and most sacred of the **Vedas**

Rinchen Bzangpo (B), 11th-century monk who brought Tibetan Buddhism to Ladakh

Rishabhanatha (J), name of **Adinatha**

rishi (J, H), sage

Rishyashringa (H), deer-headed sage in the **Ramayana**

Rudra Mahalaya (H), epithet of **Shiva**

Rudradeva (r), 12th-century **Kakatiya** ruler

Rudreshvara (H), name of **Shiva**

Rukmini (H), wife of **Krishna**

Ruru (B), deer hero of a **Jataka** story

Sachiya Mata (H), name of a goddess worshipped at Osian

Sadashiva (H), Eternal **Shiva**; sometimes represented as multi-headed

sadhu (H), ascetic

Sahadeva (H), a **Pandava** hero of the **Mahabharata**

sahasra linga (H), **linga** on which a 'thousand' miniature lingas are represented

Sama (B), hero of a **Jataka** story

Samadhishvara (H), Lord of Meditation; name of **Shiva** worshipped at Chitorgarh

Sambhavanatha (J), name of the third **Tirthankara**

Samkhapala (B), serpent hero of a **Jataka** story

samsara (B, J, H), eternal transmigration of the soul

Samvara (B), emanation of **Akshobhya**

Sangameshvara (H), name of **Shiva**, usually given to a **linga** installed at a confluence of two rivers

Sangha (B), ascetic order founded by **Buddha**

sannyasi (H), a wandering ascetic; final stage in the ideal life of a man

Sapta Matrika (H), the group of seven **Matrikas**

Sarangapani (H), name of **Vishnu** worshipped at Kumbakonam

Sarasvati (H, J), originally the personified river of the same name; wife of **Brahma** and goddess of knowledge, usually holds a musical instrument

Sarneshvara (H), name of **Shiva**

Sarvamangala (H), epithet of **Parvati**

Sasbahu (H), Mother-in-law, Daughter-in-law; usually refers to a pair of temples

Satavahana (d), 2nd-century-BC–3rd-century-AD dynasty of the Deccan

Sati (H), wife of **Shiva** who destroyed herself by immolation in fire

Sawai Jai Singh (r), 18th-century **Rajput** ruler of Jaipur

Sena (d), 11th–12th-century dynasty of eastern India

Senge Namgyal (r), 17th-century ruler of Ladakh

Sethupathi (d), 18th–19th-century dynasty of southern India

Shachi (H), consort of **Indra**

Shailodbhava (d), 7th–8th-century dynasty of Orissa

Shaiva (H), pertaining to the cult of **Shiva**

Shaiva Bhakta (H), devotee of **Shiva**

Shakti (B, H), Energy; female divinity

often associated with **Shiva**; also a name of a cult associated with various goddesses

Shakya (d), 6th-century-BC dynasty of eastern India

Shakyamuni (B), Sage of the Shakyas; title of **Buddha**

shalagrama (H), stone containing fossils, worshipped as a form of **Vishnu**

Shankara (H), epithet of **Shiva**

Shankara, Shankaracharya (H), 9th-century **Shaiva** philosopher

shankha (H), conch shell held by **Vishnu**

Shanti Durga (H), name of a goddess worshipped at Ponda

Shantinatha, Shantishvara (J), sixteenth of the twenty-four **Tirthankaras**, distinguished by the deer emblem

Shariputra (B), disciple of **Buddha**

Sharneshvara (H), name of **Shiva**

Shasta (H), local deity in the Kerala region, sometimes identified with **Ayanar**

Shastra (H), traditional treatise prescribing norms of human conduct and practice; often includes subjects like temple building, making of images and rituals of worship

Shatrughna (H), half-brother of **Rama** in the **Ramayana**

Shatrughneshvara (H), name of **Shiva**

Shesha (H), serpent who supports **Vishnu**

Sheshagiri (H), **Shesha**'s mountain; home of **Vishnu**

Sheth Hathisingh, 19th-century temple patron in Ahmadabad

Shibi (B), pigeon hero of a **Jataka** story

Shishireshvara (H), name of **Shiva**

Shitala (H), goddess of smallpox

Shitalanatha (J), name of the tenth **Tirthankara**

Shitaleshvara (H), name of **Shiva** worshipped at Calcutta

Shiva (H), principal deity of one of the major Hindu cults; generally worshipped as a **linga**, but also represented in a variety of forms, such as the dancer (**Nataraja**), the teacher (**Dakshinamurti**), the wandering ascetic (**Bhikshatanamurti**) and the terrifying destroyer (**Bhairava**); usually shown with his consorts **Devi**, **Parvati** or **Ganga**; father of **Ganesha** and **Karttikeya**

Shivaji (r), 17th-century **Maratha** leader

Shivakamasundari (H), epithet of **Parvati** worshipped at Chidambaram

Shivalaya (H), temple dedicated to **Shiva**

Shivaratri (H), night festival (February–March) dedicated to **Shiva**

Shobhanatha (J), name of **Sambhavanatha**

Shri, Shridevi (H), goddess who embodies prosperity and beauty; name of **Lakshmi**

Shri Yantra (B, H), diagrammatic form of the **Tantric** goddess

Shridhara (H), title of **Vishnu**

Shrinathji (H), image of **Krishna** worshipped at Nathdwara

Shrivaishnava (H), name of a **Vaishnava** cult

shrivatsa (J), diamond-like tuft of hair on the chest of a **Tirthankara**

Shrutadevi (J), epithet of **Sarasvati**

Shuddhodhana (B), father of **Buddha**

Shunga (d), 2nd–1st-century-BC dynasty of central and eastern India

Shurpanakha (H), sister of **Ravana**, attacked by **Lakshmana** in the **Ramayana**

Shvetambara (J), one of the two principal Jain sects, the monks of which wear white robes

Shyama, Shyama Raya (H), name of **Krishna**

Siddha, Siddhara (J, H), a sage or saint

Siddhartha (B), personal name of **Buddha**

Siddheshvara (H), name of **Shiva**

Simhala (B), princely hero of a **Jataka** story

Simhanatha (H), epithet of **Narasimha**

Sisodiya (d), **Rajput** rulers of Udaipur

Sita (H), wife of **Rama**, personification of female devotion; in the **Ramayana** epic she is abducted by **Ravana** but rescued by **Rama**

Sivali (B), wife of **Mahajanaka** in a **Jataka** story

Skanda (H), son of **Shiva** and **Parvati**, leader of the army of the gods; also known as **Karttikeya**, **Kumara** and **Subrahmanya**

Skanda Purana (H), one of the **Puranas**

Solanki (d), 10th–13th-century dynasty of western India

soma (H), sacred drink of the **Vedas**

Somanatha, Someshvara (H), celebrated **linga** at Prabhas Patan, after which other **lingas** were named

Somanatha (r), 13th-century **Hoysala** military general

Somaskanda (H), group of **Shiva**, **Uma** and **Skanda** images

Somavamshi (d), 9th–11th-century dynasty of central and eastern India

Sthalapurana (H), **Purana** pertaining to a particular temple or sacred locality

Subhadra (H), sister of **Krishna**, wife of **Arjuna**

Subrahmanya (H), epithet of **Skanda**

Sugriva (H), king of the monkeys who helped **Rama** in the **Ramayana**

Suhadevi (H), name of **Devi**

Sujata (B), maiden who offered rice to **Buddha** after his enlightenment

Sundara (H), a Tamil **Shaiva** saint

Sundaravarda Perumal (H), name of **Vishnu** worshipped at Uttaramerur

Sundareshvara (H), title of **Shiva** worshipped at Madurai

Surya (H), Sun; solar deity who rides in a seven-horsed chariot

Sutasoma (B), lioness heroine of a **Jataka** story

svami, swami (H), holy man; also used as a suffix for temple deities

Svarnajaleshvara (H), form of **Shiva**

svastika (B, J, H), 'swastika' emblem

tala (B, J, H), face-length for sacred images

Talagirishvara (H), name of **Shiva** worshipped at Panamalai

Tantra (B, H), esoteric texts which expound methods by which salvation may be easily achieved; often emphasize female power and sexual symbolism

Tantric (B, H), pertaining to the **Tantras**

Tara (B), Star; divine **Shakti** especially associated with **Avalokiteshvara**

Tarakanatha (H), name of **Shiva** worshipped at Tarakeswar

Tathagata (B), epithet of **Buddha**; sometimes represented as a group of four **Buddhas**

Tej Bahadur (S), ninth Sikh **Guru**

Tejapala, 13th-century **Solanki** temple patron

thangka (B), cloth painted with a Tibetan **Mahayana** deity; gigantic thangkas are displayed at festival times

Theravada (B), Old Ones; original Buddhist sect

Tipu Sultan (r), 18th-century Muslim ruler of Mysore

tirtha (J, H), holy spot

Tirthankara (J), Ford-Maker; title given to twenty-four saviours or teachers, the worship of whom lies at the core of Jainism

Tirumala (r), 16th-century **Nayaka** ruler of Madurai

Tiruvengalanatha (H), name of **Venkateshvara**, an aspect of **Vishnu**

Trailokyanatha (J), Lord of the Three Worlds; title of **Mahavira**

Travancore Rajas (d), 16th–19th-century rulers of Kerala

tribhanga (B, H), favourite triple-bended posture for standing figures of deities

Trilochana (H), Three-Eyed; epithet of **Shiva**

Trilokanatha (H), Lord of Three Worlds; epithet of **Shiva**

Trimbukeshvara (H), name of **Shiva** worshipped at Trimbak

Trimurti (H), triad of Hindu divinities, **Brahma**, **Vishnu** and **Shiva**

Tripura (H), demon of the three cities

Tripurantaka (H), name of **Shiva** as destroyer of **Tripura**

Trishala (J), mother of **Mahavira**

trishula (H), trident held by **Shiva**

Trivikrama (H), incarnation of **Vishnu** pacing out the universe by three gigantic steps

Tsongkhapa (B), 15th-century founder of the **Gelugpa** sect

Tulsi Das (H), translator of the **Ramayana** epic into Hindi

Tyagaraja (H), name of **Shiva** worshipped at Tiruvarur

Udayaditya (r), 11th-century **Paramara** ruler

Udayeshvara (H), name of **Shiva** worshipped at Udayapur

Uma (H), epithet of **Parvati**

Undeshvara (H), name of **Shiva** worshipped at Bijolia

Upanishads (H), ancient philosophical texts considered as part of the **Vedas**

Urvashi (H), a celestial nymph

Utpala (d), 8th–9th-century dynasty of Kashmir

Uttareshvara (H), name of **Shiva**

Vadakkunnatha (H), name of **Shiva** worshipped at Trichur

vahana (J, H), vehicle; mount or carrier of a deity

Vaidyanatha (H), name of **Shiva** worshipped at Baijnath

Vaikuntha (H), composite form of **Vishnu** shown with boar (**Varaha**) and lion (**Narasimha**) heads; also name of heaven in which **Vishnu** resides

Vairochana (B), a manifestation of **Adi Buddha**

Vaishishtha (J), name of a Jain sage

Vaishnava (H), pertaining to the cult of **Vishnu**

vajra (B, H), thunderbolt weapon held by some deities

Vajrabhairava (B), terrifying guardian deity holding the thunderbolt (**vajra**)

Vajradhara (B), a manifestation of **Adi Buddha**

Vajrapani (B), **Bodhisattva** holding the thunderbolt

Vajrayana (B), Vehicle of the Thunderbolt; name of a **Tantric** sect

Vakataka (d), 4th–5th-century dynasty of the Deccan

Vali (H), monkey ruler killed by **Rama** in the **Ramayana** epic

Vallabha (H), name of **Krishna**; also of a **Vaishnava** teacher and the sect that he founded

Valmiki (H), sage who composed the **Ramayana** epic

Vamana (H), dwarf incarnation of **Vishnu**

Vanmikanatha (H), name of **Shiva** worshipped at Tiruvarur

Varadaraja (H), epithet of **Vishnu**, especially worshipped at Kanchipuram

Varaha (H), boar incarnation of **Vishnu**, rescued the goddess **Bhu**

Varahi (H), female aspect of **Varaha**, one of the **Matrikas**

Vardnamana (J), name of **Mahavira**

Varkari (H), **Vaishnava** sect that worships **Vithoba**

Varuna (H), guardian of the west, shown with a **makara** signifying his association with water

Varunani, Varuni (H), consort of **Varuna**

Vastu Shastra (H), treatise on architecture, including temple building

Vastupala, 13th-century **Solanki** temple patron

Vasudeva (H), epithet of **Krishna** or **Vishnu**

Vayu (H), guardian of the north-west

Veda (H), oldest known religious texts; these include hymns to different divinities such as **Agni**, **Indra** and **Varuna**, who were later incorporated into Hindu cults

Vedic (H), pertaining to the **Vedas**

Venkataramana, Venkateshvara (H), Lord of the Venkata Hills; title of **Vishnu** worshipped at Tirumala

Vessantara (B), princely hero of a **Jataka** story

Vidhurapandita (B), royal hero of a **Jataka** story

Vidyaranya, Vidyashankara (H), **Shaiva** saint in the line of **Shankaracharya**

Vijaya Narayana (H), name of **Vishnu**

Vijayaditya (r), 8th-century **Early Chalukya** ruler

Vijayanagara (d), 14th–17th-century dynasty of the Deccan and southern India

Vikrama (H), mythical hero, lover of the nymph **Urvashi**

Vikramaditya (r), legendary king of Ujjain; 8th-century **Early Chalukya** ruler

Vimala, 11th-century **Solanki** minister

Virabhadra (H), vengeful form of **Shiva**

Virattaneshvara (H), name of **Shiva** worshipped at Tiruttani

Virupaksha (H), epithet of **Shiva** worshipped at Hampi (Vijayanagara)

Vishalakshi (H), name of **Parvati**, consort of **Vishvanatha**

Vishnu (H), principal cult deity in Hinduism; creator and preserver of universal order; appears in a series of ten incarnations (**Dashavatara**), as well as in a variety of other forms; is associated with **Lakshmi** and **Bhudevi**

Vishnupada (H), footprint of **Vishnu**, especially revered at Gaya

Vishnuvardhana (r), 12th-century **Hoysala** ruler

Vishvakarma (H), mythical architect of the heavens

Vishvamitra (H), a sage in the **Ramayana**

Vishvanatha, Vishveshvara (H), Lord of the Universe; celebrated **linga** of **Shiva** worshipped at Varanasi and after which other **lingas** were named

Vishvarupa (H), Omniform; aspect of **Vishnu** represented with multiple heads and arms

Vitthala, Vithoba (H), form of **Vishnu** worshipped at Pandharpur

Vivekananda (H), disciple of **Ramakrishna**, founder of the order named after this saint

Vrishabhanatha (J), name of **Adinatha**

vyala (H), lion-like fantastic beast

Wadiyar (d), 17th–20th-century dynasty of Mysore

Western Ganga (d), 9th–11th-century dynasty of southern India

Yadava (d), 11th–14th-century dynasty of the northern Deccan

yajna (H), sacrificial fire ceremony

yaksha (B, J, H), a demi-god, originally associated with nature in folk religion

yakshi, yakshini (B, J, H), female form of **yaksha**, often associated with Jain divinities

yali (H), lion-like fantastic beast

Yama (H), god of death, judge of the living; guardian of the south

Yameshvara (H), name of **Shiva**

Yamuna (H), goddess personifying the Yamuna river

yantra (B, J, H), magical diagram used in meditation

Yashoda (H), foster-mother of **Krishna**

Yashovarman (r), 8th-century **Pratihara** ruler

Yellamma (H), local folk goddess

Yoga (H), school of philosophy which concentrates on different mental and physical disciplines

yogi (H), practitioner of **Yoga**

yogini (B, H), **Tantric** goddess, manifestation of **Shakti**; sometimes appears in a group of sixty-four (**Chaunsath Yogini**)

yoni (H), vulva; sexual emblem of **Devi**, often serving as a pedestal for the **linga**

INDEX OF SITES

Sites in **bold** are described separately; other sites are only referred to incidentally.
Sites marked with an asterisk (★) also appear in Volume II. Page numbers in **bold** indicate the principal Gazetteer entry.

PHOTOGRAPHIC CREDITS

American Institute of Indian Studies: pages 36, 65, 99 top and bottom, 100 top and bottom, 143 top and bottom, 144 bottom, 146, 206–7, 210 top, 260–1, 266, 268 bottom, 269 top, 322 top, 323 top and bottom, 325 top, 412 bottom, 413 top and bottom, 415, 417

Anthony Hutt, Scorpion Archives: page 105

Archaeological Survey of India: pages 30, 50, 72, 213 top and bottom, 320 top, 419 top and bottom

Bender, Rainer J.: page 327

Berkson, Carmel: pages 101, 147, 269 bottom

Chetwode, Penelope: page 102 bottom

Fass, Virginia: page 270 top

Gollings, John: page 325 bottom

Gorbeck, Jeffrey: pages 314–15, 411 bottom

Gunn, Seona: page 102 top

Harle, J. C.: page 414

Higgott, Andrew: page 104

Huntingdon, John and Susan: page 209

India Office Library: pages 264, 319, 321, 326

Kersting, A. F.: pages 78, 103 top and bottom, 148, 210 bottom, 270 bottom, 411 top, 412 top

Lannoy, Richard: page 62

Mc Cutchion, David: pages 142, 144 top, 145 bottom left and right, 149 top and bottom, 208 bottom, 211, 212 top, 265 top and bottom, 266, 267 top left and right, 320 bottom, 322 bottom, 324 top and bottom

Michell, George: pages 145 top, 202–3, 212 bottom, 268 top, 418

O'Connor, Bill: pages 14, 96–7

Peerless, Anne and Bury: Slides Resources and Picture Library pages 141, 208 top, 271, 416

Robert Harding Picture Library: pages 406–7

Smart, Ellen: page 3

Younger, Christine: page 44

Wilson, J. H. C.: pages 20, 138–9

MAP CREDITS

Regional maps and Map of India by Ellie King. All town and district maps by Nigel White. Building plans by K. R. Ravindran.